The Motorola MC68000 Microprocessor Family: Assembly Language, Interface Design, and System Design

Thomas L. Harman

School of Sciences and Technologies
University of Houston, Clear Lake

Barbara Lawson

Prentice-Hall, Inc., Englewood Cliffs, New Jersey 07632

Library of Congress Cataloging in Publication Data

Harman, Thomas L.
    The Motorola MC 68000 microprocessor family.

    Includes index.
    1. Motorola 68000 (Microprocessor) 2. Motorola 68000
(Microprocessor)–Programming. 3. Assembler language
(Computer program language) 4. Microcomputers.
I. Lawson, Barbara. II. Title.
QA76.8.M6895H37 1985   001.64   84-11480
ISBN 0-13-603960-X

Editorial/production supervision: *Raeia Maes*
Cover design: *Photo Plus Art*
Manufacturing buyer: *Gordon Osbourne*

Printed in the United States of America

10   9   8   7

ISBN 0-13-603960-X   01

Prentice-Hall International, Inc., *London*
Prentice-Hall of Australia Pty. Limited, *Sydney*
Editora Prentice-Hall do Brasil, Ltda., *Rio de Janeiro*
Prentice-Hall Canada Inc., *Toronto*
Prentice-Hall of India Private Limited, *New Delhi*
Prentice-Hall of Japan, Inc., *Tokyo*
Prentice-Hall of Southeast Asia Pte. Ltd., *Singapore*
Whitehall Books Limited, Wellington, *New Zealand*

Contents

Preface

The introduction of the Motorola MC68000 family of microprocessors ushered in a new generation of processors. This family includes the MC68000 and the MC68010. Both are single-chip microprocessors designed to function as the central processing units of sophisticated computer systems. The characteristics and uses of these Motorola processors are treated in detail in this book. For these processors, the book covers assembly language, programming, interface design, and system design.

One important purpose of the book is to introduce the student or the practicing computer professional to all of the significant aspects of design using the MC68000. In addition, the book can serve as a reference in which topics are organized according to function and importance for the design of programs, interfaces, or systems.

This book is organized into three parts as indicated in the Chapter Descriptions below. The first four chapters present the MC68000 family to the reader and also cover other introductory material. Chapters 5 through 9 treat assembly language programming techniques for the processors. Chapters 10 through 12 are concerned with system design and development for MC68000-based computer systems. Appendices I through V summarize pertinent material about the MC68000, MC68008, and MC68010. Finally, selected answers to problems given in the chapters are included at the end of the book.

A detailed summary of the major topics covered in the book, a list of the acronyms used in the book, a list of programs by topic, and a list of additional materials that may be used in conjunction with this book are given on the following pages.

CHAPTER DESCRIPTIONS

Chapters 1 through 4 introduce the reader to the MC68000 family of products, micro-computers, fundamentals of machine arithmetic, and the MC68000 central processing unit.

- Chapter 1 presents a number of applications of the Motorola MC68000 micro-processor. The hardware and software support for the MC68000 family of integrated circuit devices is also described.

- Chapter 2 discusses the organization of typical microcomputer systems. The function of the major system components (CPU, memory, input/output) is described and the importance of the CPU word length and addressing range is presented. Three views of the system as seen by the system designer, the assembly language programmer, and the interface designer are given.

- Chapter 3 explains the internal representation of numbers and characters as used in MC68000 systems. Binary, decimal, and floating-point notations are treated along with details of arithmetic operations. The ASCII code for alphanumeric characters is also presented.

- Chapter 4 is devoted to a discussion of the characteristics of the MC68000 processor. The MC68000 is first introduced as an integrated circuit chip before its characteristics as a programmable processor are presented. The organization of memory in a typical MC68000-based system is also covered.

Chapters 5 through 9 are devoted to programming techniques using the MC68000. The assembly language for the processor is used to explain the many capabilities of the MC68000.

- Chapter 5 introduces the MC68000 assembly language. Software development, assembly language features, and the various addressing modes of the MC68000 are covered.

- Chapter 6 presents three important categories of instructions for the MC68000. Instructions for data transfer, program control, and subroutines are treated.

- Chapter 7 contains explanations and program examples concerning the arithmetic capability of the MC68000. Binary arithmetic, decimal arithmetic, and conversions between ASCII, binary, and BCD are covered.

- Chapter 8 introduces the logical instructions, shift and rotate instructions, and bit-manipulation instructions.

- Chapter 9 completes the study of basic programming techniques. Methods of creating position independent code are covered. Program examples are given for manipulation of data structures, including arrays and lists. More advanced subroutine techniques are presented.

Chapters 10, 11, and 12 are devoted to aspects of the MC68000 that determine the operation of the computer system. Chapters 10 and 11 are of concern to the system designer and the programmer who create supervisor programs. Chapter 12 covers I/O programming and details of hardware design.

- Chapter 10 considers the processor's various states and modes of operation. The assembly language instructions to control the processor and examples of initialization procedures are presented.
- Chapter 11 covers exception processing. The exceptions include interrupts, traps, and various error conditions recognized by the CPU during program execution.
- Chapter 12 presents the interfacing requirements and I/O programming for MC68000 systems.

Appendices I through V contain summary material. Appendix I contains the ASCII character codes and a table of powers of 2 and 16. Appendix II, Appendix III, and Appendix IV contain a summary of the MC68000 family characteristics, the assembly language instruction set, and the machine language instruction set for the MC68000, MC68008, and MC68010. Appendix V presents the memory map for Motorola's Design Module.

SUMMARY OF MAJOR TOPICS

General Programming

Data Types	Chapter 3
Machine Language	Section 4.5
Memory Addressing	Section 4.6
Assembly Language	Chapter 5
Summary	Appendices

MC68000 Processor

Addressing Modes	Sections 4.4, 5.3, and 9.2
Instruction Set	
Introduction	Section 4.3
Major Instructions	Chapters 6, 7, and 8
Register Set	Sections 4.2 and 10.2
Summary	Appendices

Programming Techniques

Arithmetic and Logical	
Data Types	Chapter 3
Condition Codes	Section 6.3 and 7.1
Arithmetic Operations	Chapter 7

Summary   Appendix IV
LOOP Mode Operation   Appendix IVG

LIST OF ACRONYMS

ACIA	Asynchronous Communications Interface Adapter
ASCII	American Standard Code for Information Interchange
ALU	Arithmetic and Logic Unit
BCD	Binary Coded Decimal
CAD	Computer Aided Design
CAM	Computer Aided Manufacturing
CPU	Central Processing Unit
CRT	Cathode-Ray Tube
DIP	Dual-in-Line Package
DMA	Direct Memory Address
I/O	Input and Output
MMU	Memory Management Unit
MOS	Metal-Oxide Semiconductor
PIA	Peripheral Interface Adapter
PLA	Programmed Logic Array
PTM	Programmer Timer Module
RAM	Random Access Memory (Read/Write)
ROM	Read Only Memory
SSI	Small Scale Integration
VLSI	Very Large Scale Integration

LIST OF PROGRAMS BY TOPIC

General

Arithmetic

Lists and Tables

System Operation: I/O, Interrupts, and Traps

ADDITIONAL MATERIAL

The processor manuals provide a more complete treatment of certain characteristics of the processor than is covered in this book. The User's Manual for the MC68000 is available from Prentice-Hall. A manual for the MC68010 can be obtained from Motorola Semiconductor Products Inc., Austin, Texas.

Since development systems vary considerably, the reader should refer to the reference manuals for the specific system on which programs are being developed. These manuals include the Assembly Language Reference Manual for the specific assembler being used, as well as the manuals that describe the use of the system, i.e., how to edit, assemble, and execute programs. Similarly, the hardware manuals for the system and the manufacturer's data sheets for specific components should be used because these documents cover details peculiar to any specific item.

ACKNOWLEDGMENTS

A number of people have made special contributions to this book. The material was developed over several semesters with many helpful suggestions for improvement from the students in the Microcomputer Design Class at the University of Houston, Clear Lake. In particular, Alice Burke, Diane Grafton, Judy Meier, and Ken Wood were very helpful.

The original manuscript was produced with the Text and Document Processor for the Hewlett Packard HP3000 computer system. Barbara Kipfer and Anna Mae Bozsin are to be thanked for their efforts in preparing the finished manuscript. Also, Tony Adams, Linda Dunn, and Mike Shelly acted as word processor operators for much of the project. Danny, Mike, Ric, and Saaid, of the University Computer Center, were also of great help in producing the final document. Others involved in the production include Becky Phillips, Dennis Pleticha, and Carol Lowry.

We wish to thank Mike Collins and James Farrell III, of Motorola, for their careful proofreading of the manuscript and other help. Diana Barber also acted as proofreader. Of course, the staff of Prentice-Hall did a fine job of putting the book into production. Our sincere appreciation goes to all these people who were involved in one way or another in the project.

Finally, our families are to be thanked for their patience and support during the long process of producing a textbook. We apologize to any other persons who helped in the endeavor but were not cited here. Please send any comments or criticisms to the authors in care of Prentice-Hall, Inc., Englewood Cliffs, New Jersey, 07632.

T. L. Harman
B. Lawson

1

Introduction

A decade of advances in integrated circuit technology was crowned by the announcement in 1980 of the commercial availability of the Motorola MC68000 *microprocessor.* This microprocessor and several others, which are identified as *16-bit microprocessors,* function as the central processing units (CPUs) of computers, but they have been scaled down so that the tens of thousands of circuit elements of the processor fit on a silicon chip about one-fourth of an inch (6.4 millimeters) on a side. When suitably packaged and electrically connected to other integrated circuits, which serve as memory for data and program storage and include input and output circuitry, the processor chip is the central element in a *microcomputer* system. The dimensions of the system may be 12 inches by 12 inches by 0.75 inch (30 by 30 by 1.9 centimeters) before it is enclosed in a cabinet to provide physical protection. The addition of a power supply and suitable peripheral devices such as cathode-ray tube (CRT) terminals yields a computer system capable of being programmed to accomplish a wide variety of tasks. The microprocessor itself controls the detailed operation of the system at the hardware level and performs the arithmetic, logical, or other operations required for the application involved. Figure 1.1 shows the basic hardware elements of a typical microcomputer system useful for personal or small business applications.

The excitement generated by the introduction of the MC68000 and other microprocessors of its class was not caused by the promise of small, low-cost computer systems. Such systems, based on previous microprocessors, were already commercially available. Rather, the greatly enhanced capability of these 16-bit microprocessors caused attention to be focused on the wide variety of potential applications for microcomputers. These processors definitely rival and sometimes exceed the ability of the central processing units of many minicomputers. Their speeds of operation, as an an-

1

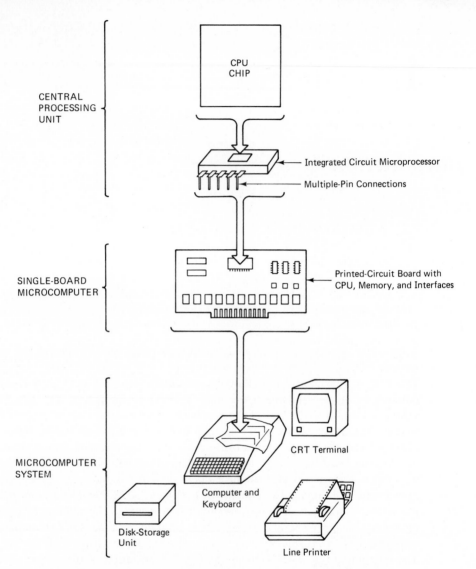

CENTRAL
PROCESSING
UNIT

SINGLE-BOARD
MICROCOMPUTER

MICROCOMPUTER
SYSTEM

CPU
CHIP

Integrated Circuit Microprocessor

Multiple-Pin Connections

Printed-Circuit Board with
CPU, Memory, and Interfaces

CRT Terminal

Computer and
Keyboard

Disk-Storage
Unit

Line Printer

Figure 1.1   A typical microcomputer system. (Courtesy of Motorola, Inc.)

cillary but vital feature of these integrated processors, is comparable with earlier systems costing many times as much. Advancements in processor design and integrated circuit technology over several decades formed the basis for the production of microprocessors capable of supporting applications of almost any complexity and speed requirement. Such requirements had previously been served only by minicomputers.

The development of programs (software) for these microcomputers is also proceeding at a rapid pace. A number of operating systems and related programs are available for MC68000-based computers, including software supplied by Motorola as well as that created by independent suppliers. The combination of software and the extensive line of hardware components offered by Motorola and other manufacturers form a "family" of products that support the development of MC68000-based systems.

This introductory chapter first presents a number of systems that use the MC68000 as the central processing unit. These systems include products such as a controller for robotics applications, as well as powerful computer systems which support extensive software development of programs for any application. This chapter also describes how the development of these products is greatly facilitated by the software and hardware support available for the MC68000 family.

1.1 APPLICATIONS OF THE MOTOROLA MC68000

Despite its small physical size, the Motorola MC68000 processor has the capability and speed of operation necessary to function as the central processor in a computer designed for very sophisticated applications. A sampling of these applications is presented in this section to indicate the range of products that may be designed based on the MC68000. Those cited are summarized in Table 1.1, which lists the area of application, the specific application, and the manufacturer of the product. In most cases, the example cited represents an increase in product capability at a lower cost than that of similar products designed and implemented using computer technology available prior to the introduction of the MC68000. Many of the capabilities of the MC68000 which allow development of such products are discussed in later chapters.

TABLE 1.1   APPLICATIONS OF THE MC68000

Area	Application	Manufacturer
Education	Teaching aid or evaluation module	Motorola Semiconductor Products, Phoenix, Ariz.
Data communications	Networking	Apollo Computer, Chelmsford, Mass.
Development of software	Software development	WICAT Systems, Orem, Utah
Graphics	Color graphics terminal	Chromatics, Tucker, Ga.
Industry	Robotics	Automatix Inc., Billerica, Mass.
Science and engineering	Desktop computer	Hewlett-Packard, Palo Alto, Calif.
Multiuser applications	Development System-EXORmacs	Motorola Semiconductor Products, Phoenix, Ariz.

Education. A photograph of the Motorola Design Module (MEX68KDM), which represents a *single-board computer,* is shown in Figure 1.2. The addition of a power supply and peripheral units to this module produces a low-cost computer system similar in concept to that shown in Figure 1.1. In the photograph, the MC68000 appears in the left center. It is connected to the other elements of the system by copper signal lines that are a part of the printed-circuit board which supports the various inte-

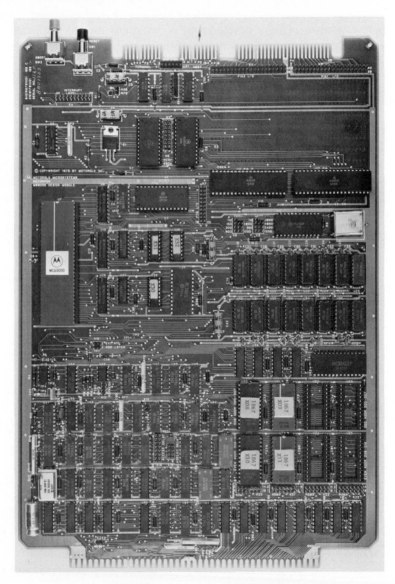

Figure 1.2   MC68000 design module. (Courtesy of Motorola, Inc.)

grated circuits. Other devices on the board represent memory units and interfacing circuits. The user communicates with the module via a CRT terminal attached by cable to a connector at the edge of the board.

The Design Module may be used to evaluate the characteristics of the MC68000 CPU during program development and execution. These programs may be created using a simple operating system which is provided in read-only memory (ROM) chips on the module. Since no assembler or compiler is provided, programs must be written (coded) in machine language. Alternatively, programs can be created on another system which generates machine-readable code for the MC68000 (e.g., with cross-assemblers). The executable code can then be loaded into the memory of the Design Module for execution. Both of these approaches to software development are described elsewhere in the book. For present purposes, it should be noted that the Design Module represents the necessary hardware to provide the CPU, memory, and interfacing capability of a computer system all on a single printed-circuit board.

Data communications.   The Apollo system is cited in Table 1.1 as an example of a networking application of the MC68000. This system takes advantage of the capability of the processor to operate with a number of computers sharing both information and peripheral devices such as large disk storage units.

The network can consist of a number of individual workstations (computers) connected in a serial fashion into what is sometimes called a "ring" configuration. Each individual user at one of the computers can use that workstation without regard to other activity in the network. Each local computer is a general-purpose computer incorporating Motorola MC68000 processors. Each node in the network has access to data or programs stored anywhere else in the system.

The workstations in the network represent the type of computer system that can be designed using the MC68000. Each display is a high-resolution CRT unit suitable for computer graphics applications. Software can be developed in one of several high-level languages to meet a particular requirement, such as that for a computer-aided-design (CAD) terminal for engineering applications. The MC68000 processors at each workstation provide the processing capability to support such applications and also allow communication with other workstations and the peripheral units shared by all.

Software development systems.   Figure 1.3 shows the WICAT Systems Model 150 computer, which is based on the MC68000. The manufacturer describes it as a workstation; it is ideal as a small business system, a dedicated personal computer, or a local computer within a network. The computer is available with several operating systems and a number of high-level language compilers to support software development.

The model pictured can be further enhanced by the addition of a number of peripheral devices. The floppy disk unit, shown in Figure 1.3, is part of the basic terminal. Other, larger-capacity disk units are available. Additional terminals can also be added to form a multiuser system that will allow simultaneous development of software by several programmers.

Figure 1.3   The WICAT development system. (Courtesy of WICAT Systems.)

Graphics.   Microprocessors such as the MC68000 have an important application in the area of computer graphics. Graphics terminals, such as the Chromatics color graphic system shown in Figure 1.4, allow much of the complex mathematical processing required for picture presentation and manipulation to be accomplished at the terminal rather than by a connected host computer. The system shown allows the development of programs for graphics applications and includes disk storage for the programs. In MC68000 assembly language, a program may call (as subroutines) a number of primitive graphics routines which are supplied in read-only memory (ROM). For example, there are routines to create figures on the screen or to allow control of the colors being displayed. Since the routines in ROM reduce the need for detailed knowledge of the hardware operation, programming is simplified in many applications.

Industry.   Microprocessors with the capability of performing complex arithmetic operations and the sophisticated decision making needed in control systems are suitable for a number of industrial applications. Figure 1.5 shows a welding system manufactured by Automatix. This programmable arc welder is controlled by the MC68000-based AI32 controller shown in the photograph. The system is pro-

Figure 1.4   Chromatics CGC 7900 color graphics terminal. (Courtesy of Chromatics, Inc.)

grammed in a high-level language suitable for welding and other computer-aided-manufacturing (CAM) applications. Automatix also manufactures a programmable visual inspection system using the AI32 as the controller. The power and flexibility of the MC68000 as a CPU allows a basic product such as the robot controller to be reprogrammed to adapt it to a variety of applications.

Science and engineering.   Computers used to solve scientific and engineering problems need a powerful arithmetic capability and must execute programs written in a high-level language such as Pascal. The Hewlett-Packard desktop computer (Model 36 or HP9836A) cited in Table 1.1 is based on the MC68000 and satisfies the needs of many scientific and engineering applications. In addition to

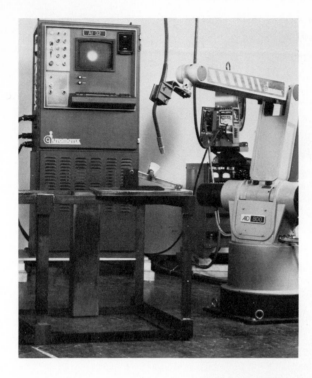

Figure 1.5 Robovision® II arc welding system. (Courtesy of Automatix Inc.)

supporting several high-level languages, including Pascal, the HP9836A allows MC68000 assembly language programs to be developed. The desktop unit shown in Figure 1.6 has a graphical display for curve plotting of the results.

Multiuser applications.   Most of the applications presented in Table 1.1 constitute single-user systems in which the speed and capability of the MC68000 microprocessor is used to satisfy the requirements of a particular product. Such use of microprocessors in products is typical and has been the rule since their inception. However, for applications such as time sharing which involve several users simultaneously, the minicomputer was the logical choice because of the number and variety of operating systems available. More sophisticated applications than those exhibited here require the development of system software, including operating systems, with the capability to share the hardware resources of the system between a number of users. Such software is difficult and expensive to develop and, unless the microcomputer was based on a previously available minicomputer, very few microprocessor-based systems of the 1970s had multiuser capability. The LSI-11 (Digital Equipment Corporation), for example, is a microcomputer system with many of the characteristics of the powerful PDP-11 minicomputer. This computer has operating systems available which allow multiuser program development.

The generation of microprocessors that includes the MC68000 are now being utilized in many multiuser systems. The MC68000 has the necessary hardware and

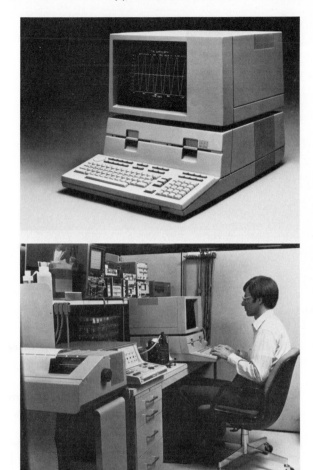

Figure 1.6   HP9836A desktop computer. (Courtesy of Hewlett Packard.)

software support that makes such multiuser systems feasible. The WICAT system shown previously, for example, can be expanded to support up to eight users simultaneously when the necessary peripheral equipment is added to the basic unit. The EX-ORmacs system pictured in Figure 1.7 is another example of a powerful multiuser system. In the full configuration, eight users may simultaneously develop software on this MC68000-based computer system from Motorola.

Summary of applications.   The applications for the MC68000 selected here represent only a small sampling of the products that can be based on this processor. Its speed of operation, large addressing capability, and modern architecture make the MC68000 an excellent choice for the CPU in products requiring a powerful processor. From the product manufacturers' viewpoint, however, the MC68000 processor is only one element in the computer system on which the product is based. The system

Figure 1.7   The Motorola EXORmacs system. (Courtesy of Motorola, Inc.)

software and hardware devices available for an MC68000-based system also influence the suitability of the MC68000 to meet particular product requirements.

1.2 THE MC68000 FAMILY

The MC68000 was chosen as the central processing unit in the products described in Section 1.1 for a variety of economic and technical reasons. The specific capabilities of the MC68000 were without doubt important in the choice, particularly when the finished product exhibits enhanced performance when compared to similar predecessors employing a less powerful processor. Another vital factor in the choice for most manufacturers of products is the *support* given to the processor line. This support comes from the manufacturer of the processor and a number of other sources. The support consists of hardware, software, development systems, and other items. Such support is provided to enable a product manufacturer to design, build and test, and produce the product in the most economical manner. Also, as technological advances allow improvement of performance and lower cost for the product, the manufacturer must modify the product in various ways to remain competitive. The *family* concept, as applied to microcomputer systems, assures that the processor line is adequately supported and is improved with time. One who is familiar with the basic processor (MC68000) has little trouble learning the characteristics of newer processors and various items that constitute other members of the family.

Table 1.2 summarizes many of the support criteria to be discussed in this section. The processor line of integrated circuits contains processors, circuits to facilitate

TABLE 1.2   SUPPORT FOR THE MC68000 FAMILY BY MOTOROLA
AND INDEPENDENT MANUFACTURERS

Type	Support
Processors and support circuits	
MC68000 family	Basic processor and enhanced versions available in various packages and speeds of operation
Peripheral interface circuits	Circuits for interfacing CPU to a wide range of peripheral devices
Special devices	Devices for floating-point mathematics, network control, and other applications
Software	
Operating systems	Various operating systems for real-time applications, time sharing, or special purposes
Development software	Editors, assemblers, compilers, debugging programs
Applications software	Special-purpose programs for accounting, engineering analysis, etc.
Documentation	Manuals, application notes, data sheets
Development	
Development systems	Complete systems for software development and hardware/ software integration
Single-board computer modules	Processing units, memory modules, and other complete hardware subsystems

design of interfaces, and special devices to improve the performance of a computer system. The software support for the MC68000 family consists of operating systems, development programs, and other programs collectively termed *system software* as well as certain applications programs. For those users developing applications software, a number of development systems are available to facilitate software production. In addition to allowing the creation and testing of software, a few development systems aid the integration of the applications software with the prototype hardware of a system developed by the user. This capability is vital if the final product is a complete system, as was the case with many of the examples presented in Section 1.1.

1.2.1 The MC68000 Processor and Related Chips

A processing unit of a microcomputer consists of the CPU and a number of auxiliary integrated circuits (chips) for interfacing but does not include the memory chips. The chips are connected together on a circuit board which typically resembles the Motorola Design Module shown in Section 1.1. Overall capability and the speed of operation of the system is basically determined by the characteristics of the CPU when input or output (I/O) transfers of data are not required during execution of a program. When I/O transfers are required, the flexibility of the system to communicate with various peripheral devices depends on the type of interfacing chips provided with the system.

To allow the greatest range of applications, Motorola and other suppliers produce a number of different central processing units and interfacing chips. As the family of chips evolves, enhanced processors and additional interfacing chips will become available.

Beyond the MC68000. Processor manufacturers respond to increasing needs of product manufacturers and to technological advances by enhancing the design of a microprocessor such as the MC68000 and producing new versions. Later versions, such as the MC68010, are distinguished from the basic MC68000 by their numerical designation. These processors are normally compatible with the MC68000 in many ways but offer different features. For example, members of the MC68000 processor family are available with different physical packaging, different operating temperature ranges, and with various speeds of operation. Otherwise, their instruction set and their electrical characteristics are identical to those of the MC68000. Other processors in the family may show more significant differences, as is the case with several advanced versions of the MC68000. The evolution of the family by year of introduction of each processor is shown in Figure 1.8. Table 1.3 describes the characteristics of the various versions.

The range of operational speed available in the MC68000 family is evident in the Motorola processors designated as MC68000L4, MC68000L6, MC68000L8, MC68000L10, and MC68000L12. The last numeric designation indicates the number

GENEALOGY OF THE M68000 PROCESSOR FAMILY

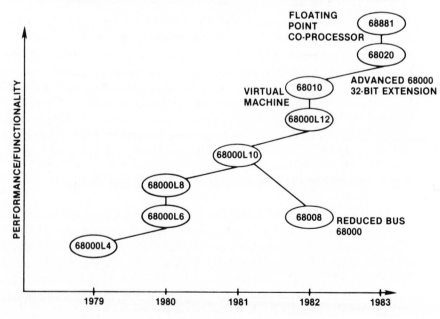

Figure 1.8 Motorola processors. (Courtesy of Motorola, Inc.)

TABLE 1.3 M68000 FAMILY OF PROCESSORS

Processor*	Characteristics or use
MC68000L4, MC68000L6, MC68000L8, MC68000L10, MC68000L12	Different speeds of operation indicated by the suffix
MC68010	Capability to support virtual memory
MC68020	32-bit data bus
MK68200 (Mostek)	Microcomputer version based on the MC68000 with on-chip memory
MC68008	8-bit data bus

*Note: Processors are manufactured by Motorola unless otherwise specified.

of operations per second in millions (the L12 represents 12.5 million operations per second). For example, the L12 device will execute the same program 1.25 (12.5/10) times as fast as the L10, 1.56 (12.5/8) times as fast the L8, and so on. In a given product, the replacement of the CPU by a faster (or slower) processor will change the performance proportionally if the speed of operation is determined by the processor alone.

The Motorola MC68010 and the MC68020 processors represent enhanced versions of the MC68000. The MC68010 is intended to be used in applications requiring virtual memory so that programs may be written which are independent of the physical memory system of the microcomputer. The MC68020 has a 32-bit data bus which classifies it as a 32-bit microprocessor, whereas the MC68000 has a 16-bit data bus. In other respects, the enhanced processors are practically identical to the MC68000. The floating-point co-processor in Figure 1.8 is used with the MC68020 to increase the capability of a system used for scientific or engineering applications.

Motorola has also introduced the MC68008, which is an 8-bit data bus version of the MC68000. This processor retains most of the characteristics of the original MC68000 but is designed for applications employing 8-bit data transfers. This reduction in the number of data signal lines reduces the cost of a system or product and simplifies the interface to certain peripheral units. An important advantage over earlier 8-bit processors in such an application is that the MC68008 executes programs written for the MC68000.

The Mostek MK68200 listed in Table 1.3 is a microcomputer version of a processor based on the MC68000 design. The processor chip contains memory storage as well as the CPU. The instruction set of the MK68200 differs from that of the MC68000, and hence programs written for the MC68000 cannot be executed by the MK68200 microcomputer. Mostek spokesmen claim, however, that programmers familiar with the MC68000 instruction set can readily learn to program the MK68200.

The MC68000 family of processors provides a choice for a system designer in that the designer can select the CPU that best fits the requirements of an application.

TABLE 1.4   INTERFACING DEVICES FOR THE MC68000
FAMILY

Interface chips	Use	Manufacturer
Intelligent Peripheral Controller	General-purpose interface device (MC68120)	Motorola
DMA Controller	Direct memory access (MC68450)	Motorola
Memory Management Unit	Memory protection and segmentation (MC68451)	Motorola
Disk Controller	Bulk storage control (SC68454)	Signetics
Network Controller	Communications controller for networks (MK68590)	Mostek

Motorola and other manufacturers also produce a variety of interfacing chips which simplify the interfacing task of computer system development. The purpose of these chips is to minimize the need for specialized hardware design.

Interface chips for the MC68000 family.   A sampling of the numerous types of interfacing chips for the MC68000 family is listed in Table 1.4. The first item listed is referred to by Motorola as an Intelligent Peripheral Controller (MC68120) and serves as the interface between the MC68000 CPU and a wide range of peripheral units. This chip is programmable to provide a flexible input and output capability under the control of the CPU. The others listed in Table 1.4 are also programmable, with each chip responding to coded instructions according to its design and purpose.

1.2.2 Software Support for the MC68000 Family

After the hardware of a computer system is constructed, programs must be developed to control the overall operation of the system. The various programs that are executed by the microcomputer are referred to, generically, as software to distinguish them from the physical equipment (hardware) of the system. For our purposes, it is convenient to discuss three categories or "levels" of software, as shown in Table 1.5.

At the level closest to the hardware, the *operating system* manages the hardware resources of the system. The operating system is frequently called the *executive* or *supervisor program.* At the next level lies the *development software* used by the programmer to create and debug applications programs. The *applications software* is written to tailor the computer system to solve a specific task. In the MC68000 family, an exten-

TABLE 1.5 SOFTWARE LEVELS

Level	Examples
Applications software	Programs tailored to solve a specific problem
Development software	Editor, assembler, or compiler to create applications programs
Operating system	Program to control CPU, input/output, and disk storage (files)
Hardware level	CPU, interfacing chips, memory, and peripheral devices

sive list of software products is available from both Motorola and from independent software suppliers. The discussion in this subsection is restricted to operating systems and development software provided by Motorola as defined in Table 1.6.

Motorola operating systems.   The VERSAdos Operating System is supplied by Motorola with the EXORmacs computer system pictured in Section 1.1. It is a multiuser operating system with extensive file management capability for the storage of programs and data files on disk units. It is considered to be a general-purpose operating system since it supports program development and can also be used as the operating system for applications employing the EXORmacs computer.

For a specific application, the RMS68K Real-Time Operating System is available to enable the computer to respond quickly to external events, as required by a

TABLE 1.6 SYSTEM SOFTWARE FROM MOTOROLA

System software	Use
Operating systems	
VERSAdos	General-purpose operating system
RMS68K	Real-time executive
Development software	
Text editor	Create and edit programs
Assembler and debug program	Translate and debug assembly language programs
FORTRAN, Pascal compilers	Compile high-level language programs
Linkage editor	Link separate machine language programs
Cross-software	
Cross-assembler	Create MC68000 machine language programs on another computer
Simulator	Simulate execution of cross-assembled programs

process-control application. RMS68K is intended primarily to support execution of the application programs required in a real-time situation.

Development software.
Under the control of the operating system, various programs to aid software development can be executed on a general-purpose computer system. Motorola software for development, as listed in Table 1.6, includes a text editor, language translators, and various utility programs. The text editor is used to create and edit the program under development before it is translated into machine language statements by the appropriate language translators. An assembler and several high-level language compilers can be purchased from Motorola to allow a selection of computer languages.

Several special-purpose programs, often called utility programs, supplement the development software for the MC68000 family. A debug program is a useful tool for isolating programming errors (bugs) by allowing execution of a small portion of a program and testing the effects. The linkage editor serves to combine program modules that have been assembled (or compiled) separately so that a complete program ready for execution by the MC68000 is created.

During program development, the operating system is used to control program execution as well as input and output operations such as printing the program text or the results after execution. The file management capability allows programs under development to be stored (or loaded into memory for execution) using the disk storage unit of the computer. These features of the operating system are required by the development software and may also be used by the applications programs if needed. In the latter case, the applications programs are intended to be executed with a particular operating system.

Cross-software for development.
In the previous discussion, it was assumed that the applications programs were developed and targeted for execution on the same MC68000-based system. An alternative approach allows applications programs to be created on another computer and translated into executable (machine language) programs for the MC68000. This technique, called *cross-development,* is possible for assembly language programs using the Motorola Cross-Assembler listed in Table 1.6. Several versions of the Cross-Assembler, including versions for the Digital Equipment Corporation PDP-11 minicomputers and the IBM 370 series of large computers, are available.

To execute the cross-assembled program, the machine language instructions can be processed by either a *simulator* program or an MC68000-based computer system. With a simulator, the operation of the MC68000 is simulated on the cross-development computer. This approach is useful when the MC68000 system hardware is not available but the programs must be tested. In effect, the simulator provides a software model of the MC68000 processor. However, hardware dependent aspects such as timing must be tested on the target MC68000-based computer. This is accomplished by transferring the cross-assembled program from the development system to the memory of the target system.

1.2.3 Development Systems

The MC68000 family elements described in the preceding two subsections can be combined with appropriate peripheral devices to create a computer system that is suitable for a software development system. The EXORmacs system, shown in Figure 1.7, is such a system. It includes disk units and a printer and can be used by up to eight users. Once applications programs are designed, they can be created, debugged, and tested on the development system. If the completed programs are to be executed on the development system itself, the testing assures that the entire system meets the requirements of the application. For example, with the proper applications software, the EXORmacs might serve as a business system with the capability to do inventory control, job scheduling, and other required tasks.

When hardware design and development is required for an application, the development effort must include integration of the application software with the hardware of the target computer. The target computer is usually a different computer than the one chosen for the application development system. Integration consists of extensive testing of the software components that control the hardware created for the target system. In typical applications, such hardware may consist of special-purpose interfaces. This hardware includes interfacing circuitry that is not available as part of the Motorola family of interfacing chips. When using the family devices, an operating

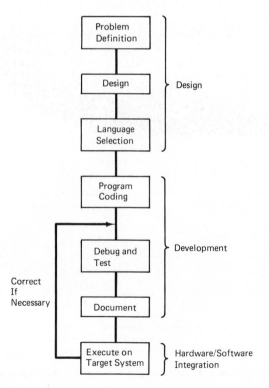

Figure 1.9   Software production.

Figure 1.10   Development system for hardware/software integration. (Courtesy of Motorola, Inc.)

system for the target computer which includes programs to control the hardware can be chosen so that a minimum amount of development and testing is needed. If no operating system is to be included with the target system, development of interfacing programs for the family chips must be created or purchased and integrated into the target system. This is frequently the case when the target is a product such as a laboratory instrument that performs computer processing.

The software production cycle for the development of programs that require hardware/software integration is shown in simplified form in Figure 1.9. If the programs execute correctly on the development system, as far as they can be tested on it,

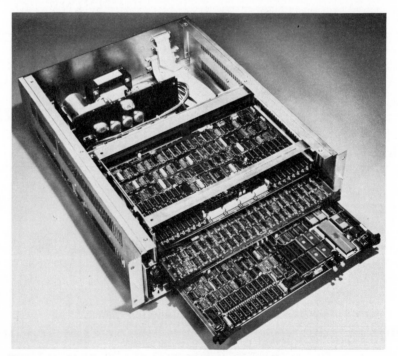

Figure 1.11   Modular construction of a computer system. (Courtesy of Motorola, Inc.)

TABLE 1.7 BOARD-LEVEL PRODUCTS FROM MOTOROLA

Module line	Typical modules
VERSAmodules	Single-board microcomputer, memory modules, floppy disk controller
VMEmodules	Single-board computer, memory modules, magnetic tape drive controller

Note: The module line is far more extensive; only a few modules are listed as typical.

they are then transferred to the target computer for further testing with the actual hardware of the final product. Errors are corrected until the product performs as required.

Figure 1.10 shows a development station which includes the connection between a single-board computer (target computer) and the development system. For hardware/software integration, program execution on the target system is controlled with the development system via appropriate commands entered by the user. These commands allow debugging of the entire target system, much as the debug program discussed previously allows debugging of programs executed on the development system itself. For example, single instructions or a small portion of the program can be executed on the target system. Then information for debugging purposes can be displayed for the user.

1.2.4 Board-Level Computer Modules

The "chips" discussed in Section 1.2.1 form the basic elements, together with other necessary circuits, for the hardware implementation of a computer system. The CPU, interfacing chips, and memory chips are electrically connected on one or more circuit boards to create the hardware of the processing system and memory storage. A manufacturer of a product or a computer system with adequate engineering and manufacturing facilities can design, test, and manufacture the complete boards if necessary, purchasing only the necessary chips from a supplier such as Motorola. However, a preferred approach in many cases is to purchase board-level modules from Motorola or other sources.[1] The manufacturer then only has to assemble the product using the modules that suit the application.

Figure 1.11 shows a computer system assembled from board-level modules. Such a system will typically contain a single-board computer as the processing unit, together with modules containing memory and perhaps other modules to control pe-

[1]Motorola claims that the board-level approach to product development is preferable to custom board design if fewer than 500 units are being produced.

ripheral devices. Two module lines that provide the circuit boards to construct a product based on the MC68000 CPU are listed in Table 1.7. Details of how the chips on each board are connected and how the modules themselves are connected together are presented in Chapter 2, where bus structures for computer systems are discussed.

FURTHER READING

The applications for the MC68000 in this chapter represent but a sampling of the many products that use the processor. New products based on the MC68000 are announced monthly in many electronics and computer journals, such as *Byte, Electronic Design, EDN, Mini-Micro Systems, IEEE Computer,* and others.

MC68000-family products from Motorola are described in a number of publications from that company. In particular, new product announcements appear in *Motorola Semiconductor Data Update* and *Motorola System News,* listed below. These periodic publications are available by subscription from Motorola. The *Motorola Microprocessor Software Catalog* is a catalog of software products for the MC68000 family, including operating systems, development software, and applications programs from independent suppliers as well as from Motorola.

The article by Monahan discusses the Hewlett-Packard Model 36 (HP9836A) desktop computer. An important feature of the article is the analysis of the MC68000 used by Hewlett-Packard designers to choose the processor.

A complete discussion of software and hardware development is given in the textbook edited by Tseng. The EXORmacs system is presented as an example of a development system.

MONAHAN, JOHN, "Tight Squeeze—The HP Series 200 Model 16," *Byte,* **8**, No. 6 (June 1983), 110–125.

Motorola Microprocessor Software Catalog. Motorola Inc., Phoenix, Ariz.

Motorola Semiconductor Data Update. Motorola Inc., Phoenix, Ariz.

Motorola System News. Motorola Inc., Phoenix, Ariz.

TSENG, VINCENT, ed., *Microprocessor Development and Development Systems.* New York: McGraw-Hill, 1982.

2

Microcomputer and Microprocessor Characteristics

Microcomputer systems operate on sequences of binary digits (bits) which represent either coded machine instructions to be executed by the CPU or a data value to be transferred, transformed, or otherwise manipulated. The ease and speed with which the CPU and other elements of the system treat the binary sequences determine the basic characteristics of the computer system. Is it fast? Can it handle large numbers of data values as well as large programs? Is it cost effective for a particular application? These questions and similar ones can be answered at least in part by examining the structure of the system and the capability of the CPU.

The microcomputer system can be characterized in terms of its CPU, memory elements, and I/O circuits, all of which are connected electrically by a system bus. When the microcomputer is considered functionally without regard to the precise physical structure, the system may be described in terms of its *organization*. This organizational view focuses on the major elements of the system, such as the CPU and memory, and their interconnections. The system designer or assembly language programmer is concerned with the system at this level. At the hardware level, the layout of the Design Module discussed in Chapter 1 is typical of the physical arrangement of the components on a single circuit board. In contrast to the organizational view, more detailed descriptions of the hardware are needed by the interface designer, who must know precise electrical and mechanical details about the system components. This chapter concentrates on the organization of typical microcomputer systems.

Two important characteristics of the CPU, which are useful in determining its capabilities, are its *word length* for data and its *addressing range*. The word length refers to the number of bits in a data item that may be transferred at one time (in parallel) between the CPU and other elements of the system. The addressing range defines the number of memory locations addressable by the CPU. The Motorola MC68000, for example, has a word length of 16 bits and an addressing range of over 16 million memory locations.

This chapter defines the most common microcomputer organizations and describes the major elements of a microcomputer system. The differences between typical 8-bit, 16-bit, and 32-bit processors are then illustrated by describing their word lengths and addressing ranges. These descriptions pertain to systems used to perform basic computer functions such as instruction execution and input/output operations. The information in these first two sections is presented to acquaint the reader with a microprocessor in its role as CPU. Emphasis is on the interaction between the various components of the computer.

The final section in this chapter presents three views of the microcomputer and introduces the characteristics of the MC68000 and similar microprocessors. These views are those of the system designer, the assembly language programmer, and the interface designer. The MC68000 was developed to satisfy three needs: as a CPU in a computer system, as a programmable processor, and as a hardware chip.

2.1 MICROCOMPUTER ORGANIZATION AND BUS STRUCTURE

The elements of a simple microcomputer are shown in Figure 2.1. This block diagram shows the microprocessor (CPU), a memory unit, and I/O circuitry. The CPU communicates with other elements of the system via parallel signal lines which, taken together, constitute the internal system bus.[1] In Figure 2.1, the bus is shown separated functionally into *address* signal lines, *data* signal lines, and *control* signal lines. These signal lines serve to connect the CPU electrically to circuits for the purpose of transferring data into and out of the microcomputer as well as to connect a memory unit holding instructions and data for the processor.

The system may be constructed in a number of ways using components of the microprocessor family described in Chapter 1. At the most elementary level, individual integrated circuit chips for the CPU, memory elements, and I/O circuits can be combined by a hardware designer using knowledge of the electrical characteristics of each element. A higher-level approach, representing board-level design, is implemented by combining a single-board computer with various other circuit boards which con-

---

[1] Parallel signal lines indicate that each signal line may be used simultaneously with the others and independently to transfer electrical signals representing information. These 16 data signal lines would allow the simultaneous transfer of 16 bits. In contrast, a serial data line would require 16 transfers of one bit at a time to accomplish the same thing.

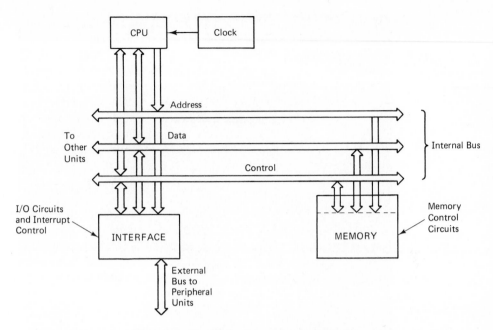

Figure 2.1   Simplified microcomputer organization.

tain memory subsystems and I/O subsystems. Construction of microcomputers from modules such as the Motorola VERSAmodules follow this board-level design approach. A module of the sort used in this type of design is shown in Figure 2.2. The internal bus connector and connectors for I/O transfer are at the bottom of this single-board or "monoboard" computer.

Figure 2.3 illustrates a possible structure for a board-level system. The modules "plug in" to connectors in a chassis containing the bus structure and a power supply. Additional modules, such as an arithmetic unit for scientific applications or I/O modules for special purposes, can be added to enlarge the system. The organization is defined by the system designer, who specifies the memory and the I/O capability necessary to meet the needs of a given application.

The completed hardware system could serve as the basis for a variety of products, from an automatic welding machine to a general-purpose computer. Software would be developed to meet specific requirements. A portion of the software in machine language might be stored in a read-only memory, so it cannot be altered after the system is complete. Such code is sometimes called *firmware,* as indicated in Figure 2.3. In later chapters, some differences between software design for read/write memories and read-only memories are explored.

In a board-level system, interfaces to special peripheral units may be required. Since the manufacturer of the other modules may not supply the unique interface

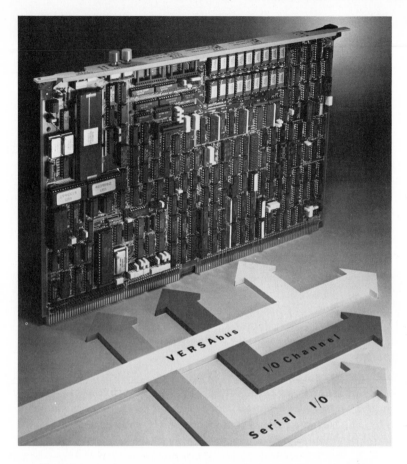

Figure 2.2   A microcomputer plug-in module. (Courtesy of Motorola, Inc.)

needed, a custom interface may be developed by an interface designer. The integration of the hardware and the software routines for these special interfaces is a vital part of the system development.

2.1.1 The Central Processing Unit and Clock

The CPU controls and coordinates all activities in the microcomputer. It executes machine language instructions, fetched from the memory unit, and performs all the arithmetic, logical, or other operations required by the instructions. The CPU can *read* data values (operands) from memory or *write* values into memory by sending the appropriate electrical signals (commands) via the internal bus. The CPU can also initiate

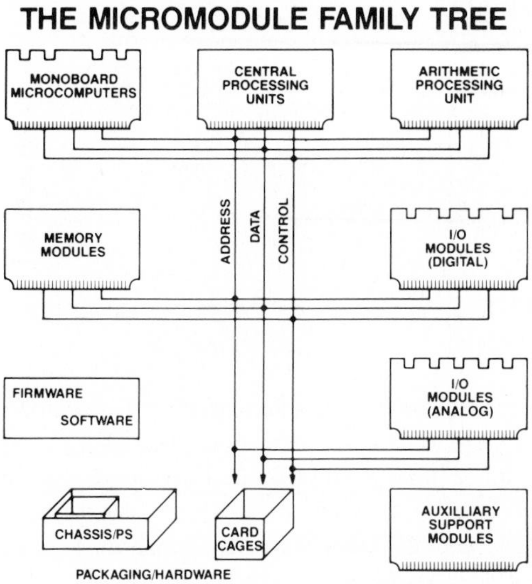

THE MICROMODULE FAMILY TREE

Figure 2.3 Board-level implementation of a microcomputer. (Courtesy of Motorola, Inc.)

an I/O operation to transfer data to or from peripheral devices. The external bus shown in Figure 2.1 connects the system to one or more peripheral units and allows the CPU to perform such I/O operations.

The occurrence of events is precisely coordinated by the system clock. The clock "ticks" to indicate the passage of a time interval, perhaps as short as one millionth of a second. In each interval, the CPU or one of the other components of the system performs a precise function, such as presenting a data value on the data signal lines. The rate at which the clock runs (number of ticks per second) determines the fundamental speed of operation of the system. Doubling the clock rate should double the operational speed of the system unless other factors, such as memory response time, limit the speed. The maximum clock rate for the system is determined by the CPU. Versions of the MC68000 are available with different maximum clock rates, as discussed in Chapter 1. A more precise definition of the system clock for MC68000 systems is given in Chapter 12.

2.1.2 The Memory Unit

In the single-memory system shown in Figure 2.1, the memory unit holds both instructions and data to be used by the CPU. Each memory cell in the memory unit contains one bit and the memory cells are organized as shown in Figure 2.4. Each memory location containing m bits is referenced by a positive number, its *address,* which indicates the position of that location in memory. The CPU can reference an individual memory location via the address signal lines and can control the operation

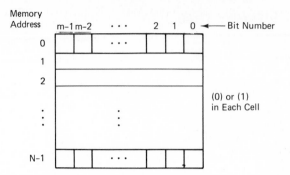

Figure 2.4   Memory organization for an *m*-bit memory.

of the memory with selected control lines. The memory itself is organized into information units, each known as a *word*. The word sizes range from 8 bits, called a *byte* in microcomputers, to 64 bits or more in large computers. For convenience in comparing the information storage capabilities of different memories, a word is usually divided into a number of bytes. The MC68000 memory word, for example, is 16 bits or two bytes, as shown in Figure 2.5. The MC68000 is a *byte-addressable* CPU since it can address either one of the two bytes (bits 0–7 or bits 8–15) of a memory word. It can also address word locations, consisting of two bytes, beginning at even addresses in memory.

The *contents* of any memory location can be obtained from memory on the data signal lines (CPU read) or the value on the data signal lines can be stored into the addressed location (CPU write). Actual operation of the memory unit is directed by memory control circuits not shown in Figures 2.4 and 2.5. The memory length, given as N locations in Figure 2.4, is typically a power of 2, such as 1024 or 4096. In general, the number of locations is $2^k = N$, where k is an integer. The MC68000 uses 24 bits to represent an address. Thus the MC68000 can address 2^{24} different memory locations, each containing a byte of information. Its word address capability is therefore 2^{23} 16-

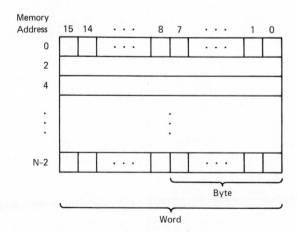

Figure 2.5   Organization of memory in an MC68000 system.

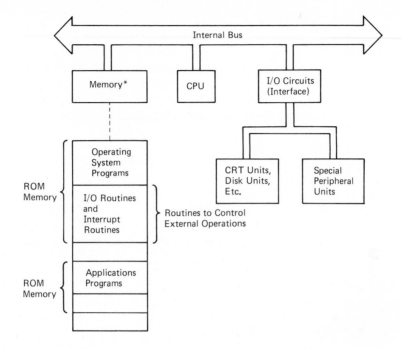

*Memory Areas not designated ROM are Read/Write areas.

Figure 2.6   Hardware and software organization for a microcomputer-based product.

bit words. Memory length is often given as a multiple of 1024 locations, which is termed 1K of memory.

The number of bits that can be transferred at the same time (in parallel) is determined by the number of data signal lines connecting the memory and the CPU. A typical 8-bit microcomputer has eight data lines and the memory is organized in bytes. The MC68000 has a 16-bit-wide data path which allows either a byte transfer on eight lines or a two-byte transfer (16 bits) on the 16 signal lines.

A possible organization of the programs in memory for a typical microcomputer-based product is shown in Figure 2.6. The operating system and the applications programs are assumed to be stored in a ROM for this example. The read/write memory holds values that are likely to be changed during the course of operation of the product. An alternative approach used in most general-purpose systems is to store the bulk of the programs on an external disk unit and load the memory with appropriate programs as needed. The operating system controls the use of the disk in this case.

Notice that the operating system and its routines to handle I/O and interrupts is separated from the applications programs and their read/write memory area. If an application program requires data transfer to external units, the transfer is typically controlled by the operating system to ensure orderly operation of the system.

2.1.3 Input/Output

The I/O circuitry shown in Figure 2.6 is controlled by the CPU to allow transfers of data between the internal bus and an external bus connecting peripheral devices to the system. Such interfacing circuitry is designed to meet the needs of the peripheral device. Also, the operation of the external bus is generally independent of the CPU operation in terms of speed and data path width. A CRT terminal, for example, normally requires data bits to be transferred in a serial manner at a rate that is very slow compared to the rate at which data values can be transferred in parallel on the internal system bus. The major function of the I/O circuitry in this case is to resolve this mismatch in speed and format. The interrupt control lines (not shown) from the interface circuitry notify the processor when the device is ready.

Peripheral devices of the microcomputer shown are addressed by the CPU in the same manner as the memory is addressed since the memory unit and I/O unit are effectively in parallel. Systems designed in this manner are said to have *memory-mapped I/O* because the CPU accesses memory and I/O circuits based on these addresses only. This scheme is discussed further in Chapter 12, which deals with the input/output capability of the MC68000.

2.1.4 The Internal Bus

The microcomputers discussed in this section are said to have a *single-bus* architecture since memory units and I/O units share the same bus with the CPU. This concept was introduced by Digital Equipment Corporation in their PDP-11 family of minicomputers and is used extensively in microcomputer systems. The number of signal lines devoted to addresses and data and control signals essentially determines the capability of the single-bus system, since all transfers of data or instructions occur over these signal paths. Each signal line can assume two states, and n lines taken in parallel represent 2^n states in an n-bit word. The MC68000 actually has 64 signal lines to accommodate addresses and data and control signals in addition to several other functions.

EXERCISES

2.1.1. Compare board-level with chip-level design of a microprocessor-based product. Include technical and financial considerations. Reference to manufacturers' literature to answer the question is encouraged.

2.1.2. The MC68000L4 (4 MHz) can execute an instruction to clear a register in 1.5 microseconds. How fast can the same instruction be executed by the
 (a) MC68000L8 (8 MHz)?
 (b) MC68000L10 (10 MHz)?
 (c) MC68000L12 (12.5 MHz)?

2.1.3. Semiconductor read/write memory is called *random access memory* (RAM). A typical chip might contain an array of 16K X 1 bits. A memory is composed of RAM chips by arranging n chips in parallel to form an *n*-bit memory. Show the physical layout and addressing for a 64K x 8-bit memory composed of 16K x 1 RAM chips.

2.2 MICROPROCESSOR WORD LENGTH AND ADDRESSING RANGE

Processors such as the MC68000 are classified as 16-bit microprocessors because they have 16 data signal lines for data transfers. For currently available processors in this class, the number of addressing lines is between 16 and 32. The 24 address lines of the MC68000 allow the processor to address over 16 million byte-length memory locations. The capabilities and characteristics of microprocessors based on their word length and addressing range are discussed in this section.

2.2.1 Word Length

The number of bits that represent the length of the most commonly used data word is often used to define the *word length* of a microcomputer. Although other definitions can be applied, the *m-bit computer* is defined here as one whose main data paths external to the processor are parallel *m*-bit paths. Thus, as an integer number, the *m*-bit word transferred between the processor and other elements of the system, such as memory, can represent 2^m numbers in the decimal range 0 to $2^m - 1$. An 8-bit word length allows only 256 values in the range 0 to 255. The MC68000 data word of 16 bits allows 65,536 values. Internally, the MC68000 CPU can operate on data values 8, 16, or 32 bits in length.

The significance of the word length is revealed by examining the numerical range. Generally, the design, the intended purpose, and the efficiency of a processor can be surmised from the word length, at least for general-purpose processors. All the information transferred to and from the processor, including the binary-coded instruction patterns, are multiples of the *m*-bit data word in length. Since these *m*-bit quantities allow 2^m different combinations to be assigned to the bit pattern, there is a possibility of 2^m instructions, data values, or other entities encoded in some desirable way. In itself, the *m*-bit length is not a great limitation. By proper programming, a quantity can be represented as two or more *m*-bit values combined to form multiple-word-length entities. An 8-bit processor can generally operate on 8-bit, 16-bit, or 32-bit quantities treated 8 bits at a time. The penalty for multiple-word operations is a loss of operating speed compared to operations using only 8-bit quantities. A 16-bit processor can obviously transfer 16-bit quantities at least twice as fast as an 8-bit unit using two transfer cycles, all other things being equal. In the microprocessor arena, word lengths of 4, 8, 16, and 32 bits serve to classify the majority of processors. The MC68008 described in Chapter 1 is more difficult to classify in this scheme since it has eight data lines but otherwise performs as the MC68000 does.

2.2.2 Addressing Range

Another characteristic of a microprocessor which determines its capability is the *addressing range* of the processor. Each instruction and data value transferred via the data lines of a processor is located by an address that designates the exact position of the item in memory. The addressing range determines the size of the largest program or the maximum number of data values the processor may address. If the signal paths for an address are parallel k-bit paths, the processor can address 2^k separate locations.

As stated previously, the MC68000 can address 2^{24} byte locations. Except for 32-bit microprocessors, the address length of k bits is longer than the data word length of m bits for most processors. For example, the MC68000 has $k = 24$ and $m = 16$. A 32-bit address, as in the MC68020, is considered sufficient for almost all applications since the CPU could address over 4.2 *billion* locations. Many 8-bit processors employ a 16-bit address length allowing 2^{16} or 65,536 locations to be referenced, with each location considered to contain an 8-bit value representing a data value, an instruction, or another item. Today this addressing range is considered inadequate or at least inconvenient for many of the applications to be satisfied with 16-bit microprocessors.

Table 2.1 lists characteristics of typical microcomputers with 8-bit, 16-bit, and 32-bit word lengths. The decimal range of a number for the given data word length is shown in the first row. Then follows the number of address signal lines and the memory length as indicated. Memory length is often given as a multiple of 1024 (2^{10}) locations, which is termed 1K of memory. Thus 16 address lines would allow 65,536 locations, or 64K of memory.

Example 2.1

As an illustration of the use of the internal system bus, assume that a processor with 16 address lines and 16 data lines is to execute an instruction. The instruction is 32 bits long. It is stored in two 16-bit words at locations 10 and 12 of memory as shown in Table 2.2. The hypothetical instruction written in mnemonic form is CLR 100. This instruction sets the contents of memory location 100 to zero, which is represented as a 16-bit string of {0}'s in location 100. The first 16-bit word of the instruction contains the operation and

TABLE 2.1 CHARACTERISTICS OF TYPICAL MICROCOMPUTERS

Characteristic	8-bit family	16-bit family	32-bit family
Decimal range of data	0 to 255	0 to 65,535	0 to 4,294,967,295
Number of address lines	14 to 16	16 to 24	32
Typical memory length (1K = 1024 bytes)	16K to 64K	64K to over 16 million (16,384K)	Any size up to 4,194,304K

Note: The 16-bit family includes the MC68000 and similar processors.

TABLE 2.2 MEMORY CONTENTS
FOR CLR 100 INSTRUCTION

Memory address (decimal)	Memory contents (binary)
10	0100 0010 0111 1000
12	0000 0000 0110 0100
14	(Next instruction)
.	.
.	.
.	.

Note: The even locations contain one 16-bit word which is considered as two 8-bit byte locations.

indicates that the address of the location involved follows in the next word. The address 100 is stored in binary at location 12.

Figure 2.7 shows the state of the signal lines with increasing time as the processor executes the instruction. The instruction fetch requires two read cycles by the CPU to determine the operation and the location to be cleared. For each read operation, the memory responds by presenting the contents of the addressed location on the data lines. There is a slight delay while the data signal lines change to the new value. The CPU then decodes the CLR instruction and executes it by writing zeros into location 100 of memory, via the data signal lines, after the control signal to write is given. The next instruction is then fetched and executed.

The 16-bit memory locations are given even addresses in this example rather than consecutive values because processors such as the MC68000 can address 8-bit operands in memory. Thus word location 10 contains two bytes at locations 10 and 11. Each instruction consists of one or more 16-bit words.

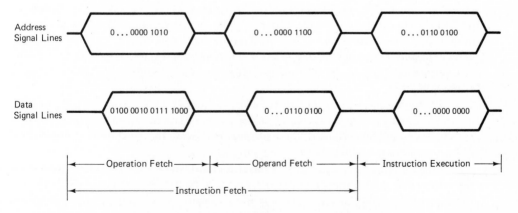

Figure 2.7 Signal line states with increasing time.

The timing sequence of Figure 2.7 is typical for a processor executing a simple instruction such as CLR. Although the functional operation is similar to that shown, the execution of this instruction by the MC68000 would in fact be more complicated. This is discussed briefly in Chapter 4, where the instruction prefetch characteristic of the MC68000 is considered. Actually, the MC68000 CPU would first read the contents of location 100 before zeros are written there when the clear (CLR) instruction is executed. However, the preceding description of the operation is adequate for our present purpose.

EXERCISES

2.2.1. The MC68000 can address byte (8 bits), word (16 bits), or longword (32 bits) operands. For each operand length, draw a diagram showing the organization of an eight-byte buffer in memory starting at location 1000. Label the bit positions and addresses. A buffer is an area of memory that holds data temporarily during I/O transfers.

2.2.2. How many bits (address lines) are necessary to address a memory with
   (a) 4096 locations?
   (b) 65,536 locations?
   (c) 16,777,216 locations?

2.2.3. What is the largest program (in bytes) for a microprocessor with
   (a) 16 addressing lines?
   (b) 20 addressing lines?
   (c) 24 addressing lines?

2.2.4. The MC68000 has 24 addressing lines and can address each 8-bit byte in memory. How many addressing lines would be needed if the MC68000 could address only 16-bit words?

2.3 THREE VIEWS OF THE MICROPROCESSOR

Modern microprocessors such as the MC68000 are incorporated into computer systems to control the overall operation of the system. These processors are capable of directing system activity by executing programs and performing the necessary input/output functions. Furthermore, the modern processors separate the processing into *supervisor* and *user* states or modes, allow memory management and protection, and detect various types of errors. These capabilities are not common for earlier processors of the 8-bit class.

Programming features of the 16-bit processors include a general and powerful instruction set as well as a number of different ways to reference an operand in memory (addressing modes). Many of these processors provide the capability to support special programming techniques and debugging aids.

Interaction of the processor and the other hardware elements of the system is via the system bus, where transfers of control signals, addresses, and data occur. The capability and flexibility of the processors in this regard is determined by the functions of the signal lines from the processor. For example, sophisticated I/O and interrupt

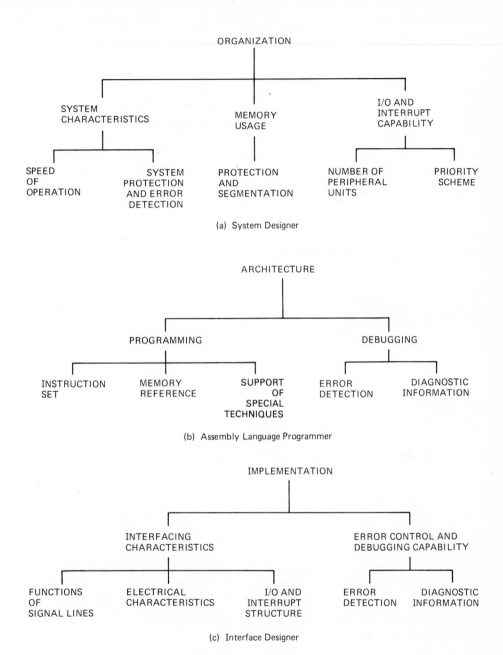

(a) System Designer

(b) Assembly Language Programmer

(c) Interface Designer

Figure 2.8   Three views of the processor.

capabilities alleviate the need to provide a great deal of special hardware in a complex system.[2] Most 16-bit processors provide the state of the processor and other relevant information to external circuits as the processor operates, a feature that simplifies the hardware design.

The features of 16-bit processors that help meet system, programming, and interfacing requirements of complex systems are presented briefly in this section. Although the material is somewhat general, it forms the basis for understanding many of the characteristics of the MC68000 family. Figure 2.8 summarizes three different views of a microprocessor. The system designer, assembly language programmer, and the interface designer each focus on different aspects of the processor, so these views may coincide or even conflict in some instances. Obviously, the assembly language programmer and the interface designer have the same goals in debugging a prototype system, but their approach to producing a correct product may differ considerably.

2.3.1 System Design

The system designer is concerned with the overall operation of the system, including its performance and reliability. The designer also determines the memory usage and how the memory areas occupied by the operating system will be protected if read/ write memory is used. This protection is vital if the system is used for developing software, in which addressing errors and runaway programs may exist. When many peripheral units are attached to the system, the design of the I/O portion of the system is critical to assure proper coordination between programs and hardware during data transfers. Table 2.3 summarizes the aspects of system design covered in this section.

System characteristics.   One important criterion used to measure the performance of a microcomputer is its speed of operation while executing a given program. A key element, although not the only one, in determining the speed of operation is the maximum rate at which the CPU executes instructions. As discussed in Section 1.2, the MC68000 is produced in versions providing a wide selection of operational speeds. The MC68000L12, for example, can execute 12.5 million processor cycles per second, whereas the MC68000L8 executes only 8 million. These relative speeds are useful in comparing the performance of different systems based on different versions of the processor.

To prevent errors in applications programs from affecting the overall operation of the system (or each other), the MC68000 provides two modes of processor execution: the *supervisor* mode and the *user* mode. Programs executing in the supervisor mode have full control of the processor and system functions. As expected, the operat-

---

[2]In our discussions, an interrupt is taken to be a signal originating external to the microcomputer which causes a transfer of control from an executing program to a special program designed to perform the processing required in response to the interrupt. After completion of the interrupt processing, control returns to the program that was interrupted.

TABLE 2.3 SYSTEM CONSIDERATIONS

Characteristic	Purpose
System	
Speed of operation	One measure of system performance
System protection (supervisor versus user modes)	To prevent user programs from interfering with the operating system
Error detection	To detect and isolate various errors through traps and interrupts
Memory usage and protection	
Separation of programs and restricted access to certain memory areas	To prevent user programs from interfering with memory allocated to the operating system or other user programs
I/O and interrupt capability	
Number of peripheral units allowed and interrupt priority	To determine the I/O capability of the system, (e.g., number of devices and response times for data transfer)

ing system executes in the supervisor mode. This includes all of its routines to handle I/O and interrupts.[3] Typically, applications programs execute in the user mode. In this mode certain processor instructions and perhaps certain memory areas are inaccessible to the applications program. The selection of the mode for various programs is determined by the system designer and the transitions between the two modes are carefully controlled.

Figure 2.9 shows an example of system operation versus time in which control is passed to a user program and returned to the operating system. The return to the su-

---

[3]A routine is usually a short program segment intended to accomplish one specific operation (e.g., transferring a data value or similar operation).

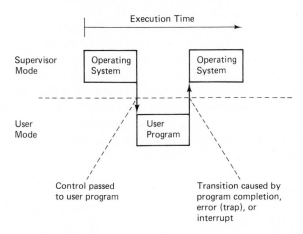

Figure 2.9 Processor states.

pervisor mode may be caused by program completion, an error detected by the CPU, or an interrupt.

Processors such as the MC68000 allow certain errors occurring during program execution in either mode to be detected and *trapped*. The trap mechanism passes control of the processor from the program causing the trap to a routine of the system software that processes the error. The execution of an illegal instruction is an example of an operation that causes a trap.[4] In the MC68000, an attempt to divide by zero in an arithmetic operation will also cause a trap.

Certain hardware errors can be detected by using the interrupt mechanism.[5] The system could be designed to process an interrupt caused by power failure as an example. The interrupt routine would typically cause the CPU to save information which allows a program to be restarted where it was interrupted after power returns.

Interrupts may occur at any time, asynchronous with program execution. Traps, on the other hand, occur only as a result of execution of program instructions.

Memory usage and protection.   Since the MC68000 has the capability to address 2^{24} byte locations, very few systems are limited by a lack of memory space. In most systems, both the operating system and the applications programs can be held in memory without conflict. The system designer determines the allocation of memory by specifying the required number of locations for each program. Particularly in those systems used for program development or multiuser applications, a method must be available which prevents an executing program from accessing (reading from or writing into) any memory locations not assigned to that program. This protection is usually provided to the operating system's memory space to prevent access by programs executing in the user mode.

In MC68000-based systems, the memory can be protected in this way by memory management circuits such as the Memory Management Unit (MC6845l) discussed in Section 1.2. The MC68000 indicates the type of access as supervisor or user via three of its control signal lines. Simultaneously, memory management circuits compare the memory location being addressed to the valid range for the mode assigned to the program. A violation is indicated by an interrupt from the memory management circuitry to the CPU. Thus, if the CPU provides the mode and address for each memory access as the MC68000 does, the protection of memory areas is easily accomplished. None of the earlier microprocessors of the 8-bit class provided this feature.

The MC68010 processor and the Memory Management Unit can be combined to provide the hardware support for both memory protection and virtual memory. A virtual memory system has the advantage that a system with a relatively small physical memory space can be used with programs of any size, at least theoretically. Several

---

[4]An illegal instruction is a machine language instruction with a bit pattern not recognized by the CPU.

[5]The MC68000 also has several other means of detecting hardware errors, which are discussed in a later section of this chapter.

references in the Further Reading section for this chapter discuss virtual memory systems with the MC68010 and the MC68000.

I/O and interrupt capability.   The system designer will specify the number and type of peripheral devices necessary to satisfy the requirements of an application. Subsequent design of the I/O subsystem becomes complicated when many devices are attached because different units have different time requirements to complete data transfers. For example, a line printer is much slower in printing characters than a disk unit is in storing them. Due to these timing variations, the system is typically designed so that each device can issue an *interrupt request* via several of the control signal lines from the interface to the CPU. A request is issued when the device is ready to receive or transmit data or when an error condition is detected. From the point of view of an executing program, the interrupt causes a break in execution until the interrupt routine completes the data transfer or other processing. Such routines execute in the supervisor mode in an MC68000-based system.

The interrupt mechanism is a primary determinant of the I/O capability of a system when a number of peripheral devices are attached to the microcomputer. In processors such as the MC68000, multilevel interrupt circuitry is part of the CPU. Physically, this means that several (three for the MC68000) control lines are dedicated to interrupt requests from external devices. The eight (2^3) possible interrupt requests are arranged in priority so that a higher-priority interrupt will interrupt a routine executing due to a lower-level interrupt request. In theory, eight interrupt routines could be in various states of execution at the same time in an MC68000-based system.

At each interrupt level, a number of devices could be given the same priority. External circuitry is required, in this case, to resolve conflicts if two or more devices interrupt on the same level at the same time or if several interrupts are pending (waiting for the interrupt routine at this level to complete). The Motorola CPU is capable of handling up to 192 devices distributed according to the system requirements across its eight interrupt levels. However, such a configuration would require extensive hardware design to control the devices that could interrupt at the same CPU interrupt level.

2.3.2 Assembly Language Programming

The ease with which a program may be created, debugged, and tested to satisfy a specific application depends largely on the characteristics of the processor, rather than on the development software, if the program is written in assembly language. Editors, assemblers, and other development aids vary in quality and efficiency, but a good development system cannot make up for an inadequate processor. Processors of the MC68000 class are adequate for most applications due to their powerful instruction sets, numerous addressing modes, and other special features not typically found in earlier microprocessors. Table 2.4 summarizes several of the characteristics of a micro-

TABLE 2.4 PROGRAMMING CONSIDERATIONS

Characteristic	Purpose
Programming	
Instruction set	Determines efficiency and ease of programming
Addressing modes	Indicates the capability to allow creation of data structures in memory
Special instructions	Convenient for creation of modern sophisticated programs and systems
Debugging	
Error detection and diagnostic information	Useful to isolate certain errors and determine the cause

processor which are used to determine the capability of the processor in satisfying the programming requirements of sophisticated software.[6]

Programming.   The *instruction set* of a microprocessor is the collection of all the machine language instructions available to the programmer. Each instruction can be described by its operation or function and the number and type of operands it manipulates. For example, the binary addition instruction of the MC68000 adds two signed integers. The MC68000 also allows subtraction, multiplication, and division of two such integers. In addition, instructions to add and subtract decimal numbers are provided.[7] Thus the MC68000 has a fairly complete set of instructions to operate on numerical operands.

In contrast, earlier 8-bit microprocessors had a more restricted set of instructions for arithmetic operations. Divide and multiply instructions were not available, for example. Routines based on the operations of addition and subtraction were created to accomplish the tasks, such as performing multiplication by repeated addition. In most cases, the equivalent instructions of the 16-bit processors as compared to the 8-bit class are more powerful and efficient. This simplifies programming and increases the speed of execution of equivalent programs. One such example was given in Section 2.1 when data word length was discussed. The MC68000 can perform arithmetic operations on operands considered either 8 bits, 16 bits, or 32 bits in length. When 8-bit processors had equivalent instructions, the operand length was typically only 8 bits.

The number and type of instructions (including the allowed operands) are exam-

[6]The term *computer architecture* is sometimes used to refer to the complete set of characteristics of a computer system that are important to the programmer. A description of the architecture would include a definition of the overall organization of the system as well as a complete discussion of the programming characteristics of the CPU. The processor's instruction set and addressing modes constitute two of the most important characteristics of the CPU for this description.

[7]Decimal numbers are represented in memory as coded bit sequences in a representation called binary-coded decimal. Chapter 3 discusses the types of operands allowed with MC68000 instructions.

ined for their capability and flexibility when comparing processors. If the operands are held in memory, the address of an operand may be specified in an instruction as a 24-bit integer. This method of directly addressing each operand is usually called *absolute addressing.* Other methods of addressing operands are possible and these addressing schemes are called *addressing modes.* The MC68000, for example, has 14 distinct addressing modes. Thus MC68000 instructions must specify not only the operation to be performed, but also the addressing mode used to refer to each operand addressed by the instruction. The CPU calculates an absolute address, sometimes called the *effective address* in this context, for each operand as the instruction executes. In terms of the number of addressing modes, the MC68000 system is more like a large computer than a microcomputer since previous microprocessors usually had restricted addressing capability. For example, a variety of data structures, such as lists and arrays, can easily be created in memory with the addressing modes of the MC68000.

In addition to having a powerful and flexible instruction set, the MC68000 has a number of special instructions not always found in other processors. These instructions are of great value in certain applications, of which only a few are introduced here. For example, the MC68000 has a set of bit-manipulation instructions which allow operations on individual bits within an 8-bit or 32-bit operand. The selected bits can be tested, set (to {1}), or cleared (to {0}) by the bit instructions. Such operations are important when the status of a device is indicated or set as a binary value (i.e., representing ON or OFF status).

Modern programming techniques dictate that programs be modular for ease of debugging and testing. Each module performs a concisely defined function, and a complete program is created by linking the modules together.[8] The MC68000 has a number of instructions to support modular programming, including instructions to invoke subroutines (modules). Additionally, the MC68000 allows parameters to be easily transferred between modules via its LINK instruction.[9] This instruction combines several operations which normally require a short program segment to accomplish on other processors.

A number of instructions of the MC68000 are useful for controlling system operation. For example, when a TRAP instruction is executed in a user mode program, control is returned to the supervisor mode. This is useful in invoking operating system routines from a user program. Another instruction, the TAS (Test And Set operand), allows several processors to share a common memory area in a multiprocessor application without danger of simultaneous access to an addressed memory location in the area.

The examples of MC68000 capabilities as a programmable processor cited only begin to indicate its power and versatility. Many of the remaining chapters are devoted to exploring its instruction set and related concepts in more detail.

---

[8]In FORTRAN programs, the modules are called *subroutines.* Parameters such as addresses or data values are passed between modules during program execution.

[9]LINK is the assembly language mnemonic for the instruction.

Debugging.   The MC68000 incorporates several features to aid in the debugging and testing of programs. The mechanism to detect an error is a trap that occurs when an instruction causing an error executes. For example, an illegal instruction or an attempt to divide by zero causes a trap. Certain addressing errors and arithmetic conditions can also cause traps. When trapping occurs, control is passed to a specific routine of the operating system which performs any required processing for the type of error detected. Information about the status of the processor and the address of the offending instruction are saved when a trap occurs, to facilitate diagnosis of the problem.

2.3.3 Interface Design

The interface designer is concerned with the *implementation* of the computer system in designing and debugging interfaces. The functional and electrical characteristics of the processor signal lines determine the design of the circuitry that connects the processor to external devices. The functional aspects of the signal lines determine their purpose. The electrical characteristics include the timing properties of the signals, the voltage levels, and other details of importance to circuit designers. When interface design is discussed in this textbook, the emphasis is on the functional approach rather than the electrical details. This subsection considers the interfacing characteristics and hardware debugging features of the MC68000 as listed in Table 2.5.

Interfacing.   Figure 2.10 shows a simplified diagram of the MC68000 which illustrates the major classes of signal lines which are connected to the system bus. These signal lines are physically connected to the processor by the 64 pins of its integrated circuit package.[10] Twenty-three signal lines are used to address a memory word,

[10]The physical configuration of the MC68000 is described in detail in Chapter 4. The package discussed is approximately 3 inches by 1 inch and is supported by pins about 0.1 inch long.

TABLE 2.5 INTERFACING CONSIDERATIONS

Characteristic	Purpose
Interfacing	
Availability of processor mode to external circuits	Indication of supervisor or user mode to external circuits for memory management or other purposes
Bus control	Allows shared bus systems
I/O capability and priority interrupt scheme	Determines design of interfaces to meet specific requirements
Error control and debugging	
Hardware error detection and diagnostic information	Aids in debugging or recovery from error
CPU-generated error signal	Indicates a faulty CPU or system error

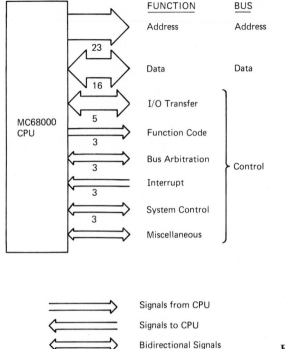

Figure 2.10   Signal lines of the MC68000.

and one of the five I/O transfer control lines indicates whether an 8-bit (one byte) or 16-bit (one word) location is selected. The 16 data lines transfer data values in either direction, as indicated by the double arrows (bidirectional). Four of the five I/O transfer control signals initiate processor reads or writes from the addressed location, while one line allows the external circuitry to acknowledge the processor's request. For normal data transfers, the address bus, data bus, and the five I/O transfer control lines are involved. The three function code lines indicate the processor mode and are used to determine whether a supervisor program or a user program is making the transfer request.

The three control lines designated for bus arbitration allow an external circuit to take control of the internal system bus by issuing a request to the CPU. When acknowledged by the MC68000, the processor is electrically isolated from the bus. Three interrupt lines accept requests from external circuits and the requests are encoded into priority levels. Three other signals for system control are used to detect external errors or to allow the CPU to indicate that it has failed. Other miscellaneous signals include the clock signal and electrical connections for power.

Since the MC68000 and similar microprocessors are typically incorporated into complex systems requiring memory protection and a large number of peripheral units, the processor is designed to accommodate such requirements. Figure 2.11 shows a mi-

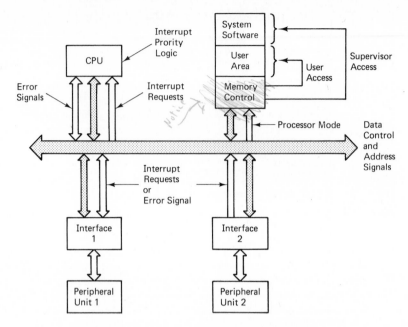

Figure 2.11   Microcomputer system bus structure.

crocomputer system with the signals for memory management, interrupt requests, and error indications separately indicated. As shown, the mode of the processor (supervisor or user) is used by the memory control circuits to address the correct area of memory. If a program in the user mode attempts to read or write in the supervisor area of memory, an error signal would be generated by the memory control circuitry and appropriate action taken by an error routine executed by the CPU.

The bus arbitration control lines are not shown explicitly in Figure 2.11. These three lines determine which device on the system bus will be the master, that is, which will control I/O transfers and similar operations. Such arbitration is required when several processors share the same bus or when any device other than the CPU is capable of initiating I/O transfers on the bus. The direct memory access chips discussed in Chapter 1 are devices of this type.

The interrupt request signals shown in Figure 2.10 are processed by the interrupt circuitry of the CPU. The CPU determines the priority of the interrupt and passes control to the interrupt routine corresponding to the highest-priority peripheral unit that is requesting service. Upon completion of that routine, control passes back to the program that was interrupted.

Error control and debugging.   Various error signals can be generated by the interface circuitry in Figure 2.11 or perhaps even by the CPU itself. The MC68000 can issue an error signal when it detects that the system cannot continue to operate correctly due to a critical external failure or to a CPU failure. This feature can be vital in a multiprocessor system where one faulty processor must be isolated when other processors in the system detect an error that could have a system-wide effect. Upon detecting failure, the CPU indicates the problem on one of the three system control signal lines. It then ceases to process instructions and another device or CPU must take control of the system.

If a hardware error is indicated, the CPU saves information in memory about the condition of the system when the error occurred. The information defines the status of the processor, the type of operation in progress, and similar data at the time the error occurred. This information can be used in certain cases to allow the system to recover from a hardware error during operation. Of course, such information is also valuable to the interface designer in debugging the hardware.

Example 2.2

A typical use of the error detection capability of the MC68000 is to determine when an external device fails to respond to an I/O transfer request. Once the request is made, a timing circuit in the system could indicate the elapsed time until the device acknowledges the request via the I/O transfer control lines. If no acknowledgment occurs within a specified time (usually several milliseconds), an error signal from the "watchdog" timing circuits would be placed on one of the system control lines to the processor. The processor's error-handling routine would then determine the next action. If the failure is critical, the processor could retry the I/O transfer or indicate a system failure on another system control line.

EXERCISES

2.3.1. Discuss the differences between a trap and an interrupt. Include both hardware and software considerations.

2.3.2. What are the possible consequences of allowing the CPU to execute illegal instructions?

2.3.3. The MC68000 requires 44 clock cycles to respond to an interrupt. At 10 MHz, each clock cycle is one-tenth of a microsecond and so the response time is 4.4 microseconds. Assume that three interrupt routines require the following total execution time after the interrupt is recognized:
   (a) R1 = 20 microseconds
   (b) R2 = 30 microseconds
   (c) R3 = 20 microseconds
   The priority levels are such that R3 has the highest priority and R1 has the lowest. What is the possible range of time for each routine to be executed when the corresponding interrupt occurs?

2.3.4. Each instruction of the MC68000 is at least 16 bits in length and occupies one word in memory. An absolute address can occupy 16 bits or 32 bits in memory. What are the possible lengths, in words, of MC68000 instructions, including their operand addresses? Instructions can have none, one, or two operands.

2.3.5. Explain the use of the supervisor and user modes. Tell which programs execute in each mode, and why.

FURTHER READING

Listed below are a number of works on the topics introduced in this chapter. References are separated into general, systems design, programming, and interface design categories for convenience. A list of articles and publications about the MC68000 and the MC68010 is also given.

Noyce and Hoff discuss the historical development of microprocessors at Intel, where the first commercial version was produced in 1971. Eckhouse and Morris, Tanenbaum, and Wakerly discuss computer organization and programming. The text by Eckhouse discusses the PDP-11 system (Digital Equipment Corporation) and can serve as a background text for understanding the MC68000 since the processors are very much alike. Tanenbaum covers not only the MC68000 but also other processors. He gives a complete discussion of virtual memory systems including an example using the MC68000. A number of microprocessors, including the MC68000, are discussed by Wakerly.

Details of microcomputer systems design are covered in the works by Carson, Ogdin, and Peatman. The first two are tutorial and consist mainly of article reprints from computer journals.

The history and fundamentals of many programming languages are covered in Sammet's large book (785 pages). Allen's tutorial text covers programming languages, development software, operating systems, and other aspects of microcomputer software. An introduction to interface design is presented by Artwick. The text by Peatman also covers aspects of interface design.

A number of articles have been written about the MC68000 family in computer journals. Three are listed here. The reader should refer to the latest issue of the journals to keep abreast of the rapidly changing microcomputer area. The three articles listed cover the MC68000 and its support. The latest publications from Motorola should be consulted for specific details about their product lines since even the journal articles tend to be outdated quickly when specific product information is needed.

The MC68010 is treated in some detail in the article by MacGregor and Mothersole referenced below. Its capability in a virtual memory system is described by two designers from Motorola.

General

ECKHOUSE, RICHARD H., JR., and L. R. MORRIS, *Minicomputer Systems,* 2nd ed. Englewood Cliffs, N.J.: Prentice-Hall, 1979.

NOYCE, ROBERT N., and M. E. HOFF, JR., "A History of Microprocessor Development at Intel," *IEEE MICRO,* **1,** No. 1 (February 1981), 8–21.

TANENBAUM, ANDREW S., *Structured Computer Organization,* 2nd ed. Englewood Cliffs, N.J.: Prentice-Hall, 1984.

WAKERLY, JOHN F., *Microcomputer Architecture and Programming.* New York: Wiley, 1981.

Systems Design

CARSON, JOHN H., *Tutorial: Design of Microprocessor Systems.* Silver Spring, Md.: IEEE Computer Society, 1979.

OGDIN, CAROL ANNE, *Tutorial: Microcomputer System Design and Techniques.* Silver Spring, Md.: IEEE Computer Society, 1980.

PEATMAN, JOHN B., *Microcomputer-Based Design.* New York: McGraw-Hill, 1977.

Assembly Language

ALLEN, BELTON E., *Tutorial: Microcomputer System Software and Languages.* Silver Spring, Md.: IEEE Computer Society, 1980.

SAMMET, JEAN E., *Programming Languages: History and Fundamentals.* Englewood Cliffs, N.J.: Prentice-Hall, 1969.

Interface

ARTWICK, BRUCE A., *Microcomputer Interfacing.* Englewood Cliffs, N.J.: Prentice-Hall, 1980.

MC68000

DE LAUNE, J., and T. SCANLON, "Supporting the MC68000," *Mini-Micro Systems,* XIII, No. 8 (August 1980), 95–102.

KISTER, JACK, and I. ROBINSON, "Development System Supports Today's Processors and Tomorrow's," *Electronics,* 53, No. 3 (January 31, 1980), 81–88.

MACGREGOR, DOUGLAS, and DAVIS S. MOTHERSOLE, "Virtual Memory and the MC68010," *IEEE MICRO,* 3, No. 3 (June 1983), 24–39.

Motorola Microprocessors Data Manual. Motorola Semiconductor Products Inc., Austin, Tex. (Data sheets for Motorola products.)

Motorola Semiconductor Data Update, Motorola Semiconductor Products Inc., Austin, Tex. (This publication announces the latest Motorola products.)

STRITTER, EDWARD, and T. GUNTER, "A Microprocessor Architecture for a Changing World: The Motorola 68000," *IEEE Computer,* 12, No. 2 (February 1979), 43–52.

3

Representation of Numbers and Characters

The digital computer has the capability of storing and processing information of interest to the programmer. The information is stored in memory as sequences of binary digits which are processed by the CPU. For example, the machine language instructions discussed in Chapter 2 represent information that controls the operation of the computer system. *Programs,* consisting of these instructions, operate on other binary sequences of *data* which represent information that has been stored for processing. This chapter explores the storage methods commonly used to represent numbers and characters for MC68000-based computer systems.

Numbers that are interpreted as positive or negative integers or fractions may be represented in memory in many ways. The most common number system used to represent numbers in microcomputers is the *two's-complement* system, which represents signed numbers as binary (base 2) values. The MC68000 provides instructions for addition, subtraction, multiplication, and division of these binary numbers. These two's-complement numbers form a fundamental *data type* for the MC68000.

Decimal numbers can also be added and subtracted with instructions of the MC68000 if the decimal values are coded into binary by a scheme called *binary-coded decimal* (BCD). To incorporate both positive and negative numbers, the *ten's-complement* system is used.

Many engineering and scientific applications require a large range for numbers which are represented in a *floating-point* format. This binary equivalent of scientific notation, which uses a mantissa and an exponent to represent a number, is employed and sometimes required in MC68000-based systems. No MC68000 instructions are available to manipulate these numbers directly, so floating-point routines must be provided to perform arithmetic operations when required. However, the MC68020 CPU with its floating-point co-processor will have floating-point instructions, so that programming will be greatly simplified. The floating-point format used in the MC68020 system is discussed in this chapter.

Text is stored in memory by assigning a specific bit pattern to each character in the alphabet. The *ASCII code* is the most popular code used to represent characters in microcomputer systems. As with floating-point numbers, any processing of the ASCII-coded characters is via software routines since the MC68000 has no instructions that operate specifically on characters.

The basic characteristics of the data types commonly used in MC68000 systems are discussed in this chapter. Machine instructions to manipulate the data types and various other programming considerations are discussed in later chapters. In particular, arithmetic operations are treated in detail in Chapter 7.

3.1 NUMBER REPRESENTATION

This section discusses the representation of positive and negative integers and fractions. A general formulation with the base or radix r for each number representation is presented and then applied to the discussion of binary values with $r = 2$ and other bases as appropriate. The generalized presentation is useful for conversion of numbers from one base to another and techniques of numerical analysis. Representation of binary numbers in the sign-magnitude, one's-complement, and two's-complement systems are presented. Decimal representations for the nine's-complement and ten's-complement systems are also presented.

3.1.1 Nonnegative Integers

A nonnegative integer in base r is written in positional notation as

$$N_r = (d_{m-1} d_{m-2} \cdots d_0)_r \qquad (3.1)$$

where each digit d_i has one of the distinct values $[0, 1, 2, \ldots, r-1]$ and m represents the base 10 or decimal number of digits in the integer. Thus the number 324 would have $d_0 = 4$, $d_1 = 2$, and $d_2 = 3$ in Equation 3.1 and could be written as

$$N_{10} = 324_{10}$$

For numbers in base 10, the subscript is omitted if no confusion could result from its omission. The form specified by Equation 3.1 is generally referred to as *positional* notation. The position of the digit starting from the rightmost digit represents a power of the base r; that is, 324 represents 4 ones (4×10^0), 2 tens (2×10^1), and 3 hundreds (3×10^2). Mathematically, the value of the number is calculated as

$$N_r = d_{m-1} r^{m-1} + d_{m-2} r^{m-2} + \cdots + d_1 r + d_0$$

$$= \sum_{i=0}^{m-1} d_i r^i \qquad (3.2)$$

in which the digits are restricted in value such that $0 \leq d_i \leq r - 1$. Thus the number 324 can be calculated as

$$324 = 3 \times 10^2 + 2 \times 10^1 + 4 \times 1$$

The arithmetic operations in Equation 3.2 could be carried out in any number base and this equation is frequently used to determine the decimal equivalent of a number in another base.

Table 3.1 lists the range of possible values of the digits in the hexadecimal, decimal, octal, and binary number systems. The decimal system is, of course, used primarily for ordinary arithmetic by human beings, and the binary system is used for computer arithmetic. Octal and hexadecimal representations are convenient for writing long binary numbers. For example,

$$01011010_2 = 5A_{16} = 132_8$$

The decimal value of the number represented in these bases is obtained from Equation 3.2 by converting the base r digits to decimal equivalents such that

$$N = 5 \times 16^1 + 10 \times 1$$
$$= 1 \times 8^2 + 3 \times 8^1 + 2 \times 1$$
$$= 90_{10}$$

The hexadecimal digits [A, B, ... F] represent the decimal numbers [10, 11, ... 15] in the conversion from hexadecimal to decimal.

Example 3.1

Consider the largest m-digit positive integer in positional notation,

$$N_r = ((r - 1)(r - 1) \cdots (r - 1))_r,$$

as in $(1111 \ldots 1111)_2$ or $(9999 \ldots 9999)_{10}$ with m digits each. The sum of Equation 3.2 indicates that the decimal value is

$$N = (r - 1) \sum_{i=0}^{m-1} r^i$$

which is an easily summed geometric series. The result is $r^m - 1$. For example, an 8-bit binary number has a maximum value of $2^8 - 1$, or 255.

Positive fractional values. The positional representation defined by Equation 3.1 is valid for integers only. If a fraction is to be represented, a radix point in the base r is used to separate the integer from the fractional part of the number. The radix point is called the *binary point* in base 2 and the *decimal point* in base 10. Thus 324.14 has the value

$$3 \times 10^2 + 2 \times 10^1 + 4 \times 1 + 1 \times 10^{-1} + 4 \times 10^{-2}$$

TABLE 3.1 DIGITS IN VARIOUS NUMBER
SYSTEMS

Number system	Base r	Digits
Hexadecimal	16	0, 1, 2, 3, 4, 5, 6, 7, 8, 9, A, B, C, D, E, F
Decimal	10	0, 1, 2, 3, 4, 5, 6, 7, 8, 9
Octal	8	0, 1, 2, 3, 4, 5, 6, 7
Binary	2	0, 1

In general, a k-digit positive fraction is written with a leading radix point as

$$.(d_{-1} d_{-2} \cdots d_{-k})_r, \tag{3.3}$$

with the value

$$.n_r = d_{-1}r^{-1} + d_{-2}r^{-2} + \cdots + d_{-k}r^{-k} \tag{3.4}$$

where the negative subscript for the digits indicates the appropriate negative power of r.

Internally, the processor performs arithmetic on integers without taking into account the position of the radix point. It is then possible to interpret the internal value of a fraction by writing $.n_r$ in the form

$$.n_r = r^{-k} \times (d_{-1} d_{-2} \cdots d_{-k}) \tag{3.5}$$

with the value in parentheses treated as an integer value. For example, the number $.1000_2 (0.5_{10})$ can be written as

$$2^{-4} \times (1000.)_2 = 2^{-4} \times 8$$

both of which have the value 0.5, as expected. The scaling factor r^{-k} has the effect of shifting the radix point k positions to the left. Thus $.n_r r^k$ may be used internally as an integer operand and the final result scaled by r^{-k}. For example, the addition of the binary values $.1000 (0.5_{10})$ and $.0100 (0.25_{10})$ can be accomplished as

$$
\begin{array}{r}
1000. \times 2^{-4} \\
+ \underline{0100. \times 2^{-4}} \\
1100. \times 2^{-4}
\end{array}
$$

The machine addition results in 1100_2 or 12 decimal, and the programmer must apply the scale factor to obtain the correct arithmetic result:

$$12 \times 2^{-4} = 0.75$$

In addition and subtraction, each scaled value must have the same scaling factor. The choice of the scaling factor may cause the radix point to be at the right of the number (integer), at the left (fraction), or anywhere within the number. Thus the value 0.5 in four-digit binary could be written as a fraction

$.1000_2$

as an integer with scaling 2^{-4} as

$(1000.)_2 \times 2^{-4}$

or as a mixed quantity scaled arbitrarily: for example,

$(10.00)_2 \times 2^{-2}$

When the radix point is fixed for a particular problem and the programmer must take the scaling into account, the system is called a *fixed-point* representation. All integer operations with the MC68000, such as addition or subtraction, assume that the scaling factor is 2^0. Therefore, the binary point is on the right. The importance of Equation 3.5 is that both for analysis and for machine operations, a fractional value may be treated as an integer during all the intermediate steps of a computation. The appropriate scale factor can be applied as the last step when the actual numerical value is desired.

Example 3.2

The first example showed that the largest m-digit integer for unsigned integers has the value $r^m - 1$. Thus the largest 16-bit (binary) integer

$1111\ 1111\ 1111\ 1111_2$

has the value

$2^{16} - 1 = 65{,}535$

in decimal representation. The largest 16-bit fraction

$.1111\ 1111\ 1111\ 1111_2$

has the decimal value

$2^{-16} \times 65{,}535 = 0.99998474$

This is obtained by scaling the 16-bit fraction as

$2^{-16} \times (2^{16} - 1) = 1 - 2^{-16}$

and performing the arithmetic on a calculator with a sufficient number of decimal places.

EXERCISES

3.1.1.1. Convert the binary number

0100.0110_2

to decimal.

3.1.1.2. What is the decimal value of

$$1111\ 1111\ .\ 1111\ 1111\ 1111\ 1111_2$$

to five decimal places in the fraction?

3.1.1.3. Compute the decimal value of the following numbers.
  (a) 130_9
  (b) 120_5
  (c) 0.7632_8
  (d) $F00A_{16}$

3.1.1.4. If

$$111_x = 31_{10}$$

what is the base x?

3.1.1.5. Compute the largest integer representable in a 32-bit computer word. Give the answer as a decimal value.

3.1.2. Representation of Signed Numbers

The positive integers, including zero, can be conveniently represented as shown in Section 3.1.1. However, to represent the complete set of integers, which includes positive integers, zero, and negative integers, a notation for negative values is necessary. In ordinary arithmetic, a negative number is represented by prefixing the magnitude (or absolute value) of the number with a minus sign. Thus -5 is a negative integer with a magnitude of 5. For hand calculations, the use of separate symbols to indicate positive $(+)$ and negative $(-)$ numbers is convenient. Computer arithmetic circuits to manipulate positive and negative integers are also simplified if one of the digits in the positional notation of a number is used to indicate the sign of the integer. Two such possible representations of signed integers are *sign-magnitude* notation and *complement* notation. In both notations, the most significant digit on the left in the positional form of the number indicates the sign. Negative fractions can also be represented in either of these systems. For fractions, the sign digit is written to the left of the radix point.

The binary arithmetic instructions of the MC68000 operate directly only on integers in two's-complement notation if signed integers are considered. Integers in other binary notations or fractions must be manipulated by programs designed for that purpose. The treatment of decimal numbers by the CPU is discussed in Section 3.2 although the mathematical representation of decimal numbers is first introduced in this section.

Sign-magnitude representation.   The sign-magnitude representation of a number in positional notation has the form

$$N_r = (d_{m-1}d_{m-2}\cdots d_1d_0)_r$$ (3.6)

where the sign of the number is indicated by the most significant (leftmost) digit:

$$d_{m-1} = \begin{cases} 0 & \text{if } N_r \geq 0 \\ r-1 & \text{if } N_r < 0 \end{cases}$$ (3.7)

Thus, using the sign-magnitude representation, 1011_2 and 9003 are four-digit negative numbers in the binary and decimal systems, respectively. The magnitude of the number, written $|N_r|$, is

$$|N_r| = \sum_{i=0}^{m-2} d_i r^i \tag{3.8}$$

where only the first $m - 1$ digits from the right are considered. The positive version of a number differs from the negative only in the sign digit, and the digits $(d_{m-2}d_{m-3} \cdots d_1 d_0)$ indicate the magnitude. According to the definitions and Equation 3.8, the four-digit number $0011_2 = 3$, and $1011_2 = -3$. The number of digits, including the sign digit, in the representation must be specified or confusion could result. For example, 1011_2 in an eight-digit representation is assumed to be $0000\ 1011_2$, which has the decimal value 11. For binary values, a negative fraction in sign-magnitude notation has a leading digit of 1 followed by the fractional part. Thus 1.100_2 is the number -0.5.

Example 3.3

The number 16 is written in a 16-bit binary system as

$$0000\ 0000\ 0001\ 0000_2$$

The number -16 has the sign-magnitude representation

$$1000\ 0000\ 0001\ 0000_2$$

Complement representation. Most microprocessors, including the MC68000, have arithmetic instructions that operate on negative numbers represented in a *complement* number system.[1] In these systems, positive numbers have the same representation as in sign-magnitude notation, but the negative numbers are formed by computing the complement of the number according to the rules of the specific system being used. The two most common complement systems are the *radix-complement* and the *diminished radix-complement* systems. The general theory of these systems will be presented first. Then the two's and ten's complements of numbers will be discussed as examples of radix-complement numbers. The one's and nine's complements are examples of diminished radix-complement systems for base 2 and base 10, respectively.

In general form, the radix complement of an m-digit number is computed mathematically as

$$N'_r = r^m - N_r \tag{3.9}$$

where N'_r is the radix complement of the base r number N_r. In the machine computation, only m-digit values can be represented. If any operation produces a result that

---

[1]Complement representations have an advantage over sign and magnitude notation because the sign digit does not have to be treated in a special way during addition and subtraction. This simplifies the arithmetic circuits of the CPU somewhat, as is discussed in several references in the Further Reading section of this chapter.

requires more than m digits, the higher-order digit is ignored. This is taken to be an out-of-range condition. A machine error of this type is called *overflow*.

The two radix-complement systems used with the MC68000 instructions are the two's-complement and the ten's-complement systems. The two's complement of a number N_2 given by Equation 3.9 using 2 as the base r is

$$N'_2 = 2^m - N_2 \qquad (3.10)$$

Thus the four-digit two's-complement form of -1 is

$$N'_2 = 2^4 - 1 = 1\ 0000 - 0001 = 1111_2$$

If the number and its complement are added:

```
  0001    N
+ 1111    N'
1 0000
```

the result is 0 to four digits, as expected. In a two's-complement system, negative values always have a leading digit of 1 and positive values have 0 as the leading digit. Thus $+4 = 0100_2$ and $-4 = 1100_2$. If addition is performed in a four-digit representation on two positive numbers, the result must not be greater than 7 or overflow occurs. This limits the range of the m-bit positive numbers to the decimal value $2^{m-1} - 1$. In the case of 4-bit numbers, the addition of $4 + 5$ in binary yields

```
  0100
+ 0101
  1001₂
```

which is a negative number in two's-complement notation. The magnitude as derived from Equation 3.9 would be

$$N_2 = 2^4 - 1001 = 1\ 0000 - 1001 = 0111_2$$

which is $+7$ in decimal, clearly an error. In the MC68000, an indication is given when such an overflow occurs and the programmer must make provisions in the program for such occurrences.

In the ten's-complement system, the ten's complement of a number N is formed as

$$N' = 10^L - N \qquad (3.11)$$

in an L-digit representation. For four digits, -1 is represented as

$$N' = 10^4 - 1 = (10{,}000 - 1) = 9999$$

The MC68000 has arithmetic instructions to operate on numbers represented in the ten's-complement system.

The diminished radix complement is computed as

$$\bar{N}_r = r^m - N_r - 1 \qquad (3.12)$$

which is one less than the radix-complement value computed by Equation 3.9. The diminished radix complement, or simply complement as it is usually called, is the one's complement for binary values and the nine's complement for decimal numbers. The four-digit decimal value 0002 has the complement

$$\bar{N}_r = (10^4 - 0002) - 1 = 9999 - 0002 = 9997 \tag{3.13}$$

From the complement, the radix complement is formed by adding 1, as a comparison of Equations 3.12 and 3.9 shows.

Table 3.2 lists the radix complement for four-digit binary and decimal numbers. The one's- and nine's-complement values are also presented for comparison. Notice that in the nine's- and ten's-complement notation, the negative values have leading digits in the range 5 through 9. The sign digit is not unique as it is in the case of two's-complement negative values.

Example 3.4

The radix complement of a number is easily computed by complementing each digit [subtracting it from $(r - 1)$] and adding 1 to the result formed from the complemented digits. Thus the value -2 is represented as follows in various four-digit systems:

$$
\begin{aligned}
&\text{2's complement:} &&-2 = (1111 - 0010) + 1 = 1110_2 \\
&\text{10's complement:} &&-2 = (9999 - 0002) + 1 = 9998 \\
&\text{16's complement:} &&-2 = (FFFF - 0002) + 1 = FFFE_{16}
\end{aligned}
$$

TABLE 3.2 COMPLEMENT SYSTEMS

Value	One's	Two's	Value	Nine's	Ten's
7	0111	0111	4999	4999	4999
6	0110	0110	4998	4998	4998
5	0101	0101	.	.	.
4	0100	0100	.	.	.
3	0011	0011	.	.	.
2	0010	0010	0002	0002	0002
1	0001	0001	0001	0001	0001
0	0000	0000	0000	0000	0000
-0	1111	—	-0000	9999	—
-1	1110	1111	-0001	9998	9999
-2	1101	1110	-0002	9997	9998
-3	1100	1101	.	.	.
-4	1011	1100	.	.	.
-5	1010	1011	.	.	.
-6	1001	1010	.	.	.
-7	1000	1001	-4999	5000	5001
-8	—	1000	-5000	—	5000

Example 3.5

For a fraction of length k digits, the radix complement is computed by complementing each digit and adding r^{-k} (not 1) to the result. Thus the number

$$0101.01_2 = 5.25$$

has as its complement the value

$$1010.10_2$$

Its radix or two's-complement representation would be

$$\begin{array}{r} 1010.10 \\ +\quad .01 \\ \hline 1010.11_2 \end{array}$$

where the value 2^{-2} is added to the one's complement of the number since $k = 2$. Similarly, the fraction 0.01_2 has complement 1.10_2 and two's complement 1.11_2.

Number range.   The range of integers (or fractions) for a given number system is specified by the smallest and largest values that can be represented. For positive integers represented in m digits, for example, there are r^m possible values with a numerical range of 0 to $r^m - 1$. For the 8-bit representation of a positive binary integer, the range is 0 to $2^8 - 1$, or 0 to 255. The range of signed integers in an m-digit representation still allows r^m values, but one-half of these values are negative numbers.

The maximum positive integer in sign-magnitude, one's-complement, or two's-complement representation is

$$(0111 \ldots 111)_2$$

where $(m - 1)$ 1's are shown. The maximum decimal value is thus $2^{m-1} - 1$, considering the discussion in Example 3.1. In an 8-bit representation, the largest positive number is $2^7 - 1$, or 127. In sign-magnitude notation, the most negative value is

$$(1111 \ldots 111)_2 = -(2^{m-1} - 1)$$

The most negative one's-complement number $(100 \ldots 00)_2$ has the same decimal value. Both of these systems allow a positive and a negative value of zero since the "positive" zero

$$(000 \ldots 000)_2$$

has negative values of $(1000 \ldots 000)_2$ and $(1111 \ldots 111)_2$ in the sign-magnitude and one's-complement notations, respectively. In the two's-complement notation, however, only one value of zero is allowed since the two's complement of the number 0 is the same value to m bits. Since there are a total of 2^m values for each m-bit representation, the two's-complement notation allows one more negative value than the others.

The two's complement of the positive value

$$(011 \ldots 111)_2$$

is the negative number

$$(100\ldots001)_2 = -(2^{m-1} - 1)$$

for m bits. The integer

$$(100\ldots000)_2$$

must then represent -2^{m-1} with no positive counterpart.

The m-digit ten's complement allows 10^m values in the range

$$-10^m/2 \quad \text{to} \quad 10^m/2 - 1$$

as from -5000 to $+4999$ in the four-digit representation shown in Table 3.2. The positive values are

$$0, 1, 2, \ldots, 499\ldots99$$

for m digits and the negative values are represented as

$$999\ldots999, 999\ldots998, \ldots, 500\ldots001, 500\ldots000$$

with values $-1, -2, \ldots$. The nine's complement representation of the negative numbers has a negative 0 and consequently one less nonzero negative value than the ten's-complement notation allows, that is, a range from

$$-10^m/2 + 1 \quad \text{to} \quad 10^m/2 - 1$$

In this case, the magnitude of the number is restricted so that

$$|N| \leq 10^m/2 - 1$$

which causes the most significant digits of 0, 1, 2, 3, or 4 to indicate a positive number and the digits 5, 6, 7, 8, or 9 to indicate a negative value.

Example 3.6

The largest positive number for an m-digit radix-complement number in base r is

$$(1/2) \times r^m - 1$$

since there are $(1/2) \times r^m$ positive integers, including zero. Thus the two's-complement maximum value is

$$(1/2) \times 2^m - 1 = 2^{m-1} - 1$$

while the ten's-complement number has the maximum value of

$$(1/2) \times 10^m - 1$$

as indicated in the previous discussion. The four-digit binary number allows values up to $+7$ in the two's-complement system, while the four-digit decimal value has a largest positive value of 4999.

Example 3.7

Applying the formulas for the most negative and most positive numbers in m-bit representations gives the following results:

Representation	Most negative	Most positive
Sign-magnitude	$-2^{m-1} + 1$	$2^{m-1} - 1$
One's complement	$-2^{m-1} + 1$	$2^{m-1} - 1$
Two's complement	-2^{m-1}	$2^{m-1} - 1$

For a 16-bit representation, the sign-magnitude and one's-complement numbers range from $-32{,}767$ to 32,767, and the two's-complement numbers range from $-32{,}768$ to 32,767.

If a signed, binary fraction is represented as

$$(b_0.b_{-1} \cdots b_{-(k-1)})_2$$

the range is determined by scaling by $2^{-(k-1)}$. For example, the 8-bit fraction in two's-complement representation has the range -1 to $1 - 2^{-7}$. The binary values in this range are

```
1.000 0000    (−1)
1.000 0001
•
•
•
0.000 0000    (0)
•
•
•
0.111 1110
0.111 1111    (1 −2^-7)
```

EXERCISES

3.1.2.1. Find the two's-complement representation of the following numbers.

(a) -0647_{16} to 16 bits

(b) -11_{10} to 16 bits

(c) -00101.110_2 to 8 bits

3.1.2.2. The most negative two's-complement number is $100\ldots0_2$ for m bits. What value results when the two's complement of the number is taken?

3.1.2.3. In the two's-complement notation, the sign bit has the weight -2^{m-1} for an m-bit integer. Determine the procedure to extend the m-bit number to $2m$ bits for (a) a positive number and (b) a negative number. This is called *sign extension.*

3.1.2.4. Represent the given numbers in the notation specified.
(a) Nine's complement of 653.72 with five digits
(b) -223_{16} in sign-magnitude form with four hexadecimal digits
(c) $-3/8$ in one's-complement form with 8 bits, including the sign bit.

3.1.2.5. Determine the range of numbers for the sign-magnitude, one's-complement, and two's-complement forms for an m-bit representation if
(a) $m = 8$
(b) $m = 16$
(c) $m = 32$

3.1.2.6. If the largest positive number in a four-digit, ten's-complement representation is limited to 999 (i.e., three digits), determine the corresponding range and representation of the negative numbers. Note that negative numbers always begin with 9 as the sign digit when the magnitude of the numbers is limited in this way.

3.1.3 Conversions between Representations

The number systems of most interest to computer users are the binary, octal, decimal, and hexadecimal systems. Although the internal machine representation in microcomputers is binary, the other representations are important for the convenience of the user. In this regard, the conversions of numbers in other bases to decimal, and vice versa, are frequently required.

Conversion between arbitrary number bases is sometimes necessary, although in computer work, the conversions between binary, octal, and hexadecimal systems are of greatest importance. Fortunately, conversions between these bases are straightforward.

Conversion to decimal for positive numbers. The number N_r in base r can be represented in decimal as

$$N.n = D_{m-1}r^{m-1} + \cdots + D_0 + D_{-1}r^{-1} + \cdots + D_{-k}r^{-k} \tag{3.14}$$

where the D_i are the equivalent values in the base 10 of the digits in base r. The number is converted by multiplying each digit by the appropriate power of r and adding each result to the sum. The number is designated here as $N.n$ to emphasize the fact that it has an integral as well as a fractional part.

Example 3.8

To convert $11\ 1110_2$ to decimal, the value is computed as a series from Equation 3.2 or 3.14 with the result

$$
\begin{aligned}
N &= 1 \times 2^5 + 1 \times 2^4 + 1 \times 2^3 + 1 \times 2^2 + 1 \times 2^1 + 0 \\
&= 32 + 16 + 8 + 4 + 2 \\
&= 62
\end{aligned}
$$

Example 3.9

The value of 0.502_8 in decimal is

$$0.n = 5 \times 8^{-1} + 0 + 2 \times 8^{-3}$$
$$= 0.6250 + 0.003906250$$
$$= 0.62890625_{10}$$

as determined by Equation 3.4 or 3.14.

Conversions from decimal to any number base.   To convert a decimal number by hand to a number in another base, it is convenient to work in the decimal system with the series representation of the number. Conversion of a positive integer is accomplished by repeated division by the new radix using successive remainders as digits in the new system. A fraction is converted by repeated multiplication by the radix, with the resulting integer parts of the products taken as digits of the result.

Example 3.10

To convert 3964_{10} to octal, the number is repeatedly divided by 8, as follows:

$$3964/8 = 495 + (4/8)$$
$$495/8 = 61 + (7/8)$$
$$61/8 = 7 + (5/8)$$
$$7/8 = 0 + (7/8)$$

The remainders of each division, represented by the numerators of each fraction, are digits in the resulting answer. The order of these digits is the reverse of the order in which they were obtained. Thus, in the example above,

$$3964_{10} = 7574_8$$

Example 3.11

The number 0.78125_{10} is converted to a hexadecimal fraction as follows:

$$0.78125 \times 16 = 12.0 + 0.5$$
$$0.5 \times 16 = 8.0 + 0$$

The result is therefore $0.78125_{10} = .C8_{16}$.

To understand the theory of these conversions, write Equation 3.14 in the form

$$N = ((\cdots((d_{m-1}r + d_{m-2})r + d_{m-3})r + \cdots + d_1)r + d_0)$$

for the integer part and set it equal to the decimal value it represents. Then divide N by the base desired. Using 8 as the base in Example 3.10, the first remainder is the octal value d_0. Continuing to divide the whole numbers (quotients) by the base successively yields $d_0, d_1, d_2, \ldots, d_{m-1}$, in that order. Try the fractional part of Equation 3.14 in a similar manner with negative powers of r to see how the value in Example 3.11 was computed.

Conversion of a number from any base to another. A number written in base r_1 can be converted to a number in base r_2 by performing the arithmetic operations in a base other than decimal. For human computation a more acceptable method is to convert the selected number to decimal from base r_1 and then convert the result from decimal to base r_2.

Example 3.12

Converting 112_3 to base 5 is accomplished by converting 112_3 to decimal:

$$1 \times 3^2 + 1 \times 3^1 + 2 = 9 + 3 + 2 = 14_{10}$$

Then the decimal number 14 is converted to base 5 in the form

$$14/5 = 2 + (4/5)$$
$$2/5 = 0 + (2/5)$$

or $14_{10} = 24_5$. Thus $112_3 = 24_5$.

Conversion of positive numbers with bases that are powers of 2. If the relationship between a number base r_1 and another base r_2 is of the form

$$r_2 = r_1{}^L$$

where L is a positive or negative integer, conversion between the bases is particularly simple using positional notation. In particular, since the binary, octal, and hexadecimal bases are related as

$$16 = 2^4$$
$$8 = 2^3$$

the conversion from binary to octal or binary to hexadecimal requires only the grouping of the binary digits by threes or fours, respectively. The conversion from octal to binary or hexadecimal to binary requires that each octal or hexadecimal digit be replaced by its binary equivalent.

Conversion between octal and hexadecimal numbers is best accomplished by using the binary representation as an intermediate step since the bases 8 and 16 are not related.

Example 3.13

Conversion of the binary number $1011\ 0111.0010\ 1_2$ to octal requires grouping the digits by threes, starting with the least significant or rightmost binary digit for the integer portion but starting with the most significant or leftmost digit for the fractional portion. Thus the conversion proceeds as

$$(010)\ (110)\ (111) \, . \, (001)\ (010) = 267.12_8$$

where extra binary digits of zero were added at each end to yield legitimate octal digits before conversion.

Conversion of negative numbers from binary to decimal.   The conversion of a positive binary number to decimal is easily achieved by the power series method shown previously. The conversion of negative numbers in one's-complement or two's-complement notation can also be achieved in this manner when the sign bit is given the proper decimal value or weight. As an example, consider the following negative numbers in 8-bit two's-complement representation and their decimal equivalents:

$$1111\ 1111_2 = -1$$
$$1111\ 1110_2 = -2$$

$$\cdot$$
$$\cdot$$
$$\cdot$$

$$1000\ 0001_2 = -127$$
$$1000\ 0000_2 = -128$$

By associating the leading digit with $-2^7\ (-128)$ and adding the positive positional value of the remaining digits, the proper decimal value results. Thus the decimal value of an 8-bit negative number in two's-complement notation is

$$-2^7 + d_6 \times 2^6 + d_5 \times 2^5 + \cdots + d_0$$

when the negative number in its positional form is

$$(1d_6d_5d_4 \cdots d_0)_2$$

By inspecting the positive values, the general case for both positive and negative two's-complement numbers may be derived to compute the decimal equivalent as

$$N = -d_{m-1} \times 2^{m-1} + \sum_{i=0}^{m-2} d_i \times 2^i \tag{3.15}$$

with $d_{m-1} = 0$ for a positive value or $d_{m-1} = 1$ when the number is negative. From this equation, the 8-bit number $1000\ 0010_2$ has the decimal value

$$N = -2^7 + 0 + \cdots + 1 \times 2^1 + 0 = -126$$

with sign bit $d_7 = 1$. The number $0000\ 0010_2$ with $d_7 = 0$ has the value

$$-0 \times 2^7 + 0 + \cdots + 1 \times 2^1 + 0 = +2$$

In essence, Equation 3.15 represents a compact notation for computation of the decimal value of an m-bit number in the two's-complement system. The decimal weights

TABLE 3.3 VALUES OF THE SIGN BIT

	Weight in decimal	
Representation	Integer (m bits)	Fraction (k bits with sign)
One's complement	$1 - 2^{m-1}$	$2^{-(k-1)} - 1$
Two's complement	-2^{m-1}	-1

of the leading digit for one's-complement and two's-complement integers and fractions are given in Table 3.3. The magnitude of a sign-magnitude number is simply multiplied by $+1$ or -1 according to its sign.

Example 3.14

(a) The integer $1000\ 0011_2$ in sign-magnitude notation has the value

$$(-1)\ (0 \times 2^6 + \cdots + 1 \times 2^1 + 1) = -3_{10}$$

since the magnitude is multiplied by -1.

(b) The number $1111\ 1001_2$ in one's-complement notation has the value

$$(1 - 2^7) + (1 \times 2^6 + 1 \times 2^5 + 1 \times 2^4 + 1 \times 2^3 + 1)$$
$$= -127 + 121 = -6_{10}$$

using the weight for the leading bit shown in Table 3.3

(c) The two's-complement number $1111\ 1001_2$ has the value

$$-2^7 + (1 \times 2^6 + 1 \times 2^5 + 1 \times 2^4 + 1 \times 2^3 + 1)$$
$$= -128 + 121 = -7_{10}$$

Example 3.15

(a) The fraction $1.001\ 0000_2$ in sign-magnitude notation has the value

$$(-1)\ (0 \times 2^{-1} + 0 \times 2^{-2} + 1 \times 2^{-3}) = -0.125_{10}$$

(b) The fraction $1.100\ 1111_2$ in one's-complement notation has the value

$$(2^{-7} - 1) + 1 \times 2^{-1} + 1 \times 2^{-4} + 1 \times 2^{-5} + 1 \times 2^{-6} + 2^{-7} \times 1)$$
$$= -0.375_{10}$$

EXERCISES

3.1.3.1. Convert the following numbers as indicated.
   (a) 1024_{10} to binary
   (b) 53000_{10} to hexadecimal
   (c) $FFFF\ FFFF_{16}$ to decimal
   (d) 35_{10} to base 5

3.1.3.2. Convert the repeating octal fraction $(0.333...)_8$ to decimal.

3.1.3.3. Show that adding 1 to the complement form of the positive number N yields the radix-complement representation $r^m - |N|$ for an m-digit number.

3.1.3.4. Convert the fraction $1.111\ 1111_2$ in two's-complement notation to its decimal value.

3.1.3.5. Using two's-complement representation, represent numbers in the range -2, $-1\frac{1}{4}$, $\ldots$, $1\frac{1}{2}$, $1\frac{3}{4}$.

3.2 BINARY-CODED DECIMAL

Many microcomputers provide instructions to perform arithmetic operations on data considered as decimal numbers. This is convenient for business processing and in representing data that are inherently decimal in nature. Thumb-wheel switches, for example, may present an output as a decimal digit encoded in binary to represent a selected digit on the switch. Many displays are designed to receive encoded decimal digits and display the result in decimal.

One decimal coding system is the *binary-coded decimal* or BCD system. In the BCD system, the first 10 binary numbers correspond to decimal digits. This is sometimes called the "natural" binary-coded decimal system.

This section discusses the binary-coded decimal system and various conversion operations with BCD numbers. The use of ten's-complement notation is convenient to represent negative BCD values, although other representations are possible. Only ten's complement is discussed here since it is the method assumed for addition and subtraction of signed decimal values performed by the MC68000 processor.

3.2.1 BCD Representation of Positive Integers

In many applications, particularly those involving financial transactions, a true representation of decimal numbers in a machine that operates on binary digits is desirable. Since any decimal digit can be represented by four binary digits, it is natural to select a binary code in which four binary digits are used for each decimal digit. Such a code is shown in Table 3.4, which lists the binary-coded decimal (BCD) representation. The possible binary values 1010_2 through 1111_2 are not used since the decimal values 10 through 15 require two BCD digits for their representation.

Each decimal digit has the value

$$D_i = b_{i3} \times 2^3 + b_{i2} \times 2^2 + b_{i1} \times 2^1 + b_{i0} \qquad (3.16)$$

where b_{ij} is the jth binary digit in the representation of the ith decimal digit. The value of the L-digit BCD number is calculated in decimal as

$$N = D_{L-1} \times 10^{L-1} + D_{L-2} \times 10^{L-2} + \cdots + D_0 \qquad (3.17)$$

TABLE 3.4   BINARY-CODED DECIMAL VALUES

BCD	Binary
0	0000
1	0001
2	0010
3	0011
4	0100
5	0101
6	0110
7	0111
8	1000
9	1001

where each D_i is formed as shown in Equation 3.16. The decimal value 95, for example, would be coded into binary as

$$1001\ 0101_2$$

and it is stored in this form. Using Equation 3.16, we have

$$D_0 = 1 \times 2^2 + 1 = 5$$

and

$$D_1 = 1 \times 2^3 + 1 = 9$$

Numbers in BCD can be added or subtracted by MC68000 instructions that perform decimal arithmetic. Therefore, the programmer does not need to be concerned with the internal representation. It is only when conversions between BCD numbers and other representations are required that the internal format must be considered.

Example 3.16

The binary number

$$0001\ 0111\ 0011\ 1001$$

has the BCD value

$$N = 1 \times 10^3 + 7 \times 10^2 + 3 \times 10^1 + 9 = 1739$$

The 16 binary digits encoded as positive BCD numbers have a range of only $0 \leq N \leq 9999$.

Example 3.17

Microprocessors that perform arithmetic operations on 8-bit (byte) and longer operands may allow such operations on "packed" BCD integers, as the MC68000 does. In this representation, two BCD digits are contained in each 8-bit value rather than storing each BCD digit in a separate byte (called *unpacked notation*).

The BCD number 3475 may be treated for the purposes of machine calculation as either packed BCD or unpacked as follows:

Decimal value		Memory (binary)
Packed	34	0011 0100
	75	0111 0101
Unpacked	03	0000 0011
	04	0000 0100
	07	0000 0111
	05	0000 0101

In the unpacked representation, the single digit is shown in a byte location with a leading 0 since the MC68000 and most other processors address memory locations containing 8 bits. The unpacked format is typically used when algorithms to perform multiplication or division of BCD numbers are employed.

EXERCISES

3.2.1.1. Show the internal machine representation (binary) of the following positive numbers in packed BCD format.
  (a) 07
  (b) 13
  (c) 99
3.2.1.2. Determine the decimal values of the following positive numbers coded in BCD format.
  (a) $0001\ 1001\ 0111\ 0000_2$
  (b) $0001\ 1111_2$
3.2.1.3. Assuming that the representation is packed BCD, compute the decimal range for the positive BCD representation of numbers using
  (a) 8 bits
  (b) 16 bits
  (c) 32 bits
3.2.1.4. Describe the test required to assure that an out-of-range condition is detected when two positive BCD integers are added (subtracted). Assume that the maximum length is L decimal digits for each BCD integer. The MC68000 has built-in hardware (condition codes) for detecting these conditions.

3.2.2. Conversion between BCD and Binary

When the machine representations as binary sequences are required, arithmetic in base 2 instead of base 10 to convert between BCD values and binary numbers, or vice versa, is convenient with the MC68000 since it has multiply and divide instructions to perform the binary arithmetic. Thus the conversion of the positive BCD number

$$(D_{L-1}D_{L-2}\cdots D_0)$$

can be accomplished by first writing Equation 3.17 in the form

$$N = (\cdots((D_{L-1}) \times 10 + D_{L-2}) \times 10 + \cdots + D_1) \times 10 + D_0$$

Converting all the digits to binary yields an equation useful for machine implementation. The binary value of the BCD number is then

$$N_2 = (\cdots((D_{L-1} \times 1010_2 + D_{L-2}) \times 1010_2 + \cdots + D_1) \times 1010_2 + D_0$$

where 1010_2 is 10 decimal and the digits D_i are used in their 4-bit binary form. First the most significant digit is multiplied by 1010_2, then the next most significant digit is added and the sum multiplied by 1010_2, and so on, until the last digit D_0 is added. The result is an m-digit binary representation of the BCD number. Programming the conversion equation is simple using the MC68000 instruction set. BCD values are sometimes converted to binary for machine processing since the CPU has an extensive set of instructions that operate on binary numbers but relatively few to manipulate BCD integers.

When it is necessary to convert binary numbers to BCD representation, the conversion is accomplished by repeated division by 10 (binary 1010). Each remainder is a BCD digit starting with the low-order digit. This is frequently done before internal binary numbers are output for display as a decimal value.

Example 3.18

Using base 2 arithmetic, 99 in BCD is converted to binary as

$$N_2 = 1001 \times 1010 + 1001 = 0110\ 0011$$

Example 3.19

The binary number $0010\ 0100_2$ is converted to the machine representation of the BCD equivalent using binary arithmetic for division as follows:

$$\frac{0010\ 0100}{1010} = 0011 + (0110)$$

$$\frac{0011}{1010} = 0 + (0011)$$

Here the remainders in parentheses represent the binary sequence

$$0011\ 0110$$

which is interpreted as 36 as a decimal equivalent.

EXERCISES

3.2.2.1. Convert $1000\ 0000_2$ to BCD by repeatedly dividing by 1010_2 in binary.

3.2.2.2. Convert the BCD number 509 to binary using both base 10 and base 2 arithmetic.

3.2.2.3. Consider the multiplication of numbers in BCD representation. Devise an algorithm to multiply a multidigit BCD value by a single-digit multiplier, assuming that only binary multiplication is possible and the digits are in unpacked form. Further assume that a BCD addition instruction is available to sum the partial results.

3.2.3 Negative BCD Integers

The MC68000 has instructions to perform arithmetic on BCD numbers represented in ten's-complement notation. As described in Section 3.1, the ten's complement of a decimal number N is formed by

$$N' = 10^L - N \qquad\qquad 3.18$$

when L digits are used to represent the number. For hand calculation, the ten's complement is easily formed by complementing the number digit by digit (nine's complement) and adding 1 to the result.

Example 3.20

The ten's complement of 1319 in a five-digit representation is

$$N' = 100,000 - 1319 = (99,999 - 1319) + 1 = 98,681$$

The BCD representation in memory would be

$$1001\ 1000\ 0110\ 1000\ 0001_2$$

Example 3.21

The ten's complement of a number can also be formed by subtracting it from 0 and ignoring the high-order borrow. Thus the ten's complement of 98,681 is

$$0 - 98,681 = 01319$$

as shown. The MC68000 instruction NBCD (negate decimal) performs this operation to form the ten's complement of a number.

EXERCISES

3.2.3.1. Determine the machine representation (binary) of the following signed BCD numbers with a word length of 16 bits.
   (a) 124
   (b) -1
   (c) -1000
   (d) 5024

3.2.3.2. What is the range of a signed BCD number that can be represented by m binary digits for
   (a) $m = 8$
   (b) $m = 16$
   (c) $m = 32$
   when the positive value is restricted to the maximum value of $10^L - 1$ for L decimal digits?

3.2.3.3. Show that the nine's complement of a BCD digit can be formed by adding 6 and then forming the one's complement of the result in binary notation.

3.3 FLOATING-POINT REPRESENTATION

The representation for numbers that we considered previously assumed that the radix point was located in a fixed position, yielding either an integer or a fraction as the interpretation of the internal machine representation. The programmer's responsibility would be to scale numerical operands to fit within a selected word length and then unscale the results to obtain the correct values. Of course, the radix point is not actually stored with the number, but its position must be remembered by the programmer. This method of representation is called *fixed-point*.

In practice, the machine value is limited to a finite range which is determined by the number of binary digits used in the representation. For a 32-bit word, the range of signed fixed-point integers is about $+2^{31}$ or $+10^{11}$. Thus the limited range of fixed-point notation is a drawback for certain applications. Furthermore, arithmetic units operating on fixed-point numbers generally have no capability of rounding results. As discussed in several references in the Further Reading section for this chapter, this limits the usefulness of fixed-point notation in scientific computing.

To overcome many of the limitations of fixed-point notation, a notation that is the counterpart of scientific notation is used for numbers in digital systems. The *floating-point* notation represents a number as a fractional part times a selected base raised to a power. In the machine representation, only the fractional part and the value of the exponent are stored. The decimal equivalent is written as

$$N.n = f \times r^e \tag{3.19}$$

where f is the fraction or *mantissa* and e is a positive or negative integer called the *exponent*. The choice for the base is usually base 2, although base 16 is sometimes used.

A number of choices are presented to the designer of a floating-point format. This applies whether the arithmetic operations are carried out by the CPU or its co-processor directly or by a software package containing routines for floating-point arithmetic. The number of formats is bewildering and only recently has an attempt been made to standardize floating-point arithmetic for computers.

The proposed IEEE standard has been adopted by Motorola for a number of their products. This IEEE standard describes precisely the data formats and other aspects of floating-point arithmetic required to provide consistent operation of a program even when it is executed on different computer systems.

3.3.1 Floating-Point Formats

The typical floating-point format stores the fraction and the exponent together in an m-bit representation. The choice for a fixed-length floating-point format is commonly 32 or 64 bits, referred to as single precision and double precision, respectively. Extended formats with $m > 64$ are occasionally used when greater range or precision is required.

Once the length of the floating-point representation is chosen, a number of choices for both the length and the format of the fraction and exponent are possible. Since either or both could be negative as well as positive, a signed fraction and a signed exponent are required. Finally, the interpretation of the bits within the floating-point representation depends on the placement of the fraction and exponent.

Many floating-point formats employ a sign-magnitude representation for the fraction. The most significant bit of the word is reserved for the sign, and this facilitates testing for a positive or negative number. The fraction is generally normalized to yield as many significant digits as possible. Thus, in a base r system, the most significant digit is in the leftmost position in the fraction. For nonzero numbers in the binary system, the leftmost digit will be a 1. As the arithmetic unit or the program shifts the digits in the fraction during arithmetic operations, the exponent is adjusted accordingly. When normalized as a base 2 value, the magnitude of the fraction is

$$0.5 \le |f| < 1 \tag{3.20}$$

unless the number is zero. The number of digits reserved for the fraction represents a compromise between the precision of the fraction and the range of the exponent. A typical single-precision format (32 bits) might contain an 8-bit exponent and a 23-bit fraction, excluding sign.

An exponent could be represented in two's complement or any other notation that allows signed values. A different alternative, which permits the exponent to be represented internally as a positive number only, is to add an offset value. This value is often called an *excess*. For this format, positive bias or offset is added to all exponents such that the number is read as

$$N.n = fr^{e' - N_b} \tag{3.21}$$

where e' is the actual value of the stored exponent and N_b is the positive offset. For an L-bit exponent in a binary base, the positive number added is usually of the form

$$N_b = 2^{L-1} \tag{3.22}$$

although the IEEE standard format discussed later uses a value of $N_b - 1$.

Example 3.22

One IBM floating-point format has the following representation for a 32-bit word:

(a) Sign as the most significant bit (leftmost bit)
(b) Next 7 bits as exponent with excess-64 or 40_{16} with radix 16
(c) Next 24 bits as fraction in base 16

Thus $+1.0$ is represented as

$$(0.1)_{16} \times 16^1$$

for which the stored exponent becomes 41_{16}. The internal representation is

$$4110\ 0000_{16}$$

Example 3.23

One PDP-11 (Digital Equipment Corporation) floating-point format uses the following conventions in a 32-bit word:

(a) Sign as the most significant bit (leftmost bit).
(b) Next 8 bits as exponent in excess-128 notation with radix 2.

(c) Next 23 bits as fraction. These 23 bits are derived from a 24-bit fraction always normalized (i.e., the leftmost bit will be a 1 in a nonzero number). The most significant bit of the normalized fraction is not stored since it is always 1.

The representation of $+12$ is thus

$$0.11_2 \times 2^{132-128}$$

and is represented internally as

$$0\ 1000\ 0100\ 1000\ 0000\ 0000\ 0000\ 0000\ 000_2$$

Notice that the leading bit of the fraction is a 1 and it is not stored with the floating-point number. This has been termed a *hidden bit* and would be restored by a floating-point hardware processor when the value is processed.

EXERCISES

3.3.1.1. Discuss the various factors that influence the choice of the exponent length, mantissa length, and choice of radix in a floating-point number. Compute the various ranges for a choice of an L-bit exponent in excess notation, a k-bit fraction, and a total length of m bits.

3.3.1.2. Express $1/32$ in binary floating-point format using an 8-bit excess-128 exponent and a 24-bit fraction with the leading bit implied. The order in the word from left to right is sign, exponent, and then fraction (PDP-11).

3.3.1.3. Convert the numbers indicated to a 32-bit floating-point representation with the characteristics: the leading bit (bit 31) is the sign of the number; the next 9 bits are the exponent in excess-256 notation and following bits are 22 bits of fraction; and a negative number is represented as the integer's two's complement of the positive floating-point number.
(a) $+16.0$ (b) -1.0

3.3.2 Standard Floating-Point Format

Although the Motorola MC68000 processor does not provide floating-point instructions, many Motorola products support the standard floating-point format proposed by the IEEE. These products include software routines, routines in read-only memory, and a co-processor chip to support floating-point arithmetic in the MC68020 systems.

The basic format allows a floating-point number to be represented in single or 32-bit format as

$$N.n = (-1)^S 2^{e'-127}(1.f) \tag{3.23}$$

where S is the sign bit, e' is the biased exponent, and f is the fraction stored normalized without the leading 1. Internally, the exponent is 8 bits in length and the stored

TABLE 3.5   IEEE STANDARD FLOATING-POINT NOTATION

	Single	Double
Length in bits		
Sign	1	1
Exponent	8	11
Fraction	23 + (1)	52 + (1)
Total	$m = 32 + (1)$	$m = 64 + (1)$
Exponent		
Max e'	255	2047
Min e'	0	0
Bias	127	1023

Note: Fractions are always normalized and the leading 1 (hidden bit) is not stored.

fraction is 23 bits long. A double-precision format allows a 64-bit representation with an 11-bit exponent and a 52-bit fraction.

Various features of these floating-point formats are presented in Tables 3.5 and 3.6. Other extended-precision formats are presented in the references in the Further Reading section of this chapter.

Example 3.24

The numbers $+1.0$, $+3.0$, and -1.0 have the following representations in the standard 32-bit format:

(a) Since $1.0 = 1.0 \times 2^0$, the internal value is $3F80\ 0000_{16}$.

TABLE 3.6   INTERNAL FORMAT BY BIT NUMBER

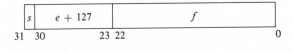

(i) Single

(ii) Double

(b) Since $3.0 = 1.5 \times 2^1$, the exponent is 128 and the fraction is 1.100_2 without the leading 1. Thus the internal value is $4040\ 0000_{16}$.

(c) Since $-1 = -1.0 \times 2^0$, the result requires the sign bit to be 1 in the representation $BF80\ 0000_{16}$.

EXERCISES

3.3.2.1. Write the internal machine representation for the following numbers in the standard floating-point single-precision format.
(a) 0.5   (b) -0.5 (c) 2^{-126}

3.3.2.2. What is the decimal value of the largest positive number that may be represented in single-precision standard format if the biased exponent is limited to a maximum of 254 when a valid number is being represented? (The value 255 is reserved for special operands.)

3.3.2.3. Express the following numbers in the internal representation using standard double-precision floating-point format.
(a) 7.0   (b) -30

3.4 ASCII REPRESENTATION OF ALPHANUMERIC CHARACTERS

Since m binary digits can represent 2^m distinct states, it is possible to assign a meaning to each possible combination of the m digits to produce a code that represents alphabetic, numeric, or other information. One of the major uses of codes is to allow human-readable input or output data to be manipulated internally by the computer. These internal binary representations are seldom desired as output except possibly for debugging purposes. Thus most computer systems will have routines (or hardware) to convert internal binary codes to readable form, and vice versa.

The code used by Motorola to represent alphanumeric characters is the ASCII (American Standard Code for Information Interchange) code, which is given in Appendix I of this text. The 7-bit codes shown in the appendix are the hexadecimal values of the ASCII characters as the values would be stored in memory. For example, the ASCII value "1" would be stored as 31_{16} or $0011\ 0001_2$.

Numbers, letters, and special characters recognized by the assembler and other Motorola system programs are stored internally in the ASCII code as 8-bit values in which one byte is used to represent one character. On output to devices such as CRT terminals or line printers, the ASCII code is transmitted unchanged. If the internal values are in binary or BCD, they must be converted to ASCII format before output for external devices that require ASCII. References in the Further Reading section give a number of examples of such conversions useful to the assembly language programmer. Programs for this purpose are given in Chapter 7 of this book.

A number of other codes are available for computer applications, each with special characteristics and advantages. Several of the references for this chapter discuss codes in more detail. Mackenzie, in particular, gives a comprehensive discussion of many of the commonly used codes and a complete presentation for the ASCII code.

Example 3.25

The ASCII character string 'INPUT' has the following internal representation:

49 4E 50 55 54

where each two digits (in hexadecimal) represent one alphabetic character.

EXERCISES

3.4.1. How many bytes of memory are required to store the text of a textbook with 100,000 words if the text is stored in ASCII code? Assume five characters per word. If a MC68000 system memory can store 2^{24} bytes, what percentage of the memory is used by the text?

3.4.2. Convert the following text into ASCII code (internal hexadecimal representation):

"THE MOTOROLA MC68000"

3.4.3. Show the machine representation of the number 255 in the following ways.
  (a) Binary
  (b) Binary-coded decimal
  (c) ASCII

3.4.4. Define the method and convert the following as directed.
  (a) 45 (BCD) to binary
  (b) 45 (BCD) to ASCII
  (c) −45 (BCD in ten's-complement notation) to ASCII assuming a three-digit BCD number with sign.

3.4.5. Can a single binary variable be used to represent the Morse code?

FURTHER READING

The books by Stein and Munro, Hwang, and Sterbenz listed below present a highly mathematical view of number representations. Sterbenz concentrates on floating-point notation. The articles in *IEEE Computer* are recommended for information on the IEEE standard format.

Weller presents a number of conversion techniques between data types of use to the assembly language programmer. The design of computer hardware and the use of various number representations for arithmetic operations is discussed by Abd-Alla and Meltzer. Mackenzie discusses the details of a large number of codes for representation of characters.

ABD-ALLA, ABD-ELFATTAH M., and ARNOLD C. MELZTER, *Principles of Digital Computer Design,* Vol. 1. Englewood Cliffs, N.J.: Prentice-Hall, 1976. (Chapter 4 presents a number of codes.)

COONEN, JEROME T., "An Implementation Guide to a Proposal Standard for Floating-Point Arithmetic," *IEEE Computer,* 13, No. 1 (January 1980), 68–79.

HWANG, KAI, *Computer Arithmetic.* New York: Wiley, 1979.

IEEE Computer, **14,** No. 3 (March 1981). (Several articles in this issue discuss the proposed floating point standard.)

MACKENZIE, CHARLES E., *Coded Character Sets: History and Development.* Reading, Mass: Addison-Wesley, 1980.

STEIN, MARVIN L., and WILLIAM D. MUNRO, *Introduction to Machine Arithmetic.* Reading, Mass.: Addison-Wesley, 1971.

STERBENZ, PAT H., *Floating-Point Computation.* Englewood Cliffs, N.J.: Prentice-Hall, 1974.

WELLER, WALTER J., *Assembly Language Programming for Small Computers.* Lexington, Mass.: Lexington Books, 1975.

4

Introduction to the MC68000

The characteristics of the MC68000 as a circuit element and a programmable processor are introduced in this chapter. These characteristics are of interest to the system designer, programmer, and interface designer. For the most part, the terminology used follows that employed by Motorola in its literature. The cover page of a 50-page product description document for the MC68000 is shown in Figure 4.1. Many of the features listed on the product sheet are discussed and explained in this chapter. The discussion also applies to the MC68010 except where differences are noted.

The product description of Figure 4.1 summarizes a number of features of the MC68000, including details of the manufacturing technology. The fabrication process is summarized by noting that the integrated circuit chip is created using the HMOS technology. Also, the chip is shown in a 64-pin package with the signal lines designated for each connection (pin). Such details are important to hardware designers and others concerned with utilizing the MC68000 as a circuit element.

Machine language or assembly language programmers are interested in the characteristics of the MC68000 as a programmable processor. The description in Figure 4.1 of the processor's register set, instruction set, and addressing modes are important for this purpose. To a large extent, these characteristics define the power and the flexibility of the processor in meeting the requirements of a programming application.

The instructions that the processor executes are coded in machine language format in memory. These instructions may be created by a programmer coding these binary sequences directly. More likely, an assembler program translates assembly language statements written in symbolic notation into machine language instructions. The assembly language programmer rarely works directly with the machine language

MOTOROLA

Advance Information

16-BIT MICROPROCESSING UNIT

Advances in semiconductor technology have provided the capability to place on a single silicon chip a microprocessor at least an order of magnitude higher in performance and circuit complexity than has been previously available. The MC68000 is the first of a family of such VLSI microprocessors from Motorola. It combines state-of-the-art technology and advanced circuit design techniques with computer sciences to achieve an architecturally advanced 16-bit microprocessor.

The resources available to the MC68000 user consist of the following:

- 32-Bit Data and Address Registers
- 16 Megabyte Direct Addressing Range
- 56 Powerful Instruction Types
- Operations on Five Main Data Types
- Memory Mapped I/O
- 14 Addressing Modes

As shown in the programming model, the MC68000 offers seventeen 32-bit registers in addition to the 32-bit program counter and a 16-bit status register. The first eight registers (D0-D7) are used as data registers for byte (8-bit), word (16-bit), and long word (32-bit) data operations. The second set of seven registers (A0-A6) and the system stack pointer may be used as software stack pointers and base address registers. In addition, these registers may be used for word and long word address operations. All seventeen registers may be used as index registers.

MC68000L4
(4 MHz)
MC68000L6
(6 MHz)
MC68000L8
(8 MHz)
MC68000L10
(10 MHz)

HMOS
(HIGH-DENSITY, N-CHANNEL,
SILICON-GATE DEPLETION LOAD)

16-BIT
MICROPROCESSOR

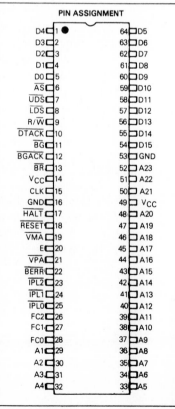

L SUFFIX
CERAMIC PACKAGE
CASE 746

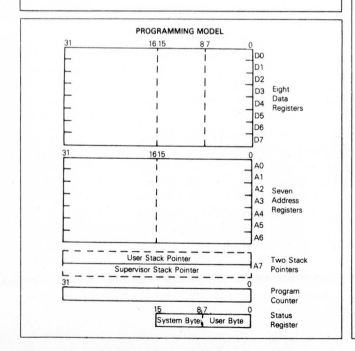

Figure 4.1 Product data for the MC68000. (Courtesy of Motorola, Inc.)

program, but a knowledge of the machine language formats is necessary for a full understanding of the capability of the processor.

This chapter first introduces the MC68000 as an integrated circuit. Subsequent sections then describe the register set, instruction set, and addressing modes, all of which define the programming model of the processor. The machine language of the MC68000 is also presented to illustrate the correspondence between the bit patterns of the instructions and the operation of the processor. The chapter concludes with a presentation of the organization of memory in an MC68000 system. Many of the features covered in this chapter are summarized briefly in Appendices II, III, and IV.

4.1 THE MC68000 AS AN INTEGRATED CIRCUIT PROCESSOR

The patent for the first integrated circuit was filed by Jack Kilby of Texas Instruments in 1959 for a device that was equivalent to several transistors and associated components. According to Motorola, the MC68000 has approximately 68,000 components that are integrated on a piece of silicon smaller than Kilby's device. Improvements in the manufacturing technology of integrated circuits over more than 20 years have resulted in a steady increase in the packing density of a chip as measured by the number of circuit elements per unit area on a single chip. There has also been an increase in the speed of operation and a lowering of power consumption per element.

Once the chip is produced, it must be packaged in a form suitable for inclusion with other integrated circuits on a printed-circuit board. The MC68000, for example, is sold in a standard package with 64 pins to connect to the system bus. The function of these signal lines and the total power consumption of the CPU as well as the mechanical attributes of the package influence the electrical and mechanical design of a system.

4.1.1 The MC68000 as an Integrated Circuit

The MC68000 is an integrated circuit characterized as a very large scale integration (VLSI) device since thousands of circuit elements are contained on a single silicon chip.[1] Circuit elements, such as transistors and resistors, are connected to form the control, storage, and interfacing circuitry of the chip itself. Figure 4.2 shows the MC68000 enlarged about 30 times before it is packaged. The actual chip is about 246 by 280 mils in size, which is about 68,000 square mils in area, 1 mil being one-thousandth of an inch. It also contains about 68,000 transistors, quite a coincidence. The regions of the chip are illustrated in Figure 4.3. A large ROM area on the chip is used to store *microcode,* which causes the execution of machine language instructions at the

---

[1]Kilby's device would be considered today as an example of small scale integration (SSI) since it contained fewer than 10 transistors. VLSI devices, such as the MC68000, have several thousand transistors.

circuit level. The execution units and the arithmetic and logic unit (ALU) perform various operations on addresses and data. These values can be transferred through the buffers, the bus control logic, and the decoders between the CPU and external devices.

Instructions that cause traps or branches utilize the appropriate programmed logic array (PLA) to determine the order in which subsequent instructions are executed in the program. Logical equations are implemented in the PLAs to control the op-

Figure 4.2   Enlarged photograph of the MC68000. (Courtesy of Motorola, Inc.)

MC68000

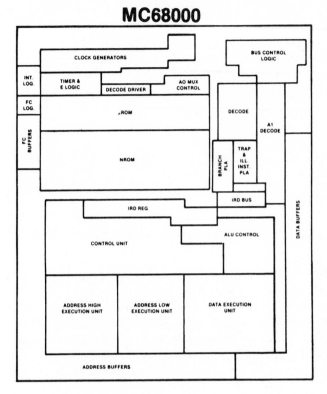

Figure 4.3 Organization of the MC68000 chip. (Courtesy of Motorola, Inc.)

eration of other circuit elements within the CPU. In this regard, a PLA is functionally similar to the ROM used for the microcode.

The method of constructing a chip is referred to as the *technology*. The name given to a particular technology broadly indicates the type of transistors (bipolar or field-effect), the fabrication procedure involved, and the characteristics of the finished device. The characteristics of integrated circuits produced by various technologies have different densities of elements per unit area, different speeds of operation, and different power consumptions.[2] Integrated circuits utilizing field-effect transistors, for example, are called metal-oxide-semiconductor (MOS) devices since they are physically constructed into three regions using different materials (metal, an oxide of silicon, and the silicon substrate or bulk region). Several transistors are combined with other circuit elements to form a cell. Each cell might hold 1 bit of information, for example. The ROM areas of the chip represent a large number of such cells taken together to form a memory.

The technology for the MC68000 is called high-density metal-oxide-semiconductor (HMOS) technology. This technique scales down the size of elements com-

---

[2]Integrated circuits are fabricated using several other technologies. Besides the MOS process used for the MC68000, the *bipolar* and the *complementary MOS* (CMOS) technologies are popular.

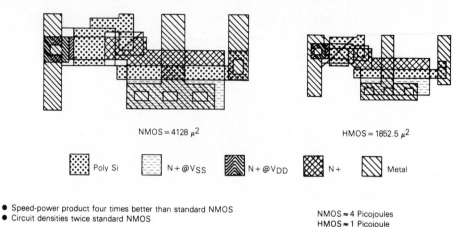

NMOS = 4128 μ^2 HMOS = 1852.5 μ^2

▦ Poly Si   ▤ N + @V$_{SS}$ ▧ N + @V$_{DD}$ ▩ N +   ▨ Metal

- Speed-power product four times better than standard NMOS
- Circuit densities twice standard NMOS

NMOS ≈ 4 Picojoules
HMOS ≈ 1 Picojoule

Figure 4.4   Comparison of MOS and HMOS. (Courtesy of Motorola, Inc.)

pared to the standard MOS process and thus increases the speed and reduces the power consumption for each transistor in the CPU.

A comparison of the MOS circuit cell used in earlier microprocessors and the HMOS cell used in MC68000 circuits is shown in Figure 4.4. The scaling or reduction from NMOS (*n*-channel MOS) circuits to HMOS by a factor of 2 yields an increase in speed of about 2 and a decrease in power by the same amount. A figure of merit for integrated circuits is the reciprocal of the speed–power product. The *speed–power product* is defined as

$$\text{product} = (\text{delay time}) \times (\text{power per element}) \tag{4.1}$$

and is measured in joules (watt-second). The delay time is the time needed for an element to change state, as from a $\{1\}$ to a $\{0\}$ in a storage cell. The speed–power product for the MC68000 is about 1 picojoule or 10^{-12} joule, which represents an improvement factor of about 4 over previous technology. The figure of merit, taken as the reciprocal of the speed–power product, is 10^{12} for the MC68000.

Other details of the MC68000 fabrication may be found in the references cited in the Further Reading section of this chapter. In fact, page 1 of the Motorola *User's Manual* (third edition) for the MC68000 describes the HMOS process. This information can be used by a system designer to compare processors and anticipate future improvements. For example, Motorola expects a reduction by a factor of 20 in the speed–power product for its processors in the near future, due to improvements in the HMOS technology. This will allow greater speed of operation and lower power consumption in systems using this improved technology.

Example 4.1

If a circuit element has a delay time of 1 nanosecond (10^{-9} second) and a switching power of 1 milliwatt (10^{-3} watt), the speed–power product is 10^{-12} joule. Scaling reduces the linear size of the element by a factor of s (where $s > 1$). This should reduce the power consumption and the delay time by a factor of s.[3] Thus the speed–power product should be divided by s^2 in the scaled circuit, compared to the product for an unscaled circuit.

4.1.2 Packaging, Signal Lines, and Power

The MC68000 is available in several different packages, which may differ in the material used or in the physical size and shape. In each package, the MC68000 has 64 signal lines that connect the processor to external circuits. Other versions of the MC68000 processor may have more (MC68020) or fewer (MC68008) connections. The technology used to fabricate the chip itself basically determines the power consumption of the CPU. However, the packaging method influences the amount of heat that can be dissipated from the chip.

Packaging.   The final step in the manufacture of the integrated circuit chip is packaging the device so that it can be protected from the environment and connected electrically to other elements in a system. The type of package determines the cost, operating temperature range, size, mechanical strength, and similar properties of the completed product. Several packages for the MC68000 are shown in Figure 4.5.

The standard package for the MC68000 is the dual-in-line package (DIP) with 64 pins, either in plastic (G10) or ceramic (L10). Motorola literature states that the plastic case is more damage resistant, while the ceramic package is usable over a wider temperature range and provides more protection from environmental factors, such as high humidity.

Figure 4.5 also shows the smaller 68 terminal chip carrier (Z10), which measures about 1 inch on a side and is 0.1 inch high. By comparison, the DIP packages are considerably larger, measuring 3 inches by 0.9 inch by 0.3 inch high. Any of the packages are mounted by soldering to a printed-circuit board or plugging into a special socket. Of the 68 connections to the chip carrier, only 64 are used for the MC68000.

Signal Lines for the MC68000.   A diagram of the MC68000 signal lines is shown in Figure 4.6. The 64 signal lines control the operation of data transfers, interrupt requests, and similar operations. A complete discussion of the meaning of each signal line is given in Chapter 12. The signal lines are introduced here simply to complete the introduction of the MC68000 chip.

From an examination of Figure 4.6 it is obvious that every one of the 64 connections to the CPU is used. This could constrain future development. For example, if Motorola desired to increase the addressing range of the MC68000, no pins would be available in the 64-pin DIP version for this enhancement. An alternative would be to design a new package with more address lines or multiplex (in time) some of the existing signal lines. The latter approach complicates the interfacing requirements, in that

---

[3]Assuming that the voltage is constant, the power is reduced by s due to the reduction in current by a factor of s. The supply voltage to the chip is 5.0 volts for the MC68000.

Figure 4.5 Packages for the MC68000 chip. (Courtesy of Motorola, Inc.)

one signal line now means different things at different times and external circuitry must be designed to decode the signals on the line. Also, the speed of operation of the processor would decrease. Future processors with 32 address lines and 32 data lines will require novel packaging to achieve maximum performance. These advanced processors may also require new technology for fabrication of the chip to achieve the necessary circuit densities.

Example 4.2

The MC68000 has 64 signal lines in its present configuration, of which 25 are used for control of the system and similar purposes. A full 32-bit version would require about 90

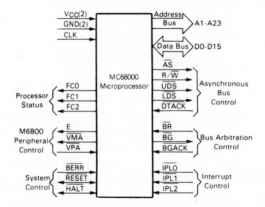

Figure 4.6 Signal lines of the MC68000. (Courtesy of Motorola, Inc.)

signal lines, including 64 for addresses and data transfer and the remainder for control purposes.

Power consumption.   The 64-pin DIP version of the MC68000 has a power consumption of about 1.5 watts. In a system with hundreds of integrated circuits, the power consumption, and consequently the heat generated, may be excessive. For example, the Motorola Design Module described in Section 1.1 requires about 20 watts of power. Since excessive heating is a major cause of chip failure, ventilation may be necessary even in a system with few devices and an apparently low power consumption.

4.1.3 Processor Design

As with many microprocessors, the circuit-level operation of the MC68000 is controlled by a *microprogrammed* sequence of instructions stored in two ROM sections within the CPU chip. As machine language instructions from external memory are fetched and decoded, they, in turn, cause the execution of a microprogram. This microprogram controls all activity on the external signal lines and all the data transfers or operations within the CPU during the execution of that instruction. Since the microprogram cannot be modified except by creating a new chip with different microcode, the user is rarely concerned with the details of the processor operations at this level. However, understanding the microcode is the only way to determine exactly what the processor is doing in response to an instruction.

One aspect of the microprogram that might effect the design of a complex system is the processor's *prefetch* operation. When one instruction is fetched by the CPU, the word in memory following the instruction word is also fetched as the instruction is being decoded and executed. This means that the processor signal lines are addressing and reading from a new location before the previous operation is finished. If hardware is being designed or debugged based on the cycle-by-cycle operation of the processor, it may be necessary to consider the microprogrammed sequence. The references in the Further Reading section discuss in more detail the prefetch feature and other aspects of the microprogram for the MC68000. Also, a brief discussion of the prefetch is presented in Appendix IV-H. The exact details of the microcoded sequence for a particular instruction can be obtained by contacting Motorola.

EXERCISES

4.1.1. The speed–power product represents the switching energy for a single element in the CPU, such as a storage cell, to change states. If the theoretical minimum switching energy for HMOS technology is 2×10^{-16} joule and the delay time is 0.02 nanosecond, what is the power per element? How much improvement is gained in the figure of merit for an ideal device over that of the present MC68000, which has a figure of merit of 10^{12}?

4.1.2. Compute the area scaling factor for the MC68000 HMOS process with that of the MOS process by comparing the areas shown in Figure 4.4.

4.2 THE MC68000 REGISTER SET

Just as the memory is used to store instructions and data associated with a program, the CPU contains storage elements called *registers,* which hold information needed for the instruction currently being processed. A register consists of one or more storage cells, each containing 1 bit of information. The *length* of the register is defined as the number of bits that may be stored or read simultaneously. A CPU contains a large number of registers, most of them used for specific purposes within the CPU. A few of these registers, called *programmable* registers, are available to the machine language or assembly language programmer via the processor's instruction set. In the MC68000, the programmable registers are the general-purpose registers, the program counter, and the status register. The basic register set of the MC68010 is the same although several new registers have been added.

The general-purpose registers of a processor hold addresses or data values being manipulated by an instruction. The *program counter* holds the address of the next instruction to be fetched from memory. The *status register* contains bits that indicate the state or status of the processor and information about the results of arithmetic or similar operations. In the MC68000, the general-purpose registers are divided into eight *data registers* and nine *address registers.* This CPU has a 32-bit program counter and a 16-bit status register.

Figure 4.7 shows the MC68000 register set and a simplified diagram of the internal and external transfer paths for the processor. The address, data, and control signal lines connect to the system bus as explained in Chapter 2. Internally, the processor contains programmable registers to hold values which are treated as data or addresses. These values can be transferred to the arithmetic and logic unit (ALU) for arithmetic computations. Data values held in the data registers of the processor can be transferred to and from memory or between the CPU and peripheral devices via the data signal lines. Values in the address registers can be placed on the address bus to reference locations in memory. These operations are controlled by machine language instructions which are fetched from memory via the data signal lines and then decoded in the instruction register. The instruction register is not part of the programmable register set of the processor since it cannot be referenced directly by MC68000 instructions.

The programmable register set of any processor may be defined in terms of its features useful to a programmer. The number, type, and length (in bits) of the registers and their connection via internal and external data paths determine the basic capability of the processor to execute instructions using these registers. In general, an

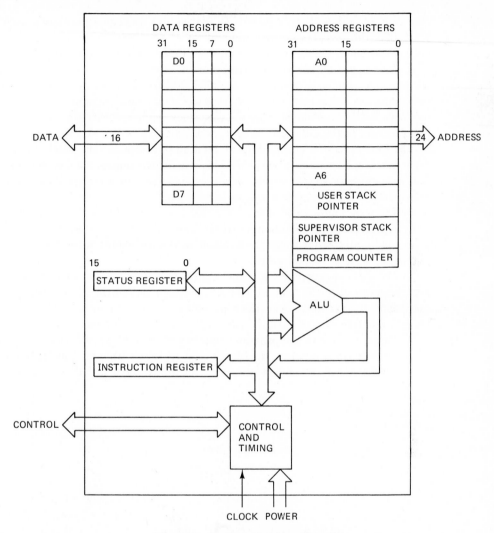

Figure 4.7   Register set and transfer paths.

increased number of available registers will simplify programming at the assembly language level. Additionally, program execution speed is increased if registers are used to hold operands since operations between registers require less processing time than do operations that reference external devices or memory.

Registers are also used to hold addresses of data items stored externally to the processor. These addresses can easily be changed during program execution by modifying the contents of the registers. Modern programming techniques favor this method of indirect register addressing rather than allowing the program to modify itself by changing an address that is part of an instruction. In many processors, such as the MC68000, the registers holding the address of an operand may be modified by the addition (or subtraction) of the contents of other registers called *index registers.*

Two of the address registers in Figure 4.7 are designed as the *user stack pointer* and the *supervisor stack pointer.* These stack pointers are used by the CPU to save return addresses and similar information on the stack during operations such as subroutine calls. In the user mode, only the user stack pointer (USP) is active and available to a program or the CPU. In the supervisor mode, the CPU uses the supervisor stack pointer (SSP) to store return addresses after an interrupt or subroutine call. However, it can also read or modify the USP. This use of two separate stack pointers assures that user mode programs cannot alter the supervisor stack area in memory and thus information for the operating system is protected.

The program counter of the MC68000 is used to address 2^{23} word (16-bit) locations in memory: over 8 million locations. The full 32-bit addressing capability of the program counter is not currently available in the MC68000 since there are a limited number of address signal lines.

The CPU also contains a status register that holds logical variables which indicate the status of the CPU and the interrupt system as well as the results of arithmetic operations. Instructions are available to test or change the contents of the status register as a program executes.

Figure 4.8 shows the programmable register set of the MC68000 and indicates the numerical designation of the bits in each register. Table 4.1 lists the registers according to their primary usage and also gives the symbolic notation used to refer to a

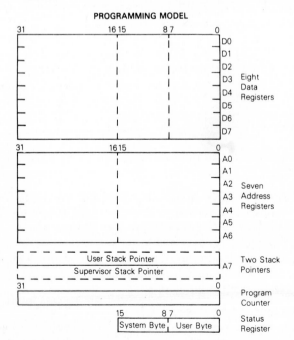

Figure 4.8 Programmable register set of the MC68000.

TABLE 4.1   REGISTER USAGE AND SYMBOLIC NOTATION

Register	Symbolic notation	Usage
Data	D0	Accumulator
	D1	Buffer register
	.	Index register
	D7	Temporary storage
Address	A0	Indirect addressing
	A1	Stack pointer
	.	Index register
	A6	
System stack pointer	A7 or SP	
User SP	A7 or USP	Subroutine calls (user mode)
Supervisor SP	A7 or SSP	Interrupt processing or subroutine calls (supervisor mode)
Program counter	PC	Instruction addressing
Status register	SR	System status, condition codes

particular register. The assembly language programmer, for example, would use this notation to designate a register in an assembly language statement. The fact that either the USP or SSP can be referred to as A7 causes no confusion since the stack pointer referenced is determined by the mode (supervisor or user) of the processor.

In order to be consistent with the register transfer notation defined in the Appendix, the contents of a register or memory location are designated here by enclosing the item in parentheses. Thus (D2) means the contents of data register D2. When selected bits of an operand are designated, the bit numbers are enclosed in brackets, with the beginning and ending bit number separated by a colon if consecutive bits are specified. For example, bits 0 through 7 of data register D1 are indicated by (D1) [7:0]. An operand designated by < operand > means that any valid operand, as determined in the discussion, may be substituted into the expression. The designation < Dn >, for example, means that any data register can be specified (i.e., any one of D0, D1, . . . , D7).

4.2.1 Data Registers

The MC68000 has eight registers designated as data registers. The registers are referred to symbolically by number as Dn, where n = 0, 1, . . . , 7. The internal bus structure of the CPU allows a byte operand (Dn) [7:0], a word operand (Dn) [15:0], or a longword operand (Dn) [31:0] to be manipulated in the data register selected. Since three lengths are possible, the processor instructions that reference a data register must indicate the operand length. Only the corresponding bits of the specified register are modified by that instruction. The portion of the register involved may be used as an accumulator, a storage register, a buffer register, or as an index register.

As accumulators, the data registers hold operands of the specified length and

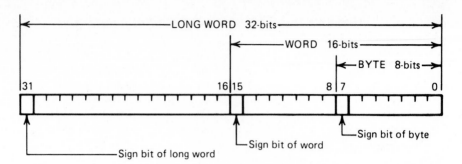

Figure 4.9 Data register format.

allow arithmetic, logical, and other operations. These registers are also used to store temporarily operands generated in other registers of the processor. The data registers act as buffer registers when data values are transferred in or out of the processor via the data signal lines. For the MC68000 with its 16 data signal lines, the possible transfers include an 8-bit or 16-bit quantity in a single transfer or a 32-bit value in two transfers of 16 bits each.

A data register can be used as an index register whose contents are added to the value in an address register to form an address of an operand. The power of this addressing capability is such that the index may be modified by any processor instruction that operates on a data register. The index value may be changed in very sophisticated ways during program execution. This usually occurs within a program loop.

Example 4.3

Figure 4.9 shows a data register of the MC68000 with the bits designated from 0 on the right to 31 on the left. The sign bit of a byte-length two's-complement number would be bit 7, as indicated. Any access of the register specifying a byte operand would affect only bits 0 through 7; the remaining bits would be unchanged. Similarly, the sign bit of a word operand is bit 15 and that of a longword operand is bit 31, as shown in the figure.

4.2.2 Address Registers

The MC68000 has nine address registers which accept word or longword values only. Seven of the address registers, symbolically designated A0, A1, ..., A6, are shared by programs in either the supervisor or the user mode, but only one of the two remaining address registers can be referenced as A7 by a program operating in a specific mode. These two registers are the system stack pointers. The other seven registers available to a program can also be used to address "private" stacks defined by the programmer.

The primary use of the address registers is to hold the address of an operand in memory. Since an address register is 32 bits in length, an address may range up to

$$2^{32} = 4,294,967,296$$

locations. In the MC68000, however, only the lower 24 bits may be output via the address signal lines of the processor. Thus, when accessing memory, an address register of the MC68000 should be considered to contain a 24-bit address.

In the MC68000, a *stack* consists of a set of contiguous memory locations addressed by a register designated as a *stack pointer*. Items stored on the stack are retrieved in reverse order, reminiscent of a push-down stack of cafeteria plates. The stack is accessed to store or retrieve data from one end only in a last-in-first-out (LIFO) manner.

Functionally, a stack pointer contains a value, designated (SP), that is used as an address to point to the top of the stack. The processor uses the value in the stack pointer to address a location from which the processor reads or to which it writes a data item. Information stored on the stack is said to be *pushed* on the stack by a processor write cycle. The item of information is retrieved by a processor read cycle which is called a *pop* or *pull* of the item.

Each address register of the MC68000 may be used as a stack pointer by a program using one of the addressing modes appropriate for stack operations. In these addressing modes, the value in the address register being used as a stack pointer is automatically changed by the proper amount after each push or pop of a data item. The data values in the stack may be either byte, word, or longword values if any of the registers designated as A0, A1, . . . , A6 are used as stack pointers.

Another use of an address register is as an index register. The index value is added to the contents of another address register to compute an effective address of an operand in memory. The same usage was defined for a data register in the preceding section. Thus the MC68000 allows both address and data registers to serve as index registers.

Example 4.4

Figure 4.10(a) shows the format of an address register of the MC68000. The address can be either 16 bits or 32 bits in length. However, the corresponding longword address would be only 24 bits in length when output to the address signal lines.

An indirect memory reference is shown in Figure 4.10(b). The address held in A1 in the example points to an operand at hexadecimal location 1000. Thus the effective address of the operand is designated as the contents of A1 or (A1).

Indexed addressing, shown in part (c) of the figure, allows the sum of two values to be used to determine the operand location. The maximum 24-bit hexadecimal address is FFFFFF.

Example 4.5

The *bottom* of the stack is the first item pushed onto the stack and the *top* of the stack is the last added. Removing (popping) an item is done from the top. A stack may grow from lower addresses to higher memory addresses, or it may grow "down" in memory. These two cases are shown in Figure 4.11(a), where the addressing required is also shown. Our notation ((SP)) means the contents of the stack (i.e., the contents of the location addressed by the stack pointer). When the stack grows down in memory toward lower addresses, (SP) points to the last item (top) and must be decremented before a push. After a

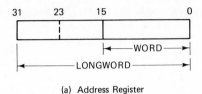

(a) Address Register

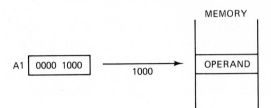

(b) Indirect Memory Reference

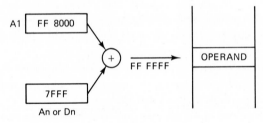

(c) Indexed Memory Reference

Figure 4.10   MC68000 address register usage.

Note: All values are in hexadecimal.

pop, (SP) must be incremented to point to the top again. The opposite is true for a stack that grows upward in memory. The increments (or decrements) are 1, 2, or 4 depending on whether the size of each item on the stack is byte, word, or longword. If an instruction specifies the *predecrement* mode of the MC68000, the CPU automatically subtracts k ($k = 1, 2,$ or 4) from (SP) before the stack pointer value is used as an address. The *postincrement* mode is used to add k to (SP) after use. These addressing modes are discussed in more detail in Section 4.4.

Figure 4.11(b) shows the stack contents before and after a push of the hexadecimal value 1234 onto a word (16-bit) stack. Before the push, the stack pointer contains the hexadecimal address 1000 in the example and the value ((SP)) is FFFF. To push the value, the stack pointer is first decremented by 2 and then used as the address of the stack location for the data value. Therefore, the item is pushed to location 0FFE.

4.2.3 System Stack Pointers

Processors such as the MC68000 save information on a stack in memory whenever the flow of control in a program is altered by a call to subroutine, a trap, or an interrupt.

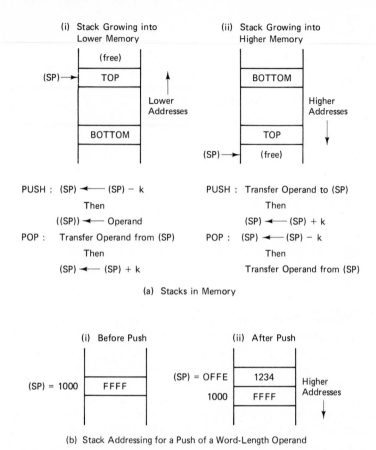

(i) Stack Growing into Lower Memory

(ii) Stack Growing into Higher Memory

PUSH : (SP) ← (SP) − k
Then
((SP)) ← Operand
POP : Transfer Operand from (SP)
Then
(SP) ← (SP) + k

PUSH : Transfer Operand to (SP)
Then
(SP) ← (SP) + k
POP : (SP) ← (SP) − k
Then
Transfer Operand from (SP)

(a) Stacks in Memory

(i) Before Push

(ii) After Push

(SP) = 1000   FFFF

(SP) = OFFE   1234
1000   FFFF

Higher Addresses

(b) Stack Addressing for a Push of a Word-Length Operand

Figure 4.11 Stack operation.

The normal flow of control causes a consecutive sequence of instructions from memory to be executed. This is accomplished in the CPU by incrementing the value of the program counter by the appropriate amount to point to the next instruction even before the current instruction has completed its execution. The next instruction is then fetched using the address in the program counter. However, when the flow of control is changed so that the next instruction in sequence is not the one to be executed, the program counter must be saved before it can be loaded with the new address. In this case, control is passed to the routine associated with the subroutine, trap, or interrupt until its task is completed. Then control must be returned to the next instruction in the preempted sequence. The transfer and return is accomplished by saving the contents of the program counter, designated (PC), on a stack before control is passed to the routine and then restoring (PC) after completion. A simplified diagram of the flow of control is shown in Figure 4.12. In the case of an interrupt or trap, the contents of the status register are also saved on the stack.

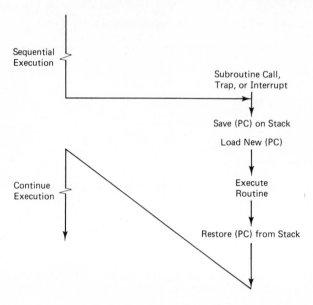

Figure 4.12   Flow of control during program execution.

In the MC68000, the situation is slightly complicated by the fact that the CPU can operate in either the supervisor or the user mode. To avoid conflicts, two separate stack areas in memory are used. In each mode, the active stack pointer, designated as the current *system stack,* contains the address of the stack location in memory. The CPU automatically determines which stack pointer to use based on the active mode. Figure 4.13 shows the method of transition between modes. The user mode can be entered only by having the operating system change to the user mode. Return to the supervisor mode is automatic when the MC68000 processes an *exception.* The exceptions as defined by Motorola include traps, interrupts, and several error conditions recognized by the CPU. The occurrence of any exception causes the appropriate routine to execute in the supervisor mode.

Table 4.2 indicates the difference between the supervisor and user modes. The modes share the general-purpose register set and the program counter. However, a user mode program cannot execute all of the instructions of the MC68000. In particular, instructions used to change the mode or control the system operation are not executable by instructions operating in the user mode. These are called *privileged instructions* and if an attempt is made to execute one by a user mode program, an exception occurs.

Figure 4.13   Transition between modes.

TABLE 4.2   SUPERVISOR VERSUS USER MODE

	Supervisor	User
Register usage	D0–D7, A0–A6, PC, USP	D0–D7, A0–A6, PC
Stack pointer	SSP	USP
Instructions	All	Restricted set
Entered by:	Exception processing	Supervisor program changing mode to user

In the supervisor mode, the active stack pointer is designated as the *supervisor stack pointer* or SSP. The system stack pointer in the user mode is the *user stack pointer* or USP.[4] Each stack accommodates only word or longword data elements which can be pushed onto the stack using the predecrement addressing mode to reference the stack pointer. Thus the stacks extend into memory locations with lower addresses as items are pushed on them. At any time after a stack access, (SP) points to the last location used. A push operation causes (SP) to be decremented by 2 for a word operand or by 4 for a longword operand before the item is stored. After an item on the stack is retrieved, (SP) is increased by 2 or 4, as required.

The system stack is used to save the contents of the program counter automatically during subroutine calls. The 32-bit contents are saved and eventually restored after the subroutine completes. During interrupt or trap processing, however, both the contents of the program counter and that of the status register are saved on the supervisor stack, as indicated in Table 4.3. Two error conditions (address error or bus error) cause seven 16-bit words to be saved on the supervisor stack to enable the programmer to investigate the cause of the error. In addition to the (PC) and (SR), the contents of the instruction register and other data are saved.

Exception processing with the MC68010 is slightly different in that at least *four* 16-bit words are saved on the supervisor stack after an exception is recognized. After an interrupt or trap, the first word pushed indicates the stack length and other information, followed by (PC) and (SR) as for the MC68000. Thus for interrupts and traps, four words are saved, including the (PC) and (SR). An address error or bus error causes a total of 29 words to be placed on the stack. This is to allow instruction continuation if the problem can be corrected by the supervisor program. Instruction continuation allows a virtual memory system to be implemented with the MC68010.

Example 4.6

Figure 4.14 shows the contents of the stacks used during the execution of a user mode program. If the program calls a subroutine, the return address is pushed on the stack using (USP) as the address that is decremented by 4 to accommodate the 32-bit (PC). If an

---

[4]In Motorola literature, the designations for USP and SSP are sometimes given as A7 and A7', respectively. In this text, the acronyms will be used.

TABLE 4.3 STACK USAGE IN SUPERVISOR
MODE FOR THE MC68000

Activity	Items saved on stack
Subroutine call	(PC) [31:0]
Interrupt or trap	(PC) [31:0]
	(SR) [15:0]
Address error or	(PC) [31:0]
bus error	(SR) [15:0]
	Instruction register [15:0]
	Access address [31:0]
	Access info [15:0]

Notes:

1. Access address is the address that was being accessed
   when the error occurred.

2. Access info:
   [2:0]: function code
   [3:3]: 0 = instruction, 1 = not an instruction
   [4:4]: 0 = write, 1 = read

3. The MC68010 has a slightly different stack format as
   described in the text.

interrupt occurs during subroutine execution, the return address within the interrupted
subroutine and the contents of the status register are saved using (SSP). The return from
the interrupt processing followed by the eventual return from the subroutine leave (USP)
and (SSP) as they were initially.

4.2.4 Program Counter

In the MC68000 family of processors, the program counter internally is 32 bits in
length, although only (PC) [23:0] can be used for addressing an instruction location in
an MC68000 system. This allows an addressing range of over 8 million words in memory. Since the MC68000 may have instructions occupying as little as one word or as
many as five words in memory, the program counter is incremented by the proper
amount automatically as the current instruction is executed.

The program counter may be modified by the programmer to change the control
sequence in several ways. The normal sequence of execution can be directly altered by
a program instruction that causes a jump or branch in the program. In this case, no
return address is saved by the CPU since control is not returned to the instruction
following the jump or branch instruction. The jump instruction thus loads the program counter with the new address and destroys its previous contents. In contrast, a
subroutine call or exception causes the current value of the program counter to be
saved on the system stack before its contents are changed to the address of the new
routine to be executed. The last instruction in a subroutine or exception routine must
be an instruction (e.g., Return) to restore the contents of the program counter.

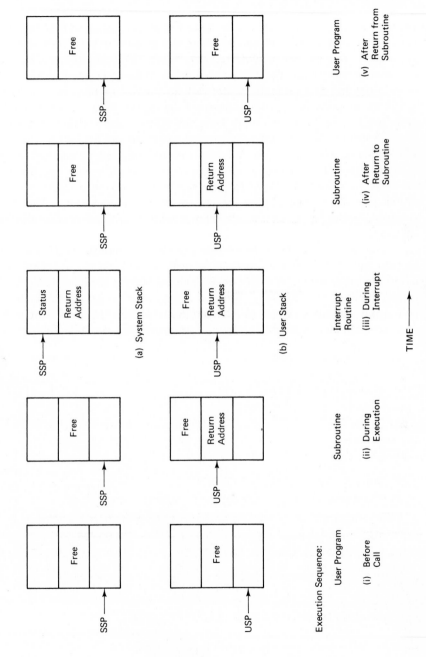

(a) System Stack

(b) User Stack

Execution Sequence:

User Program	Subroutine	Interrupt Routine	Subroutine	User Program
(i) Before Call	(ii) During Execution	(iii) During Interrupt	(iv) After Return to Subroutine	(v) After Return from Subroutine

TIME ———▶

Figure 4.14 Stack usage.

4.2.5 Status Register

During execution, a program can be described at any instant in time by its *state*. The state description contains all the information necessary to stop, then restart, the program. Specifying the instructions and data values, including the contents of the programmable register set, constitutes a complete state description. Assuming that the instructions and data values in memory are not altered if a program is suspended from execution temporarily, only the contents of the register set used by the suspended program must be saved in temporary locations. The contents of these registers must be restored before the program may execute again. In the MC68000, this register set would include selected address and data registers, the program counter, and the status register. Important information about the state of the program is contained in the status register, including its mode, the interrupt status, and the arithmetic or logical conditions that were obtained after the last instruction was executed. The "temporary" storage locations for all of this information, while a program is suspended, is usually the stack.

Figure 4.15 shows the 16-bit status register of the MC68000. The low-order 8 bits are called the *user byte* and can be read or modified by programs executing in either the supervisor or the user mode. The upper byte is called the *system byte* and can be modified only by a program in the supervisor mode. In the figure, each bit is considered separately except the interrupt mask bits SR[10:8], which are taken together as a 3-bit binary number indicating the interrupt level. The other bits are considered

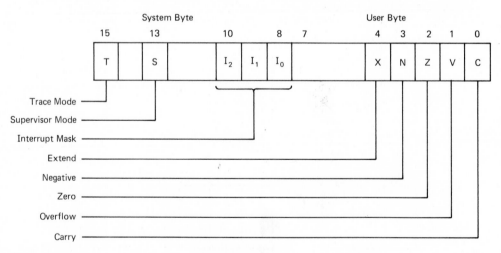

Notes:
(1) Conditions stated are true when the corresponding bit = {1}.
(2) The user byte portion of the status register is referred to as the condition code register (CCR).

Figure 4.15   MC68000 status register.

individual, with a {1} indicating that particular condition is true. Thus SR[13] = {1} indicates that a supervisor mode program is executing, and SR[13] = {0} indicates a user mode program. In practice, the operating system sets SR[13] = {0} and modifies other bits as necessary when control is passed to the user mode program. If an exception condition then occurs, the CPU operating in the supervisor mode saves the current (PC) and (SR) on the stack. The exception condition automatically changes the S bit to {1} and causes the other bits of the status register to be modified as required. As control is returned to the user program, the previous contents of the status register and program counter are pulled from the system stack and restored. When the previous contents of the program counter are restored, the user program continues execution where it left off. Thus control of the CPU mode is determined by the setting of the S bit, which provides a simple and efficient means of switching between modes.

The operating system can cause each instruction to be executed individually by setting the trace mode bit, SR[15], to {1}. After each instruction, a trap is caused and control passes to the trap-handling routine, which is typically designed to aid in debugging a user mode program.

The interrupt system of the MC68000 is controlled by three bits in the status register. These bits act as an interrupt mask for the eight-level priority-interrupt system of the MC68000. Setting these bits with a value from 0 to 6 disables or masks interrupts at the level indicated and those levels below in priority. The level 7 interrupt is referred to as a *nonmaskable interrupt* and cannot be disabled. The decimal value of the interrupt mask is 0 through 7, with priority levels in ascending order. If an interrupt occurs at a given level, the mask bits are automatically set to that level to prevent additional interrupts from that level or a level below it from being received.

The user byte of the status register contains condition codes, which are single-bit variables indicating the results of arithmetic or logical operations. These are set automatically by many of the instructions of the MC68000. For example, if an addition results in a zero sum, the Z bit is set to {1}. The other bits have similar meanings, as shown in Tables 4.4 and 4.5.

TABLE 4.4 INTERPRETATION OF CONDITION CODES

Name	Symbol	Meaning
Extend	X	Used in multiple-precision arithmetic operations; in many instructions it is set the same as the C bit.
Negative	N	Set to {1} if the most significant bit of an operand is {1}.
Zero	Z	Set to {1} if all the bits of an operand are {0}.
Overflow	V	Set to {1} if an out-of-range condition occurs in two's-complement operations.
Carry	C	Set to {1} if a carry is generated out of the most significant bit of the sum in addition. Set to {1} if a borrow is generated in subtraction.

TABLE 4.5 INTERPRETATIONS OF SYSTEM STATUS

Name	Symbol	Meaning
Trace	T	Set to {1} if the trace mode is being used (single-instruction stepping).
Supervisor	S	Set to {1} if the processor program is in the supervisor mode.
Interrupt mask	I0, I1, I2	Coded interrupt level; interrupts at level indicated and below will not be recognized (levels 1–6); level 7 is not maskable.

Example 4.7

The 8-bit operand {1XXX XXXX} would cause N = {1} if tested for a negative value. The setting of the other bits designated by X has no effect on the test. Depending on the program application, the interpretation might be: a negative two's-complement number, an unsigned binary number greater than or equal to 128, or a BCD number greater than or equal to 80.

Example 4.8

The status register contents 0700_{16} indicates the user mode with all interrupts below level 7 masked (disabled). All the condition codes are {0}. Only a level 7 interrupt will be acknowledged since it is nonmaskable. If such an interrupt occurs, the (SR) will be set to 2700_{16} during interrupt processing, indicating that the processing occurs in the supervisor mode. Upon completion of the interrupt routine, control returns to the user mode program with (SR) = 0700_{16}.

EXERCISES

4.2.1. Determine the status if the system status register contains the following hexadecimal values.
  - **(a)** 0400
  - **(b)** 2000
  - **(c)** 0004
  - **(d)** A000

4.2.2. Show the contents of the system status register after a level 4 interrupt is accepted. Assume that the status register initially contained 0 for each bit.

4.2.3. What registers must be initialized before the processor can execute a program? Consider first a supervisor mode program. What registers must the operating system initialize before control is passed to a user mode program?

4.2.4. Show the contents of the system stack if a program is interrupted by a level 1 interrupt when (PC) = $101C_{16}$. If the level 1 interrupt routine is itself interrupted by a level 2 interrupt when $(PC) = 200C_{16}$, show the changes to the system stack. Assume that initially $(SR) = 0$ and $(SSP) = 8000_{16}$.

4.3 INTRODUCTION TO THE MC68000 INSTRUCTION SET

The instruction set for the MC68000 determines the operations that are available to perform data transfer, arithmetic processing, and control program flow. Each complete MC68000 instruction consists of the following:

(a) An operation code determining the operation to be performed
(b) A designation of the length of the operand or operands
(c) Specification of the locations of any operands involved by indicating an addressing mode for each.

Figure 4.16 lists the instruction set for the MC68000 in alphabetical order. Each mnemonic represents the operation code. A letter is used to indicate a length of byte (B), word (W), or longword (L) for 8-bit, 16-bit, and 32-bit operands, respectively. For example, the symbolic instruction to add two 16-bit operands would be

ADD.W   X,Y

where X and Y designate the locations of the operands.

Instructions for the MC68000 can be classified by type or by the number of operands. The number of operands for an instruction determines whether it is classified as a single-address or double-address instruction. Classification by type groups the basic operations allowed by the processor into categories, such as those for data movement or those for arithmetic operations.

A processor instruction set is sometimes separated into types in order to compare it to instruction sets of other processors. A ... cessor with an extensive arithmetic ... ty to support mathematical progra ... so convenient for coding instructio ... elect the best instruction to perfor ... e instruction (EXG), listed in Figu ... o MC68000 registers and is more ... movement instructions that could ...

The basic types ... movement, arithmetic and logical ... em control. These categories are e ... ent, only a few instructions represe ... nce, the instruction set is also pres ...

Mnemonic	Description
ABCD	Add Decimal with Extend
ADD	Add
AND	Logical And
ASL	Arithmetic Shift Left
ASR	Arithmetic Shift Right
Bcc	Branch Conditionally
BCHG	Bit Test and Change
BCLR	Bit Test and Clear
BRA	Branch Always
BSET	Bit Test and Set
BSR	Branch to Subroutine
BTST	Bit Test
CHK	Check Register Against Bounds
CLR	Clear Operand
CMP	Compare
DBcc	Test Condition, Decrement and Branch
DIVS	Signed Divide
DIVU	Unsigned Divide
EOR	Exclusive Or
EXG	Exchange Registers
EXT	Sign Extend
JMP	Jump
JSR	Jump to Subroutine
LEA	Load Effective Address
LINK	Link Stack
LSL	Logical Shift Left
LSR	Logical Shift Right
MOVE	Move
MOVEM	Move Multiple Registers
MOVEP	Move Peripheral Data
MULS	Signed Multiply
MULU	Unsigned Multiply
NBCD	Negate Decimal with Extend
NEG	Negate
NOP	No Operation
NOT	Ones Complement
OR	Logical Or
PEA	Push Effective Address
RESET	Reset External Devices
ROL	Rotate Left without Extend
ROR	Rotate Right without Extend
ROXL	Rotate Left with Extend
ROXR	Rotate Right with Extend
RTE	Return from Exception
RTR	Return and Restore
RTS	Return from Subroutine
SBCD	Subtract Decimal with Extend
Scc	Set Conditional
STOP	Stop
SUB	Subtract
SWAP	Swap Data Register Halves
TAS	Test and Set Operand
TRAP	Trap
TRAPV	Trap on Overflow
TST	Test
UNLK	Unlink

Figure 4.16 Instruction set. (Courtesy of Motorola, Inc.)

4.3.1 The Clear Instruction

The Clear (CLR) instruction is considered a single-address arithmetic instruction which has the symbolic form

CLR.X   < EAd >

where X is B, L, or W and the < EAd > is the effective address of the destination. Zeros are transferred to the portion of the destination location specified by the operation, as shown in Table 4.6. If the destination location originally contained all 1's, executing the CLR.X instruction causes the designated portion of the location to be cleared. The operation can be defined as

(EAd) [X] ← 0 [X]

which is read: "The contents of location EAd of length X is replaced with zeros."

The description of the CLR instruction of the MC68000 is shown in Figure 4.17. This summary, taken from the Motorola *User's Manual,* presents the characteristics of the instruction in several ways. The *operation* indicates that the destination location is replaced by 0. Motorola refers to this notation as Register Transfer Language (RTL), which is summarized in Appendix IV. The assembler recognizes the CLR mnemonic and converts it and the effective address of the destination location to machine language. The valid destinations, in terms of the possible addressing modes, are listed in the table accompanying the description of the instruction. These modes are discussed in Section 4.4. Other important characteristics, such as the effect on the condition codes and the machine language format, are also given.

There are a number of ways to specify the location to be cleared by the CLR instruction. The method is chosen from among the eight valid addressing modes shown in the table at the bottom of the figure. The length of the operand at the destination location is called its *size* and is specified as byte (8 bits), word (16 bits), or longword (32 bits), with the corresponding symbolic designation B, W, or L, respectively. For example, the assembler recognizes

CLR.B   D1

TABLE 4.6 OPERATION OF THE CLR
INSTRUCTION

Instruction		Contents of the destination after instruction executes	
CLR.B	< EAd >	FFFF	FF00
CLR.W	< EAd >	FFFF	0000
CLR.L	< EAd >	0000	0000

Note: Destination contains FFFF FFFF before each instruction executes.

CLR

Clear an Operand

CLR

Operation: $0 \rightarrow$ Destination

**Assembler
Syntax:** CLR <ea>

Attributes: Size = (Byte, Word, Long)

Description: The destination is cleared to all zero bits. The size of the operation may be specified to be byte, word, or long.

Condition Codes:

X	N	Z	V	C
—	0	1	0	0

N   Always cleared.
Z   Always set.
V   Always cleared.
C   Always cleared.
X   Not affected.

Instruction Format:

15	14	13	12	11	10	9	8	7	6	5 4 3	2 1 0
0	1	0	0	0	0	1	0	Size		Effective Address Mode	Register

Instruction Fields:

Size field — Specifies the size of the operation:
00 — byte operation.
01 — word operation.
10 — long operation.

Effective Address field — Specifies the destination location. Only data alterable addressing modes are allowed as shown:

Addressing Mode	Mode	Register	Addressing Mode	Mode	Register
Dn	000	register number	d(An, Xi)	110	register number
An	—	—	Abs.W	111	000
(An)	010	register number	Abs.L	111	001
(An) +	011	register number	d(PC)	—	—
– (An)	100	register number	d(PC, Xi)	—	—
d(An)	101	register number	Imm	—	—

*Direct
Address Reg
Illegal*

Note: A memory destination is read before it is written to.

Figure 4.17   Description of the CLR instruction. (Courtesy of Motorola, Inc.)

as the instruction to clear 8 bits of register D1. To describe this operation precisely, our notation will be

$$(D1) [7:0] \leftarrow 0$$

indicating that bits 0 through 7 of register D1 are cleared. The replacement symbol ($\leftarrow$) will mean that the operand on the left is replaced by the value on the right. After the instruction executes, the contents of the destination locations are equal to zero, which is indicated as

$$(D1) [7:0] = 0$$

for this example.

Example 4.9

Several examples of the CLR instruction are given below. The addresses for the destination locations in memory are indicated as decimal values. This conforms with the assembly language notation to be discussed in Chapter 5. A word (16-bit) location in memory consists of two consecutive bytes.

Instruction symbolic form		After execution
CLR.B	D1	$(D1) [7:0] = 0$
CLR.W	D1	$(D1) [15:0] = 0$
CLR.B	1000	$(1000) = 0$
CLR.W	1000	$(1000) = 0$
		$(1001) = 0$

4.3.2 The MOVE Instruction

The fundamental data movement instruction for the MC68000 is the MOVE instruction, which is a double-address instruction written in symbolic form as

$$\text{MOVE.X} \quad <EAs>, <EAd>$$

where X = B, W, or L specifies the length or size of the operand. A copy of the source operand of length X in location <EAs> is transferred to the destination location <EAd>, leaving the source location unchanged. Both the source and destination operands are treated as though they are of length X. The MOVE instruction copies the source operand into bits [7:0], [15:0], or [31:0] for the transfer of a byte, word, or longword, respectively. The effective addresses, <EAs> and <EAd>, are computed by the processor according to the specification of the addressing mode. They may indicate processor registers or memory locations. Figure 4.18 shows the operation of the MOVE instruction for the three operand lengths. In each case, the destination and source locations contain 32-bit values, but only the specified portion of the operand is copied from the source to the destination location.

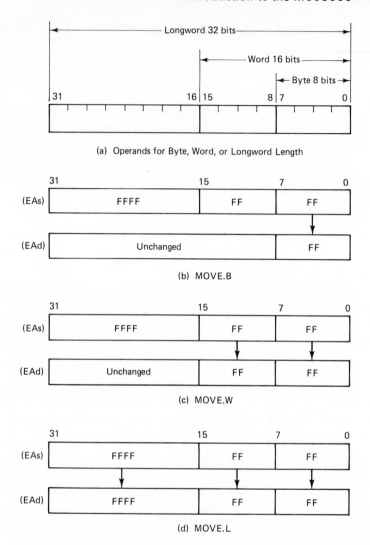

(a) Operands for Byte, Word, or Longword Length

(b) MOVE.B

(c) MOVE.W

(d) MOVE.L

Note: Source operand is FFFF FFFF$_{16}$.

Figure 4.18   Operation of the MOVE instruction.

Example 4.10

A number of examples of the MOVE instruction are shown in the following summary. In each case, the source location, data register D2, contains the hexadecimal value 0FFF 0105 before each instruction executes. The destination register D1 contains 1000 0000 in 32 bits before execution.

Instruction		Destination after execution	
MOVE.B	D2,D1	1000	0005
MOVE.W	D2,D1	1000	0105
MOVE.L	D2,D1	0FFF	0105

4.3.3 The ADD Instruction

An important arithmetic instruction is the ADD instruction. It has the form

$$ADD.X \quad <EAs>, <EAd>$$

and performs binary addition between the source operand and the destination operand of length X. In such double-address instructions which compute a result, the result is stored in the destination location according to the replacement

$$(EAd)[X] \leftarrow (EAs)[X] + (EAd)[X]$$

by execution of the instruction. The source operand is not changed by these instructions. The ADD, CLR, and MOVE instructions discussed previously are typical of the MC68000 instructions for arithmetic operations or data transfer. In such instructions, an operand location and length as well as the operation to be performed must be specified.

Example 4.11

Assume that data register D2 contains the hexadecimal value of 0FFF 0105 and D1 contains 1000 0001 before each instruction executes. The results stored in D1 are shown here for addition of operands of the length specified.

Instruction		Destination after execution	
ADD.B	D2,D1	1000	0006
ADD.W	D2,D1	1000	0106
ADD.L	D2,D1	1FFF	0106

4.3.4 Other Instruction Types

Program control instructions may modify the flow of control in a program by changing the value in the program counter and thereby causing a new sequence of instructions to be executed. For example, the Jump instruction

$$JMP \quad <EA>$$

causes program control to be transferred to the instruction contained in the location designated by the effective address <EA>. The Branch instruction

> BRA   <disp>

adds a displacement value to the contents of the program counter at the time the instruction is executed. This causes program control to be transferred within the range allowed by the value <disp>, which is either a positive or negative integer. Both the BRA (Branch Always) and JMP instructions cause unconditional transfer of control. Other branch instructions may or may not cause a branch, depending on conditions set by an arithmetic operation. For example,

> BGT   <disp>

causes a branch if the result was greater than zero. The condition is indicated by the setting of the condition code bits in the status registers. These program control instructions are discussed in detail in Chapter 6.

Instructions that control the operation of the processor or the system are generally reserved for programs operating in the supervisor mode. The instruction STOP, for example, causes the processor to discontinue fetching and executing instructions. Such instructions are discussed in more detail in Chapter 10.

EXERCISES

4.3.1. Describe the contents of each byte location affected by the instruction CLR.L 1000.

4.3.2. Before each instruction given executes, assume the following hexadecimal contents of D1, D2, and longword location 1000.

> (D1) = 0601
> (D2) = 0805
> (1000) = 1913

Determine the results of executing each of the following instructions.

(a) MOVE.B   D1,D2
(b) MOVE.B   D1,1001
(c) CLR.W   1000
(d) ADD.B   D1,D2
(e) ADD.W   1000,D1

4.4 ADDRESSING MODES FOR THE MC68000

The *addressing modes* of a CPU determine the ways in which a processor can reference an operand held in one of its registers or in memory. For each operand, the addressing mode specifies how the processor is to locate or calculate the actual address

TABLE 4.7   BASIC ADDRESSING MODES

Type	Effective address	Symbolic designation
Direct		
Register	EA = Rn	D0, D1, . . . , D7; A0, A1, . . . , A7
Absolute	EA = <address>	<decimal address> $ <hexadecimal address>
Indirect		
Address register	EA = (An)	(A0), (A1), . . . , (A7)
Predecrement	An = An − k, EA = (An)	−(An)
Postincrement	EA = (An), An = An + k	(An)+
Relative with displacement	EA = (PC) + <disp>	* + <disp>
Immediate	None	# <data>

Notes:

1. Rn refers to any register Dn or An.

2. For the predecrement and postincrement modes, k is 1, 2, or 4 for byte, word, or longword operations, respectively.

3. Angle brackets < > imply that the indicated value must be specified.

of the operand. The actual address is called the *effective address* and is determined when the instruction referencing the operand is executed.[5]

The broad categories of addressing for the MC68000 include direct addressing, indirect addressing, and addressing relative to the program counter. A special immediate mode is also provided. Table 4.7 defines these basic modes for the MC68000. In the table, the category of addressing mode and the effective address that results from instruction execution are listed. The symbolic designation is the reference to the given addressing mode recognized by a Motorola assembler. An absolute address is considered to be a decimal value unless it is preceded by "$" to indicate a hexadecimal value. The symbol "*" in a symbolic instruction references the current value of the program counter and the symbol "#" preceding a number indicates immediate addressing.

Instructions of the MC68000 may specify one or two operands in the manner described in Section 4.3. The CLR instruction, for example, may specify the destination by any of the modes indicated in Table 4.7 except immediate. The MOVE or ADD instructions require two operands, and both the source and the destination addressing modes must be specified. A number of examples in this section show how the basic addressing modes are specified symbolically. The discussion presented in this section is limited to those modes shown in Table 4.7, which represent only 8 of the 14

[5]When the CPU directly addresses the memory, an effective address is the actual or physical hardware address. In many sophisticated systems, special circuitry called *memory-mapping circuitry* is employed. This circuitry then computes the physical address that corresponds to the CPU address. The physical addresses involved depend entirely on the design of the system and are independent of programming references to operands in memory.

possible addressing modes for the MC68000. A more detailed study of the MC68000 addressing modes is given in Chapter 5 after assembly language programming is introduced.

4.4.1 Direct Addressing

The *direct* addressing modes of the MC68000 include register addressing and absolute addressing. In either case, the location or address of an operand is specified directly as part of the instruction, so that no calculation of an effective address by the CPU is necessary. For the register modes, the operand is in one of the address or data registers. In the absolute mode, the operand is in memory at a location designated by a positive integer representing its address. This address is not related to the length or size of the operand except that word and longword operands must be addressed at even locations in memory.

The basic format for the CLR instruction using register addressing is

CLR. <X>   <Dn>

where the operand of length X is cleared in register Dn, which is written specifically as one of D0, D1, . . . , D7. Thus the instruction

CLR.W   D2

clears the low-order 16 bits of register D2. The MOVE instruction requires two operands and has the form

MOVE. <X>   <Dm>,<Dn>

as, for example,

MOVE.W   D1,D2

which copies (D1) [15:0] into (D2) [15:0].

An absolute address may be specified as a decimal or hexadecimal integer in an instruction. For example, the instruction

MOVE.W   10000,D1

transfers 16 bits from word location 10000 to (D1) [15:0]. According to the conventions of Motorola assemblers, the symbolic form for the same location in hexadecimal would be

MOVE.W $2710,D1

since the value 2710_{16} corresponds to 10000 and the $ indicates hexadecimal.

Example 4.12

Being the simplest addressing schemes, the direct addressing modes were used in the preceding section to introduce important processor instructions. For example, the instruction

CLR.W   1000

specifies the *absolute* address 1000 as the destination. The address is stored with the instruction in memory. The instruction

MOVE.W   1000,D1

employs absolute addressing for the source location and register direct addressing for the destination. An instruction such as

MOVE.W   A1,D1

transfers the 16-bit address in A1 to the data register.

4.4.2 Indirect Addressing

In the MC68000, *indirect* addressing means the use of the contents of an address register as the address of an operand in memory. The contents are used as a pointer to reference the location. For example, if the instruction

MOVE.W   (A1),D1

is executed when (A1) = 1000, the 16-bit value in memory word location 1000 would be copied into (D1) [15:0]. To modify the address referenced in memory, the address register may be changed by any instruction that operates on the contents of address registers. This ability to modify the pointer in very flexible ways allows a programmer to address values in sophisticated data structures in memory. A simple example is the stack structure discussed in Section 4.3.2.

In fact, the stack structure is so common in modern programs that the MC68000 has two indirect addressing modes which are used primarily with stacks. These stacks can be created and used by employing the address register indirect with postincrement or predecrement addressing modes. To add data to a stack that grows from high memory to low memory, for example, the instruction

MOVE.W   D1,−(A1)

transfers a word from D1 to the stack after the stack pointer (A1) is decremented by two (bytes) to point to the next free memory location. A data item could be retrieved with the instruction

MOVE.W   (A1) + ,D2

which pops the word from the stack addressed by A1 and copies it to (D2) [15:0]. After the transfer, A1 is incremented by 2. The push operation, for the downward-growing stack, employs the predecrement addressing mode using A1 as the stack pointer. The pop requires the postincrement mode for the source addressing mode. Any address register of the MC68000 can be used as a stack pointer. The source location in the push or the destination location in the pop operation can be a memory location or any register of the MC68000.

Several other indirect addressing modes are provided by the MC68000. An address register containing an indirect address may be indexed by another address register or a data register. Variations on indirect addressing are described in more detail in Chapter 5.

4.4.3 Relative Addressing

A program counter *relative* address is an address that the CPU calculates by adding a displacement to the value in the program counter. The calculated effective address is then

$$EA = (PC) + <disp>$$

where the displacement value $<disp>$ is specified in the instruction. The displacement is a positive or a negative integer, so the referenced location can be higher or lower in memory relative to the instruction using this addressing mode.

An example of relative addressing is indicated by the instruction

```
BRA   * + 10
```

which, when executed, would cause a branch 10 byte locations ahead of that indicated by the program counter.[6] In the case of the BRA instruction, the value in the program counter is changed to the new address to point to the next instruction six word locations farther up in memory from the location of the BRA instructions. Relative addressing can also be used to address data values in memory.

Since the program counter contents act as a pointer to the instruction currently executing, the displacement value indicates the distance between the operand referenced in the relative mode and the instruction itself. If the program is moved in memory, the relative references in the program are still correct. When the memory references used by a program are relative, the program is said to be *position independent*. Such programs are discussed in Chapter 9. Programs with absolute references to memory locations cannot be moved unless the absolute addresses are changed to indicate the new locations.

The MC68000 also allows program counter relative addressing with indexing. In this mode, the effective address is calculated as the contents of the PC, plus a displacement value, plus the contents of an index register. Such variations on relative addressing are discussed in Chapter 5.

4.4.4 Immediate Addressing

The *immediate* addressing mode is used to specify a constant 8, 16, or 32 bits long. The constant is included in the instruction in memory. For example, the instruction

---

[6]When the branch is taken, the value in the PC is the address of the BRA instruction + 2. The BRA instruction requires two word locations in memory. Thus, the BRA instruction shown causes a branch to an instruction six word locations higher in memory than the first word of the BRA instruction itself.

ADD.W   #5,D1

adds 5 to the value in (D1) [15:0]. The instruction

MOVE.B   # 'A',(A1)

moves the ASCII value 'A' into the byte addressed by A1 in memory. The assembler recognizes the source addressing modes in these two examples as immediate. Of course, the immediate mode is never allowed as a destination mode since the destination location must be alterable (writable).

Example 4.13

The symbolic instruction

MOVE.L   # '1234',D1

causes the contents of D1 to be replaced with the hexadecimal value 3132 3334. Similarly, the instruction

MOVE.W   #$F0,D1

has the effect

$(D1)[15:0] \leftarrow F0_{16}$

An instruction with an immediate operand as a destination such as

MOVE.B   1000,#1000

would be illegal and cannot be assembled.

EXERCISES

4.4.1. Using hexadecimal values for all of your answers, determine the operation and locations affected by each of the following instructions.
(a) MOVE.W   1000,2000
(b) MOVE.W $1000,D1
(c) MOVE.B   1000,D1
(d) CLR. L $FFFFFC

4.4.2. Compare the operation of the following instructions when $(A1) = 1000$ and $(1000) = FFE0_{16}$ before each execution.
(a) MOVE.W   A1,D1
(b) MOVE.W   (A1),D1
(c) MOVE.W   1000,D1
(d) MOVE.W   #1000,D1

4.4.3. Determine the contents of the destination in hexadecimal after each instruction executes.
(a) MOVE.W   #'AB',D1
(b) MOVE.W   #$C1,D1
(c) MOVE.W   #1000,D1

4.4.4. Using only the instructions and techniques discussed thus far, write the symbolic instructions to store the low-order word of D1 into memory locations 1001 and 1002, that is, after execution (1001) = (D1) [15:8] and (1002) = (D1) [7:0].

Remember that word-length operands must start at even locations in memory and that they occupy two bytes.

4.5 MACHINE LANGUAGE FOR THE MC68000

The machine language instructions for the MC68000 consist of from one to five 16-bit words in memory. The first word is the operation word, which contains the operation code (op code) as well as the size or length and the addressing modes for any operands, if necessary. For most instructions, the op code is contained in bits 12 through 15 of the first word. Various combinations of these four bits yield 16 different op codes.

The meaning of each of these is defined in Figure 4.19. The remaining 12 bits in the operation word are used to define further the operation to be performed. Additional extension words for the machine language instructions may contain immediate data or absolute addresses for source or destination operands. A short absolute address (16 bits) requires one extra word, and a long address (32 bits) requires two. The format of the machine language instruction is shown in Figure 4.20. The extension words follow the operation code at higher memory addresses.

The formats for single- and double-address instructions are discussed in this section. As in previous sections of this chapter, the CLR, ADD, and MOVE instructions are used for specific examples. Every instruction for the MC68000 is described in Appendix IV.

4.5.1 Single-Address Instructions

The operation word for a single-address instruction is shown in Figure 4.21(a). Bits [15:6] define the operation and bits [5:0] designate the addressing mode. The effective address field is itself divided into mode and register subfields of 3 bits each. For an addressing mode employing a register, the register number (0–7) is given in the regis-

Bits 15 through 12	Operation	Bits 15 through 12	Operation
0000	Bit Manipulation/MOVEP/Immediate	1000	OR/DIV/SBCD
0001	Move Byte	1001	SUB/SUBX
0010	Move Long	1010	(Unassigned)
0011	Move Word	1011	CMP/EOR
0100	Miscellaneous	1100	AND/MUL/ABCD/EXG
0101	ADDQ/SUBQ/Scc/DBcc	1101	ADD/ADDX
0110	Bcc/BSR	1110	Shift/Rotate
0111	MOVEQ	1111	(Unassigned)

Figure 4.19 Operation codes. (Courtesy of Motorola, Inc.)

15	14	13	12	11	10	9	8	7	6	5	4	3	2	1	0
Operation Word (First Word Specifies Operation and Modes)															
Immediate Operand (If Any, One or Two Words)															
Source Effective Address Extension (If Any, One or Two Words)															
Destination Effective Address Extension (If Any, One or Two Words)															

Figure 4.20   Instruction formats. (Courtesy of Motorola, Inc.)

ter subfield. In this case, the mode subfield specifies whether direct or indirect addressing is used and the variations shown in Figure 4.22 apply. Absolute, relative, or immediate addressing modes have a fixed encoding for the entire 6-bit field.

As an example, the instruction

CLR.B   D1

specifies the destination D1 by direct register addressing. The machine language format is shown in Figure 4.21(b). For data registers, the mode in the effective address

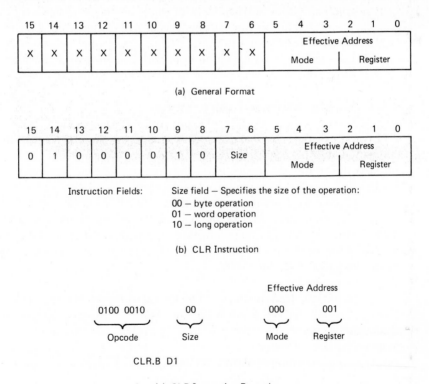

(a) General Format

(b) CLR Instruction

Instruction Fields: Size field — Specifies the size of the operation:
00 — byte operation
01 — word operation
10 — long operation

(c) CLR Instruction Example

CLR.B   D1

Figure 4.21   Single-address instructions. (Courtesy of Motorola, Inc.)

Addressing Mode	Mode	Register
Data Register Direct	000	register number
Address Register Direct	001	register number
Address Register Indirect	010	register number
Address Register Indirect with Postincrement	011	register number
Address Register Indirect with Predecrement	100	register number
Address Register Indirect with Displacement	101	register number
Address Register Indirect with Index	110	register number
Absolute Short	111	000
Absolute Long	111	001
Program Counter with Displacement	111	010
Program Counter with Index	111	011
Immediate or Status Register	111	100

Figure 4.22 Effective address encoding. (Courtesy of Motorola, Inc.)

field is {000} and the register number is {001}. The bit pattern in bits [15:8] specifies the CLR instruction. The operand size is a byte in this example and is indicated by 00 in bits [7:6]. Since only register addressing is used, the instruction requires only one word of memory.

A number of other single-address instructions, such as NEG (negate), NOT (one's complement), and NBCD (negate decimal), have the same general format as the CLR instruction. Other instructions with single operands or those with no operands may vary considerably in their machine language format from that shown for the CLR instruction. Instructions to control the processor may have no address specification but use a unique 16-bit operation word with fixed format. For example, the STOP instruction has the single hexadecimal word 4E72 as its op code.

4.5.2 Double-Address Instructions

When an instruction uses two operands, the addressing modes for both the source and destination must be specified in the operation word. If each double-address instruction encoded the addressing modes into 6 bits each, as shown previously, and specified length (byte, word, or longword) for each operand using 2 bits, a total of 14 bits of the 16-bit operation word would be taken; thus only 2 bits would remain for the op code. Since 4 bits are always used for the op code, flexibility in addressing for double-address instructions must be limited further to provide a full set of instructions. A comparison of the MOVE instruction and the ADD instruction shows the approach taken by the designers of the MC68000.

The MOVE Instruction.   The format of the MOVE instruction is shown in Figure 4.23(a) for MOVE.B, MOVE.L, and MOVE.W with bits [13:12] of the op code specifying the length. The source addressing mode is specified as before for single-address instructions. However, the destination addressing mode for MOVE reverses the mode/register encoding as shown. As an example, the format for the instruction

MOVE.W   D1,D3

is illustrated in Figure 4.23(b).

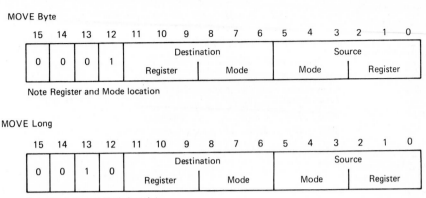

MOVE Byte

Note Register and Mode location

MOVE Long

Note Register and Mode location

MOVE Word

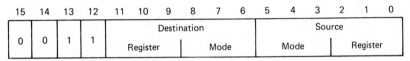

Note Register and Mode location

(a) Instruction Format

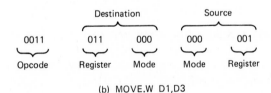

(b) MOVE.W D1,D3

Figure 4.23   MOVE instruction. (Courtesy of Motorola, Inc.)

The ADD Instruction.   The ADD instruction has the format shown in Figure 4.24(a). It requires the source or destination operand to be held in one of the data registers of the processor. The symbolic form of the ADD instruction is either

ADD.X   < EAs > , < Dn >

or

ADD.X   < Dn > , < EAd >

with X = B, W, or L, as before. In the first case, Dn specifies the destination for the result of the addition. The "op mode" bits [8:6] determine the length X and specify the destination as Dn. In the second instruction, the location specified by < EAd > is the destination and Dn is the source, so the op mode changes. An example is shown in Figure 4.24(b).

15	14	13	12	11	10	9	8	7	6	5	4	3	2	1	0
1	1	0	1	Register			Op-Mode			Effective Address Mode | Register					

Instruction Fields:

Register field — Specifies any of the eight data registers
Op-Mode field —

Byte	Word	Long	Operation
000	001	010	$(<Dn>) + (<ea>) \rightarrow <Dn>$
100	101	110	$(<ea>) + (<Dn>) \rightarrow <ea>$

(a) ADD Instruction Format

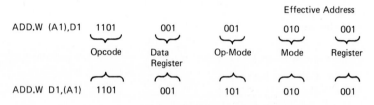

(b) ADD Instruction Encoding

Figure 4.24 ADD instruction. (Courtesy of Motorola, Inc.)

```
MC68000 ASM REV= 1.4 - COPYRIGHT BY MOTOROLA 1978           PAGE   1


 1                                   LLEN    100
 2  .                        *
 3          00001000                 ORG     $1000

 4  001000  421D                     CLR.B   (A5)+
 5  001002  4258                     CLR.W   (A0)+
 6  001004  42B80568                 CLR.L   $0568
 7  001008  423900020000            CLR.B   $00020000

 8  00100E  D800                     ADD.B   D0,D4
 9  001010  D37830E8                 ADD.W   D1,$30E8
10  001014  06420030                 ADD.W   #$30,D2

11  001018  141D                     MOVE.B  (A5)+,D2
12  00101A  3401                     MOVE.W  D1,D2
13  00101C  31C130E8                 MOVE.W  D1,$30E8
14  001020  1CFC002D                 MOVE.B  #'-',(A6)+
15  001024  21FC20002000
            0404                     MOVE.L  #$20002000,$404
16                                   END

****** TOTAL ERRORS    0--    0


SYMBOL TABLE - APPROX 1202 SYMBOL ENTRIES LEFT
```

Figure 4.25 Examples of instruction formats.

Many other double-address instructions restrict the source or destination location to be a processor register. Thus memory-to-memory operations are not allowed
except with the MOVE instruction. The MOVE instruction is therefore the most flexible of the MC68000 instructions with respect to its allowed addressing modes.

Example 4.14

Figure 4.25 shows several examples of the machine language and assembly language
forms for the CLR, ADD, and MOVE instructions. The hexadecimal values to the left of
the instruction represent the machine language code. Any immediate value or absolute
address is held in memory words following the operation word.

EXERCISES

4.5.1. Write the symbolic statements necessary to add two values in memory together and store
the results in a third location.

4.5.2. Assume that (A1) = $1000 and ($1000) = $0010 before the execution of each instruc-
tion listed. Determine the resulting action of each instruction.
  (a) CLR.B $1000
  (b) CLR.W   (A1)
  (c) MOVE.W   A1,(A1)
  (d) MOVE.W $1000,D1
  (e) MOVE.W   #$1000,D1
  (f) MOVE.B   (A1),D1
  The values are hexadecimal numbers for addresses and contents.

4.5.3. Translate the following machine language statements, given in hexadecimal, into the assembler language (symbolic) equivalent.
  (a) 4241
  (b) 200B
  (c) 103C 002E

4.5.4. Write the machine language instruction for the following symbolic instructions.
  (a) CLR.W   D0
  (b) MOVE.L   A0,D0
  (c) ADD.B   D0,D5

4.6 THE MC68000 AND MEMORY ORGANIZATION

A simplified diagram of a MC68000 system is shown in Figure 4.26, which illustrates
the 24 signal lines for addressing and 16 signal lines for data transfer or instruction
fetching by the processor. The MC68000 is considered a byte addressing processor
and each address indicates a byte (8 bits) location in memory or the address of a location associated with an interface. The range of possible addresses is called the *addressing space* of the processor. This space for the 24 address lines of the MC68000 is
shown in Figure 4.27.

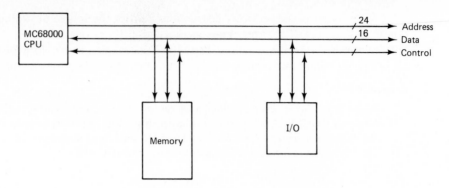

Figure 4.26   The MC68000 and memory.

The system designer can allocate the addressing space for programs, data, or I/O interfaces as necessary, but certain conventions are required for products that use the MC68000. The lower 1024 locations are reserved by the MC68000 processor for use as addresses (called *vectors* by Motorola). These addresses point to routines for servicing interrupts or processing traps. As such, they indicate the starting address of operating system routines that process exceptions in the supervisor mode. In MC68010 systems, one or more vector tables can be present and each located anywhere in memory.

Since the MC68000 can address byte, word, or longword operands, the physical organization of memory into bytes as shown in Figure 4.27 may be confusing when word or longword operands are addressed. The programmer must be aware of the relationship between the physical organization of memory into bytes and the operand length specified in an instruction. For byte-length operands, the physical address directly identifies the byte addressed. When a word or longword operand is specified in an instruction, the address identifies two or four bytes in memory, respectively.

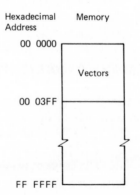

Figure 4.27   Address space for byte data.

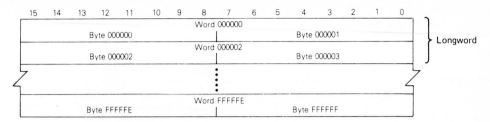

Figure 4.28   Memory organization by address. (Courtesy of Motorola, Inc.)

4.6.1 Memory Organization and Addressing

The physical byte configuration of MC68000 memory may be logically organized into words as shown in Figure 4.28. Although each byte in the word can be addressed by the processor, instructions and word operands must be referenced only at even addresses and, therefore, occupy locations designated n, n + 2, n + 4, . . . , where n is an even integer. An attempt to address a word operand at an odd boundary, as in the instruction

> MOVE.W $1001,D1

would result in an addressing error since the absolute address $1001 resides at an odd-word boundary. If a longword is referenced, two words are used and the memory addresses are designated n, n + 4, n + 8, . . . , where n is again an even integer. Thus four bytes are transferred for each longword accessed.

4.6.2 Data Organization in Memory

Data or addresses are stored in memory as illustrated in Figure 4.29. Within a byte, bit 0 is the rightmost and bit 7 is the leftmost bit. For integer data, bit 0 represents the least significant digit for either 8-bit (byte) or 16-bit (word) values. A longword is stored with the high-order 16 bits in location n and the low-order portion at location n + 2, where n is an even integer. For example, the hexadecimal value 0200 0100 is stored with (0200) at the lower memory address and (0100) at the next word location. If the value is an address, the address is stored in the same way. Binary-coded decimal (BCD) values are stored two digits per byte, as shown.

Example 4.15

> Table 4.8 shows a number of items stored in memory at the locations specified. In each case, the address and its contents are hexadecimal. The instructions CLR and MOVE require one word for their operation word. The MOVE instruction also requires an additional word to indicate the short absolute address $1000. The long address $200F6 is stored as shown, with the most significant word appearing first in memory. For example, a return address saved on the system stack would be stored in this manner. The word

Bit Data
1 Byte = 8 Bits

7	6	5	4	3	2	1	0

Integer Data
1 Byte = 8 Bits

15	14	13	12	11	10	9	8	7	6	5	4	3	2	1	0
MSB		Byte 0					LSB				Byte 1				
		Byte 2									Byte 3				

1 Word = 16 Bits

15	14	13	12	11	10	9	8	7	6	5	4	3	2	1	0
MSB							Word 0								LSB
							Word 1								
							Word 2								

1 Long Word = 32 Bits

15	14	13	12	11	10	9	8	7	6	5	4	3	2	1	0
MSB							High Order								
— Long Word 0—							Low Order								LSB
— Long Word 1 —															
— Long Word 2 —															

Addresses
1 Address = 32 Bits

15	14	13	12	11	10	9	8	7	6	5	4	3	2	1	0
MSB							High Order								
— — Address 0							Low Order								LSB
— — Address 1															
— — Address 2															

MSB = Most Significant Bit
LSB = Least Significant Bit

Decimal Data
2 Binary Coded Decimal Digits = 1 Byte

15	14	13	12	11	10	9	8	7	6	5	4	3	2	1	0
MSD	BCD 0				BCD 1		LSD	BCD 2				BCD 3			
	BCD 4				BCD 5			BCD 6				BCD 7			

MSD = Most Significant Digit
LSD = Least Significant Digit

TABLE 4.8 EXAMPLE OF MEMORY CONTENTS

Memory address	Memory contents		Meaning
Increasing			
1000	42	83	CLR.L D3
1006	11	C0	MOVE.B D0,$1000
1008	10	00	
100A	00	02	Address $200F6
100C	00	F6	
	.		
	.		
	.		
2000	20	01	Byte data
	.		(2000) = 20
	.		(2001) = 01
	.		
2008	10	21	BCD 1021_{10}

Note: Except for the BCD value 1021, all numbers are hexadecimal.

location $2000 contains $2001 in the figure, but each individual byte could be addressed. Thus the byte address $2000 contains $20 and the byte address $2001 contains $01, as shown. The instruction

  MOVE.B $2000,D1

would cause (D1) [7:0] = $20. The transfer

  MOVE.W $2000,D1

results in (D1) [15:0] = $2001.

  Finally the location $2008 contains the decimal value 1021 stored as a BCD number. The two low-order digits are stored in byte location $2009 and the two high-order digits are in location $2008. MC68000 instructions that operate on multidigit BCD numbers require this format for BCD data storage.

EXERCISES

4.6.1. Determine the decimal number of bytes, words, or longwords the MC68000 can address.

4.6.2. Show how the following numbers or characters are stored in memory if each starts at hexadecimal location 1000. The data and formats are as follows:

 (a) 10,203,040 (BCD)

 (b) 0200 00FC (hexadecimal)

 (c) 'ABCD' (ASCII)

← **Figure 4.29** Data organization in memory. (Courtesy of Motorola, Inc.)

4.6.3. The program counter contained 0002 FFF0$_{16}$ before it was transferred into memory starting at location 1002$_{16}$. What are the memory contents in each byte of the memory area where (PC) is stored?

FURTHER READING

The article by Frank and Sproull and several articles in *MC68000 Article Reprints* discuss the advantage of a microprogrammed design for the MC68000. This publication contains approximately 25 articles of interest to MC68000 users and is available from Motorola. The article by Stritter and Gunter covers many of the topics discussed in this chapter and can be found in the reprints or in the *IEEE Computer* issue of February 1979.

The textbook by Mead and Conway and the article by Pashley et al. discuss the technology involved in the fabrication of integrated circuits. The other textbooks referenced discuss the design of central processors and compare various approaches.

BELL, C. GORDON, J. C. MUDGE, and E. MCNAMARA, *Computer Engineering.* Bedford, Mass. Digital Press, 1978.

FRANK, EDWARD H., and R. F. SPROULL, "An Approach to Debugging Custom Integrated Circuits," Annual Report, Department of Computer Science, Carnegie-Mellon University, 1979–1980.

KRAFT, GEORGE D., and W. N. TOY, *Mini/Microcomputer Hardware Design.* Englewood Cliffs, N.J.: Prentice-Hall, 1979.

MC68000 Article Reprints, A-13260-1, Motorola Semiconductor Products Inc., Austin, Tex. 1981.

MEAD, CARVER, and L. CONWAY, *Introduction to VLSI Systems.* Reading, Mass. Addison-Wesley, 1980.

PASHLEY, RICHARD, et al, "H-MOS Scales Traditional Devices to Higher Performance Level," *Electronics,* **50,** No. 17 (August 18, 1977), 94–99.

STRITTER, EDWARD, and T. GUNTER, "A Microprocessor Architecture for a Changing World: The Motorola 68000," *IEEE Computer,* **12,** No. 2 (February 1979), 43–52.

5

MC68000 Assembly Language and Basic Instructions

The brief introduction in Chapter 4 to the machine language of the MC68000 should indicate the complexity involved in machine language programming. The extensive instruction set combined with the variety of addressing modes for many instructions would preclude efficient coding in machine language except for the simplest of programs. In assembly language, instructions and addresses are designated by symbolic names which the assembler program translates into the appropriate binary code. Motorola has defined a standard assembly language for the MC68000. The rules for the language specify the instruction mnemonics, symbolic addressing references, and the format for each assembly language statement. These conventions are generally followed by other suppliers of assemblers for the MC68000. Differences in assemblers must be resolved by reference to the user's manual for a particular assembler.

This chapter begins with a discussion of program development. Then the assembly language instructions for Motorola assemblers are introduced. The emphasis is on standard features common to all assemblers. Advanced programming techniques that may require the more sophisticated capabilities of an assembler are covered in later chapters.

In this chapter, a hexadecimal number in the text itself is preceded by a "$". Otherwise, numerical values are decimal. However, assembler listings and outputs from monitor sessions use hexadecimal values for addresses of memory locations and their contents. No preceding symbol is used to indicate hexadecimal notation by these programs, but the assembly language statements created by the programmer require the form $NNN to indicate a hexadecimal number as an immediate value or as a memory address of an operand.

When an address register is used as the destination location in an instruction of

an example, the instruction variations ADDA, MOVEA, SUBA, and so on, are used. Instruction variations for immediate (16 to 32 bits) and quick immediate (3 bits) are referenced as ADDI, ADDQ, SUBI, SUBQ, and so on. Most assemblers recognize instruction variations without explicitly defining the suffix. The programs explicitly use the variations for clarity. For convenience, the assembly language instruction set for the MC68000 is summarized in Appendix IV.

5.1 SOFTWARE DEVELOPMENT

Software development consists of problem analysis, software design, and program coding, followed by debugging and testing. Appropriate documentation should be provided at each stage. The programming activities are shown in simplified form in Figure 5.1, which emphasizes the cyclic or iterative nature of the process. The editor program is used to create an assembly language *source* program which is translated by the assembler.[1] At this stage in development, the assembler *listing* is used to find errors in the source program. The listing gives the assembly language source program and the machine language equivalent if no errors are detected by the assembler. Errors in the source program are indicated on the listing.

Once the program is free of assembly errors, an *object program* is produced. The object program is loaded into the target machine's memory for execution. In this simplified discussion, the object program is a machine language program.[2] Execution of the code is controlled during debugging by a program called a *monitor.* This program allows the user to cause instruction-by-instruction execution and to display intermediate results after each instruction completes. Errors in the design of the program may be detected at this stage. To correct the errors, the source program must be reedited and reassembled.

5.1.1 The Assembler and Listing

As noted previously, the assembly process checks source statements for errors. Each statement is either an MC68000 instruction, an assembler directive, or a comment. A symbolic instruction such as

    ADD.W   D1,D2

becomes an executable machine language instruction. The mnemonic ADD, the operand size, and the operand addresses are recognized by the assembler and converted to

---

[1]The details involved in executing the development software (editor, assembler, debugger) vary greatly with different systems. Also, the source and object programs are normally stored as disk files on the development system disk. The user's manual or operating system manual for a particular system will describe the procedure required to create, store, and execute programs.

[2]In practice, the object program may require processing by another program, called a *linkage editor,* before it is loaded into memory for execution. The distinction between assembly, loading, and execution operations is discussed in many of the references contained in the Further Reading section for this chapter.

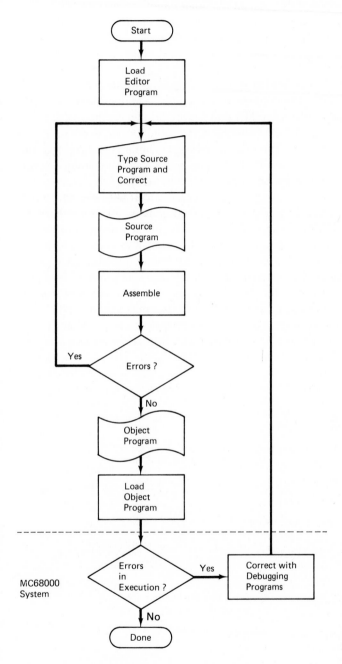

Figure 5.1 Programming a microcomputer.

binary machine code. Assembler directives, on the other hand, are instructions for the assembler, not the CPU. The origin directive, for example, specifies where the program is to be loaded into memory. As an example, the directive

ORG $1000

indicates that the program is to be loaded at the hexadecimal location $1000. Comments for the convenience of the programmer may also appear in the source program. These comments are ignored by the assembler and simply printed on the listing.

Figure 5.2 shows a typical MC68000 listing in the same format as example listings to be presented in this chapter. The first or leftmost column is the decimal line number. The second column is the hexadecimal value of the location counter at each instruction. The location counter keeps track of instruction locations during assembly much as the program counter does during program execution. If the program shown were loaded beginning at location $1000, the PC would change just as the location counter in Figure 5.2. The third column is the machine language translation showing the operation word for each instruction followed by the value of any extension words required for the instruction. Any value assigned by an assembler directive, such as the origin (ORG) statement shown, also appears in this column. The machine language translation is followed to the right by the source program statement that generated it. In our examples, the in-line comments are preceded by a semicolon. An entire line may be treated as a comment if an asterisk (*) is the first character of the line.

The simple program in Figure 5.2 sums four 16-bit integers in locations $2000, $2002, $2004, and $2006. The result is stored in (D1) [15:0]. The three directives

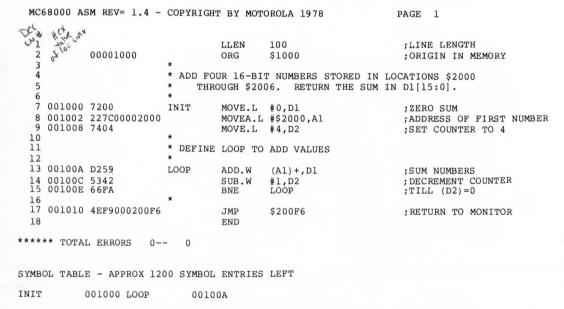

```
MC68000 ASM REV= 1.4 - COPYRIGHT BY MOTOROLA 1978              PAGE   1

   1                              LLEN    100                  ;LINE LENGTH
   2         00001000             ORG     $1000                ;ORIGIN IN MEMORY
   3                        *
   4                        * ADD FOUR 16-BIT NUMBERS STORED IN LOCATIONS $2000
   5                        *    THROUGH $2006.  RETURN THE SUM IN D1[15:0].
   6                        *
   7 001000 7200            INIT    MOVE.L  #0,D1                ;ZERO SUM
   8 001002 227C00002000            MOVEA.L #$2000,A1            ;ADDRESS OF FIRST NUMBER
   9 001008 7404                    MOVE.L  #4,D2                ;SET COUNTER TO 4
  10                        *
  11                        * DEFINE LOOP TO ADD VALUES
  12                        *
  13 00100A D259            LOOP    ADD.W   (A1)+,D1             ;SUM NUMBERS
  14 00100C 5342                    SUB.W   #1,D2                ;DECREMENT COUNTER
  15 00100E 66FA                    BNE     LOOP                 ;TILL (D2)=0
  16                        *
  17 001010 4EF9000200F6            JMP     $200F6               ;RETURN TO MONITOR
  18                                END

****** TOTAL ERRORS    0--   0


SYMBOL TABLE - APPROX 1200 SYMBOL ENTRIES LEFT

INIT        001000 LOOP          00100A
```

Figure 5.2 Typical assembly listing.

LLEN, ORG, and END define the width of the listing, the origin, and the end of the program, respectively. INIT and LOOP are labels attached to a particular line in the program so that the line can be referred to symbolically from elsewhere in the program. The labels have values assigned by the location counter. The symbol table following the program listing indicates that value.

In the program, INIT indicates the location of the first instruction. LOOP defines the start of a sequence of instructions which is repeated four times during execution to sum the values. This iteration or "loop" is terminated when the value in D2 reaches zero.

Since the program assembled correctly, it is only necessary to load it at location $1000 and execute it. This is accomplished in our examples by use of a monitor program which begins at location $200F6. After the additions are performed, control is returned to the monitor by the JMP statement.

5.1.2 Monitor Program

The Motorola debugging program used for most of the examples in this book is called MACSbug. It is referred to as a monitor program and provides three fundamental capabilities:

(a) Loading a program

(b) Executing a program

(c) Aid in debugging

The monitor itself resides in read-only memory, which is part of the MC68000 Design Module discussed in Chapter 1. The starting address of the monitor is $200F6.

Object programs may be loaded from the disk unit of a development system or from another computer if cross-development software is being used. Each system has a different procedure and MACSbug or other monitors will have features to allow program loading. These features are not discussed here since they depend so completely on the system being used. However, many of the MACSbug capabilities are provided by most other monitors.

In general, any monitor or debugging program will allow the user to initialize memory locations and processor registers, including the program counter. This monitor session is carried on interactively via a CRT terminal. Values can be changed as required during execution of the program for the purpose of testing. Monitors also allow the contents of memory locations and registers to be *displayed* by the user. This is one of the primary debugging aids available to the assembly language programmer. Finally, the monitor allows the user to stop and start execution of the program. One or more selected instructions may be executed and then the results displayed.

Table 5.1 lists a number of commands for the MACSbug monitor. The asterisk is a monitor "prompt" on the display screen and indicates that the monitor is ready to accept commands. The user enters the desired command followed by a carriage return

TABLE 5.1 MACSbug Commands

Initialize registers or memory	
*\<Rn> \<value>	(Rn) = \<value>
*OP \<start addr>	Open memory
*SM \<start addr> \<values>	Set memory
*PC \<address>	First instruction

Display registers or memory	
*\<Rn>	Display (Rn)
*DM \<start address>	Display memory
*TD	Display trace

Execute and trace	
*TD \<Rn.1>	Set display
*GO	Execute
*GO TILL \<address>	Execute until \<address>
*T	Single step

Notes:

1. * is the prompt from the monitor.
2. All values for data and addresses are hexadecimal.
3. In TD \<Rn.l>, l = 1, 2, 3, or 4 bytes of the register.
4. \<Rn> is any address or data register.
5. Numerical values are entered as \<NNN> and are hexadecimal values.

(CR) to invoke a command. Anything printed by the monitor in response to a user command is not preceded by an "*" in the examples in this chapter. Also, all addresses and contents are given in hexadecimal unless otherwise indicated. However, numerical values entered in response to monitor prompts are considered hexadecimal and are not preceded by a "$". Processor registers are designated by their symbolic names: A0, A1, . . . , A7 for address registers and D0, D1, . . . , D7 for data registers.

Example 5.1

The use of the monitor for debugging purposes is shown in Figure 5.3. As discussed previously, the program adds four 16-bit numbers in memory locations $2000 through $2006 and accumulates the sum in (D1) [15:0]. The address of the first number is loaded into A1 by the MOVEA instruction, a variation of the MOVE instruction. The four values are 1, 2, 3, 4, which are entered in memory starting at the *hexadecimal* location $2000 by the command

*OP 2000

followed by the values as shown. The Set Memory (SM) command could also be used to initialize the values. The Open Memory (OP) command in the example is followed by a Display Memory (DM) command. This causes 16 byte locations to be displayed, the last

8 of which are uninitialized. The registers to be displayed during a trace of the program are defined by the Trace Display (TD) command. In this case, three bytes of the program counter, two bytes of (D1), one byte of (D2), and all of (A1) are to be displayed as defined by the command

    *TD PC.3 D1.2 D2.1 A1.4

This command defines the registers to be traced but causes no other action. The register D1 accumulates the sum, (D2) is a counter, and (A1) points to the next operand to be added in the program loop. The use of postincrement addressing with A1 causes A1 to be incremented by 2 after each execution of the statement at LOOP.

```
MC68000 ASM REV= 1.4 - COPYRIGHT BY MOTOROLA 1978              PAGE   1


 1                                 LLEN     100                ;LINE LENGTH
 2        00001000                 ORG      $1000             ;ORIGIN IN MEMORY
 3                          *
 4                          * ADD FOUR 16-BIT NUMBERS STORED IN LOCATIONS $2000
 5                          *    THROUGH $2006.  RETURN THE SUM IN D1[15:0].
 6                          *
 7  001000 7200            INIT     MOVE.L   #0,D1            ;ZERO SUM
 8  001002 227C00002000             MOVEA.L  #$2000,A1        ;ADDRESS OF FIRST NUMBER
 9  001008 7404                     MOVE.L   #4,D2            ;SET COUNTER TO 4
10                          *
11                          * DEFINE LOOP TO ADD VALUES
12                          *
13  00100A D259            LOOP     ADD.W    (A1)+,D1         ;SUM NUMBERS
14  00100C 5342                     SUB.W    #1,D2            ;DECREMENT COUNTER
15  00100E 66FA                     BNE      LOOP             ;TILL (D2)=0
16                          *
17  001010 4EF9000200F6             JMP      $200F6           ;RETURN TO MONITOR
18                                  END

****** TOTAL ERRORS    0--    0


SYMBOL TABLE - APPROX 1200 SYMBOL ENTRIES LEFT

INIT        001000 LOOP        00100A



*OP 2000
002000 FF ?00
002001 FF ?01
002002 FF ?00
002003 FF ?02
002004 FF ?00
002005 FF ?03
002006 FF ?00
002007 FF ?04
002008 FF ?.
*DM 2000
002000  00 01 00 02 00 03 00 04 FF FF FF FF FF FF FF FF   ...............
*TD PC.3 D1.2 D2.1 A1.4
*PC 1000
*GO TILL 1010
PC=001010 D1=000A D2=00 A1=00002008
*
```

Figure 5.3 A monitor session.

Once the appropriate memory locations are initialized and the display defined, the program may be executed with the commands

*PC 1000

*GO TILL 1010

The first command sets (PC) = $1000 and the second causes the program to execute until the instruction at $1010. The command

*TD

displays the contents of the various registers of interest.

5.2 ASSEMBLY LANGUAGE CHARACTERISTICS

The source program statements, as processed by the assembler, consist of strings of ASCII characters combined to form symbols. These symbols are constructed according to the rules of the language. Each statement consists of four *fields:* label, operations, operand(s), and comments. The fields are separated by spaces or other delimiters according to the *format* required. For example, the statement

INIT   MOVE.L   # 0,D1   ; ZERO SUM

consists of the label INIT; a mnemonic instruction MOVE, which represents the operation; an operand field (# 0,D1); and a comment. In this case, the delimiter between fields is a blank or space character. At least one space is required to separate the fields. However, multiple spaces can be used. This is referred to as a *free-field format.*

Typically, the assembler first scans each source statement to determine that the formatting and symbol usage are valid. An error results if the format is incorrect or if the operation is not either a processor instruction or an assembler directive.

This subsection divides the discussion of MC68000 assembly language into two parts. The first deals with the construction of source statements representing executable instructions for the processor. The second covers assembler directives, which control the way the assembler itself operates. The characteristics discussed in this section are necessary for the creation of useful programs, although most assemblers have many additional capabilities.

5.2.1 Statement Formats

The source statements processed by the assembler must follow a precise format defining the order and relationship of the elements in the statement. The MC68000 assemblers recognize source statements composed of the following fields:

(a) Label field
(b) Operation code or directive field

TABLE 5.2 ASSEMBLY LANGUAGE FORMAT

Label field	Operation code and directive field	Operand(s) field	Comment field
[< LABEL >]	< op code > or < directive >	[< operand 1 > [, < operand 2 >]]	[< comment >]

Notes:

1. An asterisk in column 1 indicates a comment line.
2. Angle brackets indicate any valid symbol.
3. Square brackets indicate an optional field.

    (c) Operand(s) field

    (d) Comment field

Each assembly language statement consists of these elements separated by spaces.

    Table 5.2 shows the format of a general assembly language statement with optional fields enclosed in brackets. If a "*" is encountered in the first column of a statement, the entire statement is a comment. If another character is encountered in the first column, the symbol is considered to be a label, which must consist of from one to eight alphanumeric characters. In most assemblers, the first character of a symbol must be a letter (A–Z), although different assemblers have other conventions. If no label is used, the first column must contain a blank (space) if other fields are present.

    The next field encountered is interpreted as an instruction mnemonic or assembler directive. For example, in a statement without a label such as

    MOVE.W   D1,D2   ;COMMENT

the instruction mnemonic must start in column 2 or beyond. A space must precede the operands and the comment. The semicolon is not needed before the comment but is used here to enhance readability.

    Labels.   The label is optional for most instructions and directives. When one is used, it represents an address. The label is assigned the value of the location counter when the label is encountered. In statements such as

    HERE   MOVE.W   D1,D3

the label HERE defines the location of the instruction in memory after the program is loaded and can be used to define the beginning of a program segment for later reference.

Example 5.2

    Figure 5.4 shows several examples of labels used as addresses. As discussed previously, the program adds four values to form a sum. The program starts at location $1000 and

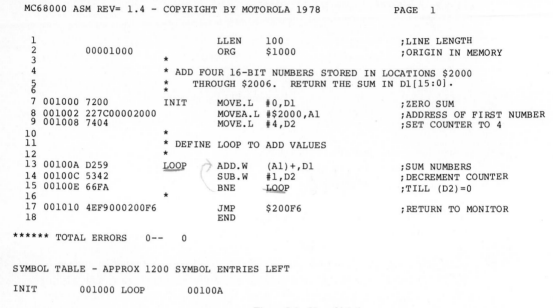

```
MC68000 ASM REV= 1.4 - COPYRIGHT BY MOTOROLA 1978          PAGE  1

  1                              LLEN    100              ;LINE LENGTH
  2        00001000              ORG     $1000            ;ORIGIN IN MEMORY
  3                        *
  4                        * ADD FOUR 16-BIT NUMBERS STORED IN LOCATIONS $2000
  5                        *    THROUGH $2006.  RETURN THE SUM IN D1[15:0].
  6                        *
  7 001000 7200            INIT    MOVE.L  #0,D1            ;ZERO SUM
  8 001002 227C00002000            MOVEA.L #$2000,A1        ;ADDRESS OF FIRST NUMBER
  9 001008 7404                    MOVE.L  #4,D2            ;SET COUNTER TO 4
 10                        *
 11                        * DEFINE LOOP TO ADD VALUES
 12                        *
 13 00100A D259            LOOP    ADD.W   (A1)+,D1         ;SUM NUMBERS
 14 00100C 5342                    SUB.W   #1,D2            ;DECREMENT COUNTER
 15 00100E 66FA                    BNE     LOOP             ;TILL (D2)=0
 16                        *
 17 001010 4EF9000200F6            JMP     $200F6           ;RETURN TO MONITOR
 18                              END

****** TOTAL ERRORS    0--    0


SYMBOL TABLE - APPROX 1200 SYMBOL ENTRIES LEFT

INIT        001000 LOOP        00100A
```

Figure 5.4   Use of labels.

initializes the sum to zero when it executes. The symbol INIT is a label associated with the first statement and has the value $1000. Another program (not shown) could use the instruction

> JMP   INIT

to begin execution of this segment. The label LOOP locates the first instruction of a repeated sequence of instructions. The loop is executed four times until the counter (D2) is decremented to zero. This label is simply for the addition sequence and would not be referenced by instructions other than the BNE instruction in the loop.

Operation codes.   The second field in the source statement must contain an instruction mnemonic or assembler directive. When the operands require a length to be specified, a length specification is included as part of the instruction field. The length specification is preceded by a period ".", which is appended to the operation code, and consists of B, W, or L to specify byte, word, or longword, respectively. For example, the instruction

> MOVE.W   D1,D2

defines word-length operands.

Operands.   Location of the operands for the instructions are accessed according to the addressing mode for each operand. The general formats for operands are shown in Table 5.3. A few instructions require no operands. Others refer to the processor registers implicitly and their execution may cause the program counter, stack pointer, or status register values to be modified. The TRAP and STOP instructions require an immediate value in the form of a decimal or hexadecimal number.

Most instructions require operands to be specified by addressing modes. Single-address instructions contain the specification of one operand. Double-address instructions contain two operands which are separated by a comma in the operand field. Processor address or data registers are designated symbolically by the letter A or D followed by the register number. Thus the instruction

> MOVE.W   A1,D1

designates A1 as the source register and D1 as the destination. Indirect addressing is specified by enclosing the address register symbol in parentheses, as in the instruction

> MOVE.W   (A1),D2

which causes the word in the location pointed to by (A1) to be copied into D2. The addressing modes are described in detail in Section 5.3.

Example 5.3

Figure 5.5 is an assembler listing showing a number of statements to illustrate the specification of operands. The RESET and RTS (Return from Subroutine) instructions require no operands. A TRAP instruction must have the trap number specified as an immediate value. Such instructions have unique requirements for operand specification.

Single-address instructions, such as CLR, require one address in the operand field. The address may be specified by any addressing mode valid for the particular instruction. Several examples are shown for specifying the operand for the CLR instruction.

TABLE 5.3   MC68000 INSTRUCTION REFERENCES

Operand	Format	Typical reference or operand	Example
None	OPR	External device	RESET
Implied	OPR	PC, SP, or SR	NOP, TRAPV, RTS
Immediate	OPR <value>	Processor control or instructions requiring a value	TRAP, STOP
Single	OPR <address>	Relative address Instruction address Operand address	BRA JMP CLR, NEG
Double	OPR <value>, <destination> OPR <source>, <destination>	Immediate value to destination or double address	ADD, MOVE

Notes:

1. OPR is any valid operation code.

2. Minor variations from the formats shown are possible.

MC68000 ASM REV= 1.4 - COPYRIGHT BY MOTOROLA 1978   PAGE 1

```
  1                                   LLEN     100
  2        00001000                   ORG      $1000
  3                          *
  4                          * MISCELLANEOUS INSTRUCTIONS
  5                          *
  6 001000 4E70                        RESET
  7                          *
  8 001002 4E4F                        TRAP     #15
  9                          *
 10 001004 4E75                        RTS
 11                          *
 12                          * SINGLE ADDRESS
 13                          *
 14 001006 4241                        CLR.W    D1              ;DATA REG. DIRECT
 15 001008 42781000                    CLR.W    $1000           ;ABSOLUTE
 16 00100C 4251                        CLR.W    (A1)            ;INDIRECT
 17 00100E 4261                        CLR.W    -(A1)           ;PREDECREMENT
 18 001010 4259                        CLR.W    (A1)+           ;POSTINCREMENT
 19 001012 42690002                    CLR.W    2(A1)           ;INDIR. WITH DISP.
 20 001016 42711002                    CLR.W    2(A1,D1.W)      ;INDIR. WITH INDEX
 21                          *
 22                          * DOUBLE ADDRESS (SOURCE ADDRESS SPECIFIED)
 23                          *
 24 00101A 3401                         MOVE.W   D1,D2           ;DATA REG. DIRECT
 25 00101C 3409                         MOVE.W   A1,D2           ;ADDR REG. DIRECT
 26 00101E 34381000                     MOVE.W   $1000,D2        ;ABSOLUTE
 27 001022 3411                         MOVE.W   (A1),D2         ;INDIRECT
 28 001024 3421                         MOVE.W   -(A1),D2        ;PREDECREMENT
 29 001026 3419                         MOVE.W   (A1)+,D2        ;POSTINCREMENT
 30 001028 34290002                     MOVE.W   2(A1),D2        ;INDIR. WITH DISP.
 31 00102C 34311002                     MOVE.W   2(A1,D1.W),D2   ;INDIR. WITH INDEX
 32
 33 001030 343C0005                     MOVE.W   #5,D2           ;IMMEDIATE
 34 001034 3438103C                     MOVE.W   *+8,D2          ;RELATIVE
 35 001038 4EF9000200F6                 JMP      $200F6          ;RETURN TO MONITOR
 36                                     END
****** TOTAL ERRORS   0--   0

SYMBOL TABLE - APPROX 1202 SYMBOL ENTRIES LEFT
```

Figure 5.5 Examples of operand specification.

The double-address MOVE instruction is shown with various addressing modes used to specify the source operand. The destination is a register in each example, although the MOVE instruction does allow other addressing modes for the destination operand.

Expressions as operands.   The assembler recognizes certain symbols in the operand field. A symbol may designate an absolute address, an immediate value, or any other valid operand. An *expression* is a combination of symbols, constants, algebraic operators, and parentheses which the assembler evaluates to determine the address or value of the operand.

To specify a constant value, sometimes called a *literal,* the immediate addressing mode is used. For most assemblers, the constants can represent either numbers or

ASCII characters. These constants are the simplest form of expressions and are specified using the definition in Table 5.4. A numerical constant can be any decimal or hexadecimal value that can be represented as an 8-bit, 16-bit, or 32-bit integer. The size specification of the instruction determines the appropriate length. A decimal number is defined by a string of decimal digits and a hexadecimal number is defined by a dollar sign ($) followed by a string of hexadecimal digits. Thus the instruction

MOVE.W   #$2000,D1

defines the 16-bit hexadecimal value 2000 as the immediate source operand.

ASCII literals consist of up to four ASCII characters enclosed in apostrophes. For example, the string 'ABCD' is recognized by the assembler and converted into the ASCII code

41 42 43 44

which occupies four bytes when stored in memory. Longer character strings cannot be used as a literal value in an expression since the size is limited by the 32-bit registers of the MC68000.

The operators for addition, subtraction, and multiplication can be used in an expression. The result of any arithmetic operation is a 32-bit integer value. The use of the unary minus ($-$) is recognized as a means to define negative numbers. For example, the immediate value -1 is computed in the instruction

MOVE.W   #$-1,D1

and is stored as $FFFF with the instruction. An equivalent specification is

MOVE.W   #$FFFF,D1

where the value $FFFF is the two's-complement number in 16 bits.

TABLE 5.4 ASSEMBLER SYMBOLS FOR EXPRESSIONS

Symbolic format	Interpretation
$ < Number >	Hexadecimal number
< Number >	Decimal number
' < String > '	ASCII string of characters
# < Number >	Immediate operand
#' < String > '	Immediate operand
In expressions	
+	Add
−	Subtract
*	Multiply
/	Divide
( )	Grouping

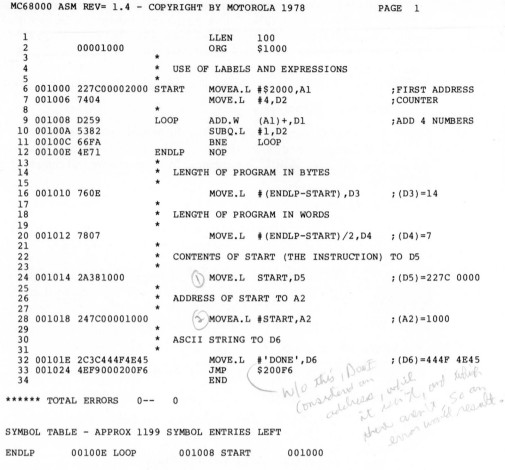

MC68000 ASM REV= 1.4 - COPYRIGHT BY MOTOROLA 1978   PAGE   1

```
 1                                  LLEN      100
 2          00001000                ORG       $1000
 3                          *
 4                          *   USE OF LABELS AND EXPRESSIONS
 5                          *
 6  001000 227C00002000 START       MOVEA.L   #$2000,A1           ;FIRST ADDRESS
 7  001006 7404                      MOVE.L    #4,D2               ;COUNTER
 8                          *
 9  001008 D259         LOOP         ADD.W     (A1)+,D1            ;ADD 4 NUMBERS
10  00100A 5382                      SUBQ.L    #1,D2
11  00100C 66FA                      BNE       LOOP
12  00100E 4E71         ENDLP        NOP
13                          *
14                          *   LENGTH OF PROGRAM IN BYTES
15                          *
16  001010 760E                      MOVE.L    #(ENDLP-START),D3   ;(D3)=14
17                          *
18                          *   LENGTH OF PROGRAM IN WORDS
19                          *
20  001012 7807                      MOVE.L    #(ENDLP-START)/2,D4 ;(D4)=7
21                          *
22                          *   CONTENTS OF START (THE INSTRUCTION) TO D5
23                          *
24  001014 2A381000                  MOVE.L    START,D5            ;(D5)=227C 0000
25                          *
26                          *   ADDRESS OF START TO A2
27                          *
28  001018 247C00001000              MOVEA.L   #START,A2           ;(A2)=1000
29                          *
30                          *   ASCII STRING TO D6
31                          *
32  00101E 2C3C444F4E45              MOVE.L    #'DONE',D6          ;(D6)=444F 4E45
33  001024 4EF9000200F6              JMP       $200F6
34                                   END
```

****** TOTAL ERRORS   0--   0

SYMBOL TABLE - APPROX 1199 SYMBOL ENTRIES LEFT

ENDLP   00100E LOOP   001008 START   001000

(handwritten annotation: W/o this 'DONE' considered an address, which it isn't, and there aren't so an error would result.)

Figure 5.6   Use of labels and expressions.

Example 5.4

The short program segment in Figure 5.6 shows various uses of labels and expressions. The labels START and ENDLP serve to define the values of the beginning and end of a group of statements in the example. The MOVEA and MOVE instructions initialize the address and counter, respectively, when the program is executed. When the addition is complete, the result is in (D1). The segment length is calculated as 14 bytes (seven words) in (D3). The length in words in (D4) is half of the length in bytes. If the machine language instructions were moved in memory without reassembly, statements referencing START as a source address or operand would be in error. The length calculations, however, would be correct.

The instruction itself at location START is moved into D5 when the source oper-

and in a MOVE instruction specifies the label only. The immediate form #START selects the address.

The final MOVE instruction transfers the ASCII string 'DONE' to D3. Note that
the immediate mode must be indicated or the value would be interpreted as an address. A
suitable I/O routine could be used to print the string to indicate completion of the program.

5.2.2 Assembler Directives

The mnemonic symbols for instruction op codes and those for the various addressing
modes are part of an internal *symbol table* used by the assembler to translate the
source statements into machine language. The user-defined symbols, such as labels,
are used to reference instructions or data within the assembly language program. The
assembler automatically keeps track of locations and offsets associated with the machine language program.

The use of symbolic forms as addresses of instructions or as operands is of valuable assistance in writing assembly language programs. This is one of the principal advantages of assembly language over machine language. However, most assemblers aid
the programmer in other ways by providing *assembler directives* which are actually
instructions to the assembler rather than for the processor. The action caused by each
directive occurs only when the source program is being assembled. The major categories of directives are for assembly control, symbol definition, data definition and storage allocation, and listing control, as shown in Table 5.5

TABLE 5.5 ASSEMBLER DIRECTIVES

Directive and format	Meaning
Assembly control	
ORG < expression >	Origin
END	End source
Symbol definition	
< label > EQU < expression >	Equate value of < label >
Data definition and storage	
[< label >] DC. < l > < value(s) >	Define constant(s)
[< label >] DS. < l > < number >	Reserve storage
Listing control	
LLEN < N >	Line length
LIST	List (default)
NOLIST	No listing
SPC < N >	< N > blank lines
PAGE	Next page

Notes:

1. Square brackets indicate an optional field.

2. < l > denotes B, W, or L.

Assembly control.   The location counter of the assembler normally begins with the value $0000 to indicate the location of the first executable instruction. This counter is increased by the appropriate amount as each instruction is assembled. If the machine language program were loaded into memory at location $0000 and executed, the program counter would follow the same sequence as the location counter as each instruction is executed in turn.

Loading programs at location $0000 is not possible in MC68000 systems since the lowest addressed area in memory is reserved for MC68000 vectors. This restriction does not apply to MC68010 systems. Use of the ORG (origin) directive allows the programmer to define the starting value of the location counter and, consequently, the first address of the program in memory. In the previous examples in this chapter the ORG directive was used to indicate that hexadecimal location $1000 was to be used to store the first machine language statement in a program.

The format of the ORG directive is

ORG   < expression >

in which the < expression > has the same meaning as previously defined. When the directive is encountered, the location counter is "loaded" with the value much as a jump (JMP) instruction changes the contents of the PC. The ORG directive can appear anywhere in the source program and can be used, for example, to divide the program into instruction and data sections. This is particularly useful if the instructions are to be held in a read-only memory and data are held in a writable memory at another starting location.

Another assembly control directive is the END directive, which is always the last source statement in a program. It causes the assembler to stop its top-to-bottom scan of the program. Any source statements after the END directive are not processed by the assembler.

Symbol definition.   An EQU directive is used to equate a number to a symbol. The value may represent an address or a constant. The format is

< label >   EQU   < expression >

where < label > is assigned the value of the expression when the statement is assembled. The expression may contain a label if it has been defined previously in the program. Thus the statement

TTYOUT   EQU $7FFF

assigns the value $7FFF to the symbol TTYOUT. The intent might be to define the address of an output buffer using a mnemonic term. Then a statement such as

MOVEA.L   #TTYOUT,A1

transfers the number $7FFF to the address register A1. If the immediate mode is not used for the source, the contents of the location are transferred. The instruction

MOVE.B   D1,TTYOUT

would move a byte from D1 to the location $7FFF, which might be the location of an output buffer, for example.

An important advantage of the EQU directive is evident when a value is defined which is referenced several times within a program. If the address TTYOUT needs to be changed in a subsequent assembly, reassembly with a new EQU set to the correct address would change the value throughout the program. This might be necessary if the program is executed on several systems, each with different buffer locations.

The EQU directive can also be used to give mathematical constants useful names, as in the statement

    ONEK   EQU   1024

which defines "ONEK" as 1024 decimal. As another example, MAXMEM could be equated to the maximum memory space available for a system. The value could be changed, if necessary, when the program is reassembled on a new system. The only drawback is that the value defined by the EQU directive is known only to the assembler and does not exist in memory. Therefore, it cannot be changed without reassembly.

Data directives.   The two directives DC (Define Constant) and DS (Define Storage) are available to initialize values in memory and reserve space in memory, respectively. The DC directive is similar to a DATA statement in FORTRAN, in which the variables defined are assigned initial values. The DS directive is similar to the DIMENSION statement, which reserves space for variables but assigns no values to them.

The Define Constant directive causes the assembler to store specified values in the location or locations associated with the location counter value at the time the DC directive is encountered during assembly. When the machine language program is loaded into memory, the locations involved have the initial values specified. For example, the statement

    INITV   DC.W   20

causes the decimal value 20 to occupy a word at location INITV. However, if the program is executed more than once and the value at INITV changes between executions, any program statement depending on the initial value of 20 may not yield the correct results when executed. Thus the DC directive should never be used to initialize a value that may be modified after the program is loaded into memory if multiple program executions depend on the initial value. A better approach to initialization of values is to reserve space for the values with a DS directive and then initialize the values with executable instructions.

Both the DC and DS directives require a length specification (B, W, or L). The length specification determines whether bytes, words, or longwords are reserved. Thus the directive

    DS.W $10

reserves 16 words in memory. The length of each constant defined by the DC directive is determined by the size specification. For example, the directive

> DC.W   LABEL+1

will store the address of LABEL plus 1 in a word location.

Listing control.   The last group of directives in Table 5.5 indicates a few of the options available to format the listing produced by the assembler. The LLEN (line length) directive determines the number of characters in the printed lines. LLEN 72 is typically used for CRT units, but longer lines with more than 72 characters may be used for line printers. The SPC directive causes the specified number of blank lines to appear on the printout to enhance readability. Other directives, such as PAGE, are usually offered to format the listing. The PAGE directive causes an advance to the top of a new page each time it is encountered. The page length depends on the printer being used and is generally set as a parameter in the operating system. One other directive (not shown in Table 5.5) is useful for MC68000 assemblers. The G directive instructs the assembler to list the contents of every location initialized by a DC directive. Otherwise, only the first locations have their values listed when the operand is a string of characters.

Generally, each option for listing has a default value for which the opposite can be specified. The NOLIST directive in Table 5.5, for example, causes the statements following it to be omitted from the listing. Its opposite, the LIST directive, is the default value and need not be specified unless the NOLIST option is to be reversed. Thus the sequence

> LIST
> (segment I)
> NOLIST
> (segment II)
> LIST
> (segment III)
> END

lists segments I and III of a program but not segment II.

Example 5.5

Figure 5.7 illustrates a program employing a number of assembler directives. The first three directives set the line length, cause printing of the values defined by the DC directives, and set the origin to $1000, respectively. The EQU directives define the constant ONE, the address of the monitor (MACSbug), and also the starting address of the program for the second ORG directive.

The first ORG directive defines the area for data storage beginning at location $1000. The executable program begins at location $2000, as specified by the directive

> ORG PROGRAM

The program clears the data locations between COMMON and the last location used for data.

```
  1                           LLEN     100
  2                           G
  3        00001000           ORG      $1000
  4        00000001  ONE      EQU      1                    ;A CONSTANT
  5        000200F6  MACSBUG  EQU      $200F6               ;MONITOR ADDRESS
  6        00002000  PROGRAM  EQU      $2000                ;STARTING ADDRESS
  7                           *
  8                           *   DATA AREA
  9                           *
 10 001000 0A        INITDT   DC.B     10,5,7               ;BYTES - DECIMAL
 10 001001 05
 10 001002 07
 11 001004 0000000A           DC.L     10,5,7               ;LONGWORDS - DECIMAL
 11 001008 00000005
 11 00100C 00000007
 12 001010 FF                 DC.B     $FF,$10,$AF          ;BYTES - HEX
 12 001011 10
 12 001012 AF
 13 001014 000000FF           DC.L     $FF,$20,$AE          ;LONGWORDS - HEX
 13 001018 00000020
 13 00101C 000000AE
 14 001020 41                 DC.B     'ABCDEFGH'           ;BYTES - ASCII
    001021 42
    001022 43
    001023 44
    001024 45
    001025 46
    001026 47
    001027 48
 15 001028 41                 DC.L     'A','BC'             ;LONGWORDS - ASCII
    001029 00
    00102A 00
    00102B 00
 15 00102C 42
    00102D 43
    00102E 00
    00102F 00
 16 001030 00001000  INITADD  DC.L     INITDT               ;ADDRESS INITDT
 17 001034 00000014  COMMON   DS.W     10                   ;10 WORDS
 18 001048 00000020  HEXVAL   DS.W     $10                  ;16 WORDS
 19 001068 00000003  BYTES    DS.B     3                    ; 3 BYTES
 20 00106C 00000000           DS       0                    ;EVEN BOUNDARY
 21                           *
 22                           * THE LENGTH IS COMPUTED BASED ON THE LAST DATA LOCATION (BYTES+3)
 23                           * MINUS THE FIRST DATA LOCATION (COMMON)
 24                           *
 25        00000037  LENGTH   EQU      (BYTES+3-COMMON)     ;NUM. OF BYTES
 26                           *
 27        00002000           ORG      PROGRAM
 28                           *
 29                           *   CLEAR COMMON VALUES
 30                           *
 31 002000 123C0037  BEGIN    MOVE.B   #LENGTH,D1           ;COUNTER
 32 002004 227C00001034       MOVEA.L  #COMMON,A1           ;ADDR. OF FIRST WORD
 33                           *
 34 00200A 12FC0000  LOOP     MOVE.B   #0,(A1)+             ;CLEAR COMMON BLOCK
 35 00200E 5301               SUBQ.B   #ONE,D1
 36 002010 66F8               BNE      LOOP
 37 002012 4EF9000200F6       JMP      MACSBUG
 38                           END

***** TOTAL ERRORS    0--    0
```

YMBOL TABLE - APPROX 1192 SYMBOL ENTRIES LEFT

```
EGIN      002000  BYTES     001068  COMMON    001034  HEXVAL    001048
NITADD    001030  INITDT    001000  LENGTH    000037  LOOP      00200A
ACSBUG    0200F6  ONE       000001  PROGRAM   002000
```

Figure 5.7 Use of directives.

The DC directives define a number of constants in the data area. Note that

    INITADD DC.L   INITDT

initializes INITADD with the address of INITDT. The instruction

    MOVE.L   #INITDT,INITADD

would accomplish the same thing, but only as the program executes.

A total of 55 bytes are reserved by the various DS directives and

    DS.B   55

would accomplish the same results. However, it is assumed that reference to the individual blocks (COMMON, HEXVAL, BYTES) is required in another program segment not shown. The final

    DS   0

directive aligns the next location address on a word (even) boundary.

EXERCISES

5.2.1. Write a routine to reserve a 20-word block of memory for storage and then initialize it to the successive values 1 through 20 upon execution.

5.2.2. Find the errors in the following program to add four 16-bit numbers in locations $2000 through $2006.

```
          ORG              $1000
          MOVE.L           $2000,A1
          MOVE.L           4,D2
          ADD.W            (A1)+,D2
          SUB.W            #ONE,D2
          BNE              LOOP
     ONE  DC.W             1
          JMP              MACSBUG
          END
```

5.2.3. Determine the values (if any) created by the following directives.
    (a) DC.B 'N IS'
    (b) DC.B 20
    (c) HERE EQU   *
    (d) DS.L 1
    (e) DC.L LABEL+2

5.2.4. Assume that EQU directives have been used to assign START the value $1000 and END the value $2000. Find the value computed by the assembler for the following expressions.
    (a) START-2
    (b) END-START
    (c) (END-START)/2
    (d) (END-START)/3
    (e) 2*END

5.3 ADDRESSING MODES FOR THE MC68000

The different addressing modes of a processor determine the variety of ways that an operand or its address may be referenced by an instruction. Generally speaking, processors employed in sophisticated applications require a large number of addressing modes to be effective and efficient. The MC68000 allows 14 different modes, which classifies it among the most powerful microprocessors in this regard. The basic addressing modes were introduced in Chapter 4, where the operation of the CPU and its

TABLE 5.6 MC68000 ADDRESSING MODES

Mode	Effective address calculation
Register direct addressing	
Data Register direct	$EA = Dn$
Address Register direct	$EA = An$
Absolute data addressing	
Absolute short	$EA =$ (next word)
Absolute long	$EA =$ (next two words)
Indirect addressing	
Address Register indirect	$EA = (An)$
Indirect with postincrement	$EA = (An); (An) \leftarrow (An) + N$
Indirect with predecrement	$(An) \leftarrow (An) - N; EA = (An)$
Indirect with displacement	$EA = (An) + <d_{16}>$
Indirect with index	$EA = (An) + (Xn) + <d_8>$
Relative addressing	
PC relative with offset	$EA = (PC) + <d_{16}>$
PC relative with index	$EA = (PC) + (Xn) + <d_8>$
Immediate data addressing	
Immediate	$DATA =$ next word(s)
Quick immediate	Inherent data
Implied addressing	
Implied Register	$EA = SR, USP, SP,$ or PC

Notes:

1. | | |
   |---|---|
   | EA | Effective address |
   | An | Address register |
   | Dn | Data register |
   | Xn | Address or data register used as index register |
   | SR | Status register |
   | PC | Program counter |
   | $<d_8>$ | 8-bit offset (displacement) |
   | $<d_{16}>$ | 16-bit offset (displacement) |
   | ( ) | Contents of |
   | $\leftarrow$ | Replaces |

2. $N = 1$ for byte, 2 for words, and 4 for longwords. If An is the stack pointer and the operand size is byte, $N = 2$ to keep the stack pointer on a word boundary.

3. The designation Ri is also used to indicate a register used for indexing. Motorola literature also uses Xi or ix for an index register as in Appendix IV.

TABLE 5.7 ADDRESSING CATEGORIES AND ASSEMBLER SYNTAX

Addressing mode	Mode	Register	Data	Mem.	Cont.	Alter.	Assembler syntax
Data register direct	000	Reg. no.	X	—	—	X	Dn
Address register direct	001	Reg. no.	—	—	—	X	An
Address register indirect	010	Reg. no.	X	X	X	X	(An)
Address register indirect with postincrement	011	Reg. no.	X	X	—	X	(An)+
Address register indirect with predecrement	100	Reg. no.	X	X	—	X	−(An)
Address register indirect with displacement	101	Reg. no.	X	X	X	X	d(An)
Address register indirect with index	110	Reg. no.	X	X	X	X	d(An,Ri)
Absolute short	111	000	X	X	X	X	NNN
Absolute long	111	001	X	X	X	X	NNNNNN
Program counter with displacement	111	010	X	X	X	—	d(PC)
Program counter with index	111	011	X	X	X	—	d(PC,Ri)
Immediate	111	100	X	X	—	—	#NNN

machine language were emphasized. In the present sections, all of the modes are discussed using the MC68000 assembly language notation.

The general classification of addressing modes includes register direct, absolute, indirect, relative, and immediate addressing. In each class, a number of variations is available for the MC68000, as indicated in Table 5.6. For each addressing mode, the processor addressing circuitry computes the effective address of any operand specified in an instruction when that instruction is fetched and decoded. The table defines how the effective address, EA, is calculated for each addressing mode.

The classification of addresses according to mode is convenient for the programmer to determine the ways in which operands can be referenced. Certain addressing modes are allowed and others forbidden to specific instructions. Motorola literature further classifies addressing into categories to simplify the discussion of those modes available for an instruction. As defined in Table 5.7, the addressing categories are *data, memory, control,* and *alterable,* referring to the operand characteristics. The significance of the categories is discussed later in this section. The table also lists the assembler syntax for each addressing mode and the effective address encoding (mode/register) used as part of the machine language format.

5.3.1 Register Direct and Absolute Addressing

In both the register direct and absolute addressing modes, the location of an operand is specified explicitly in the instruction. An MC68000 *direct address* must refer to one of the processor data or address registers. The contents of the register is the operand. An *absolute address* is a 16-bit or 32-bit memory address. In this case the contents of the location is the operand. A 16-bit address is termed "short" and a 32-bit address is considered "long."

Register direct addressing.

In effect, the processor registers represent a high-speed memory within the CPU and operations between registers require no external memory references. The two modes for register direct addressing are *data register direct* and *address register direct.* The effective address calculated is

$$EA = Dn$$

which specifies data register Dn. The address register direct mode calculates the effective address as

$$EA = An$$

when An specifies the nth address register. The instruction referring to a data register can specify a byte (B), word (W), or longword (L) length for the operand. Thus the instruction

CLR.$<X>$ D2

clears register D2 for the length $<X>$ = B or W or L. This is the typical format for a single-address instruction using a data register as the destination. An address register is considered to hold an address 16 or 32 bits long. The MC68000, however, uses only a 24-bit address to reference memory. Instructions are not available for byte operations using address registers. For example, the instruction

MOVE.$<X>$ A1,D1

will allow a size specification of only $<X>$ = W or $<X>$ = L. In addition to the size restriction, other limitations are placed on the use of an address register as the destination location.

The MC68000 allows manipulation of addresses by a group of instructions which use an address register as the destination. These instructions normally take the suffix "A" in assembly language notation. The instruction

MOVEA.L   A1,A2

transfers the 32-bit contents of A1 to A2, for example. The MOVEA (Move Address) instruction performs the same function as the MOVE instruction, but is designed to treat operands as addresses (i.e., positive numbers), indicating memory locations. Thus the data registers and address registers of the MC68000 are not considered equivalent for many operations. The differences are presented in detail in Chapter 9, where instructions that operate on addresses are considered.

Absolute short addressing.

The absolute short or 16-bit address for an operand in memory is contained in an extension word to the operation word for an instruction. The address is actually converted to a 32-bit address by extending the sign bit (bit 15) of the short address. Figure 5.8(a) shows the calculation. A 24-bit address is used to address memory with leading zeros or ones in bits [23:16], replicating the most significant bit of the extension word. The extended address is considered to be a positive 24-bit number.

Example 5.6

> Figure 5.9 shows the effect of using the short addressing mode. If the hexadecimal address is between 0 and $7FFF, the low 32K bytes of memory can be addressed. Short addresses $8000 and above are sign-extended to 24 bits, resulting in addresses in memory between $FF8000 and $FFFFFF which are the upper 32K bytes of memory addressable by the MC68000. Thus the designers of the instruction set treated these segments of memory at the extremes in a special way. Normally, the system designer specifies the lowest segment of memory for system parameters. In fact, the MC68000 processor uses the first 1024 bytes for its vectors, which define the starting addresses for trap and interrupt routines. The highest segment is reserved for I/O interfaces in many systems. The absolute short addressing mode allows efficient access to fixed locations in either of these regions.

Absolute long addressing.   As shown in Figure 5.8(b), a long address is formed from two extension words following the operation word of an instruction. Such an address can span the entire addressing space of the MC68000 memory. The

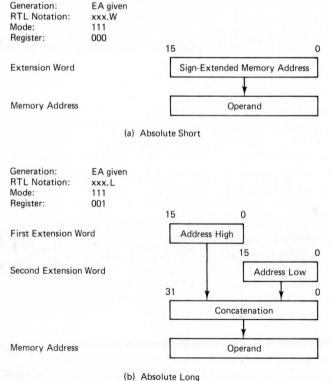

(a) Absolute Short

(b) Absolute Long

Figure 5.8 Absolute addressing. (Courtesy of Motorola, Inc.)

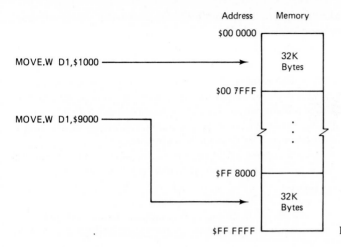

Figure 5.9 Absolute short addressing.

magnitude of the absolute address specified in the assembly language statement determines whether the short or long absolute addressing mode is used. The instruction

    MOVE.W $12000,D1

requires absolute long addressing for the source operand because the address requires more than 16 bits. An instruction such as

    MOVE.B $3FFF,$12000

specifies both absolute modes. The source address could be given as $0000 3FFF, which would force most assemblers to use the long absolute mode. Reference to the

TABLE 5.8 REGISTER AND ABSOLUTE ADDRESSING

Machine language (hexadecimal)	Instruction		After execution
2406	MOVE.L	D6,D2	(D2) = (D6)
4240	CLR.W	D0	(D0) [15:0] = 0
2640	MOVEA.L	D0,A3	(A3) = (D0)
1038 2001	MOVE.B	$2001,D0	(D0) [7:0] = ($2001)
21FC 0002 14AA 0024	MOVE.L	$214AA,$24	($24) = ($214AA)
21F8 0534 0528	MOVE.L	$0534,$0528	($0528) = ($0534)

assembly language manual of the particular assembler being used will determine how these addresses are handled and translated into machine language.

Example 5.7

Table 5.8 shows a few of the addressing modes just discussed as they would be used in instructions. The table also lists the machine language statements as they are stored in memory. The instructions specifying register modes are one word in length and are the most efficient for storage and execution. As noted previously, the mnemonic MOVEA is used as the operation code when the destination is an address register.

In the absolute modes, the address is independent of the operand length except that word or longword operands must be addressed at even locations. The instruction

    MOVE.L $0534,$0528

copies the 32-bit value in locations $0534 through $0537 into four bytes beginning at address $0528 since longword operands are specified. However, both addresses are short absolute addresses.

5.3.2 Indirect Addressing

Five indirect addressing modes are available for the MC68000 to reference an operand that is part of a data structure in memory. All five modes use an address register to hold the basic address, which can then be modified in various ways to compute the effective address of a specific operand. Unlike the absolute addresses that are defined when the program is assembled, the indirect address is computed as the program executes. Address register indirect, register indirect with displacement, and register indirect with indexing are discussed in this subsection. The postincrement and predecrement indirect modes are discussed in Section 5.3.3.

Address register indirect.   Any of the eight address registers of the MC68000 may be used to address indirectly an operand in memory. The effective address is calculated as

    EA = (An)

when the nth register is designated. The contents of the selected address register are used as the operand address when an instruction using this mode executes. To load the register, an instruction such as

    MOVEA.L   # < addr > ,A1

transfers the address < addr > to A1. Then, reference to (A1), as in the instruction

    MOVE.W   (A1),D1

would move the 16-bit value contained at location < addr > into D1. The specification of the address used as the source in the MOVEA instruction can be by any of the

MOVEA.L	#$1000, A1	; START OF LIST: 1
CLR.L	D1	; ZERO THE INDEX
	.	
	.	
	.	
LOOP MOVE.W	8(A1, D1.L), D2	; ITEM TO D2:2 . . N
	.	
	.	; PROCESS
	.	
ADD.W	#2, D1	; NEXT ITEM
(Branch to LOOP if not done)		
	.	
	.	
	.	; continue

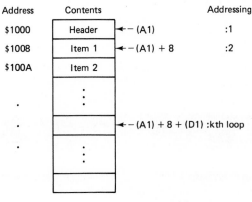

(a) Program Segment

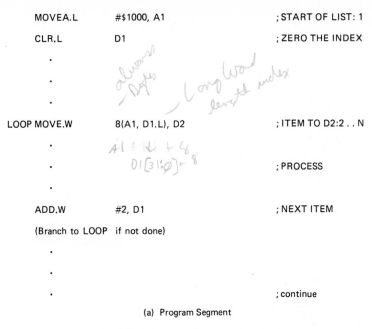

(b) Memory Reference

Figure 5.12 Indirect addressing with indexing.

changed automatically as the instructions using the modes execute. Thus no time is wasted increasing index values by program instructions as with the indirect with indexing addressing mode. Perhaps the most important use for these modes is to manipulate operands in a stack in memory as discussed in Chapter 4. However, many other data manipulation operations are simplified though the use of these modes.

The effective address for each mode is calculated as shown in Figure 5.13. In the postincrement mode, the address in An is used before An is incremented by 1, 2, or 4 for byte, word, or longword operands, respectively. This mode allows a program to

Generation: EA = (An)
An = An + N

RTL Notation: An @ +
Mode: 011
Register: n

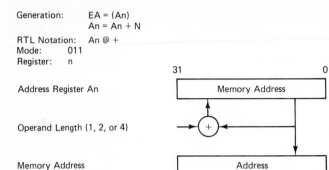

Address Register An

Operand Length (1, 2, or 4)

Memory Address

(a) Postincrement

Generation: An = An − N
EA = (An)

RTL Notation: An @ −
Mode: 100
Register: n

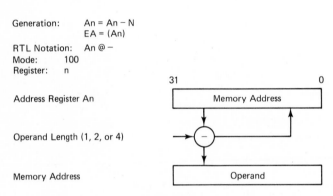

Address Register An

Operand Length (1, 2, or 4)

Memory Address

(b) Predecrement

Figure 5.13 Predecrement and postincrement addressing. (Courtesy of Motorola, Inc.)

address consecutive values stored at increasingly higher addresses in memory. In the predecrement mode, An is decremented first, then used as a pointer to a memory location.

The assembler recognizes the predecrement mode as −(An) and the postincrement as (An)+. In the instruction

MOVE.W   −(A1),(A2)+

a word is moved from location (A1)−2 to location (A2). If the instruction is executed again, the source address is one word lower in memory and the destination one word higher than the original values. This is typical usage in program loops in which the autoindexed instruction is repeatedly executed until the condition to quit looping is met.

These modes are also used to move blocks of data from one memory segment to another when statements such as

MOVE.W   (A1)+,(A2)+

are used in a loop. Here (A1) designates the first block and (A2) the second. The addressing in this case is equivalent to using

> MOVE.W   (A1),(A2)
>
> ADD.L   #2,A1
>
> ADD.L   #2,A2

where both the source and destination addresses are incremented by 2 after the transfer since the operands are two bytes in length.

Example 5.10

> The simple program segment in Figure 5.14 moves a 32-byte block of data from location $2000 to location $3000, but in reverse order. The order of the data is reversed by starting the transfer from the first byte of the source block using postincrement addressing to the last byte of the destination block with predecrement addressing. The byte at $2000 is moved to $301F, the byte at $2001 is moved to $301E, and so on. Register D1 is used as a counter for the loop and registers A1 and A2 contain the addresses of the blocks.

5.3.4 Relative Addressing

The relative addressing modes of the MC68000 allow an operand address to be calculated with respect to the value in the program counter. The *program counter relative with displacement* addressing mode allows a 16-bit integer value to be added to the value in the PC to compute the effective address. If the displacement is not fixed but must be altered during program execution, the *program counter relative with index* mode may be used. The effective address is the sum of the address in the PC, an 8-bit integer that is sign-extended, and the contents of the index register. The calculation of the effective address for these two modes is shown in Figure 5.15(a). Each mode requires one extension word for the displacement in the instruction and the value in the program counter is the address of the extension word when the effective address is computed.

The assembler automatically treats any branch instruction (BRA, BGT, etc.) as an instruction using relative addressing with displacement. The distance between the branch instruction and the destination is computed as an offset from the contents of the program counter. A forced reference to the (PC) occurs in statements such as

> ADD.W   *+$10,D1

where the operand is in a location eight words (16 bytes) past the location of the extension word of the ADD instruction. The operand is added to the contents of D1 [15:0]. The symbol "*" indicates the location counter to the assembler and the instruction is assembled using PC relative with displacement addressing. In this example instruction, the operand is nine words or 18 bytes past the location of the operation word of the ADD instruction.

MC68000 ASM REV= 1.4 - COPYRIGHT BY MOTOROLA 1978   PAGE   1

```
 1                              LLEN    100
 2      00001000                ORG     $1000
 3                          *
 4      000200F6     MACSBUG     EQU     $200F6              ;MONITOR ADDRESS
 5                          *
 6                          *  MOVE 32 BYTES FROM $2000 TO $3000 REVERSING THEIR ORDER
 7                          *
 8 001000 123C0020             MOVE.B   #32,D1             ;SET COUNTER TO 32
 9 001004 227C00002000         MOVEA.L  #$2000,A1          ;SET UP ADDRESSES
10 00100A 247C00003020         MOVEA.L  #$3020,A2          ;  FOR TRANSFER
11                          *
12 001010 1519        LOOP     MOVE.B   (A1)+,-(A2)        ;MOVE NEXT BYTE
13
14 001012 04010001             SUBI.B   #1,D1              ;DECREMENT COUNT
15 001016 66F8                 BNE      LOOP               ;CONTINUE UNTIL COUNT = 0
16                          *
17 001018 4EF9000200F6         JMP      MACSBUG            ;RETURN TO MONITOR
18                              END
```

****** TOTAL ERRORS   0--   0

SYMBOL TABLE - APPROX 1200 SYMBOL ENTRIES LEFT

LOOP   001010 MACSBUG   0200F6

```
*TD
PC=001000 SR=2000 US=00007F00 SS=00007FFE
D0=00000000 D1=00000020 D2=00000000 D3=00000000
D4=00000000 D5=00000000 D6=00000000 D7=00000000
A0=00000000 A1=00000000 A2=00003000 A3=00000000
A4=00000000 A5=00000000 A6=00000000 A7=00007FFE
---------------------------------------------------------
*DM 2000 20
002000  00 01 02 03 04 05 06 07 08 09 0A 0B 0C 0D 0E 0F   ...............
002010  10 11 12 13 14 15 16 17 18 19 1A 1B 1C 1D 1E 1F   ...............
*G TILL 1018
PC=001018 SR=2004 US=00007F00 SS=00007FFE
D0=00000000 D1=00000000 D2=00000000 D3=00000000
D4=00000000 D5=00000000 D6=00000000 D7=00000000
A0=00000000 A1=00002020 A2=00003000 A3=00000000
A4=00000000 A5=00000000 A6=00000000 A7=00007FFE
---------------------------------------------------------
*DM 3000 20
003000   1F 1E 1D 1C 1B 1A 19 18 17 16 15 14 13 12 11 10   ...............
003010   0F 0E 0D 0C 0B 0A 09 08 07 06 05 04 03 02 01 00   ...............
*
```

Figure 5.14   Examples of postincrement and predecrement addressing.

The relative with index addressing mode causes the effective address to be computed as

$$EA = (PC) + (Ri) [X] + \langle d_8 \rangle$$

where the length of the index register is either 16 bits or 32 bits, indicated by $X = W$ or L, respectively. The fixed displacement is a signed 8-bit value. It is contained in an extension word in the instruction, as shown in Figure 5.15(b).

Generation: EA = (PC) + d
RTL Notation: PC @ (d)
Mode: 111
Register: 010

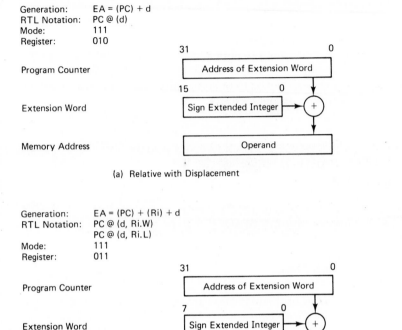

(a) Relative with Displacement

Generation: EA = (PC) + (Ri) + d
RTL Notation: PC @ (d, Ri.W)
               PC @ (d, Ri.L)
Mode: 111
Register: 011

Figure 5.15 Relative addressing.
(Courtesy of Motorola, Inc.)

(b) Relative with Index

The relative modes of addressing are described in more detail in Chapter 9, particularly when position-independent coding is discussed. It should be noted that different assemblers may reference the relative addressing modes differently. One Motorola assembler (the resident assembler) allows references such as

ADD.W $10(PC),D1

which forces the relative mode for the address of the source. The * + $10 reference would also be recognized by this assembler.

5.3.5 Immediate and Implied Addressing

The immediate addressing mode for the MC68000 allows byte, word, or longword values to be used as constants in an instruction. The byte or word-length values require one extension word, and the long value adds two words to the instruction in memory. The assembler recognizes the immediate mode in instructions such as

MOVE.W   #50,D2

by the symbol "#" and the instruction moves 50 (decimal) into the low-order word of D2. As defined previously, hexadecimal values are specified with "$" and ASCII characters are enclosed within apostrophes.

Some MC68000 instructions do not require an operand to be specified and other instructions affect processor registers without explicitly referencing them in the instructions. These *implicit* references can be to the program counter, the status register, or the stack pointer. For example, the instruction

RTS

which returns from a subroutine to the calling program uses the stack pointer to retrieve the return address from the stack. The instruction

BSR   < address >

does not explicitly reference the stack pointer or the program counter, but modifies both during its execution. These types of instructions have an addressing mode which is implied.

5.3.6 Addressing Categories

The individual addressing modes of the MC68000 are further characterized into four groups of *addressing categories*. These categories refer to the characteristics of the operand being addressed. As defined in Figure 5.16, the categories are *data, memory, control,* and *alterable*. The data category includes every mode but address register direct addressing. This is logical since the operand in an address register is assumed to be an address, not a data item, in this context. Except for register direct addressing, the other addressing modes can all refer to an operand in memory. However, all the memory references are not considered alterable. An immediate value is obviously not alterable. Also, relative addressing modes do not refer to an alterable operand. This means that the relative modes cannot be used to define destination addresses that are to be written (altered). For example, a MOVE instruction requires an alterable destination, which excludes the immediate and relative modes according to Figure 5.16.

The programmer uses the category information to determine which addressing modes are allowed for particular instructions. For example, according to the description found in the Motorola *User's Manual* or Appendix IV, the CLR instruction allows only data-alterable addressing modes for the destination operand. This excludes the address registers and relative addresses as destinations according to Figure 5.16. Thus the instruction

CLR   A1

is not allowed. In the discussion of the instructions in later chapters, the allowed addressing will be described in terms of these categories.

A few observations on the categories in Figure 5.16 should be noted:

(a) Instructions that require data-alterable addressing cannot use address registers as operands.

Effective address modes may be categorized by the ways in which they may be used. The following classifications will be used in the instruction definitions.

Data   If an effective address mode may be used to refer to data operands, it is considered a data addressing effective address mode.

Memory   If an effective address mode may be used to refer to memory operands, it is considered a memory addressing effective address mode.

Alterable If an effective address mode may be used to refer to alterable (writable) operands, it is considered an alterable addressing effective address mode.

Control   If an effective address mode may be used to refer to memory operands without an associated size, it is considered a control addressing effective address mode.

Addressing Mode	Mode	Register	Addressing Categories				Assembler Syntax
			Data	Mem	Cont	Alter	
Data Reg Dir	000	reg no.	X	–	–	X	Dn
Addr Reg Dir	001	reg no.	–	–	–	X	An
Addr Reg Ind	010	reg no.	X	X	X	X	(An)
Addr Reg Ind w/Postinc	011	reg no.	X	X	–	X	(An)+
Addr Reg Ind w/Predec	100	reg no.	X	X	–	X	–(An)
Addr Reg Ind w/Disp	101	reg no.	X	X	X	X	d(An)
Addr Reg Ind w/Index	110	reg no.	X	X	X	X	d(An, Ri)
Absolute Short	111	000	X	X	X	X	XXX
Absolute Long	111	001	X	X	X	X	XXXXXX
Prog Ctr w/Disp	111	010	X	X	X	–	d(PC)
Prog Ctr w/Index	111	011	X	X	X	–	d(PC, Ri)
Immediate	111	100	X	X	–	–	#XXX

Figure 5.16   Addressing categories. (Courtesy of Motorola, Inc.)

(b) The relative addressing modes reference operands that are not alterable (writable) by MC68000 instructions.

(c) Address register indirect addressing is allowed for all instructions that take operands. The same comment applies to the other modes which are considered to encompass all four categories.

EXERCISES

5.3.1. List some reasons why operands addressed relative to the program counter can be read and manipulated but their locations cannot be written.

5.3.2. The MC68000 does not allow the CLR instruction to specify an address register as a destination. Is the restriction on using CLR with address registers a problem? How does a program address location 0?

5.3.3. Discuss the various addressing modes in terms of values to be defined before assembly and those that can be defined or changed during program execution. (Assume that the program will not change its own instructions in memory.)

5.3.4. Discuss the advantages and disadvantages of the absolute short addressing mode compared to the absolute long addressing mode.

5.3.5. If (A1) = $1000, determine the operand address for the following instructions.
 (a) CLR.B $FFFF (A1)
 (b) MOVE.B (A1)+,D1
 (c) MOVE.W −(A1),D1

5.3.6. What do these instructions accomplish?
 (a) MOVE.L 4 (A0),(A0)
 (b) MOVE.W $9000,D1
 (c) MOVE.B 0(A0,D1),D1

5.3.7. Compare the absolute short addressing mode with the indirect displacement mode when the displacement value is $8000.

FURTHER READING

The book edited by Vincent Tseng discusses the various aspects of software and hardware development for microcomputers. The Motorola EXORmacs system is presented in some detail. Barron's short but lucid text describes in detail the operation of an assembler. The three books on programming all cover the assembly language of the MC68000. Kane et al.'s book includes a large number of examples.

BARRON, D. W., *Assemblers and Loaders.* 2nd ed. New York: American Elsevier, 1972.

KANE, GERALD, DOUG HAWKINS, and LANCE LEVENTHAL, *68000 Assembly Language Programming.* Berkeley, Calif.: Osborne (McGraw-Hill), 1981.

SCANLON, LEO J., *The 68000: Principles and Programming.* Indianapolis, Ind.: Howard W. Sams, 1981.

TSENG, VINCENT, ed., *Microprocessor Development and Development Systems.* New York: McGraw-Hill, 1982.

WAKERLY, JOHN F., *Microcomputer Architecture and Programming.* New York: Wiley, 1981.

6

Data Transfer, Program Control, and Subroutines

Several chapters are devoted to a discussion of the assembly language instruction set of the MC68000. The purpose of these chapters is to analyze each instruction in detail and illustrate its use in assembly language programs. These discussions begin in this chapter. The instructions and their variations are separated into categories based on the operation performed. The instructions listed in Table 6.1 for *data transfer, program control,* and *subroutine usage* are discussed in this chapter. Instructions for arithmetic, logical, and similar operations are presented in subsequent chapters.

The MOVE instruction is the primary instruction in the data transfer category. It does not have many restrictions on the location and length of operands which can be transferred between the CPU and memory. Two variations of this instruction are also listed in Table 6.1. They are distinguished from the MOVE instruction by adding a letter suffix, Q or M, to form MOVEQ or MOVEM. The MOVEQ "quick" form is a one-word instruction to load a data value into a data register. The MOVEM instruction is a variation that allows the contents of a selected group of registers to be transferred to or from consecutive memory locations. These two variations may be more efficient than the MOVE instruction for some purposes.

Instructions for program control are used to define the flow of control within a program. The BRA and JMP instructions cause unconditional transfer of control. The Bcc and DBcc instructions branch when certain conditions, which are defined by the condition codes, are met. The CMP instruction and its variations, which are listed in Table 6.1, are included in the discussion in this chapter because they set the condition codes based on the values of the operands.

Subroutines may be called with the BSR or JSR instructions. The execution of a RTR or RTS instruction in the subroutine causes control to be returned to the calling

TABLE 6.1   SELECTED INSTRUCTIONS

Data transfer	
MOVE	Move
MOVEQ	Move Quick (immediate)
MOVEM	Move Multiple Registers
EXG	Exchange Registers
SWAP	Swap Data Register Halves
Program control	
Unconditional	
BRA	Branch Always
JMP	Jump
Conditional branch and compare	
Bcc	Branch Conditionally
DBcc	Test Condition, Decrement, and Branch
CMP	Compare
CMPI	Compare Immediate
CMPM	Compare Memory
TST	Test
Subroutine	
BSR	Branch to Subroutine
JSR	Jump to Subroutine
RTR	Return and Restore (CCR)
RTS	Return from Subroutine

program. The saving and restoring of the return address is handled automatically by the CPU when the call and return instructions are executed in the proper sequence.

In this chapter the instructions are defined in terms of the assembler syntax, operand length, valid addressing modes, and the effect on the condition codes. The entire instruction set is presented in Appendix IV.

6.1 DATA TRANSFER

The instructions MOVE, MOVEQ, MOVEM, EXG, and SWAP represent data transfer instructions. The MOVE instruction is the most flexible and, consequently, the most frequently used. The quick variation, MOVEQ, transfers an 8-bit data value to a designated data register. MOVEM has the letter suffix M designating "multiple." It is used to save the contents of a selected group of registers in memory or to restore their contents from memory. The EXG and SWAP instructions transfer data between and within registers.

Table 6.2 summarizes the instructions covered in this section. For each instruc-

TABLE 6.2 INSTRUCTIONS FOR DATA TRANSFER

Instruction	Syntax	Operand length (bits)	Addressing modes		Condition codes affected
			Source	Destination	
Move	MOVE.\<l\> \<EAs\>,\<EAd\>	8, 16, 32	All[2]	Data alterable	N, Z V = {0}, C = {0}
Move Quick	MOVEQ #\<d$_8$\>,\<Dn\>	32	Immediate (sign-extended)	Dn	N, Z V = {0}, C = {0}
Move Multiple Registers	MOVEM.\<l$_1$\> \<list\>,\<EA\> MOVEM.\<l$_1$\> \<EA\>,\<list\>	16 or 32 16 or 32	Register list Control or postincrement	Control alterable or predecrement Register list	None None
Exchange Registers	EXG \<Rx\>,\<Ry\>	32	Rx	Ry	None
Swap Register Halves	SWAP \<Dn\>	16	(Dn)[31:16] ⟶ (Dn)[15:0]	—	N,Z V = {0}, C = {0}

Notes:

1. \<EA\>   effective address
   \<l\>   B, W, or L
   \<l$_1$\>   W, or L
   \<Rn\>   Any Dn or An
   \<list\>   register list

2. If the operand size is a byte, \<An\> cannot be a source.

tion, the listings show the assembler syntax, the valid operand lengths, the possible addressing modes, and the condition codes affected by the instruction. When a number of modes are possible for the source or destination operand, the addressing modes are defined in terms of the addressing categories introduced in Chapter 5. The data-alterable category excludes address register direct, relative, and immediate addressing. Control-alterable addressing prohibits register direct, postincrement, predecrement, relative, and immediate addressing. The control category does not include the register direct, postdecrement, predecrement, or immediate modes.

6.1.1 The MOVE Instruction

The MOVE instruction transfers data between registers, between registers and memory, or between different memory locations. The format is

     MOVE.<l>   <EAs>,<EAd>

in which <l> = B, W, or L, indicating 8-bit, 16-bit, or 32-bit operands, respectively. Only the portion of the destination location specified by <l> is replaced in the operation

     (EAd) [l] ← (EAs) [l]

where [l] designates the appropriate bits affected. If An is specified as a source operand, the length must be a word or longword (W or L) since byte operations on address registers are not allowed. The destination addressing mode must be data alterable, which excludes address registers and relative addresses. The instruction variation MOVEA transfers values to address registers.

     The value transferred by the MOVE instruction is treated as a signed integer of the specified length. Condition codes N and Z are set as a result of the operation and V and C are set to {0}. Thus tests on the operand for negative or zero values are possible immediately following a MOVE instruction. For example, the sequence

     MOVE.W   LENGTH,D1

     BEQ   DONE

causes a branch to the instruction at DONE if the contents of location LENGTH were zero since BEQ (Branch if Equal Zero) branches when Z = {1}. Otherwise, program execution continues with the next instruction. This sequence could be used, for example, to manipulate a data table of given length. If the length held in location LENGTH is zero, the instructions to manipulate the data values are skipped and control is passed to the instruction labeled DONE.

     The instruction

     MOVE.B   #$FF,D1

sets Z = {0} since the immediate value is not zero, but also sets N = {1} because the 8-bit value is considered negative.

The MOVE instruction is used in most of the example programs in this book, so specific examples of its use are not given here. Instead, variations of the MOVE instruction are presented in the next subsection and the MOVE instruction is compared with each variation.

6.1.2 Variations of MOVE

The MOVEQ instruction is a one-word instruction which has the symbolic form

   MOVEQ $\# <d_8>, <Dn>$

where $<d_8>$ is an 8-bit constant. The 8-bit value is sign-extended to 32 bits and transferred to Dn. This instruction is very efficient when loading a data register with a constant in the decimal range -128 to $+127$. It executes in only four machine cycles, which is why it is called "quick." Standard MOVE instructions require more cycles for all transfers except register-to-register transfers. The condition codes are affected by the MOVEQ instruction exactly as they are for the MOVE instruction, allowing a test for zero or negative.

   The instruction to clear a register

   MOVEQ   #0,D1

has the same effect as CLR.L D1 since both instructions affect the full 32 bits of the register. There is no basic difference in efficiency or operation between these instructions.

   Another variation of the MOVE instruction is MOVEM, which transfers data between processor registers and memory locations. The instruction has the symbolic form

   MOVEM. $<l_1>$ $<$ list $>, <$ EA $>$

where the registers in the $<$ list $>$ are to be moved to memory locations beginning at address $<$ EA $>$; the low-order word or the whole register contents is moved if $<l_1> = $ W or L, respectively. The syntax for the $<$ list $>$ is shown in Table 6.3(a). Thus the instruction

   MOVEM.W   D0/D1/A2–A4,$1100

transfers the low-order contents of D0, D1, A2, A3, and A4 to locations $1100, $1102, $1104, $1106, and $1108, respectively. To restore the register values, the format is

   MOVEM. $<l_1>$ $<$ EA $>, <$ list $>$

where $<l_1>$ and $<$ list $>$ have the same meaning as before.

   When the destination for a MOVEM instruction is memory, only control-alterable addressing modes or the predecrement mode are allowed. This excludes register direct, postincrement, and program counter relative addressing for the destination $<$ EA $>$. In the control modes, the data registers are stored in the first locations of the specified memory area followed by the address registers, regardless of the order speci-

TABLE 6.3 MOVEM INSTRUCTION

(a) Register list
    (1) Selected registers are separated by "/" (e.g., D1/D3/D4)
    (2) Consecutive registers are specified by "–" (e.g., D1–D4)

(b) Transfer order

Order	Type

D0–D7, A0–A7
    into higher address
	1. Register to memory
	    (control-alterable)
	 2. Memory to register

A7–A0, D7–D0
    into lower addresses
	Register to memory
	    (predecrement)

fied in the register list. The predecrement mode is used to store the register contents on a stack growing downward in memory and the order of storage is reversed. That is, address registers are stored first, followed by data registers.

A transfer from memory to the registers allows only control-alterable modes or postincrement addressing for the source operands. The registers are transferred in the order D0, D1, ..., A0, ..., A7, regardless of the order in the list. The storage addresses are assumed to increase in memory. The postincrement addressing pops the designated registers off the stack. Table 6.3(b) summarizes the transfer order for the various cases.

Example 6.1

The MOVEM instruction is used in several ways in the program shown in Figure 6.1. The first MOVEM saves the low-order contents of D4, D3, D2, and D1 on the system stack. The second MOVEM transfers four words from locations $1100, $1102, $1104, and $1106 to registers D1, D2, D3, and D4, respectively. The numbers are added and the sum stored in location $1108. The registers are then restored from the stack in the reverse order from that in which they were stored.

6.1.3 Internal Data Transfer

The instruction EXG exchanges the 32-bit longword in the source register with that in the destination register. The registers involved can be data registers, address registers, or an address register and a data register. The instruction format is

    EXG   <Rx>,<Ry>

where the contents of Rx and Ry are exchanged. Only 32-bit exchanges are allowed and the condition codes are not affected.

The EXG instruction removes the need for temporary storage of register contents when 32-bit operands in two registers must be interchanged. The use of the exchange instruction is illustrated in Example 6.2.

MC68000 ASM REV= 1.4 - COPYRIGHT BY MOTOROLA 1978   PAGE   1

```
 1                              LLEN    100
 2      00001000               ORG     $1000
 3                        *
 4      000200F6   MACSBUG EQU     $200F6                ;MONITOR ADDRESS
 5                        *
 6                   * USE OF MOVEM INSTRUCTION
 7                        *
 8 001000 48A77800            MOVEM.W D1-D4,-(SP)        ;SAVE REGISTERS ON STACK
 9 001004 4CB8001E1100        MOVEM.W $1100,D1-D4        ;LOAD DATA
10                        *
11 00100A D441               ADD.W    D1,D2             ;ADD THE NUMBERS
12 00100C D642               ADD.W    D2,D3
13 00100E D843               ADD.W    D3,D4
14                        *
15 001010 31C41108            MOVE.W   D4,$1108          ;SAVE THE RESULT
16                        *
17 001014 4C9F001E            MOVEM.W (SP)+,D1-D4        ;RESTORE REGISTERS
18                        *
19 001018 4EF9000200F6        JMP      MACSBUG           ;RETURN TO MONITOR
20                        *
21                              END
```

****** TOTAL ERRORS   0--   0

SYMBOL TABLE - APPROX 1201 SYMBOL ENTRIES LEFT

MACSBUG   0200F6

Figure 6.1   Use of MOVEM instruction.

The SWAP instruction exchanges the low-order word with the high-order word in a single register. The instruction has the form

SWAP   < Dn >

in which only a data register can be specified. The condition codes are set according to the full 32-bit result to test for negative or zero.

Example 6.2

The program shown in Figure 6.2 illustrates two methods of exchanging the contents of two registers, A0 and D1. In the first method, the contents of register D1 are saved in a temporary location in memory. Then D1 can be loaded with the value in A0 and, finally, A0 can be loaded with the original contents of D1 from the temporary memory location. The second method uses the EXG instruction to accomplish the same operation in one instruction.

EXERCISES

6.1.1. Why must the MOVE instruction clear the condition codes C and V?

6.1.2. Write a routine to find the largest value of a set of 16-bit integers stored in consecutive locations in memory by comparing numbers in order and exchanging a smaller one for a

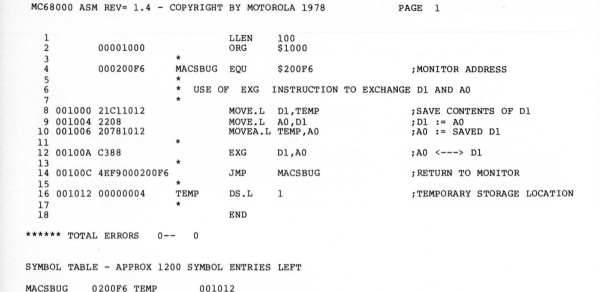

```
MC68000 ASM REV= 1.4 - COPYRIGHT BY MOTOROLA 1978               PAGE   1


  1                                   LLEN    100
  2          00001000                 ORG     $1000
  3                          *
  4          000200F6        MACSBUG   EQU     $200F6              ;MONITOR ADDRESS
  5                          *
  6                          *  USE OF  EXG  INSTRUCTION TO EXCHANGE D1 AND A0
  7                          *
  8  001000 21C11012                   MOVE.L  D1,TEMP            ;SAVE CONTENTS OF D1
  9  001004 2208                       MOVE.L  A0,D1              ;D1 := A0
 10  001006 20781012                   MOVEA.L TEMP,A0            ;A0 := SAVED D1
 11                          *
 12  00100A C388                        EXG    D1,A0              ;A0 <---> D1
 13                          *
 14  00100C 4EF9000200F6               JMP     MACSBUG            ;RETURN TO MONITOR
 15                          *
 16  001012 00000004         TEMP      DS.L    1                  ;TEMPORARY STORAGE LOCATION
 17                          *
 18                                     END


****** TOTAL ERRORS   0--   0


SYMBOL TABLE - APPROX 1200 SYMBOL ENTRIES LEFT

MACSBUG    0200F6 TEMP          001012
```

Figure 6.2 Use of EXG instruction.

larger one in a processor register until the register contains the largest one. Try it with and without use of the EXG instruction.

6.1.3. A stack with N words has its first element at location BOTTOM. Write the instructions to transfer the word values to another stack. Let both stacks grow down in memory.

6.1.4. What advantage does MOVEM have over a series of MOVE instructions to save register contents in memory?

6.1.5. Think of possible uses of the SWAP instruction. Remember that the second most significant byte in a 32-bit register is not directly accessible. What type of instruction is needed to access any particular byte in a 32-bit register?

6.2 PROGRAM CONTROL

In every sophisticated program, it is necessary to select which sequence of instructions to execute based on the results of computations. Thus the flow of control will follow different paths through the program depending on these computations. In some cases, the transfer of control is *unconditional.* For example, the statement

JMP   MACSBUG

which was the last executable statement in several of our previous examples, serves to return control to the monitor program unconditionally. Other programs require *conditional* transfer of control which is based on the results of an arithmetic or other operation. These operations set the condition codes of the MC68000 status register. The conditional branch instructions test these condition codes to determine whether a branch is required.

Two MC68000 instructions, BRA and JMP, cause unconditional transfer of control. The branch instruction BRA is limited in the range of memory locations that can be bypassed and allows only relative addressing to determine the branch distance or displacement in memory. The Bcc (Branch Conditionally) instruction allows one of 14 conditions to be specified. If the selected condition is met, program execution continues at the branch location designated in the instruction. The MC68000 also has a more complicated DBcc (Test Condition, Decrement, and Branch) instruction, which is useful for conditional branching in an iterative program structure. These branch instructions and those instructions that compare the test operands are discussed in this section. The setting of the condition codes and the MC68000 instructions that affect them are listed in Appendix IV.

6.2.1 Unconditional Branch and Jump

The instructions BRA (Branch Always) and JMP (Jump) cause unconditional transfer of control by changing the value in the program counter, as shown in Table 6.4. Anytime a branch or jump occurs, the new instruction address must be on a word (even) boundary or an addressing error will occur. The JMP instruction differs from the BRA instruction because the jump may be to anywhere in memory while the range of the BRA transfer is limited to a displacement of an 8-bit or 16-bit signed integer. Additionally, the jump address may be specified by different addressing modes, but branch addressing is always relative to the program counter.

BRA instruction.   The form of the BRA instruction is

BRA   < disp >

which allows either an 8-bit or a 16-bit displacement. For an 8-bit displacement, the branch range is −126 byte locations to +129 byte locations from the BRA instruction location since the value (PC) is the current instruction location plus 2 when the new value is calculated. In the case of a 16-bit displacement, the range is −32,766 to

TABLE 6.4 UNCONDITIONAL BRANCH AND JUMP

Syntax	Operation	Address modes
BRA < disp >	(PC) = (PC) + < disp >	Relative
JMP < EA >	(PC) = (EA)	Control modes

Notes:
1. In BRA < disp >, < disp > is a signed 8-bit or 16-bit integer.
2. (PC) is the BRA instruction location + 2.
3. Condition codes are not affected.

+32,769 bytes. The value of the displacement is determined automatically by the assembler when the displacement is specified as a label in the form

BRA   <label>

If the displacement to the location specified by <label> exceeds the branch range, the JMP instruction must be used instead.

JMP instruction.   The JMP instruction has the form

JMP   <EA>

where EA specifies the location of the next instruction to be executed. Only control addressing modes are allowed, which eliminates register direct and autoindexing modes. An indirect jump in the form

JMP   (An)

takes the address of the next instruction from the contents of An. This indirect jump can be used to create jump tables, as shown in the following example.

Example 6.3

The program segment shown in Figure 6.3 shows how a jump table may be created in memory. The table contains the addresses of specific sequences of instructions. The address of the proper sequence to execute is selected by a code that specifies the entry in the table. The address is then loaded from the table into an address register and an indirect jump is executed using the register contents. In this example, the code is simply the number of the entry.

The table starting address must be loaded into A0 and the entry number 0, 1, 2, . . . into D0 before execution of the program segment. Each address is assumed to be held in a longword, so the entry number is multiplied by 4 to index into the table. The table has the following format:

Entry number	Address	Memory contents
0	(A0)	First address
1	(A0) + 4	Second address
.	.	.
.	.	.
.	.	.
n	(A0) + 4 * (D0)	nth address

The initial values in A0 and D0 are first transferred to A1, and D1, respectively, so the original contents are saved. Multiplying the contents of D1 by 4 with an unsigned multiply instruction (MULU) gives the offset from the starting address. The contents are

MC68000 ASM REV= 1.4 - COPYRIGHT BY MOTOROLA 1978   PAGE   1

```
  1                                    LLEN    100
  2            00001000                ORG     $1000
  3                               *
  4                               *   JUMP TABLE EXAMPLE
  5                               *     INPUT :  (D0.W) = ENTRY NUMBER
  6                               *              (A0.L) = TABLE ADDRESS
  7                               *
  8  001000 2248                      MOVEA.L A0,A1          ;SAVE STARTING ADD. OF TABLE
  9  001002 3200                      MOVE.W  D0,D1          ;SAVE ENTRY NUMBER
 10                               *
 11  001004 C2FC0004                  MULU    #4,D1          ;COMPUTE INDEX INTO TABLE
 12  001008 24711800                  MOVEA.L 0(A1,D1.L),A2  ;MOVE JUMP ADDRESS
 13  00100C 4ED2                      JMP     (A2)           ;TRANSFER CNTL. TO JMP ADDR.
 14                               *
 15            00002000                ORG     $2000
 16                               *
 17            00003000      SCHED     EQU     $3000         ;SET UP   DUMMY SUBROUTINES
 18            00004000      QUEUE     EQU     $4000
 19            00005000      DISP      EQU     $5000
 20            00006000      TIMER     EQU     $6000
 21                               *
 22  002000 00003000      TABLE     DC.L    SCHED         ;JUMP TABLE
 23  002004 00004000                DC.L    QUEUE
 24  002008 00005000                DC.L    DISP
 25  00200C 00006000                DC.L    TIMER
 26                               *
 27                                    END
```

****** TOTAL ERRORS   0--   0

SYMBOL TABLE - APPROX 1197 SYMBOL ENTRIES LEFT

```
DISP       005000 QUEUE      004000 SCHED       003000 TABLE     002000
TIMER      006000
```

Figure 6.3   Jump table example.

located and transferred to A2 using address register indirect with index addressing for the source operand in the instruction

> MOVEA.L   0(A1,D1.L),A2

where the 16-bit value in D1 is the index value. The indirect jump address has now been determined. Then the transfer of control is caused by the JMP instruction.

After the jump, the original contents of the PC are lost, so no return is possible in the program as shown. To transfer control and return from a segment addressed by the table, a subroutine call could be used with indirect addressing to specify the beginning location.

6.2.2 Branch Conditionally

The Bcc instructions allow selection of a control path in a program based on conditions:

> IF (condition is true)
>   THEN (branch to new sequence)
>   ELSE (execute next instruction)

The new sequence of instructions may be at either higher or lower memory addresses relative to the branch instruction. The assembly language format for the general conditional branch is

Bcc   < label >

which uses program counter relative addressing. The displacement added to the value of the program counter to cause branching can be either an 8-bit or a 16-bit signed integer. Some assemblers accept Bcc.S to force an 8-bit displacement (short) when possible.

Figure 6.4 illustrates the operation of the Bcc instructions. Arithmetic operations as well as a number of other instructions set the condition codes based on the result of the particular operation. If the condition is true, the displacement value is added to the value in the program counter. At this time, the PC contains the conditional branch instruction address plus 2. The possible conditions are listed in Figure 6.5 together with the condition code settings that cause a branch. The instruction format indicates how the conditions are coded in machine language.

If an arithmetic instruction or a **MOVE** instruction is executed, the condition codes indicate the arithmetic conditions that apply to the destination operand. For instance, in the addition

ADD. <l>   X,Y

the destination value, which can be of length $<l> = $ B, W, or L, is the sum. The contents of the destination, designated (Y), may represent a signed or unsigned integer. In the case of an unsigned integer, the result may have been zero $(Z = \{1\})$ or nonzero $(Z = \{0\})$. If the sum is too large, it is indicated by a carry $(C = \{1\})$. Signed

Instructions:

Arithmetic, MOVE,
CMP, TST, or
others

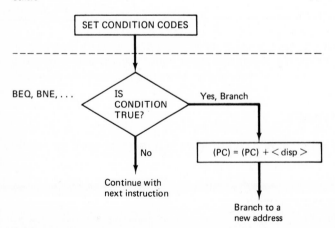

Figure 6.4 Operation of Bcc instructions.

CC	carry clear	0100	$\overline{C}$		LS	low or same	0011	$C + Z$
CS	carry set	0101	C		LT	less than	1101	$N \cdot \overline{V} + \overline{N} \cdot V$
EQ	equal	0111	Z		MI	minus	1011	N
GE	greater or equal	1100	$N \cdot V + \overline{N} \cdot \overline{V}$		NE	not equal	0110	$\overline{Z}$
GT	greater than	1110	$N \cdot V \cdot \overline{Z} + \overline{N} \cdot \overline{V} \cdot \overline{Z}$		PL	plus	1010	$\overline{N}$
HI	high	0010	$\overline{C} \cdot \overline{Z}$		VC	overflow clear	1000	$\overline{V}$
LE	less or equal	1111	$Z + N \cdot \overline{V} + \overline{N} \cdot V$		VS	overflow set	1001	V

Condition Codes: Not affected

Instruction Format:

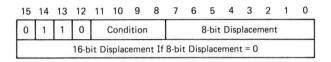

Notes:
   (1) $\overline{X}$ as a condition code means X = {0} is a TRUE condition, i.e., $\overline{X}$ = {1} .
   (2) "+" means LOGICAL OR.
   (3) "·" means LOGICAL AND.

Figure 6.5 Conditional branch instructions.

arithmetic could yield an out-of-range condition (V = {1}) or a positive, zero, or negative sum. The possible tests for signed and unsigned integers are listed in Table 6.5.

After a MOVE instruction, the condition codes may be examined, but no out-of-range condition is possible. The condition codes C and V are cleared so that C = {0} and V = {0} after the transfer. As indicated in the table, except for the test for zero or nonzero, different condition tests apply to unsigned than signed integers. This section introduces the branching conditions required in both cases. Further discussion of the programming techniques for arithmetic operations is presented in Chapter 7.

Branch if zero or nonzero.   The conditional instructions BEQ and BNE are logical opposites. After a preceding instruction sets the condition codes, the instruction

   BEQ   <label>

will branch if the result was zero. Branching on a nonzero condition would require

   BNE   <label> .

Both instructions are valid for either signed or unsigned arithmetic and represent the only conditional branches that may be used with either.

Branches with unsigned integer arithmetic.   Unsigned arithmetic involves the positive integers and zero. Addresses should be treated as unsigned numbers. The only condition codes that should be tested after an addition or subtraction of unsigned integers are zero (Z) and carry (C).

The condition code C = {1} indicates that a carry occurred in addition because

TABLE 6.5 CONDITIONAL TESTS

	Conditions for branch	
Instructions	Unsigned	Signed
ADD. <1> X,Y	(Y) = 0 BEQ	(Y) = 0 BEQ
or		
SUB. <1> X,Y	(Y) ≠ 0 BNE	(Y) ≠ 0 BNE
or		
MOVE. <1> X,Y		(Y) ≥ 0 BPL
		(Y) < 0 BMI
Out of range for	C = {1} BCS	V = {1} BVS
arithmetic instructions	C = {0} BCC	V = {0} BVC

Note: For the MOVE instruction with signed integers as operands, BGE, BLT, BGT, and BLE are also valid.

the sum was too large for the specified length of the operand. In subtraction, a carry bit set to {1} represents a borrow because the subtrahend was larger than the minuend. In either case, the result is not a valid unsigned integer. When arithmetic with unsigned integers is performed, the test for Branch on Carry Set (BCS) or Branch on Carry Clear (BCC) can be used to select between paths in the program.

The Bcc instruction is most often used to create loops in a program to perform the iterative parts of the algorithm being implemented. The Branch on Condition instruction is used to exit the loop. For example, the simplest form of iteration occurs when the number of repetitions is known. In several previous programming examples, the termination of a loop relied on a counter value being decremented from the number of iterations required to zero. Then the BNE LOOP instruction following the decrement (SUB #1,Dn in most cases) instruction caused the looping to terminate when (Dn) = 0. If the branch instruction is the last statement in the loop, the loop is considered *posttested* and has the general form

        REPEAT
            (body of loop)
        UNTIL (count is zero)

These loops execute the instructions in the body of the loop at least once. The FORTRAN loop

        DO 10   I = 1,20
            (body of loop)
        10 CONTINUE

is a loop of this type. Other types of loop structures are shown in examples elsewhere in the book.

Example 6.4

The program shown in Figure 6.6 adds two arrays or vectors of unsigned 16-bit integers. The program computes X(I) + Y(I) and saves the sum in X(I) for each element in the arrays. The length of the arrays is input in D0 and the addresses of the arrays are input in A0 and A1. After each addition, the C condition code is checked. If the C bit is {1}, an overflow occurred and the low-order word of D0 will contain the value $FFFF.

In the program, (D1) is used as a counter and also as an index value into the arrays. After D1 is loaded with the word count and tested for zero, the value in D1 is multiplied by 2 to yield a byte count. The LSL (logical shift left) instruction accomplishes the multiplication. In the loop, the counter and index in D1 are decremented by 2 and tested before each addition is performed. The BMI (Branch If Minus) instruction is used so the last addition is performed when (D1) = 0. Address register indirect with index addressing is used to select the values to be added. Notice that the last elements in the arrays are added first since (D1) begins in the loop with the byte count minus 2 as an index and decrements to zero. If no overflow occurs, the BCC instruction returns control to the first instruction in the loop. Otherwise, an error is indicated.

Branching with signed arithmetic.   If the values being manipulated are two's-complement numbers, the condition codes N, Z, and V are applicable. After arithmetic operations, V = {1} indicates an out-of-range condition. The instruction BVS branches when V = {1} and BVC branches when V = {0}. If the result is valid, the operand may be tested for a zero, nonzero, positive, or negative value. After a

```
MC68000 ASM REV= 1.4 - COPYRIGHT BY MOTOROLA 1978             PAGE  1


   1                              LLEN    100
   2      00001000                ORG     $1000
   3                       *
   4      000200F6        MACSBUG  EQU     $200F6                  ;MONITOR ADDRESS
   5                       *
   6                       *   COMPUTE SUMS OF UNSIGNED INTEGER ARRAYS
   7                       *      INPUT : (A0.L) = X ARRAY OF 16-BIT NUMBERS
   8                       *              (A1.L) = Y ARRAY OF 16-BIT NUMBERS
   9                       *              (D0.W) = NUMBER OF ELEMENTS IN ARRAYS
  10                       *      OUTPUT : (D0.W) = $FFFF IF ERROR OCCURRED
  11                       *
  12  001000 48E760C0      SUM      MOVEM.L  D1-D2/A0-A1,-(SP)     ;SAVE REGISTERS
  13  001004 3200                   MOVE.W   D0,D1                 ;SET UP COUNTER
  14  001006 67000014               BEQ      ERROR                ;IF ZERO, EXIT WITH ERROR
  15  00100A E349                   LSL.W    #1,D1                ;COUNT BYTES INSTEAD OF WORDS
  16  00100C 5541          LOOP     SUBQ.W   #2,D1                ;DECREMENT INDEX
  17  00100E 6B000010               BMI      DONE                 ;EXIT WHEN (D1) < 0
  18  001012 34311000               MOVE.W   0(A1,D1.W),D2        ;GET Y VALUE
  19  001016 D5701000               ADD.W    D2,0(A0,D1.W)        ;ADD X := X + Y
  20                       *
  21  00101A 64F0                   BCC      LOOP                 ;NO OVERFLOW, CONTINUE
  22                       *
  23  00101C 303CFFFF      ERROR    MOVE.W   #$FFFF,D0            ;SET STATUS TO ERROR
  24  001020 4CDF0306      DONE     MOVEM.L  (SP)+,D1-D2/A0-A1    ;RESTORE REGISTERS
  25  001024 4EF9000200F6           JMP      MACSBUG              ;RETURN TO MONITOR
  26                                END

****** TOTAL ERRORS   0--   0


SYMBOL TABLE - APPROX 1197 SYMBOL ENTRIES LEFT

DONE      001020 ERROR      00101C LOOP      00100C MACSBUG    0200F6
SUM       001000
```

Figure 6.6 Overflow checking for unsigned arithmetic.

MOVE instruction, V = {0} and BGE, BLT, BGT, and BLE also perform valid tests according to the logic equations from Figure 6.5. When V = {0}, BGE has the same effect as BPL.

6.2.3 Branching after CMP or TST

The instructions CMP (Compare) and TST (Test) are used to set the condition codes based on operand values. Then conditional branch instructions can be used to direct the flow of control in the program. The instruction

CMP   X,Y

compares two operands by performing the computation

(Y) − (X)

to set the condition codes N, Z, V, and C. The instruction

TST   Y

evaluates one operand by performing the computation (Y) − 0, which always clears V and C but sets N and Z based on the result. Both of these instructions set the condition codes but do not modify the operands. The instructions discussed in this section are listed in Table 6.6. The CMP instruction has variations Compare Immediate (CMPI) and Compare Memory (CMPM), as shown.

The compare instruction

CMP.<l>   <EA>,<Dn>

subtracts the source operand from the contents of the specified data register. The computation

(Dn) − (EA)

is performed without modifying the operand and the length <l> of each operand can be defined as B, W, or L. If the source is an address register, the operand length is restricted to word or longword.

The CMPI (Compare Immediate) instruction compares an immediate value to an operand referenced by a data-alterable addressing mode. This excludes the address register direct and relative addressing modes. Byte, word, or longword operands are allowed. For example, the instruction

CMPI.B   #5,$2000

compares the value 5 with the contents of the byte at location $2000. Unlike the CMP instruction, the CMPI instruction may reference memory locations as the destination.

The CMPM (Compare Memory) instruction is used to compare sequences of bytes, words, or longwords in memory. Only the postincrement addressing mode is allowed for both operands. The instruction

CMPM.B   (A1)+,(A2) +

TABLE 6.6 COMPARE AND TEST INSTRUCTIONS

| Instruction | Syntax | Addressing modes | | Operation | Condition codes affected |
		Source	Destination		
Compare	CMP.<l> <EA>,<Dn>	ALL	<Dn>	(Dn) − (EA)	N, Z, V, C
Compare immediate	CMPI <l> # <d>,<EA>	d	Data alterable	(EA) − d	N, Z, V, C
Compare memory	CMPM.<l> (Am)+,(An)+	(Am)+	(An)+	((An)) − ((Am))	N, Z, V, C
Test	TST.<l> <EA>	—	Data alterable	(EA) − 0	N, Z, C = {0}, V = {0}

Notes:

1. <l> denotes B, W, or L.
2. If An is the source for CMP, only word (W) or longword (L) operands are allowed.

compares the bytes addressed by A1 and A2 and then increments the addresses to point to the next bytes.

The TST (Test) instruction has the format

TST. <l>   < EA >

where <l> can be B, W, or L and < EA > can be specified by all but the address register direct or relative addressing modes. The instruction sets the Z and N condition codes based on the value of the operand. However, V and C are always cleared.

The valid conditional branches after the TST instruction for an unsigned integer operand are BEQ and BNE. These conditions for a zero or nonzero value are also valid for signed integers. Since the TST instruction clears the C and V condition codes, a number of other tests for signed integers are also valid. After the instruction

TST   X

the conditional branch instructions BGT, BLT or BMI, BGE or BPL, and BLE can be used when the location X contains a signed integer.

When a Bcc instruction follows a CMP instruction in the sequence

CMP   X,Y
Bcc   < label >

the comparison made is

IF (Y) "condition cc" (X)
        THEN branch to < label >
        ELSE continue

For example, the instruction sequence

CMP.W   D1,D2
BGE   DONE

checks if the 16-bit value in D2 is greater than or equal to the 16-bit value in D1. If so, the branch is taken to DONE.

The TST instruction compares an operand with zero in a similar manner. Thus the sequence

TST.W   D2
BEQ   DONE

has the logic

IF (D2) [15:0] equals 0
        THEN branch to DONE
        ELSE continue

Table 6.7 lists the Bcc instructions that would cause a branch if executed after the CMP or TST instruction. The tests for Branch on Less Than (BLT) and Branch

TABLE 6.7 Bcc INSTRUCTIONS WITH CMP AND TST

Instruction	Result	Branch condition	
		Unsigned	Signed
CMP X, Y	$(Y) = (X)$	BEQ (Equal)	BEQ (Equal)
	$(Y) \neq (X)$	BNE (Not Equal)	BNE (Not Equal)
	$(Y) > (X)$	BHI (High)	BGT (Greater Than)
	$(Y) \geq (X)$	BCC (Carry Clear)	BGE (Greater or Equal)
	$(Y) < (X)$	BCS (Carry Set)	BLT (Less Than)
	$(Y) \leq (X)$	BLS (Low or Same)	BLE (Less Than or Equal)
TST X	$(X) = 0$	BEQ	BEQ
	$(X) \neq 0$	BNE	BNE
	$(X) > 0$	BNE	BGT
	$(X) < 0$	—	BLT, BMI
	$(X) \geq 0$	—	BGE, BPL
	$(X) \leq 0$	—	BLE

Notes:

1. In CMP   X,Y; the destination is a data register.

2. TST sets C = {0} and V = {0}.

3. BMI (Branch on Minus) is the same as BLT, and BPL (Branch on Plus) is the same as BGE when V = {0}.

on Minus (BMI) as well as BGE and BPL are equivalent after a TST instruction because the overflow bit V is cleared.

Both CMP and TST can be used with either signed or unsigned integer interpretations. However, the processor always performs the computation in two's-complement arithmetic. Therefore, the valid conditional branch instructions are different for the two interpretations of integers.

Example 6.5

The sample program in Figure 6.7 compares two tables of bytes addressed by A1 and A2. D1 contains the number of bytes in each table and D2 contains a status word or "flag" to indicate if the tables are the same. The flag is initialized to a default value of zero to indicate unequivalent values before the comparison begins. If all corresponding bytes of the two tables are equal, a value of $+1$ is entered into D2 by the last instruction before returning to the monitor program. If the number of bytes is zero, D2 will be left with the initialized zero value. Such a program is typically used to compare two strings of ASCII characters to see if they are equal.

Before comparison, a TST instruction determines if D1 has a nonzero byte count. Within the loop, the bytes addressed by A1 and A2 are compared and the addresses are automatically incremented. If any two bytes are not equal, the first BNE instruction causes a branch and the test ends. After each successful compare, the counter value in D1 is decremented. Looping continues until the counter reaches zero. If all the bytes are equal, D2 will be set to 1 by the instruction at label EQUAL. Before the program can be executed, A1, A2, and D1 must all be initialized with the proper input values.

Example 6.6

The program shown in Figure 6.8 compares 16-bit positive integers in an array previously stored in locations NUM1, NUM1 + 2, and so on, and leaves the largest one in D1. Register D3 is used as a counter to determine when all the numbers have been tested. The count of numbers is assumed to be in D3 before the program executes.

Since positive numbers only are considered, BLS (Branch Lower or Same) is used to test if a value in D2 is smaller than the assumed maximum held in D1. If so, the loop is tested for completion. If the new value in D2 is larger than the "maximum" in D1, the register contents are exchanged.

```
MC68000 ASM REV= 1.4 - COPYRIGHT BY MOTOROLA 1978            PAGE   1


 1                                  LLEN    100
 2          00001000                ORG     $1000
 3                          *
 4          000200F6        MACSBUG EQU     $200F6                  ;MONITOR ADDRESS
 5                          *
 6                          * COMPARE TWO STRINGS
 7                          * INPUTS : (A1.L) = ADDRESS OF FIRST STRING
 8                          *          (A2.L) = ADDRESS OF SECOND STRING
 9                          *          (D1.B) = NUMBER OF BYTES IN THE STRINGS
10                          *
11                          * OUTPUT : (D2.W) = 0 : NOT EQUAL
12                          *                   1 : EQUAL
13                          *
14 001000 48E74060         COMPARE MOVEM.L D1/A1-A2,-(SP)          ;SAVE REGISTERS
15 001004 4242                     CLR.W   D2                      ;SET FAULT STATUS
16 001006 4A01                     TST.B   D1                      ;IF LENGTH IS ZERO
17 001008 67000010                 BEQ     DONE                    ; THEN BRANCH TO FINISH
18                          *
19 00100C B509             LOOP    CMPM.B  (A1)+,(A2)+             ; ELSE IF TWO BYTES ARE
20                          *                                      .NOT EQUAL
21 00100E 6600000A                 BNE     DONE                    ;   THEN BRANCH TO FINISH
22 001012 5301                     SUBQ.B  #1,D1                   ;   ELSE DECREMENT COUNTER
23 001014 66F6                     BNE     LOOP                    ;LOOP IS NOT FINISHED
24 001016 343C0001         EQUAL   MOVE.W  #1,D2                   ;SET STATUS TO EQUAL
25                          *
26 00101A 4CDF0602         DONE    MOVEM.L (SP)+,D1/A1-A2          ;RESTORE REGISTERS
27                          *
28 00101E 4EF9000200F6             JMP     MACSBUG                 ;RETURN TO MONITOR
29                                  END

****** TOTAL ERRORS    0--   0


SYMBOL TABLE - APPROX 1197 SYMBOL ENTRIES LEFT

COMPARE    001000 DONE       00101A EQUAL       001016 LOOP       00100C
MACSBUG    0200F6
```

Figure 6.7 Use of CMP and TST instructions.

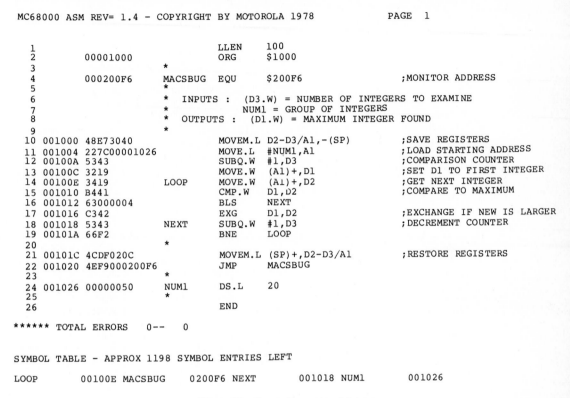

```
MC68000 ASM REV= 1.4 - COPYRIGHT BY MOTOROLA 1978                PAGE  1

  1                                 LLEN    100
  2          00001000               ORG     $1000
  3                          *
  4          000200F6       MACSBUG  EQU    $200F6                ;MONITOR ADDRESS
  5                          *
  6                          *  INPUTS :  (D3.W) = NUMBER OF INTEGERS TO EXAMINE
  7                          *            NUM1 = GROUP OF INTEGERS
  8                          *  OUTPUTS : (D1.W) = MAXIMUM INTEGER FOUND
  9                          *
 10 001000 48E73040                 MOVEM.L D2-D3/A1,-(SP)       ;SAVE REGISTERS
 11 001004 227C00001026             MOVE.L  #NUM1,A1             ;LOAD STARTING ADDRESS
 12 00100A 5343                      SUBQ.W  #1,D3               ;COMPARISON COUNTER
 13 00100C 3219                      MOVE.W  (A1)+,D1            ;SET D1 TO FIRST INTEGER
 14 00100E 3419            LOOP      MOVE.W  (A1)+,D2            ;GET NEXT INTEGER
 15 001010 B441                      CMP.W   D1,D2               ;COMPARE TO MAXIMUM
 16 001012 63000004                  BLS     NEXT
 17 001016 C342                      EXG     D1,D2               ;EXCHANGE IF NEW IS LARGER
 18 001018 5343            NEXT      SUBQ.W  #1,D3               ;DECREMENT COUNTER
 19 00101A 66F2                      BNE     LOOP
 20                          *
 21 00101C 4CDF020C                 MOVEM.L (SP)+,D2-D3/A1       ;RESTORE REGISTERS
 22 001020 4EF9000200F6   ,         JMP     MACSBUG
 23                          *
 24 001026 00000050        NUM1     DS.L    20
 25                          *
 26                                 END

****** TOTAL ERRORS   0--   0

SYMBOL TABLE - APPROX 1198 SYMBOL ENTRIES LEFT

LOOP        00100E MACSBUG    0200F6 NEXT        001018 NUM1        001026
```

Figure 6.8 Comparing unsigned integers.

6.2.4 DBcc Instruction

The Test, Decrement, and Branch instruction is a powerful instruction for control of loop structures. The basic format is

DBcc   < Dn >, < label >

which designates three parameters: the condition "cc", a data register, and a displacement. The displacement is represented here as a label in an assembly language program. The syntax and the various conditions for the instruction are shown in Figure 6.9.

The DBcc instruction can cause a loop to be terminated when either the specified condition, cc, is TRUE or when the count held in < Dn > reaches −1. Each time the instruction is executed, the value in Dn is decremented by 1. The flowchart for the instruction in Figure 6.10 illustrates the conditions that cause the next instruction in sequence to be executed.

Test Condition, Decrement
and Branch

DBcc $<$ Dn $>$, $<$ disp $>$ (1)   Test "cc"

(2)   If "cc" TRUE, Next Instruction
ELSE

(Dn) [15:0] = (Dn) [15:0] − 1
IF (Dn) [15:0] = −1,
next instruction
ELSE (PC) = (PC) + $<$ disp $>$

Notes:
  (1) (PC) is instruction address +2.
  (2) $<$ disp $>$ is a signed 16-bit integer that is sign-extended.

(a) Syntax and Operation

CC	carry clear	0100	$\overline{C}$		LS	low or same	0011	$C + Z$
CS	carry set	0101	C		LT	less than	1101	$N \cdot \overline{V} + \overline{N} \cdot V$
EQ	equal	0111	Z		MI	minus	1011	N
F	false	0001	0		NE	not equal	0110	$\overline{Z}$
GE	greater or equal	1100	$N \cdot V + \overline{N} \cdot \overline{V}$		PL	plus	1010	$\overline{N}$
GT	greater than	1110	$N \cdot V \cdot \overline{Z} + \overline{N} \cdot \overline{V} \cdot \overline{Z}$		T	true	0000	1
HI	high	0010	$\overline{C} \cdot \overline{Z}$		VC	overflow clear	1000	$\overline{V}$
LE	less or equal	1111	$Z + N \cdot \overline{V} + \overline{N} \cdot V$		VS	overflow set	1001	V

Condition Codes: Not affected

Instruction Format:

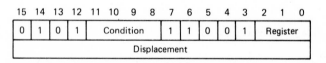

15	14	13	12	11	10	9	8	7	6	5	4	3	2	1	0
0	1	0	1		Condition			1	1	0	0	1		Register	
Displacement															

(b) Conditions and Instruction format

Figure 6.9   DBcc instruction.

Fourteen of the logical conditions tested by DBcc are the same as those for the Bcc instruction discussed previously. However, the DBcc is sometimes called a "Don't Branch on Condition" instruction. If the condition is TRUE, no branch is taken, which is the opposite operation from that of the Bcc instruction. A loop structure with the DBcc terminating the loop has the logic

REPEAT
      (body of loop)
UNTIL (condition)

For example, the sequence of instructions with the structure

        LOOP . . .
            (body of loop)
        TST   X   ;Test for zero
        DBEQ   < Dn >,LOOP   ;LOOP IF NOT ZERO

will continue to loop until the contents of location X are zero or until the count in Dn
has been exhausted. The TST instruction sets the condition codes based on the value
(X). The DBcc tests the conditions and decrements < Dn > if the condition is false

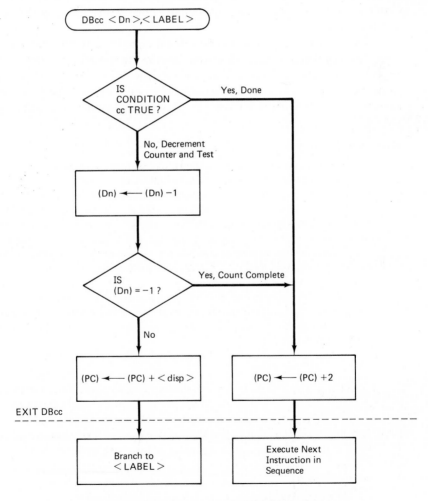

Figure 6.10   Operation of the DBcc instruction.

but does not affect the condition codes. When the specified condition is true or when $\langle Dn \rangle$ contains -1, the loop is terminated. If the example program above needed to loop (branch) on the X equal 0 condition, the opposite logical condition, DBNE, should be used. Then if X is zero, a branch is taken to LOOP; otherwise, execution continues to the next instruction.

In addition to the 14 testable conditions which are used by both DBcc and Bcc instructions, the DBcc has two other conditions, TRUE(T) and FALSE(F). The DBT instruction never branches. Its logical opposite, the DBF, always branches unless the count is exhausted. For the DBF instruction, no condition is tested. The DBF instruction replaces the "decrement and test for zero" sequence frequently used to terminate a loop.[1] There is one difference, however. Since the counter must reach -1 before looping stops, the initial value of the counter must be one less than the number of iterations required.

The register specified to hold the count contains a 16-bit integer with a decimal value between 0 and 65,535. Assuming that the register initially contained the integer value N and also that the condition cc is not true, then in a posttested loop, the count would be N, N $-$ 1, N $-$ 2, . . . , 0 before the loop is exited; thus N $+$ 1 iterations are executed. To loop N times, the counter register should contain the value N$-$ 1 initially.

Example 6.7

The two short program segments shown in Figure 6.11 compare the use of the Bcc and DBcc instructions. Each program tests a table containing (N $+$ 1) word-length operands to locate a nonzero entry. Before execution, address register A1 must contain the first address of the table and D1 contains N. In the first segment, a nonzero entry addressed by (A1) causes a branch to label DONE1. The address of the nonzero entry is (A1) -2 since postincrement addressing is used in the TST instruction. If no nonzero entries are found, (D1) is decremented until it reaches -1, upon which the BPL instruction terminates the loop. Thus, if (D1) $= -1$ after the program segment is complete, the table contains all zero values.

The instruction to test for a nonzero value and those to decrement and test the loop count in the first program can be replaced with a single DBcc instruction. The second segment in Figure 6.11 shows the instructions to test the (N $+$ 1) locations for a nonzero value as before.

EXERCISES

6.2.1. Discuss the use of a jump table if the program is in read-only memory but the routines to be executed may have a different starting address in different systems.

6.2.2. Compare the use of indirect addressing in the following instructions.
  (a) JMP   (A2)
  (b) MOVEA   (A2),A1

[1]Some MC68000 assemblers use the form "DBRA" instead of the mnemonic DBF.

```
MC68000 ASM REV= 1.4  - COPYRIGHT  BY  MOTOROLA  1978          PAGE   1


     1                      LLEN    100
     2  00001000            ORG     $1000
     3                  *
     4  000200F6    MACSBUG EQU     $200F6          ;MONITOR ADDRESS
     5                  *
     6                  *   COMPARISON OF DBCC AND BCC OPERATION
     7                  *   INPUTS : (D1.W) = LENGTH OF TABLE - 1
     8                  *            (A1.L) = ADDRESS OF TABLE
     9                  *   OUTPUTS : (A1.L) = ADDRESS OF NONZERO ENTRY
    10                  *             (D1.W) = $FFFF ; NO NONZERO ENTRIES
    11                  *
    12                  *   BCC OPERATION
    13                  *
    14  001000 4A59     LOOP1   TST.W   (A1)+
    15  001002 66000006          BNE     DONE1           ;BRANCH  IF NOT EQUAL ZERO
    16  001006 5341              SUBQ.W  #1,D1
    17  001008 6AF6              BPL     LOOP1           ;BRANCH  IF COUNTER  IS  NOT NEGATIVE
    18  00100A 5589     DONE1   SUBQ.L  #2,A1
    19  00100C 4EF9000200F6      JMP     $200F6
    20                  *
    21  00002000          ORG     $2000
    22                  *
    23                  *   DBCC OPERATION
    24                  *
    25  002000 4A59     LOOP2   TST.W   (A1)+
    26  002002 56C9FFFC          DBNE    D1,LOOP2        ;BRANCH  IF NONZERO  OR COUNTER
    27                  *                                ;IS NEGATIVE
    28  002006 5589     DONE2   SUBQ.L  #2,A1
    29  002008 4EF9000200F6      JMP     MACSBUG         ;RETURN  TO MONITOR
    30                          END

****** TOTAL ERRORS  0-- 0

SYMBOL TABLE - APPROX 1197 SYMBOL ENTRIES LEFT

DONE1    00100A DONE2    002006 LOOP1    001000 LOOP2    002000
MACSBUG  0200F6
```

Figure 6.11 Comparison of Bcc and DBcc.

185

6.2.3. If the instruction

> CMP.W   I,J

has been executed, specify the instruction that will perform the following.
(a) branch to ZERO if I = J
(b) branch to LESS if I < J
(c) branch to MORE if I > J
where ZERO, LESS, and MORE are statement labels.

6.2.4. Rewrite the sequence

> LOOP . . .
>   (body of loop)
>   SUB.W   #1,CNT
>   BNE   LOOP

to use a DBcc instruction.

6.2.5. Write the assembly language program to implement the FORTRAN loop

> DO 10   I = 1,20
>   (body of loop)
> 10   CONTINUE

6.2.6. Write the assembly language program equivalent to the following:

> SUM = 0
> I = MAXVAL
> 10 SUM = SUM + I
> I = I − 1
> IF (I .NE. 0) GOTO 10

Assume that MAXVAL was defined previously. Test the program for the three values MAXVAL = 10, 1, and 0. Modify the program to take into account the case for MAX-VAL = 0.

6.2.7. Since the MOVE and TST instructions always set the condition code V = {0}, show that BGE, BLT, BGT, and BLE are valid as branches after a MOVE or TST instruction when signed integers are moved. Also show that BGE is the same as BPL and that BLT is the same as BMI in this case.

6.3 SUBROUTINE USAGE WITH THE MC68000

The *subroutine* is a sequence of instructions which is treated as a separate program module within a larger program. The subroutine can be "called" or executed one or more times as the program executes. Generally, the subroutines associated with a program accomplish specific tasks, each of which represents a simpler procedure than that of the entire program. In fact, subroutines are called *procedures* in the Pascal language. Each module or single subroutine should be self-contained, that is, be testable by itself independently of the calling program. When the subroutine is called during execution of a program, its instructions are executed and control is then returned to the next instruction in sequence following the call to the subroutine.

The location of the first instruction of a subroutine is called its *starting address*. This must be defined in each program calling the subroutine. If the subroutine and the calling program are assembled at the same time, the subroutine starting address can be defined by a label at its first instruction. If the subroutine and calling program are not assembled together, the subroutine starting address must be explicitly defined in the call instruction.[2]

The MC68000 instructions to call and return from a subroutine are shown in Table 6.8. The BSR (Branch to Subroutine) and JSR (Jump to Subroutine) instructions perform calls. In each case, execution causes the longword address of the instruction following the call to be pushed onto the system stack. Execution then continues at the subroutine starting address. No other information is saved by the call, so it is the programmer's responsibility to preserve any register contents, including the contents of the status register if these are modified by the subroutine. These may be saved before the call and restored after the return, but a well-designed subroutine will save the values and restore them before returning. The latter approach is more reasonable since there are typically multiple calls to a single subroutine. Also, if subroutines are designed separately, the programmer designing the calling program may not be aware of what registers are modified by the subroutine unless good documentation is available. Therefore, our examples will show subroutines whose execution is *transparent* to the calling program except for modification of registers used to return values calculated by the subroutine.

Two return instructions are available for the MC68000. The RTR (Return and Restore) is used when the condition codes held in the condition code register (CCR) have been saved on the stack by the subroutine. Otherwise, RTS (Return from Subroutine) is used to simply load the program counter with the return address from the stack.

The instructions for calling and returning and their use with simple subroutine structures are discussed in this section. A more detailed look at subroutines is given in Chapter 9, where various methods of passing data between calling programs and subroutines is discussed. In the present discussion it is assumed that parameters are passed in processor registers.

6.3.1 Invoking Subroutines

The instructions BSR and JSR cause a transfer of control to the beginning address of a subroutine. In the Branch to Subroutine statement

BSR   < label >

---

[2]If a subroutine has several entry points, each address must be defined. Also, when independent programs are assembled separately, the external or "global" references are usually defined when the modules are linked together.

TABLE 6.8 INSTRUCTIONS FOR SUBROUTINE USAGE

Instruction	Syntax	Operation	Comments
Branch to Subroutine	BSR $<$disp$>$	1. $(SP) \leftarrow (SP) - 4; ((SP)) \leftarrow (PC)$ 2. $(PC) \leftarrow (PC) + <$disp$>$	$<$disp$>$ is 8-bit or 16-bit signed integer
Jump to Subroutine	JSR $<$EA$>$	1. $(SP) \leftarrow (SP) - 4; ((SP)) \leftarrow (PC)$ 2. $(PC) \leftarrow (EA)$	$<$EA$>$ is a control addressing type
Return and Restore Condition Codes	RTR	1. $(CCR) \leftarrow ((SP))[7:0]; (SP) \leftarrow (SP) + 2$ 2. $(PC) \leftarrow ((SP)); (SP) \leftarrow (SP) + 4$	$(CCR) = (SR)[7:0]$
Return from Subroutine	RTS	$(PC) \leftarrow ((SP)); (SP) \leftarrow (SP) + 4$	—

Notes:
1. SP denotes the system stack pointer.
2. CCR is the condition code register, that is, $(SR)[7:0]$.
3. PC is the program counter.

the < label > operand causes the assembler to calculate the displacement between the BSR instruction and the instruction identified by < label >. This displacement is added during execution to the current contents of the program counter (the BSR location plus 2) to calculate the starting location of the subroutine. The displacement is stored as a 16-bit integer in two's-complement notation. The BSR operates in the same manner as the BRA instruction discussed in Section 6.2.1 except that the address of the instruction following the BSR is saved on the system stack. Similarly, the JSR (Jump to Subroutine) is identical to the JMP instruction except for the saving of the return address. The addressing range of the JSR instruction is unlimited and any control addressing mode can be used. Thus the absolute modes, the relative modes, and the indirect addressing modes, except postincrement and predecrement, are allowed to specify the starting address. For example, the instruction

    JSR   4(A5)

uses indirect with displacement addressing and causes a jump to the instruction four bytes past the address in A5. The return to the instruction following the BSR or JSR calling the subroutine is accomplished by executing a RTR or RTS instruction in the subroutine.

Figure 6.12 shows the general structure of the subroutine call. The call decrements (SP) by 4 and saves (PC) at location $7FFA. In the subroutine, the first statement saves the contents of the status register on the stack at location $7FFB just below (in memory) the two words containing the return address. The MOVEM.L instruction pushes all 32 bits of each register specified by the list onto the stack using predecrement addressing. Sixty bytes between $7FBC and $7FF7 are used. After processing, the registers are restored by the last MOVEM instruction before the return. The RTR instruction restores the condition codes to the status register, leaving the upper byte of SR unchanged before returning. If the condition codes had not been saved upon entry into the subroutine, the return would be through the RTS instruction. This instruction simply loads the return address from the stack into the program counter.

Figure 6.13 shows the stack contents before, during, and after the call to SUBR. The (PC) always occupies two words of the stack. The 16-bit contents of the status register are saved in the next (lower) word in memory. Then each register is saved when the MOVEM instruction is executed. The system stack pointer now points to the new TOP of stack, and the stack can be used by interrupt routines or during calls to other subroutines. After the subroutine has completed its processing, the return instruction should leave the stack pointer at its original value.

6.3.2 Program Structure

Large programs may be divided into a number of subroutines to accomplish specific tasks. This type of program structuring has the advantage of simplifying program testing and improving maintainability. The execution time is longer than that for a similar program without subroutines, due to the time required by the calling and return se-

```
 1                          LLEN   100
 2       00001000           ORG    $1000
 3                      *
 4                      *  MAIN PROGRAM
 5                      *
 6  001000 4EB81008         JSR    SUBR
 7                      *
 8  001004 4E722000         STOP   #$2000
 9
10                      *  SUBROUTINE
11                      *
12  001008 40E7        SUBR   MOVE.W   SR,-(SP)          ;SAVE CONDITION CODES
13  00100A 48E7FFFE           MOVEM.L D0-D7/A0-A6,-(SP)  ;SAVE REGISTERS
14                      *
15  00100E 4E71               NOP
16                      *
17  001010 4CDF7FFF           MOVEM.L (SP)+,D0-D7/A0-A6  ; RESTORE REGISTERS
18                      *
19                      *  RETURN AND RESTORE CONDITION CODES
20                      *
21  001014 4E77               RTR
22                             END

****** TOTAL ERRORS   0--   0
```

190

```
SYMBOL TABLE - APPROX 1201 SYMBOL ENTRIES LEFT

SUBR      001008

*TD
PC=001000 SR=2000 US=00007F00 SS=00007FFE
D0=00000000 D1=11111111 D2=22222222 D3=33333333
D4=44444444 D5=55555555 D6=66666666 D7=77777777
A0=AAAA0000 A1=AAAA1111 A2=AAAA2222 A3=AAAA3333
A4=AAAA4444 A5=AAAA5555 A6=AAAA6666 A7=00007FFE
                                                              _____

*G TILL 100E
PC=00100E SR=2000 US=00007F00 SS=00007FBC
D0=00000000 D1=11111111 D2=22222222 D3=33333333
D4=44444444 D5=55555555 D6=66666666 D7=77777777
A0=AAAA0000 A1=AAAA1111 A2=AAAA2222 A3=AAAA3333
A4=AAAA4444 A5=AAAA5555 A6=AAAA6666 A7=00007FBC
                                                              _____

*DM 7FBC 42
007FBC  00 00 00 00  11 11 11 11  22 22 22 22  33 33 33 33   ........""""3333
007FCC  44 44 44 44  55 55 55 55  66 66 66 66  77 77 77 77   DDDDUUUUffffwwww
007FDC  AA AA 00 00  AA AA 11 11  AA AA 22 22  AA AA 33 33   ..........""..33
007FEC  AA AA 44 44  AA AA 55 55  AA AA 66 66  20 00 00 00   ..DD..UU..ff....
007FFC  10 04 00 00  61 00 61 00  61 00 61 00  61 00 61 00   ................
*G TILL 1004
PC=001004 SR=2000 US=00007F00 SS=00007FFE
D0=00000000 D1=11111111 D2=22222222 D3=33333333
D4=44444444 D5=55555555 D6=66666666 D7=77777777
A0=AAAA0000 A1=AAAA1111 A2=AAAA2222 A3=AAAA3333
A4=AAAA4444 A5=AAAA5555 A6=AAAA6666 A7=00007FFE
                                                              _____

*
```

Figure 6.12 Structure of a subroutine module.

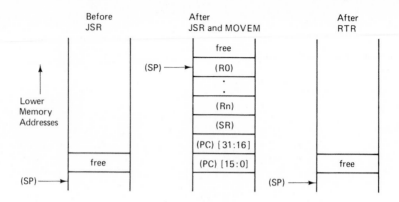

Note: Ri indicates an Address Register or a Data Register.

Figure 6.13   Stack usage during subroutine call.

quence for each subroutine. In most cases, the requirement for modularity is more important than minimizing execution time.

The possible structure of a program to read characters from a keyboard, convert them to BCD, and then process the numerical values is shown in Figure 6.14. The program begins by initializing values and then calls the first subroutine to read or input the characters as they are typed. After a string of characters is input, each is tested by a second subroutine. This test consists of checking each to see that it is a valid ASCII numeric character and converting valid characters to BCD. If an invalid character is detected, an error subroutine is called to display an invalid data message on the CRT screen. If no errors were detected, the BCD data can be processed further by additional subroutines.

Example 6.8

The subroutine shown in Figure 6.15 converts an ASCII decimal string ending with a carriage return character ($0D) to BCD digits. These are then stored in sequential bytes in memory. The overall operation of the module is as follows:

> IF [the ASCII string addressed by (A1) is valid]
> 　THEN [convert it to a BCD string addressed by (A2)]
> 　ELSE [set error condition (D1) = −1]

The starting address of the ASCII string in A1 and that of the resulting decimal string in A2 are assumed to be supplied before the module is executed by the **JSR ASCBCD** instruction. Subroutines **INIT** and **INPUT** (not shown) would read the characters and define these addresses. As the point of the example is to illustrate subroutines structures, the theory of the conversion is not discussed here. Section 7.6 specifically covers conversions between ASCII and BCD.

Subroutine ASCBCD tests each character for an ASCII value between 30_{16} and 39_{16}, or 0–9 as a decimal digit. If valid, each BCD character is stored in the byte addressed by (A2) until the count is exhausted. This routine also saves the contents of the registers it uses.

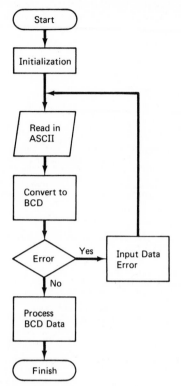

Figure 6.14 An example program structure.

If the character string $31, $32, $33, $34, $0D ('1234') starts at location (A1) = $2000, the result for (A2) = $200A is $01, $02, $03, and $04 in locations $200A through $200D with the low-order word of (D2) = 4. These digits could now be used for decimal arithmetic or converted to binary as required for further processing.

After the conversion is completed, (D1) is tested to determine if an error occurred. If not, the program transfers control to subroutine PROCESS (not shown). Otherwise, subroutine BADDATA (not shown) is called to output an error message. Then the sequence starts over.

EXERCISES

6.3.1. If the instruction

    BSR   SUB1

is located at address $3012 and the label SUB1 is at $3022, define the machine language instruction for

    BSR   SUB1

Refer to Apendix IV for the machine language format.

```
1                             LLEN    100
2           00001000          ORG     $1000
3                       *
4           00001100  INIT    EQU     $1100              ;SET UP DUMMY SUBROUTINES
5           00001200  INPUT   EQU     $1200
6           00001300  BADDATA EQU     $1300
7           00001400  PROCESS EQU     $1400
8                       *
9                       * MAIN PROGRAM
10                      *   ...
11 001000 4EB81100          JSR     INIT               ;PERFORM INITIALIZATION
12 001004 4EB81200  INLOOP  JSR     INPUT              ;READ IN ASCII
13                      *
14 001008 227C00002000      MOVE.L  #ASCII,A1          ;SET UP ADDRESSES
15 00100E 247C0000200A      MOVE.L  #BCD,A2            ;    FOR ASCBCD
16                      *
17 001014 4EB8102E          JSR     ASCBCD             ;CONVERT TO BCD
18 001018 4A01              TST.B   D1                 ;CHECK FOR ERROR
19 00101A 67000008          BEQ     GOOD               ;NONE,SKIP TO PROCESS
20                      *   ...
21 00101E 4EB81300          JSR     BADDATA            ;OUTPUT ERROR MESSAGE
22 001022 60E0              BRA     INLOOP             ;TRY AGAIN
23                      *
24 001024 4EB81400  GOOD    JSR     PROCESS
25                      *   ...
26 001028 4E71              NOP
27                      *   ...
28 00102A 4E722000          STOP    #$2000
29                      *
30                      *
31                      * CONVERT ASCII TO BCD
32                      * INPUT : (A1.L) = ADDRESS OF ASCII STRING
33                      *         (A2.L) = ADDRESS TO STORE BCD
34                      *
35                      * OUTPUT : (D1.B) = 0 : NO ERRORS DETECTED
36                      *                 NOT 0 : INVALID CHARACTER OR OVERFLOW DETECTED
37                      *          (D2.W) = LENGTH OF ASCII STRING
38                      *
39         0000000D  CR      EQU     $0D                ;CARRIAGE RETURN
40                      *
41 00102E 48E78060  ASCBCD  MOVEM.L D0/A1-A2,-(SP)     ;SAVE REGISTERS
42 001032 4201              CLR.B   D1                 ;SET STATUS TO SUCCESS
43 001034 4242              CLR.W   D2                 ;SET LENGTH COUNT TO 0
44                      *
45 001036 1019      LOOP    MOVE.B  (A1)+,D0           ;GET FIRST ASCII CHARACTER
46 001038 0C00000D          CMPI.B  #CR,D0             ;IF CHAR = CARRIAGE RETURN
47 00103C 67000020          BEQ     DONE               ;    THEN FINISHED
48 001040 04000030          SUBI.B  #'0',D0            ;IF CHAR < $30
49 001044 6D000014          BLT     ERROR              ;    THEN INVALID CHARACTER, ERROR EX
50 001048 0C000009          CMPI.B  #9,D0              ;IF CHAR > $39
51 00104C 6E00000C          BGT     ERROR              ;    THEN INVALID CHARACTER, ERROR EX
52 001050 14C0              MOVE.B  D0,(A2)+           ;SAVE BCD
53 001052 5242              ADDQ.W  #1,D2              ;INCREMENT LENGTH COUNT
54 001054 65000004          BCS     ERROR              ;OVERFLOWED COUNTER, ERROR EXIT
55 001058 60DC              BRA     LOOP               ;CONTINUE WITH NEXT CHARACTER
56                      *
57 00105A 123CFFFF  ERROR   MOVE.B  #-1,D1             ;SET ERROR STATUS
58 00105E 4CDF0601  DONE    MOVEM.L (SP)+,D0/A1-A2     ;RESTORE REGISTERS
59 001062 4E75              RTS
60                      *
61         00002000          ORG     $2000              ;DATA AREA
62 002000 0000000A  ASCII   DS.B    10                 ;DUMMY ASCII STRING
63 00200A 0000000A  BCD     DS.B    10                 ;DUMMY STORAGE FOR BCD
64                      *
65                              END
```

****** TOTAL ERRORS   0--   0

SYMBOL TABLE - APPROX 1191 SYMBOL ENTRIES LEFT

ASCBCD	00102E ASCII	002000 BADDATA	001300 BCD	00200A
CR	00000D DONE	00105E ERROR	00105A GOOD	001024
INIT	001100 INLOOP	001004 INPUT	001200 LOOP	001036
PROCESS	001400			

Figure 6.15 Subroutine usage: ASCII-to-BCD conversion.

6.3.2. Draw a diagram of the stack for the module in Example 6.8 if (SP) = $7FFE initially.

6.3.3. In the MC68000, what limits the number of subroutines that may be nested? A "nested" subroutine is one called by another subroutine.

FURTHER READING

A number of works discuss assembly language programming in a manner that is useful to the MC68000 programmer. In particular, the book by Kane et al., listed below, gives a number of good examples of programs for the MC68000. Many of the textbooks written about the PDP-11 system can be applied to the study of the MC68000 if the differences between the processors are taken into account. For instance, the instruction

    CMP   A,B

for the PDP-11 evaluates (A) – (B), which is the reverse of the MC68000. The texts by Eckhouse and Morris and by Lewis explain many of the aspects of assembly language programming for the PDP-11. Programs for the PDP-11 can be converted to MC68000, and vice versa, by a programmer familiar with both machines. The Further Reading section for Chapter 5 lists other references which provide more details about assembly language programming and the operation of assemblers.

ECKHOUSE, RICHARD H., JR., and L. R. MORRIS, *Minicomputer Systems,* 2nd ed. Englewood Cliffs, N.J.: Prentice-Hall, 1979.

KANE, GERALD, DOUG HAWKINS, and LANCE LEVENTHAL, *68000 Assembly Language Programming.* Berkeley, Calif.: Osborne (McGraw-Hill), 1981.

LEWIS, HARRY R., *An Introduction to Computer Programming and Data Structures Using MACRO-11.* Reston, Va.: Reston, 1981.

7

Arithmetic Operations

This chapter is concerned with arithmetic operations on numbers. Numerical data are used for identification of locations by their addresses and for representation of quantities such as temperatures or bank balances. In any case, the fundamental operations of addition, subtraction, multiplication, and division of numbers are essential in algorithms that are designed to process numerical data. Almost all programs incorporate some form of arithmetic operation.

The number system used in microprocessors is binary. The internal use of binary arithmetic and our external interpretation of the results as decimal numbers cause no problems if suitable conversion routines are available. Decimal values may be converted to ASCII code for input to the computer system and then be converted to binary for processing. The reverse conversions may be applied for output. A problem does arise in certain cases, however, due to the finite length of the machine representation. Stated another way, the length in bits of an integer value is a measure of the largest integer representable in a given format. Thus a 16-bit representation limits the magnitude of a positive integer to $2^{16} - 1$. Each operation, such as the addition of two 16-bit numbers, carries with it the danger of exceeding the maximum allowable value. The tests for such a condition and the means for extending the precision when necessary are two important aspects of the study of arithmetic operations using computers.

A review of the topics in Chapter 3 is suggested before or during the study of this chapter. Many of the mathematical details of binary and decimal arithmetic presented there are not repeated here. The setting of the condition codes resulting from execution of MC68000 instructions is summarized in Appendix IV.

7.1 *SOME DETAILS OF BINARY ARITHMETIC*

In the MC68000, the binary representation of operands can be 8, 16, or 32 bits in length. Numerically, positive integer values range from 0 to $2^m - 1$, where $m = 8, 16$, or 32. For signed integers, the range is -2^{m-1} to $+2^{m-1} - 1$ in two's-complement notation. In adding or subtracting m-bit integers, various out-of-range conditions can occur and these are indicated by condition code bits of the processor. The case of unsigned integers is treated differently from that for signed integers since the interpretation of the condition codes changes.

Consider the addition of two unsigned m-digit integers. For example, the 8-bit addition of 125 and 200 yields

Binary

$$
\begin{array}{r}
0111 \quad 1101 \\
+\,1100 \quad \underline{1000} \\
\hline
(1) \quad 0100 \quad 0101
\end{array}
$$

or an 8-bit result of 69 with a carry. This addition in the MC68000 would cause the carry condition code C to be set to $\{1\}$ to indicate the overflow. Similarly, subtraction with a subtrahend larger than the minuend is indicated by a borrow out of the $(m + 1)^{st}$ place. In the MC68000, the borrow indication is also C = $\{1\}$. Thus, whenever the carry bit is $\{1\}$ after addition or subtraction of unsigned integers, the m-bit result is incorrect and the programmer must decide on the appropriate action.

When integers in two's-complement notation are added or subtracted, the carry bit is ignored and the overflow (V) bit is checked for an out-of-range condition. For an m-bit representation, the positive range is only 0 to $2^{m-1} - 1$, so the addition of two positive numbers must not exceed that value. For example, the 8-bit addition of $+\,125$ and $+\,127$ yields

Binary

$$
\begin{array}{r}
0111 \quad 1101 \\
+\,0111 \quad \underline{1111} \\
\hline
1111 \quad 1100
\end{array}
$$

which is -4!   The overflow condition, V = $\{1\}$, is also indicated. The problem which arises is that two positive numbers which were added together produced a negative result. Similarly, if the addition of two negative values produces a positive result, the V condition code is again set to $\{1\}$. This mathematical condition is termed *underflow* and means the result is too small (too negative) to be represented. However, the V or overflow bit indicates the error, and reference to out-of-range conditions in the machine is usually called "overflow." If the operands are of opposite sign, no out-of-range condition can occur. When subtraction is performed, the V bit set to $\{1\}$ again indicates an erroneous result.

In the MC68000, division and BCD arithmetic can also yield out-of-range re-

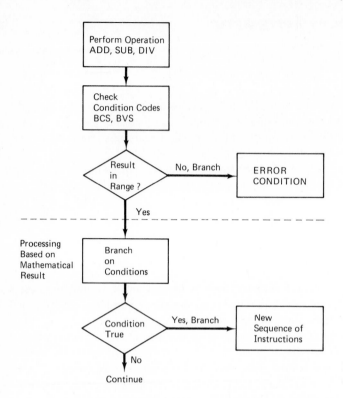

Figure 7.1 Testing for out-of-range conditions.

sults. The conditions for these cases are covered in the appropriate sections of this chapter. In summary, the condition codes must be checked after an arithmetic operation to determine if an out-of-range condition occurred. Figure 7.1 indicates the procedure used to check for valid numbers. An error condition indicates that the m-bit representation is not valid. Either the result is rejected or a multiple-precision representation is required.

Conditional tests.   The BCS (Branch if Carry Set) following the arithmetic instruction causes a branch if a carry occurred during addition or a borrow occurred during subtraction of unsigned integers. BVS (Branch if Overflow Set) branches when an out-of-range condition occurs during arithmetic with two's-complement integers. It is recommended that such tests (or the opposite logic of BCC or BVC) be used before other conditional tests are executed.

When conditional branch instructions are executed after arithmetic instructions, the conditional tests as described in Chapter 6 must be used with care. Consider the addition just shown of $+125$ and $+127$ for 8-bit signed numbers. The condition codes after the ADD instruction would be

$$Z = \{0\}, N = \{1\}, C = \{0\}, V = \{1\}$$

indicating nonzero, negative, no carry, and overflow, respectively. The result is in error mathematically, but the BMI instruction would cause a branch since it tests only for $N = \{1\}$. Worse yet, BGE would branch but BPL would not. BGE branches whenever N and V condition codes are the same, but BPL branches when $N = \{0\}$ without testing any other condition codes.

If no out-of-range condition is present, the conditional tests operate as shown in Figure 7.2(a). Here BPL and BGE are equivalent for valid signed integers, as are BMI

Instruction	Branch Condition	Result
UNSIGNED ADD, SUB $C = \{0\}$	BEQ BNE	$X = 0$ $X \neq 0$
SIGNED ADD, SUB $V = \{0\}$	BEQ BNE BPL, BGE BLE BMI, BLT BGT	$X = 0$ $X \neq 0$ $X \geq 0$ $X \leq 0$ $X < 0$ $X > 0$

(a) Signed and Unsigned Tests

Mnemonic	Condition	Encoding	Test
T	true	0000	1
F	false	0001	0
HI	high	0010	$\overline{C} \cdot \overline{Z}$
LS	low or same	0011	$C + Z$
CC (HS)	carry clear	0100	$\overline{C}$
CS (LO)	carry set	0101	C
NE	not equal	0110	$\overline{Z}$
EQ	equal	0111	Z
VC	overflow clear	1000	$\overline{V}$
VS	overflow set	1001	V
PL	plus	1010	$\overline{N}$
MI	minus	1011	N
GE	greater or equal	1100	$N \cdot V + \overline{N} \cdot \overline{V}$
LT	less than	1101	$N \cdot \overline{V} + \overline{N} \cdot V$
GT	greater than	1110	$N \cdot V \cdot \overline{Z} + \overline{N} \cdot \overline{V} \cdot \overline{Z}$
LE	less or equal	1111	$Z + N \cdot \overline{V} + \overline{N} \cdot V$

(b) Condition Code Tests

Figure 7.2 Conditional branches for valid numbers.

and BLT. Figure 7.2(b) shows the conditions and the tests on the condition code. The "encoding" specifies the condition in the machine language instruction. The instruction sequence in Figure 7.1 is followed in most of the examples in this chapter where the possibility of an out-of-range condition may occur.

EXERCISES

7.1.1. Compare the use of the Bcc instructions after arithmetic operations with their use after the MOVE, CMP, and TST instructions, as discussed in Chapter 6.

7.1.2. Show that BGE and BPL yield opposite results when overflow occurs.

7.1.3. Determine the result of subtracting $-32,768$ from $16,384$ using 16-bit two's-complement arithmetic.

7.1.4. Show that subtraction can be accomplished with binary numbers by adding the two's complement of the subtrahend to the minuend.

7.2 ADDITION AND SUBTRACTION

Binary addition is performed on 8-, 16-, or 32-bit operands with the ADD instruction and its variations, as shown in Table 7.1. Similarly, byte, word, or longword operands can be subtracted with the SUB instruction. The NEG instruction forms the two's complement (negative) of the operand specified. These three instructions and their variations are used to perform basic arithmetic on binary integers. As seen in Table 7.1, each instruction has restrictions on the addressing modes allowed. In the operation of each instruction, which is defined in Table 7.2, the destination operand of specified length is replaced by the result. This is the sum for ADD, the difference for SUB, or the negative value when NEG is executed. The condition codes N, Z, V, and C are set according to the result. The X (extend) condition code is also set.

Addition.   The assembly language format of the ADD instruction is

ADD. $<l>$ $<EA>,<Dn>$

when the destination operand is held in a data register. The source is specified as a byte, word, or longword operand ($<l>$ = B, W, or L) unless the source is an address register, in which case the length is restricted to word or longword operands. Thus the instruction

ADD.B   D1,D5

replaces (D5) [7:0] with the sum (D5) [7:0] + (D1) [7:0]. Only the specified length of the destination is affected.

TABLE 7.1   ARITHMETIC INSTRUCTIONS ADD, SUB, AND NEG

Syntax	Addressing modes	
	Source	Destination
Addition or subtraction		
ADD.<l> <EA>,<Dn> SUB.<l> <EA>,<Dn>	All[1]	Dn
ADD.<l> <Dn>,<EA> SUB.<l> <Dn>,<EA>	Dn	Memory alterable
ADDI.<l> #<d>,<EA> SUBI.<l> #<d>,<EA>	#<d>	Data alterable
ADDQ.<l> #<d_3>,<EA> SUBQ.<l> #<d_3>,<EA>	#<d_3>[2]	Alterable[3]
Negate		
NEG.<l> <EA>	—	Data alterable

Notes:

1. If the source effective address in the instructions ADD or SUB is an address register, the operand length is word or longword.
2. <d_3> is a value between 1 and 8.
3. If An is a destination, only word or longword operations are allowed. In this case, the condition codes are not affected.
4. <l> denotes B, W, or L in all the instructions except as in notes 1 and 3.
5. Except as in note 3, all the condition codes are affected by the instructions.

The addition of the value in a data register to an operand in memory is also allowed. For example, the instruction

ADD.L   D1,(A1)

adds the 32-bit contents of D1 to the contents of the location addressed by Al. The destination operand cannot, however, be the contents of an address register or be addressed by program counter relative addressing.

Several variations of the ADD instruction shown in Figure 7.2 are ADDI (Add Immediate) and ADDQ (Add Quick). The immediate format can add an 8-, 16-, or 32-bit constant to a data-alterable location. This excludes an address register or a PC relative address for the destination. The ADDI instruction adds a specified constant to a destination location, while the ADD instruction operates only between registers and memory. Thus the instruction

ADDI.B   #20,(A1)

is used to add 20 to the byte addressed by Al as an example.

The ADDQ instruction adds an immediate value between 1 and 8 to the speci-

TABLE 7.2 ARITHMETIC INSTRUCTION OPERATION

Instruction	Operation
ADD.<l> <EAs>,<EAd>	(EAd) [l] ← (EAs)[l] + (EAd)[l]
SUB.<l> <EAs>,<EAd>	(EAd) [l] ← (EAd)[l] − (EAs)[l]
NEG.<l> <EA>	(EA) [l] ← 0 − (EA)[l]

Notes:

1. <EAs> and <EAd> are the source and destination effective addresses, respectively.

2. <l> denotes B, W, or L.

3. [l] indicates corresponding bits in the operation.

fied destination location. Any alterable destination location is allowed, including an address register. Destinations addressed by the PC relative mode are prohibited. In the cases where An is the destination, the condition codes are not affected, but the whole register (32 bits) is changed. Arithmetic operations with addresses are considered in Chapter 9.

It should be noted that some assemblers select the appropriate variation of an ADD instruction without the programmer specifying it. For instance, the instruction

        ADD   #1,D4

may be interpreted as an ADDI instruction or an ADDQ instruction by certain assemblers. The practice of letting the assembler choose the variation is not always wise if consistency in program documentation and machine language instruction length is desired.

Example 7.1

The subroutine shown in Figure 7.3 adds a column (vector elements) of 16-bit integers to form either a 16- or a 32-bit sum. Before the subroutine is called, D1 holds the number of integers to be summed and A1 contains the starting address of the column. If the length of the column is zero, D3 contains −1 after the subroutine executes. Otherwise, the low-order word of D3 contains zero if the sum is contained in 16 bits or +1 if the sum requires 32 bits. Each time a carry occurs in the addition of a new value to D2, 1 is added to the upper word of D2 to form the proper sum.

The purpose of the program might be to use word (rather than longword) operations in subsequent processing if a 16-bit sum is the result. This would reduce the memory storage needed and be more efficient in time if memory accesses are made. A longword access to memory requires two read or write cycles by the processor since there are only 16 data signal-lines.

Subtraction.   The instructions SUB, SUBI, and SUBQ are exact counterparts of the addition instructions. They calculate the difference between the destination operand (minuend) and the source operand (subtrahend). This difference replaces the byte, word, or longword portion of the destination location as specified by the instruction.

If an address register is the destination in a SUBQ instruction, the immediate value can be a word or a longword operand. If the length is word, the immediate value is sign-extended to 32 bits before the subtraction is performed. For example, the instruction

SUBQ.W   #1,A1

has the effect of subtracting 1 from the entire contents of Al. Therefore, both ADDQ and SUBQ affect the 32-bit contents of a destination address register.

All the condition code bits are affected by a subtraction instruction unless the subtraction is made from an address register. The condition $C = \{1\}$ indicates a borrow in unsigned subtraction. In signed arithmetic, N, Z, and V bits set to 1 indicate a negative number, zero, and an overflow condition, respectively.

```
MC68000 ASM REV= 1.4 - COPYRIGHT BY MOTOROLA 1978              PAGE   1


 1                                   LLEN    100
 2          00001000                 ORG     $1000
 3                           *
 4                           *   ADD 16-BIT UNSIGNED INTEGERS
 5                           *
 6                           *   INPUT :   (D1.W) = NUMBER OF INTEGERS
 7                           *             (A1.L) = STARTING ADDRESS OF INTEGERS
 8                           *
 9                           *   OUTPUT : (D3.W) = -1 : NUMBER OF INTEGERS IS ZERO
10                           *                      0 : 16-BIT SUM IN D2 [15:0]
11                           *                      1 : 32-BIT SUM IN D2 [31:0]
12                           *            (D2.L) = SUM
13                           *
14  001000 48E74040   ADDUNS        MOVEM.L D1/A1,-(SP)        ;SAVE REGISTERS
15                           *
16  001004 4282                     CLR.L   D2                ;SUM:=0
17  001006 363CFFFF                 MOVE.W  #-1,D3            ;SET STATUS TO ERROR
18  00100A 5341                     SUBQ.W  #1,D1             ;SET UP LOOP COUNTER
19  00100C 6D000016                 BLT     DONE
20  001010 4243                     CLR.W   D3                ;SET STATUS TO 16-BIT SUM
21                           *
22  001012 D459         LOOP        ADD.W   (A1)+,D2
23  001014 6400000A                 BCC     ENDLP             ;IF NO OVERFLOW, THEN SKIP
24  001018 068200010000             ADDI.W  #$10000,D2        ;ELSE ADD 1 TO UPPER WORD
25  00101E 7601                     MOVEQ.W #1,D3             ;SET STATUS TO 32-BIT SUM
26  001020 51C9FFF0     ENDLP       DBRA    D1,LOOP           ;CONTINUE
27  001024 4CDF0202     DONE        MOVEM.L (SP)+,D1/A1       ;RESTORE REGISTERS
28  001028 4E75                     RTS
29                                  END

****** TOTAL ERRORS   0--   0


SYMBOL TABLE - APPROX 1198 SYMBOL ENTRIES LEFT

ADDUNS      001000 DONE     001024 ENDLP     001020 LOOP      001012
```

Figure 7.3 Addition routine for 16- or 32-bit sums.

Negation.   The NEG instruction replaces a data-alterable destination location of specified length with the result of the calculation

$$0 - (\text{destination})$$

thus forming the two's-complement value. As an example, if location $1000 contains the value 1, the instruction

NEG.B $1000

replaces the value with $FF. The only case in which an overflow can occur is when the value negated is -2^{m-1}, since this number has no positive equivalent in two's-complement notation.

```
MC68000 ASM REV= 1.4 - COPYRIGHT BY MOTOROLA 1978              PAGE  1


 1                              LLEN    100
 2        00001000              ORG     $1000
 3                        *
 4                        * SUM OF DIFFERENCES OF TWO COLUMNS OF 16-BIT
 5                        * INTEGERS
 6                        *
 7                        * INPUT : (D1.W) = LENGTH OF THE COLUMNS
 8                        *         (A1.L) = ADDRESS OF FIRST COLUMN
 9                        *         (A2.L) = ADDRESS OF SECOND COLUMN
10                        *
11                        * OUTPUT : (D3.W) = ABSOLUTE VALUE OF RESULT
12                        *          (D4.W) = 0 : ERROR OCCURRED
13                        *                  -1 : RESULT IS NEGATIVE
14                        *
15 001000 48E76060    SUMDIF  MOVEM.L D1/D2/A1/A2,-(SP)    ;SAVE REGISTERS
16 001004 4243                CLR.W   D3                   ;SUM := O
17 001006 4244                CLR.W   D4                   ;SET DEFAULT STATUS TO ERROR
18 001008 4A41                TST.W   D1                   ;IF COLUMNS ARE EMPTY
19 00100A 67000022            BEQ     DONE                 ;THEN RETURN WITH ERROR
20                        *
21 00100E 3419        LOOP    MOVE.W  (A1)+,D2             ;COMPUTE
22 001010 945A                SUB.W   (A2)+,D2             ; ((A1)) - ((A2))
23 001012 D642                ADD.W   D2,D3                ;SUM THE DIFFERENCES
24 001014 69000018            BVS     DONE                 ;ON OVERFLOW, EXIT WITH ERROR
25 001018 5341                SUBQ.W  #1,D1                ;DECREMENT COUNT
26 00101A 66F2                BNE     LOOP                 ;LOOP UNTIL FINISHED
27                        *
28 00101C 4A43                TST     D3                   ;IF RESULT IS POSITIVE
29 00101E 6C00000C            BGE     POS                  ;THEN PROCESS IT
30 001022 383CFFFF            MOVE.W  #-1,D4               ;ELSE SET STATUS TO NEGATIVE
31 001026 4443                NEG.W   D3                   ;TAKE ABSOLUTE VALUE
32 001028 60000004            BRA     DONE
33                        *
34 00102C 7801        POS     MOVEQ.W #1,D4                ;SET STATUS TO POSITIVE
35 00102E 4CDF0606    DONE    MOVEM.L (SP)+,D1/D2/A1/A2    ;RESTORE REGISTERS
36 001032 4E75                RTS
37                              END

****** TOTAL ERRORS   0--   0


SYMBOL TABLE - APPROX 1198 SYMBOL ENTRIES LEFT

DONE      00102E LOOP      00100E POS     00102C SUMDIF     001000
```

Figure 7.4   Routine to compute the sum of differences.

Example 7.2

The subroutine shown in Figure 7.4 sums the differences between two columns or vectors of integers addressed by (A1) and (A2). The length of the columns is initially held in D1. If the length of the columns is zero or an overflow occurs, then (D4)[15:0] is set to 0 to indicate the error. Otherwise, the differences between corresponding entries in the columns are accumulated in the low-order word of D3. Once the summation is complete, the result is tested for positive or negative. If the result is negative, the NEG instruction is used to determine the magnitude of the number. A program using this routine must first check the status output in D4 for an error condition. If no error is indicated, the magnitude of the sum of the differences is held in the low-order word of D3. The program might then convert the magnitude to decimal ASCII and prefix the sign to the printed results.

EXERCISES

7.2.1. Assume that (D1) = $0000 FFFF before each instruction below executes. Determine the results, including the setting of the condition codes after the following:
   (a) ADDI.B #1,D1
   (b) ADDQ.L #1,D1
   (c) SUBQ.B #1,D1
   (d) NEG.W   D1
   (e) SUB.L   D1,D1

7.2.2. Show that using only one carry bit after an m-bit unsigned addition is sufficient to assure that no information is lost.

7.2.3 For an m-bit subtraction operation N3 = N2 − N1, show that the proper result is obtained when N1 is negative and N2 is positive, if the sum of the magnitudes of N1 and N2 is equal to or less than $2^{m-1} - 1$. Refer to Chapter 3 for the two's-complement formulas.

7.2.4. Write a routine to multiply two unsigned 16-bit integers by using repeated addition.

7.2.5. Modify the program of Example 7.2 to compute the sum of the absolute value of the differences between the two columns of numbers.

7.3 MULTIPLICATION AND DIVISION

Instructions for integer multiplication and division are included in the instruction set of most of the 16-bit microprocessors. The MC68000 provides separate instructions for multiplication and division of unsigned integers and for multiplication and division of two's-complement integers. This section presents these instructions and discusses the operations, numerical ranges, and possible errors involved in their use. Table 7.3 shows the syntax and the operations of the DIV (divide) instruction and the MUL (multiply) instruction. The suffix "U" for unsigned integers or "S" for signed integers must be specified each time they are used. The multiplicand for the multiplication operation and the divisor for the division operation are specified by a 16-bit source oper-

TABLE 7.3   MULTIPLY AND DIVIDE INSTRUCTIONS

Syntax	Operation
Multiplication	
MULU <EA>,<Dn>	(Dn)[31:0] ← (Dn)[15:0] * (EA)[15:0]
MULS <EA>,<Dn>	
Division	
DIVU <EA>,<Dn>	(Dn) [31:0]/(EA)[15:0];
DIVS <EA>,<Dn>	(Dn)[15:0] ← quotient
	(Dn)[31:16] ← remainder

Notes:

1. Only data addressing modes are allowed for the source address <EA> (i.e., An is prohibited).

2. In division, a zero divisor causes a *trap*; an overflow is indicated by $V = \{1\}$.

3. In signed division, a remainder has the sign of the dividend.

and. Only address register direct addressing is prohibited for the source. The multiplier and dividend are always held in data registers.

Unsigned multiplication. The MULU instruction multiplies two unsigned 16-bit operands to yield a 32-bit product. For example, the instruction

    MULU $10,D2

with (D2)[15:0] = $0002 results in (D2) = $0000 0020 or 32 decimal. Since the 16-bit multiplicand and multiplier may each range from 0 to 65,535, the product cannot exceed 4,294,836,225, which is less than $2^{32} - 1$. Therefore, no overflow is possible and the condition code bits C and V are always cleared after the MULU instruction. N and Z are set according to the result. In the case of unsigned integers, $N = \{1\}$ indicates that the product equals or exceeds 2^{31} in magnitude.

Signed multiplication. When signed integers are multiplied, the result is positive or negative depending on the signs of the multiplicand and multiplier. The range of each is -2^{15} to $+2^{15} - 1$, or $-32,768$ to $+32,767$. If the two most negative values are multiplied, the result is 1,073,741,824, or 2^{30}. The largest possible negative result is

$$-2^{15} \times (2^{15} - 1) = -1,073,709,056$$

Therefore, no out-of-range condition can occur for a 32-bit product, and both V and C are always cleared. For MULS, the N bit indicates a negative product when $N = \{1\}$, as expected. If the result is zero, then $Z = \{1\}$. The instruction

    MULS   # -1,D2

with (D2)[15:0] = $0002 results in (D2) = $FFFF FFFE, or -2 in two's-complement notation. The N bit is set to indicate a negative result.

Example 7.3

Although the use of a single multiply instruction cannot result in an overflow, the use of these instructions in an equation that requires several multiplies could produce a result that exceeds an allowable maximum magnitude. For example, to calculate the sum of squares as

$$Z = \sum_{i=i}^{N} (X_i^2 + Y_i^2)$$

the individual products cannot overflow in 32 bits, although the sum of several terms or the entire sum can. The program in Figure 7.5 computes the sum of squares of N pairs of signed 16-bit integers. The numbers are stored in the order

$$X(1), Y(1), X(2), Y(2), .. , X(N), Y(N)$$

as a table or column of 16-bit words whose first address is given by (Al) when the program is entered. The length N is assumed to be in the low-order 16-bits of D1. The 32-bit result is accumulated in D3 unless an error occurs. After execution, an error is indicated by (D4)[15:0] = -1 and any program making use of the result should check the status in D4 before the result is accepted. The address register indirect with displacement mode

```
MC68000 ASM REV= 1.4 - COPYRIGHT BY MOTOROLA 1978            PAGE  1


   1                              LLEN    100
   2         00001000             ORG     $1000
   3                         *
   4                         * SUM OF SQUARES
   5                         *
   6                         * INPUT :   (D1.W) = LENGTH OF COLUMN
   7                         *           (A1.L) = ADDRESS OF COLUMN OF NUMBERS
   8                         *                    STORED X1,Y1,X2,Y2,...,XN,YN
   9                         *
  10                         * OUTPUT:   (D3.L) = RESULT
  11                         *           (D4.W) = 0 : SUCCESSFUL
  12                         *                   -1 : ERROR
  13                         *
  14 001000 48E76040         SUMSQ    MOVEM.L  D1/D2/A1,-(SP)     ;SAVE REGISTERS
  15 001004 4283                      CLR.L    D3                 ;SUM := 0
  16 001006 383CFFFF                  MOVE.W   #-1,D4             ;SET DEFAULT TO ERROR
  17 00100A 5341                      SUBQ.W   #1,D1              ;IF LENGTH IS ZERO
  18 00100C 6D000022                  BLT      DONE               ;THEN EXIT WITH ERROR
  19                         *
  20 001010 34290000         LOOP     MOVE.W   0(A1),D2           ;COMPUTE
  21 001014 C5C2                      MULS     D2,D2              ;XN**2
  22 001016 D682                      ADD.L    D2,D3              ;ADD TO SUM
  23 001018 69000016                  BVS      DONE               ;ON ERROR EXIT
  24 00101C 34290002                  MOVE.W   2(A1),D2           ;COMPUTE
  25 001020 C5C2                      MULS     D2,D2              ;YN**2
  26 001022 D682                      ADD.L    D2,D3              ;ADD TO SUM
  27 001024 6900000A                  BVS      DONE               ;ON ERROR, EXIT
  28 001028 5889                      ADD.L    #4,A1              ;INCREMENT TO NEXT PAIR
  29 00102A 51C9FFE4                  DBRA     D1,LOOP            ;DECREMENT COUNTER AND CONTINUE UNTI
  30                         *
  31 00102E 4244                      CLR.W    D4                 ;SET STATUS TO SUCCESS
  32 001030 4CDF0206         DONE     MOVEM.L  (SP)+,D1/D2/A1     ;RESTORE REGISTERS
  33 001034 4E75                      RTS
  34                                  END

****** TOTAL ERRORS   0--   0


SYMBOL TABLE - APPROX 1199 SYMBOL ENTRIES LEFT

DONE       001030 LOOP      001010 SUMSQ      001000
```

Figure 7.5 Sum-of-squares program.

is used to address the operands, so if an overflow occurs, (Al) points to the current pair of operands.

Unsigned division.   The MC68000 instruction DIVU performs the division

$$Y/W = Q + R/W$$

where Y is a 32-bit unsigned integer, W is a 16-bit unsigned integer, Q is a 16-bit quotient, and R is a 16-bit remainder. For example, the instruction

DIVU   #2,D1

divides the 32-bit operand in D1 by 2. The result, as indicated in Table 7.3, is a quotient in the low-order word of D1 and the remainder, or zero, in the upper word of D1. Thus, if D1 contained $0000 0005 before the instruction executed, the result is (D1) = $0001 0002 since $5/2 = 2 + 1/2$.

Two special conditions may arise when performing a division operation:

(a) division by zero, or

(b) an overflow of the quotient.

Both of these situations are indicated by error conditions. Exception processing in a trap routine occurs in the case of division by zero. An overflow can occur because the range of the dividend is 0 to $2^{32} - 1$ but the length of the quotient is only 16 bits. Obviously, dividing an integer greater than $2^{16} - 1$ by 1 would cause an overflow. Or, more generally, if the dividend exceeds the divisor in magnitude by 2^{16} or greater, an overflow will occur. The overflow is indicated by $V = \{1\}$ even though unsigned arithmetic is being performed. If overflow occurs, the operands are not changed.

Signed division.   The instruction DIVS executes in the same manner as the DIVU instruction, but the operands are signed integers. Motorola's convention is that the sign of the remainder, if any, is the same as the sign of the dividend. Thus the instruction

DIVS   #3,D1

with (D1) = $FFFF FFF6 calculates $-10/3$ with the result

(D1) = $FFFF FFFD

or $Q = -3$ and $R = -1$. The condition code N is set to $\{1\}$ to indicate that the quotient is negative.

In signed division, the quotient can range from -2^{15} to $+2^{15} - 1$. Therefore, overflow will occur unless the magnitude of the 32-bit dividend is less than 2^{15} times that of the divisor. The V bit is set to $\{1\}$ if overflow occurs. A trap occurs if a divisor is zero.

Remainder in division.   Consider the unsigned division

$$Y/W = Q + R/W$$

where R/W is the remainder, which must be less than 1. Therefore, R/W has the representation

$$d_{-1} \times 10^{-1} + d_{-2} \times 10^{-2} + \cdots$$

and the positional number Y/X can be written

$$Q \cdot d_{-1} d_{-2} \cdots$$

as long as the division operation did not overflow. If only the fraction is considered, multiplying R/W by 10 yields d_{-1} as the first integer with a remainder of

$$d_{-2} \times 10_{-1} + \ldots$$

Successive multiplications of R by 10 followed by a division by W yields the decimal digits as the quotient for as many places as desired. As an example, 22/7 is 3.142..., which approximates π to three decimal places. The divisions and multiplications yield

$$22/7 = 3 + 1/7$$
$$10/7 = 1 + 3/7$$
$$30/7 = 4 + 2/7$$
$$20/7 = 2 + 6/7$$

and so on until the result 3.142... is computed. Of course, the operations will be done in binary in the computer, but each digit can be converted to binary-coded decimal or ASCII for output if desired. The exercises in this section consider such conversions.

Example 7.4

The subroutine shown in Figure 7.6 computes the average of a series of numbers stored in vector or column form and addressed by Al. If the number of values, which is in D1, is not zero, the 32-bit sum is formed in D3. The sum is then divided by the number of values and the low-order word of D3 contains the quotient and any remainder is in the high-order word.

EXERCISES

7.3.1. Determine the quotient and the remainder in the following divisions when the instruction listed is executed with the dividend and divisor as shown.
   (a) 10/5; DIVU
   (b) −10/5; DIVU
   (c) −10/5; DIVS
   (d) −5/2; DIVS

```
MC68000 ASM REV= 1.4 - COPYRIGHT BY MOTOROLA 1978                    PAGE   1


  1                                    LLEN    100
  2          00001000                  ORG     $1000
  3                            *
  4                            * COMPUTATION OF AVERAGE
  5                            *
  6                            * INPUT :    (A1.L) = ADDRESS OF SERIES OF 16-BIT NUMBERS
  7                            *            (D1.W) = LENGTH OF SERIES
  8                            *
  9                            * OUTPUT :   (D3)[15:0] = AVERAGE
 10                            *            (D3)[31:16] = REMAINDER OF SUM/LENGTH
 11                            *
 12 001000 48E76840    AVG              MOVEM.L D1-D2/D4/A1,-(SP)      ;SAVE REGISTERS
 13                            *
 14 001004 4A41                         TST.W   D1                    ;IF LENGTH = 0
 15 001006 67000014                     BEQ     DONE                  ;THEN FINISHED
 16                            *
 17 00100A 4282                         CLR.L   D2
 18 00100C 4283                         CLR.L   D3                    ;SUM;=0
 19 00100E 3801                         MOVE.W  D1,D4                 ;SET COUNTER
 20 001010 5344                         SUBQ.W  #1,D4                 ;TO LENGTH - 1
 21                            *
 22 001012 3419        LOOP             MOVE.W  (A1)+,D2              ;LOOP TO SUM NUMBERS
 23 001014 D682                         ADD.L   D2,D3
 24 001016 51CCFFFA                     DBRA    D4,LOOP
 25                            *
 26 00101A 87C1                         DIVS    D1,D3                 ;SUM/LENGTH
 27                            *
 28 00101C 4CDF0216    DONE             MOVEM.L (SP)+,D1-D2/D4/A1     ;RESTORE REGISTERS
 29 001020 4E75                         RTS
 30                                     END

****** TOTAL ERRORS    0--    0


SYMBOL TABLE - APPROX 1199 SYMBOL ENTRIES LEFT

AVG          001000 DONE          00101C LOOP          001012
```

Figure 7.6   Program for averaging values.

The negative values should be written in two's-complement notation to perform the divisions.

7.3.2. Suppose two signed integers are multiplied by the MULU instruction. Show that unsigned binary multiplication will cause an error if one or both of the numbers are negative. Test this by multiplying $(-1) \times (-1)$ in two's-complement notation but with unsigned multiplication. How can the result be corrected?

7.3.3. If $N_2 < 2^m \times N_1$ in the unsigned binary division N_2/N_1, prove that overflow cannot occur if the dividend has $2m$ bits and the quotient is m bits.

7.3.4. Write a routine to compute a 32-bit quotient and a 32-bit remainder when overflow occurs with the DIVU instruction. The result can be obtained by writing Y/W as

$$(Y2 \times 2^{16} + Y1)/W$$

where Y2 is the upper 16 bits of the dividend and Y1 represents the lower 16 bits.

7.4 MULTIPLE-PRECISION ARITHMETIC

In scientific measurements, the term *accuracy* refers to the correctness of a measurement, that is, to its freedom from mistake or error. *Precision* refers to the amount of detail used to represent a measurement. For numerical values, the amount of precision is usually expressed by giving the number of significant digits in the numerical value. If a quantity is judged to have insufficient precision for a given application, additional significant digits may be used to produce a more precise result.

Arithmetic units in microprocessors operate on a maximum of m digits when performing arithmetic operations. We shall call this maximum length the *single-precision* length. The MC68000 maximum single-precision length is 32 bits, but 8-bit or 16-bit quantities can also be handled. Sequences of greater length cannot be handled as a single arithmetic operand by the processor. Therefore, to extend the precision, several m-digit operands can be considered mathematically as a single value. If k operands were combined, the value would be $k \times m$ digits long. Double-precision values, for example, have $k = 2$. Thus the MC68000 double-precision length would be 2×32, or 64 bits.

Arithmetic operations with multiple-precision operands are performed by using the processor instructions on each m-digit portion of the values, and then combining the results. This procedure yields the correct answer when mathematical details such as carries or borrows between the intermediate results are treated properly.

The MC68000 provides special instructions to facilitate addition, subtraction, and negation of double-precision integers. This section is concerned primarily with the use of two 32-bit values to yield 64-bit double-precision numbers.

The instruction ADDX (Add with Extend), SUBX (Subtract with Extend), and NEGX (Negate with Extend) are defined in Table 7.4. The difference between these extended instructions and the instructions for addition, subtraction, and negation dis-

TABLE 7.4   EXTENDED ARITHMETIC INSTRUCTIONS

	Addressing modes	
Syntax	Source	Destination
Add or Subtract Extended		
ADDX. <l> <Dm>,<Dn>	<Dm>	<Dn>
SUBX. <l> <Dm>,<Dn>		
ADDX. <l> −(Am),−(An)	Predecrement	Predecrement
SUBX. <l> −(Am),−(An)		
Negate with Extend		
NEGX. <l> <EA>	—	Data alterable

Note: <l> denotes B, W, or L.

TABLE 7.5 OPERATION OF EXTENDED INSTRUCTIONS

Instruction	Operation
ADDX.$<l>$ $<$src$>$,$<$dst$>$	(dst)[l] $\leftarrow$ (src)[l] + (dst)[l] + X
SUBX.$<l>$ $<$src$>$,$<$dst$>$	(dst)[l] $\leftarrow$ (dst)[l] $-$ (src)[l] $-$ X
NEGX.$<l>$ $<$EA$>$	(EA)[l] $\leftarrow$ 0 $-$ (EA) [l] $-$ X

Notes:

1. C, N, and V condition code bits set as for any arithmetic operation.

2. Z is cleared if the result is nonzero; otherwise, it is unchanged.

3. X is set the same as the C bit.

4. $<l>$ denotes B, W, or L.

5. [l] indicates corresponding bits in the operation.

cussed previously is the use of the condition code bits X and Z by the extended operations.

As shown in Table 7.5, the extended instructions utilize the X (Extend) bit in their operation. If the X bit was set by a previous operation, the instructions ADDX, SUBX, and NEGX take this setting into account when they are executed. The primary use of the extend bit is to add a carry (ADDX) or subtract a borrow (SUBX) when the upper m bits of a double-precision value are being manipulated. The carry or borrow would have resulted from the single-precision operation on the lower m bits. For example, the sequence

ADD.L   D1,D3

ADDX.L   D2,D4

adds the double-precision value in D2/D1 to the 64-bit value in D4/D3. The X bit is set to {1} if the addition of the low order portions (D1 and D3) caused a carry. The second instruction adds the carry value to the sum.

In the case of arithmetic instructions, the X bit is set to the same value as the C bit. In general, most MC68000 instructions that are not used for arithmetic operations do not affect the X bit, so the C bit and the X bit should not be considered the same. For example, if D4 in the example just given was tested for zero by the instruction

TST.L   D4

the carry bit would be cleared but the X bit (set by the ADDX instruction) would not be changed.

The zero condition code bit, Z, is also treated in a special way by the extended instructions. The setting of Z, after an extended instruction is executed, is based on both the previous setting of the Z bit and the value of the current operand. Consider the 64-bit integer

$0000\ 0000\ 0000\ 0001_{16}$

in which the lower 32-bit value is nonzero. If each 32-bit half is tested for zero separately, Z would be set to {0} for the low-order portion. However, Z would become {1} when the high-order portion is tested. If a conditional test is subsequently made, the results would be based on a zero value!

To obtain the correct results for double-precision conditions, the instructions ADDX, SUBX, and NEGX set the Z bit according to the logical equation

$$Z = Z_2 \text{ AND } Z_1$$

in which *both* Z_1 and Z_2 must be {1} to set $Z = \{1\}$. Here Z_1 was the setting before the extended instruction was executed and Z_2 is the result from the extended operation. This is assumed to involve the high-order portion of a double-precision operand, as in the instruction sequence just given for addition. Thus if $Z_1 = \{0\}$, then $Z = \{0\}$ regardless of the setting of Z_2. Only if both portions of the double-precision value are zero will Z be set to {1}. In the example of the 64-bit number, $Z = \{0\}$ indicates that the result is nonzero when the value is computed using the extended instructions.

A double-precision integer can be written in positional notation as

$$(b_{2m-1}b_{2m-2}\ldots b_m b_{m-1}\ldots b_0)$$

where the digits $b_0 b_1 \ldots b_{m-1}$ represent the single-precision length. Two double-precision operands N_1 and N_2 can be written as

$$N_1 = N_{1U} + \text{N}_{1L}$$

and

$$N_2 = N_{2U} + N_{2L}$$

where N_{iL} refers to digits 0 through $m - 1$ and N_{iU} refers to the digits m through $2m - 1$, with $i = 1$ or 2. This notation will be used, when it is necessary, to distinguish the lower-precision from the upper-precision portions of a value.

7.4.1 Addition and Subtraction

The sequences of instructions to perform double-precision addition or subtraction require that the operation ADD be followed by ADDX or SUB be followed by SUBX. For addition, any carry generated from the ADD of the lower portion is indicated by both the C and the X condition code bits. The upper sum is then computed by ADDX, which adds the X bit into the result. A carry generated when the ADDX instruction executes indicates an unsigned result which is too large for the double-precision representation. If signed integers are being represented, an overflow condition is indicated by the condition code bit $V = \{1\}$.

When double-precision integers are subtracted, any borrow required by the low-order subtraction is indicated by the X bit. This is subtracted from the difference of the high-order values. A high-order out-of-range condition is indicated after SUBX executes by C = {1} for unsigned integers or V = {1} if signed integers were subtracted.

The sequence

NEG
NEGX

performs negation of a double-precision integer when NEG operates on the lower-precision portion and NEGX on the upper-precision portion. An overflow indication (V = {1}) occurs if the most negative integer is negated.

Example 7.5

Examples of multiple-precision operations are shown in Figure 7.7. For simplicity the single-precision lengths are eight binary digits. The states of the relevant condition codes are also shown after each portion of the multiple-precision operation. In each case, the lower 8 bits of the operands are treated first, and this is followed by the extended instruction operating on the upper 8 bits.

Example 7.6

The subroutine shown in Figure 7.8 adds two columns or vectors of N unsigned integers element by element. If X[i] represents the locations of the ith element in the first array and Y[i] is the corresponding element in the second, the operation is

$$(Y[i]) \leftarrow (X[i]) + (Y[i])$$

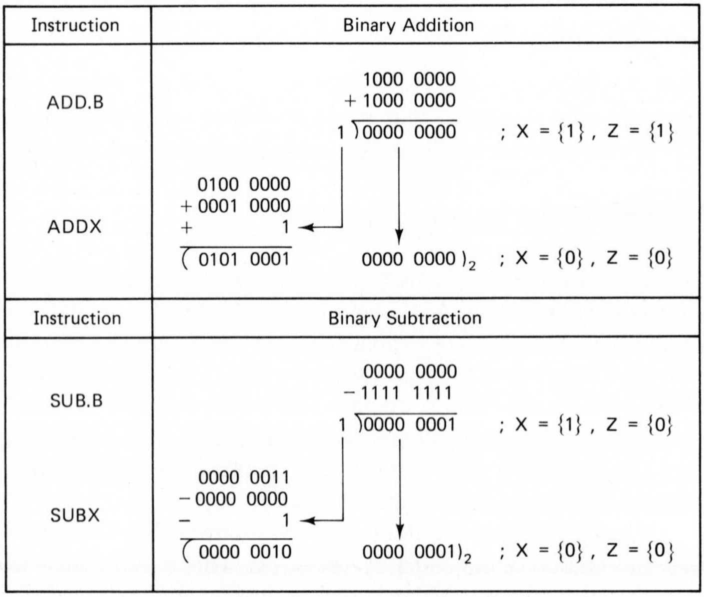

Instruction	Binary Addition
ADD.B	1000 0000 + 1000 0000 1)0000 0000 ; X = {1}, Z = {1}
ADDX	0100 0000 + 0001 0000 + 1 ◄──┘ (0101 0001 0000 0000)₂ ; X = {0}, Z = {0}
Instruction	Binary Subtraction
SUB.B	0000 0000 − 1111 1111 1)0000 0001 ; X = {1}, Z = {0}
SUBX	0000 0011 − 0000 0000 − 1 ◄──┘ (0000 0010 0000 0001)₂ ; X = {0}, Z = {0}

Figure 7.7 Multiple-precision operations.

```
MC68000 ASM REV= 1.4 - COPYRIGHT BY MOTOROLA 1978          PAGE  1


  1                                    LLEN    100
  2         00001000                   ORG     $1000
  3                           *
  4                           * ADD TWO SERIES OF 64-BIT NUMBERS
  5                           *   Y(I) <-- Y(I) + X(I)    FOR I = 1,N
  6                           *
  7                           * INPUTS :  (A1.L) = LAST ADDRESS OF FIRST ARRAY+4
  8                           *           (A2.L) = LAST ADDRESS OF SECOND ARRAY+4
  9                           *           (A3.L) = ADDRESS OF LAST ELEMENT IN
 10                           *                    SECOND ARRAY   (ADDRESS OF Y(N))
 11                           *
 12                           * OUTPUTS:  (A2.L) = ADDRESS OF SUMS
 13                           *           (D1.B) = 0 : ERROR DETECTED
 14                           *                    NOT 0 : SUCCESSFUL
 15                           *
 16                           * NOTES:
 17                           *  1.  64-BIT NUMBERS ARE STORED THIS WAY:
 18                           *
 19                           *      XN [63:32]
 20                           *      XN [31:0]      FIRST LONGWORD ADDRESS
 21                           *      .
 22                           *      .
 23                           *      .
 24                           *      X1 [63:32]
 25                           *      X1 [31:0]      LAST LONGWORD ADDRESS
 26                           *
 27                           *  2.  A1 AND A2 POINT TO X1+4
 28                           *      A3 POINTS TO XN [63:32]
 29                           *
 30 001000 48E78060  SERIES   MOVEM.L D0/A1-A2,-(SP)     ;SAVE REGISTERS
 31 001004 4201               CLR.B   D1                 ;SET STATUS TO FAILURE
 32 001006 2021      LOOP     MOVE.L  -(A1),D0
 33 001008 D1A2               ADD.L   D0,-(A2)
 34 00100A D589               ADDX.L  -(A1),-(A2)
 35 00100C 6500000A           BCS     ERROR              ;OVERFLOW
 36 001010 B7CA               CMPA.L  A2,A3              ;IF NOT LAST NUMBER
 37 001012 63F2               BLS     LOOP               ;THEN CONTINUE
 38                  *                                    ELSE FINISHED
 39 001014 123CFFFF           MOVE.B  #-1,D1             ;SET STATUS TO SUCCESS
 40 001018 4CDF0601  ERROR    MOVEM.L (SP)+,D0/A1-A2     ;RESTORE REGISTERS
 41 00101C 4E75               RTS
 42                           END

****** TOTAL ERRORS   0--   0


SYMBOL TABLE - APPROX 1199 SYMBOL ENTRIES LEFT

ERROR      001018 LOOP       001006 SERIES      001000
```

Figure 7.8 Multiple-precision addition program.

with $i = 1, 2, \ldots, N$. In memory, each 64-bit integer is stored with the least significant 32 bits at the *higher* address of two longword locations. The values are stored with the last element, X[N] or Y[N], at the lowest memory address and each array requires $2N$ longword locations or $8N$ bytes. This storage scheme takes advantage of the predecrement addressing capability of the MC68000 using extended instructions.

When the subroutine is entered, A1 and A2 should point to the next longword location following the first and second array, respectively. Address register A3 must contain the address of the last element in the second array (i.e., it should point to Y[N]).

If no overflow occurs, the additions continue until (A2) = (A3) to indicate the location of the last value to be added. The Compare Address (CMPA) instruction might change the C condition code but leaves X unaffected. When the two addresses are equal, the branch higher test is FALSE and the loop is terminated. In programs where the state of the X bit must be preserved but the C bit is used for conditional tests, having separate C and X bits is an advantage since the X bit does not have to be saved before the compare operations.

7.4.2 Multiplication

The MC68000 instructions MULU and MULS form a 32-bit product when two 16-bit numbers are multiplied. In order to multiply 32-bit operands to yield a 64-bit product, the multiply instruction can be used repeatedly to form partial products. These partial products are added together to produce the result. For example, consider the multiplication

$$(x + y) \times (w + z) = x \times w + y \times w + x \times z + y \times z$$

which requires four multiplications and four additions. Double-precision multiplication is similar in theory if y and z represent the lower-precision values of the operands and x and w the upper. In machine computation, however, the magnitude ranges of the different partial products is not the same and this must be taken into account. The appropriate calculation can be determined for unsigned numbers by writing the double-precision operand in the form

$$N = N_U \times 2^m + N_L$$

This is a $2m$ digit number in which N_U and N_L are the m-digit integers formed by the upper and lower portions, respectively. The product of two double-precision integers N_1 and N_2 becomes

$$N_1 \times N_2 = 2^{2m} \times (N_{2U} \times N_{1U}) + 2^m \times (N_{2L} \times N_{1U} + N_{2U} \times N_{1L}) + N_{2L} N_{1L}$$

The total length of the product is $4m$ digits and each partial product has $2m$ digits. The machine algorithm that performs the multiplication operation must align the partial products properly before adding them in the same manner that multiplication by hand is achieved. For example, multiplying 1201 times 1501 involves four partial products. Each product after the first must be shifted left by one decimal place. The MC68000 instructions for shifting (discussed in Chapter 8) can be used to align the partial results, or the SWAP instruction can be used, as shown in Example 7.8.

When multiple-precision signed integers are multiplied, the scheme just described for unsigned integers fails if one or both of the operands to be multiplied is negative. A mathematical investigation using the two's-complement representation as described in Chapter 3 yields an algorithm that is suitable for this case. Several references in the Further Reading section at the end of this chapter discuss the approach. An alternative approach is to change the sign of (negate) any negative operands and

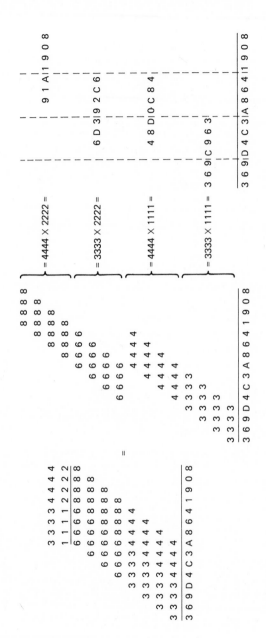

Figure 7.9 32-bit multiply example.

Note: All values are hexadecimal.

```
MC68000 ASM REV= 1.4  -  COPYRIGHT BY MOTOROLA 1978                    PAGE    1

             1                          LLEN    120
             2           00001000       ORG     $1000
             3                  *
             4                  *  32 X 32 BIT MULTIPLY
             5                  *
             6                  *  INPUT :  (D1.L) = FIRST VALUE
             7                  *           (D2.L) = SECOND VALUE
             8                  *
             9                  *  OUTPUT :  (D2/D1)[63:0] = RESULT OF D1 * D2
            10                  *
            11  001000 48E71C00  MULR    MOVEM.L D3/D4/D5,-(SP)      ;SAVE REGISTERS
            12                  *
            13  001004 2601              MOVE.L  D1,D3              ;COPY MULTIPLICAND
            14  001006 2801              MOVE.L  D1,D4
            15  001008 2A02              MOVE.L  D2,D5              ;COPY MULTIPLIER
            16  00100A 4844              SWAP    D4
            17  00100C 4845              SWAP    D5
            18                  *
            19  00100E C2C2              MULU    D2,D1              ;PARTIAL 1 :  NUM1[15:0]  * NUM2[15:0]
            20  001010 C4C4              MULU    D4,D2              ;PARTIAL 2 :  NUM1[31:16] * NUM2[15:0]
            21  001012 C6C5              MULU    D5,D3              ;PARTIAL 3 :  NUM2[31:16] * NUM1[15:0]
            22  001014 C8C5              MULU    D5,D4              ;PARTIAL 4 :  NUM2[31:16] * NUM1[31:16]
            23                  *
            24  001016 4841              SWAP    D1                 ;
            25  001018 D242              ADD.W   D2,D1
            26  00101A 4285              CLR.L   D5
            27  00101C D985              ADDX.L  D5,D4              ;CARRY 1
            28  00101E D243              ADD.W   D3,D1
            29  001020 D985              ADDX.L  D5,D4              ;CARRY 2
            30  001022 4841              SWAP    D1
            31                  *
            32  001024 4242              CLR.W   D2
            33  001026 4243              CLR.W   D3
            34  001028 4842              SWAP    D2
            35  00102A 4843              SWAP    D3
            36  00102C D483              ADD.L   D3,D2
            37  00102E D484              ADD.L   D4,D2
            38                  *
            39  001030 4CDF0038          MOVEM.L (SP)+,D3/D4/D5
            40  001034 4E75              RTS
            41                          END

****** TOTAL ERRORS    0--    0

SYMBOL TABLE - APPROX 1201 SYMBOL ENTRIES LEFT

MULR     001000
```

Figure 7.10 Double-precision multiply routine.

correct the sign after peforming unsigned multiplication. The program to accomplish this is left as an exercise.

Example 7.7

Figure 7.9 shows the multiplication of two 32-bit integers in hexadecimal, which produces a 64-bit result. The partial sums are shown aligned as they must be for computer implementation of the algorithm.

Example 7.8

The subroutine shown in Figure 7.10 multiplies

$$(D1) \times (D2)$$

as 32-bit unsigned integers and returns a 64-bit product in (D2)/(D1). Here D2 holds the upper 32 bits and D1 the lower 32 bits. Two observations must be noted to understand the program fully. First, the unsigned multiply instruction MULU and the ADD.W instruction operate only on the low-order 16 bits of the registers used as operands. Thus the SWAP instruction is required to move the high-order 16 bits into the low-order portion of a register, where they can be multiplied or added. Second, a diagram showing the contents of the registers involved during execution of the program is almost manadatory to create such a program. The version shown here is from Motorola; however, comments were added.

EXERCISES

7.4.1 Determine the range of unsigned integers, fractions, and signed integers for a 64-bit representation. Express the answers as powers of 10.

7.4.2. Modify the double-precision multiplication routine to multiply two's-complement integers. (Determine the sign of the result based on the signs of the factors; then perform the multiplication on the absolute values.)

7.5 DECIMAL ARITHMETIC

The MC68000 provides instructions for addition, subtraction, and negation of decimal values represented in binary-coded decimal (BCD). This code was defined in Chapter 3 and this section applies many of the mathematical principles presented there. The three instructions for BCD arithmetic are defined in Table 7.6. The instructions allow addition, subtraction, and negation of BCD values. For each instruction the operand length is 8 bits, which represents two BCD digits. For example, the Add Decimal with Extend (ABCD) instruction

ABCD   D1,D2

performs decimal addition between byte-length operands. The operation is

$$(D2)[7:0] \leftarrow (D1)[7:0] + (D2)[7:0] + X$$

TABLE 7.6 DECIMAL ARITHMETIC INSTRUCTIONS

Syntax	Operation
Addition	
ABCD \<Dm\>,\<Dn\>	(Dn)[7:0] ← (Dn)[7:0] + (Dm)[7:0] + X
ABCD −(Am),−(An)	(dest) ← (dest) + (src) + X
Subtraction	
SBCD \<Dm\>,\<Dn\>	(Dn)[7:0] ← (Dn)[7:0] − (Dm)[7:0] − X
SBCD −(Am),−(An)	(dest) ← (dest) − (src) − X
Negation	
NBCD \<EA\>	(EA) ← 0 − (EA) − X

Notes:

1. All operations perform decimal arithmetic on two BCD digits.
2. N and V condition code bits are undefined.
3. C is set if a decimal carry (or borrow) occurs.
4. Z is cleared if the result is nonzero; otherwise it is unchanged.

Notice that this instruction adds the value of the X condition code bit into the sum to facilitate multiple-precision additions. However, the X bit must be cleared before the first ABCD is executed. After the addition operation, X = {1} indicates that a decimal carry occurred because the sum was greater than 99. The Z bit is cleared if the sum is not zero. Otherwise, it is unchanged to allow tests for zero to be performed after multiple-precision operations. The Subtract Decimal with Extend (SBCD) operates similarly, but the source operand and the value of the X bit are both subtracted from the destination value.

The operations of the BCD instructions are similar to those for extended-precision arithmetic as far as the use of condition code bits is concerned. The exception lies in the fact that the N and V bits are not defined for BCD operations. Moreover, the BCD instructions restrict the operand length to 8 bits and the addressing modes to data register direct or predecrement for BCD addition and subtraction. The instruction Negate Decimal with Extend (NBCD) forms the ten's complement of a two-digit operand when X = {0} before the operation. If X = {1}, NBCD forms the nine's complement. It allows any data-alterable addressing mode for the effective address in the symbolic form

NBCD \<EA\>

This excludes an operand in an address register or one addressed relative to the program counter.

Example 7.9

Table 7.7 shows the effect of decimal addition and subtraction for various operands and condition code settings. Addition of the values 65 and 17 yields 82 if the X bit is cleared or 83 if it is set. Adding 42 and 77 yields a result of 19 with an indication of a carry. The proper value of 119 would require an additional BCD digit. The incorrect nonzero indication that results for the addition of 0 and 0 without the Z bit set is also shown.

Subtraction of two BCD digits yields a correct result for unsigned numbers in the range 0 to 99 or signed numbers between -10 and $+9$. The subtraction of the unsigned numbers 77 minus 32 yields 45 as expected. But 17 minus 65 leaves the ten's-complement result of -48 (52) with a borrow indication. If the X bit is set before the operation, the nine's complement of -48 (51) results when 65 is subtracted from 17. When two equal values are subtracted with the X bit set, the result is 99 or the nine's complement of 0 with a borrow indication.

Multiple-precision decimal arithmetic.   Operations on BCD numbers with more than two digits are normally performed on operands held in memory rather than in a register. This is because the ABCD and SBCD instructions can operate only on the low-order byte of a data register. If a decimal string of digits is held in a data register, the rotate instructions introduced in Chapter 8 would be needed to shift the digits being manipulated to the low-order byte. This is avoided by performing memory-to-memory operations using predecrement addressing. For example, the instruction

        ABCD $-(A1),-(A2)$

first decrements (A1) by 1 and then (A2) by 1. Then the two digits in the addressed byte locations plus the X bit value are added into the destination location addressed by A2. To perform operations on more-than-two-digit numbers, a decimal string is stored

TABLE 7.7   EXAMPLE OF BCD OPERATIONS

(a) Addition: ABCD   (src), (dest)

Before execution				After execution		
(src)	(dest)	X	Z	(dest)	X	Z
65	17	0	1	82	0	0
65	17	1	1	83	0	0
42	77	0	0	19	1	0
0	0	0	0	00	0	0

(b) Subtraction: SBCD   (src), (dest)

Before execution			After execution	
(src)	(dest)	X	(dest)	X
32	77	0	45	0
65	17	0	52	1
65	17	1	51	1
35	35	1	99	1

Note: The contents of the source and destination locations are decimal values.

in memory with the least significant two digits at the highest byte address. Thus the decimal number 123456 at location $1000 would be stored as follows:

(1000) = 12
(1001) = 34
(1002) = 56

An addition or subtraction of this value should start with the beginning address initialized at $1003 when the predecrement modes are used.

Example 7.10

The program in Figure 7.11 adds two six-digit BCD integers. Initially, the addresses of the operands as just described are stored in A1 and A2. The sum is left in the location addressed by A2. The X bit must be cleared and the Z bit must be set before the addition begins. If the result is nonzero, the Z bit will be cleared by the addition. If the integers are restricted to positive values, the C bit indicates an overflow condition after the additions.

```
MC68000 ASM REV= 1.4 - COPYRIGHT BY MOTOROLA 1978                PAGE   1


  1                                LLEN     100
  2         00001000               ORG      $1000
  3                         *
  4                         * BCD ADDITION
  5                         *
  6                         * INPUTS :   (A1.L) = ADDRESS OF 6-DIGIT BCD NUMBER
  7                         *            (A2.L) = ADDRESS OF 6-DIGIT BCD NUMBER
  8                         *
  9                         * OUTPUTS :  (A2.L) = ADDRESS OF 6-DIGIT BCD RESULT
 10                         *
 11                         * NOTES:
 12                         *   1.  BCD NUMBERS ARE STORED 2 DIGITS/BYTE
 13                         *       BCD [6:5]
 14                         *       BCD [4:3]
 15                         *       BCD [2:1]
 16                         *
 17                         *   2.  ADDRESS REGISTERS POINT TO BCD [2:1] + 1
 18                         *       SO THAT PREDECREMENT ADDRESSING CAN BE
 19                         *       USED
 20                         *
 21 001000 48E70060         ADDBCD   MOVEM.L A1/A2,-(SP)           ;SAVE REGISTERS
 22 001004 44FC0004                  MOVE.W  #4,CCR                ;CLEAR X BIT , SET Z BIT
 23 001008 C509                      ABCD    -(A1),-(A2)           ;ADD THE BCD NUMBERS
 24 00100A C509                      ABCD    -(A1),-(A2)
 25 00100C C509                      ABCD    -(A1),-(A2)
 26 00100E 4CDF0600                  MOVEM.L (SP)+,A1/A2           ;RESTORE REGISTERS
 27 001012 4E75                      RTS
 28                                  END

****** TOTAL ERRORS   0--   0


SYMBOL TABLE - APPROX 1201 SYMBOL ENTRIES LEFT

ADDBCD      001000
```

Figure 7.11 Six-digit BCD addition.

EXERCISES

7.5.1. Express the following BCD numbers in binary using 4 digits. Show the machine representation using ten's-complement notation.

    (a) $+37$

    (b) -37

    (c) -1319

7.5.2. Using the MC68000 formats, perform the following operations on BCD integers.

    (a) $1754 - 1319$

    (b) $9375 + 3470$

    How are the results in part (b) interpreted when only four-digit unsigned integers are allowed?

7.5.3. Perform the addition 127 plus 299 using binary arithmetic but with the values in BCD notation. Adjust the binary result by adding "6" to any digit greater than 9 and add the carry to the next-higher digit. (The Motorola MC68000 BCD instructions perform this decimal adjustment automatically.)

7.5.4. Write a subroutine to add or subtract two BCD integers with up to eight digits each. Signed integers are represented in ten's-complement notation. What is the decimal range of the valid integers? What is the decimal range of their sum or difference?

7.5.5 Write a subroutine to multiply two four-digit positive BCD numbers in MC68000 format. The routine might perform multiplication by repeated addition, or an algorithm can be devised to perform decimal multiplication.

7.6 CONVERSIONS BETWEEN ASCII, BINARY, AND BCD

The standard representations for the MC68000 include binary and BCD for integers and ASCII for characters. For input and output ASCII is generally the code used for data being transferred between the computer system and peripheral devices such as line printers or CRT terminals. Conversions between these representations are therefore frequently required since the arithmetic processing requires binary or BCD values in memory.

    Figure 7.12(a) shows the typical steps to convert a decimal number in ASCII to a binary representation. The ASCII characters for the decimal digits are first converted to binary numbers in the range 0–9. The 4 bits for each digit are also the BCD value in memory. Then the string of BCD digits is converted to a binary number. This conversion takes into account the positional value of each BCD digit. For example, the ASCII string '123' as an input value is stored in memory as $31, $32, and $33. This is converted to three BCD digits, 1, 2, and 3, and then to the binary value 0111 1011.

    The output of binary values that are to be printed as decimal numbers requires the opposite conversion from binary to BCD and then to ASCII. Of course, the binary value in memory could be printed in binary, hexadecimal, or another code. The binary

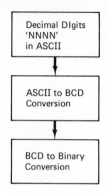

(a) Conversion of Input Data

Meaning	Binary Representation in Memory	To Convert to ASCII	ASCII in Memory
Decimal Digits 0–9 (BCD)	0000 0000 0000 0001 ⋮ 0000 1001	Add 0011 0000₂ ($30)	$30–$39
Hexadecimal Digits 0–9	0000 0000 0000 0001 ⋮ 0000 1001	Add $30	$30–$39
Hexadecimal Digits A–F	0000 1010 0000 1011 ⋮ 0000 1111	Add $37	$41–$46

(b) Decimal or Hexadecimal to ASCII for Output

Figure 7.12   Conversions of data values.

number in the input example just given has the hexadecimal value 7B. This could be output in ASCII as $37, $42.

The examples in this subsection use a table-lookup scheme to convert a hexadecimal digit to ASCII or BCD and a subroutine to convert a string of BCD digits to binary. The table in Figure 7.12(b) shows the ASCII equivalents for decimal and hexadecimal digits.

Example 7.11

Figure 7.13 shows a subroutine to determine the ASCII or BCD value of a hexadecimal digit stored in the low-order 4 bits of D1. If (D2) [7:0] contains a 0 upon entry, the ASCII code is placed in the low-order byte of D2. The value is found by addressing the table ASCTAB and indexing based on the hexadecimal digit in D1. If (D2) [7:0] is 1 upon entry, the BCD digit corresponding to the hexadecimal digit is placed in D2. The value is obtained from the table BCDTAB.

Example 7.12

If a string of decimal digits is stored as $D_{n-1}D_{n-2}\cdots D_0$ in separate bytes in memory, the conversion to binary is easily accomplished since the numerical value is

$$(\cdots(D_{n-1} \times 10 + D_{n-2}) \times 10 + \cdots + D_1 \times 10) + D_0$$

as explained in Chapter 3. The binary sum is formed by computing the terms in parentheses using binary arithmetic and adding each term into the total. Figure 7.14 shows a subroutine to accomplish this conversion. On entry, the decimal digits are assumed to be stored right-justified in the byte locations addressed by Al. If no out-of-range condition occurs, the binary value is returned in D1.

```
MC68000 ASM REV= 1.4 - COPYRIGHT BY MOTOROLA 1978              PAGE  1


 1                              LLEN    100
 2          00001000            ORG     $1000
 3                          *
 4                          * HEXADECIMAL TO BCD/ASCII
 5                          *
 6                          * INPUT :   (D2.B) = 0 : ASCII REQUESTED
 7                          *                   NOT 0 :  BCD REQUESTED
 8                          *           (D1.W) = HEXADECIMAL DIGIT TO CONVERT
 9                          *
10                          * OUTPUT :  (D2.B) = BCD OR ASCII
11                          *
12                          *
13                          *
14 001000 2F09      CONVERT  MOVE.L  A1,-(SP)           ;SAVE REGISTER
15 001002 227C0000101C       MOVE.L  #ASCTAB,A1         ;ASSUME ASCII WAS REQUESTED
16 001008 4A02               TST.B   D2                 ;CHECK REQUEST
17 00100A 67000008           BEQ     INDEX              ; IF BCD REQUESTED
18 00100E 227C0000102C       MOVE.L  #BCDTAB,A1         ;THEN CHANGE TO BCD TABLE
19                          *
20 001014 14311000   INDEX    MOVE.B  0(A1,D1.W),D2     ;LOOK UP VALUE
21 001018 225F               MOVE.L  (SP)+,A1           ;RESTORE REGISTERS
22 00101A 4E75               RTS
23 00101C 30        ASCTAB   DC.B    '0123456789ABCDEF'
24 00102C 00        BCDTAB   DC.B    0,1,2,3,4,5,6
25 001033 07                 DC.B    7,8,9,$10,$11
26 001038 12                 DC.B    $12,$13,$14,$15
27                          END

****** TOTAL ERRORS   0--   0


SYMBOL TABLE - APPROX 1198 SYMBOL ENTRIES LEFT

ASCTAB     00101C BCDTAB     00102C CONVERT     001000 INDEX      001014
```

Figure 7.13 Table lookup for hexadecimal conversion.

```
MC68000 ASM REV= 1.4 - COPYRIGHT BY MOTOROLA 1978              PAGE   1

  1                               LLEN    100
  2        00001000               ORG     $1000
  3                          *
  4                          * BCD TO BINARY
  5                          *
  6                          * INPUTS :  (D2.W) = NUMBER OF DIGITS IN BCD NUMBER
  7                          *           (A1.L) = ADDRESS OF THE MOST SIGNIFICANT
  8                          *                         BCD DIGIT
  9                          *
 10                          * OUTPUTS : (D1.L) = BINARY VALUE
 11                          *           (D4.W) = 0 :  ERROR DETECTED
 12                          *                    NOT 0 :   SUCCESSFUL
 13                          *
 14                          * NOTES:
 15                          *  1.  BCD DIGITS ARE STORED ONE/BYTE AND ARE
 16                          *       VALID
 17                          *  2.  ONLY POSITIVE BCD NUMBERS ARE ALLOWED
 18                          *
 19                          *
 20                          *
 21 001000 48E73040  BCDBN   MOVEM.L D2/D3/A1,-(SP)        ;SAVE REGISTERS
 22 001004 4281              CLR.L   D1                    ;VALUE := 0
 23 001006 4244              CLR.W   D4                    ;SET DEFAULT TO ERROR
 24 001008 4A42              TST.W   D2                    ;IF LENGTH IS ZERO
 25 00100A 67000024          BEQ     DONE                  ; THEN EXIT WITH ERROR
 26                     *
 27 00100E D219      LOOP    ADD.B   (A1)+,D1              ;ADD TO VALUE
 28 001010 5342              SUBQ.W  #1,D2                 ;DECREMENT COUNTER
 29 001012 67000018          BEQ     SUCCESS               ; IF FINISHED , EXIT
 30                     *
 31 001016 E389              LSL.L   #1,D1                 ;MULTIPLY BY TWO
 32 001018 6B000016          BMI     DONE                  ; ON OVERFLOW , EXIT
 33                     *
 34 00101C 2601              MOVE.L  D1,D3                 ;SAVE THE RESULT OF MULTIPLY
 35 00101E E589              LSL.L   #2,D1                 ;MULTIPLY BY FOUR (VALUE * 8)
 36 001020 6B00000E          BMI     DONE                  ; ON OVERFLOW , EXIT
 37                     *
 38 001024 D283              ADD.L   D3,D1                 ;VALUE = VALUE * 10
 39 001026 6B000008          BMI     DONE                  ; ON OVERFLOW , EXIT
 40                     *
 41 00102A 60E2              BRA     LOOP                  ;PROCESS NEXT DIGIT
 42 00102C 383C0001  SUCCESS MOVE.W  #1,D4                 ;SET STATUS TO SUCCESS
 43 001030 4CDF020C  DONE    MOVEM.L (SP)+,D2/D3/A1        ;RESTORE REGISTERS
 44 001034 4E75              RTS
 45                          END

****** TOTAL ERRORS   0--   0


SYMBOL TABLE - APPROX 1198 SYMBOL ENTRIES LEFT

BCDBN      001000 DONE       001030 LOOP       00100E SUCCESS      00102C
```

Figure 7.14   BCD-to-binary conversion.

EXERCISES

7.6.1. Write a subroutine to convert an ASCII string to signed binary representation when the range of the input can be up to eight decimal digits plus a sign.

7.6.2 Write a subroutine to convert a string of binary digits to ASCII.

7.6.3. To convert from binary to decimal, it is possible to follow the procedure shown in this section using the decimal expansion for the number to be converted. Repeatedly dividing the number by 10 will yield the decimal digits, as remainders, in ascending order. Write a subroutine to convert a 16-bit unsigned integer to the equivalent BCD value.

7.6.4. Write a routine to convert a string of ASCII digits to BCD when the input string contains a decimal point ($2E). Determine the number of digits and leave the scale factor in a register; that is, determine the number of decimal places and store the BCD number as an integer.

FURTHER READING

Knuth's volume on seminumerical algorithms contains a number of useful algorithms and other information for those doing sophisticated mathematical programming. Grappel lists a 32-bit divide routine for the MC68000 in his article. A number of such routines are available and Motorola representatives usually have a repertoire for customers. The textbook by Stein and Monro presents the rigorous basis for machine arithmetic.

GRAPPEL, ROBERT D., "68000 Routine Divides 32-Bit Numbers," *EDN,* **26**, No. 5 (March 4, 1981), 161–162.

KNUTH, DONALD E., *The Art of Computer Programming,* Vol. 2: *Seminumerical Algorithms,* Reading, Mass.: Addison-Wesley, 1968.

STEIN, MARVIN L., and WILLIAM D. MONRO, *Introduction to Machine Arithmetic,* Reading, Mass.: Addison-Wesley, 1971.

8

Logical and Bit Operations

This chapter introduces three new categories of MC68000 instructions: logical instructions, shift and rotate instructions, and bit-manipulation instructions. The *logical operations* treat an operand as a collection of separate logical variables. This category includes the instructions AND, OR, EOR (Exclusive OR), and NOT. The second category includes the instructions ASL, ASR, LSL, and LSR to *shift* the bits within an operand. Both arithmetic shifts and logical shifts are provided. The instructions ROL, ROR, ROXL, and ROXR rotate the bits of an operand in a cyclic fashion.

Instructions for *bit manipulation* form a separate category of instructions for the MC68000. Separate instructions are provided to test, set to {1}, clear, and change an individual bit within an operand. In order, they have the mnemonics BTST, BSET, BCLR, and BCHG. Two other instructions show the result of a conditional test by modifying an indicator variable called a flag. They are the Scc (Set According to Condition) and the TAS (Test and Set) instructions.

8.1 LOGICAL OPERATIONS

In some applications, it is convenient to treat each bit in an operand as an individual logical variable. The condition code register, for example, contains five independent bits and the bits may be tested singly. Each logical variable has only two possible states, which are defined variously according to the application as TRUE or FALSE, ON or OFF, or {1} or {0}, among other possibilities. Therefore, the m-bit computer word holds m logical variables. In the MC68000, logical instructions may operate on 8, 16, or 32 such variables simultaneously.

If x and y are considered to be logical variables, the truth tables of Table 8.1 define the operations that correspond to MC68000 logical arithmetic. A collection of m logical variables is written in positional notation

$$(x_{m-1} x_{m-2} \cdots x_0)$$

as it would be stored in an m-bit word. This is called an m-tuple of variables. For example, the MC68000 instruction

    NOT.W   X

will complement each bit of an operand containing 16 logical variables, in the memory location addressed by X. The other MC68000 instructions for logical operations perform their operation between the logical variables in the source location and those in the destination. The result is stored in the destination location. Thus the operation

    AND.W   D1,D2

leaves the results of the operation between 16 variables in D1 and 16 variables in D2 in the low-order word of D2. The operation performed is

    (D2)[15:0]←(D2)[15:0] AND (D1)[15:0]

The logical instructions are listed in Table 8.2, which shows the assembler syntax and addressing modes for each instruction. The instructions with suffix "I" allow only an immediate value for the source operand. None of the instructions operate on address registers. Also, no memory-to-memory operations are possible with the AND, EOR, and OR instructions. The condition code bits C and V are always cleared after any logical operation and the N and Z bits are set according to the result. The Z bit would be set to {1} if the result is all zeros. The N bit is set to {1} if the most significant bit of the result is a {1}.

The AND and OR instructions allow the same addressing modes for their operands. For either instruction, if the destination is a data register, the source operand is addressed by any data mode. This allows all the source addressing modes except address register direct addressing. Alternatively, if Dn contains the source operand, the

TABLE 8.1 RESULTS OF LOGICAL OPERATIONS

x	y	NOT x	x AND y	x OR y	x EOR y
0	0	1	0	0	0
0	1	1	0	1	1
1	0	0	0	1	1
1	1	0	1	1	0

Note: x and y are logical variables. The results for each operation are defined by the "truth" table for the operation. For example, (x OR y) is true or {1} if either x or y or both is {1}.

TABLE 8.2 INSTRUCTIONS FOR LOGICAL OPERATIONS

Syntax	Addressing modes	
	Source	Destination
Logical AND		
AND.<l> <EA>,<Dn>	Data	<Dn>
AND.<l> <Dn>,<EA>	<Dn>	Memory alterable
ANDI.<l> #<d>,<EA>	<d>	Data alterable
Logical OR		
OR.<l> <EA>,<Dn>	Data	<Dn>
OR.<l> <Dn>,<EA>	<Dn>	Memory alterable
ORI.<l> #<d>,<EA>	<d>	Data alterable
Exclusive OR		
EOR.<l> <Dn>,<EA>	<Dn>	Data alterable
EORI.<l># <d>,<EA>	<d>	Data alterable
NOT		
NOT.<l> <EA>	—	Data alterable

Notes:

1. <l> denotes B, W, or L.
2. <d> is an 8-, 16-, or 32-bit logical variable as an immediate value.
3. The condition code bits C and V are always cleared; N and Z are set according to the result.
4. The destination location is modified according to the result.

destination must be addressed by a memory-alterable mode. Thus only register direct and program counter relative addressing are prohibited for the destination.

The ANDI and ORI instructions use an immediate value as the source operand and any data-alterable location for the destination. For example, the instruction

    ANDI.W   #$000F,D1

clears all but the low-order 4 bits of D1. This instruction might be used to isolate a single BCD digit for subsequent mathematical calculations, for example. If the operand is held in memory, it may be addressed by all the addressing modes except PC relative.

The EOR (Exclusive OR) instruction has slightly different addressing restrictions not conforming to the requirements for AND and OR. It requires a data register for the source location. Also, the destination must be a data-alterable location, as was the case for both ANDI and ORI. The immediate form, EORI, has the same addressing requirements for the destination operand. It is used to perform the Exclusive OR between an immediate value and an operand in either a data register or in memory. Clearly, the regularity in addressing of most MC68000 instructions is missing among its logical instructions to some extent.

The NOT instruction complements each bit of an operand in a data register or in memory using any type of memory addressing except PC relative. The NOT can be interpreted as either forming the logical NOT, if the operand is composed of *m* logical variables, or the one's complement, if the operand is considered to be a number. The mathematical description of the one's-complement operation was given in Chapter 3.

System control using logical instructions.   The immediate forms of ANDI, EORI, and ORI can reference the status register or the condition code register[1] as the destination operand. These forms are usually used for system control and will be discussed in Chapter 10. The reader is referred to that chapter for a complete discussion.

Example 8.1

Table 8.3 shows several examples of logical instructions operating on various operands. For simplicity, the examples limit the operand length to 8 bits and show only immediate-to-register or register-to-register operations. Before each instruction executes, the low-order byte of D1 contains the value {1101 0001}, which represents eight logical variables. Similarly, (D2) [7:0] = {1101 0101} initially.

The ANDI instruction, as used in the example, serves to "mask" or set to zero the low-order 4 bits of D1. The ORI instruction does the opposite by setting the designated bits (bits 0 and 1) to {1} and leaving the other bits in the destination unchanged. After either of these instructions execute, condition code bit N would be set to {1} in the examples shown.

The NOT instruction inverts the low-order 8 bits of D1. If the original value in D1 is interpreted as the decimal number −46 in 8-bit, one's-complement notation, the inversion produces +46, as expected.

The Exclusive OR (EOR) instruction causes a logical variable in the result to be set to {1} when the two variables in the corresponding bit positions of the operands are different. For example, if D1 contains the first reading of 8 status bits taken from an external device and D2 contains a second reading taken later, any change in status would be indicated by a nonzero result (Z = {0}) after the EOR operation. If the readings had been the same, the result would have been all zeros with Z = {1}. A conditional branch

---

[1] Condition code register (CCR) refers to the low-order byte of the status register (SR[7:0]).

TABLE 8.3 EXAMPLES OF LOGICAL OPERATIONS

Instruction	Operands	Result
ANDI.B #$F0,D1	{1111 0000} AND {1101 0001}	(D1)[7:0] = {1101 0000}
ORI.B #03,D1	{0000 0011} OR {1101 0001}	(D1)[7:0] = {1101 0011}
NOT.B D1	NOT {1101 0001}	(D1)[7:0] = {0010 1110}
EOR.B D1,D2	{1101 0001} EOR {1101 0101}	(D2)[7:0] = {0000 0100}

Note: (D1)[7:0] = {1101 0001} and (D2)[7:0] = {1101 0101} before each instruction executes.

TABLE 8.4   TRUTH TABLE FOR DECODER

Input		Output			
B	A	Y0	Y1	Y2	Y3
0	0	0	1	1	1
0	1	1	0	1	1
1	0	1	1	0	1
1	1	1	1	1	0

Notes:

Y0 = NOT (NOT A AND NOT B) = A OR B
Y1 = NOT (A AND NOT B) = NOT A OR B
Y2 = NOT (NOT A AND B) = A OR NOT B
Y3 = NOT (A AND B) = NOT A OR NOT B

instruction such as BEQ or BNE could be used after the EOR instruction to determine the subsequent program path.

Example 8.2

To illustrate the use of logical instructions with various addressing modes, this example implements the equations for a "two-line to four-line decoder" using MC68000 instructions. One of four possible output values is determined by the value of two input variables. The input variables are two logical variables, designated as A and B in the example. They are stored in memory in two consecutive bytes with B first and are addressed by (A1). The output is to be four variables designated Y0, Y1, Y2, and Y3 stored in four consecutive bytes addressed by (A2). All the logical variables are right-justified in their locations. That is, the variable {A} has the memory representation {0000 000A}. The truth table and the equations are shown in Table 8.4, which shows that only one output can be {0} for each pair of inputs. If A and B together are interpreted as a two-digit binary number, {BA}, then Yn = {0} when the value of the input is n, for n = 0, 1, 2, or 3. All the other output variables are {1}. Hence the output line corresponding to the value of the inputs is selected. In this case, the selected line is considered "TRUE" or "ON" when its value is {0}.

The subroutine in Figure 8.1 first transfers A and B to the low-order bytes of D0 and D1, respectively. The complement of each input is then formed in the low-order bit of another register. Each equation for Yn is coded in a straightforward way. The computed result is stored in memory using the appropriate displacement from the base address held in A2.

EXERCISES

8.1.1. Write a simple subroutine to convert ASCII values to BCD, and vice versa, using logical instructions. The conversion was discussed in Chapter 7.

MC68000 ASM REV= 1.4 - COPYRIGHT BY MOTOROLA 1978   PAGE   1

```
 1                              LLEN    100
 2          00001000            ORG     $1000
 3                        *
 4                        * 2 TO 4 LINE DECODER
 5                        * INPUT : (A1.L) = ADDRESS OF 2 BYTES CONTAINING LOGICAL VARIABLES
 6                        *         (A2.L) = ADDRESS OF 4 BYTES FOR DECODED VALUES
 7                        * OUTPUT : 4 BYTES DECODED INTO (A2)
 8                        *
 9                        * NOTE :  LOGICAL VARIABLES ARE STORED IN THE LS BIT OF THE BYTE
10                        *
11          00000000      A     EQU     0
12          00000001      B     EQU     1
13          00000000      Y0    EQU     0
14          00000001      Y1    EQU     1
15          00000002      Y2    EQU     2
16          00000003      Y3    EQU     3
17                        *
18  001000 48E7F800      DECODER MOVEM.L D0-D4,-(SP)         ;SAVE REGISTERS
19                        *
20  001004 10290000              MOVE.B  A(A1),D0            ;GET A
21  001008 12290001              MOVE.B  B(A1),D1            ;GET B
22                        *
23  00100C 1400                  MOVE.B  D0,D2
24  00100E 4602                  NOT.B   D2
25  001010 02020001              ANDI.B  #01,D2              ;COMPLEMENT OF A
26                        *
27  001014 1601                  MOVE.B  D1,D3
28  001016 4603                  NOT.B   D3
29  001018 02030001              ANDI.B  #01,D3              ;COMPLEMENT OF B
30                        *
31  00101C 1800                  MOVE.B  D0,D4
32  00101E 8801                  OR.B    D1,D4
33  001020 15440000              MOVE.B  D4,Y0(A2)           ;A .OR. B
34                        *
35  001024 1802                  MOVE.B  D2,D4
36  001026 8801                  OR.B    D1,D4
37  001028 15440001              MOVE.B  D4,Y1(A2)           ;NOT A .OR. B
38                        *
39  00102C 1800                  MOVE.B  D0,D4
40  00102E 8803                  OR.B    D3,D4
41  001030 15440002              MOVE.B  D4,Y2(A2)           ;A .OR. NOT B
42                        *
43  001034 8602                  OR.B    D2,D3
44  001036 15430003              MOVE.B  D3,Y3(A2)           ;NOT A .OR. NOT B
45                        *
46  00103A 4CDF001F              MOVEM.L (SP)+,D0-D4          ;RESTORE REGISTERS
47  00103E 4E75                  RTS
48                                END
```

****** TOTAL ERRORS   0--   0

SYMBOL TABLE - APPROX 1197 SYMBOL ENTRIES LEFT

```
A         000000 B          000001 DECODER   001000 Y0        000000
Y1        000001 Y2         000002 Y3        000003
```

Figure 8.1   Program for a two-line to four-line decoder.

8.1.2. Improve the decoder program used as an example in this section. Make the program more general to allow four-line to 16-line decoding.

8.1.3. Write a subroutine to exchange the contents of two *m*-bit words in memory using only the EOR instruction and appropriate data transfer instructions.

8.2 SHIFT AND ROTATE INSTRUCTIONS

The shift and rotate instructions of the MC68000 move the bits in an operand to the right or left a designated number of places. The three different possibilities provided include:

(a) Arithmetic shifts
(b) Logical shifts
(c) Rotates

Arithmetic shifts to the left in effect multiply a signed binary integer by a power of 2. Arithmetic right shifts accomplish division by powers of 2. Of course, the shifted number must be within a valid range or the result is in error. Logical shifts are used to shift an *m*-tuple of logical variables right or left. The rotate instructions cause bits shifted off one end of the *m*-tuple to reappear at the other end in a *cyclic* shift.

Figure 8.2 shows the operation of the arithmetic shifts (ASL, ASR), the logical shifts (LSL, LSR), and the rotate instructions (ROL, ROR). The rotate instructions have extended variations for shifting multiple-precision operands. The instructions

Instruction	Operand Size	Operation
ASL	8, 16, 32	X/C ← ← ← 0
ASR	8, 16, 32	→ → X/C
LSL	8, 16, 32	X/C ← ← ← 0
LSR	8, 16, 32	0 → → → X/C
ROL	8, 16, 32	C ← ←
ROR	8, 16, 32	→ → C
ROXL	8, 16, 32	C ← ← ← X ←
ROXR	8, 16, 32	X → → → C

Figure 8.2 Shift and rotate instructions. (Courtesy of Motorola, Inc.)

ROXL and ROXR include the X bit in the cyclic shift. The assembler language syntax for the instructions is presented in Table 8.5.

Three different formats are available to designate the shift count and the operand to be shifted. The count can be held in a register or specified as an immediate value for operands in a data register. A one-place shift of a word-length operand in memory is allowed. These are shown in Table 8.6. For example, the instruction

   LSR.W   D3,D2

shifts the 16-bit operand in the low-order word of D2 to the right by the number of places designated in D3. The number in D3 is treated as modulo 64, so shifts from 0 to 63 places are possible. Of course, after 16 logical shifts left or right in a word-length operand, the value left in the low-order word contains all zero bits. The instruction

   LSL.W   #5,D3

perform a left, logical shift of the low-order word of D3 by five places. An immediate shift length can range from 1 to 8. The third form of specifying operands allows a word-length operand in memory to be shifted or rotated one place at a time. Any op-

TABLE 8.5   ASSEMBLY LANGUAGE SYNTAX FOR SHIFT
AND ROTATE INSTRUCTIONS

Arithmetic shift left	Arithmetic shift right
ASL.<l> <Dm>,<Dn>	ASR.<l> <Dm>,<Dn>
ASL.<l> #<d>,<Dn>	ASR.<l> #<d>,<Dn>
ASL <EA>	ASR <EA>
Logical shift left	Logical shift right
LSL.<l> <Dm>,<Dn>	LSR.<l> <Dm>,<Dn>
LSL.<l> #<d>,<Dn>	LSR.<l> #<d>,<Dn>
LSL <EA>	LSR <EA>
Rotate left	Rotate right
ROL.<l> <Dm>,<Dn>	ROR.<l> <Dm>,<Dn>
ROL.<l> #<d>,<Dn>	ROR.<l> #<d>,<Dn>
ROL <EA>	ROR <EA>

Notes:

1. <l> denotes B, W, or L when <Dn> is the destination; <Dm> or #<d> specifies the shift count.

2. When the destination is a memory location, only word-length operands are allowed for <EA>.

3. Only memory-alterable addressing modes are allowed for <EA>, excluding register direct and PC relative addresses.

4. ROXL and ROXR have the same syntax as the rotate instructions.

5. Condition code bits N and Z are set according to the result; V is cleared except by ASL.

TABLE 8.6   OPERAND FORMATS FOR SHIFTS AND ROTATE

Operand format	Shift count	Destination
$<Dm>,<Dn>$	(Dm); range 0–63	(Dn)[l]
$\#<d>,<Dn>$	$\#<d>$; range 1–8	(Dn)[l]
$<EA>$	1	(EA)[15:0]

Notes:

1. $<l>$ in B, W, or L for register operands.
2. [l] indicates corresponding bits in the operation.
3. $<EA>$ is a memory-alterable address.
4. A shift count of zero in Dm has a special meaning.

erand referenced by a memory-alterable addressing mode may be manipulated. For example, the instruction

> ASR   (A2)

performs a single-place, right arithmetic shift on the 16-bit operand addressed by A2.

A shift instruction using the shift count held in the data register performs *dynamic shifting* since the shift count may be changed under program control. A shift count of zero will affect only the condition codes, as shown in Appendix IV. For a nonzero shift count, the arithmetic and logical shifts preserve the last bit shifted off in the C and X bits. The rotate instructions affect only the C bit. Rotate with extend operations shift the previous value of the X bit into one end of the operand while saving the latest value rotated out the other end in the C and X bits.

After any shift or rotate operation, the N and Z condition codes are set according to the result, just as they were set for the arithmetic operations. The overflow condition code V is set to {0} after every operation except an arithmetic left shift. The ASL instruction multiplies the operand by 2^r if it is shifted r bits left. If the result exceeds the numerical range of a signed m-bit operand, V set to {1} indicates an out-of-range condition. For unsigned numbers, the carry bit C set to {1} indicates an overflow after an ASL instruction.

Example 8.3

Several shift and rotate instructions are shown in Table 8.7. The results shown in the table assume that the low-order byte of D1 contained the binary value {1110 0101} and that the X bit was {0} before each instruction was executed.

In the case of the ASR instruction, the sign bit is extended to the right at each shift. The orginal number was -27 in two's-complement notation. It becomes -14 and then -7 after successive shifts, thus simulating integer division by 2 each time. Note that -14, however, is not the expected result of the integer division of -27 by 2. Use of the DIVS instructions would result in a quotient of -13 and a remainder of -1. This truncation in the wrong direction will occur whenever an odd, negative integer is shifted to the right.

The LSL instruction, with a shift count of 4, shifts the low-order 4 bits of the byte

TABLE 8.7   EXAMPLE OF SHIFT AND ROTATE OPERATIONS

Instruction	Before (D1)[7:0]	After (D1)[7:0]	C	X
ASR.B #2,D1	{1110 0101}	{1111 1001}	0	0
LSL.B #4,D1	{1110 0101}	{0101 0000}	0	0
ROR.B #4,D1	{1110 0101}	{0101 1110}	0	—
ROXR.B #1,D1	{1110 0101}	{0111 0010}	1	1

Note: X = {0} before each instruction executes.

to the upper 4 bits. The N condition code bit would be set to {1} to indicate that the most significant bit is nonzero.   Rotating a byte four places to the right with the ROR instruction swaps 4 bits and leaves each unchanged. Rotating the original value with X = {0} one place to the right with the ROXR instruction causes a zero to be shifted into the most significant bit. The bit shifted off the right end is saved in both C and X. Notice from Figure 8.2 that if X = {1} before the ROXR executed, the most significant bit of the operand would become {1}.

Example 8.4

The subroutine shown in Figure 8.3 multiplies the 32-bit positive integer in D4 by a positive power of 2 specified in data register D1. The number is passed to the subroutine in

```
MC68000 ASM REV= 1.4 - COPYRIGHT BY MOTOROLA 1978          PAGE  1


 1                              LLEN    100
 2         00001000             ORG     $1000
 3                         *
 4                         * POWER OF TWO MULTIPLY
 5                         *    INPUT : (D1.B) = POWER OF TWO TO MULTIPLY BY
 6                         *            (D4.L) = INTEGER TO BE MULTIPLIED (MUST BE POSITIVE)
 7                         *
 8                         *    OUTPUT : (D5/D4)[64:0] = RESULT
 9                         *             (D2.B) = 0 : SUCCESS
10                         *                     -1 : ERROR DETECTED
11                         *
12 001000 2F01      POWER2    MOVE.L  D1,-(SP)         ;SAVE REGISTER
13 001002 4285                CLR.L   D5               ;ZERO RESULT
14 001004 143CFFFF            MOVE.B  #-1,D2           ;SET DEFAULT TO ERROR
15                         *
16 001008 E38C      LOOP      LSL.L   #1,D4            ;SHIFT LEFT (MULTIPLY BY 2)
17 00100A E395                ROXL.L  #1,D5            ;SHIFT CARRY OUT OF D4 INTO D5
18 00100C 6500000A            BCS     DONE             ;IF CARRY OUT OF D5, EXIT WITH ERROR
19 001010 04010001            SUBI.B  #1,D1            ;DECREMENT COUNT
20 001014 66F2                BNE     LOOP             ;    UNTIL (D0) = 0
21                         *
22 001016 4202                CLR.B   D2               ;SET STATUS TO SUCCESS
23                         *
24 001018 221F      DONE      MOVE.L  (SP)+,D1         ;RESTORE REGISTER
25 00101A 4E75                RTS
26                         *
27                           END

****** TOTAL ERRORS    0--   0


SYMBOL TABLE - APPROX 1199 SYMBOL ENTRIES LEFT

DONE       001018 LOOP       001008 POWER2      001000
```

Figure 8.3   Program to multiply a number by 2^N

D4 and the 64-bit result is held in registers D5 and D4. If the result causes a carry out of D5, the low-order byte of D2 is set to -1 to indicate the overflow. Otherwise, the error flag in D2 is zero. The loop is an example of dynamic shifting since the power of 2 in D1 is used as a counter and is decremented after each shift.

EXERCISES

8.2.1. Why do the MC68000 instructions allow shifts of up to 63 places when the longest operand is only 32 bits?

8.2.2. State in words and use an equation to define the conditions for an error when a *signed* integer is shifted left or right by the ASL or ASR instructions. Consider both even and odd integers.

8.2.3. Determine the numerical value when the binary number

{1110 0101}

is shifted left three places.

8.2.4. Show that the correct rule for doubling a one's-complement number is a left cyclic shift.

8.2.5. How can the two upper bytes in a 32-bit register be accessed for use by a MC68000 instruction operating on a byte-length operand?

8.2.6. Write subroutines that pack and unpack 4-bit operands into byte-length values. Assume that the operands are held in memory.

8.2.7. Modify the subroutine shown in Example 8.4 to multiply signed integers by 2^N.

8.2.8. Write a subroutine to multiply a signed integer by 2^r, where r can be positive or negative. If a negative value is truncated by right shifts, correct the result for proper integer division if necessary.

8.3 BIT-MANIPULATION AND FLAG-SETTING INSTRUCTIONS

It is convenient in many applications to employ a logical variable to indicate one of two possible results of an operation. A logical variable used in this way is called a *flag*. The flag variable indicates that a condition has occurred and is used to communicate this fact to a routine that must test the flag variable. For example, the flags that indicate the results of arithmetic operations for the MC68000 collectively form the condition code register. In this case, a conditional branch instruction may test one or more condition codes to determine subsequent action. Another common application of a flag is to indicate the status of a peripheral device. The status would determine if the device were "busy" or ready to accept data transfers. Usually, a single bit is set by the device when it is ready and this information is used by the processor to begin the transfer of data. In such an application, the logical variable can be termed an *event flag* and it serves to synchronize the operation of the processor with the external device. The MC68000 instructions to test, set, clear, or change a single bit within an operand are useful for manipulating such flag bits as well as for other operations.

Another important use of logical variables is to communicate information between independent programs or between routines of an operating system or other sophisticated software systems. The conditions for which a flag would be set or cleared can be very complicated and involve a number of conditional tests. The MC68000 provides a Set According to Condition (Scc) instruction which allows a variable to be set to indicate a TRUE or FALSE result based on the condition code values.

When operating system routines or several processors share an area of memory, a synchronization problem can occur if a routine or processor can access a memory area or location during the time another routine or processor is using this same memory area or location. For example, this can occur in a real-time system where the program execution sequence is controlled in part by external events, signaled to the processor as an interrupt. In a multiprocessor system, the synchronization problem requires a partial hardware solution if the processors act independently. The Test and Set instruction is useful for such situations.

8.3.1 Bit-Manipulation Instructions

The MC68000 bit-manipulation instructions operate on a single bit in a Data Register or in memory. Each instruction tests a specified bit and sets only the Z condition code bit based on the value. As a logical variable, the Z bit indicates the *complement* of the designated bit. The BTST (Bit Test) instruction sets the Z bit according to the state of the tested bit. The instructions BCHG, BCLR, and BSET set the Z bit accordingly and then cause the designated bit to be changed, cleared, and set to {1}, respectively. The bit-manipulation instructions are shown in Table 8.8.

The number of the bit to examine is either contained in a data register for "dynamic" specification or it is specified as an immediate value in the instruction. For example, if

(D1) = $0000 0001
    and
(D2) = $0000 88FF

to specify bit 1 of register D2, the instruction

BCHG   D1,D2

first causes the Z condition code to be set to {0}, the complement of (D2)[1]. Then the operand in D2 becomes $0000 88FD since bit 1 of D2 is complemented by the operation. The value in D1 should be a number between 0 and 31 because the destination is another data register. The instruction

BCLR   #1,D2

would have the same effect on D2.

TABLE 8.8 BIT-MANIPULATION INSTRUCTIONS

	Syntax	Operation
Bit Change		
BCHG	$<Dn>,<EA>$	Z = NOT(bn)
BCHG	#$<bn>,<EA>$	THEN bn ← NOT(bn)
Bit Clear		
BCLR	$<Dn>,<EA>$	Z = NOT(bn)
BCLR	#$<bn>,<EA>$	THEN bn ← {0}
Bit Set		
BSET	$<Dn>,<EA>$	Z = NOT(bn)
BSET	#$<bn>,<EA>$	THEN bn ← {1}
Bit Test		
BTST	$<Dn>,<EA>$	Z = NOT(bn)
BTST	#$<bn>,<EA>$	

Notes:

1. If $<Dn>$ is the destination, the length is 32 bits; otherwise, the length of the destination operand is one byte.
2. $<bn>$ is the bit number of the operand.
3. BTST allows all addressing modes for the destination except address register direct (data modes only).
4. BCHG, BCLR, and BSET allow only data-alterable addressing modes for the destination.

When the operand is held in memory, only a byte-length operand is allowed. The BCHG, BCLR, and BSET instructions allow only data-alterable addressing modes. Therefore, address register direct and program counter relative addressing is prohibited. The BTST instruction, however, allows all addressing modes except address register direct.

Example 8.5

The subroutine shown in Figure 8.4 generates odd parity for a single ASCII character held in a location addressed by Al and leaves the result in the same location. The odd-parity bit (bit 7) is defined to be {0} when the number of {1} bits in the character is odd. Otherwise, the parity bit is set to {1} so that the number of nonzero bits in the byte is always an odd number.

The routine begins by setting (D0) = $FF indicating that the parity bit should be {1}. In the loop, encountering a {0} bit has no effect and the next bit in sequence is tested. The bits are tested in order 6, 5, 4, 3, 2, 1, and 0. When a {1} bit is found, (D0) is complemented. Since (D0) was initialized to indicate that a parity bit was needed, finding 1,3, or 5 bits with value {1} will cause the routine to complement the initial value in D0. Otherwise, if 0, 2, 4, or 6 bits have the value {1}, (D0) will indicate that the parity bit must be set to {1}. The BSET instruction accomplishes this.

```
MC68000 ASM REV= 1.4 - COPYRIGHT BY MOTOROLA 1978                PAGE  1


  1                              LLEN    100
  2          00001000            ORG     $1000
  3                         *
  4                         * PARITY GENERATOR
  5                         * INPUT : (A1.L) = ADDRESS OF CHARACTER
  6                         *
  7                         * OUTPUT : PARITY BIT (BIT 7) ADDED TO CHARACTER AT (A1)
  8                         *
  9 001000 48E7C000   PARITY    MOVEM.L D0/D1,-(SP)          ;SAVE REGISTERS
 10 001004 123C0006             MOVE.B  #6,D1               ;SET UP COUNTER
 11 001008 103C00FF             MOVE.B  #$FF,D0             ;PARITY INDICATOR = 1'S
 12                         *
 13 00100C 0311       LOOP      BTST    D1,(A1)             ;CHECK BIT
 14 00100E 67000004             BEQ     NEXT                ;IF NOT ZERO
 15 001012 4600                 NOT.B   D0                  ;   THEN COMPLEMENT PARITY INDICATOR
 16 001014 51C9FFF6   NEXT      DBRA    D1,LOOP             ;CONTINUE, UNTIL (D1) = -1
 17                         *
 18 001018 4A00                 TST.B   D0                  ;IF PARITY SHOULD BE 0
 19 00101A 67000006             BEQ     DONE                ;   THEN SKIP (DO NOT CHANGE BIT)
 20 00101E 08D10007             BSET    #7,(A1)             ;   ELSE SET PARITY BIT
 21                         *
 22 001022 4CDF0003   DONE      MOVEM.L (SP)+,D0/D1         ;RESTORE REGISTERS
 23 001026 4E75                 RTS
 24                         *
 25                              END

****** TOTAL ERRORS    0--   0


SYMBOL TABLE - APPROX 1198 SYMBOL ENTRIES LEFT

DONE        001022 LOOP       00100C NEXT       001014 PARITY      001000
```

Figure 8.4 Subroutine to generate an odd-parity bit.

8.3.2 Set According to Condition Instruction

The instruction Scc sets all 8 bits of a destination location to $\{1\}$'s if the condition "cc" is true. Otherwise, the byte is set to all $\{0\}$'s when the condition is false. The conditions (carry clear, carry set, etc.) are the same as those for the DBcc instruction discussed in Chapter 6. For example, if the Z condition code bit is $\{1\}$, the instruction Set if Equal (to zero)

     SEQ   D1

writes $FF into the low-order byte of D1, indicating a TRUE condition to any program testing the flag in D1.

The destination $<EA>$ for the instruction must be a data-alterable location. Thus all addressing modes except address register direct and program counter relative are allowed.

After the operand is set to all $\{1\}$'s or all $\{0\}$'s, its condition might be tested using the TST.B instruction, which sets $Z = \{1\}$ when the flag has the value $\{0000\ 0000\}$. In fact, all of the logical instructions operating on a byte-length operand can be used to manipulate the logical variable created by the Scc instruction. For example, if D1 contains the value $FF from the SEQ instruction just shown, the instruction

    EORI.B   #$FF,D1

causes $Z = \{1\}$ and reverses the flag.

8.3.3. Test and Set Instruction

The TAS instruction is used to test and modify a byte-length operand held either in a data register or in memory. Its operation is defined in Figure 8.5(a) and the instruction has the symbolic form

    TAS   <EA>

If (EA) = 0
   THEN set Z = {1}
   ELSE set Z = {0} , N = {1}

If (EA)[7] = {1}
   THEN set N = {1}
   ELSE set N = {0}

Set (EA)[7] = {1}

Notes:
  (1) (EA) is a byte-length operand addressed by data alterable
      addressing modes.
  (2) The read-modify-write cycle is indivisible.

    (a) TAS Operation   (TAS <EA>)

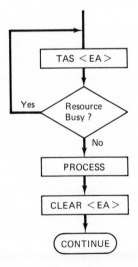

    (b) Typical Usage   **Figure 8.5**   TAS instruction.

If the operand is zero, the condition code bit Z is set to {1}. Otherwise, the Z bit is cleared. If bit 7 of the operand is {1}, N is set to {1}. In this regard, TAS operates much like the TST (Test) instruction operating on a byte value. However, after the operand is examined by the TAS instruction and N and Z are set accordingly, the most significant bit of the operand is set to {1}.

For example, if the byte used as a flag and addressed by Al has the initial value of $00, the instruction

TAS   (A1)

causes Z = {1} and changes the operand to $80 after the instruction is executed. If the initial zero value indicated that a memory area or other resource was free for use, the Z condition code bit indicates this after the TAS instruction has executed. However, now the flag has been altered. A subsequent test of the flag would indicate that the resource is in use. This subsequent test might be made by another program running concurrently (perhaps activated by an interrupt) or by another processor in a multiprocessor system.

Notice that if a flag variable set to $80 is tested in a loop such as

```
LOOP  TAS     (A1)      ;test flag
      BNE     LOOP      ;branch back if not clear
```

the next instruction in sequence cannot be executed until some other program or processor clears the flag. When the flag is already set as in this example, the TAS instruction does not change it.

As noted in Figure 8.5(a), the operand being tested by TAS cannot be held in an address register or be referenced using program counter relative addressing. Also, the C and V bits are always cleared by the TAS operation. The flowchart in Figure 8.5(b) shows a typical use of the TAS instruction, followed by a conditional test. Here a program is testing to determine if some resource such as a line printer or memory area is available to it. The conditional test is most likely implemented by a conditional branch instruction which causes looping until the flag is clear. With such usage, the processor executing the test is busy executing the loop until either an interrupt occurs which allows the flag to be cleared or until another processor clears it.

If the resource being shared is critical to the continued execution of the program making the test, a wait loop is necessary with the TAS instruction. After the resource is made available, processing can continue utilizing the resource. The flag should be cleared after processing is completed to release the resource for other users. Thus the TAS instruction may be used as a means to set flags used to communicate between processes, such as real-time routines, or interrupt routines of an operating system. It has further use, however, to *synchronize* accesses to a shared resource when timing is a consideration. It is the synchronization aspect of the TAS instruction that is critically important in many multiprocessor systems in which several processors share resources such as memory areas.

Synchronization with the TAS instruction.

The TAS instruction is used to prevent access to a shared resource by other programs when one program has control of the resource. This is sometimes termed *lockout*. When hardware access to the shared resource is possible, as in a multiprocessing system, a problem could arise if two processors examine the flag simultaneously and both consider the resource to be available. To prevent this, the TAS instruction has an indivisible, read–modify–write cycle. Once the operand is addressed by the MC68000 executing the TAS instruction, the system bus is not available to any other device, including another processor, until the instruction completes. The first processor executing the TAS instruction controls the shared resource until the flag is cleared. Thus accesses are synchronized at the hardware level. Details of the hardware operation of the MC68000 are discussed in Chapter 12.

Example 8.6

The subroutine shown in Figure 8.6 illustrates the use of the TAS instruction to allocate and lock a block of memory locations for the calling program. The memory is segmented into eight blocks of 256 bytes with the blocks numbered 0, 1, 2, ..., 7. The first byte of each block contains a flag or "lock" used by the TAS instruction.

On entry to the subroutine, the label FREEMEM must define the start of the free-space area. Up to eight 256-byte memory blocks are examined to determine whether one is available for use. If a free block is located, its lock byte is set by TAS, its address is

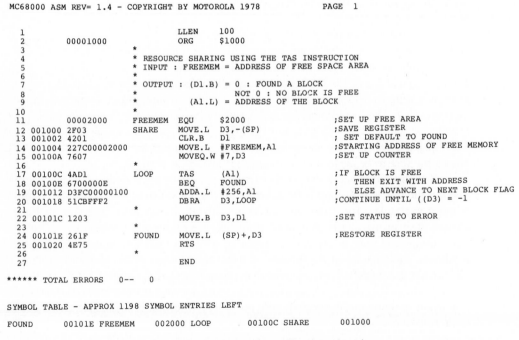

```
MC68000 ASM REV= 1.4 - COPYRIGHT BY MOTOROLA 1978              PAGE  1


   1                              LLEN    100
   2         00001000             ORG     $1000
   3                         *
   4                         * RESOURCE SHARING USING THE TAS INSTRUCTION
   5                         * INPUT : FREEMEM = ADDRESS OF FREE SPACE AREA
   6                         *
   7                         * OUTPUT : (D1.B) = 0 : FOUND A BLOCK
   8                         *                   NOT 0 : NO BLOCK IS FREE
   9                         *          (A1.L) = ADDRESS OF THE BLOCK
  10                         *
  11         00002000    FREEMEM   EQU     $2000                ;SET UP FREE AREA
  12 001000 2F03         SHARE     MOVE.L  D3,-(SP)             ;SAVE REGISTER
  13 001002 4201                   CLR.B   D1                   ; SET DEFAULT TO FOUND
  14 001004 227C00002000           MOVE.L  #FREEMEM,A1          ;STARTING ADDRESS OF FREE MEMORY
  15 00100A 7607                   MOVEQ.W #7,D3                ;SET UP COUNTER
  16                         *
  17 00100C 4AD1         LOOP      TAS     (A1)                 ;IF BLOCK IS FREE
  18 00100E 6700000E               BEQ     FOUND                ;   THEN EXIT WITH ADDRESS
  19 001012 D3FC00000100           ADDA.L  #256,A1              ;   ELSE ADVANCE TO NEXT BLOCK FLAG
  20 001018 51CBFFF2               DBRA    D3,LOOP              ;CONTINUE UNTIL ((D3) = -1
  21                         *
  22 00101C 1203                   MOVE.B  D3,D1                ;SET STATUS TO ERROR
  23                         *
  24 00101E 261F         FOUND     MOVE.L  (SP)+,D3             ;RESTORE REGISTER
  25 001020 4E75                   RTS
  26                         *
  27                              END

****** TOTAL ERRORS   0--   0


SYMBOL TABLE - APPROX 1198 SYMBOL ENTRIES LEFT

FOUND     00101E FREEMEM    002000 LOOP      00100C SHARE      001000
```

Figure 8.6 Memory allocation subroutine.

returned in A1 and D1 is set to {0} to indicate a free block was found. If no free block is located, D1 is returned with a nonzero value.

EXERCISES

8.3.1. Give the bit test needed to determine the following:
  (a) An integer is even.
  (b) A signed integer m bits long is negative.
  (c) A character is an uppercase or lowercase ASCII alphabetic character.

8.3.2. Compare the following instructions with their equivalent bit manipulation instructions:
  (a) ANDI.W   #$7FFF,D2
  (b) ORI.W   #$8000,D2
  (c) EORI.W   #$8000,D2
  (d) TST.W   D2

8.3.3. Give the steps needed to generate the arithmetic (or logical) values {1} and {0} from the TRUE and FALSE conditions set by Scc instructions.

8.3.4. Write a subroutine to change a string of alphabetic characters (ASCII) from uppercase to lowercase, or vice versa. See Appendix I, which contains the character set.

8.3.5. Compare the hardware and software operation of the

> TAS   < EA >

instruction with the

> BSET   #7, < EA >

instruction. Determine under what conditions a busy-wait loop using the TST and BNE instructions followed by the BSET instruction rather than TAS might not be sufficient to provide a lock of a shared resource. Consider both single- and multiple-processor systems.

8.3.6. Let a "bit map" contain N bits, indicating the availability of N 256-byte blocks of memory. If a bit is {0}, the block is free. Assume that the bit map is held in memory at a fixed location and the first address of the contiguous memory area is known. Write a subroutine to find the first collection of k contiguous blocks. Return the starting address of these blocks and set the proper bits in the bit map to {1} to indicate the memory blocks are in use. If fewer than k blocks are found or if k is not an integer between 1 and N, return an error indication to the calling program.

FURTHER READING

A number of the textbooks referenced in previous chapters deal with logical and bit operations (Eckhouse and Morris, Tannenbaum, and Wakerly, for example). The mathematics of shifting is discussed by Stein and Munro, as referenced in Chapter 3.

Discussions of the concept of interlocking shared resources are generally found in texts dealing with operating systems. The article by Denning, listed here, defines in greater detail some of the concepts introduced in this chapter.

DENNING, PETER J., "Third Generation Computer Systems," *Computing Surveys,* **3**, No. 4 (December 1971), 175–216.

9

Programming Techniques

In the preceding chapters, the MC68000 instruction set was introduced by separating the instructions into categories. These categories discussed instructions that are used to create programs to move data, perform calculations, or provide simple functions. For the most part, these programs were designed to satisfy a particular application, such as ASCII-to-binary conversion. In contrast, this chapter explores various programming techniques that are useful in creating more sophisticated programs. The emphasis is on the powerful addressing capability of the MC68000.

Some MC68000 instructions, such as DIVU and MULU, prohibit operations on address registers directly. This restriction is very slight since address registers and data registers can be easily exchanged. In addition, however, the MC68000 provides special instructions to manipulate addresses. These instructions are introduced in the first section since they provide the flexibility necessary for advanced programming techniques.

One special technique involves the creation of *position-independent code.* Program counter relative addressing and base register addressing can be used in programs so that they will execute independent of their starting address in memory.

Manipulation of typical *data structures* such as arrays and lists involves the use of advanced programming methods. Although only a few of the many topics concerning the creation and manipulation of data structures is discussed in this chapter, the power and flexibility of the MC68000 instructions are revealed.

Subroutines were introduced in Chapter 6 as a common technique to aid the programmer in creating modular programs. The linkage between a calling program and a subroutine via the return address on the system stack was discussed there in some detail. Passing data values or addresses between program modules was accomplished using processor registers to hold the values. More sophisticated methods of transferring data values are discussed in this chapter. The techniques to create a stack frame (LINK and UNLK instructions) and to write reentrant subroutines are also presented.

9.1 INSTRUCTIONS THAT MANIPULATE ADDRESSES

Except for values in registers or values specified by the immediate mode of addressing, operands of MC68000 instructions are referenced by their addresses. A distinction is also made between data and addresses because they have separate output signal lines and are held in data registers and address registers, respectively. The address signal lines specify a location in memory (or in the I/O space of the system) and the separate data signal lines are used to transfer values. Internally, both data values and addresses can be manipulated with various processor instructions.

The MC68000 instruction set provides instructions to operate specifically on addresses. These include instructions to perform a comparison of two addresses (CMPA), to perform arithmetic operations (ADDA, SUBA), and to transfer addresses (MOVEA, LEA, PEA). Except for the CMPA instruction, these instructions do not alter the condition code register.

For all operations involving addresses, the valid address range for the MC68000 is 0 to $FFFFFF (hexadecimal) due to the limit of 24 address lines. For instructions that allow word-length operands, the 16-bit addresses are sign-extended to 32 bits before being used by the instructions. Therefore, short addresses (16 bits) have a valid range of either 0 to $7FFF or $FF8000 to $FFFFFF.

9.1.1 Arithmetic Address Manipulation

The instructions ADDA (Add Address), SUBA (Subtract Address), and CMPA (Compare Address) operate on a source operand that can be addressed by any mode. However, the destination operand must be held in an address register. The syntax and operation for these instructions are shown in Table 9.1. These instructions are similar to the ADD, SUB, and CMP operations on data values.

The ADDA instruction adds a value in a register or memory to the value in the destination address register. A common use of the ADDA instruction is to add a constant, which is specified by the immediate addressing mode, to the value in the address register involved. For example, the instruction

    ADDA.L   #20,A1

increments (A1) by 20 when it is executed. In a loop, the instruction allows A1 to address every twentieth element in a data structure. The instructions that operate on addresses provide a much greater flexibility, however, since the source operand can be specified by any addressing mode. For example, an instruction in the form

    ADDA.L   A2,A2

TABLE 9.1   OPERATION OF ADDA, SUBA, and CMPA

Instruction	Syntax	Operation	Condition codes affected
Add Address	ADDA.$<$l$>$ $<$EA$>$,$<$An$>$	(An) ← (An) + (EA)	None
Subtract Address	SUBA.$<$l$>$ $<$EA$>$,$<$An$>$	(An) ← (An) − (EA)	None
Compare Address	CMPA.$<$l$>$ $<$EA$>$,$<$An$>$	(An) − (EA)	N, Z, V, C

Notes:

1. $<$l$>$ denotes W or L only.

2. If a word operand (W) is specified, it is sign-extended to 32 bits.

3. All addressing modes are allowed for $<$EA$>$.

doubles the value in A2. This could be used to convert an entry number held in A2 to an index that references a table of 16-bit words. For example, if (A2) = \$100 indicates the 256th word in a memory block, then 2 × \$100, or \$200, is the address of that word as an offset (in bytes) from the starting location of the block.

The SUBA instruction forms the difference between a destination address register and the source operand. The instruction

     SUBA.L   D1,A1

leaves the 32-bit value of

     (A1) − (D1)

in A1. Like the ADDA instruction, SUBA does not modify the condition codes.

The CMPA instruction is used to determine the order of two addresses (lower, equal, or higher). The condition codes are set in the same manner as for the CMP instruction discussed in Chapter 6. Addresses should be considered as unsigned integers and tests on the C bit and the Z bit have the interpretation as explained in Chapter 6. The tests BHI (higher), BLS (lower or same), BNE (not equal), or BEQ (equal) are also useful to implement tests comparing addresses. For example, the instructions

     CMPA.L   A2,A1   ;form (A1) − (A2)
     BHI   LOOP   ;branch if (A1) > (A2)

cause a branch if (A1) is larger than (A2). Otherwise, a branch is not taken.

The CMPA instruction calculates

     (destination) − (source)

and sets the condition codes based on the result. Table 9.2 summarizes the conditional branch instructions that are valid after a CMPA instruction.

The instruction variations ADDQ (Add Quick) and SUBQ (Subtract Quick) can also be used to add and subtract a constant in the range 1 to 8 from the contents of an address register. The source operand is the immediate value of the constant as dis-

TABLE 9.2   COMPARISON OF ADDRESSES

Instruction	Branch	True condition
CMPA.L A1,A2	BHI (higher)	(A2) > (A1)
	BLS (lower or same)	(A2) ≤ (A1)
	BCC (high or same)	(A2) ≥ (A1)
	BCS (low)	(A2) < (A1)
	BNE (not equal)	(A2) ≠ (A1)
	BEQ (equal)	(A2) = (A1)

cussed in Chapter 7. These instructions represent one-word instructions that are used to efficiently increment or decrement an address.

Example 9.1

The subroutine of Figure 9.1 counts the number of negative 8-bit integers in a block or table of consecutive memory bytes. The starting address of the block is passed to the subroutine in A0, and A1 must contain the address of the last byte + 1 upon entry. Each byte is then tested and the count accumulated in the low-order word of D0.

In each loop, A0 is incremented by 1 with the ADDA instruction. The testing ter-

```
MC68000 ASM REV= 1.4 - COPYRIGHT BY MOTOROLA 1978              PAGE   1


 1                                    LLEN    100
 2            00001000                ORG     $1000
 3                          *
 4                          * DETERMINE THE NUMBER OF NEGATIVE BYTES IN A BLOCK
 5                          *
 6                          * INPUT :  (A0.L) = STARTING ADDRESS OF BLOCK
 7                          *          (A1.L) = ENDING ADDRESS OF BLOCK + 1
 8                          *
 9                          * OUTPUT :  (D0.W) = NUMBER OF NEGATIVE BYTES
10                          *
11 001000 2F08             CNTNEG    MOVE.L  A0,-(SP)            ;SAVE REGISTER
12 001002 4240                       CLR.W   D0
13                          *
14 001004 4A10             LOOP      TST.B   (A0)                ;IF BYTE IS NOT NEGATIVE,
15 001006 6A000004                   BPL     NEXT                ;   THEN PROCESS NEXT BYTE
16 00100A 5240                       ADDQ.W  #1,D0               ;   ELSE COUNT IT
17 00100C D1FC00000001 NEXT         ADDA.L  #1,A0               ;INCREMENT TO NEXT BYTE
18 001012 B1C9                       CMPA.L  A1,A0               ;IF NOT FINISHED,
19 001014 6DEE                       BLT     LOOP                ;   THEN CONTINUE
20 001016 205F                       MOVE.L  (SP)+,A0            ;RESTORE REGISTER
21 001018 4E75                       RTS
22                                   END

****** TOTAL ERRORS    0--    0


SYMBOL TABLE - APPROX 1199 SYMBOL ENTRIES LEFT

CNTNEG      001000 LOOP       001004 NEXT       00100C
```

Figure 9.1   Examples of address manipulation.

minates when the value in the addressing register A1 becomes equal to the final address in A1.

9.1.2 Transfer of Addresses

The MOVEA, LEA, and PEA instructions are used to transfer addresses. The MOVEA (Move Address) instruction loads an address register with an operand that can be held in a register or memory location or be specified as an immediate value. The LEA (Load Effective Address) instruction computes the effective address of a location in memory and transfers the address value to an address register. The PEA (Push Effective Address) instruction calculates an effective address and pushes it onto the system stack. LEA and PEA differ from most instructions because the effective address calculated for an operand is transferred rather than the contents of the addressed location. The syntax and addressing modes for these three instructions that transfer addresses are shown in Table 9.3.

Move address instruction.   The MOVEA instruction has the symbolic form

MOVEA. $<l>$ $<EA>, <An>$

where $<l>$ = W or L and $<EA>$ is designated by any addressing mode. The operation results in the transfer

(An)[31:0] ← (EA)

with any 16-bit references being sign-extended to 32-bit quantities before the transfer. When a data register, an address register, or a memory location is the source, the contents of it are transferred. The instruction

MOVEA.L   TABLE,A1

moves the 32-bit word at location TABLE into A1. The value in this location is considered an address, and TABLE in the discussion might refer to the first address of a table of addresses. Register A1 can then be used to reference the value pointed to by the address at location TABLE. For example, if the MOVEA instruction given above is followed with the instruction

MOVE.W   (A1),D1

the 16-bit word referenced by the operand (address) at location TABLE is transferred to the low-order word of D1. The two operations thus perform the transfer

(D1) [15:0] ← ((TABLE) [31:0]) [15:0]

In contrast, when the immediate mode is used with a label, the address is moved. In the instruction

MOVEA.L   #TABLE,A1

TABLE 9.3 INSTRUCTIONS TO TRANSFER ADDRESSES

Instruction	Syntax	Operand length (bytes)	Addressing modes	
			Source	Destination
Move Address	MOVEA.<l> <EA>,<An>	16 or 32	All	An
Load Effective Address	LEA <EA>,<An>	32	Control modes	An
Push Effective Address	PEA <EA>	32	Control modes	−(SP)

Notes:

1. Condition codes are not affected.

2. <l> denotes W or L only.

3. For word-length operands, the source operand is sign-extended to 32 bits, and all 32 bits are loaded into the address register.

the address of the location TABLE, which is the source operand, is transferred to A1. Thus the immediate form loads the address of the table itself. Without the immediate symbol, the MOVEA instruction would be used to load the first address within a table of addresses starting at location TABLE into A1.

Load effective address.   The LEA instruction is used to calculate an effective address based on the source addressing mode and transfer it to an address register. The symbolic form is

LEA   < EA >,An

where < EA > is specified by a control addressing mode. Thus register direct, postincrement, and predecrement addressing is not allowed. The instruction

LEA   TABLE,A1

results in the operation

(A1) [31:0] ← TABLE

where TABLE is an address in an assembly language program. This instruction is equivalent to the MOVEA instruction with the immediate form of the source operand address.

When other addressing modes are used for the source operand in the LEA instruction, the instruction performs a function that is not possible with other data transfer instructions. The LEA instruction allows an address to be calculated during program execution and transferred to an address register.

Consider the instruction sequence

```
LEA       2(A1,D1.W),A0     ;CALCULATE ADDRESS
MOVE.W    (A0),D2           ;PUT VALUE IN D2
MULU      #4,D2             ;4 × VALUE
MOVE.W    D2,(A0)           ;SAVE IT
```

This sequence first calculates an address based on the indirect with indexing addressing mode as

(A1) + (D1) [15:0] + 2

and transfers it into A0. The operand addressed by (A0) is moved into D2, modified, and saved. The indirect reference (A0) is more efficient in the use of memory than the indirect with indexing reference 2(A1,D1.W), which requires an extension word for the displacement to its instruction. Also, fewer machine cycles are required to calculate the indirect address than to calculate the indirect with index address. Without the LEA instruction, both move instructions would need the indexed addressing to calculate the operand location.

Push effective address.   The PEA instruction calculates an effective address and uses the system stack as the destination. The symbolic form

PEA   <EA>

causes a 32-bit effective address to be calculated for an operand specified by one of the control addressing modes. The value calculated is pushed onto the stack by the CPU using the sequence

$$(SP) \leftarrow (SP) - 4$$
$$((SP)) \leftarrow <EA>$$

where the system stack pointer is first decremented by 4 and then used to point to the longword location for <EA>.

Example 9.2

Table 9.4 shows the results of executing the PEA, LEA, and MOVEA instructions. For the PEA instruction, the stack pointer is initialized to $0000 7FFE. The instruction pushes (A0) as shown. Since the system stack is used, the more significant bytes of A0 are stored at lower memory addresses. LEA loads A0 with the source operand itself. To accomplish a similiar result, MOVEA with an immediate value would be used. In the next example, if the source operand were specified for MOVEA as an absolute address rather than immediate, the contents of the word location at $8000 would be transferred to A0. As it is, the immediate value $8000 is sign-extended to $FFFF 8000 before it is used.

Example 9.3

Figure 9.2 lists the instruction sequences that are equivalent to LEA and PEA. In each case, A0 holds the first address of a table representing blocks of byte-length operands in memory. The low-order word of D0 is an index to select the starting address of a particu-

TABLE 9.4 ADDRESS MANIPULATION EXAMPLES

Memory contents (hexadecimal)	Instruction	Results
4850	PEA (A0)	($7FFA) = $00
		($7FFB) = $00
		($7FFC) = $10
		($7FFD) = $20
41F9 0001 2345	LEA $00012345,A0	(A0) = $0001 2345
307C 8000	MOVEA.W #$8000,A0	(A0) = $FFFF 8000

Note: Initially, (A0) = $0000 1020 and (SP) = $0000 7FFE.

MC68000 ASM REV= 1.4 – COPYRIGHT BY MOTOROLA 1978   PAGE 1

```
 1                              LLEN    100
 2      00001000                ORG     $1000
 3                      *
 4      0000000A        OFFSET  EQU     10
 5                      *
 6                      * COMPARISON OF LEA AND PEA
 7                      *
 8                      * INPUT : (A0.L) = ADDRESS OF TABLE
 9                      *         (D0.W) = INDEX INTO TABLE
10                      *         OFFSET = BYTE WITHIN ELEMENT OF PREDEFINED TABLE
11                      *
12                      * OUTPUT : (A1.L) = EFFECTIVE ADDRESS (LEA)
13                      *
14                      * OPERATION OF THE LEA TO LOAD THE ADDRESS OF AN ELEMENT
15                      *
16 001000 43F0000A              LEA     OFFSET(A0,D0.W),A1
17                      *
18                      * LOAD THE ADDRESS OF AN ELEMENT WITHOUT USING LEA
19                      *
20 001004 2248                  MOVE.L  A0,A1
21 001006 D2C0                  ADDA.W  D0,A1
22 001008 D2FC000A              ADDA.W  #OFFSET,A1
23                      *
24                      * OPERATION OF THE PEA TO SAVE AN ADDRESS
25                      *
26 00100C 4870000A              PEA     OFFSET(A0,D0.W)
27                      *
28                      * SAVE AN ADDRESS WITHOUT USING PEA
29                      *
30 001010 2248                  MOVE.L  A0,A1
31 001012 D2C0                  ADDA.W  D0,A1
32 001014 D2FC000A              ADDA.W  #OFFSET,A1
33 001018 2F09                  MOVE.L  A1,-(SP)
34                      *
35                              END
```

****** TOTAL ERRORS   0--   0

SYMBOL TABLE – APPROX 1201 SYMBOL ENTRIES LEFT

OFFSET   00000A

Figure 9.2   Comparison of LEA and PEA.

lar block when added to (A0). The OFFSET selects the address of a particular byte when used to calculate the effective address.

EXERCISES

9.1.1. Let (A1) = $0000 1000 before each of the following instructions is executed. Compute the address in A1 after each instruction executes.
  (a) ADDA.W   #$2000,A1
  (b) ADDA.L   #$9000,A1
  (c) SUBA.W   #$2000,A1

9.1.2. Let the hexadecimal values in A0 and A1 be

> (A0) = \$0000 1000
> (A1) = \$0001 1F00

before the operation

> CMPA.W A0,A1

Which conditional branch statements following the compare will cause a branch?

9.1.3. If the instruction

> LEA 1(A1,D1.W),A2

is executed with

> (D1) = \$0000 8000
> (A1) = \$0000 1FFF

what is the address loaded into A2?

9.1.4. How can LEA or PEA be used to debug a program by verifying the addresses from which data are fetched?

9.1.5. The MC68000 allows indirect addressing only using an address register. Suppose that it is desired to hold an indirect address in a given memory location which itself is indirectly addressed. Show how the LEA instruction is used to access the indirect address if the address is at location ADDR1. Then generalize the concept to allow two levels of indirect addressing with the addresses in memory.

9.2 POSITION-INDEPENDENT CODE AND BASE ADDRESSING

In most of the previous programming examples, the program occupied fixed locations in memory and the starting address was defined by the origin (ORG) directive of the assembler. If these programs were to be moved to another area in memory, reassembly with a new origin would be required. The fact that the programs cannot be moved or relocated in memory without reassembly is inconvenient in some cases. It is not acceptable at all for ROM-based programs. In these cases, the programs must be able to be relocated after they are assembled.[1] Some operating systems may need to relocate an applications program even after its execution has already started.

A program is said to be *statically position independent* if it can be loaded and executed from any starting address in memory. Most programs in ROM are statically position independent since the starting address of the ROM program is defined by the system designer based on the requirements of the system. A floating-point routine in ROM, for example, may have a starting address of \$2000 in one system and start at location \$10000 in another. Perhaps the second system requires a much greater con-

---

[1]Relocation using a linkage editor is discussed in a number of the references in the Further Reading section for this chapter.

tinguous RAM area. Writing *position-independent code* is a technique of coding a routine so that the starting address is arbitrary. A major difference in this type of program is that it does not contain any absolute addresses except those dictated by hardware definitions such as I/O device addresses.

  Dynamic position independence allows a program to be moved after it has begun execution. This is required in systems with *virtual* memory. Stated simply, the virtual memory system permits programs to be written without regard to the limitations of the physical memory. If relocation is required, the operating system and memory management circuitry control the actual (physical) addressing automatically.

  Position independence is provided in MC68000 programs by several addressing modes. All program counter relative addresses are position independent. Also, address register indirect with index or displacement addressing can be used to create position independent code in a scheme called *base register* addressing.

9.2.1 Position-Independent Code with (PC)

When a location referenced in a program is at a fixed distance from the instruction making the reference, the program counter relative addressing mode can be used to create position-independent code. As long as the relative displacement is not changed, the program will execute correctly anywhere in memory. If all memory references use PC relative addressing, the program will be *dynamically* position independent since the effective addresses will be calculated as each instruction executes. Moving the program and restarting it at the point where it was temporarily suspended will not cause a problem as long as the program and data are moved together as a block. Unfortunately, it is difficult to write MC68000 programs that use only the PC relative addressing mode since destination operands in memory cannot be referenced this way by most instructions.

  Table 9.5 shows the type of instructions and memory references which are inherently position independent. Any of the conditional branch instructions or BRA use program counter with displacement addressing, allowing up to a 16-bit signed dis-

TABLE 9.5   POSITION-INDEPENDENT REFERENCES

Category	Addressing mode

Branch instructions
  BRA
  Bcc
  DBcc
	PC relative with displacement

Immediate instructions
  Logical (ORI, ANDI, EORI)
  Arithmetic (ADDI, SUBI, CMPI, ADDQ, SUBQ)
  Transfers (MOVEI)
	Immediate

Absolute reference to fixed locations	Absolute long, Absolute short
Relative memory references	PC relative with displacement, PC relative with index

TABLE 9.6   RELATIVE ADDRESSING FOR
INSTRUCTIONS

Source	Destination
ADD, ADDA	BRA, Bcc, DBcc
AND	BSR
CHK	BTST
CMP, CMPA	JMP, JSR
DIV	
LEA	
MOVE, MOVEA	
MOVEM	
MUL	
OR	
PEA	
SUB, SUBA	

placement. Immediate values are obviously unaffected by moving a program. Fixed addresses have system-defined values which are not changed. These are typically defined in the program using the Equate (EQU) directive. In addition, relative memory addresses using (PC) can be used by the programmer to ensure that the code is position independent.

As shown in Table 9.6, most of the MC68000 instructions that specify two operands allow only the source operand to be designated by the PC relative addressing mode. Thus the instruction

    MOVE.W   X,Y

could have only X specified as PC relative. The destination location for BRA, Bcc, DBcc, BTST, JMP, or JSR, however, can be specified by a PC relative mode. Basically, the MC68000 does not allow an operand that can be altered to be referenced by PC relative addressing. The MC68000 designers consider a reference using the PC to be a reference to a program instruction, not a data reference.[2] The only exception is the Bit Test (BTST) instruction.

Assemblers may differ in the manner in which relative addressing is specified by the programmer. The Motorola Cross-Assembler, for example, requires that the directive RORG (relative origin) be used in place of the ORG directive. Following the RORG directive, instructions that reference labels defined in the program will be automatically assembled using PC relative addressing instead of absolute addressing. Motorola's Resident Structured Assembler requires that the suffix "(PC)" be append-

---

[2]This distinction is explained when the function code lines of the MC68000 are discussed in Chapter 12.

ed to a label to force PC relative addressing or that the directive OPT PCS (PC relative option) be used. The manual for the system being used will define the specific
procedure. Our examples will use the Cross-Assembler to create position-independent
code using the RORG directive.

Example 9.4

Figure 9.3 shows two subroutines that compare the use of absolute and relative addresses.
In the first routine starting at ABSMOVE, the starting address of the block or buffer of
bytes is defined by BUFABS. The absolute location is $1016 and it is part of the machine
language instruction at $1004 to load the address into A1. If the program with the buffer
is moved in memory, the address of the buffer must be changed.

In contrast, when the buffer location is referenced relatively as in the subroutine
RELMOVE, only the offset is specified in the LEA instruction at $1004. Since
(PC) = $1006 when the address is calculated and the offset is $0E, a little hand calcula-
tion will show that (A1) = $1014, as it should before the loop is entered.

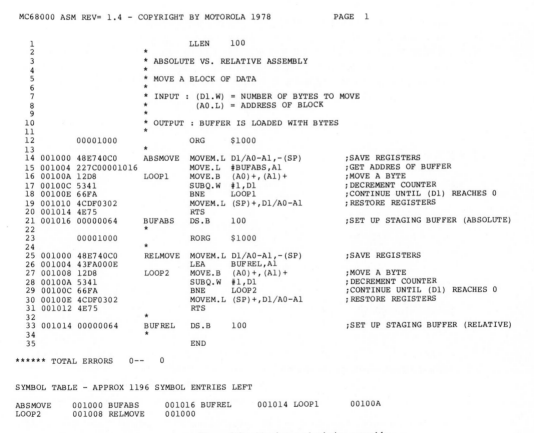

```
MC68000 ASM REV= 1.4 - COPYRIGHT BY MOTOROLA 1978              PAGE  1


 1                              LLEN    100
 2                         *
 3                         * ABSOLUTE VS. RELATIVE ASSEMBLY
 4                         *
 5                         * MOVE A BLOCK OF DATA
 6                         *
 7                         * INPUT : (D1.W) = NUMBER OF BYTES TO MOVE
 8                         *         (A0.L) = ADDRESS OF BLOCK
 9                         *
10                         * OUTPUT : BUFFER IS LOADED WITH BYTES
11                         *
12       00001000              ORG     $1000
13                         *
14 001000 48E740C0     ABSMOVE  MOVEM.L D1/A0-A1,-(SP)    ;SAVE REGISTERS
15 001004 227C00001016          MOVE.L  #BUFABS,A1        ;GET ADDRES OF BUFFER
16 00100A 12D8         LOOP1    MOVE.B  (A0)+,(A1)+       ;MOVE A BYTE
17 00100C 5341                  SUBQ.W  #1,D1             ;DECREMENT COUNTER
18 00100E 66FA                  BNE     LOOP1             ;CONTINUE UNTIL (D1) REACHES 0
19 001010 4CDF0302              MOVEM.L (SP)+,D1/A0-A1    ; RESTORE REGISTERS
20 001014 4E75                  RTS
21 001016 00000064     BUFABS   DS.B    100               ;SET UP STAGING BUFFER (ABSOLUTE)
22                         *
23       00001000              RORG    $1000
24                         *
25 001000 48E740C0     RELMOVE  MOVEM.L D1/A0-A1,-(SP)    ;SAVE REGISTERS
26 001004 43FA000E              LEA     BUFREL,A1
27 001008 12D8         LOOP2    MOVE.B  (A0)+,(A1)+       ;MOVE A BYTE
28 00100A 5341                  SUBQ.W  #1,D1             ; DECREMENT COUNTER
29 00100C 66FA                  BNE     LOOP2             ;CONTINUE UNTIL (D1) REACHES 0
30 00100E 4CDF0302              MOVEM.L (SP)+,D1/A0-A1    ; RESTORE REGISTERS
31 001012 4E75                  RTS
32                         *
33 001014 00000064     BUFREL   DS.B    100               ;SET UP STAGING BUFFER (RELATIVE)
34                         *
35                              END

****** TOTAL ERRORS   0--   0


SYMBOL TABLE - APPROX 1196 SYMBOL ENTRIES LEFT

ABSMOVE   001000 BUFABS    001016 BUFREL     001014 LOOP1     00100A
LOOP2     001008 RELMOVE   001000
```

Figure 9.3 Absolute and relative assembly.

9.2.2 Base Register Addressing

In the discussion of position-independent code, the program counter was used as a *base address* to which a displacement and pos.ibly an index value was added to locate an operand in memory. The address register indirect with displacement and the address register indirect with index addressing modes of the MC68000 can be used to accomplish *base register* addressing using any of the address registers. As the instruction using base register addressing executes, the operand location is calculated by adding an offset to the base address.

In MC68000 programs, the base register addressing is typically used to access data in an array or similar structure or to pass the base address of a data area to a subroutine. This addressing method is particularly useful when the relative position of a data item can be located by a displacement or an index value but the starting address of the structure is not known at the time of assembly.

Example 9.5

Figure 9.4 illustrates the possibility of segmenting memory into blocks using base register addressing. Registers A1, A2, and A3 address different segments. Memory references in a program using A1 reference the first segment, and an index value could be added to access a specific location. Similarly, the other address registers could be used to locate data or instructions in other segments. If a segment were moved, the operating system would reload the proper address register with the new starting address.

EXERCISES

9.2.1. Consider the simple program segment

```
            RORG    0           ;SYMBOLS ARE RELATIVE
START       MOVE.W  FIRST,D1
            ADD.W   SECOND,D1
            MOVE.W  D1,RESULT
            RTS
FIRST       DC.W    1
SECOND      DS.W    1
RESULT      DS.W    1
            END
```

The program attempts to calculate

$$(RESULT) = (FIRST) + (SECOND)$$

but will not work. Also, the program cannot be moved in memory from location 0000. Correct the program so that it will work anywhere in memory.

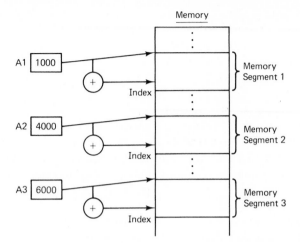

Memory

Figure 9.4   Base addressing.

9.2.2. Show that the following program is statically position independent:

```
        ORG     0
START   LEA     *+0,A0              ;Get PC
        ADDA.L  #(DATA-START),A0    ;Relocate pointer
        MOVE.W  #19,D1             ;Counter
LOOP    ADD.W   (A0)+,D2           ;Sum array
        DBF     D1,LOOP
        RTS
DATA    DS.W    20
        END
```

Show that the pointer to the data array (A0) contains the proper address of DATA after the program is moved. DBRA is also used for DBF in many assemblers.

9.2.3. Suppose that the instructions

```
LEA     Y(PC),A1
ADD.W   X(PC),(A1)
```

are used to create position-independent code. Relative addresses are specified for both the source X and destination Y. After execution of the LEA instruction, A1 contains the address of Y calculated from the (PC) value plus displacement. Show that the program is not dynamically position independent. (*Hint:* Consider the case when the program is moved after the LEA executes but before the ADD instruction executes.)

9.2.4. Compare indexed addressing with base register addressing. In the MC68000, the two addressing modes are identical as far as machine language code is concerned but have different purposes. Discuss the use of each.

9.2.5. Write a position-independent program to sum the values in five locations reserved by a DS directive in the program. Test it by writing another program that moves the program to sum the values and executes it after it is moved.

9.3 DATA STRUCTURES

The fundamental data types for the MC68000 are signed or unsigned integers, BCD integers, and Boolean variables. They are considered to be fundamental or primitive data types because MC68000 instructions are available to manipulate them directly. In contrast, strings of characters must be created and manipulated in algorithms that are devised by the programmer. These represent a data type not available at the assembly language level. The definition of new data types and the logical relationship defining their organization leads to the study of *data structures.*

An *array* is an example of a data structure. Arrays consist of a set of items of a single data type stored in contiguous locations in memory. The terms "array" and "table" are usually used synonymously. Arrays of numbers and tables of addresses have been used in examples of previous chapters. In this section, the concepts are generalized for both single- and multidimensional arrays.

The *linked list* is another type of data structure useful in many applications. This structure allows data items to be stored in noncontiguous storage locations using pointers to indicate the location of the next item in the list. The MC68000, with its extensive address manipulation capability, is well suited for programs using linked lists. Review of the MC68000 addressing modes described in Chapter 5 may be helpful.

9.3.1 One-Dimensional Arrays

The one-dimensional array is a structure consisting of a collection of items in which each element is identified uniquely by an index value corresponding to its position in the array. Since each item in the array is of the same data type, the structure is homogeneous. In mathematics, the one-dimensional array of numbers is called a *vector,* with the position of each element specified by a subscript. If the first subscript is arbitrarily chosen as 1, the vector elements are

$$V_1, V_2, \ldots, V_N$$

for an N-element vector. The FORTRAN convention begins the vector with subscript 1 and has elements

$$V(1), V(2), \ldots, V(N)$$

where V(i) indicates the address of element V_i. Languages such as Pascal or ALGOL allow arbitrary specification of the first index. In assembly language, complete flexibility is available. For this discussion, V_i will refer to the ith element itself and V(i) will be the address of the ith element.

Address calculation.   Sequential storage of the elements of a one-dimensional array allows each element to be easily referenced according to its address. If an N-element array X starts at location X(1) and each element occupies C bytes, then the jth element has the address

$$X(j) = X(1) + C * (j - 1)   1 \leq j \leq N$$

where C is a constant.[3] The array length in bytes is

$$length = (X(N) - X(1)) + C$$

when X(N) and X(1) represent the last and first addresses of the elements, respectively. Table 9.7 shows the address calculations for various arrays, and Figure 9.5 illustrates the general relationship in memory.[4]

Array addressing with the MC68000.   Addressing elements of an array is accomplished using the indirect or relative addressing modes of the MC68000. If the starting or base address of an array is held in an address register, the indirect modes can be used to locate elements in the array as shown in Table 9.8. When the program counter is used to perform relative addressing, a displacement value or an index plus displacement value is added to the (PC) to reference an element of the array. The fixed displacement is calculated by the assembler when relative addressing is specified in an

[3] If X(0) is the first address, then the jth element has address $X(j) = X(0) + c \times j; j = 0, 1, 2, \dots,$ N−1.

[4] There is no reason that the array could not have elements with higher indices occupying lower memory addresses and thus have the physical ordering be opposite the logical ordering. In this case, the equations given in this section would require modification.

TABLE 9.7   ONE-DIMENSIONAL ARRAY ADDRESSING

Size of Element in table	C	jth Location	Length of array (bytes)
Byte	1	$X(j) = X(1) + (j - 1)$	N
Word	2	$X(j) = X(1) + 2 * (j - 1)$	$2N$
Longword	4	$X(j) = X(1) + 4 * (j - 1)$	$4N$
Strings (fixed length)	k	$X(j) = X(1) + k * (j - 1)$	$k \times N$

Notes:

1. N is the number of elements each of length C bytes.
2. The index range is $1 \leq j \leq N$. The first address is X(1), containing the value X_1.

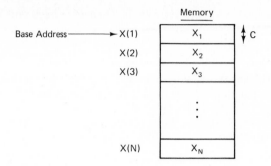

Notes:
(1) C is the length of one element in bytes.
(2) X(k) is the address of element X_k.

Figure 9.5 Array storage in memory.

instruction and the array storage is allocated with a Define Storage (DS) directive at a labeled statement.

The postincrement addressing mode can be used to reference array elements in sequence. For byte, word, or longword elements, the postincrement addressing mode allows an element to be examined and manipulated, after which the address register contains the address of the next element in the array. The instruction

    MOVE.W   (A1)+,D1

transfers the 16-bit value addressed by A1 to (D1) [15:0]. Register A1 is then incremented by 2 to point to the next value in the array. For an array whose elements are stored at decreasing memory locations from the base address, the predecrement mode permits the array to be scanned in the reverse order.[5] Without additional programming, only byte, word, or longword elements may be addressed with these modes in a sequential fashion.

The address register indirect with displacement mode can be used to address a specific element in an array. The address register holds the base address of the array and the displacement specifies the relative position of the element as an offset. The displacement is a 16-bit signed integer. This mode is often used to compare elements in separate arrays.

As an example, consider two arrays with word-length elements. If (A1) points to the first element X(1) and (A2) points to Y(1), the instruction sequence

    MOVE.W   4(A1),D1   ;(X(3))
    MOVE.W   4(A2),D2   ;(Y(3))
    CMP.W   D1,D2   ;COMPARE: (Y(3)) − (X(3))

_____

[5] The predecrement and postincrement modes are useful for manipulating stacks and queues of byte, word, or longword entries. These are *dynamic* arrays since the length varies with program execution. Several of the references in the Further Reading section at the end of this chapter discuss these structures in detail.

compares Y_3 and X_3 located at addresses $Y(3)$ and $X(3)$, respectively. Notice that the third element is located by a four-byte offset from the base address according to the addressing equation for $X(j)$ previously given. The offset in the indirect mode and in the program counter relative with displacement mode cannot be modified after the program is assembled, so the use of these modes does not allow indexing through an array.

Flexibility is provided by using either the address register indirect with index or PC relative with index addressing mode. In these modes, the base address consists of a register value (address register or PC) and possibly a sign-extended 8-bit displacement value. The index into the array may be calculated before it is used by evaluation of an index *expression* of any complexity. For example, in the instruction

MOVE.W   0(A1,D1.W),D1

the base address is held in A1 and the low-order 16-bit value in D1 contains the index. The value in D1 could be calculated by any mathematical expression before it is used as an index. If the 16-bit index is not sufficient, a long index of 32 bits may be specified according to the discussion of these addressing modes given in Chapter 5.

Example 9.6

The subroutine ERRMSG in Figure 9.6 calculates the address of a specified element in an array consisting of five elements, each 13 bytes in length. The array of error messages begins at location TABLE and an offset from that address is calculated according to the value in the low-order byte of D0. The address of the element is calculated by multiplying the error number by 13 and adding this value to the base address in A0. The addressing equation in this example would be

$$TABLE(k) = TABLE + 13 \times (k)$$

where $k = 0, 1, 2, 3,$ or 4 is the error number.

TABLE 9.8 MC68000 ARRAY ADDRESSING

MC68000 Addressing mode	Typical use
Predecrement	To address byte, word, or longword elements in descending sequence
Postincrement	To address byte, word, or longword elements in ascending sequence
(PC) with displacement or (An) with displacement	To locate an element at a fixed position from the base address
(PC) with index or (An) with index	To locate an element at an arbitrary postion using an index register

```
 1                                  LLEN    100
 2          00001000                ORG     $1000
 3                            *
 4                            * ERROR MESSAGES
 5                            *
 6                            * INPUT : (D0.B) = ERROR NUMBER BETWEEN 0 AND 4
 7                            *
 8                            * OUTPUT : (A0.L) = ADDRESS OF THE CORRESPONDING ERROR MESSAGE
 9                            *
10  001000 2F01      ERRMSG   MOVE.L  D1,-(SP)         ;SAVE REGISTER
11  001002 41F81012           LEA     TABLE,A0         ;GET ADDRESS OF START OF TABLE
12  001006 323C000D           MOVE.W  #13,D1           ;13 BYTES PER STRING
13  00100A C0C1               MULU    D1,D0
14  00100C D0C0               ADDA.W  D0,A0            ;COMPUTE INDEX
15  00100E 221F               MOVE.L  (SP)+,D1         ;RESTORE REGISTER
16  001010 4E75               RTS
17                      *
18                      * DEFINE TABLE OF ERROR MESSAGES
19                      *
20  001012 4F         TABLE    DC.B    'OVERFLOW     '
21  00101F 55                  DC.B    'UNDERFLOW    '
22  00102C 53                  DC.B    'SUBSCRIPT    '
23  001039 5A                  DC.B    'ZERO DIVIDE  '
24  001046 55                  DC.B    'UNIMPLEMENTED'
25                      *
26                              END
```

****** TOTAL ERRORS   0--   0

SYMBOL TABLE - APPROX 1200 SYMBOL ENTRIES LEFT

ERRMSG   001000 TABLE   001012

Figure 9.6 Addressing of an array element.

```
 1                                  LLEN    100
 2          00001000                ORG     $1000
 3                            *
 4                            * SORT A TABLE OF 8-BIT VALUES
 5                            *
 6                            * INPUT : (A0.L) = ADDRESS OF TABLE TO SORT
 7                            *         (D0.L) = NUMBER OF ENTRIES IN TABLE (NUM)
 8                            *
 9  001000 48E7FFFE   SORT     MOVEM.L D0-D7/A0-A6,-(SP)   ;SAVE REGISTERS
10  001004 5380                SUBQ.L  #1,D0
11  001006 2600                MOVE.L  D0,D3            ;COUNTER 1 = NUM - 2
12  001008 4201       SORT10   CLR.B   D1               ;FLAG = 0
13  00100A 2800                MOVE.L  D0,D4            ;COUNTER 2 = NUM - 2
14                      *
15  00100C 4DF04800   SORT20   LEA     0(A0,D4.L),A6
16  001010 1C2EFFFF            MOVE.B  -1(A6),D6        ;GET VALUE (CNT2 + 1)
17  001014 BC2E0000            CMP.B   0(A6),D6         ;IF VALUE(CNT2+1) >= VALUE(CNT2)
18  001018 6C000010            BGE     SORT30           ;    THEN SKIP
19  00101C 123800FF            MOVE.B  $FF,D1           ;SET FLAG
20  001020 1D6E0000FFFF        MOVE.B  0(A6),-1(A6)     ;SWAP KEYS
21  001026 1D460000            MOVE.B  D6,0(A6)
22                      *
23  00102A 4A01       SORT30   TST.B   D1               ;IF FLAG /= 0
24  00102C 5384                SUBQ.L  #1,D4            ;DECREMENT CNT2
25  00102E 66DC                BNE     SORT20           ;    AND LOOP
26                      *
27  001030 4A01                TST.B   D1               ;IF FLAG /= 0
28  001032 5383                SUBQ.L  #1,D3            ;THEN DECREMENT CNT1
29  001034 66D2                BNE     SORT10           ;    AND LOOP
30                      *
31  001036 4CDF7FFF            MOVEM.L (SP)+,D0-D7/A0-A6 ;RESTORE REGISTERS
32  00103A 4E75                RTS
33                              END
```

****** TOTAL ERRORS   0--   0

SYMBOL TABLE - APPROX 1198 SYMBOL ENTRIES LEFT

SORT   001000 SORT10   001008 SORT20   00100C SORT30   00102A

Figure 9.7 Sorting example.

Example 9.7

The subroutine of Figure 9.7 performs a "bubble" sort on an array of 8-bit values. When completed, the routine leaves the largest value in the first location with the following values in descending numerical order. The starting address, holding the first value of the array, is supplied in A0 and D0 should contain N, the number of elements in the array. The array is sorted by comparing elements starting with the last value in the array for each pass.

This routine uses (D0) to set up two counters in D3 and D4. The inner loop at SORT20 uses the counter in D4 to index into the array and retrieve the elements to sort. The inner loop exchanges elements until the branch condition is true. Then if any elements were exchanged, it is indicated by the flag in D1 set to $FF. The outer loop is then used to check for elements to exchange again. If the operation of the subroutine is not clear from the program comments, more detailed explanations on bubble sorts are given in the references in the Further Reading section for the chapter.

9.3.2 Two-Dimensional Arrays

A generalization of the one-dimensional array is a higher-dimensional array of elements. The elements in the multidimensional array are specified by more than one subscript, as is shown in Table 9.9(a) for the two-dimensional $M \times N$ array. Table 9.9(b) shows the 3×3 array as a specific example. In this notation, M is the number

TABLE 9.9   MULTIDIMENSIONAL ARRAYS

(a) General form

$$
\begin{array}{cccc}
X_{11} & X_{12} & \cdots & X_{1N} \\
X_{21} & X_{22} & \cdots & X_{2N} \\
\cdot & \cdot & & \cdot \\
\cdot & \cdot & & \cdot \\
\cdot & \cdot & & \cdot \\
X_{M1} & X_{M2} & \cdots & X_{MN}
\end{array}
$$

(b) 3×3 Example

$$
\begin{array}{ccc}
X_{11} & X_{12} & X_{13} \\
X_{21} & X_{22} & X_{23} \\
X_{31} & X_{32} & X_{33}
\end{array}
$$

(c) Column-major storage of a 3×3 array starting at location $1000

	Address (hexadecimal)	Array element
X(1,1)	$1000	X_{11}
X(2,1)	$1002	X_{21}
X(3,1)	$1004	X_{31}
X(1,2)	$1006	X_{12}
X(2,2)	$1008	X_{22}
X(3,2)	$100A	X_{32}
X(1,3)	$100C	X_{13}
X(2,3)	$100E	X_{23}
X(3,3)	$1010	X_{33}

of horizontal rows and N is the number of vertical columns. The element in the ith row and jth column is designated X_{ij}, where $1 \leq i \leq M$ and $1 \leq j \leq N$. X(i,j) represents the address in memory of the element X_{ij} in the form X (row, column). An $M \times N$ array has $M \times N$ elements. The row index has a range of M values and the column index has a range of N values regardless of the starting indices. Questions pertinent to structuring the data in memory concern the method of storage by row and by column as well as the techniques necessary to compute the address of an element.

Array storage.   If the $M \times N$ array X is stored sequentially by rows in addresses beginning with X(1,1) as

   X(1,1), X(1,2), . . ., X(1,N), X(2,1), . . ., X(2,N), . . ., X(M,N)

the storage is said to be in *row-major* form. An alternative scheme is *column-major* form with successive element addresses

   X(1,1), X(2,1), . . ., X(M,1), X(1,2), . . ., X(M,2), . . ., X(M,N)

as shown in Table 9.9(c). The figure shows the storage for a 3×3 array of words in the MC68000 memory starting at location $1000. This column-major form is required in standard FORTRAN and will be used for our examples in this subsection.

Once the storage form is chosen, the indices for a specific element can be computed in several ways. The *address polynomial* for an $M \times N$ array has the form

$$X(i,j) = \text{base address} + C_1 \times (j - i) + C_2 \times (i - 1)$$

for a two-dimensional array with the first address at location X(1,1). When the constants C_1 and C_2 are properly chosen, address calculation is straightforward on a processor with a multiply instruction.[6]

---

[6] In some cases, to save the time required by multiplication or to allow dynamic (during execution) allocation of array storage, special addressing methods are used. These include the use of a "dope vector" describing the array characteristics or addressing by indirection in which the row (or column) addresses are held in a table. This subject is developed further in several of the references in the Further Reading section at the end of this chapter.

TABLE 9.10   MULTIDIMENSIONAL ARRAY ADDRESSING

Array storage	Address X(i,j)
Column-major storage X(1,1), X(2,1), . . .	Bo + C * [(i − 1) + M × (j − 1)]
Row-major storage X(1,1), X(1,2), . . .	Bo + C * [(j − 1) + N × (i − 1)]

Notes:

1. Bo is the base address of array X(i,j) with elements C bytes in length.
2. The indices range as follows:
      rows: $1 \leq i \leq M$
      columns: $1 \leq j \leq N$

Table 9.10 shows the address polynomials for arrays with elements of length C bytes. The address of X_{ij} in an array stored by column-major form is

$$X(i,j) = Bo + C \times [(i - 1) + M \times (j-1)]$$

in which

$$1 \leq i \leq M \quad \text{and} \quad 1 \leq j \leq N$$

and Bo is the base address. This addressing method is easily implemented with the MC68000 using indirect addressing with indexing if elements in a fixed column (or row) are being selected. If both indices are varied, one address must be calculated separately and added to the value of the effective address computed with indexed addressing.

Example 9.8

When the address of an element in a two-dimensional array is calculated, two indices must be added to the starting or base address. The address register indirect with index and the PC relative with index addressing modes of the MC68000 allow two separate offsets and calculate the effective address as

$$<EA> = (R) + (Rn) + <d_8>$$

The register R here could be either an address register in the indirect mode or the program counter for the relative mode. The index register Rn is either an address register or data register. The displacement value $<d_8>$ is limited to an 8-bit signed integer. Figure 9.8 shows the use of this addressing method for an array stored in column-major form. If the number of bytes per element is 1, the address calculation becomes

$$X(i,j) = Bo + [(i - 1) + M \times (j - 1)]$$

The base address and one index can be stored in registers. The second index can be specified as the 8-bit offset in the address register indirect with index addressing mode. In the figure, the offset selects the row and remains fixed. The 3×3 array begins at hexadecimal location $1000, which is stored in A1, and the register D1 contains the column index $(j - 1) \times M$, which is $0006. The instruction

        MOVE.B   1(A1,D1.L),D2

transfers element X_{23} to the low-order byte of D2. To select A_{2j} from another column, (D1) must be changed to indicate the column offset, which is computed as $3 \times (j - 1)$ with $j = 1, 2,$ or 3.

Example 9.9

The subroutine in Figure 9.9 performs a binary search of a table or array for a word-length bit pattern called a key value. The table is composed of M entries which are each N bytes long. The starting address of the table is supplied in A0 and the key to locate is in D0[7:0]. The low-order word of D1 contains the length (N) of each entry and D2[15:0] contains the number of entries (M) in the table.

If the search is successful, the address of the key value is returned in A6. Otherwise, A6 contains a zero. Since a binary search is being performed, the data are assumed to be sorted numerically in the table being searched.

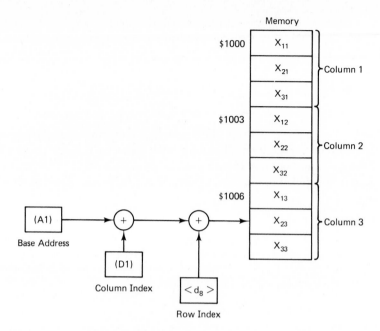

Example: Load X_{23} into D2
           MOVE.B 1(A1, D1.L),D2   ;(D2)[7:0] ◄── ((A1) + (D1) + 1)

           (A1) = $0000 1000 (Base)
           (D1) = $0000 0006 (Column index = (j − 1)*M)
           $< d_8 >$ =   .1   (Row index = i − 1)

Figure 9.8   Fixed-element addressing.

9.3.3 Linked Lists

When dealing with arrays, the successor of an item being addressed is located by add-ing a constant to the address of the present item. For example, in a one-dimensional array

$$X(j + 1) = X(j) + C$$

where C is the number of bytes occupied by each element. The elements, ordered suc-cessively, occupied contiguous blocks of memory, as shown in Figure 9.10. In compar-ison, the *linked list* is a data structure that does not require contiguous storage of its elements. The linked list is treated in an introductory manner in this subsection. Ad-vanced operations on such lists, including management of the memory space occupied by the list and ordering of list elements, is discussed in several of the references in the Further Reading section at the end of the chapter.

The sketch in Figure 9.11(a) shows a sample linked list of five items. Each ele-

MC68000 ASM REV= 1.4 - COPYRIGHT BY MOTOROLA 1978   PAGE 1

```
 1                              LLEN    100
 2       00001000               ORG     $1000
 3                         *
 4                         * SEARCH SUBROUTINE DOES A BINARY SEARCH OF A TABLE
 5                         * INPUT : (A0.L) = TABLE TO SEARCH
 6                         *         (D0.B) = KEY TO SEARCH FOR
 7                         *         (D1.W) = LENGTH OF EACH ENTRY IN TABLE
 8                         *         (D2.W) = NUMBER OF ENTRIES IN TABLE   (END)
 9                         *
10                         * OUTPUT : (A6.L) = ADDRESS OF ITEM IN TABLE WITH VALUE OF
11                         *                   KEY (OR ZERO)
12                         *
13 001000 48E7FFFC     SEARCH    MOVEM.L D0-D7/A0-A5,-(SP)    ;SAVE REGISTERS ON STACK
14 001004 5342                   SUBQ.W  #1,D2               ;INIT :  END (D2)
15 001006 4283                   CLR.L   D3                  ;        BEGIN (D3)
16 001008 2C43                   MOVE.L  D3,A6               ;        OUTPUT VALUE
17                         *
18 00100A B642         SER10     CMP.W   D2,D3               ;IF BEGIN >= END
19 00100C 6E000028               BGT     EXIT                ;   THEN EXIT
20 001010 3803                   MOVE.W  D3,D4               ;   ELSE COMPUTE
21 001012 D842                   ADD.W   D2,D4               ;        INDEX = (BEGIN
22                         *                                                  + END)/2
23                         *                                 ENDIF
24 001014 E24C                   LSR.W   #1,D4
25 001016 3A04                   MOVE.W  D4,D5               ;COMPUTE ADDRESS
26 001018 CAC1                   MULU    D1,D5               ;INDEX IN TABLE OF KEY
27                         *                                  * ENTRY LENGTH
28 00101A B0305000               CMP.B   0(A0,D5),D0         ;IF KEY >= ENTRY
29 00101E 6C000008               BGE     SER20               ;   THEN BRANCH TO MODIFY
30                         *                                          BEGIN
31 001022 5344                   SUBQ.W  #1,D4               ;   ELSE SET
32 001024 3404                   MOVE.W  D4,D2               ;        END = INDEX - 1
33 001026 60E2                   BRA     SER10               ;   TRY AGAIN
34                         *
35                         *                                 ENDIF
36 001028 67000008     SER20     BEQ     SUCCESS             ;IF KEY = TABLE ENTRY
37                         *                                   THEN BRANCH TO UPDATE
38                         *                                        OUTPUT
39 00102C 5244                   ADDQ.W  #1,D4               ;   ELSE
40 00102E 3604                   MOVE.W  D4,D3               ;        BEGIN = INDEX + 1
41 001030 60D8                   BRA     SER10               ;        TRY AGAIN
42                         *
43                         *                                 ENDIF
44 001032 4DF05000     SUCCESS   LEA     0(A0,D5.W),A6       ;SAVE OUTPUT ADDRESS
45 001036 4CDF3FFF     EXIT      MOVEM.L (SP)+,D0-D7/A0-A5   ;RESTORE REGISTERS
46 00103A 4E75                   RTS
47                               END
```

****** TOTAL ERRORS   0--   0

SYMBOL TABLE - APPROX 1197 SYMBOL ENTRIES LEFT

EXIT   001036 SEARCH   001000 SER10   00100A SER20   001028
SUCCESS   001032

Figure 9.9 Search routine.

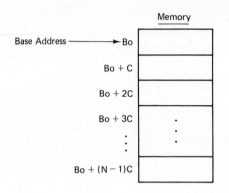

Notes:
(1) Bo is the base address.
(2) Each element is C bytes long.

Figure 9.10 Sequential array storage.

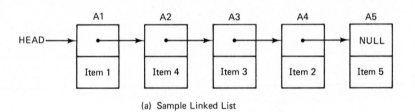

(a) Sample Linked List

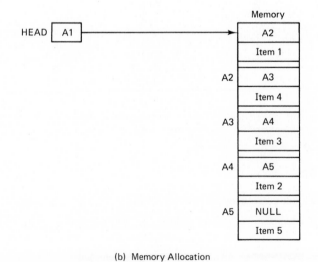

(b) Memory Allocation

Figure 9.11 Allocation for an unordered linked list.

ment in the list contains both a pointer (address) or a *link* to the next element in the list and the data item. The list shown has a *one-way* link since only an item's successor can be found. Also, the sample list is unordered since the data items do not follow one another in numerical order. The pointer to the list is stored at address HEAD. The last element, item 5 in the figure, contains a special symbol. It is designated NULL to indicate the end of the list. A NULL value of zero, for example, could be used in MC68000 programs since no data item would be stored at location 0000. If location HEAD contains the value NULL, the list is empty. Figure 9.11(b) illustrates how the sample list could be stored in memory.

Example 9.10

Figure 9.12 shows a subroutine that creates a linked list in a free area of memory with beginning address AVAIL. The nodes or elements in the list are each eight bytes in length and the list will be initialized to contain 10 entries. The loop starting at label LINK computes the address of the next node in the list and then stores the address as the link to that node. After the loop terminates, the last link that was stored is rewritten with a NULL value.

The monitor listing shows the contents of memory before and after this subroutine is executed. After execution the HEAD has been initialized to point to AVAIL and the links have been stored.

EXERCISES

9.3.1. Write a subroutine to return the sine of an angle in degrees when an angle from 0 to 360 degrees is specified. Use a lookup table with a 1-degree resolution in angle. Assume that the table with starting address SINE is already provided and contains 16-bit values for the sines of angles from 0 to 89 degrees. If the angle is greater than 90 degrees, compute the sine of the angle using trigonometric identities. (*Note:* The value could be calculated using the Taylor series expansion for SIN(X):

$$\text{SIN}(X) = X - (X^3/3!) + (X^5/5!) - \cdots$$

The series method will yield the sine value to any accuracy but is far slower than the table lookup if the table has sufficient resolution. Create an abbreviated table of sine values and test your routine.

9.3.2. Write a subroutine to clear a three-dimensional array *without* calculating the three-dimensional address polynomial. Assume that the array is stored in column-major form and the subroutine is passed the starting address, the size of the array ($M \times N \times O$), and the number of bytes in each element.

9.3.3. Write a routine to multiply two 2×2 matrices.

9.3.4. Write the address polynomial for a *k*-dimensional array if $I_1, I_2, I_3, \ldots, I_k$ are the indices and $L_1, L_2, L_3, \ldots, L_k$ are the lengths.

9.3.5. Write a subroutine to remove an entry from the top of the linked list created in Example 9.10. What happens if the list is empty [i.e., (HEAD) = NULL]?

MC68000 ASM REV= 1.4 - COPYRIGHT BY MOTOROLA 1978   PAGE 1

```
1                              LLEN    100
2        00001000              ORG     $1000
3                      *
4        00000000      NULL    EQU     0                       ;SET UP VALUE FOR NULL
5                      *
6                      * CREATE A LINKED LIST
7                      *
8                      * INPUT : AVAIL IS THE ADDRESS OF A FREE BLOCK OF MEMORY
9                      *         HEAD IS THE POINTER TO THE TOP OF THE LINKED STACK
10                     *
11                     * OUTPUT : LINKS ARE STORED IN THE BLOCK AT AVAIL AND
12                     *          HEAD POINTS TO THE FIRST NODE IN THE LIST
13                     *
14 001000 48E7C0C0     LNKLST  MOVEM.L D0-D1/A0-A1,-(SP)        ;SAVE REGISTERS
15 001004 41F8102A             LEA     AVAIL,A0
16 001008 21C81026             MOVE.L  A0,HEAD                  ;SET HEAD TO POINT TO AVAIL
17 00100C 7008                 MOVE.L  #8,D0                    ;SET UP BYTES/NODE
18 00100E 720A                 MOVE.L  #10,D1                   ;SET UP NUMBER OF NODES
19                     *
20 001010 2248         LINK    MOVE.L  A0,A1                    ;NODE ADDRESS INTO A1
21 001012 D1C0                 ADD.L   D0,A0                    ;COMPUTE NEXT NODE
22 001014 2288                 MOVE.L  A0,(A1)                  ;STORE LINK TO NEXT NODE
23 001016 5381                 SUBQ.L  #1,D1                    ;DECREMENT NUMBER OF NODES
24 001018 66F6                 BNE     LINK                     ;UNTIL COUNT REACHES ZERO
25                     *
26 00101A 22BC00000000         MOVE.L  #NULL,(A1)               ;REWRITE LAST LINK
27                     *
28 001020 4CDF0303             MOVEM.L (SP)+,D0-D1/A0-A1        ;RESTORE REGISTERS
29 001024 4E75                 RTS
30                     *
31 001026 00000004     HEAD    DS.L    1                        ;POINTER TO TOP OF LINKED STACK
32 00102A 00000050     AVAIL   DS.L    20                       ;MEMORY BLOCK FOR LINKED STACK
33                     *
34                             END
```

****** TOTAL ERRORS   0--   0

SYMBOL TABLE - APPROX 1198 SYMBOL ENTRIES LEFT

```
AVAIL      00102A HEAD      001026 LINK       001010 LNKLST       001000
NULL       000000
```

```
*DM 1026 50
001026  FF FF FF FF FF FF FF FF FF FF FF FF FF FF FF FF    ................
001036  FF FF FF FF FF FF FF FF FF FF FF FF FF FF FF FF    ................
001046  FF FF FF FF FF FF FF FF FF FF FF FF FF FF FF FF    ................
001056  FF FF FF FF FF FF FF FF FF FF FF FF FF FF FF FF    ................
001066  FF FF FF FF FF FF FF FF FF FF FF FF FF FF FF       ...............
*TD
PC=001000 SR=2004 US=00007F00 SS=00007FFE
D0=00000000 D1=00000000 D2=00000000 D3=00000000
D4=00000000 D5=00000000 D6=00000000 D7=00000000
A0=00000000 A1=00000000 A2=00000000 A3=00000000
A4=00000000 A5=00000000 A6=00000000 A7=00007FFE
----------------------------------------------------------------
*G TILL 1024
PC=001024 SR=2004 US=00007F00 SS=00007FFE
D0=00000000 D1=00000000 D2=00000000 D3=00000000
D4=00000000 D5=00000000 D6=00000000 D7=00000000
A0=00000000 A1=00000000 A2=00000000 A3=00000000
A4=00000000 A5=00000000 A6=00000000 A7=00007FFE
----------------------------------------------------------------
*DM 1026 50
001026  00 00 10 2A 00 00 10 32 FF FF FF FF 00 00 10 3A    ...*...2.......:
001036  FF FF FF FF 00 00 10 42 FF FF FF FF 00 00 10 4A    .......B......J
001046  FF FF FF FF 00 00 10 52 FF FF FF FF 00 00 10 5A    .......R......Z
001056  FF FF FF FF 00 00 10 62 FF FF FF FF 00 00 10 6A    .......b......j
001066  FF FF FF FF 00 00 10 72 FF FF FF FF 00 00 00 00    .......r........
*
```

Figure 9.12 Subroutine to create a linked list.

9.4 SUBROUTINE USAGE AND ARGUMENT PASSING

The use of *subroutines* or procedures is an important programming technique to create modular programs in which each subroutine performs a specific task within the overall program. The method of transfer of control between the calling program and the subroutine is called *subroutine linkage.* In the MC68000, the call to the subroutine is performed by the instruction

JSR   <SUBR>

which first causes the return address within the calling program to be pushed onto the system stack. Then control is transferred to the subroutine at address <SUBR>. The address may be specified by any of the control addressing modes of the MC68000. Thus transfer of control is accomplished very simply in the MC68000. When data must be passed between the calling program and the subroutine, a number of methods are available to transfer the information. The method is selected when the program is designed, and this choice constitutes an important part of the program design.

The information needed by the subroutine is defined in terms of *parameters* which allow the subroutine to handle general cases rather than operate on specific values. Each call to the subroutine allows different values, called *arguments,* to be supplied for the parameters. Some typical FORTRAN subroutine references are shown in Figure 9.13. The subroutine is named SUBR and has the parameters A, B, and C. It may be called with various arguments as long as the arguments are the same data type (integer, floating-point, etc.) as the parameters in the subroutine definition. The names or values of the arguments are arbitrary. The symbolic names for the arguments in the example are actually addresses assigned by the compiler. The specific values 1.0 and 3.0 in the second call can be substituted to take advantage of the flexibility of the FORTRAN language. In assembly language, the distinction between actual values and the addresses of arguments is important.

The mechanics of defining parameters and transmitting arguments to subroutines are more complex in assembly language. Processor registers, the system stack, or fixed locations in memory may hold arguments. Also, the LINK and UNLK instructions of the MC68000 can be used to create *stack frames* as a subroutine is called. This frame is a block of memory reserved on the stack which holds the return address, arguments, and local variables, if any. Recursive subroutines can be implemented using this method of data handling in the subroutine.

9.4.1 Passing Arguments to Subroutines

The parameters, which define the arguments to be transferred between a subroutine and the calling program, can be data values, addresses, or combinations of both. When only a small number of arguments are to be transferred, they are passed directly between the programs in processor registers. When many variables are passed or when a data structure such as an array is being referenced, the address of the group of variables or data structure is transferred. The distinctions here have broad significance in

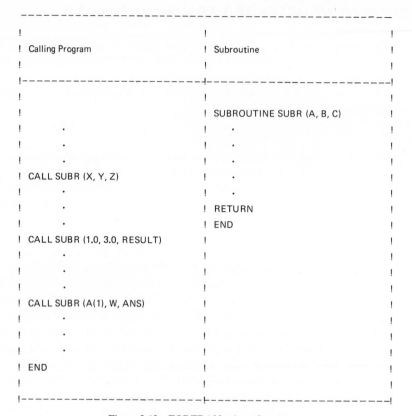

Figure 9.13   FORTRAN subroutine usage.

many high-level language programs when the operation of the compiler is considered. In assembly language, the distinction between values and addresses is important because the method of passing the parameters determines how the arguments are accessed.

Several techniques used to pass values or addresses between programs are listed in Table 9.11. The calling program sets up the calling sequence, including the definition of the arguments to be transferred to the subroutine. The subroutine then accesses the arguments for processing and possibly returns values or addresses to the calling program. The arguments passed to the subroutine are defined as the *input parameters*. The results are values or addresses corresponding to the *output parameters* for the subroutine. Of course, a combination of the techniques listed in Table 9.11 could be used when a complicated set of input and output parameters are defined.

Register transfer.   The simplest method of passing arguments is using the MC68000 register set. Data values can be passed in any of the eight data registers. Similarly, the address registers can be used to pass addresses that may point to data

TABLE 9.11 METHODS TO PASS ARGUMENTS

Type	Description	Comments
Register	The calling routine loads predefined registers with values or addresses.	Number of parameters is limited Dynamic
Stack	The calling routine pushes values or addresses on the stack.	Return address must be saved during processing and restored before return
Parameter areas	Memory areas are defined which contain the values or addresses.	Static, if areas are defined during assembly Dynamic, if base address of area is passed in a register
In-line	Values or addresses are stored following the call. The subroutine computes the location of the parameters.	Static

values or may contain the starting addresses of data structures. The register passing scheme has the advantages of simplicity, small memory requirements, and minimum execution time. The number of arguments that can be passed is limited to the number of registers available: 15 for the MC68000. The designer of the subroutine and the calling routine need only agree on which registers are used to pass the arguments. For example, the instruction sequence

```
MOVE.W     VALUE,D1     ;DATA
MOVEA.L    ADDTAB,A1    ;POINTER
LEA        HEAD,A2      ;ADDRESS OF HEAD
JSR        SUBR
```

sets up a 16-bit value in D1, the address pointer in location ADDTAB in A1 and the address HEAD in A2. The subroutine SUBR can then access the values in the registers directly to perform its function.

Stack transfer.   A stack can be used to pass arguments by having the calling routine push values or addresses on the stack before the call. A private stack, which can be defined in MC68000 programs using address register A0, A1, . . ., or A6 to represent the stack pointer, could be used. The values are pushed using the predecrement or postincrement mode of addressing in the calling program. Popping the arguments in the subroutine allows access to the values or addresses. For a private stack, the modification of the stack pointer during execution does not affect system operation and is handled at the discretion of the programmer. The sequence to set up A1 as the stack pointer and pass two values might be

```
LEA        STACKP,A1    ;ADDRESS OF STACK IN A1
MOVE.W     VAL1,(A1)+   ;PUSH FIRST VALUE
```

```
MOVE.W    VAL2,(A1)+    ;PUSH SECOND VALUE
JSR       SUBR
```

where STACKP is the BOTTOM of the stack in memory and the stack increases into higher memory locations. The subroutine accesses the values by the sequence

```
MOVE.W    −(A1),D2      ;SECOND VALUE
MOVE.W    −(A1),D1      ;FIRST VALUE
```

if the object is to load the values into data registers. The stack pointer A1 now contains its original value STACKP. In this example, the argument in register A1 contained the address of a data structure (the stack) in memory.

When the system stack is used to pass arguments, the return address is at top of the stack when the subroutine begins execution. This value must be removed before the subroutine can extract the arguments from the stack. When the processing of the subroutine is complete, the return address must be placed back on the top of the stack before the RTS instruction can be executed. The calling sequence for this method of parameter passing could be

```
PEA       ADDR        ;PUSH ADDRESS
MOVE.W    VAL1,−(SP)  ;PUSH VALUE
JSR       SUBR
```

The address ADDR is placed on the stack first, then the value in location VAL1, and finally the return address. Since (PC) is at the top of the stack, it can be saved and then restored before the return. The sequence to accomplish this might be

```
MOVE.L    (SP)+,A1      ;SAVE (PC) TEMPORARILY
MOVE.W    (SP)+,D1      ;GET DATA
MOVEA.L   (SP)+,A2      ;GET ADDRESS
            .
            .                         ;PROCESS
            .
MOVE.L    A1,−(SP)      ;RESTORE (PC)
RTS
```

Since this method is typically used by a program in the user mode, the active stack pointer is the USP. Modifying the stack pointers does not interfere with interrupt processing and similar system operations that use the supervisor stack pointer (SSP).

Memory locations for arguments.   When large numbers of parameters are to be passed, a *parameter area* can be set up in memory. This area contains, in a predetermined sequence, the values or addresses that are accessed by the subroutine after it has been passed the starting address of the area. The same area could be used by several subroutines requiring different parameters as long as the area is large enough to hold the maximum number of arguments.

Another use of this method is common in systems which have subroutines in ROM such as the MACSbug monitor described in Chapter 5. The parameter area in RAM (Random Access read/write Memory) memory is defined according to the system requirements and the address is passed to the subroutines to use as a base address in accessing the arguments.[7]

The calling program could set up a parameter area in the following way:

```
MOVE.W      VAL1,PRMAREA        ;STORE DATA
MOVE.W      VAL2,PRMAREA+2      ;SECOND WORD
               .
               .
               .
MOVE.W      VAL5, PRMAREA+8     ;FIFTH WORD
LEA         PRMAREA,A1          ;PUSH ADDRESS
JSR         SUBR
               .
               .
               .
PRMAREA     DS.W 5              ;RESERVED AREA
END
```

in which five words are defined as parameters. The subroutine could access the values using indirect addressing with displacement. For example, the instruction

```
MOVE.W 6(A1),D1
```

transfers the fourth value to D1. Many variations are possible to define the parameter areas in memory.

In-Line coding.   Another method of passing values to a subroutine is to code the values following the call to the subroutine. This method, called *in-line coding,* defines argument values which are constant and will not change after assembly. These values can be defined by DC directives following the call. Consider the instruction sequence

```
JSR    SUBR
DC.W 1                 ;IN-LINE ARGUMENT
```

The 32 bits of (PC) are pushed on the system stack by the subroutine call. This address points to the location of the *argument* in the instruction sequence. The following sequence can be executed by the subroutine to load the argument into the low-order word of D1 and point the return address on the stack to the word beyond the value:

```
MOVEA.L   (A7),A0     ;GET PC VALUE
MOVE.W    (A0)+,D1    ;GET ARGUMENT, INCREMENT
```

---

[7] Another version, used when FORTRAN "common" areas are specified, defines the address of the parameter area to both the calling program and the subroutine during compilation.

```
                            ;PUSH NEW RETURN ADDRESS
MOVEA.L    · A0,(A7)
                 ·          ;PROCESS
                 ·

RTS
```

The first instruction loads the (PC) into A0 from the stack. Register A0 then addresses the argument and is incremented by 2 after D1 is loaded. After A0 is incremented,
it points to the next instruction in the calling program following the in-line argument.
The next instruction in the subroutine pushes the correct return address on the stack,
overwriting the value saved by the JSR instruction. The RTS instruction is used here
to restore (PC) and return control to the calling program. The reference to A7 indicates the system stack pointer: either USP or SSP depending on whether the program
mode is user or supervisor, respectively.

9.4.2 Stack Frames

One of the principal issues in the design of subroutines involves the concept of *trans-
parency*. Simply stated, when a subroutine finishes executing, it should have no "visi-
ble" effect except as defined by its linkage to the calling program. For example, a
subroutine should not change the values in any registers, unless a register is used to
return a result. In the previous example programs, this was accomplished by pushing
the contents of the registers used by the subroutine on the stack upon entry to the
subroutine. The values were restored before returning to the calling program. The return address was automatically saved and restored by the JSR and RTS instructions.

The use of the system stack to save and restore the return address and the contents of registers used within the subroutine assured that the details of the subroutine
operation were transparent to the calling program. If a subroutine itself made a subroutine call, the use of the stack for temporary storage of register contents by each
subroutine and for each return address allowed such nesting of subroutine calls without difficulty. This concept of using the stack to store data temporarily during subroutine execution can be extended by defining a *stack frame*.

The stack frame is a block of memory in the stack that is used for return addresses, input parameters, output parameters, and local variables. It is the area of the
stack accessed by a subroutine during its execution. Local variables are those values
used during the subroutine execution that are not transferred back to the calling routine. A loop counter, for example, which changes as the subroutine performs each iteration might be defined as a local variable. On each call to the subroutine, a new set of
parameters, local variables, and return addresses can be accessed by a subroutine using the stack frame technique. If the subroutine is called before it is completely finished, the values in the stack frame will not be destroyed.

MC68000 stack frames.   In multiprogramming systems, several independent tasks may use the same subroutine. For example, two CRT terminals may be

connected to the system but share the same I/O routine. As the operating system switches control between the terminals, it is possible that the I/O routine of one is interrupted and control passed to the other terminal temporarily. All the data associated with the first terminal used by the I/O routine must be saved so that when the first terminal regains control, the I/O routine begins where it left off. Such usage requires *reentrant* routines in which no data in the program memory itself changes value during execution. Any values that change are placed on the stack for storage. Thus the program or code is separated completely from the data on which it operates. A special case is the *recursive* routine, which calls itself and so is self-reentrant. The stack frame allows reentrant and recursive routines to be created easily.

The stack frame is created by the calling program and the subroutine using the MC68000 instructions LINK and UNLK. The syntax and operation of these instructions are shown in Table 9.12. Access to variables on the stack by the subroutine is accomplished by using offsets (or indexing) from a base register called a *frame pointer*. Although the stack pointer may change value as items are pushed or popped, the frame pointer does not change during the subroutine's execution. Figure 9.14 illustrates a possible sequence in the calling program and the operation of the subroutine. Figure 9.15 shows the stack contents for this example. Many variations are possible according to the application. In the case shown, the calling routine first reserves N bytes on the stack for arguments to be returned by the subroutine. Then an input value and an address are pushed on the stack. The JSR instruction pushes the return address and transfers control to the subroutine. At this point, the stack contains N bytes of space for the result, the 32-bit contents of location ARG, the address X, and the return address.

The subroutine first executes the LINK instruction to create a stack frame and define the frame pointer. This instruction saves the value of $<An>$ on the stack and replaces $<An>$ with the value of the stack pointer using A1 in our example. The frame pointer thus points to the *bottom* of the local area for the subroutine. Then the displacement is added to the stack pointer so that (SP) points M bytes farther down in memory. Local variables are stored in this area and accessed by displacements from the value in the frame pointer. Once the input arguments are processed and the outputs are stored on the stack, the UNLK instruction is executed. This instruction as defined in Table 9.12 releases the local area and restores the stack pointer contents so that it points to the return address.

Specifically, the UNLK instruction first loads (SP) with the value in the frame pointer A1, which points to the old value of A1 saved on the stack by the LINK instruction. Then A1 is restored to its previous value using the autoincrement mode of addressing so that (SP) now points to the return address. The RTS instruction returns control to the calling program, with (SP) indicating the location of the top of the parameter area set up by this program as indicated in Figure 9.15. The calling routine then adds 8 to (SP) by the instruction

        LEA   8(SP),SP

which skips over the input parameter area and leaves (SP) pointing to the output argu-

TABLE 9.12   OPERATION OF LINK AND UNLK

Instruction	Syntax	Operation
Link	LINK $<$An$>$,#$<$disp$>$	1. (SP) $\leftarrow$ (SP) $-$ 4; ((SP)) $\leftarrow$ (An)
		2. (An) $\leftarrow$ (SP)
		3. (SP) $\leftarrow$ (SP) $+$ $<$disp$>$
Unlink	UNLK $<$An$>$	1. (SP) $\leftarrow$ (An)
		2. (An) $\leftarrow$ ((SP)); (SP) $\leftarrow$ (SP) $+$ 4

Note: $<$disp$>$ is a 16-bit signed integer. A negative displacement is specified to allocate stack area.

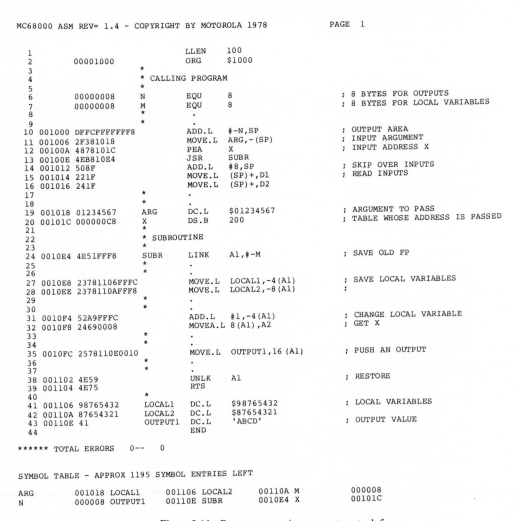

```
MC68000 ASM REV= 1.4 - COPYRIGHT BY MOTOROLA 1978          PAGE  1


     1                            LLEN    100
     2      00001000              ORG     $1000
     3                       *
     4                       * CALLING PROGRAM
     5                       *
     6      00000008     N    EQU     8                ; 8 BYTES FOR OUTPUTS
     7      00000008     M    EQU     8                ; 8 BYTES FOR LOCAL VARIABLES
     8                       *    .
     9                       *    .
    10 001000 DFFCFFFFFFF8      ADD.L   #-N,SP          ; OUTPUT AREA
    11 001006 2F381018          MOVE.L  ARG,-(SP)       ; INPUT ARGUMENT
    12 00100A 4878101C          PEA     X               ; INPUT ADDRESS X
    13 00100E 4EB810E4          JSR     SUBR
    14 001012 508F              ADD.L   #8,SP           ; SKIP OVER INPUTS
    15 001014 221F              MOVE.L  (SP)+,D1        ; READ INPUTS
    16 001016 241F              MOVE.L  (SP)+,D2
    17                       *    .
    18                       *    .
    19 001018 01234567     ARG  DC.L    $01234567       ; ARGUMENT TO PASS
    20 00101C 000000C8     X    DS.B    200             ; TABLE WHOSE ADDRESS IS PASSED
    21                       *
    22                       * SUBROUTINE
    23                       *
    24 0010E4 4E51FFF8     SUBR LINK    A1,#-M          ; SAVE OLD FP
    25                       *    .
    26                       *    .
    27 0010E8 23781106FFFC      MOVE.L  LOCAL1,-4(A1)   ; SAVE LOCAL VARIABLES
    28 0010EE 2378110AFFF8      MOVE.L  LOCAL2,-8(A1)   ;
    29                       *    .
    30                       *    .
    31 0010F4 52A9FFFC          ADD.L   #1,-4(A1)       ; CHANGE LOCAL VARIABLE
    32 0010F8 24690008          MOVEA.L 8(A1),A2        ; GET X
    33                       *    .
    34                       *    .
    35 0010FC 2578110E0010      MOVE.L  OUTPUT1,16(A1)  ; PUSH AN OUTPUT
    36                       *    .
    37                       *    .
    38 001102 4E59              UNLK    A1              ; RESTORE
    39 001104 4E75              RTS
    40                       *    .
    41 001106 98765432     LOCAL1  DC.L    $98765432    ; LOCAL VARIABLES
    42 00110A 87654321     LOCAL2  DC.L    $87654321    ;
    43 00110E 41           OUTPUT1 DC.L    'ABCD'       ; OUTPUT VALUE
    44                            END

****** TOTAL ERRORS   0--   0


SYMBOL TABLE - APPROX 1195 SYMBOL ENTRIES LEFT

ARG       001018 LOCAL1   001106 LOCAL2    00110A M        000008
N         000008 OUTPUT1  00110E SUBR      0010E4 X        00101C
```

Figure 9.14   Program operation to create a stack frame.

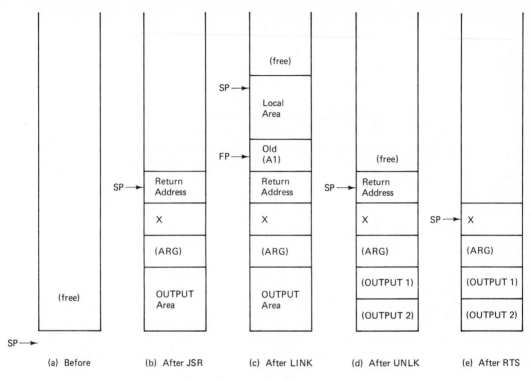

Figure 9.15 Stack contents using stack frame.

ments. These arguments now represent input values to the calling program. After these are popped, the stack pointer has its original contents.

EXERCISES

9.4.1. Compare the passing of addresses rather than data values as arguments when a subroutine processes an array.

9.4.2. Discuss the advantages and disadvantages of in-line parameter passing.

9.4.3. The dynamic nature of the stack used to hold arguments can result in a considerable savings of memory space when compared to the assignment of individual parameter areas for each subroutine. How does one compute the required maximum size of the stack to hold parameters?

9.4.4. Write a subroutine to compare two multiple-precision integers (64 bits) and place the largest value in a given location. Pass the addresses on the stack with the first integer in location N1, the second in N2, and the result to be placed in location MAX. Be sure to correct the stack pointer value to "collapse" the stack before the subroutine returns control to the calling program.

9.4.5. Compare the instruction sequence

      LEA $2000,A3

      LEA $1FF0,SP

with the instruction

      LINK   A3,$-$10

if (SP) = $2000 when the LINK instruction is executed.

9.4.6. Write a program that produces the sum and the average value of N positive 16-bit integers stored in a fixed area of memory. Use a stack frame to pass all the parameters between the program segments.

FURTHER READING

Position-independent coding is discussed in most textbooks written about the PDP-11 computer. In particular, Tanenbaum explains this technique and also includes discussions of base register addressing and dynamic relocation of programs. Stritter and Gunter discuss a number of the MC68000 instructions used in this chapter. Knuth gives an excellent discussion of data structures, as well as subroutine usage, with emphasis on assembly language programming. The stack frame technique is well discussed in Wakerly's book, which includes MC68000 programming examples.

KNUTH, DONALD E., *The Art of Computer Programming,* Vol. 1: *Fundamental Algorithms.* Reading, Mass.: Addison-Wesley, 1969.

STRITTER, EDWARD, and TOM GUNTER, "A Microprocessor Architecture for a Changing World: The Motorola 68000," *IEEE Computer,* **12,** No. 2 (February 1979), 43–52.

TANENBAUM, ANDREW S., *Structured Computer Organization*, 2nd ed. Englewood Cliffs, N.J.: Prentice-Hall, 1984.

WAKERLY, JOHN F., *Microcomputer Architecture and Programming.* New York: Wiley, 1981.

10

System Operation

The previous chapters have considered the MC68000 applications programs. The emphasis was, therefore, on the instruction set of the MC68000 and programming techniques. The next three chapters discuss the operation of MC68000 systems, emphasizing the interaction between the various components. These components include the operating system or supervisor program, the CPU, memory, and associated hardware.

The CPU can be running a program *normally,* processing an *exception,* or simply waiting in a *halted* state for a signal to reset the system. The reset sequence is associated with system initialization and is initiated by external circuitry. The operation of the system reset is shown in Figure 10.1(a). The initial values of certain registers and the vector addresses associated with system operation are initialized by the system hardware and the supervisor program. Then control is passed to an applications program which operates as illustrated in Figure 10.1(b). Program execution continues until its task is complete or a supervisor service is required. The program may cause a trap to return control to the supervisor in order to perform a service, such as inputting or outputting data.

The trap is an example of a condition that causes exception processing in the supervisor mode, as shown in Figure 10.1(c). Each exception initiates execution of the appropriate exception routine. Upon completion of the routine, control may be returned to the program that was executing when the exception occurred. The exact sequence depends completely on the design of the system.

This chapter discusses MC68000 system operation in the various states. Instructions used for system control and initialization are included. Exception processing is covered in Chapter 11 using program examples. System design considerations and in-

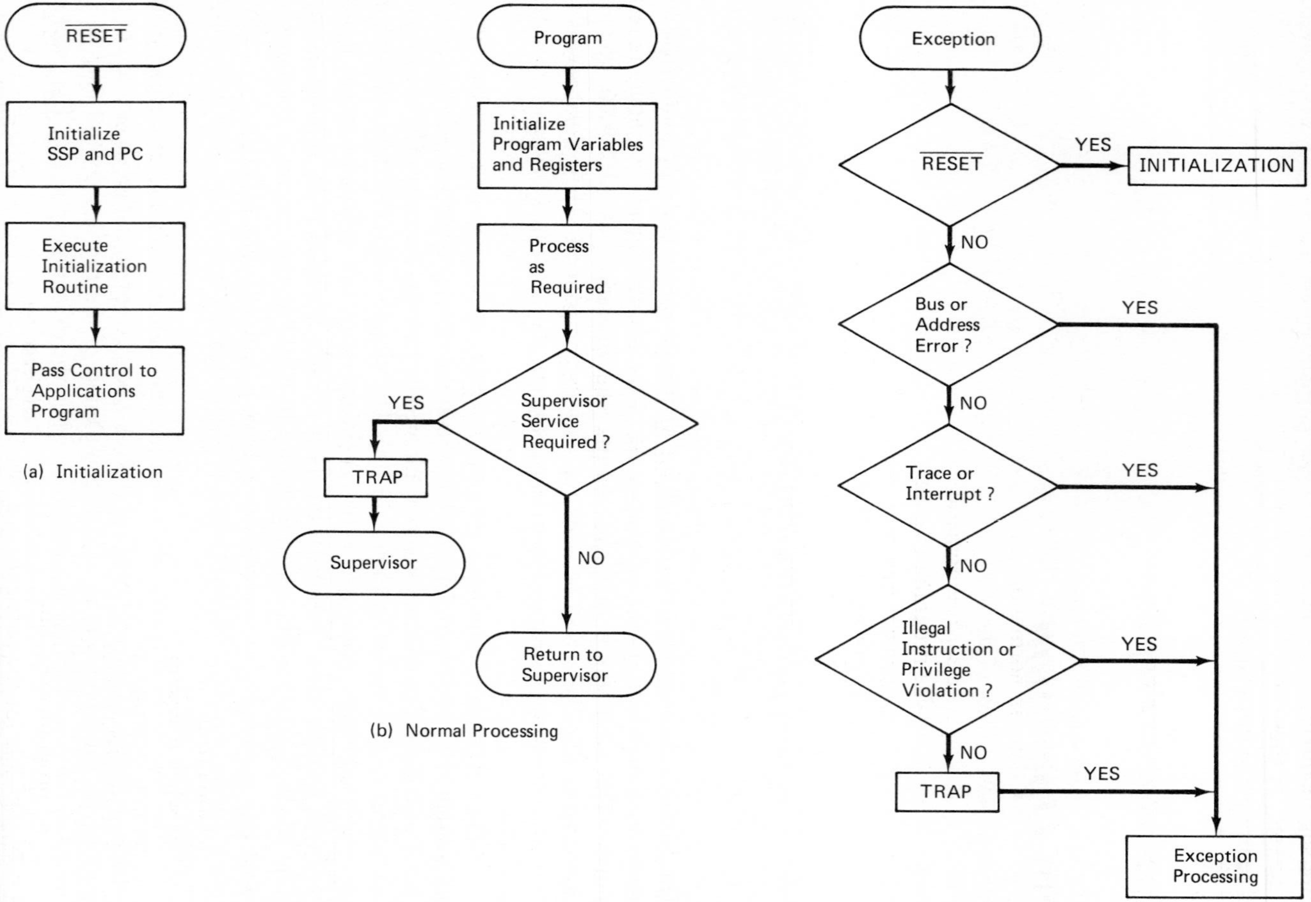

Figure 10.1 System operation.

(a) Initialization

RESET → Initialize SSP and PC → Execute Initialization Routine → Pass Control to Applications Program

(b) Normal Processing

Program → Initialize Program Variables and Registers → Process as Required → Supervisor Service Required?

Supervisor Service Required? — YES → TRAP → Supervisor

Supervisor Service Required? — NO → Return to Supervisor

(c) Exception

Exception → RESET?

RESET — YES → INITIALIZATION

RESET — NO → Bus or Address Error?

Bus or Address Error? — YES → Exception Processing

Bus or Address Error? — NO → Trace or Interrupt?

Trace or Interrupt? — YES → Exception Processing

Trace or Interrupt? — NO → Illegal Instruction or Privilege Violation?

Illegal Instruction or Privilege Violation? — YES → Exception Processing

Illegal Instruction or Privilege Violation? — NO → TRAP → Exception Processing

terfacing requirements are discussed in Chapter 12. A review of Chapters 2 and 4 is suggested, as those chapters contain preliminary discussions of many of the concepts to be presented in the following text.

10.1 PROCESSOR STATES AND MODES

The MC68000 operates in one of three processing states: normal, exception, or halted. When a program is executing, the processor operation is further described by its mode or privilege state. In normal operation, the mode is either supervisor or user, as determined by the setting of the status bit ("S" bit) in the status register. When an exception occurs, the processor is automatically put in the supervisor mode. The states and modes affect both the programming and the hardware operation of the system. Programming aspects are considered here, and a discussion of the external electrical activity of the processor is presented in Chapter 12.

10.1.1 Normal, Exception, and Halted States

Table 10.1 summarizes the three states of the processor. The *normal* state is associated with program execution in either the supervisor or the user mode. In this state, the processor is fetching instructions and operands from memory to process. Programs not associated with exception processing always execute in the normal state. The state is typically entered after initialization of the system. Unless a hardware failure is detected, the state of the processor changes only when an exception occurs.

The only special case during operation in the normal state is the *stopped* condition. Here the processor no longer executes instructions but waits for an external event to initiate continued execution. A stopped condition in the normal state occurs when the instruction

STOP   # <d_{16}>

is executed. The 16-bit immediate value <d_{16}> replaces the contents of the status register and the (PC) is advanced to point to the next instruction. Until an interrupt or other event is recognized, the processor stops fetching and executing instructions. The STOP instruction must be executed by a program in the supervisor mode or a privilege violation (trap) will occur.[1] Processor activity resumes when an interrupt is recognized or when a system reset is performed. In practice, the STOP instruction can be considered a "wait for interrupt" instruction used only in special applications.

The *exception* state is entered when a reset, hardware error condition, trace, interrupt, or trap is recognized. The processor is automatically placed in the supervisor mode and program execution begins at the location in memory indicated in the exception vector table for the particular exception that occurred. The addresses in the table

[1] A trace exception will occur if the trace condition is indicated when the STOP instruction is executed.

TABLE 10.1 PROCESSOR STATES AND MODES

State	Condition	CPU Activity
Normal	Processing	Supervisor or user mode program executing
	Stopped	Waiting for interrupt
Exception	Reset	Initialization
	Interrupt	Interrupt acknowledge and processing
	Trap	Trap processing
	Trace	Single instruction trace
Halted	System error condition	No activity

are supplied when the system is initialized. When a program is executing in the user mode, only exception processing can change the mode to the supervisor mode.

The *halted* state provides system protection by causing the CPU to cease all external signaling activity. As explained in Chapter 12, the processor halts if certain types of errors are detected while the processor is already processing another error. These error conditions should occur only after a catastrophic hardware failure for which recovery is not possible, so a system reset is necessary to restart the halted processor. During the halted state, the CPU indicates its condition on the system bus via a signal line explicitly for this purpose. External circuitry or an operator must then determine whether to restart the halted processor.

A processor in the stopped condition or halted state cannot be restarted by a program since external signal lines control the CPU activity after one of these conditions has occurred. In contrast, during normal or exception processing, a program controls the operation of the processor. The distinction between supervisor mode and user mode programs is important when the processor operates in the normal state. During normal operations, the mode defines the privilege conditions for a program.

10.1.2 Supervisor and User Modes

Some of the differences between the supervisor mode and the user mode of the MC68000 were presented in earlier chapters. The use of a separate stack pointer for each mode and other important distinctions are listed in Table 10.2. Basically, the supervisor mode represents the level with more privilege. A program in this mode may execute any MC68000 instruction and may change the status register and user stack pointer. User mode programs are allowed a restricted instruction set with no privilege to execute certain instructions which control the operation of the system.

As indicated in Table 10.2, the supervisor mode is entered when any exception is recognized by the CPU. A program operating in the supervisor mode can change to the user mode by modifying the status bit, $(SR)[13]$, in the status register. Whenever

TABLE 10.2 DISTINCTIONS BETWEEN SUPERVISOR AND USER MODES

	Supervisor mode	User mode
Enter mode by	Recognition of a trap, reset, or interrupt	Clearing status bit "S"
System stack pointer	Supervisor stack pointer	User stack pointer
Other stack pointers	User stack pointer and registers A0–A6	Registers A0–A6
Status bits available		
Read	C, V, Z, N, X, I_0–I_2, S, T	C, V, Z, N, X, I_0–I_2, S, T
Write	C, V, Z, N, X, I_0–I_2, S, T	C, V, Z, N, X
Instructions available	All, including:	All except those listed
	STOP	under supervisor mode
	RESET	
	MOVE to SR	
	ANDI to SR	
	ORI to SR	
	EORI to SR	
	MOVE USP to < An >	
	MOVE to USP	
	RTE	
Function code line FC2 =	1	0

$(SR)[13] = \{1\}$, the processor is operating in the supervisor mode and the transition to user mode can be accomplished by setting $(SR)[13] = \{0\}$. Because only the supervisor program may change modes, the instructions listed in the table that indicate SR as destination are privileged instructions. In addition, the contents of the user stack pointer (USP) can only be transferred or changed by a program in the supervisor mode. Attempted execution of a privileged instruction by a user mode program causes a trap that indicates a privilege violation.

In the user mode, an MC68000 program may use the MOVE instruction to read the contents of the entire status register, but it may write only to the condition code register (CCR), or $(SR)[7:0]$. The other system control instructions, STOP, RESET, and RTE, are also privileged. The MC68010 processor differs from the MC68000 in that it allows no user mode access to the supervisor part of the status register $(SR)[15:8]$. It allows a user program to read or write using the condition code register only.

Finally, the function code signal-lines indicate the processor mode to external devices. These signal lines are used as the basis for memory protection and for control of external interrupt circuitry.[2]

---

[2]These lines indicate the supervisor or user mode and program or data reference for an executing program. They also indicate the acknowledgment of an interrupt by the MC68000. The use of the function code signal lines for system protection is discussed in Chapter 12.

EXERCISES

10.1.1. Draw a diagram showing the possible states of the MC68000 and the transitions between them.

10.1.2. Compare the stopped condition with the halted state.

10.1.3. Discuss possible applications for the STOP instruction and the stopped condition of the processor.

10.1.4. List the protection mechanisms provided for a MC68000 system and define the purpose and possible application of each. Include both hardware and software considerations.

10.2 SYSTEM CONTROL INSTRUCTIONS

Special MC68000 instructions are provided to change the system operation dynamically in some way. The primary group of these instructions are privileged instructions that can be executed only in the supervisor mode. These include instructions to change the contents of the status register (SR) or the user stack pointer (USP). Another group of system control instructions is available for user mode programs to modify the contents of the condition code register (CCR). In an MC68000 system, a user mode program can also examine the contents of the status register but cannot modify it. For completeness, the Return From Exception (RTE) and the RESET instructions are also considered in this section. However, applications of these two system control instructions are described more completely in the next two chapters.

10.2.1 Status Register Modification

Table 10.3 lists the instructions available to a supervisor mode program that can modify the contents of the status register. The logical instructions (ANDI, EORI, ORI) operate in the manner described in Chapter 8. However, in this application, the destination location is the status register, which makes them privileged instructions. Each of these instructions performs the logical operation designated using the 16-bit immediate value and the entire contents of the status register.

The MOVE instruction is used to transfer the source operand to the status register, thereby replacing the previous contents. In the form

        MOVE   <EA>,SR

The effective address <EA> is specified by any data addressing mode which includes all addressing modes except address register direct. To transfer the contents of the status register to a memory location or a data register, the instruction

        MOVE.W   SR,<EA>

is used. This instruction is available to both supervisor and user mode programs in MC68000 systems. The MC68010 restricts this move from SR instruction to supervi-

TABLE 10.3 INSTRUCTIONS TO MODIFY THE PROCESSOR STATUS

Syntax		Operation
ANDI.W	# $<d_{16}>$,SR	$(SR) \leftarrow (SR) \text{ AND } <d_{16}>$
EORI.W	# $<d_{16}>$,SR	$(SR) \leftarrow (SR) \text{ EOR } <d_{16}>$
MOVE.W	$<EA>$,SR	$(SR) \leftarrow (EA)$
ORI.W	# $<d_{16}>$,SR	$(SR) \leftarrow (SR) \text{ OR } <d_{16}>$

Notes:

1. All instructions are privileged.

2. MOVE to SR requires a data addressing mode for $<EA>$.

sor mode programs. A new instruction, move from CCR, is provided for user mode programs.

Example 10.1

Figure 10.2 shows the MC68000 status register as it is divided into user byte SR[7:0] and system byte SR[15:8]. The values in the AND and OR column are given in hexadecimal. The AND mask clears any bit in the status register which corresponds to a {0} in the mask. The OR of (SR) with the bit pattern shown as {ENABLE} sets the corresponding bit to {1}. Thus the instruction

ANDI   #$7FFF, SR

sets T = {0} to disable the trace mode but does not affect the other bits. The instruction

ORI   #$8000,SR

enables the trace mode. The use of the supervisor mode bit is similar. When bit 13 is {0}, the processor is operating in the user mode.

The interrupt level value $\{I_2, I_1, I_0\}$ is not treated as a logical variable but as a 3-bit integer. A value of 0, {000}, indicates that all interrupt levels will be accepted with increasing priority from 1 to 7. During interrupt processing, the value indicates the current level as explained in Chapter 11. Interrupts at that level and below are ignored. The instruction

ANDI   #$F8FF,SR

enables all interrupt levels by setting the interrupt bits to {000}. The interrupt levels are disabled by the instruction

ORI   #$0700,SR

which disables all interrupts below level 7 since a level 7 interrupt cannot be masked (disabled).

Operations on the user byte or CCR are also shown in Figure 10.2. The immediate values listed do not affect the system byte when used with the ANDI or ORI instructions as shown. The instruction

ANDI   #$FF00,SR

15	14	13	12	11	10	9	8	7	6	5	4	3	2	1	0	← Bit Number
T		S			I_2	I_1	I_0				X	N	Z	V	C	

← ————— System Byte ————— → ← ————— User Byte ————— →

Condition	Status Bit	AND {MASK}	OR {ENABLE}
Trace Mode	(SR) [15] = T	{7FFF}	{8000}
Supervisor Mode	(SR) [13] = S	{DFFF}	{2000}
Interrupt Level	(SR) [10:8] = level	{F8FF}	{0700}
Extend	(SR) [4] = X	{FFEF}	{0010}
Negative	(SR) [3] = N	{FFF7}	{0008}
Zero	(SR) [2] = Z	{FFFB}	{0004}
Overflow	(SR) [1] = V	{FFFD}	{0002}
Carry	(SR) [0] = C	{FFFE}	{0001}

Notes:
(1) SR [15: 8] is System Byte; SR [7:0] is User Byte or CCR.
(2) ((SR) AND {MASK}) sets bit to {0} ; ((SR) OR {ENABLE}) sets bit to {1} .
(3) For the interrupt level, the value $\{I_2 I_1 I_0\}$ is interpreted as a 3-bit code.

Figure 10.2   Status register operation.

would clear the CCR, for example. Thus use of ANDI with the {MASK} value shown clears the corresponding bit to {0} in the CCR. The bit is set to {1} when ORI is used with the immediate value given as {ENABLE} in Figure 10.2.

10.2.2 User Stack Pointer Manipulation

A program executing in the supervisor mode can save, restore, or change the contents of the user stack pointer. The privileged instruction

MOVE.L   USP, < An >

copies (USP) into address register An. The opposite transfer has the form

MOVE.L   < An >,USP

and is used to initialize or modify (USP). In each case, a 32-bit transfer occurs.

As would be expected, only a program operating in the supervisor mode has control of the contents of the user stack pointer. Therefore, the address of the user stack must be loaded into USP by the supervisor program during initialization. The proper address could be tranferred to < An > and then to the user stack pointer by the instructions

> MOVEA.L   #USERSTK, < An >
>
> MOVE.L   < An > ,USP

where USERSTK is the address of the bottom of the user's stack.

10.2.3 Status Register Access in User Mode

The instructions listed in Table 10.4 are available to user mode programs. The logical instructions allow the contents of the CCR to be modified using the 8-bit immediate value. For example, the instruction

> ORI.B   #$01,CCR

sets the carry bit $C = \{1\}$ and does not modify any other condition code bits. The entire contents of the CCR can be modified by the instruction

> MOVE.W   < EA > ,CCR

in which $(< EA >)[7:0]$ contains the new condition code bits for the CCR. The addressing for < EA > requires a data addressing mode which allows all modes except address register direct. Note that the operation requires a word operand but only the low-order byte is used to update the condition codes. This means that the address of the operand < EA > must be an even address in memory.

TABLE 10.4   USER MODE ACCESS TO (SR)

Syntax		Operation
Modify CCR		
ANDI.B	#$< d_8 >$,CCR	$(SR)[7:0] \leftarrow (SR)[7:0]$ AND $< d_8 >$
EORI.B	#$< d_8 >$,CCR	$(SR)[7:0] \leftarrow (SR)[7:0]$ EOR $< d_8 >$
MOVE.W	$< EAs >$,CCR	$(SR)[7:0] \leftarrow (EAs)[7:0]$
ORI.B	#$< d_8 >$,CCR	$(SR)[7:0] \leftarrow (SR)[7:0]$ OR $< d_8 >$
Move SR		
MOVE.W	SR, $< EAd >$	$(EA) \leftarrow (SR)$

Notes:

1. MOVE to CCR requires a data addressing mode for < EAs > , the source.
2. MOVE SR to < EAd > requires a data-alterable addressing mode for < EAd > , the destination. This is not allowed in MC68010 systems.
3. CCR is (SR)[7:0].

An MC68000 user mode program can also transfer the contents of the status register by executing the instruction

MOVE.W   SR, < EA >

where < EA > is a data-alterable location which excludes address register direct and program counter relative addressing. As pointed out previously, this is a privileged operation in MC68010 systems.

10.2.4 RTE Instruction

The Return from Exception instruction (RTE) is a privileged instruction used to load the status register and the program counter with values stored on the supervisor stack. The operation of the RTE instruction for the MC68000 is

(a) Load (SR)

(SR) [W] ← ((SSP))   ;POP (SR)
(SSP) ← (SSP) + 2   ;POINT TO (PC)

(b) Load (PC)

(PC)[L] ← ((SSP))   ;POP (PC)
(SSP) ← (SSP) + 4

as shown in Figure 10.3. The RTE is most frequently used as the last instruction in an exception-handling routine since (PC) and then (SR) are pushed on the supervisor stack when an exception occurs. The RTE instruction is also used to pass control to a

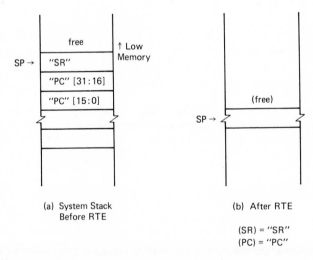

(a) System Stack
     Before RTE

(b) After RTE

(SR) = "SR"
(PC) = "PC"

Figure 10.3   Operation of RTE instruction.

Note: "SR" and "PC" are values to replace the current (SR) and (PC), respectively.

user mode program during the system initialization procedure, as discussed in the next section.

As indicated in Section 4.2, the MC68010 stack contents during an exception can occupy either 4 or 29 words of the stack area in memory. Thus the RTE instruction of the MC68010 does not operate in the manner just described. The reader should consult the MC68010 manual from Motorola for specific details. The operation shown in Figure 10.3 applies then only to the MC68000 processor.

10.2.5 RESET Instruction

The RESET instruction is a privileged instruction used to reset external interfaces during system initialization. Its execution asserts a signal line used as an indication to external circuitry that the processor is requesting initialization of the appropriate interfaces. The exact function of the RESET instruction in terms of system operation is determined by the hardware design of the system. Most of the peripheral chips of the MC68000 family respond to this instruction (via a reset signal line) by initializing their internal circuitry.

EXERCISES

10.2.1. Determine the effect of the following instructions.
    (a) MOVE.W   #$0400,SR
    (b) ANDI.W   #$DFFD,SR
    (c) MOVE.W   #$2700,SR
    (d) EORI.W   #$2000,SR
    The instructions are executed by a program in the supervisor mode.

10.2.2. What is the effect of the following instructions executed by a program in the user mode?
    (a) MOVE.W   #$000C,CCR
    (b) ANDI.B   #$01,CCR
    (c) EORI.W   #$2700,SR

10.2.3. Write the sequence of instructions to initialize (USP) to hexadecimal value $7FFF.

10.2.4. Why does a user mode program in an MC68000 system need to be able to transfer the contents of (SR)? How does a user mode program test the entire contents of the CCR? How does the MC68010 allow the user to check (CCR)?

10.3 SYSTEM INITIALIZATION

A *system initialization* sequence is used to place the system in a known state or condition before any application program is executed. The sequence normally begins with a reset signal supplied by external circuitry to cause the hardware to assume its initial

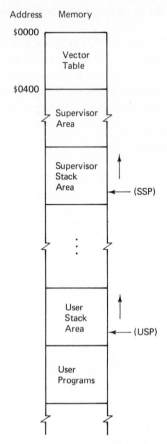

Figure 10.4 Initial memory layout.

state. Then an initialization routine is executed to initialize all constants, addresses, and other data values associated with the system operation. The initialization routine is usually held in read-only memory and can be executed automatically after a system reset. This routine not only initializes the data used for the system but may also cause the loading of the operating system from an external storage device such as a disk unit. The exact procedure, of course, depends on the hardware configuration and the application of the system. In this section the basic initialization procedure for MC68000-based systems is described according to the requirements of the processor.

Initialization may produce the typical memory layout as shown in Figure 10.4. The vector table in MC68000 systems is lowest in memory and contains the addresses of exception routines. The SSP and USP point to the bottom of the supervisor stack area and the user stack area, respectively. The amount of space reserved for the program and stack areas is determined when the software system is designed. Enough space must be allocated so that the various areas do not overlap during operation. The stacks shown in Figure 10.4 are system stacks and grow toward lower memory locations as return addresses, register contents, and other data are pushed onto the stack.

Once the system is initialized and the various programs to be executed are load-ed into memory, the supervisor program passes control to an applications program. The techniques for transfer of control are also covered in this section.

In MC68010 systems, the exception vector table may be relocated in memory. The processor contains a "vector base register" whose contents are added to the vector location (offset) in the table to compute the effective address of the vector in memory. During the initialization sequence, the instruction MOVEC (Move to/from Control Register) of the MC68010 is used to initialize to contents of the vector base register.

10.3.1 Initialization Procedure

For convenience of discussion, the initialization procedure is separated into two phases. In the first phase, the MC68000 CPU hardware is reset and causes execution of the routine at the location indicated by the initial value of the program counter. This portion of the initialization is fixed by the processor design and cannot be altered. The second phase begins when the initialization routine of the supervisor program executes.

Reset and initialization of the processor.   Initialization is accomplished by an external device asserting the $\overline{\text{RESET}}$ signal line to the CPU. The sequence of events is shown in Figure 10.5, in which the processor first sets the status register contents to indicate the supervisor mode and masks all interrupts. Then, in sequence, the

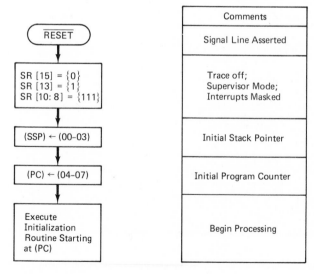

Notes:
(1) If an error occurs while the (SSP) and (PC) values are being fetched, the processor will enter the halted state.
(2) $\overline{\text{RESET}}$ is a signal line to the CPU.

Figure 10.5   Reset operation.

supervisor stack pointer and the program counter are initialized from the first eight bytes in memory. If no errors occur, program execution begins at the location defined by the program counter contents. The entire procedure up to this point requires about 100 milliseconds.

In most systems, the lower memory locations which hold the vector addresses are in volatile memory. Therefore, if power is lost, the contents of such locations should be considered destroyed. During a system reset, the MC68000 or MC68010 processor reads longword location (00–03) for the supervisor stack pointer value and location (04–07) for the program counter value. These eight bytes must be interpreted as permanent values. Therefore, external circuitry must be designed to accomplish

Vector Number(s)	Dec	Address Hex	Space	Assignment
0	0	000	SP	Reset: Initial SSP[2]
	4	004	SP	Reset: Initial PC[2]
2	8	008	SD	Bus Error
3	12	00C	SD	Address Error
4	16	010	SD	Illegal Instruction
5	20	014	SD	Zero Divide
6	24	018	SD	CHK Instruction
7	28	01C	SD	TRAPV Instruction
8	32	020	SD	Privilege Violation
9	36	024	SD	Trace
10	40	028	SD	Line 1010 Emulator
11	44	02C	SD	Line 1111 Emulator
12[1]	48	030	SD	(Unassigned, Reserved)
13[1]	52	034	SD	(Unassigned, Reserved)
14[1]	56	038	SD	(Unassigned, Reserved)
15	60	03C	SD	Uninitialized Interrupt Vector
16-23[1]	64	040	SD	(Unassigned, Reserved)
	95	05F		–
24	96	060	SD	Spurious Interrupt[3]
25	100	064	SD	Level 1 Interrupt Autovector
26	104	068	SD	Level 2 Interrupt Autovector
27	108	06C	SD	Level 3 Interrupt Autovector
28	112	070	SD	Level 4 Interrupt Autovector
29	116	074	SD	Level 5 Interrupt Autovector
30	120	078	SD	Level 6 Interrupt Autovector
31	124	07C	SD	Level 7 Interrupt Autovector
32-47	128	080	SD	TRAP Instruction Vectors[4]
	191	0BF		
48-63[1]	192	0C0	SD	(Unassigned, Reserved)
	255	0FF		–
64-255	256	100	SD	User Interrupt Vectors
	1023	3FF		–

NOTES:
1. Vector numbers 12, 13, 14, 16 through 23, and 48 through 63 are reserved for future enhancements by Motorola. No user peripheral devices should be assigned these numbers.
2. Reset vector (0) requires four words, unlike the other vectors which only require two words, and is located in the supervisor program space.
3. The spurious interrupt vector is taken when there is a bus error indication during interrupt processing. Refer to Paragraph 5.5.2.
4. TRAP #n uses vector number 32 + n.

Figure 10.6 Vector table for the MC68000 system. (Courtesy of Motorola, Inc.)

TABLE 10.5   TYPICAL SYSTEM INITIALIZATION PROCEDURE

Operation	Comments
Initialize addresses for vectors as required.	Locations $0008–$03FC (32-bit addresses)
Load any supervisor routines needed.	Load from disk unit
Initialize contents of any memory locations needed by the supervisor.	As needed
Initialize all peripheral services for the system.	As needed: RESET instruction for peripheral devices and other I/O control commands
Initialize USP.	(USP) ← user stack address
Push starting address for user mode program.	((SSP)) ← start of program
Push status for user mode program.	((SSP)) ← user (SR)
Transfer control to user mode program.	RTE

Notes:

1. Exception-handling routines have fixed starting addresses. These addresses are used to initialize the vectors.

2. After hardware initialization, the CPU is in the supervisor mode with all interrupts masked. Execution of the initialization begins at the address specified in location $0004.

3. Initialization of an MC68010 system is similar although the vector table may be relocated.

this.[3] The initialization routine which is then executed can initialize the remaining values in the other vector locations and perform other necessary processing. In MC68010 systems, the vector table may be relocated in memory.

    Initialization routine.   The initialization routine prepares the system for execution of the supervisor program. This preparation includes loading vector addresses into the locations shown in Figure 10.6 and initializing any external devices. When the routine completes, control may be passed to a supervisor routine, which determines which application program is to be executed. If there is no supervisor, control is passed directly to the application program immediately after initialization of the system is complete.

    The initialization routine for the MC68000 usually performs the series of operations shown in Table 10.5, although many variations are possible for a specific application. After the system is properly initialized, the user stack pointer, status register, and program counter contents are set to pass control to the application program, which is assumed to operate in the user mode in the sequence shown in Table 10.5. As shown in that table, the supervisor program controls all systems operations and the initial setting of the stack pointer for the application program. If the memory utilization is

---

[3]To initialize the values, the addresses could be translated by special circuits to an address in read-only memory, as is done with the Motorola Design Module. In any case, the first eight byte locations must not be volatile locations when accessed by the CPU for initialization. The reset sequence is initiated in the Design Module by a pushbutton which causes the $\overline{\text{RESET}}$ signal line of the CPU to be asserted.

also controlled by the supervisor, the application programs would be loaded into memory before control is passed to the user.

10.3.2 Initialization Example

The brief initialization routine in Figure 10.7 is loaded with a starting address just above the vector table from $0000 to $03FF. First, assembler directives are used to initialize the vector addresses for an interrupt error (level 0) and several other interrupt levels. The vector for TRAP #0 is initialized with address EXEC. A user pro-

```
MC68000 ASM REV= 1.4 - COPYRIGHT BY MOTOROLA 1978               PAGE   1


   1                          LLEN    120
   2                  *
   3                  * PERFORM SYSTEM INITIALIZATION
   4                  *
   5        00007000  XPTERR  EQU     $7000          ;ADDRESS FOR SPURIOUS INTERRUPT HANDLER
   6        00007100  IOXPT   EQU     $7100          ;ADDRESS FOR I/O INTERRUPT HANDLER
   7        00007200  TMXPT   EQU     $7200          ;ADDRESS FOR TIMER INTERRUPT HANDLER
   8        00007300  PEXPT   EQU     $7300          ;ADDRESS FOR PARITY ERROR INTERRUPT HANDLER
   9        00007400  PFXPT   EQU     $7400          ;ADDRESS FOR POWER FAIL INTERRUPT HANDLER
  10                  *
  11        00007500  EXEC    EQU     $7500          ;ADDRESS OF EXECUTIVE SUPERVISOR CALL
  12                  *
  13        00007000  USERSTK EQU     $7000          ;USER STACK
  14        00001000  USERIN  EQU     $1000          ;USER STARTING ADDRESS
  15                  *
  16                  * LOAD 68000 INTERRUPT VECTORS
  17                  *
  18        00000060          ORG     $060
  19 000060 00007000          DC.L    XPTERR         ;SPURIOUS INTERRUPT LEVEL 0
  20                  *
  21        00000070          ORG     $070
  22 000070 00007100          DC.L    IOXPT          ;I/O INTERRUPT LEVEL 4
  23 000074 00007200          DC.L    TMXPT          ;TIMER INTERRUPT LEVEL 5
  24 000078 00007300          DC.L    PEXPT          ;PARITY ERROR INTERRUPT LEVEL 6
  25 00007C 00007400          DC.L    PFXPT          ;POWER FAIL INTERRUPT LEVEL 7
  26                  *
  27                  * LOAD 68000 TRAP VECTORS
  28                  *
  29        00000080          ORG     $080
  30 000080 00007500          DC.L    EXEC           ;SUPERVISOR CALL TRAP VECTOR
  31                  *
  32                  * INITIALIZE USER
  33                  *
  34        00000400          ORG     $400
  35 000400 207C00007000      MOVE.L  #USERSTK,A0    ;GET USER STACK ADDRESS
  36 000406 4E60              MOVE.L  A0,USP         ;   AND LOAD IT INTO USER SP
  37                  *
  38                  * SAVE USER STARTING ADDRESS AND STATUS REGISTER ON THE SUPERVISOR STACK
  39                  *
  40 000408 2F3C00001000      MOVE.L  #USERIN,-(SP)
  41 00040E 3F3C0000          MOVE.W  #0,-(SP)       ;MODE=USER,INTERRUPT MASK=000
  42                  *
  43                  * TRANSFER CONTROL TO USER PROGRAM
  44                  *
  45 000412 4E73              RTE
  46                          END

****** TOTAL ERRORS   0--   0


SYMBOL TABLE - APPROX 1195 SYMBOL ENTRIES LEFT

EXEC      007500 IOXPT     007100 PEXPT     007300 PFXPT     007400
TMXPT     007200 USERIN    001000 USERSTK   007000 XPTERR    007000
```

Figure 10.7 Initialization routine.

gram executing a TRAP #0 instruction will return control to the supervisor or executive program at this address.

The initialization routine loads the USP with address USERSTK. Then the starting address of the user mode program USERIN is pushed. Next, the user status $0000 is pushed on the stack. All interrupt levels are enabled and user mode is selected. After the execution of RTE, the user mode program begins to execute.

EXERCISES

10.3.1. Assume that lower memory is volatile RAM. List (or diagram) the decision required by external circuitry to allow the CPU to address nonvolatile ROM locations during the reset sequence. Assume that the reset vectors are held in ROM beginning at hexadecimal location $20000. The initial (SSP) is $06B8 and the initial (PC) is $20008.

10.3.2. The instruction sequence

```
MOVE.W    #$0000,SR

JMP       USER
```

could be used to transfer control to a program at location USER. Why is the approach using RTE better? Consider the case when the memory is segmented (and protected) into supervisor program space and user program space.

10.3.3. Write an initialization routine to execute a special user mode program upon recognition of a level 7 interrupt at vector address $07C. The user mode program begins at location $2000 and the interrupt routine is located at $1000.

FURTHER READING

The following article by Cates describes the circuitry that is required to translate the initial vector addresses from locations $0000–$0007 to an area of memory occupied by ROM.

CATES, RON L., "Mapping an Alterable Reset Vector for the MC68000," *Electronics,* **55**, No. 15 (July 28, 1982).

11

Exception Processing

The exception processing capability of the MC68000 is provided to assure an orderly transfer of control from an executing program to the supervisor program. Exceptions may be broadly divided into those caused by an instruction, including an unusual condition arising during its execution, and those caused by external events. Those in the first category are called *traps* and represent exceptional conditions caused by the program itself that are detected by the CPU. Hardware error exceptions and *interrupts* are caused by external events and these exceptions are initiated by circuitry outside the CPU. The hardware error is termed a *bus error* by Motorola.

Table 11.1 lists the MC68000 exceptions and their causes. The program exceptions are divided into those generated by the TRAP instruction, instructions used to test program conditions, unimplemented instructions, tracing, and various error conditions. Externally generated exceptions include bus errors and interrupts from external devices.

Figure 11.1 illustrates the processing sequence for most exceptions. Briefly stated, the processor enters the supervisor mode with tracing off and executes the exception routine at the address in the exception vector table. The previous values in the program counter and status register are saved on the supervisor stack so that a return from exception (RTE) can be performed when processing is complete. For certain exceptions, such as interrupts, the processing is slightly different and will be discussed in the appropriate section of this chapter. The vector number and its memory address for each exception are listed in Figure 11.2. These addresses are loaded during system initialization.

In MC68010 systems, at least four words are saved on the system stack when an

302

TABLE 11.1 MC68000 EXCEPTIONS

Type	Cause
Trap instruction: TRAP # \<N\> ; N = 0, 1, ... , 15	Sixteen trap routines may be defined and used by the program
Program checks: DIVS, DIVU	Trap when divisor is zero
Instructions TRAPV	Trap if overflow condition is detected
CHK \<EA\>,\<Dn\>	Trap if register value is out of bounds
Unimplemented instruction	Trap if op code is {1010} or {1111}
Trace exception	Single instruction trace
Error conditions Privilege violation	Trap if user mode program attempts to execute privileged instruction
Illegal instruction	Trap if op code is unrecognized
Address error	Trap if access of a word or longword location with odd address
Bus error	Externally generated exception request
Halt	Double error condition halts processor
Interrupt system Autovector	Automatic vectoring for seven levels of priority
Vectored	192 user interrupt vectors; priority determined by hardware design

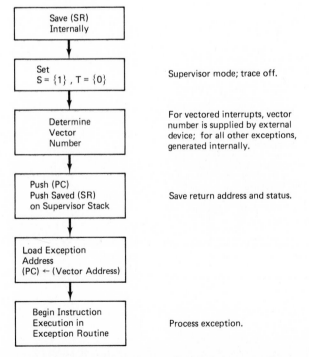

Save (SR) Internally

Set S = {1} , T = {0}   Supervisor mode; trace off.

Determine Vector Number   For vectored interrupts, vector number is supplied by external device; for all other exceptions, generated internally.

Push (PC) Push Saved (SR) on Supervisor Stack   Save return address and status.

Load Exception Address (PC) ← (Vector Address)

Begin Instruction Execution in Exception Routine   Process exception.

Note: Processing for reset, interrupts, address error, and bus error is slightly different from that shown.

Figure 11.1 Exception processing sequence.

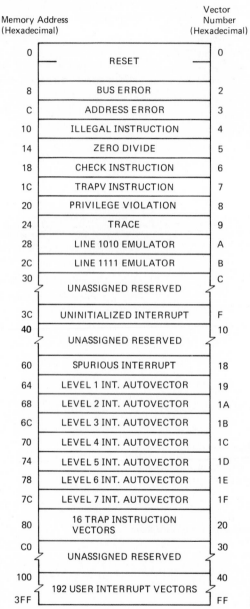

Figure 11.2 Vector allocation.

exception is recognized as discussed in Section 4.2. The vector address in memory is calculated by adding the contents of the vector base register to the vector offset. In Figure 11.2 the vector offset is computed as four times the vector number. The vector base register of the MC68010 must first be initialized as described in Section 10.3.

The discussions of MC68000 exception processing in this chapter apply to the MC68010 in almost every detail. The MC68010 exception stack is four words long for all exceptions but address errors and bus errors. In these two cases, 29 words of information are saved on the stack. Unless the exception stack is being manipulated during exception processing, the exact stack format is not of concern to the programmer. Also, after initialization, the vector address for the various exceptions is determined automatically by the MC68010. Therefore, programming routines to handle most of the exceptions is the same for both the MC68000 and the MC68010.

11.1 EXCEPTIONS CAUSED BY PROGRAM EXECUTION

As each instruction is executed, the processor tests the instruction to determine if an exception condition is generated. These exceptions are called *traps* and are caused by normal program execution. These exceptions are categorized as shown in Table 11.2 into those caused by either one of the following:

(a) Program control instructions
(b) Instructions to check program conditions

TABLE 11.2 PROGRAM TRAPS

Type of trap	Cause of trap	Vector address	Comments
Program control TRAP instruction	Normal execution	$080–$0BC	Normal operation to call executive program. (PC) value is next instruction location.
Unimplemented instruction	Normal execution	$028 or $02C	Op code {1010} or {1111} (PC) locates unimplemented instruction.

Program condition
  CHK
	Range checked is
	  out of bounds
		$018	The exception routine can attempt to recover from the condition and return control to the program or abort program.

DIVS or DIVU	Divisor is zero	$014	
TRAPV	Execution with V = {1}	$01C	(PC) value is next instruction location.

A TRAP instruction is used to return control to the supervisor program. The traps caused by division, TRAPV or CHK, indicate a program error. Two unimplemented instruction traps are available to allow the design of special routines.

The operation sequence of each type of trap is the same as far as the application program is concerned. Upon detection of a trap condition, the processor saves the contents of the status register (internally) and enters the supervisor mode with the trace condition off. Then the contents of the program counter and the saved value of the status register are pushed on the supervisor stack. After the vector address is calculated, program control is passed to the trap routine beginning at the address specified by the vector.

If control is to be returned to the program that caused the exception, the trap routine executes an RTE instruction which restores the contents of the status register and program counter from the stack. For traps caused by unimplemented instructions, the contents of the program counter which is saved indicate the location of the instruction causing the trap. In order to return to the next instruction in sequence, the saved (PC) must be modified by the exception-handling routine for the unimplemented instructions.

11.1.1 The TRAP Instruction

Execution of the TRAP instruction with the format

$$\text{TRAP} \quad \# < \text{vector} >$$

first causes the contents of the program counter and the status register, in that order, to be pushed on the supervisor stack. Then processing begins at the address specified in the vector location. The value $< \text{vector} >$ is an integer in the range 0–15 and is used to calculate the hexadecimal vector address as follows:

$$\text{vector address} = 80_{16} + 4* < \text{vector} >$$

The exception processing begins at the location loaded into the program counter with

$$(PC) \leftarrow (\text{vector address})$$

where each address is 32 bits in length. For convenience, the vector addresses are listed in Table 11.3. These locations must be initialized before the TRAP is executed.

The TRAP instruction has numerous uses. For a program operating in the user mode, its execution may return control to the supervisor program at the location of the designated trap routine. The 16 possible traps allow a user mode program to call the supervisor for processing, which must be executed at the supervisor level. For ex-

TABLE 11.3 TRAP VECTOR ADDRESSES

TRAP # <N> instruction	Vector address (hexadecimal)
TRAP #0	80
TRAP #1	84
TRAP #2	88
TRAP #3	8C
TRAP #4	90
TRAP #5	94
TRAP #6	98
TRAP #7	9C
TRAP #8	A0
TRAP #9	A4
TRAP #10	A8
TRAP #11	AC
TRAP #12	B0
TRAP #13	B4
TRAP #14	B8
TRAP #15	BC

Note: Vector number is decimal.

ample, a call via the TRAP instruction might be used to input or output data using peripheral devices which are controlled by the supervisor. In effect, the trap is a software interrupt. This mechanism could be used in debugging operations to simulate interrupts. The TRAP instruction is also a means of returning control to the supervisor mode after the applications task is completed.

Example 11.1

Figure 11.3 contains a program segment in a real-time executive (supervisor) which can be invoked by the user through a

    TRAP #0

instruction. Information is coded following the TRAP using a DC.W instruction to define a 16-bit integer (function number) which selects the particular executive service being requested by the user. The function number is an integer 0, 1, 2, or 3.

The segment starting at EXEC first disables all interrupts by calling subroutine DIALL (not shown) and then saves the user's registers on the stack. Then the return address within the user's program is retrieved from the stack. This address points to the location following the TRAP instruction which contains the 16-bit function number. The function number is validated and a jump table used to obtain the address of the selected

MC68000 ASM REV= 1.4 - COPYRIGHT BY MOTOROLA 1978   PAGE 1

```
 1                              LLEN     120
 2          00000080           ORG      $080
 3 000080  00001000            DC.L     EXEC              ;INITIALIZE TRAP 0
 4          00001000           ORG      $1000
 5                         *
 6          00000010  EEXEC    EQU      $10               ; ERROR CODE IN EXECUTIVE
 7          00004000  DIALL    EQU      $4000             ; DUMMY ROUTINE TO DISABLE INTERRUPTS
 8          00004100  DISP     EQU      $4100             ; DUMMY ROUTINE TO DISPATCH
 9          00004200  INTSCH   EQU      $4200             ; DUMMY ROUTINE TO SAVE INTERRUPTED TASKS
10          00004300  SCHED    EQU      $4300             ; DUMMY ROUTINE TO PERFORM SCHEDULING
11          00004400  RTERRX   EQU      $4400             ; DUMMY ROUTINE FOR ERROR PROCESSING
12                         *
13                         * EXEC
14                         *
15                         * THIS ROUTINE DETERMINES THE EXECUTIVE FUNCTION
16                         * REQUESTED AND TRANSFERS CONTROL TO IT.  EXEC PLACES
17                         * 15 REGISTERS ON THE STACK AND USES A JUMP TABLE
18                         * TO PASS CONTROL ON TO THE APPROPRIATE FUNCTION.  IT
19                         * PASSES THE ADDRESS OF THE FUNCTION REQUEST DATA IN A0
20                         * AND THE FUNCTION CODE * 4 IN D1.
21                         *
22                         * EXEC EXECUTES AT THE SYSTEM LEVEL AND IS INVOKED
23                         * AS FOLLOWS:
24                         *      TRAP      #0        .
25                         *      DC.W      #FUNCTION (0=DISP,1=SCHED,2=TMSCH,3=INTSCH)
26                         *      DC.      ADDITIONAL DATA AS DEFINED BY EACH FUNCTION
27                         *
28                         * EXEC INVOKES THE FOLLOWING ROUTINES:
29                         *      DIALL  - DISABLE INTERRUPTS
30                         *      DISP   - DISPATCHER
31                         *      INTSCH - INTERRUPTED TASK SCHEDULER
32                         *      RTERRX - RTE ERROR EXIT
33                         *      SCHED  - TASK SCHEDULER
34                         *
35                         * EXEC USES THE FOLLOWING DATA:
36                         *      EEXEC  - ERROR CODE IN EXEC (I.E. ILLEGAL FUNCTION)
37                         *      ERRAD  - ERROR ADDRESS
38                         *      ERRCD  - ERROR CODE
39                         *      EXECTB - EXECUTIVE CONTROL JUMP TABLE
40                         *      EXTBLN - EXECUTIVE CONTROL TABLE LENGTH
41                         *
```

Figure 11.3   Example of TRAP usage.

executive routine. This address is pushed on the stack and a return is executed to transfer control to the selected function.

Error processing occurs when an illegal function number is detected. The address of the error in the user program and the error code are saved before control is transferred to the error processing routine.

11.1.2 Divide-by-Zero Trap and TRAPV

Certain arithmetic errors in an applications program can be detected and trapped by the CPU. In particular, execution of a signed divide (DIVS) or unsigned divide (DIVU) instruction with a divisor of zero automatically causes a trap through vector address $14. An overflow condition ($V = \{1\}$) will cause a trap if the instruction TRAPV is executed. Processing in this case begins at the address located by the vector at $1C. In the design of most systems, control is not returned to the program having an error when one of the arithmetic traps occurs.

```
42 001000 61002FFE    EXEC    BSR     DIALL              ; DISABLE INTERRUPTS
43 001004 48E7FFFE            MOVEM.L D0-D7/A0-A6,-(A7)  ; SAVE REGISTERS
44 001008 206F003E            MOVE.L  62(A7),A0          ; GET PC (POINTS TO FUNCTION REQUEST DATA)
45 00100C 4281               CLR.L   D1
46 00100E 3218                MOVE.W  (A0)+,D1           ; GET FUNCTION NO. REQUESTED
47 001010 0C410004            CMPI.W  #EXTBLN,D1         ; IS FUNCTION LEGAL?
48 001014 6C0C                BGE.S   EXEC10             ; NO, PROCESS ERROR
49 001016 43F81038            LEA     EXECTB,A1          ; ELSE, GET FUNCTION
50 00101A E589                LSL.L   #2,D1              ; REQUESTED'S ADDRESS
51 00101C D3C1                ADD.L   D1,A1              ; (FUNC. NO. * 4 + TABLE ADDRESS)
52 00101E 2F11                MOVE.L  (A1),-(A7)         ; AND PLACE ON STACK
53                   *
54                   * EXECUTE 'RETURN' TO FUNCTION WHOSE ADDRESS WAS STACKED
55                   *
56 001020 4E75                RTS
57                   *
58                   * ERROR DETECTION PROCESSING
59                   *
60 001022 4CDF7FFF    EXEC10  MOVEM.L (A7)+,D0-D7/A0-A6  ; RESTORE REGISTERS
61 001026 21EF0002104C        MOVE.L  2(A7),ERRAD        ; GET ADDRESS OF ERROR INTO DATA BLOCK
62 00102C 21FC00000010
         1048                 MOVE.L  #EEXEC,ERRCD       ; STORE ERROR CODE
63 001034 4EF84400            JMP     RTERRX             ; RTE ERROR EXIT
64                   *
65                   * EXECUTIVE CONTROL JUMP TABLE AND OTHER DATA
66                   *
67        00000004    EXTBLN  EQU     4                  ; EXECUTIVE CONTROL TABLE LENGTH
68 001038 00004100    EXECTB  DC.L    DISP               ; DISPATCHER
69 00103C 00004300            DC.L    SCHED              ; SCHEDULER
70 001040 00004300            DC.L    SCHED              ; TIMED SCHEDULER
71 001044 00004200            DC.L    INTSCH             ; INTERRUPTED TASK SCHEDULER
72 001048 00000004    ERRCD   DS.L    1                  ; ERROR CODE
73 00104C 00000004    ERRAD   DS.L    1                  ; ERROR ADDRESS
74                           END
****** TOTAL ERRORS   0--   0


SYMBOL TABLE - APPROX 1191 SYMBOL ENTRIES LEFT

DIALL     004000  DISP     004100  EEXEC    000010  ERRAD    00104C
ERRCD     001048  EXEC     001000  EXEC10   001022  EXECTB   001038
EXTBLN    000004  INTSCH   004200  RTERRX   004400  SCHED    004300
```

Figure 11.3 continued

Example 11.2

Figure 11.4 shows an example of processing a "divide by zero" trap. The first section stores the address of the trap handler routine in the trap vector location at $14. Next, a short program segment at $1000 causes a divide by zero to occur to test the trap routines. Finally, the trap handler routine begins at $4000 and sets the quotient to a particular value based on the value of the dividend, either the most positive or most negative integer allowed.

11.1.3 CHK Instruction

The Check Register Against Bounds instruction (CHK) has the symbolic form

CHK   <EA>,<Dn>

where <EA> is designated by a data addressing mode. This allows all addressing modes except address register direct. This instruction determines if the 16-bit contents

```
MC68000 ASM REV= 1.4 - COPYRIGHT BY MOTOROLA 1978              PAGE  1

 1                              LLEN    100
 2                        *
 3          000200F6       MACSBUG  EQU    $200F6             ; ADDRESS OF MONITOR
 4                        *
 5                        * THIS PROGRAM CAUSES A DIVIDE BY ZERO AND HAS
 6                        * THE PROCESSING TO LOAD THE QUOTIENT WITH THE
 7                        * LARGEST REPRESENTABLE NUMBER HAVING THE SIGN
 8                        * OF THE DIVIDEND
 9                        *
10          00000014              ORG    $14                 ; SET UP THE ADDRESS FOR
11 000014 00004000               DC.L   ZDIV                ; FOR ZERO DIVIDE PROCESSING
12                        *
13          00001000              ORG    $1000
14                        *
15                        * EXECUTE A DIVIDE BY ZERO WITH
16                        *    D0 = DIVISOR
17                        *    D1 = DIVIDEND
18                        *
19 001000 303C0000               MOVE.W  #0,D0              ; SET DIVISOR TO 0
20 001004 83C0                   DIVS    D0,D1              ; DIVIDE D1 BY D0
21 001006 4EF9000200F6           JMP     MACSBUG            ; EXIT TO MONITOR
22                        *
23                        * ZERO DIVIDE PROCESSING
24                        *
25                        * IF DIVIDEND IS NEGATIVE
26                        *    THEN SET QUOTIENT TO $FFFF (MOST NEGATIVE)
27                        *    ELSE SET QUOTIENT TO $7FFF (MOST POSITIVE)
28                        *
29          00004000              ORG    $4000
30                        *
31 004000 203C0000FFFF  ZDIV     MOVE.L  #$FFFF,D0          ; SET D0 TO MOST NEGATIVE
32 004006 4A81                   TST.L   D1                 ; IF D1 IS NEGATIVE
33 004008 6B000008               BMI     ZDIV01             ;    THEN SKIP TO EXIT
34 00400C 203C00007FFF           MOVE.L  #$7FFF,D0          ;    ELSE SET D0 TO MOST POSITIVE
35 004012 4E73         ZDIV01    RTE
36                              END

****** TOTAL ERRORS   0--   0


SYMBOL TABLE - APPROX 1199 SYMBOL ENTRIES LEFT

MACSBUG   0200F6 ZDIV      004000 ZDIV01      004012
```

Figure 11.4 Divide by zero trap.

of $<Dn>$ is between 0 and the value contained in $<EA>$ and causes a trap if the contents of $<Dn>$ are not within this range. The upper bound held in (EA) is treated as a 16-bit, two's-complement integer. The operation is as follows:

IF $0 < (Dn) [15:0] \leq (EA)$, THEN continue
    ELSE *trap* and
        set $N = \{1\}$ if $(Dn) [15:0] < 0$ or
        set $N = \{0\}$ if $(Dn) [15:0] > (EA)$

The exception routine begins at the address in location $18 if the trap is taken. The CHK instruction is typically placed in a program after the calculation of an offset or an index value to assure that the limits of the value are not exceeded. This facilitates testing whether an array address fits within the dimensions of the array when the address register indirect with indexing addressing mode is used to locate array elements. For example, the sequence

MOVE. B   0(A1,D1.W),D2
CHK   #99,D1

would trap if (D1) [15:0] exceeded 99 decimal. If Al held the base address of the array with 100 byte-length elements, the addressing range of the MOVE instruction is limited to values within this array. The addressing of arrays in FORTRAN is not always protected in this manner, but array boundary checking is typically provided in languages such as Pascal.[1]

Other uses of the CHK instruction include the testing of the space used by a stack or keeping a program from accessing data outside its designated space. For these applications, a value in an address register must be transferred to a data register in order to perform the bounds check.

11.1.4 Unimplemented Instruction Trap

The CPU recognizes instructions whose first bits are {1010} ($A) or {1111} ($F) as *unimplemented instructions*. These op codes are available to the programmer to cause execution of special routines that appear to be additional "macroinstructions" added to the MC68000 instruction set. Typical examples include routines for floating-point software, string manipulation, and fast Fourier transform algorithms. The other 12 bits in a word-length instruction with either of these op codes can be used to select the various options as interpreted by the special routines.

To cause the {1010} trap using vector location $2B, the directive

    DC.W $A000

could be inserted in the program where the trap is required. Similarly, the directive

    DC.W $F000

would cause a trap using the vector at $2C. After the trap occurs, the value of the program counter saved on the supervisor stack points to the unimplemented instruction. The address can be obtained using the instruction

    MOVEA.L   2(SP),Al

which skips over the contents of the status register saved on the stack and loads Al with the value saved for the PC. This value can be used to locate the unimplemented instruction to decode any other bits used to select options for the trap routine.

EXERCISES

11.1.1. If the instruction

        TRAP #1

is located at location $1004 and executes when (SR) = $A000 and (SP) = $7FFE, show the contents of the system stack before and after the TRAP instruction executes. Initialize the TRAP #1 vector so that the trap routine starts at location $1100.

---

[1]Whether or not array boundary checking is provided depends on the compiler and the system being used. In some cases, boundary checking is an optional feature of a compiler.

11.1.2. Write a program that pushes word-length values on the user stack beginning at location $1000. If the stack length is 10 words maximum, use the CHK instruction to return control to the supervisor program when the stack overflows.

11.1.3. Write a signed division routine that will accept a divisor of zero. If the dividend is positive, load the quotient with the largest positive integer when the zero divide occurs. If the dividend is negative, set the quotient to the most negative number. Define the register used for the dividend in the user program. Why is it not possible to correct a division routine in which the location of the dividend is arbitrary?

11.1.4. Emulate a "macroinstruction" that moves a string of characters of arbitrary length from one area of memory to another. Assume that D1 holds the length, A1 the start of the string, and A2 the destination location for the first character to be moved.

11.2 THE TRACE EXCEPTION

In testing a microcomputer system, it is sometimes desirable to execute instructions one at a time with the processor suspending execution between instructions. This single instruction mode of operation is provided by the trace feature of the MC68000.[2] Rather than suspending operation, the MC68000 causes execution of a trace routine after each instruction is executed whenever the trace status bit (SR) [15] or T = {1}. The vector holding the address of the first instruction of the trace routine is held in longword location $24. Figure 11.5 shows the general operation of the trace feature.

The trace operates for programs executing in either the supervisor mode or the user mode. However, the trace bit (T) can be changed only by an instruction executed in the supervisor mode. The return to the program being traced is accomplished by executing an RTE instruction, which should be the last instruction in the trace routine.

The trace routine is typically designed to display or record the contents of all the registers and memory locations that affect program execution or processing. These values may be output to a terminal or similar device to allow a programmer to follow

---

[2]An alternative is *single-cycle* operation in which execution is suspended after each access to memory. The $\overline{\text{HALT}}$ signal line of the MC68000 can be used for this purpose if the proper circuitry is employed to implement it.

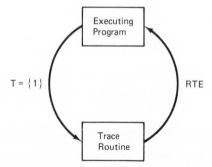

Figure 11.5 Trace operation.

changes in register contents or other values as the program executes each instruction in turn.

EXERCISES

11.2.1. Write a simple trace routine to print the contents of all the processor registers when the trace exception is taken. Test the tracing by writing a simple program in which each instruction is traced. (*Note:* The routine to print values is provided by the supervisor program in most systems. You may have to convert the hexadecimal values on the stack to ASCII for printing.)

11.3 ERROR CONDITIONS CAUSING TRAPS

The MC68000 is designed to protect the system from errors that could cause unpredictable behavior. The errors that cause traps are listed in Table 11.4. The privilege violation, illegal instruction, or address error traps usually occur when a program is being debugged. The bus error and the halted state typically indicate a hardware failure in the system. Recovery from any of these errors is usually not possible or desirable until the offending program or hardware is corrected.

In MC68010 systems, the bus error condition is used to implement virtual memory. If the processor were to attempt to access a location in the virtual memory space

TABLE 11.4   ERRORS CAUSING TRAPS

Errors	Cause	Comments
Privilege violation	In user mode; attempt to execute privileged instruction	If S = {0}, attempt to execute: STOP, RESET, RTE, MOVE USP, ANDI to SR, EORI to SR, ORI to SR, or MOVE to SR
Illegal instruction	Bit pattern of op code not recognized	(PC) value on stack is address of illegal instruction
Address error	Attempted word access at odd address	Stack contains (PC), (SR), op word, access address, and status word (seven words)
Bus error	External request	Same stack contents as for address error
Halted state	Address or bus error during processing of bus error, address error, or reset	Reset required to restart processor

Note: The address error or bus error exception in the MC68010 uses 29 words of the stack to allow instruction continuation after the exception is processed.

that is not residing in physical memory, a page fault would occur. The access to that location is temporarily suspended while the necessary program segments or data are fetched from secondary storage and placed in physical memory. Then the suspended access is completed. If the bus error is used to signal the page fault, the MC68010 can continue instruction execution of the suspended instruction after the physical memory has been updated.

11.3.1 Privilege Violations

If a program operating in the user mode attempts to execute a *privileged* instruction, a trap using the vector at location $20 is caused. The value of the PC saved on the stack is the address of the first word of the instruction causing the violation.

11.3.2 Illegal Instruction

The *illegal instruction* trap, with vector at location $10, is used to protect the system from the effects of incorrect machine code or a localized memory failure. The value of the PC saved on the stack points to the illegal instruction that caused the trap.

11.3.3 Address Error

If the processor attempts to access a word operand, longword operand, or an instruction at an odd address, an *address error* exception is generated using the vector at location $0C. Before the exception routine is executed, the following information is saved on the stack:

(a) The value of (PC), which may be advanced beyond the address of the first word of the instruction causing the error
(b) The value of (SR)
(c) The contents of the instruction register
(d) The address being accessed
(e) A status information word

The order and format of this information on the stack are shown in Figure 11.6. The information saved would not normally allow recovery from the error but is useful to aid in diagnosis of the problem.

Example 11.3

Figure 11.7 shows the printed output for a trace routine provided by the Motorola MACSbug monitor program used with the Motorola MC68000 Design Module. The assembly language program shown causes an addressing error when the second instruction is executed. The first instruction, executed in the supervisor mode with trace (T command), yields the register contents shown. When the address error occurs, the supervisor

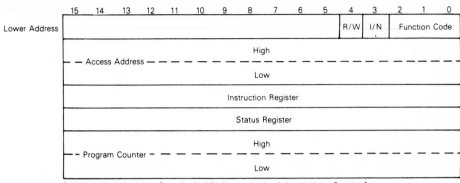

R/W (read/write): write = 0, read = 1. I/N (instruction/not): instruction = 0, not = 1

Figure 11.6 Stack contents after an address error. (Courtesy of Motorola, Inc.)

```
MC68000 ASM REV= 1.4 - COPYRIGHT BY MOTOROLA 1978          PAGE  1


1                           LLEN    100
2        00002000           ORG     $2000
3                     *
4                     * CREATE AN ADDRESSING ERROR
5                     *
6  002000 307C3001          MOVE.W  #$3001,A0        ; PUT AN ILLEGAL ADDRESS IN A0
7  002004 3010              MOVE.W  (A0),D0          ; TRY TO ACCESS IT
8                           END

****** TOTAL ERRORS    0--    0


SYMBOL TABLE - APPROX 1202 SYMBOL ENTRIES LEFT



       *TD
       PC=002000 SR=2004 US=00007F00 SS=00008000
       D0=00000000 D1=00000000 D2=00000000 D3=00000000
       D4=00000000 D5=00000000 D6=00000000 D7=00000000
       A0=00000000 A1=00000000 A2=00000000 A3=00000000
       A4=00000000 A5=00000000 A6=00000000 A7=00008000
       ----------------------------------------------------------------
       *G
       TRAP ERROR
       *TD
       PC=003001 SR=3015 US=00007F00 SS=00007FF8
       D0=00000000 D1=00000000 D2=00000000 D3=00000000
       D4=00000000 D5=00000000 D6=00000000 D7=00000000
       A0=00003001 A1=00000000 A2=00000000 A3=00000000
       A4=00000000 A5=00000000 A6=00000000 A7=00007FF8
       ----------------------------------------------------------------
       *DM 7FF8 10
       007FF8   30 10 20 04 00 00 20 06 61 00 61 00 61 00 61 00   0..............
       *
```

Figure 11.7 Address error example.

stack pointer at $7FFE is used to address the stack and store the error information into lower memory locations.

The trace exception was not taken because the address error exception has a higher priority. Instead, a TRAP ERROR is indicated by the monitor address error exception routine. The Display Memory (DM) command is used to print the relevant stack contents.

11.3.4 Bus Error

The bus error exception is generated when external circuitry reports the error via a processor signal line. The exact cause is determined by the hardware design of the system. Programmatically, the bus error is treated exactly as the address error just described but uses the vector at location $08. The stacked information is the same as for the address error exception. More details on the bus error and its system consequences are discussed in Chapter 12.

11.3.5 Halted State

If an address error or a bus error occurs during the processing of an address error, bus error, or system reset, the processor is halted. This response to double errors prevents the processor from unpredictable behavior when a catastrophic failure in the system is indicated. One of the processor signal lines is activated to indicate this condition to external devices.

EXERCISES

11.3.1. Write an address error routine to decode the information saved on the stack and output it to the user. (*Note:* The output routine to print the information is part of the supervisor program and depends on the system being used.)

11.3.2. Describe several ways an illegal instruction trap could occur in a system.

11.3.3. Assume that an illegal (odd) address is stored in the address error vector location. What would happen to the system if the processor detects an address error during execution of a program?

11.4 INTERRUPT PROCESSING BY THE MC68000

The interrupt system of the MC68000 allows an external device to interrupt the processor execution and causes program control to be passed to an interrupt-handling routine. This section is concerned with the programming aspects of the interrupt sequence for the MC68000, including the priority scheme for interrupts and the processor operation during interrupt processing. A discussion of the signal lines used for interrupt requests and acknowledgments is presented in Chapter 12.

An interrupt request from an external device can occur at one of seven levels of priority which is determined by the value presented on the three interrupt signal lines of the processor. Priorities are assigned to interrupts so that level 1 is lowest and level 7 is highest. These priorities allow a routine that is processing a lower-level interrupt to be interrupted by a higher-level interrupt request. After the highest-level interrupt processing is completed, control returns to the next-lower-level interrupt routine that is waiting to complete execution. Once all of the interrupt requests are processed, control finally returns to any program that was interrupted.

From the processor's point of view, an interrupt is an externally generated request for exception processing. The interrupt request may be considered active, pending, or disabled. An *active* request is processed immediately after the completion of any instruction currently executing provided that no higher priority exceptions take precedence. The request is *pending* if the processor is currently processing a higher-priority exception. Pending requests will be serviced when the higher-priority processing completes unless the processor enters the halted state. If an interrupt level is

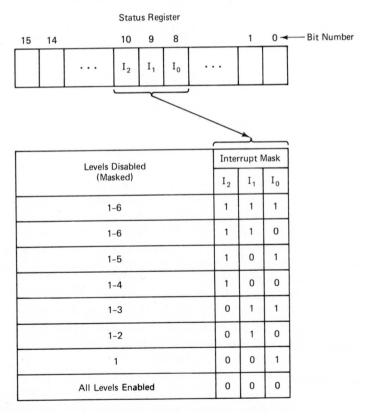

Figure 11.8   Interrupt mask for the MC68000.

TABLE 11.5   VECTOR TABLE FOR INTERRUPT ROUTINES

Vector number (decimal)	Memory location (hexadecimal)	Name
15	$003C	Uninitialized interrupt vector
24	$0060	Spurious
25	$0064	Level 1 autovector
26	$0068	Level 2 autovector
27	$006C	Level 3 autovector
28	$0070	Level 4 autovector
29	$0074	Level 5 autovector
30	$0078	Level 6 autovector
31	$007C	Level 7 autovector
⋮	⋮	⋮
64	$0100	User interrupt vector 1
65	$0104	User interrupt vector 2
⋮	⋮	⋮
255	$03FC	User interrupt vector 192

Notes:

1. Vector 15 should be provided by an uninitialized external device if the CPU requests a vector number.

2. A spurious interrupt occurs when the CPU detects an error during interrupt processing.

disabled, an interrupt request at that level is ignored until the level is enabled by changing the interrupt mask in the status register, (SR) [10:8].

The interrupt system is initialized by a supervisor program during system initialization by loading the starting addresses of each interrupt routine to be used into the appropriate location in the vector table. This initialization is performed with all interrupt levels disabled except level 7, which cannot be disabled. The interrupt levels are enabled just before control is passed from the supervisor program to the first application program to be executed.

The interrupt mask bits are shown in Figure 11.8 which includes the mask value for each level. In general, when the interrupt request is at the level masked or less, the interrupt request will not be accepted. The level 7 request is an exception to this rule and will be processed regardless of the setting of the interrupt mask. If the mask is set to {000}, all interrupt levels are enabled.

The vector table for interrupts is shown in Table 11.5. The spurious interrupt vector is used when the processor recognizes an interrupt request but some error condition exists externally. Rapid changes in the interrupt-level signal lines (unstable value) or an indication of a bus error from an external device during an interrupt request will cause a spurious interrupt. Otherwise, the starting address of the interrupt routine for levels 1 through 7 will be taken from the appropriate vector location. The two classifications of interrupts are autovector and user interrupts. Selection between these modes of operation for the interrupt system is determined entirely by external circuitry. In either case, the address of the interrupt is calculated as four times the vector number. The difference in hardware operation has no effect on the design of interrupt routines.

11.4.1 Interrupt Processing

If the processor is executing instructions in the normal state, an interrupt request that is acknowledged and becomes active causes a sequence of events designed to pass control to a designated interrupt routine. This routine processes the interrupt as required,

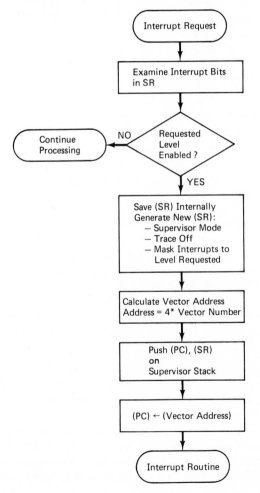

Figure 11.9 Interrupt processing.

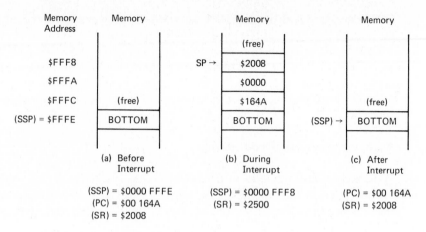

Figure 11.10   System stack during interrupt processing.

and then returns control to the interrupted program. This sequence of events is shown in Figure 11.9. The operations are performed by the hardware until control is passed to the interrupt routine. The processing required in the interrupt routine is entirely dependent on the application.

Use of interrupts for I/O programming is considered in Section 12.2. A program example in that section initializes and defines an interrupt routine for a programmable timer chip.

Example 11.4

During the processing of a trap or interrupt, the contents of both the program counter (PC) and the status register (SR) are saved on the system stack. The supervisor stack pointer is the active stack pointer since the exception processing forces the system into the supervisor mode. The contents of the PC are pushed first and then the 16-bit status register contents are pushed. Therefore, at least three words of the system stack are used for each response to an interrupt by the MC68000 processor. As discussed previously, the MC68010 uses at least four words of the stack.

As shown in Figure 11.10, an interrupt occurring when the initial contents of selected registers have the values

(SR) = $2008
(PC) = $00 164A
(SSP) = $0000 FFFE

causes a push of (PC) and then (SR) into the longword location $FFFA and the word location $FFF8, respectively. The interrupt routine may continue to use the system stack as required as long as (SSP) is restored to the value $0000 FFF8 before executing an RTE instruction to return control to the interrupted program. To return, (SR) are pulled from word location $FFF8 and (PC) is restored from longword location $FFFA. Then processing continues with the instruction at location $00 164A. If the interrupt request is at autovectored level 5, the interrupt routine begins execution with

$$(PC) = (\$0074)$$
$$(SR) = \$2500$$

which allows execution at the vectored location with interrupts at level 5 and below disabled.

Example 11.5

External signal lines determine whether the interrupt mode is *autovector* or *user interrupt*. The user interrupt is also called simply a vectored interrupt request. When the autovector mode is requested by an external device, the CPU automatically provides the vector location. Otherwise, in the user interrupt (vectored) mode, the external device must provide the vector number. This number is multiplied by 4 to give the address of the exception vector. The way that the vector number is supplied to the CPU from the external device is discussed in Chapter 12.

In either case, the programmer must know the following information to program an interrupt routine:

(a) The vector number (or address)

(b) The priority assigned by the hardware design of the system for masking or unmasking vectored interrupts (the priority for autovectors is fixed)

(c) Details of the functional operation of the interrupt routine as determined by the hardware requirements

The location of the interrupt routine is typically decided during the software design phase and the priority for each interrupt is determined by the system requirements, primarily the timing constraints of external devices. The interrupt priority is important to the programmer only if the interrupt routine manipulates the interrupt mask.

EXERCISES

11.4.1. What are some system applications for the level 7, nonmaskable interrupt?

11.4.2. How many user interrupt vectored plus autovectored interrupt vectors are available according to the exception vector table? The vector number is an 8-bit integer allowing 256 entries to address the exception vector table, but not all entries can be associated with interrupts according to the table. Or can they? In other words, is a designer forbidden from using vectors 0 through 23 or vectors 32 through 47 as interrupt vectors?

11.4.3. Write an interrupt routine to update a real-time clock. The clock should give the time of day in hours, minutes, and seconds. Assume that a level 4 interrupt occurs once per second.

11.5 EXCEPTION PRIORITY

Exceptions can be categorized according to their priorities, which are fixed by the design of the processor and cannot be changed. Motorola divides exceptions into group 0, group 1, and group 2, in descending order of priority. Figure 11.11 lists the priority groups, the exceptions contained in each group, and the processing that occurs. The highest-priority exception is the reset exception, which causes system initialization. If this exception occurs, any other processing is immediately terminated. All the other exceptions are processed according to priority if two or more occur simultaneously.

If a group 0 exception is detected, the instruction being executed is aborted, possibly before it has completed execution. The instruction will complete its current hardware cycle, and then exception processing will begin. Within group 0, reset exceptions have the highest priority, followed by bus errors and, finally, address errors.

In group 1, the trace exception has the highest priority if the instruction being traced executes to completion. If execution is not completed because the instruction caused an illegal instruction trap or privilege violation trap, the trace exception will not occur. If an interrupt is pending following an instruction to be traced, the trace exception is processed first.

The exceptions in group 2 have no priorities within the group since only one instruction executes at a time. The execution of these instructions will always be completed unless a group 0 exception occurs during their execution. If the program and system are operating properly, only a reset exception would cause these instructions to be aborted.

EXERCISES

11.5.1. Describe the processing that occurs under the following conditions:
  (a) An illegal instruction is detected when the trace bit is $\{1\}$.
  (b) A bus error occurs during a TRAP instruction.
  (c) An interrupt occurs while an instruction is executing with $T = \{1\}$.
  Which routine gets final control?

Group	Exception	Processing
0	Reset Bus Error Address Error	Exception processing begins at the next minor cycle
1	Trace Interrupt Illegal Privilege	Exception processing begins before the next instruction
2	TRAP, TRAPV, CHK Zero Divide	Exception processing is started by normal instruction execution

Figure 11.11 Priority groups for exceptions. (Courtesy of Motorola, Inc.)

FURTHER READING

The article by Hemenway and that by Starnes listed here discuss exception processing for the MC68000. Hemenway's article gives an example of an interrupt routine to service a terminal. Both of these articles are also reprinted in *MC68000 Article Reprints* (see the Further Reading section for Chapter 4).

The article by Grappel gives an interesting application of the trace feature of the MC68000. His program calculates a histogram of memory usage as a program is traced.

GRAPPEL, ROBERT D., "MC68000 Charts Its Own Memory Usage," *EDN* 25, No. 21 (November 20, 1980), 115–117.

HEMENWAY, JACK, and ROBERT GRAPPEL, "Use MC68000 Interrupts to Supervise a Console," *EDN,* 25, No. 11 (June 5, 1980), 183–186.

STARNES, THOMAS W., "Handling Exceptions Gracefully Enhances Software Reliability," *Electronics,* 53, No. 20 (September 11,1980), 153–157.

12

Interfacing and I/O Programming

This chapter discusses interfacing requirements and input/output programming for MC68000 systems. First, the general characteristics of interfaces are defined to describe typical MC68000 systems. Today, these systems are designed using peripheral chips to provide much of the interface circuitry. The programming of a few of these I/O chips is covered as their special requirements are defined. Basic techniques for programming the interfacing devices considered here apply to many of those available. Interfaces and I/O programming are presented in the first two sections of this chapter.

During system design, calculation of the timing requirements for programs is sometimes important to predict system performance. The exact time taken by any instruction or the time to initiate exception processing can be determined by using the instruction execution times published in the Motorola *User's Manual* for the MC68000. A number of examples in Section 12.3 show how these times may be used to determine timing in MC68000 systems.

Understanding of the signal lines of the CPU is necessary to design interfaces that connect to the system bus. Various signal lines are used for data transfer, memory protection and management, interrupt processing, bus control, and the detection of hardware errors. The MC68000 also provides special signal lines used to control peripheral chips from the 8-bit M6800 family of products by Motorola. Section 12.4 treats the CPU signal lines from the hardware designer's point of view.

12.1 INTERFACE DESIGN

Figure 12.1 shows the organization of a typical computer system, emphasizing the role played by the interfacing circuitry. This interface electrically connects the internal sys-

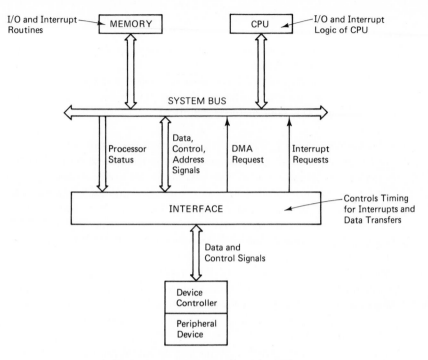

Figure 12.1   Typical interface organization.

tem bus with the device controller and resolves differences in timing or formats between the CPU and the external device. The CPU, through its logical circuitry and I/O routines, controls the operation of the system. The I/O routines prepare the interface for data transfers with the peripheral device, which itself is controlled by the device controller.

When the device is initialized and ready for transfer, it can perform its function, such as transmitting a character to the CPU or memory. Transfers to the CPU usually involve an interrupt request. High-speed transfers of blocks of characters are accomplished with DMA requests. If the device uses a direct memory access (DMA) technique, for example, the transfer request passes through the interface to the bus control circuits and the memory.

The functional characteristics of an interface depend entirely on its application. For standard operations such as serial transfer of data to CRT terminals or parallel transfer to tape drives and disc units, the interface and perhaps part of the device controller are typically packaged together as a peripheral chip. When the interface is used to connect special-purpose devices, a custom interface may be required.

12.1.1 Functional Design of Interfaces

Most standard peripheral devices are connected to a system using peripheral chips to supply the interfaces. Therefore, it is important to understand the general principle of operation of these chips, which function as *programmable* interfaces. Such interfaces require initialization and act under the control of an I/O routine. The design, integration, and testing of these interfaces and the associated routines require cooperation between the hardware designer and the programmer.

Table 12.1 lists some of the items to be specified when describing the functional operation of an interface. This functional description is normally prepared by the hardware designer, who includes details of the programming required for the interface.

The functional description begins with a discussion of the purpose of the interface. This is governed by the requirements of the system design, particularly the type of peripheral device involved. Operational modes are described by defining the operation of the circuitry needed to perform initialization and data transfers. Timing considerations and similar hardware aspects of the interface must also be described.

Electrical and physical characteristics of the interface are also included in the functional description. The electrical details are dictated by the system bus and the electrical requirements of the device controller. Such details include specification of the voltage levels, rate of change of signals (rise times), and the like. The physical considerations include environmental requirements and space limitations on the circuit boards involved. The temperature and humidity ranges for the environment determine the type of chip and the packaging required for integrated circuit chips. The size of the circuit boards influences the number of chips and their placement on a board. Most designs involve standard-size circuit boards which plug into connectors to the system bus. As pointed out in Chapter 4, the MC68000 itself is available in a number of different packages to meet various physical requirements.

Once the mode of operation of an interface has been specified, the programming requirements can be defined. An interface is controlled by sequences of logical variables or binary values written to the interfacing circuitry by an I/O routine. A sequence must be defined for each mode of operation. For example, the programming procedure to reset the interface and initialize it to some known state must be described. Programming a data transfer includes determining if the interface is ready for the transfer, performing the transfer, and checking for errors.

Finally, a test procedure for the interface is defined. This usually includes a

TABLE 12.1 FUNCTIONAL DESIGN OF INTERFACES

Purpose of the interface
Modes of operation
   Initialization
   Data transfers
Timing
Electrical characteristics
Physical characteristics
Programming: sequence of data and commands transferred
Test procedure

hardware procedure to verify that the interface is functional as well as the steps for testing of the interface under program control. The peripheral chips available as part of the MC68000 family of products serve to simplify the design and programming interfaces.

12.1.2 Peripheral Chips as Interfaces

The MC68000 family includes a number of peripheral chips for interfacing. These integrated circuits provide the interface to particular peripheral devices and eliminate a great deal of the hardware design associated with interfacing. These chips are designed to connect to the MC68000 system bus directly or with a minimal amount of additional circuitry.

Peripheral chips are programmed by writing into or reading from registers internal to the chips. The addresses of these registers are in the I/O space of the system. For MC68000 systems, these addresses appear to be memory locations because of the memory-mapped I/O scheme of the MC68000.

Figure 12.2 shows the structure of a typical peripheral chip. The output side of the peripheral chip has data and control lines designed to transfer control information and data to a peripheral device. The signal lines on the input side are used to select or "enable" the chip and transfer data between the CPU and internal registers of the chip. Each internal register has an I/O address defined during the system design. The address decoder shown enables the chip when an internal register address is placed on the address lines by the CPU.[1] The read/write control lines from the I/O control logic

[1]In certain peripheral chips, the control and status registers have the same address. This is accomplished by using the "read" signal line to select a read-only status register. Similarly, the write signal line would be used to select the write-only control register. Many of the peripheral chips for the MC68000 family have this feature.

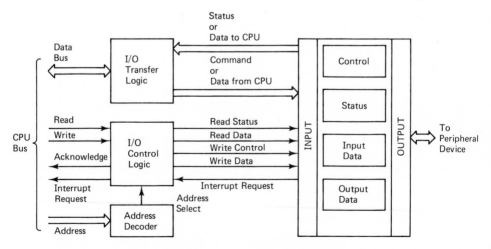

Figure 12.2   A typical peripheral chip.

circuitry then select a particular register of the chip. After the peripheral chip acknowledges the request from the CPU, the I/O transfer logic acts as a buffer for data between the data bus and the peripheral chip.

The control register receives a sequence of bits from the CPU to control the chip's operation. For example, the MC68000 instruction

MOVE.B   # $<d_8>$,CREG

could be used to transfer 8 bits to the control register at address CREG. Various bits in the command byte $<d_8>$ typically determine whether a transfer operation is input or output and whether interrupts from the chip are enabled or not.

A status register on the chip contains information about the transfer or about the chip. Bits in this register might indicate whether the chip is ready for data transfer, as well as the interrupt status and error conditions. An 8-bit status could be read with the instruction

MOVE.B   SREG,D1

if SREG is the address of the status register on the chip.

Two data registers are shown on the chip in Figure 12.2. One receives data from the peripheral device and the other stores data to be transmitted to it. The input data

Product	Device No.	Title
MPU	MC68000	16 Bit MPU
	MC68008	16 Bit MPU with 8 Bit Data Bus
	MC68010	16 Bit Virtual Memory MPU
	MC68020	32 Bit MPU
MMU	MC68451	Memory Management Unit (MMU)
Math Processor	MC68881	Floating Point Co-Processor (FPCP)
Bus Controllers	MC68452	Bus Arbitration Module (BAM)
	MC68153	Bus Interrupter Module (BIM)
DMA Controllers	MC68440	DMA Controller (2-Channel) (DDMA)
	MC68450	DMA Controller (4-Channel) (DMAC)
General Purpose I/O	MC68230	Parallel Interface Timer (PI/T)
	MC68901	Multi-Function Peripheral (MFP)
Peripheral Controller	MC68120	Intelligent Peripheral Controller (IPC)
Data Communications	MC68561	Multi-Protocol Communications Controller II (MPCCII)
	MC68562	Dual Univeral Serial Communications Controllers
	MC68564	Serial Input/Output (SIO)
	MC68652	Multi-Protocol Communications Controller (MPCC)
	MC68653	Polynomial Generator Checker (PGC)
	MC68661	Enhanced Programmable Communications Interface (EPCI)
	MC68681	Dual Universal Asynchronous Receiver/Transmitter (DUART)
Disk Controller	MC68465	Floppy Disk Controller (FDC)

Figure 12.3   MC68000 family chips. (Courtesy of Motorola, Inc.)

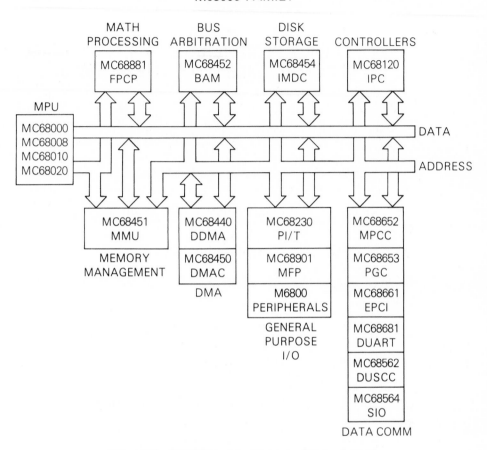

Figure 12.4   MC68000 system. (Courtesy of Motorola, Inc.)

register is read in a manner similar to that used to read the status register. The CPU writes to the output data register as it does to the control register.

12.1.3 MC68000 System Support Chips

The chips in the family of MC68000 products are listed in Figure 12.3. Their connections to the address and data bus of the CPU are illustrated in Figure 12.4. Each of these support chips fulfills a specific interfacing function and is programmed according to its unique requirements. Notice that when a memory management unit (MMU) is included in the system, it controls the addresses output on the address lines. In addition, a number of peripheral chips from the MC6800 8-bit family that are directly compatible with the MC68000 are listed in Figure 12.5.

M6800 FAMILY PERIPHERALS THAT ARE DIRECTLY COMPATIBLE WITH THE MC68000

MCM6810	128 X 8 Bit Static RAM
MC6821	Peripheral Interface Adapter
MC6840	Programmable Timer Module
MC6843	Floppy Disk Controller
MC6845	CRT Controller
MC6847	Video Display Generator
MC6850	Asynchronous Communication Interface Adapter
MC6852	Synchronous Serial Data Adapter
MC6854	Advanced Data Link Controller
MC6859	Data Security Device
MC6860	0 to 600 bps Digital Modem
MC6862	2400 bps Modulator
MC68488	General Purpose Interface Adapter

Figure 12.5   M6800 family chips. (Courtesy of Motorola, Inc.)

EXERCISES

12.1.1. MC68000 systems use memory-mapped I/O for data transfer. Another scheme is called *isolated I/O*. With this technique, separate instructions for I/O are part of the CPU instruction set. Typically, there are several I/O instructions (IN or OUT) and 256 possible I/O locations or *ports*. These ports are accessed by separate signal lines which are not part of the system address bus. Describe the advantages and disadvantages of each scheme in terms of the system flexibility and the hardware requirements for interfacing.

12.1.2. Describe the steps in the program and the hardware sequence needed to initialize an interface to receive a byte of data from an external device. Define the operation of the interface and the use of its registers after the byte is received. What sequence is required of the processor itself to read the byte?

12.1.3. Refer to Motorola literature to describe the purpose and operation of the peripheral chips available for MC68000 systems.

12.2 I/O PROGRAMMING

The use of memory-mapped I/O in MC68000 systems allows a great flexibility to the designer of I/O routines. Any instruction that references memory can be used to control or transfer data to and from a peripheral interface. The powerful instruction set and the various addressing modes of the MC68000 can be applied to I/O programming. In addition, two special instructions are available to control and access peripheral chips. These are introduced first in this section.

A general discussion of I/O transfers follows which differentiates between CPU initiated transfers and device initiated transfers. Motorola's Design Module is used to illustrate the I/O capability of various peripheral chips. The peripheral chips that are discussed are not described in complete detail; however, the manufacturer's literature about the chip can be referenced for further information.

12.2.1 RESET and MOVEP Instructions

The two instructions listed in Table 12.2 are used to control or access peripheral interfaces. The RESET instruction asserts a CPU signal line which is used to cause interfaces to assume their initial hardware state. This instruction can be executed only in the supervisor mode and does not affect the processor state. Execution continues with the next instruction.

The MOVEP (Move Peripheral Data) instruction transfers a word or longword value between a data register and *alternate* bytes of memory. This instruction is used to access peripheral chips whose register addresses are successive even or odd byte addresses in memory. For example, the instruction

    MOVEP.L   D1,0(A1)

TABLE 12.2   RESET AND MOVEP INSTRUCTIONS

Syntax	Operation
RESET	RESET signal line asserted
MOVEP. $<l>$ $<Dn>, <d_{16}>(An)$	Transfer to (EA), (EA + 2), ...
MOVEP. $<l>$ $<d_{16}>(An), <Dn>$	Transfer from (EA), (EA + 2), ...

Notes:

1. RESET is a privileged instruction.
2. $<l>$ is W or L for MOVEP.

transfers four bytes from D1 to every other byte beginning at the first byte addressed by (A1). The high-upper byte, (D1) [31:24], is transferred to location (A1); the middle-upper byte, (D1) [23:16], to byte address (A1) + 2; and so on. This method to access interface registers is used for the M6800 family of peripheral chips and for some 16-bit peripheral chips from Motorola.

12.2.2 I/O Transfer Techniques

I/O transfers are divided into those initiated by the CPU and those initiated by the peripheral device and its controller. Table 12.3 lists transfer techniques in these categories and defines the required initialization and program operation. Before transfers begin, an I/O routine executed by the CPU performs the initialization for the interface.

The *unconditional* transfer requires that the peripheral device be ready for trans-

TABLE 12.3   I/O TRANSFER TECHNIQUES

Type of transfer	Initialization by program	Program operation
CPU-initiated transfer		
Unconditional	None	Transfer data
Conditional	Set up device for direction of transfer	Test status of device and wait until ready; then transfer
Device-initiated transfer		
Interrupt transfer	1. Set up device for I/O transfer with interrupt 2. Enable interrupts	1. Transfer data when interrupt occurs 2. Clear interrupt request after transfer
DMA	1. Set up device for I/O transfer 2. Load DMA registers (a) Count (b) Address 3. Issue command to begin	Process end-of-block interrupt

Note: Conditional I/O is sometimes called programmed I/O or polled I/O.

fers at all times. A common example of this type of transfer is found in systems where the "device" is a unit to display numbers or characters. The I/O routine simply transfers the data with a MOVE instruction to the proper address. Circuitry of the display unit is used to convert the binary word from the CPU to the proper display format. Another use of this method is to read a group of switches whose settings are coded into binary sequence.

Conditional transfers are sometimes called *programmed I/O* or *polled I/O*. The operation of these transfers is illustrated in Figure 12.6. Once the interface is initialized, the I/O routine repeatedly checks the status register of the chip until the status indicates the device is ready. The routine then transfers the data to the peripheral chip. Since the CPU is in a wait loop until the device is ready, the usefulness of this transfer is limited. For example, a conditional transfer could be used to write into a control register during initialization of the interface.

For devices that transmit or receive data very slowly compared to the execution times of the I/O routines, interrupt controlled transfer is preferred. This transfer method is shown is Figure 12.7. The interface is first initialized to transfer data. Then the CPU executes other programs until an interrupt occurs. When control is passed to the interrupt routine, a test of the peripheral chip status for errors is made. If an error is detected, the appropriate action is taken. Otherwise, the transfer occurs. Afterward, the interrupt request from the interface must be cleared before the next transfer can occur. This will usually be done automatically when the status register of the peripheral chip is read.

When a device is capable of transferring blocks of data at high speeds, the direct memory access (DMA) method of transfer is frequently used. A DMA interface typi-

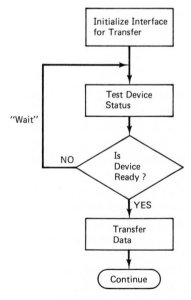

Figure 12.6 Conditional transfer.

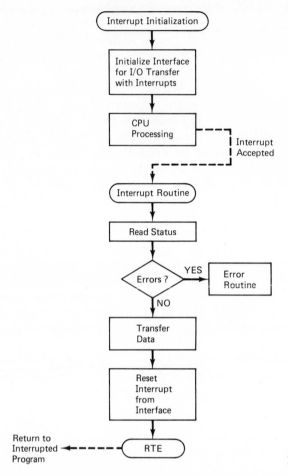

Figure 12.7   Interrupt-controlled transfer.

cally contains two programmable registers. A counter register contains the number of values to transfer and an address register contains the starting address of the block. The initialization program loads these registers and sends a command sequence to initiate the transfer. The CPU is then free to process other programs. The transfer of data between the interface and memory is entirely controlled by DMA circuitry without the intervention of the CPU.

For each DMA transfer of a data value, the DMA circuitry requests use of the system bus. The CPU relinquishes the bus for the time of transfer, which is usually one bus cycle. During the transfer, the DMA interface controls the memory just as the CPU normally does. Typically, less than one bus cycle out of five is used for DMA transfers. This "cycle stealing" has little effect on system performance in most cases. For comparison, the MC68000 requires at least four bus cycles to fetch an instruction. Upon completion of the transfer of an entire block of data, the DMA circuitry causes

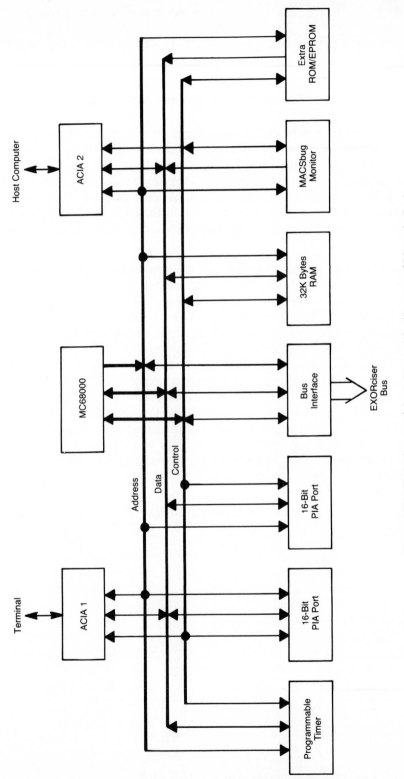

Figure 12.8 Block diagram of the design module. (Courtesy of Motorola, Inc.)

an interrupt. The CPU may now process the input data or initiate the next DMA output.

12.2.3 I/O Features of the Design Module

The MC68000 Design Module is used as single-board computer to create and test prototype systems. A block diagram of this module is shown in Figure 12.8. The MACSbug monitor is contained in ROM and the RAM storage is provided by 16K × 1 chips arranged as 32K bytes of memory. Two peripheral chips for serial transfers, two for parallel transfers, and a programmable timer are provided. The memory locations used to interface with the module are shown in Table 12.4. These assignments are used in the program examples. A memory map for the module is also given in Appendix V.

Motorola MC6850 ACIA.   The Asynchronous Communications Interface Adapter (ACIA) is a M6800 family chip with the numerical designation MC6850. This chip, as shown in Figure 12.9, transmits or receives serial data when connected to an external device. Internally, the chip receives serial bits as input and converts them to 8-bit parallel data bytes for the CPU data bus. For output, the ACIA converts 8-bit data bytes from the CPU to serial bits for transmission to the device.

The chip has four addressable registers for status, control, received data (input), and transmitted data (output). A CPU write to location $3FF01 or $3FF21 of the Design Module loads the control register of ACIA1 or AC1A2, respectively. The status registers share the same addresses as the control registers. A CPU read from location $3FF01 or $3FF21 transfers the status from the selected ACIA. The transmit data register and receive data register share the same address in a similar manner. A CPU read of location $3FF03 (ACIA1) or $3FF23 (ACIA2) reads the receive data register

TABLE 12.4   DESIGN MODULE MEMORY ASSIGNMENT

Item	Address
RAM area (32K bytes)	0–$7FFF
MACSbug (8K bytes)	$20000–$21FFF
ACIA1	$3FF01; $3FF03
ACIA2	$3FF21; $3FF23
PIA1	$3FF41; $3FF43 $3FF45; $3FF47
PIA2	$3FF40; $3FF42 $3FF44; $3FF46
PTM	$3FF61–$3FF6F (odd bytes)

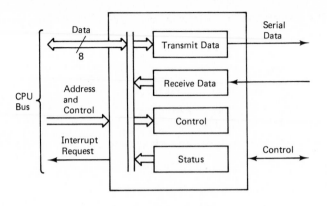

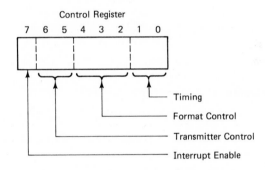

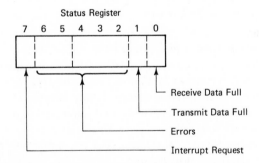

Figure 12.9   Simplified diagram of the ACIA.

of the addressed ACIA. A CPU write to either of these addresses loads a byte into the transmit data register for output.

Example 12.1

The short program segment of Figure 12.10 illustrates the method of conditional I/O transfer with an ACIA. In the example, the status of the chip is tested or polled until it has received a character. When its data register is full, the character is transferred to the

```
MC68000 ASM REV= 1.4 - COPYRIGHT BY MOTOROLA 1978            PAGE   1

    1                             LLEN    100
    2                       *
    3      00000001   SOH      EQU    $01
    4      0003FF01   ACIA     EQU    $3FF01
    5      000200F6   MACSBUG  EQU    $200F6
    6                       *
    7      00001000            ORG    $1000
    8                       *
    9                       * THIS LOOP CONTINUOUSLY POLLS THE ACIA CHIP UNTIL A
   10                       * CONTROL-A IS DETECTED, THEN IT EXITS TO THE MONITOR
   11                       *
   12 001000 43F90003FF01 LOOP   LEA    ACIA,A1
   13 001006 1211             MOVE.B (A1),D1           ; READ STATUS
   14 001008 02010001         ANDI.B #1,D1
   15 00100C 67F2             BEQ.S  LOOP             ; IF RDRF = 0 JUST LOOP
   16 00100E 12290002         MOVE.B 2(A1),D1          ; READ CHARACTER
   17 001012 0201007F         ANDI.B #$7F,D1
   18 001016 0C010001         CMPI.B #SOH,D1
   19 00101A 66E4             BNE.S  LOOP             ; IF CTRL A, CONTINUE LOOPING
   20 00101C 4EF9000200F6     JMP    MACSBUG          ; ELSE, EXIT TO MAXBUG
   21                         END

****** TOTAL ERRORS   0--   0


SYMBOL TABLE - APPROX 1198 SYMBOL ENTRIES LEFT

ACIA       03FF01 LOOP      001000 MACSBUG    0200F6 SOH         000001
```

Figure 12.10   ACIA programming example.

low-order byte of CPU register D1. If the character received is a control-A ($01), then control is returned to the monitor. Otherwise, looping continues while the program waits for another character.

Motorola MC6820 PIA.

The Motorola chip designated MC6820 is the Peripheral Interface Adapter (PIA), which is capable of interfacing with two separate devices. As shown in Figure 12.11, the chip receives or transmits data in a parallel fashion to an external device. It also accepts interrupt requests from the device and causes a CPU interrupt request if initialized to do so. The three registers shown in the figure are referred to as control register A (CRA), data direction register A (DDRA), and data register A (DRA). The corresponding registers for port B (CRB, DDRB, and DRB) are not shown.

These registers and their addresses on the Design Module for PIA1 are given in Table 12.5. The registers are each 8 bits in length. For I/O transfers without interrupts, CRA[2] or CRB[2] selects between the corresponding data register (bit $2 = \{1\}$) or data direction register (bit $2 = \{0\}$). When the data direction register is selected, the eight data lines to the peripheral device can be individually assigned for input (bit $i = \{0\}$) or output (bit $i = \{1\}$). Thus the instruction sequence

```
MOVE.B   #$00,$3FF45      ;CLEAR CRA, SELECT DDRA
MOVE.B   #$FF,$3FF41      ;OUTPUT
```

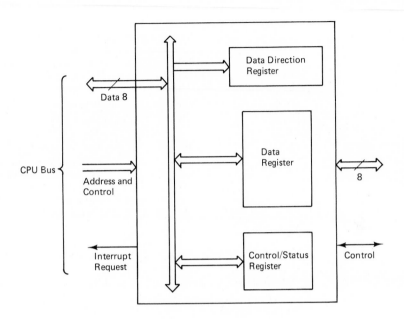

(a) PIA Diagram Showing One Port Only

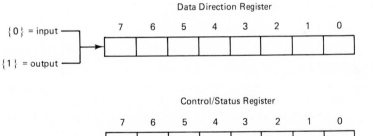

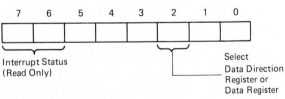

Note: Bits 0, 1, and 3, 4, 5 are used to specify the operation of control lines to
the external device and enable interrupt requests.

(b) PIA Register Format

Figure 12.11   Simplified diagram of the PIA.

TABLE 12.5 PIA1 REGISTERS AND ADDRESSES (DESIGN MODULE)

Register	Address	Purpose
Data direction		To program peripheral data
DDRA	$3FF41	lines for input or output
DDRB	$3FF43	({0} = input; {1} = output)
Data		
DRA	$3FF41	Data buffers—
DRB	$3FF43	read or write
Control		
CRA	$3FF45	1. Write to select data
CRB	$3FF47	direction register or data
		register (bit 2); program
		control lines; enable
		interrupts
		2. Read status

Notes:

1. Read of a data register clears the corresponding interrupt request from an external device.

2. Only bits [5:0] of a control register can be written. The entire register can be read.

programs the eight data lines associated with side A for output. Values could be output to the data lines by the instructions

```
MOVE.B   #$04,$3FF45   ;SELECT DRA
MOVE.B   D1,$3FF41     ;OUTPUT (D1) [B]
```

which transfer the low-order byte from D1 to DRA and thus to the output lines.

Example 12.2

The program segment of Figure 12.12 will initialize the PIA to accept an input value on Port A (DRA) and output the 8-bit value on Port B (DRB). The PIA address $3FF41 is first stored in A0. Then both control registers (CRA and CRB at locations $3FF45 and $3FF47) are cleared and the data direction registers are selected. The MOVEP instruction initializes both simultaneously.

After Port A is programmed for input and Port B for output, the data registers are selected by setting bit 2 = {1} in both control registers. If a nonzero value is detected in the loop labeled RTEST, the value is transmitted to DRB for output. The logical right shift by eight places in the loop is necessary to place the input value in the low-order byte of D3. In the example, the status register of the PIA was not read since interrupts were not used. Also, the initialization shown is used to disable interrupts and program the PIA. It is not equivalent to a hardware reset of the chip as would be caused by execution of the RESET instruction.

Motorola MC6840 PTM.   The Programmable Timer Module (PTM) on the Design Module is used to measure time intervals and perform other functions. In fact, the PTM can be employed as the basis of a variety of measurement circuits, in-

```
MC68000 ASM REV= 1.4 - COPYRIGHT BY MOTOROLA 1978              PAGE   1


  1                             LLEN     100
  2         00001000            ORG      $1000
  3                        *
  4                        *   PIA EXAMPLE
  5                        *
  6         0003FF41    PIAADR   EQU      $3FF41
  7         000200F6    MACSBUG  EQU      $200F6
  8                        *
  9                        * AFTER INITIALIZATION, PORTA(DRA) IS READ.
 10                        * WHEN A NONZERO CHARACTER IS DETECTED,
 11                        *  THE VALUE IS OUTPUT TO PORTB(DRB).
 12                        *
 13                        ***********************************
 14                        *
 15                        * INITIALIZE; CLEAR CRA AND CRB
 16                        *   SELECT DDRA AND DDRB.
 17                        *
 18 001000 207C0003FF41             MOVEA.L #PIAADR,A0
 19 001006 303C0000                 MOVE.W  #0000,D0
 20 00100A 01880004                 MOVEP.W D0,4(A0)
 21                        *
 22                        *
 23                        * PORTA INPUT; PORTB OUTPUT.
 24                        *   THEN SELECT DATA REGISTERS.
 25                        *
 26 00100E 323C00FF                 MOVE.W  #$00FF,D1       ;DDRA=00; DDRB=FF
 27 001012 343C0404                 MOVE.W  #$0404,D2
 28 001016 03880000                 MOVEP.W D1,0(A0)
 29 00101A 05880004                 MOVEP.W D2,4(A0)        ;CRA,CRB  BIT2=1
 30                        *
 31                        * TEST FOR NONZERO VALUE
 32                        *
 ₃3 00101E 07080000    RTEST    MOVEP.W 0(A0),D3           ; GET DRA VALUE
 34 001022 E04B                     LSR     #8,D3
 35 001024 0C430000                 CMP.W   #0,D3          ; DRA IN (D3)[7:0}
 36 001028 67F4                     BEQ     RTEST
 37                        *
 38                        * OUTPUT NONZERO VALUE
 39                        *
 40 00102A 07880000                 MOVEP.W D3,0(A0)
 41                        *
 42 00102E 4EF9000200F6             JMP     MACSBUG
 43                        *
 44                             END

****** TOTAL ERRORS    0--    0


SYMBOL TABLE - APPROX 1199 SYMBOL ENTRIES LEFT

MACSBUG    0200F6 PIAADR    03FF41 RTEST        00101E
$
```

Figure 12.12 PIA programming example.

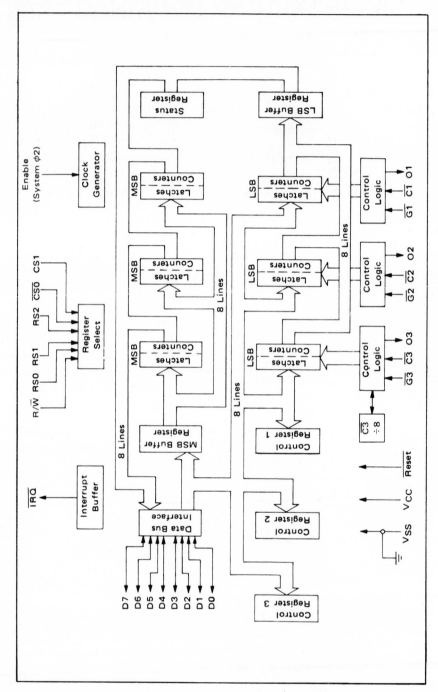

Figure 12.13 PTM block diagram. (Courtesy of Motorola, Inc.)

cluding an event counter, frequency counter, or a pulse generator. The chip contains three independent 16-bit counters that are referred to as *timers* and are illustrated in Figure 12.13.

A timer can be programmed for specific applications by writing the mode of operation into its control register. These control registers are designated CR1, CR2, and CR3 for the three timers. For example, to cause timer 1 to count down from a given initial value, CR1 must be initialized and the count loaded into the 16-bit counter. In hardware, this actually occurs with two 8-bit write cycles since only eight data lines from the system bus are connected to the chip. Loading the 16-bit value in two write cycles is accomplished with the MC68000 MOVEP instruction.

The time between intervals at which the counter value is decremented depends on the period of the clock signal to the chip. Using the Motorola Design Module, the period of the signal at the chip is ten times longer than the period of the system clock for the CPU. This is determined by the hardware design of the system. In the simplest operating mode, when the count has the initial decimal value N and T is the time in seconds between counts, the elapsed time until the count reaches zero is

$$Tc = N \times T \text{ seconds}$$

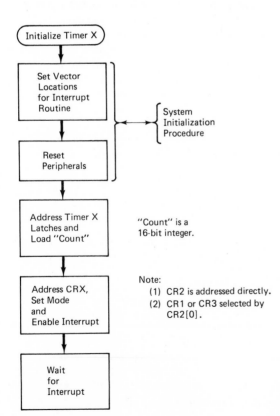

"Count" is a 16-bit integer.

Note:
(1) CR2 is addressed directly.
(2) CR1 or CR3 selected by CR2[0].

Figure 12.14 PTM initialization for interrupt-controlled timing.

Other modes of operation require different expressions to calculate the elapsed time.

When the count reaches zero, the timer will cause an interrupt request to the CPU if the control register for that timer had bit 6 set to {1} during initialization. An interrupt bit is also set to {1} in the status register, corresponding to the timer whose count reached zero.

The initialization sequence for interrupt-controlled timing is shown in Figure 12.14. CR2 is accessed by writing to its location directly. To access CR1 or CR3, bit 0 of CR2 must be set first. The setting of CR2[0] and the addresses associated with the PTM on the Design Module are shown in Table 12.6. The interrupt request from the timer is cleared by reading the status register of that timer followed by a CPU read of the timer value itself. Both reads are necessary in order to clear the interrupt request.

Example 12.3

The program of Figure 12.15 illustrates the initialization and interrupt handling for an interval timer using a Motorola MC6840 PTM. The interval timer handles multiple requests for scheduling delays by setting up and maintaining a stack of delay requests.

The PTM register addresses are equated to variable names for easier reference and the actual code for subroutines, which are not directly involved in the timer processing, is omitted. Level five is designated as the interrupt level for the timer and the corresponding vector location is set to the address of the timer interrupt handler TMXPT.

The timed schedule stack is a linked list of entries containing delay counts and is referenced through the dummy node at TSCHST. Entries available for use are maintained on a stack pointed to by AVTSCH. An example of these data structures is shown in Figure 12.16 in which there is one entry on the timer stack and two entries available.

The initialization segment of the program (INIT) sets the timed schedule stack to empty and links an area of memory to form the available entry area. Then the timer initialization is performed.

TABLE 12.6   PTM REGISTERS AND ADDRESSES (DESIGN MODULE)

Timer	Write control register CRX	Write (initialize) count MSB	LSB	Read timer MSB	LSB
Timer 1	$3FF61; CR2[0] = {1}	$3FF65	$3FF67	$3FF65	$3FF67
Timer 2	$3FF63	$3FF69	$3FF6B	$3FF69	$3FF6B
Timer 3	$3FF61; CR2[0] = {0}	$3FF6D	$3FF6F	$3FF6D	$3FF6F

Notes:

1. All addresses in hexadecimal.

2. Status register; read $3FF63.

3. CR2[0] controls access to CR1 or CR3.

4. MSB is the most significant byte. LSB is the least significant byte.

```
1                              LLEN    120
2                      *
3                      * PROGRAMABLE TIMER REGISTERS ADDRESSES
4                      *
5          0003FF61    TCTRL1  EQU     $3FF61              ; PTM CONTROL REGISTER 1 (OR 3)
6          0003FF63    TCTRL2  EQU     $3FF63              ; PTM CONTROL REGISTER 2
7          0003FF63    TSR     EQU     $3FF63              ; PTM STATUS REGISTER
8          0003FF65    TIMER1  EQU     $3FF65              ; PTM TIMER 1 COUNTER (ACCESS VIA MOVEP)
9          0003FF69    TIMER2  EQU     $3FF69              ; PTM TIMER 2 COUNTER (ACCESS VIA MOVEP)
10         0003FF6D    TIMER3  EQU     $3FF6D              ; PTM TIMER 3 COUNTER (ACCESS VIA MOVEP)
11                     *
12         00004000    DIALL   EQU     $4000               ; DUMMY ROUTINE TO DISABLE INTERRUPTS
13         00004100    TIMOUT  EQU     $4100               ; DUMMY ROUTINE TO PROCESS DELAY COMPLETION
14                     *
15                     * INTERRUPT VECTOR
16                     *
17         00000074            ORG     $074
18 000074 000010BA            DC.L    TMXPT               ; LEVEL 5 INTERRUPT
19                     *
20                     * TIMED SCHEDULE STACK POINTER
21                     *
22                     * THE POINTER TO THE TIMED SCHEDULE STACK POINTS TO THE TOP
23                     * OF A STACK OF ENTRIES EACH OF WHICH HAS THE FOLLOWING FORMAT:
24                     *    LINK        4 BYTES
25                     *    ADDRESS OF
26                     *      DELAY COUNT
27                     *    ENTRY       4 BYTES
28                     *                -------
29                     *    TOTAL/ENTRY 8 BYTES
30                     *
31         00001000            ORG     $1000
32 001000 00000004    TSCHST  DS.L    1
33                     *
34                     * TIMED SCHEDULE STACK AVAILABLE POOL
35                     *
36         0000000A    TSCHLN  EQU     10                  ; NUMBER OF TIMER STACK ENTRIES
37 001004 00000004    AVTSCH  DS.L    1
38 001008 00000050            DS.B    8*TSCHLN            ; 8 BYTES * NO. ENTRIES
39                     *
40                     * INIT
41                     *
42                     * INIT USES THE FOLLOWING DATA:
43                     *    AVTSCH - TIMED SCHEDULE STACK AVAILABLE POOL
44                     *    TCTRL1 - PTM CONTROL REGISTER 1 OR 3
45                     *    TCTRL2 - PTM CONTROL REGISTER 2
46                     *    TIMER1 - FIRST TIMER COUNTER
47                     *    TIMER2 - SECOND TIMER COUNTER
48                     *    TSCHLN - TIMED SCHEDULE STACK LENGTH
49                     *    TSCHST - TIMED SCHEDULE STACK
50                     *
51                     * TIMED SCHEDULE STACK INITIALIZATION
52                     *
53 001058 21FC00000000
          1000         INIT    MOVE.L  #0,TSCHST           ; SET POINTER TO EMPTY
54                     *
55                     * LINK AVAILABLE POOL FOR TIMED SCHEDULING
56                     *
57 001060 41F81004             LEA     AVTSCH,A0           ; LOAD POINTER ADDRESS
58 001064 7008                 MOVE.L  #8,D0               ; LOAD BYTES/ENTRY
59 001066 720A                 MOVE.L  #TSCHLN,D1          ; LOAD NUMBER OF ENTRIES
60 001068 61000034             BSR     LINK
61                     *
62                     * LOAD TIMER 1 AND 2 PTM COUNTERS
63                     *
64 00106C 207C0003FF69 INIT05  MOVE.L  #TIMER2,A0          ; GET ADDRESS OF TIMER 2
65 001072 203C000003E7         MOVE.L  #999,D0             ; GET LOAD COUNT (1000D-1)
66 001078 01880000             MOVEP.W D0,0(A0)            ; LOAD TIMER 2 COUNT
67 00107C 207C0003FF65         MOVE.L  #TIMER1,A0          ; GET ADDRESS OF TIMER 1
68 001082 303C0013             MOVE.W  #19,D0#             ; GET LOAD COUNT (5000/CYCTM)
69 001086 01880000             MOVEP.W D0,0(A0)            ; LOAD TIMER 1 COUNT
70                     *
71                     * LOAD CONTROL REGISTER 2 TO ENABLE TIMER 2 USING
72                     * AN INTERNAL CLOCK AND TO SWITCH TO CONTROL REGISTER 1
73                     *
74 00108A 13FC0083
          0003FF63             MOVE.B  #$83,TCTRL2
```

Figure 12.15   PTM programming example.

```
75                    *
76                    * LOAD CONTROL REGISTER 1 TO ENABLE IRQ AND BEGIN COUNTING
77                    *
78 001092 13FC0040
       0003FF61               MOVE.B    #$40,TCTRL1
79 00109A 4EF8109A    WAIT     JMP       WAIT                      ; LOOP TO WAIT FOR INTERRUPT
80                    *
81                    * LINK
82                    *
83                    * THIS ROUTINE LOOPS THROUGH A BUFFER WHOSE POINTER IS
84                    * PASSED IN A0, STORING LINKS IN THE FIRST 4 BYTES
85                    * OF EACH ENTRY (NO. OF ENTRIES SPECIFIED BY D1 AND
86                    * LENGTH SPECIFIED BY D0.)
87                    *
88 00109E 2248        LINK     MOVE.L    A0,A1
89 0010A0 5888                 ADD.L     #4,A0
90 0010A2 2288                 MOVE.L    A0,(A1)                   SET POINTER TO FIRST ENTRY
91 0010A4 2248        LIN010   MOVE.L    A0,A1                     COPY ADDRESS OF ENTRY
92 0010A6 D1C0                 ADD.L     D0,A0                     ADD LENGTH OF ENTRY (NEXT ENTRY ADDRESS)
93 0010A8 2288                 MOVE.L    A0,(A1)                   STORE LINK TO NEXT ENTRY
94 0010AA 048100000001         SUBI.L    #1,D1                     ALL ENTRIES DONE?
95 0010B0 66F2                 BNE       LIN010                    NO, DO NEXT
96 0010B2 22BC00000000         MOVE.L    #0,(A1)                   ELSE, EMPTY LAST LINK
97 0010B8 4E75                 RTS
98                    *
99                    * TMXPT
100                   *
101                   * THIS ROUTINE CHECKS WHETHER THE TIMER STACK
102                   * IS EMPTY AND EXITS IF IT IS.  IF NOT, THE CURRENT
103                   * TASK IS STACKED AND EACH ENTRY IN THE TIMER STACK
104                   * IS DECREMENTED BY ONE COUNT.  IF ANY OF THE DELAYS ARE
105                   * UP, THE ENTRY IS REMOVED FROM THE TIMER STACK AND LINKED
106                   * INTO THE SCHEDULE QUEUE.
107                   *
108                   * TMXPT EXECUTES AT THE SYSTEM LEVEL AND IS INVOKED
109                   * FROM AN INTERRUPT LEVEL 5.
110                   *
111                   * TMXPT INVOKES THE FOLLOWING ROUTINES:
112                   *     DIALL  - DISABLE INTERRUPTS
113                   *     DISP   - DISPATCHER INVOKED THROUGH TRAP #0
114                   *          INTSCH - INTERRUPTED TASK SCHEDULER
115                   *     TIMOUT - PROCESS EXPIRATION OF TIME DELAY
116                   *
117                   * TMXPT USES THE FOLLOWING DATA:
118                   *     AVTSCH - TIMED SCHEDULE STACK AVAILABLE POOL
119                   *     TIMER1 - FIRST TIMER COUNTER
120                   *     TSCHST - TIMED SCHEDULER STACK
121                   *     TSR    - TIMER STATUS REGISTER
122                   *
123 0010BA 2F08       TMXPT    MOVE.L    A0,-(A7)                  ; SAVE REGISTER OF STACK
124 0010BC 2F00                MOVE.L    D0,-(A7)
125 0010BE 207C0003FF63        MOVE.L    #TSR,A0                   ; GET ADDRESS OF PTM STATUS
126 0010C4 1010                MOVE.B    (A0),D0                   ; READ STATUS
127 0010C6 207C0003FF65        MOVE.L    #TIMER1,A0                ; GET ADDRESS OF TIMER 1 COUNTER
128 0010CC 01080000            MOVEP.W   0(A0),D0                  ; READ TIMER 1 BUFFER
129 0010D0 201F                MOVE.L    (A7)+,D0                  ; RESTORE REGISTER FROM STACK
130 0010D2 205F                MOVE.L    (A7)+,A0
131 0010D4 4AB81000            TST.L     TSCHST                    ; IS TIMER STACK EMPTY?
132 0010D8 6602                BNE.S     TM010                     ; NO, CHECK EACH ENTRY
133                   *
134                   * RETURN TO USER
135                   *
136 0010DA 4E73                RTE
137                   *
138                   * TIMED ENTRIES EXIST, SO PROCESS
139                   *
140 0010DC 61002F22   TM010    BSR       DIALL                     ; DISABLE INTERRUPTS
141 0010E0 4E40                TRAP      #0                        ; INVOKE INTSCH TO STACK CURRENT TASK
142 0010E2 0003                DC.W      #3
143 0010E4 41F81000            LEA       TSCHST,A0                 ; GET TOP OF STACK
144 0010E8 2850       TM015    MOVE.L    (A0),A4                   ; GET ADDRESS OF ENTRY
145 0010EA 2614                MOVE.L    (A4),D3                   ; SAVE LINK TO NEXT ENTRY
146 0010EC 246C0004            MOVE.L    4(A4),A2                  ; GET ADDRESS OF COUNT
147 0010F0 049200000001        SUBI.L    #1,(A2)                   ; DECREMENT COUNT BY ONE
148 0010F6 6614                BNE.S     TM020                     ; NON-ZERO, SO PROCESS NEXT ENTRY
149 0010F8 302A0004            MOVE.W    4(A2),D0                  ; ZERO, GET PRIORITY OF ENTRY
150 0010FC 61003002            BSR       TIMOUT                    ; PERFORM EXPIRATION PROCESSING
151 001100 2094                MOVE.L    (A4),(A0)                 ; TAKE ENTRY OUT OF TIMER STACK
152 001102 28B81004            MOVE.L    AVTSCH,(A4)               ; LINK ENTRY BACK WITH AVAIALBLE
153 001106 21CC1004            MOVE.L    A4,AVTSCH                 ; MAKE IT THE TOP OF AVAILABLE
154 00110A 2848                MOVE.L    A0,A4                     ; MAKE CURRENT NODE = PREVIOUS
```

Figure 12.15 continued

346

```
155                         *
156 00110C 4A83     TM020    TST.L   D3              ; END OF STACK?
157 00110E 6704              BEQ.S   TM030           ; YES, EXIT
158 001110 204C              MOVE.L  A4,A0           ; SET TO PROCESS NEXT ENTRY
159 001112 60D4              BRA     TM015           ; PROCESS NEXT
160                         *
161 001114 4E40     TM030    TRAP    #0              ; DISPATCH
162 001116 0000              DC.W    #0
163                         *
164                          END

****** TOTAL ERRORS    0--    0


SYMBOL TABLE - APPROX 1183 SYMBOL ENTRIES LEFT

AVTSCH    001004  DIALL     004000  INIT      001058  INIT05    00106C
LIN010    0010A4  LINK      00109E  TCTRL1    03FF61  TCTRL2    03FF63
TIMER1    03FF65  TIMER2    03FF69  TIMER3    03FF6D  TIMOUT    004100
TM010     0010DC  TM015     0010E8  TM020     00110C  TM030     001114
TMXPT     0010BA  TSCHLN    00000A  TSCHST    001000  TSR       03FF63
WAIT      00109A
```

Figure 12.15 continued

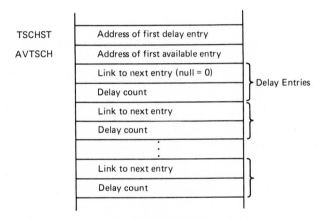

(a) Timed Scheduling Stack Formats

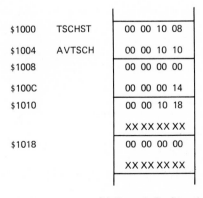

(b) Example Configuration

Figure 12.16 Data structure for PTM example.

347

The timer's delay equation can be expressed in terms of the counts and clock rates as

$$\text{Length of Delay} = 2 \times \text{TIMER2} \times \text{TIMER1} \times \text{Clock Rate}$$

but for a timer on the design module,

$$\text{Clock Rate} = 10 \times \text{Processor Cycle Time}$$

Therefore, if a 0.05 second delay is desired,

$$0.05 \text{ sec} = 2 \times \text{TIMER2} \times \text{TIMER1} \times 10 \times \text{Processor Cycle Time}$$

If the count TIMER2 is chosen to be fixed at 1000 and an 8-MHz processor is used, then

$$5.0 \times 10^7 \text{ ns} = 2 \times 10^3 \times \text{TIMER1} \times 10 \times 125$$

TIMER1 can then be calculated as

$$\text{TIMER1} = \frac{5.0 \times 10^7}{2 \times 10^3 \times 10 \times 125} = 20$$

During initialization, in the mode of operation being discussed here, timer 2 is loaded with 999 and timer 1 with 19 because the counters will decrement until they reach zero. Control register 2 is loaded with $83 to enable timer 2's output and to set up the chip to allow initialization of control register 1. Control register 1 is then loaded with $40 to enable interrupts and start the countdown. When an interrupt occurs, a new count-down is automatically begun and the interrupt processing is started.

The timing interrupt handler (TMXPT) first reads the status and timer count of the programmable timer chip in order to reset the timer interrupt. TMXPT then checks whether or not the timed schedule stack (TSCHST) is empty and returns to the user if it is.

If entries exist in the timed schedule stack, TMXPT invokes the interrupted task scheduler to stack the "currently executing" (the interrupted) task. TMXPT then search-es the timed schedule stack and decrements the delay counts of each entry. If any of the delay times expires, the entry is removed from the timed schedule stack and TIMOUT is called to process the time out. When all the entries have been processed by TMXPT, the dispatcher is invoked.

This example combines a number of techniques discussed in previous chapters. The program segment could be part of a real-time executive in which a number of different tasks require separate time delays. The stack structure is used to hold the data values. The PTM is programmed for interrupt controlled transfer. TRAP #0 is used within the interrupt routine to invoke other supervisor routines (not shown).

EXERCISES

12.2.1. Compare interrupt, DMA, and conditional transfer with respect to each of the follow-ing.

     (a) System speed of operation

(b) Programming complexity

(c) Interface complexity

12.2.2. Assume that CPU processing takes 10 microseconds per byte of data transferred. Which method of data transfer would be best for the following devices with the data transfer rates given in bytes per second?

(a) 1000 (communications link)

(b) 10,000 (tape unit)

(c) 1,000,000 (disk unit)

12.2.3. Draw the flowchart for a conditional I/O transfer routine when a string of characters is to be transferred. If a character is ready every 0.1 second, compute the time required to input 10 characters if the CPU processing time is 10^{-5} second per character. This timing is typical of a slow terminal.

12.2.4. Use the MC68000 MOVEP instruction to transfer a table of values from one area of memory to either another area of memory or to a peripheral device. The table of values has M bytes located in consecutive even addresses which are to be deposited at consecutive odd addresses. Move four bytes at a time and assume that M is divisible by 4.

12.2.5. Write routines to do the following.

(a) Output a string of characters using TRAP #5 to initialize the ACIA and transmit the characters using conditional I/O. The call is

```
TRAP  #5      ;OUTPUT STRING
DC.W  #2
```

Let (A5) indicate the starting address of the string and (A6) − 1 indicate the address of the last character. The routine should transmit a carriage return and line feed as the last two characters.

(b) Input a string using the ACIA with the call

```
TRAP  #5      ;INPUT string
DC.W  #1
```

where (A5) contains the starting address to store the input buffer. The string ends with a carriage return which should not be stored. The last character of the buffer should be pointed to by (A6) − 1 when the routine is complete.

12.2.6. Modify the program in Exercise 5 to use interrupt processing for input and output.

12.2.7. Design and test a timing feature for programs using the PTM. The routine should compute the time required for the program to execute (optional program if your system has a PTM or a real-time clock).

12.3 INSTRUCTION EXECUTION TIMES

The MC68000 CPU timing is controlled by a master clock. This clock is a circuit that generates a periodic sequence of pulses which synchronize all changes in the input and output signal lines. The timing of all the operations of the MC68000 are determined by the number of clock pulses required for the operation. If the number of pulses per second or pulse rate is increased (decreased), the speed of operation of the processor is increased (decreased).

Figure 12.17 shows the clock signal for MC68000 systems. The table lists the cycle time for several versions of the processor. All the processors will operate at a minimum pulse rate of 2×10^6 pulses per second except the 12.5-MHz version, which has a minimum of 4×10^6 pulses per second. The maximum pulse rate for any version is the reciprocal of the cycle time.[2] The MC68000L8 (8 MHz) version, for example, operates with a frequency between 2 and 8 MHz. The cycle time corresponding to this range has a maximum of 500 nanoseconds and a minimum of 125 nanoseconds.

The cycle time, designated t_c in the text, is used to calculate the execution time of MC68000 instructions and other operations, such as interrupt response time. The calculation is based on the time to fetch an instruction, compute the effective addresses, and fetch or store the operand. The times for the MC68000 instruction set are listed in Appendix IV. A short summary is given in Table 12.7.

From Table 12.7, the time to read or write a word from memory requires $4t_c$ since a minimum of four clock pulses are necessary to complete the operation. In practice, the time could be longer if the memory cannot respond in the minimum time. The source effective address can be calculated with no delay for register operations or up to $16t_c$ for a long operand being addressed by an absolute long address. This long word operation takes two reads ($8t_c$) to fetch the address and two more reads to fetch the operand ($8t_c$), for a total of 16 cycles.

[2]The frequency of operation in hertz is considered the reciprocal of the cycle time. More precisely, it refers to the frequency of the fundamental sinusoidal wave in a Fourier series analysis of the clock pulse train.

Characteristic	Symbol	4 MHz		6 MHz		8 MHz		10 MHz		12.5 MHz		Unit
		Min	Max	Min	Max	Min	Max	Min	Max	Min	Max	
Frequency of Operation	F	2.0	4.0	2.0	6.0	2.0	8.0	2.0	10.0	4.0	12.5	MHz
Cycle Time	t_{cyc}	250	500	167	500	125	500	100	500	80	250	ns
Clock Pulse Width	t_{CL}	115	250	75	250	55	250	45	250	35	125	ns
	t_{CH}	115	250	75	250	55	250	45	250	35	125	
Rise and Fall Times	t_{Cr}	—	10	—	10	—	10	—	10	—	5	ns
	t_{Cf}	—	10	—	10	—	10	—	10	—	5	

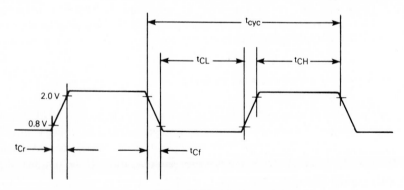

Figure 12.17   Clock waveform.

TABLE 12.7 INSTRUCTION EXECUTION TIME
(MC68000)

Operation	Time
Write to memory	$4t_c$ word
	$8t_c$ longword
Read from memory	$4t_c$ word
	$8t_c$ longword
Calculate effective address	0 to $12t_c$ byte, word
of source and fetch operand	0 to $16t_c$ longword
Instruction execution	$4t_c$ to $158t_c$
(including instruction fetch)	
Interrupt response	$44t_c$
TRAP instruction	$38t_c$

Instruction execution, including the fetch of the op code, requires at least four cycles. The DIVS instruction is one of the longest executing instructions. It requires a maximum of 158 cycles to execute. Interrupt processing requires 44 cycles before the interrupt routine begins executing. This does not include any time required for the present instruction to complete. The TRAP instruction takes 38 cycles to push (PC) and (SR) onto the system stack and replace the contents of the PC with the TRAP vector contents.

Although the general principles presented in this section apply also to the MC68010, the exact timing of MC68010 instructions are available in the MC68010 manual from Motorola. A number of the MC68010 instructions have improved execution time as compared to those of the MC68000. The MC68010 also has a "loop mode" feature using the DBcc instruction. Under certain conditions, the mode allows a one-word length instruction to be executed in a loop without fetching the instruction repeatedly from memory.

Example 12.4

The instruction to transfer a 32-bit immediate value

> MOVE.L $\# <d_{32}>,(An)$

requires 20 cycles according to the information in the MC68000 *User's Manual* (see Appendix IV). This is calculated as follows:

Instruction fetch	$4t_c$
Fetch of immediate value	$8t_c$
Store operand	$8t_c$
	$\overline{20t_c}$

For the 10-MHz version of the MC68000, the time required is

$$t = 20 \times 10^{-7} \text{ seconds}$$

or 2 microseconds.

EXERCISES

12.3.1. Compute the minimum response time in microseconds for an interrupt with the following processors.
  (a) MC68000L6
  (b) MC68000L8
  (c) MC68000L12

12.3.2. **(a)** What is the worst-case timing for interrupt response if an instruction is just beginning to be fetched as the interrupt occurs?
  (b) What is this time for the 8-MHz version of the MC68000?

12.3.3. Use the No Operation (NOP) instruction of the MC68000 to create a delay loop with variable delays from 100 microseconds to 1 second. The NOP requires four cycles, including fetching and execution.

12.4 HARDWARE CONSIDERATIONS

The electrical connection between elements in a MC68000 system is via the system bus. The bus contains address signal lines, data signal lines, and control signal lines. A few miscellaneous signal lines, such as a clock signal, power (+5 volts), and a ground reference, are also included. All of the peripheral devices and the processor are connected in parallel to the bus signals. In most applications, the MC68000 processor acts as the system controller and determines the use of the bus for transfer of data and control signals. The MC68000 signal lines and the dual-in-line pin (DIP) configuration is shown in Figure 12.18. The signal lines are defined by function, mnemonic, and characteristics in Figure 12.19. The signal lines that are described as "three-state" in the table are put in a high-impedance or hi-Z state when the processor relinquishes the use of the bus to other devices. These signal lines are, effectively, disconnected electrically from the bus when in this state.

An understanding of the use of the MC68000 signal lines for fundamental operations is necessary in order to design interfaces. Data transfer operations and the use the function code lines during processor accesses to memory are described in this section. This information is particularly important to the system designer when a memory management scheme is used to protect and segment various areas of memory. The interrupt hardware sequence, the control of the bus by other devices, and interfacing to the 8-bit M6800 family devices are also discussed.

It should be emphasized that the information in this section describes the functional operation of the MC68000 signal lines. The precise timing diagrams needed by an interface designer are not presented. The source of these diagrams is Motorola's data sheets for the MC68000, containing the electrical specifications for the device. The minimum and maximum times for signal changes and those times between changes on different signal lines (to determine allowable timing margins) are given in the data sheets.

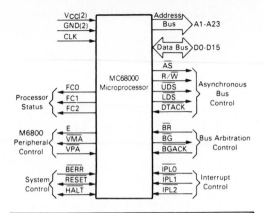

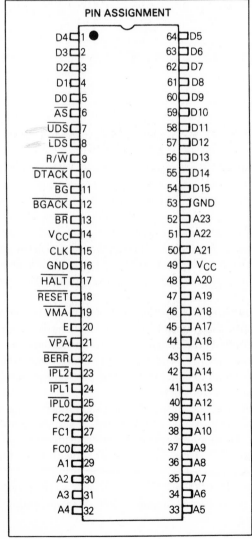

Figure 12.18 Input and output signals of the MC68000. (Courtesy of Motorola, Inc.)

Signal Name	Mnemonic	Input/Output	Active State	Three State
Address Bus	A1-A23	Output	High	Yes
Data Bus	D0-D15	Input/Output	High	Yes
Address Strobe	$\overline{AS}$	Output	Low	Yes
Read/Write	R/$\overline{W}$	Output	Read-High Write-Low	Yes
Upper and Lower Data Strobes	$\overline{UDS}$, $\overline{LDS}$	Output	Low	Yes
Data Transfer Acknowledge	$\overline{DTACK}$	Input	Low	No
Bus Request	$\overline{BR}$	Input	Low	No
Bus Grant	$\overline{BG}$	Output	Low	No
Bus Grant Acknowledge	$\overline{BGACK}$	Input	Low	No
Interrupt Priority Level	$\overline{IPL0}$, $\overline{IPL1}$, $\overline{IPL2}$	Input	Low	No
Bus Error	$\overline{BERR}$	Input	Low	No
Reset	$\overline{RESET}$	Input/Output	Low	No*
Halt	$\overline{HALT}$	Input/Output	Low	No*
Enable	E	Output	High	No
Valid Memory Address	$\overline{VMA}$	Output	Low	Yes
Valid Peripheral Address	$\overline{VPA}$	Input	Low	No
Function Code Output	FC0, FC1, FC2	Output	High	Yes
Clock	CLK	Input	High	No
Power Input	V_{CC}	Input	–	–
Ground	GND	Input	–	–

*Open Drain

Figure 12.19 Signal lines of the MC68000. (Courtesy of Motorola, Inc.)

The signal lines of the MC68010 are identical to those of the MC68000. However, the use and timing of the MC68010 signal lines are not always the same as for the MC68000. In particular, the function code signal lines of the MC68010 have a more general use.

Before discussing various hardware operations, the conventions used to specify the signal lines must be presented. Further detail of hardware design are presented in several references in the Further Reading section at the end of the chapter. The electrical characteristics of the MC68000 are summarized in Appendix II of this text.

Designation of signal lines. The electrical signals generated or received by the MC68000 may be specified in terms of their electrical characteristics and also by their functional or logical use. These electrical characteristics include the voltage level, current requirements, and speed of switching. Other characteristics of the signal generated by the processor or by an external device and propagated along the signal lines of the system bus must also be considered.

The processor and external devices respond to the signals according to the state of the signal. A signal line with two states is designated as active/inactive, HIGH/LOW, true/false, or {1}/{0}. These four designations are considered equivalent when the electrical characteristics are TTL (transistor-transistor logic) compatible and the positive-true logic definition is employed.

All the signal lines of the MC68000 are TTL compatible, so the processor can be electrically connected to any TTL chip as long as certain loading conditions are recognized. Since the TTL family is the most popular logic type employed today for interfacing circuitry, the MC68000 processor is easily connected to a large number of TTL circuits which are available to implement various logical functions. The TTL signal line is considered to be in the LOW state when its steady-state voltage is 0 volts with respect to the ground reference. The TTL HIGH state is indicated by a voltage level with respect to a ground of 5 volts. The power-supply voltage for a TTL system, designated V_{CC}, is typically 5.0 volts. Any TTL line designated by its functional name (usually a mnemonic) is considered to be active or true or indicate a logical $\{1\}$ when the voltage level is HIGH. Similarly, the line is inactive or false or indicates a $\{0\}$ when the voltage level is LOW. Any signal, designated as the logical NOT of its function, represents the opposite conditions. In this case, a LOW voltage represents an active or true or $\{1\}$ state and these signals will be designated with a bar (logical NOT symbol) above them.

Thus the data lines of the MC68000 are designated D0, D1, . . . , D7 with a TTL HIGH on any line representing an $\{1\}$ and a TTL LOW representing a $\{0\}$. On the other hand, the signal line $\overline{\text{AS}}$ (Address Strobe) in a TTL HIGH state indicates that the address strobe is not asserted (not active or not true). When the voltage is LOW on the $\overline{\text{AS}}$ line, the address strobe line is asserted (active or true). This use of an active-LOW signal is quite common with TTL logic and provides better immunity to electrical noise under certain conditions. Such a line is often referred to as an "active-low" signal line and is spoken of as "Address Strobe NOT." In print, such a distinction is not necessary since the form $\overline{\text{AS}}$ indicates the logical operation of the signal line.

12.4.1 Data Transfer Operations

The read and write operations of the MC68000 processor are presented here. A read operation requires that data from an external device or memory be placed on the bus in response to signal lines controlled by the MC68000. During a write operation the processor presents data on the bus to be stored in memory or output to an external device. The processor controls the bus to initiate data transfer operations in either direction, but waits for the selected device to acknowledge the transfer request. Such data transfer operations are termed *asynchronous* because the timing of the memory or peripheral device determines the timing of the transfer rather than the CPU timing. These devices are typically slower to transfer data than the processor.

The MC68000 operation, as bus master, for a read cycle of a byte or a word is illustrated in Figure 12.20. The read lines (R/$\overline{\text{W}}$), the address lines, and the function code lines are asserted (set to their true values) before the transfer request. Then address strobe signal line ($\overline{\text{AS}}$) is asserted (held LOW), followed by the proper data strobe signal line ($\overline{\text{UDS}}$ or $\overline{\text{LDS}}$ or both) to select the upper 8 bits, the lower 8 bits, or all 16 bits of the data signal lines. The device presents data on the data signal lines and asserts the data transfer acknowledge signal ($\overline{\text{DTACK}}$) when it is ready. The processor then reads the data value, negates its strobe signals, and waits for the $\overline{\text{DTACK}}$

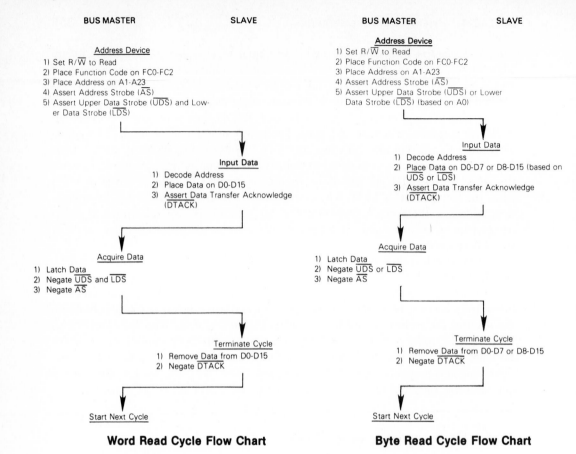

BUS MASTER   SLAVE   BUS MASTER   SLAVE

Address Device

1) Set R/$\overline{W}$ to Read
2) Place Function Code on FC0-FC2
3) Place Address on A1-A23
4) Assert Address Strobe ($\overline{AS}$)
5) Assert Upper Data Strobe ($\overline{UDS}$) and Lower Data Strobe ($\overline{LDS}$)

Input Data

1) Decode Address
2) Place Data on D0-D15
3) Assert Data Transfer Acknowledge ($\overline{DTACK}$)

Acquire Data

1) Latch Data
2) Negate $\overline{UDS}$ and $\overline{LDS}$
3) Negate $\overline{AS}$

Terminate Cycle

1) Remove Data from D0-D15
2) Negate $\overline{DTACK}$

Start Next Cycle

Word Read Cycle Flow Chart

Address Device

1) Set R/$\overline{W}$ to Read
2) Place Function Code on FC0-FC2
3) Place Address on A1-A23
4) Assert Address Strobe ($\overline{AS}$)
5) Assert Upper Data Strobe ($\overline{UDS}$) or Lower Data Strobe ($\overline{LDS}$) (based on A0)

Input Data

1) Decode Address
2) Place Data on D0-D7 or D8-D15 (based on $\overline{UDS}$ or $\overline{LDS}$)
3) Assert Data Transfer Acknowledge ($\overline{DTACK}$)

Acquire Data

1) Latch Data
2) Negate $\overline{UDS}$ or $\overline{LDS}$
3) Negate $\overline{AS}$

Terminate Cycle

1) Remove Data from D0-D7 or D8-D15
2) Negate $\overline{DTACK}$

Start Next Cycle

Byte Read Cycle Flow Chart

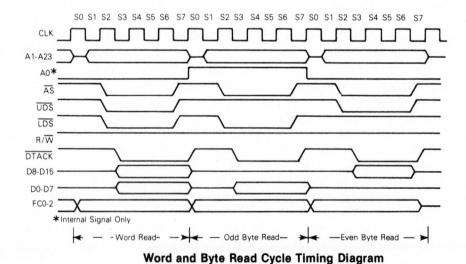

Word and Byte Read Cycle Timing Diagram

Figure 12.20 Read operations. (Courtesy of Motorola, Inc.)

356

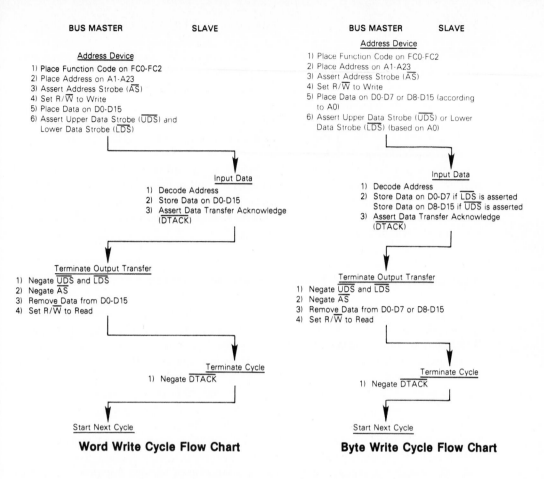

BUS MASTER   **SLAVE**

<u>Address Device</u>

1) Place Function Code on FC0-FC2
2) Place Address on A1-A23
3) Assert Address Strobe ($\overline{AS}$)
4) Set R/$\overline{W}$ to Write
5) Place Data on D0-D15
6) Assert Upper Data Strobe ($\overline{UDS}$) and
Lower Data Strobe ($\overline{LDS}$)

                      <u>Input Data</u>

         1) Decode Address
         2) Store Data on D0-D15
         3) Assert Data Transfer Acknowledge
            ($\overline{DTACK}$)

<u>Terminate Output Transfer</u>

1) Negate $\overline{UDS}$ and $\overline{LDS}$
2) Negate $\overline{AS}$
3) Remove Data from D0-D15
4) Set R/$\overline{W}$ to Read

                    <u>Terminate Cycle</u>

        1) Negate $\overline{DTACK}$

<u>Start Next Cycle</u>

Word Write Cycle Flow Chart

BUS MASTER   **SLAVE**

<u>Address Device</u>

1) Place Function Code on FC0-FC2
2) Place Address on A1-A23
3) Assert Address Strobe ($\overline{AS}$)
4) Set R/$\overline{W}$ to Write
5) Place Data on D0-D7 or D8-D15 (according
to A0)
6) Assert Upper Data Strobe ($\overline{UDS}$) or Lower
Data Strobe ($\overline{LDS}$) (based on A0)

                      <u>Input Data</u>

         1) Decode Address
         2) Store Data on D0-D7 if $\overline{LDS}$ is asserted
            Store Data on D8-D15 if $\overline{UDS}$ is asserted
         3) Assert Data Transfer Acknowledge
            ($\overline{DTACK}$)

        <u>Terminate Output Transfer</u>

    1) Negate $\overline{UDS}$ and $\overline{LDS}$
    2) Negate $\overline{AS}$
    3) Remove Data from D0-D7 or D8-D15
    4) Set R/$\overline{W}$ to Read

                    <u>Terminate Cycle</u>

        1) Negate $\overline{DTACK}$

<u>Start Next Cycle</u>

Byte Write Cycle Flow Chart

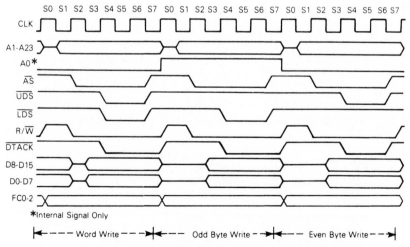

*Internal Signal Only

Word Write — Odd Byte Write — Even Byte Write

Word and Byte Write Cycle Timing Diagram

Figure 12.21   Write operations. (Courtesy of Motorola, Inc.)

signal line to be negated. The processor then initiates the next cycle. The functional timing diagram for the read operations is also shown in Figure 12.20. The read cycle is four clock cycles long if the device responding negates $\overline{\text{DTACK}}$ in the fourth clock cycle. Otherwise, wait states one clock cycle in length are generated until the device responds. The CPU will wait even if the device never responds unless external circuitry indicates that the device did not respond in the allotted time. This type of circuitry is sometimes called a "watchdog" timer.

The write operation is defined in Figure 12.21 and is similar to the read cycle just described. The read/write signal line being LOW indicates a write request for the CPU. The processor does not remove valid data from the data signal lines until the device acknowledges the transfer with $\overline{\text{DTACK}}$ negated. The write operation requires a minimum of four clock cycles to complete.

12.4.2 Function Code Lines and Memory Usage

The signal lines FC0 FC1, and FC2 present a function code to external devices or memory indicating the type of activity occurring on the address or data signal lines. The function code indicates the processor mode (supervisor or user) and the type of access (data or program) each time the processor initiates a read or write operation. The code also indicates if an interrupt is being acknowledged.

Figure 12.22 lists the electrical state of the function code signal lines of the MC68000 for each type of reference. The states not specified are not defined. The processor mode is always determined by the setting of the supervisor status bit in the status register, (SR)[13]. The distinction between data and program references is determined by the addressing mode and the instruction being executed. Table 12.8 defines the addressing modes which cause the selection of various function code states during normal execution.

Using the function code lines to select memory areas, the system memory can be segmented into supervisor and user space. These spaces, in turn, can be segmented into program and data areas. A simplified scheme to accomplish this is shown in Figure 12.23. Each distinct function code allows a selected memory block, or group of blocks, to be accessed using a decoder and selection circuitry. More sophisticated memory protection, including write protection of certain memory areas, can be designed using the MC68451 Memory Management Chip from Motorola. This chip sep-

FC2	FC1	FC0	Cycle Type
Low	Low	Low	(Undefined, Reserved)
Low	Low	High	User Data
Low	High	Low	User Program
Low	High	High	(Undefined, Reserved)
High	Low	Low	(Undefined, Reserved)
High	Low	High	Supervisor Data
High	High	Low	Supervisor Program
High	High	High	Interrupt Acknowledge

Figure 12.22 Function code references. (Courtesy of Motorola, Inc.)

TABLE 12.8 ADDRESSING MODES AND FUNCTION CODES

Function code reference	Addressing modes
Data	All indirect modes, unless used with JMP or JSR instructions
	Absolute modes, unless used with JMP or JSR instructions
Program	Relative modes
	Indirect and absolute modes with JMP or JSR instructions

arates supervisor and user space and also protects memory based on the address signal lines.

The function code signal lines of the MC68000 respond to internally generated conditions within the CPU and the use of these signals is not alterable. Therefore, if memory is protected as shown in Figure 12.23, the supervisor program could not access the user's data or program space unless special logic circuits were included to rec-

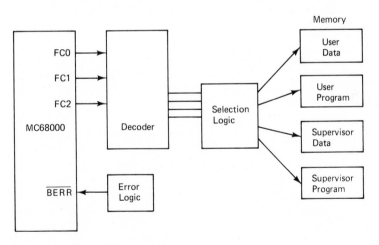

Notes:
(1) The decoder asserts a single line corresponding to the binary value of the Function Code bits.
(2) The selection logic enables selected memory blocks. It could be used to allow a Supervisor Program to access all of memory, for example, but still restrict user's access to the proper block.
(3) The error logic is necessary to indicate an error if the wrong block is accessed.
(4) Address, data, and control signal lines to memory are not shown.

Figure 12.23 Memory protection.

ognize the supervisor mode access. By way of contrast, the MC68010 allows a supervisor program to define the memory space being accessed by specifying the function code.

12.4.3 Interrupt Processing

The MC68000 interrupt circuitry allows seven levels of interrupt priorities, numbered from 1 to 7, with level 7 being the highest priority. By adding external circuitry, an essentially unlimited number of devices may be connected at the same interrupt level. The subpriorities within any CPU interrupt level must be determined by special circuitry. As described in Chapter 11, the MC68000 interrupt circuitry accommodates both user vectored interrupts and autovectored interrupts.

In the user interrupt vectored mode, Motorola allows 192 vectors to be distribut-

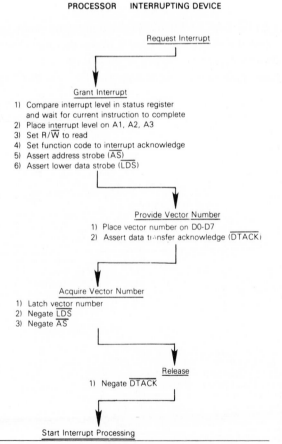

PROCESSOR   INTERRUPTING DEVICE

Request Interrupt

Grant Interrupt
1) Compare interrupt level in status register and wait for current instruction to complete
2) Place interrupt level on A1, A2, A3
3) Set R/$\overline{W}$ to read
4) Set function code to interrupt acknowledge
5) Assert address strobe ($\overline{AS}$)
6) Assert lower data strobe ($\overline{LDS}$)

Provide Vector Number
1) Place vector number on D0-D7
2) Assert data transfer acknowledge ($\overline{DTACK}$)

Acquire Vector Number
1) Latch vector number
2) Negate $\overline{LDS}$
3) Negate $\overline{AS}$

Release
1) Negate $\overline{DTACK}$

Start Interrupt Processing

Figure 12.24 Interrupt sequence in vectored mode. (Courtesy of Motorola, Inc.)

ed among the seven priority levels as determined by the system designer. The seven autovector interrupts have vectors at fixed locations in the exception vector table (locations $064 through $07C). The CPU selects the proper autovector location based on the priority level requested by the external device.

An interrupt request is made to the CPU by encoding the interrupt request level, as a binary number, on the three interrupt request signal lines ($\overline{\text{IPL0}}$, $\overline{\text{IPL1}}$, $\overline{\text{IPL2}}$). An autovector interrupt is requested when the interface asserts the Valid Peripheral Address ($\overline{\text{VPA}}$) signal line in addition to the requested level. If $\overline{\text{VPA}}$ is not asserted, the number used to calculate the location of the vector in the exception vector table must be supplied by the peripheral device. If the interface does not respond to the interrupt acknowledge sequence from the CPU, a "spurious interrupt" processing routine is executed (vector location $60).

The interrupt system of the MC68000 responds to the three signal lines, $\overline{\text{IPL0}}$ to $\overline{\text{IPL2}}$, to service an interrupt request. The external device encodes the priority level on the signal lines as

$$\text{level} = \overline{\text{IPL2}} \times 2^2 + \overline{\text{IPL1}} \times 2^1 + \overline{\text{IPL0}}$$

where a LOW signal is considered a {1} and a HIGH signal a {0} in the equation. A level of zero indicates there is currently no interrupt request.

The sequence of processor and external device operations for *vectored* interrupts is shown in Figure 12.24. In the sequence, the processor places the interrupt level acknowledged on the three address signal lines (A1–A3) and indicates an interrupt acknowledge by outputting the function code {111}. For the vectored case shown, the external device should respond to the read request of the processor with the *vector number* on the lower data signal lines (D0–D7). The vector number is converted to an address in the interrupt vector table. After the transfer is complete, the processor begins interrupt processing. Figure 12.25(a) shows the timing for the interrupt request and acknowledge sequence.

An alternative mode of operation is for the processor to provide the vector address in the *autovector* mode, which requires less complicated circuitry in the interface. The timing of that operation is shown in Figure 12.25(b). The external device requests autovectoring by asserting $\overline{\text{VPA}}$ (LOW). The priority of interrupts and the use of interrupt lines $\overline{\text{IPL0}}$ to $\overline{\text{IPL2}}$ is identical to that for vectored interrupts as just described.

12.4.4 Bus Control and Bus Error

Control of the MC68000 system bus can be taken over by an external device in several ways. One method is for the external device to assert the $\overline{\text{HALT}}$ signal line. As long as it is held LOW, the processor keeps its address, data, and function code signal lines in the high-impedance state, which allows other bus activity independent of the processor. When the $\overline{\text{HALT}}$ signal is again negated, the processor resumes execution. An

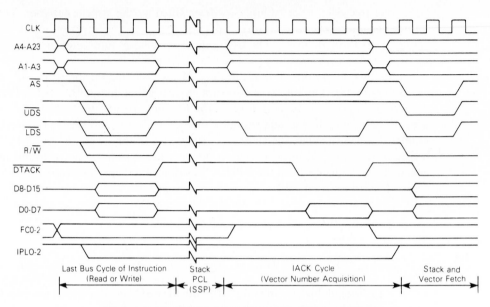

(a) Interrupt Acknowledge Sequence Timing Diagram

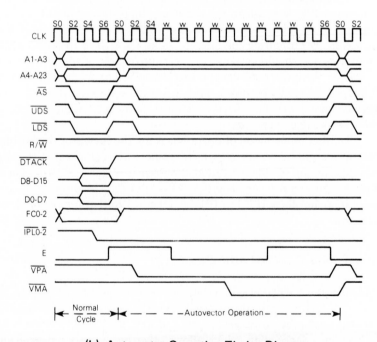

(b) Autovector Operation Timing Diagram

Figure 12.25   Interrupt timing. (Courtesy of Motorola, Inc.)

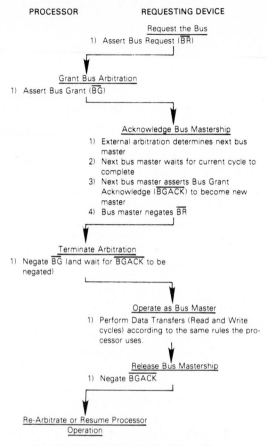

PROCESSOR   REQUESTING DEVICE

Request the Bus
1) Assert Bus Request ($\overline{BR}$)

Grant Bus Arbitration
1) Assert Bus Grant ($\overline{BG}$)

Acknowledge Bus Mastership
1) External arbitration determines next bus master
2) Next bus master waits for current cycle to complete
3) Next bus master asserts Bus Grant Acknowledge ($\overline{BGACK}$) to become new master
4) Bus master negates $\overline{BR}$

Terminate Arbitration
1) Negate $\overline{BG}$ (and wait for $\overline{BGACK}$ to be negated)

Operate as Bus Master
1) Perform Data Transfers (Read and Write cycles) according to the same rules the processor uses.

Release Bus Mastership
1) Negate $\overline{BGACK}$

Re-Arbitrate or Resume Processor Operation

(a) Bus Arbitration Cycle Flow-Chart

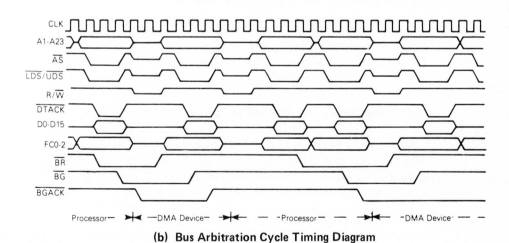

(b) Bus Arbitration Cycle Timing Diagram

Figure 12.26 Bus arbitration. (Courtesy of Motorola, Inc.)

alternative method is for an external device to control the bus through the use of the MC68000's bus arbitration logic. In most cases, this is the better approach.[3]

The bus arbitration feature of the MC68000 allows another device to request use of the bus, as shown in Figure 12.26(a). Asserting the Bus Request signal ($\overline{\text{BR}}$) will force the processor to assert the Bus Grant signal ($\overline{\text{BG}}$) after it completes its current bus cycle. If a number of external devices can request control of the bus and each acts as master, external circuitry must be provided to determine their priority. Once the requesting device is in control, the Bus Grant Acknowledge signal ($\overline{\text{BGACK}}$) is held LOW and the bus is used by the device as necessary. When the operations are complete, the device negates the $\overline{\text{BGACK}}$ signal and the MC68000 then resumes control of the bus. Figure 12.26(b) shows the timing sequence for a device requesting DMA access by cycle stealing from the processor. This represents a typical application for the bus arbitration capability of the MC68000.

Bus error and halt. If an external device detects an error, the device can assert the Bus Error signal line ($\overline{\text{BERR}}$). This signal line held LOW causes the bus error exception to be processed. This exception causes exception processing in the manner described in Chapter 11. In general, no recovery by the exception routine is possible from a bus error in MC68000 systems. However, diagnostic information is saved on the supervisor stack. In addition to the values (PC) and (SR), the contents of the instruction register, the address that was being accessed, and the function codes are saved. This information is useful to diagnose the error. The use of the bus error signal of the MC68010 was discussed previously in connection with virtual memory.

Except for an occasional error caused by excessive noise on the signal lines for a brief period during an operation, a bus error generally indicates a serious failure in the system. In fact, if a bus error is signaled without the $\overline{\text{HALT}}$ while the MC68000 is processing an address error, another bus error, or a $\overline{\text{RESET}}$ exception, the processor will halt.

If an external device asserts both $\overline{\text{BERR}}$ and $\overline{\text{HALT}}$ simultaneously, the MC68000 will try to rerun the previous bus cycle unless the cycle is caused by the TAS instruction. By design, the TAS instruction has an indivisible read–modify–write cycle. The processor will rerun the cycle as many times as requested.

12.4.5 Interfacing to MC6800 Family Chips

The signal activity previously described between the CPU and a device for data transfer is commonly termed *handshaking*. Using this method, every CPU activity is acknowledged (via the signal line $\overline{\text{DTACK}}$), by the device and vice versa. The transfer is asynchronous because the speed of operation is determined by the response of the de-

---

[3]The MC68000 can be operated in a single-cycle mode, which is the hardware equivalent of the trace mode for single-instruction execution. The circuitry to accomplish this using the $\overline{\text{HALT}}$ signal line is discussed in the MC68000 *User's Manual.*

vice and is not based on a fixed number of cycles of the system clock. In contrast, the 8-bit M6800 peripheral chips are designed to transfer data synchronously based on cycles of an enabling signal (E), which acts as a clock for these chips. The MC68000 provides this signal as a constant-frequency clock that has one-tenth the frequency of the system clock. For example, the 10-MHz version of the MC68000 provides a 1-MHz clock on its enable signal line when the CPU is running at its maximum speed.

As shown in Figure 12.27, the 8-bit chip requests synchronous transfer by asserting Valid Peripheral Address ($\overline{\text{VPA}}$). The CPU then asserts Valid Memory Address ($\overline{\text{VMA}}$) after setting up the other signal lines for ordinary transfer. The CPU

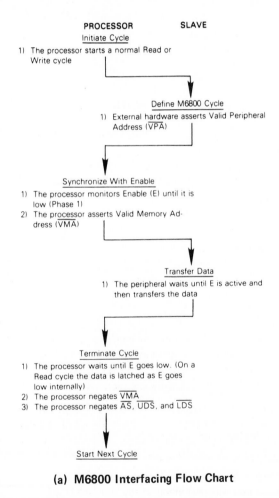

(a) **M6800 Interfacing Flow Chart**

Figure 12.27   MC68000 operation with M6800 peripheral chips. (Courtesy of Motorola, Inc.)

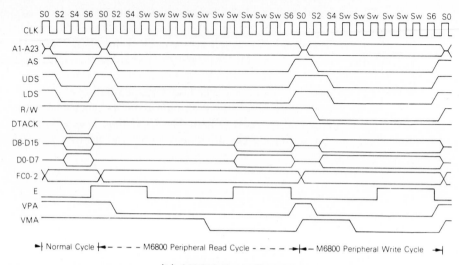

(b) M6800 Cycle Operation

Figure 12.27 continued

uses a number of wait states to synchronize with the enable signal, which has a period of 10 CPU cycles.

EXERCISES

12.4.1 The instruction

> MOVE.B   D1,$2001

is executed. Define the value or condition for the address lines, data strobe lines, and other signal lines as the operand is transferred to memory.

12.4.2. Determine the type of memory reference that occurs and the values of the function code lines for each of the following instructions.

(a) MOVE.W	D1,(A1)	;IN USER MODE
(b) JSR	(A1)	;IN USER MODE
(c) MOVE.W	D1,DISP (PC)	;IN SUPERVISOR MODE
(d) CLR.L	$2000	;IN SUPERVISOR MODE

12.4.3. In Chapter 9 it was shown that the use of PC relative addresses for an alterable destination location was prohibited. If the memory is segmented into program space and data space, could such destination addressing be used even if the PC addressing modes were allowed to specify memory locations as destinations? How is position-independent code achieved in a system with protected memory?

12.4.4. What vector address in the exception vector table is being requested by a device that supplied vector number 64 in response to an interrupt? Could an interface supply vector numbers between 2 and 47, and if so, what problems might arise in the system?

12.4.5. Define the operation of the system if the interrupt request lines receive the following levels:

$\overline{IPL2}$ is LOW
$\overline{IPL1}$ is HIGH
$\overline{IPL0}$ is HIGH

Define the sequence of operation and the values on the address lines and the function code lines.

FURTHER READING

The textbook by Gibson and Liu and that by Newell provide an introduction to many of the topics covered in this chapter. Both texts discuss the M6800 peripheral chips and programming considerations. Stockton's article discusses interfacing to peripheral chips with the MC68000. The article by Von Glahn gives a design example using the MC68000 with RAM. The reader is also referred to *Application Notes* and *Engineering Bulletins* from Motorola. These publications treat various aspects of system and hardware design with the MC68000.

GIBSON, GLENN A., and YU-CHENG LIU, *Microcomputers for Engineers and Scientists.* Englewood Cliffs, N.J.: Prentice-Hall, 1980.

NEWELL, SYDNEY B., *Introduction to Microcomputers.* New York: Harper & Row, 1982.

STOCKTON, JOHN, "Learn the Timing and Interfacing of MC68000 Peripheral Circuits," *Electronic Design,* **20,** No. 23 (November 8, 1979), 58–64.

VON GLAHN, PETER, "Capable Support IC's Ease Dynamic RAM Interfacing," *EDN,* **27,** No. 15 (August 4, 1982), 145–154.

Appendix I

ASCII Character Set and Powers of Two and Sixteen

TABLE I.1 ASCII CHARACTER SET

Character	Comments	Hex value
NUL	Null or tape feed	00
SOH	Start of heading	01
STX	Start of Text	02
ETX	End of Text	03
EOT	End of Transmission	04
ENQ	Enquire (who are you, WRU)	05
ACK	Acknowledge	06
BEL	Bell	07
BS	Backspace	08
HT	Horizontal Tab	09
LF	Line Feed	0A
VT	Vertical Tab	0B
FF	Form Feed	0C
RETURN	Carriage Return	0D
SO	Shift Out (to red ribbon)	0E
SI	Shift In (to black ribbon)	0F
DLE	Data Link Escape	10
DC1	Device Control 1	11
DC2	Device Control 2	12
DC3	Device Control 3	13
DC4	Device Control 4	14
NAK	Negative Acknowledge	15
SYN	Synchronous Idle	16
ETB	End of Transmission Block	17
CAN	Cancel	18
EM	End of Medium	19
SUB	Substitute	1A
ESC	Escape, prefix	1B
FS	File Separator	1C
GS	Group Separator	1D
RS	Record Separator	1E
US	Unit Separator	1F
SP	Space or Blank	20

TABLE I.1   (continued)

Character	Comments	Hex value
!	Exclamation point	21
"	Quotation marks (dieresis)	22
#	Number sign	23
$	Dollar sign	24
%	Percent sign	25
&	Ampersand	26
'	Apostrophe (acute accent, closing single quote)	27
(	Opening parenthesis	28
)	Closing parenthesis	29
*	Asterisk	2A
+	Plus sign	2B
,	Comma (cedilla)	2C
-	Hyphen (minus)	2D
.	Period (decimal point)	2E
/	Slant	2F
0	Digit 0	30
1	Digit 1	31
2	Digit 2	32
3	Digit 3	33
4	Digit 4	34
5	Digit 5	35
6	Digit 6	36
7	Digit 7	37
8	Digit 8	38
9	Digit 9	39
:	Colon	3A
;	Semicolon	3B
<	Less than	3C
=	Equals	3D
>	Greater than	3E
?	Question mark	3F
@	Commercial at	40

TABLE I.1   (continued)

Character	Comments	Hex value
A	Upper-case letter A	41
B	Upper-case letter B	42
C	Upper-case letter C	43
D	Upper-case letter D	44
E	Upper-case letter E	45
F	Upper-case letter F	46
G	Upper-case letter G	47
H	Upper-case letter H	48
I	Upper-case letter I	49
J	Upper-case letter J	4A
K	Upper-case letter K	4B
L	Upper-case letter L	4C
M	Upper-case letter M	4D
N	Upper-case letter N	4E
O	Upper-case letter O	4F
P	Upper-case letter P	50
Q	Upper-case letter Q	51
R	Upper-case letter R	52
S	Upper-case letter S	53
T	Upper-case letter T	54
U	Upper-case letter U	55
V	Upper-case letter V	56
W	Upper-case letter W	57
X	Upper-case letter X	58
Y	Upper-case letter Y	59
Z	Upper-case letter Z	5A
[	Opening bracket	5B
\	Reverse slant	5C
]	Closing bracket	5D
^	Circumflex	5E
—	Underline	5F

TABLE I.1   (continued)

Character	Comments	Hex value
'	Quotation mark	60
a	Lower-case letter a	61
b	Lower-case letter b	62
c	Lower-case letter c	63
d	Lower-case letter d	64
e	Lower-case letter e	65
f	Lower-case letter f	66
g	Lower-case letter g	67
h	Lower-case letter h	68
i	Lower-case letter i	69
j	Lower-case letter j	6A
k	Lower-case letter k	6B
l	Lower-case letter l	6C
m	Lower-case letter m	6D
n	Lower-case letter n	6E
o	Lower-case letter o	6F
p	Lower-case letter p	70
q	Lower-case letter q	71
r	Lower-case letter r	72
s	Lower-case letter s	73
t	Lower-case letter t	74
u	Lower-case letter u	75
v	Lower-case letter v	76
w	Lower-case letter w	77
x	Lower-case letter x	78
y	Lower-case letter y	79
z	Lower-case letter z	7A
{	Opening brace	7B
|	Vertical line	7C
}	Closing brace	7D
~	Equivalent	7E
	Delete	7F

TABLE I.2   POWERS OF TWO AND SIXTEEN

16^k 2^n	n	k	2^{-n}
1	0	0	1.0
2	1		0.5
4	2		0.25
8	3		0.125
16	4	1	0.062 5
32	5		0.031 25
64	6		0.015 625
128	7		0.007 812 5
256	8	2	0.003 906 25
512	9		0.001 953 125
1 024	10		0.000 976 562 5
2 048	11		0.000 488 281 25
4 096	12	3	0.000 244 140 625
8 192	13		0.000 122 070 312 5
16 384	14		0.000 061 035 156 25
32 768	15		0.000 030 517 578 125
65 536	16	4	0.000 015 258 789 062 5
131 072	17		0.000 007 629 394 531 25
262 144	18		0.000 003 814 697 265 625
524 288	19		0.000 001 907 348 632 812 5
1 048 576	20	5	0.000 000 953 674 316 406 25
2 097 152	21		0.000 000 476 837 158 203 125
4 194 304	22		0.000 000 238 418 579 101 562 5
8 388 608	23		0.000 000 119 209 289 550 781 25
16 777 216	24	6	0.000 000 059 604 664 775 390 625
33 554 432	25		0.000 000 029 802 322 387 695 312 5
67 108 864	26		0.000 000 014 901 161 193 847 656 25
134 217 728	27		0.000 000 007 450 580 596 923 828 125
268 435 456	28	7	0.000 000 003 725 290 298 461 914 062 5
536 870 912	29		0.000 000 001 862 645 149 230 957 031 25
1 073 741 824	30		0.000 000 000 931 322 574 615 478 515 625
2 147 483 648	31		0.000 000 000 465 661 287 307 739 257 812 5
4 294 967 296	32	8	0.000 000 000 232 830 643 653 869 628 906 25

Appendix II

MC68000 Characteristics

TABLE IIA.1 SIGNAL SUMMARY

Signal Name	Mnemonic	Input/Output	Active State	Three S
Address Bus	A1-A23	Output	High	Yes
Data Bus	D0-D15	Input/Output	High	Yes
Address Strobe	$\overline{AS}$	Output	Low	Yes
Read/Write	$R/\overline{W}$	Output	Read-High Write-Low	Yes
Upper and Lower Data Strobes	$\overline{UDS}$, $\overline{LDS}$	Output	Low	Yes
Data Transfer Acknowledge	$\overline{DTACK}$	Input	Low	No
Bus Request	$\overline{BR}$	Input	Low	No
Bus Grant	$\overline{BG}$	Output	Low	No
Bus Grant Acknowledge	$\overline{BGACK}$	Input	Low	No
Interrupt Priority Level	$\overline{IPL0, IPL1, IPL2}$	Input	Low	No
Bus Error	$\overline{BERR}$	Input	Low	No
Reset	$\overline{RESET}$	Input/Output	Low	No*
Halt	$\overline{HALT}$	Input/Output	Low	No*
Enable	E	Output	High	No
Valid Memory Address	$\overline{VMA}$	Output	Low	Yes
Valid Peripheral Address	$\overline{VPA}$	Input	Low	No
Function Code Output	FC0, FC1, FC2	Output	High	Yes
Clock	CLK	Input	High	No
Power Input	V_{cc}	Input	—	—
Ground	GND	Input	—	—

*Open Drain

TABLE IIA.2 DATA STROBE CONTROL OF DATA BUS

$\overline{\text{UDS}}$	$\overline{\text{LDS}}$	R/$\overline{\text{W}}$	D8-D15	D0-D7
High	High	—	No Valid Data	No Valid Data
Low	Low	High	Valid Data Bits 8-15	Valid Data Bits 0-7
High	Low	High	No Valid Data	Valid Data Bits 0-7
Low	High	High	Valid Data Bits 8-15	No Valid Data
Low	Low	Low	Valid Data Bits 8-15	Valid Data Bits 0-7
High	Low	Low	Valid Data Bits 0-7*	Valid Data Bits 0-7
Low	High	Low	Valid Data Bits 8-15	Valid Data Bits 8-15*

*These conditions are a result of current implementation and may not appear on future devices.

TABLE IIA.3 FUNCTION CODE OUTPUTS

FC2	FC1	FC0	Cycle Type
Low	Low	Low	(Undefined, Reserved)
Low	Low	High	User Data
Low	High	Low	User Program
Low	High	High	(Undefined, Reserved)
High	Low	Low	(Undefined, Reserved)
High	Low	High	Supervisor Data
High	High	Low	Supervisor Program
High	High	High	Interrupt Acknowledge

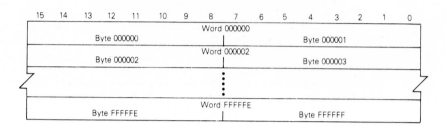

Word Organization In Memory

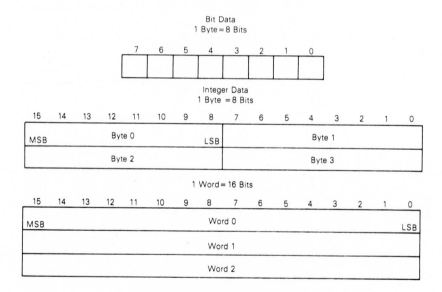

Data Organization In Memory

1 Long Word = 32 Bits

| 15 | 14 | 13 | 12 | 11 | 10 | 9 | 8 | 7 | 6 | 5 | 4 | 3 | 2 | 1 | 0 |

MSB

High Order

— Long Word 0 — — — — — — — — — — — — — — — — — — —

Low Order   LSB

— Long Word 1 —

— Long Word 2 —

Addresses
1 Address = 32 Bits

| 15 | 14 | 13 | 12 | 11 | 10 | 9 | 8 | 7 | 6 | 5 | 4 | 3 | 2 | 1 | 0 |

MSB

High Order

— — Address 0 — — — — — — — — — — — — — — — — — — —

Low Order   LSB

— — Address 1 — — — — — — — — — — — — — — — — — — —

— — Address 2 — — — — — — — — — — — — — — — — — — —

MSB = Most Significant Bit
LSB = Least Significant Bit

Decimal Data
2 Binary Coded Decimal Digits = 1 Byte

| 15 | 14 | 13 | 12 | 11 | 10 | 9 | 8 | 7 | 6 | 5 | 4 | 3 | 2 | 1 | 0 |

MSD

| BCD 0 | BCD 1 | LSD | BCD 2 | BCD 3 |
| BCD 4 | BCD 5 | | BCD 6 | BCD 7 |

MSD = Most Significant Digit
LSD = Least Significant Digit

APPENDIX IIC: EXCEPTION VECTOR ASSIGNMENTS

Vector Number(s)	Dec	Address Hex	Space	Assignment
0	0	000	SP	Reset: Initial SSP[2]
	4	004	SP	Reset: Initial PC[2]
2	8	008	SD	Bus Error
3	12	00C	SD	Address Error
4	16	010	SD	Illegal Instruction
5	20	014	SD	Zero Divide
6	24	018	SD	CHK Instruction
7	28	01C	SD	TRAPV Instruction
8	32	020	SD	Privilege Violation
9	36	024	SD	Trace
10	40	028	SD	Line 1010 Emulator
11	44	02C	SD	Line 1111 Emulator
12[1]	48	030	SD	(Unassigned, Reserved)
13[1]	52	034	SD	(Unassigned, Reserved)
14[1]	56	038	SD	(Unassigned, Reserved)
15	60	03C	SD	Uninitialized Interrupt Vector
16-23[1]	64	040	SD	(Unassigned, Reserved)
	95	05F		—
24	96	060	SD	Spurious Interrupt[3]
25	100	064	SD	Level 1 Interrupt Autovector
26	104	068	SD	Level 2 Interrupt Autovector
27	108	06C	SD	Level 3 Interrupt Autovector
28	112	070	SD	Level 4 Interrupt Autovector
29	116	074	SD	Level 5 Interrupt Autovector
30	120	078	SD	Level 6 Interrupt Autovector
31	124	07C	SD	Level 7 Interrupt Autovector
32-47	128	080	SD	TRAP Instruction Vectors[4]
	191	0BF		
48-63[1]	192	0C0	SD	(Unassigned, Reserved)
	255	0FF		—
64-255	256	100	SD	User Interrupt Vectors
	1023	3FF		—

NOTES:
1. Vector numbers 12, 13, 14, 16 through 23, and 48 through 63 are reserved for future enhancements by Motorola. No user peripheral devices should be assigned these numbers.
2. Reset vector (0) requires four words, unlike the other vectors which only require two words, and is located in the supervisor program space.
3. The spurious interrupt vector is taken when there is a bus error indication during interrupt processing. Refer to Paragraph 5.5.2.
4. TRAP #n uses vector number 32 + n.

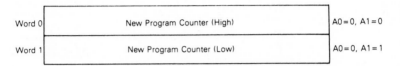

Figure IIC.1   Exception vector format (Courtesy of Motorola, Inc.)

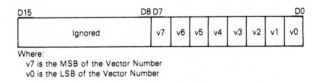

Figure IIC.2   Peripheral vector number format (Courtesy of Motorola, Inc.)

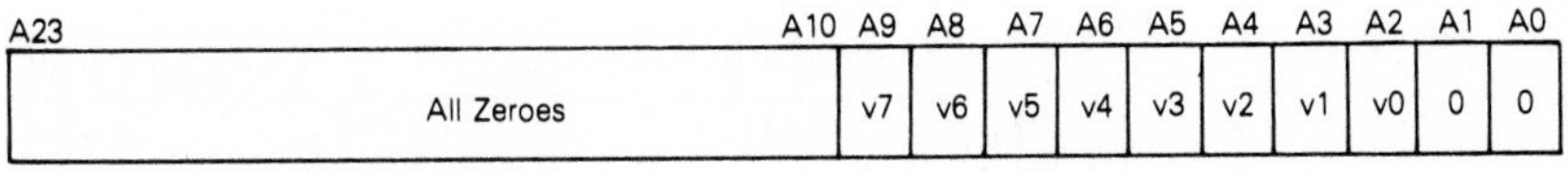

Figure IIC.3   Address translated from 8-bit vector number. (Courtesy of Motorola, Inc.)

APPENDIX IID: PROGRAMMING MODEL

TABLE IID.1 REGISTER SET

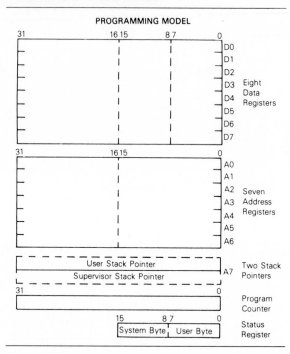

TABLE IID.2 STATUS REGISTER

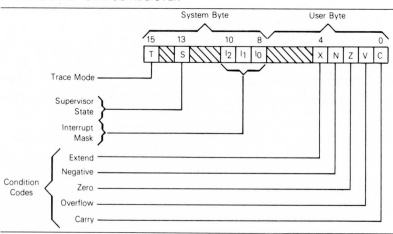

Appendix III

Assembly Language

TABLE III.1 CHARACTER SET

The character set recognized by the Motorola MC68000 Resident Structured Assembler is a subset of ASCII (American Standard Code for Information Interchange, 1968). The characters listed below are recognized by the assembler, and the ASCII Code.

1. The upper case letters A through Z
2. The integers 0 through 9
3. Four arithmetic operators: + − * /
4. The logical operators: >> << & !
5. Parentheses used in expressions ( )
6. Characters used as special prefixes:

    # (pound sign) specifies the immediate mode of addressing
    $ (dollar sign) specifies a hexadecimal number
    ' (apostrophe) specifies an ASCII literal character

7. The special characters used in macros: < > \ @
8. Three separating characters:

    SPACE
    , (comma)
    . (period)

9. A comment in a source statement may include any characters with ASCII hexadecimal values from 20 (SP) through 5F (__).
10. Character used as a special suffix:

    : (colon) specifies the end of a label

TABLE III.2 ASSEMBLER INSTRUCTION SET

Mnemonic	Operation	Assembler syntax	Cond. codes				
			X	N	Z	V	C
ABCD	Add Decimal With Extend	ABCD Dy,Dx ABCD —(Ay),—(Ax)	*	U	*	U	*
ADD	Add Binary	ADD <ea>,Dn ADD Dn,<ea>	*	*	*	*	*
ADDA	Add Address	ADDA <ea>,An	—	—	—	—	—
ADDI	Add Immediate	ADDI #<data>,<ea>	*	*	*	*	*
ADDQ	Add Quick	ADDQ #<data>,<ea>	*	*	*	*	*
ADDX	Add Extended	ADDX Dy,Dx ADDX —(Ay), —(Ax)	*	*	*	*	*
AND	AND Logical	AND <ea>,Dn AND Dn,<ea>	—	*	*	0	0
ANDI	AND Immediate	ANDI #<data>,<ea>	—	*	*	0	0
ASL, ASR	Arithmetic Shift	ASd Dx,Dy ASd #<data>,Dy ASd <ea>	*	*	*	*	*
Bcc	Branch Conditionally	Bcc <label>	—	—	—	—	—
BCHG	Test a Bit and Change	BCHG Dn,<ea> BCHG #<data>,<ea>	—	—	*	—	—
BCLR	Test a Bit and Clear	BCLR Dn,<ea> BCLR #<data>,<ea>	—	—	*	—	—
BRA	Branch Always	BRA <label>	—	—	—	—	—
BSET	Test a Bit and Set	BSET Dn,<ea> BSET #<data>,<ea>	—	—	*	—	—
BSR	Branch to Subroutine	BSR <label>	—	—	—	—	—
BTST	Test a Bit	BTST Dn,<ea> BTST #<data>,<ea>	—	—	*	—	—
CHK	Check Register Against Bounds	CHK <ea>,Dn	—	*	U	U	U
CLR	Clear an Operand	CLR <ea>	—	0	1	0	0
CMP	Arithmetic Compare	CMP <ea>,Dn	—	*	*	*	*
CMPA	Arithmetic Compare Address	CMPA <ea>,An	—	*	*	*	*
CMPI	Compare Immediate	CMPI #<data>,<ea>	—	*	*	*	*
CMPM	Compare Memory	CMPM (Ay)+,(Ax)+	—	*	*	*	*
DBcc	Test Condition Decrement and Branch	DBcc Dn,<label>	—	—	—	—	—
DIVS	Signed Divide	DIVS <ea>,Dn	—	*	*	*	0
DIVU	Unsigned Divide	DIVU <ea>,Dn	—	*	*	*	0
EOR	Exclusive OR Logical	EOR Dn,<ea>	—	*	*	0	0
EORI	Exclusive OR Immediate	EORI #<data>,<ea>	—	*	*	0	0
EXG	Exchange Registers	EXG Rx,Ry	—	—	—	—	—

TABLE III.2   **(continued)**

Mnemonic	Operation	Assembler syntax	X	N	Z	V	C
					Cond. codes		
EXT	Sign Extend	EXT Dn	—	*	*	0	0
JMP	Jump	JMP < ea >	—	—	—	—	—
JSR	Jump to Subroutine	JSR < ea >	—	—	—	—	—
LEA	Load Effective Address	LEA < ea >,An	—	—	—	—	—
LINK	Link and Allocate	LINK An,# < displacement >	—	—	—	—	—
LSR, LSL	Logical Shift	LSd Dx,Dy LSd # < data >,Dy LSd < ea >	*	*	*	0	*
MOVE	Move Data from Source to Destination	MOVE < ea >, < ea >	—	*	*	0	0
MOVE from SR	Move from the Status Register	MOVE SR, < ea >	—	—	—	—	—
MOVE to CC	Move to Condition Codes	MOVE < ea >,CCR	*	*	*	*	*
MOVE to SR	Move to the Status Register	MOVE < ea >,SR	*	*	*	*	*
MOVE USP	Move User Stack Pointer	MOVE USP,An MOVE An,USP	—	—	—	—	—
MOVEA	Move Address	MOVEA < ea >,An	—	—	—	—	—
MOVEM	Move Multiple Registers	MOVEM < register list >, < ea > MOVEM < ea >, < register list >	—	—	—	—	—
MOVEP	Move Peripheral Data	MOVEP Dx,d(Ay) MOVEP d(Ay),Dx	—	—	—	—	—
MOVEQ	Move Quick	MOVEQ # < data >,Dn	—	*	*	0	0
MULS	Signed Multiply	MULS < ea >,Dn	—	*	*	0	0
MULU	Unsigned Multiply	MULU < ea >,Dn	—	*	*	0	0
NBCD	Negate Decimal with Extend	NBCD < ea >	*	U	*	U	*
NEG	Two's Complement Negation	NEG < ea >	*	*	*	*	*
NEGX	Negate with Extend	NEGX < ea >	*	*	*	*	*
NOP	No Operation	NOP	—	—	—	—	—
NOT	Logical Complement	NOT < ea >	—	*	*	0	0
OR	Inclusive OR Logical	OR < ea >,Dn OR Dn, < ea >	—	*	*	0	0
ORI	Inclusive OR Immediate	ORI # < data >, < ea >	—	*	*	0	0
PEA	Push Effective Address	PEA < ea >	—	—	—	—	—
RESET	Reset External Devices	RESET	—	—	—	—	—

TABLE III.2   (continued)

Mnemonic	Operation	Assembler syntax	X	N	Z	V	C
ROL, ROR	Rotate without Extend	ROd Dx,Dy ROd # < data >,Dy ROd < ea >	—	*	*	0	*
ROXL, ROXR	Rotate with Extend	ROXd Dx,Dy ROXd # < data >,Dy ROXd < ea >	*	*	*	0	*
RTE	Return from Exception	RTE	*	*	*	*	*
RTR	Return and Restore Condition Codes	RTR	*	*	*	*	*
RTS	Return from Subroutine	RTS	—	—	—	—	—
SBCD	Subtract Decimal with Extend	SBCD Dy,Dx SBCD —(Ay),—(Ax)	*	U	*	U	*
Scc	Set according to Condition	Scc < ea >	—	—	—	—	—
STOP	Stop Program Execution	STOP #xxx	*	*	*	*	*
SUB	Subtract Binary	SUB < ea >,Dn SUB Dn, < ea >	*	*	*	*	*
SUBA	Subtract Address	SUBA < ea >,An	—	—	—	—	—
SUBI	Subtract Immediate	SUBI # < data >, < ea >	*	*	*	*	*
SUBQ	Subtract Quick	SUBQ # < data >, < ea >	*	*	*	*	*
SUBX	Subtract with Extend	SUBX Dy,Dx SUBX —(Ay),—(Ax)	*	*	*	*	*
SWAP	Swap Register Halves	SWAP Dn	—	*	*	0	0
TAS	Test and Set an Operand	TAS < ea >	—	*	*	0	0
TRAP	Trap	TRAP # < vector >	—	—	—	—	—
TRAPV	Trap on Overflow	TRAPV	—	—	—	—	—
TST	Test an Operand	TST < ea >	—	*	*	0	0
UNLK	Unlink	UNLK An	—	—	—	—	—

NOTE: For condition codes, — indicates that code is unchanged and * indicates that code is set according to the result.

Appendix IV

Machine Language Characteristics of the MC68000, MC68008, and MC68010

Appendix IV is taken from *16-Bit Microprocessor, User's Manual,* 3rd ed. and from *MC68000 16/32-Bit Microprocessor, Programmer's Reference Manual,* 4th ed. Courtesy of Motorola, Inc.

APPENDIX IVA: CONDITION CODES COMPUTATION

A.1 INTRODUCTION

This appendix provides a discussion of how the condition codes were developed, the meanings of each bit, how they are computed, and how they are represented in the instruction set details.

Two criteria were used in developing the condition codes:
- Consistency — across instruction, uses, and instances
- Meaningful Results — no change unless it provides useful information

The consistency across instructions means that instructions which are special cases of more general instructions affect the condition codes in the same way. Consistency across instances means that if an instruction ever affects a condition code, it will always affect that condition code. Consistency across uses means that whether the condition codes were set by a compare, test, or move instruction, the conditional instructions test the same situation. The tests used for the conditional instructions and the code computations are given in paragraph A.5.

A.2 CONDITION CODE REGISTER

The condition code register portion of the status register contains five bits:

N — Negative
Z — Zero
V — Overflow
C — Carry
X — Extend

The first four bits are true condition code bits in that they reflect the condition of the result of a processor operation. The X bit is an operand for multiprecision computations. The carry bit (C) and the multiprecision operand extend bit (X) are separate in the MC68000 to simplify the programming model.

A.3 CONDITION CODE REGISTER NOTATION

In the instruction set details given in Appendix B, the description of the effect on the condition codes is given in the following form:

Condition Codes:

	X	N	Z	V	C

where:

N (negative)   Set if the most significant bit of the result is set. Cleared otherwise.

Z (zero)   Set if the result equals zero. Cleared otherwise.

V (overflow)   Set if there was an arithmetic overflow. This implies that the result is not representable in the operand size. Cleared otherwise.

C (carry)   Set if a carry is generated out of the most significant bit of the operands for an addition. Also set if a borrow is generated in a subtraction. Cleared otherwise.

X (extend)   Transparent to data movement. When affected, it is set the same as the C bit.

The notational convention that appears in the representation of the condition code register is:

*   set according to the result of the operation

—   not affected by the operation

0   cleared

1   set

U   undefined after the operation

A.4 CONDITION CODE COMPUTATION

Most operations take a source operand and a destination operand, compute, and store the result in the destination location. Unary operations take a destination operand, compute, and store the result in the destination location. Table A-1 details how each instruction sets the condition codes.

Table A-1. Condition Code Computations

Operations	X	N	Z	V	C	Special Definition
ABCD	*	U	?	U	?	C = Decimal Carry $Z = Z \cdot \overline{Rm} \cdot \ldots \cdot \overline{R0}$
ADD, ADDI, ADDQ	*	*	*	?	?	$V = Sm \cdot Dm \cdot \overline{Rm} + \overline{Sm} \cdot \overline{Dm} \cdot Rm$ $C = Sm \cdot Dm + \overline{Rm} \cdot Dm + Sm \cdot \overline{Rm}$
ADDX	*	*	?	?	?	$V = Sm \cdot Dm \cdot \overline{Rm} + \overline{Sm} \cdot \overline{Dm} \cdot Rm$ $C = Sm \cdot Dm + Rm \cdot Dm + Sm \cdot \overline{Rm}$ $Z = Z \cdot \overline{Rm} \cdot \ldots \cdot \overline{R0}$
AND, ANDI, EOR, EORI, MOVEQ, MOVE, OR, ORI, CLR, EXT, NOT, TAS, TST	—	*	*	0	0	
CHK	—	*	U	U	U	
SUB, SUBI SUBQ	*	*	*	?	?	$V = \overline{Sm} \cdot Dm \cdot \overline{Rm} + Sm \cdot \overline{Dm} \cdot Rm$ $C = Sm \cdot \overline{Dm} + Rm \cdot \overline{Dm} + Sm \cdot Rm$
SUBX	*	*	?	?	?	$V = \overline{Sm} \cdot Dm \cdot \overline{Rm} + Sm \cdot \overline{Dm} \cdot Rm$ $C = Sm \cdot \overline{Dm} + Rm \cdot \overline{Dm} + Sm \cdot Rm$ $Z = Z \cdot \overline{Rm} \cdot \ldots \cdot \overline{R0}$
CMP, CMPI, CMPM	—	*	*	?	?	$V = \overline{Sm} \cdot Dm \cdot \overline{Rm} + Sm \cdot \overline{Dm} \cdot Rm$ $C = Sm \cdot \overline{Dm} + Rm \cdot \overline{Dm} + Sm \cdot Rm$
DIVS, DIVU	—	*	*	?	0	V = Division Overflow
MULS, MULU	—	*	*	0	0	
SBCD, NBCD	*	U	?	U	?	C = Decimal Borrow $Z = Z \cdot \overline{Rm} \cdot \ldots \cdot \overline{R0}$
NEG	*	*	*	?	?	$V = Dm \cdot Rm, C = Dm + Rm$
NEGX	*	*	?	?	?	$V = Dm \cdot Rm, C = Dm + Rm$ $Z = Z \cdot \overline{Rm} \cdot \ldots \cdot \overline{R0}$
BTST, BCHG, BSET, BCLR	—	—	?	—	—	$Z = \overline{Dn}$
ASL	*	*	*	?	?	$V = Dm \cdot (\overline{D_{m-1}} + \ldots + \overline{D_{m-r}})$ $\quad + \overline{Dm} \cdot (D_{m-1} + \ldots + D_{m-r})$ $C = D_{m-r+1}$
ASL (r=0)	—	*	*	0	0	
LSL, ROXL	*	*	*	0	?	$C = D_{m-r+1}$
LSR (r=0)	—	*	*	0	0	
ROXL (r=0)	—	*	*	0	?	$C = X$
ROL	—	*	*	0	?	$C = D_{m-r+1}$
ROL (r=0)	—	*	*	0	0	
ASR, LSR, ROXR	*	*	*	0	?	$C = D_{r-1}$
ASR, LSR (r=0)	—	*	*	0	0	
ROXR (r=0)	—	*	*	0	?	$C = X$
ROR	—	*	*	0	?	$C = D_{r-1}$
ROR (r=0)	—	*	*	0	0	

— Not affected
U Undefined
? Other — see Special Definition

*General Case:
$X = C$
$N = Rm$
$Z = \overline{Rm} \cdot \ldots \cdot \overline{R0}$

Sm Source Operand — most significant bit
Dm Destination operand — most significant bit
Rm Result operand — most significant bit
n bit number
r shift count

ADDI

ADDI   Add Immediate   **ADDI**

Operation: Immediate Data + (Destination) → Destination

**Assembler
Syntax:**   ADDI #<data>,<ea>

Attributes: Size = (Byte, Word, Long)

Description: Add the immediate data to the destination operand, and store the result in the destination location. The size of the operation may be specified to be byte, word, or long. The size of the immediate data matches the operation size.

Condition Codes:

X	N	Z	V	C
*	*	*	*	*

N   Set if the result is negative. Cleared otherwise.
Z   Set if the result is zero. Cleared otherwise.
V   Set if an overflow is generated. Cleared otherwise.
C   Set if a carry is generated. Cleared otherwise.
X   Set the same as the carry bit.

Instruction Format:

15	14	13	12	11	10	9	8	7	6	5	4	3	2	1	0
0	0	0	0	0	1	1	0	Size		Effective Address Mode | Register					
Word Data (16 bits)								Byte Data (8 bits)							
Long Data (32 bits, including previous word)															

Instruction Fields:

Size field — Specifies the size of the operation:
    00 — byte operation.
    01 — word operation.
    10 — long operation.

Effective Address field — Specifies the destination operand. Only data alterable addressing modes are allowed as shown:

Addressing Mode	Mode	Register	Addressing Mode	Mode	Register
Dn	000	register number	d(An, Xi)	110	register number
An	—	—	Abs.W	111	000
(An)	010	register number	Abs.L	111	001
(An) +	011	register number	d(PC)	—	—
– (An)	100	register number	d(PC, Xi)	—	—
d(An)	101	register number	Imm	—	—

Immediate field — (Data immediately following the instruction):
    If size = 00, then the data is the low order byte of the immediate word.
    If size = 01, then the data is the entire immediate word.
    If size = 10, then the data is the next two immediate words.

ADDQ

Add Quick

ADDQ

Operation: Immediate Data + (Destination) → Destination

**Assembler
Syntax:**   ADDQ #<data>, <ea>

Attributes: Size = (Byte, Word, Long)

Description: Add the immediate data to the operand at the destination location. The data range is from 1 to 8. The size of the operation may be specified to be byte, word, or long. Word and long operations are also allowed on the address registers and the condition codes are not affected. The entire destination address register is used regardless of the operation size.

Condition Codes:

X	N	Z	V	C
*	*	*	*	*

N   Set if the result is negative. Cleared otherwise.
Z   Set if the result is zero. Cleared otherwise.
V   Set if an overflow is generated. Cleared otherwise.
C   Set if a carry is generated. Cleared otherwise.
X   Set the same as the carry bit.

The condition codes are not affected if an addition to an address register is made.

Instruction Format:

15	14	13	12	11	10	9	8	7	6	5	4	3	2	1	0
0	1	0	1		Data		0		Size		Effective Address Mode			Register	

Instruction Fields:

Data field — Three bits of immediate data, 0, 1-7 representing a range of 8, 1 to 7 respectively.

Size field — Specifies the size of the operation:
    00 — byte operation.
    01 — word operation.
    10 — long operation.

Effective Address field — Specifies the destination location. Only alterable addressing modes are allowed as shown:

Addressing Mode	Mode	Register	Addressing Mode	Mode	Register
Dn	000	register number	d(An, Xi)	110	register number
An*	001	register number	Abs.W	111	000
(An)	010	register number	Abs.L	111	001
(An)+	011	register number	d(PC)	—	—
–(An)	100	register number	d(PC, Xi)	—	—
d(An)	101	register number	Imm	—	—

*Word and Long only.

ADDX · Add Extended · ADDX

Operation: (Source) + (Destination) + X → Destination

Assembler   ADDX Dy, Dx
Syntax: ADDX − (Ay), − (Ax)

Attributes: Size = (Byte, Word, Long)

Description: Add the source operand to the destination operand along with the extend bit and store the result in the destination location. The operands may be addressed in two different ways:
1. Data register to data register: the operands are contained in data registers specified in the instruction.
2. Memory to memory: the operands are addressed with the predecrement addressing mode using the address registers specified in the instruction.

The size of the operation may be specified to be byte, word, or long.

Condition Codes:

X	N	Z	V	C
*	*	*	*	*

N   Set if the result is negative. Cleared otherwise.
Z   Cleared if the result is non-zero. Unchanged otherwise.
V   Set if an overflow is generated. Cleared otherwise.
C   Set if a carry is generated. Cleared otherwise.
X   Set the same as the carry bit.

NOTE
Normally the Z condition code bit is set via programming before the start of an operation. This allows successful tests for zero results upon completion of multiple-precision operations.

Instruction Format:

15	14	13	12	11 10 9	8	7 6	5	4	3	2 1 0
1	1	0	1	Register Rx	1	Size	0	0	R/M	Register Ry

Instruction Fields:

Register Rx field — Specifies the destination register:
If R/M = 0, specifies a data register.
If R/M = 1, specifies an address register for the predecrement addressing mode.
Size field — Specifies the size of the operation:
00 — byte operation.
01 — word operation.
10 — long operation.

— Continued —

ADDX

Add Extended

ADDX

Instruction Fields: (Continued)

R/M field — Specifies the operand addressing mode:

0 — The operation is data register to data register.

1 — The operation is memory to memory.

Register Ry field — Specifies the source register:

If R/M = 0, specifies a data register.

If R/M = 1, specifies an address register for the predecrement addressing mode.

AND

AND Logical

AND

Operation: (Source)Λ(Destination) → Destination

Assembler AND <ea>, Dn
Syntax: AND Dn, <ea>

Attributes: Size = (Byte, Word, Long)

Description: AND the source operand to the destination operand and store the result in the destination location. The size of the operation may be specified to be byte, word, or long. The contents of an address register may not be used as an operand.

Condition Codes:

X	N	Z	V	C
—	*	*	0	0

N Set if the most significant bit of the result is set. Cleared otherwise.
Z Set if the result is zero. Cleared otherwise.
V Always cleared.
C Always cleared.
X Not affected.

Instruction Format:

15	14	13	12	11 10 9	8 7 6	5 4 3	2 1 0
1	1	0	0	Register	Op-Mode	Effective Address Mode	Register

Instruction Fields:

Register field — Specifies any of the eight data registers.

Op-Mode field —

Byte	Word	Long	Operation
000	001	010	(<Dn>) Λ (<ea>) → <Dn>
100	101	110	(<ea>) Λ (<Dn>) → <ea>

Effective Address field — Determines addressing mode:
If the location specified is a source operand then only data addressing modes are allowed as shown:

Addressing Mode	Mode	Register	Addressing Mode	Mode	Register
Dn	000	register number	d(An, Xi)	110	register number
An	—	—	Abs.W	111	000
(An)	010	register number	Abs.L	111	001
(An)+	011	register number	d(PC)	111	010
−(An)	100	register number	d(PC, Xi)	111	011
d(An)	101	register number	Imm	111	100

— Continued —

Effective Address field (Continued)

If the location specified is a destination operand then only alterable memory addressing modes are allowed as shown:

Addressing Mode	Mode	Register	Addressing Mode	Mode	Register
Dn	—	—	d(An, Xi)	110	register number
An	—	—	Abs.W	111	000
(An)	010	register number	Abs.L	111	001
(An)+	011	register number	d(PC)	—	—
−(An)	100	register number	d(PC, Xi)	—	—
d(An)	101	register number	Imm	—	—

Notes:
1. If the destination is a data register, then it cannot be specified by using the destination <ea> mode, but must use the destination Dn mode instead.
2. ANDI is used when the source is immediate data. Most assemblers automatically make this distinction.

ANDI

AND Immediate

Operation: Immediate Data Λ (Destination)→Destination

**Assembler
Syntax:** ANDI #<data>, <ea>

Attributes: Size = (Byte, Word, Long)

Description: AND the immediate data to the destination operand and store the result in the destination location. The size of the operation may be specified to be byte, word, or long. The size of the immediate data matches the operation size.

Condition Codes:

X	N	Z	V	C
—	*	*	0	0

N   Set if the most significant bit of the result is set. Cleared otherwise.
Z   Set if the result is zero. Cleared otherwise.
V   Always cleared.
C   Always cleared.
X   Not affected.

Instruction Format:

15	14	13	12	11	10	9	8	7	6	5	4	3	2	1	0
0	0	0	0	0	0	1	0	Size		Effective Address Mode | Register					
Word Data (16 bits)								Byte Data (8 bits)							
Long Data (32 bits, including previous word)															

Instruction Fields:

Size field — Specifies the size of the operation:
00 — byte operation.
01 — word operation.
10 — long operation.

Effective Address field — Specifies the destination operand. Only data alterable addressing modes are allowed as shown:

Addressing Mode	Mode	Register	Addressing Mode	Mode	Register
Dn	000	register number	d(An, Xi)	110	register number
An	—	—	Abs.W	111	000
(An)	010	register number	Abs.L	111	001
(An) +	011	register number	d(PC)	—	—
– (An)	100	register number	d(PC, Xi)	—	—
d(An)	101	register number	Imm	—	—

Immediate field — (Data immediately following the instruction):
If size = 00, then the data is the low order byte of the immediate word.
If size = 01, then the data is the entire immediate word.
If size = 10, then the data is the next two immediate words.

ANDI
to CCR

AND Immediate to Condition Codes

ANDI
to CCR

Operation: (Source)∧CCR → CCR

**Assembler
Syntax:** ANDI #xxx, CCR

Attributes: Size = (Byte)

Description: AND the immediate operand with the condition codes and store the result in the low-order byte of the status register.

Condition Codes:

X	N	Z	V	C
*	*	*	*	*

N   Cleared if bit 3 of immediate operand is zero. Unchanged otherwise.
Z   Cleared if bit 2 of immediate operand is zero. Unchanged otherwise.
V   Cleared if bit 1 of immediate operand is zero. Unchanged otherwise.
C   Cleared if bit 0 of immediate operand is zero. Unchanged otherwise.
X   Cleared if bit 4 of immediate operand is zero. Unchanged otherwise.

Instruction Format:

15	14	13	12	11	10	9	8	7	6	5	4	3	2	1	0
0	0	0	0	0	0	1	0	0	0	0	1	1	1	0	0
0	0	0	0	0	0	0	0	Byte Data (8 bits)							

ANDI
to SR

ANDI
to SR

AND Immediate to the Status Register
(Privileged Instruction)

Operation: If supervisor state
  then (Source)∧SR → SR
  else TRAP

Assembler
Syntax: ANDI #xxx, SR

Attributes: Size = (Word)

Description: AND the immediate operand with the contents of the status register and store the result in the status register. All bits of the status register are affected.

Condition Codes:

X	N	Z	V	C
*	*	*	*	*

N Cleared if bit 3 of immediate operand is zero. Unchanged otherwise.
Z Cleared if bit 2 of immediate operand is zero. Unchanged otherwise.
V Cleared if bit 1 of immediate operand is zero. Unchanged otherwise.
C Cleared if bit 0 of immediate operand is zero. Unchanged otherwise.
X Cleared if bit 4 of immediate operand is zero. Unchanged otherwise.

Instruction Format:

15	14	13	12	11	10	9	8	7	6	5	4	3	2	1	0
0	0	0	0	0	0	1	0	0	1	1	1	1	1	0	0
Word Data (16 bits)															

ASL, ASR   <small>Arithmetic Shift</small>   ASL, ASR

Operation: (Destination) Shifted by < count > → Destination

Assembler
Syntax:
ASd Dx, Dy
ASd #< data >, Dy
ASd < ea >

Attributes: Size = (Byte, Word, Long)

Description: Arithmetically shift the bits of the operand in the direction specified. The carry bit receives the last bit shifted out of the operand. The shift count for the shifting of a register may be specified in two different ways:
    1. Immediate: the shift count is specified in the instruction (shift range, 1-8).
    2. Register: the shift count is contained in a data register specified in the instruction.
The size of the operation may be specified to be byte, word, or long. The content of memory may be shifted one bit only and the operand size is restricted to a word.

For ASL, the operand is shifted left; the number of positions shifted is the shift count. Bits shifted out of the high order bit go to both the carry and the extend bits; zeroes are shifted into the low order bit. The overflow bit indicates if any sign changes occur during the shift.

ASL:

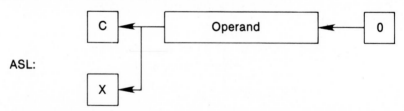

For ASR, the operand is shifted right; the number of positions shifted is the shift count. Bits shifted out of the low order bit go to both the carry and the extend bits; the sign bit is replicated into the high order bit.

ASR:

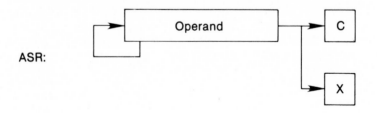

— Continued —

ASL, ASR Arithmetic Shift ASL, ASR

Condition Codes:

X	N	Z	V	C
*	*	*	*	*

N Set if the most significant bit of the result is set. Cleared otherwise.
Z Set if the result is zero. Cleared otherwise.
V Set if the most significant bit is changed at any time during the shift operation. Cleared otherwise.
C Set according to the last bit shifted out of the operand. Cleared for a shift count of zero.
X Set according to the last bit shifted out of the operand. Unaffected for a shift count of zero.

Instruction Format (Register Shifts):

15	14	13	12	11 10 9	8	7 6	5	4	3	2 1 0
1	1	1	0	Count/Register	dr	Size	i/r	0	0	Register

Instruction Fields (Register Shifts):

Count/Register field — Specifies shift count or register where count is located:

If i/r = 0, the shift count is specified in this field. The values 0, 1-7 represent a range of 8, 1 to 7 respectively.

If i/r = 1, the shift count (modulo 64) is contained in the data register specified in this field.

dr field — Specifies the direction of the shift:

0 — shift right.
1 — shift left.

Size field — Specifies the size of the operation:

00 — byte operation.
01 — word operation.
10 — long operation.

i/r field —

If i/r = 0, specifies immediate shift count.
if i/r = 1, specifies register shift count.

Register field — Specifies a data register whose content is to be shifted.

Instruction Format (Memory Shifts):

15	14	13	12	11	10	9	8	7	6	5 4 3	2 1 0
1	1	1	0	0	0	0	dr	1	1	Effective Address Mode	Register

— Continued —

ASL, ASR   Arithmetic Shift   ASL, ASR

Instruction Fields (Memory Shifts):

dr field — Specifies the direction of the shift:

0 — shift right.

1 — shift left.

Effective Address field — Specifies the operand to be shifted. Only memory alterable addressing modes are allowed as shown:

Addressing Mode	Mode	Register	Addressing Mode	Mode	Register
Dn	—	—	d(An, Xi)	110	register number
An	—	—	Abs.W	111	000
(An)	010	register number	Abs.L	111	001
(An)+	011	register number	d(PC)	—	—
−(An)	100	register number	d(PC, Xi)	—	—
d(An)	101	register number	Imm	—	—

Bcc

Branch Conditionally

Bcc

Operation: If (condition true) then PC + d → PC

Assembler
Syntax: Bcc <label>

Attributes: Size = (Byte, Word)

Description: If the specified condition is met, program execution continues at location (PC) + displacement. Displacement is a twos complement integer which counts the relative distance in bytes. The value in PC is the current instruction location plus two. If the 8-bit displacement in the instruction word is zero, then the 16-bit displacement (word immediately following the instruction) is used. "cc" may specify the following conditions:

CC	carry clear	0100	$\overline{C}$	LS	low or same	0011	$C+Z$
CS	carry set	0101	C	LT	less than	1101	$N \cdot \overline{V} + \overline{N} \cdot V$
EQ	equal	0111	Z	MI	minus	1011	N
GE	greater or equal	1100	$N \cdot V + \overline{N} \cdot \overline{V}$	NE	not equal	0110	$\overline{Z}$
GT	greater than	1110	$N \cdot V \cdot \overline{Z} + \overline{N} \cdot \overline{V} \cdot \overline{Z}$	PL	plus	1010	$\overline{N}$
HI	high	0010	$\overline{C} \cdot \overline{Z}$	VC	overflow clear	1000	$\overline{V}$
LE	less or equal	1111	$Z + N \cdot \overline{V} + \overline{N} \cdot V$	VS	overflow set	1001	V

Condition Codes: Not affected.

Instruction Format:

15	14	13	12	11	10	9	8	7	6	5	4	3	2	1	0
0	1	1	0	Condition				8-bit Displacement							
16-bit Displacement if 8-bit Displacement = 0															

Instruction Fields:

Condition field — One of fourteen conditions discussed in description.

8-bit Displacement field — Twos complement integer specifying the relative distance (in bytes) between the branch instruction and the next instruction to be executed if the condition is met.

16-bit Displacement field — Allows a larger displacement than 8 bits. Used only if the 8-bit displacement is equal to zero.

Note: A short branch to the immediately following instruction cannot be done because it would result in a zero offset which forces a word branch instruction definition.

BCHG

Test a Bit and Change

BCHG

Operation: $\sim$(<bit number>) OF Destination $\rightarrow$ Z;
$\sim$(<bit number>) OF Destination $\rightarrow$ <bit number> OF Destination

Assembler Syntax: BCHG Dn, <ea>
BCHG #<data>, <ea>

Attributes: Size = (Byte, Long)

Description: A bit in the destination operand is tested and the state of the specified bit is reflected in the Z condition code. After the test, the state of the specified bit is changed in the destination. If a data register is the destination, then the bit numbering is modulo 32 allowing bit manipulation on all bits in a data register. If a memory location is the destination, a byte is read from that location, the bit operation performed using the bit number modulo 8, and the byte written back to the location with zero referring to the least-significant bit. The bit number for this operation may be specified in two different ways:

1. Immediate — the bit number is specified in a second word of the instruction.
2. Register — the bit number is contained in a data register specified in the instruction.

Condition Codes:

X	N	Z	V	C
—	—	*	—	—

N Not affected.
Z Set if the bit tested is zero. Cleared otherwise.
V Not affected.
C Not affected.
X Not affected.

Instruction Format (Bit Number Dynamic):

15	14	13	12	11	10	9	8	7	6	5	4	3	2	1	0
0	0	0	0	Register			1	0	1	Effective Address Mode			Register		

Instruction Fields (Bit Number Dynamic):

Register field — Specifies the data register whose content is the bit number.

Effective Address field — Specifies the destination location. Only data alterable addressing modes are allowed as shown:

Addressing Mode	Mode	Register	Addressing Mode	Mode	Register
Dn*	000	register number	d(An, Xi)	110	register number
An	—	—	Abs.W	111	000
(An)	010	register number	Abs.L	111	001
(An) +	011	register number	d(PC)	—	—
– (An)	100	register number	d(PC, Xi)	—	—
d(An)	101	register number	Imm	—	—

*Long only; all others are byte only.

— Continued —

BCHG   Test a Bit and Change   BCHG

Instruction Format (Bit Number Static):

15	14	13	12	11	10	9	8	7	6	5	4	3	2	1	0
0	0	0	0	1	0	0	0	0	1	Effective Address		Mode		Register	
0	0	0	0	0	0	0	0	bit number							

Instruction Fields (Bit Number Static):

Effective Address field — Specifies the destination location. Only data alterable addressing modes are allowed as shown:

Addressing Mode	Mode	Register	Addressing Mode	Mode	Register
Dn	000	register number	d(An, Xi)	110	register number
An	—	—	Abs.W	111	000
(An)	010	register number	Abs.L	111	001
(An) +	011	register number	d(PC)	—	—
– (An)	100	register number	d(PC, Xi)	—	—
d(An)	101	register number	Imm	—	—

*Long only; all others are byte only.

bit number field — Specifies the bit numbers.

BCLR   Test a Bit and Clear   BCLR

Operation: ~(<bit number>) OF Destination)→Z;
                  0→<bit number> OF Destination

Assembler   BLCR Dn, <ea>
Syntax: BCLR #<data>, <ea>

Attributes: Size = (Byte, Long)

Description: A bit in the destination operand is tested and the state of the specified bit
is reflected in the Z condition code. After the test, the specified bit is
cleared in the destination. If a data register is the destination, then the bit
numbering is modulo 32 allowing bit manipulation on all bits in a data
register. If a memory location is the destination, a byte is read from that
location, the bit operation performed using the bit number modulo 8, and
the byte written back to the location with zero referring to the least-
significant bit. The bit number for this operation may be specified in two
different ways:
  1. Immediate — the bit number is specified in a second word of the in-
     struction.
  2. Register — the bit number is contained in a data register specified in
     the instruction.

Condition Codes:

X	N	Z	V	C
—	—	*	—	—

N   Not affected.
Z   Set if the bit tested is zero. Cleared otherwise.
V   Not affected.
C   Not affected.
X   Not affected.

Instruction Format (Bit Number Dynamic):

15	14	13	12	11	10	9	8	7	6	5	4	3	2	1	0
0	0	0	0	Register			1	1	0	Effective Address Mode ¦ Register					

Instruction Fields (Bit Number Dynamic):

Register field — Specifies the data register whose content is the bit
number.

Effective Address field — Specifies the destination location. Only data
alterable addressing modes are allowed as shown:

Addressing Mode	Mode	Register	Addressing Mode	Mode	Register
Dn*	000	register number	d(An, Xi)	110	register number
An	—	—	Abs.W	111	000
(An)	010	register number	Abs.L	111	001
(An) +	011	register number	d(PC)	—	—
− (An)	100	register number	d(PC, Xi)	—	—
d(An)	101	register number	Imm	—	—

*Long only; all others are byte only.

— Continued —

BCLR

Test a Bit and Clear

BCLR

Instruction Format (Bit Number Static):

15	14	13	12	11	10	9	8	7	6	5 4 3	2 1 0
0	0	0	0	1	0	0	0	1	0	Effective Address Mode	Register
0	0	0	0	0	0	0	0			bit number	

Instruction Fields (Bit Number Static):

Effective Address field — Specifies the destination location. Only data alterable addressing modes are allowed as shown:

Addressing Mode	Mode	Register	Addressing Mode	Mode	Register
Dn*	000	register only	d(An, Xi)	110	register number
An	—	—	Abs.W	111	000
(An)	010	register number	Abs.L	111	001
(An) +	011	register number	d(PC)	—	—
– (An)	100	register number	d(PC, Xi)	—	—
d(An)	101	register number	Imm	—	—

*Long only; all others are byte only.

bit number field — Specifies the bit number.

BRA

BRA   Branch Always   **BRA**

Operation: PC + d → PC

**Assembler
Syntax:**   BRA < label >

Attributes: Size = (Byte, Word)

Description: Program execution continues at location (PC) + displacement. Displacement is a twos complement integer which counts the relative distance in bytes. The value in PC is the current instruction location plus two. If the 8-bit displacement in the instruction word is zero, then the 16-bit displacement (word immediately following the instruction) is used.

Condition Codes: Not affected.

Instruction Format:

15	14	13	12	11	10	9	8	7	6	5	4	3	2	1	0
0	1	1	0	0	0	0	0	8-bit Displacement							
16-bit Displacement if 8-bit Displacement = 0															

Instruction Fields:

8-bit Displacement field — Twos complement integer specifying the relative distance (in bytes) between the branch instruction and the next instruction to be executed if the condition is met.

16-bit Displacement field — Allows a larger displacement than 8 bits. Used only if the 8-bit displacement is equal to zero.

Note: A short branch to the immediately following instruction cannot be done because it would result in a zero offset which forces a word branch instruction definition.

BSET

Test a Bit and Set

BSET

Operation: ~(<bit number>) OF Destination → Z
1 → <bit number> OF Destination

Assembler BSET Dn, <ea>
Syntax: BSET #<data>, <ea>

Attributes: Size = (Byte, Long)

Description: A bit in the destination operand is tested and the state of the specified bit is reflected in the Z condition code. After the test, the specified bit is set in the destination. If a data register is the destination, then the bit numbering is modulo 32, allowing bit manipulation on all bits in a data register. If a memory location is the destination, a byte is read from that location, the bit operation performed using the bit number modulo 8, and the byte written back to the location with zero referring to the least-significant bit. The bit number for this operation may be specified in two different ways:
1. Immediate — the bit number is specified in a second word of the instruction.
2. Register — the bit number is contained in a data register specified in the instruction.

Condition Codes:

X	N	Z	V	C
—	—	*	—	—

N   Not affected.
Z   Set if the bit tested is zero. Cleared otherwise.
V   Not affected.
C   Not affected.
X   Not affected.

Instruction Format (Bit Number Dynamic):

15	14	13	12	11	10	9	8	7	6	5	4	3	2	1	0
0	0	0	0	Register			1	1	1	Effective Address Mode			Register		

Instruction Fields (Bit Number Dynamic):

Register field — Specifies the data register whose content is the bit number.

Effective Address field — Specifies the destination location. Only data alterable addressing modes are allowed as shown:

Addressing Mode	Mode	Register	Addressing Mode	Mode	Register
Dn*	000	register number	d(An, Xi)	110	register number
An	—	—	Abs.W	111	000
(An)	010	register number	Abs.L	111	001
(An)+	011	register number	d(PC)	—	—
−(An)	100	register number	d(PC, Xi)	—	—
d(An)	101	register number	Imm	—	—

*Long only; all others are byte only

— Continued —

Instruction Format (Bit Number Static):

15	14	13	12	11	10	9	8	7	6	5	4	3	2	1	0
0	0	0	0	1	0	0	0	1	1	Effective Address Mode			Register		
0	0	0	0	0	0	0	0	bit number							

Instruction Fields (Bit Number Static):

Effective Address field — Specifies the destination location. Only data alterable addressing modes are allowed as shown:

Addressing Mode	Mode	Register	Addressing Mode	Mode	Register
Dn*	000	register number	d(An, Xi)	110	register number
An	—	—	Abs.W	111	000
(An)	010	register number	Abs.L	111	001
(An)+	011	register number	d(PC)	—	—
−(An)	100	register number	d(PC, Xi)	—	—
d(An)	101	register number	Imm	—	—

*Long only; all others are byte only.

bit number field — Specifies the bit number.

BSR

Branch to Subroutine

BSR

Operation: PC→ − (SP); PC + d → PC

Assembler Syntax: BSR <label>

Attributes: Size = (Byte, Word)

Description: The long word address of the instruction immediately following the BSR instruction is pushed onto the system stack. Program execution then continues at location (PC) + displacement. Displacement is a twos complement integer which counts the relative distances in bytes. The value in PC is the current instruction location plus two. If the 8-bit displacement in the instruction word is zero, then the 16-bit displacement (word immediately following the instruction) is used.

Condition Codes: Not affected.

Instruction Format:

15	14	13	12	11	10	9	8	7	6	5	4	3	2	1	0
0	1	1	0	0	0	0	1	8-bit Displacement							
16-bit Displacement if 8-bit Displacement = 0															

Instruction Fields:

8-bit Displacement field — Twos complement integer specifying the relative distance (in bytes) between the branch instruction and the next instruction to be executed if the condition is met.

16-bit Displacement field — Allows a larger displacement than 8 bits. Used only if the 8-bit displacement is equal to zero.

Note: A short subroutine branch to the immediately following instruction cannot be done because it would result in a zero offset which forces a word branch instruction definition.

BTST

Test a Bit

BTST

Operation: ~(<bit number>) OF Destination → Z

Assembler BTST Dn, <ea>
Syntax: BTST #<data>, <ea>

Attributes: Size = (Byte, Long)

Description: A bit in the destination operand is tested and the state of the specified bit is reflected in the Z condition code. If a data register is the destination, then the bit numbering is modulo 32, allowing bit manipulation on all bits in a data register. If a memory location is the destination, a byte is read from that location, and the bit operation performed using the bit number modulo 8 with zero referring to the least-signifcant bit. The bit number for this operation may be specified in two different ways:

1. Immediate — the bit number is specified in a second word of the instruction.
2. Register — the bit number is contained in a data register specified in the instruction.

Condition Codes:

X	N	Z	V	C
—	—	*	—	—

N   Not affected.
Z   Set if the bit tested is zero. Cleared otherwise.
V   Not affected.
C   Not affected.
X   Not affected.

Instruction Format (Bit Number Dynamic):

15	14	13	12	11	10	9	8	7	6	5	4	3	2	1	0
0	0	0	0	Register			1	0	0	Effective Address Mode			Register		

Instruction Fields (Bit Number Dynamic):

Register field — Specifies the data register whose content is the bit number.

Effective Address field — Specifies the destination location. Only data addressing modes are allowed as shown:

Addressing Mode	Mode	Register	Addressing Mode	Mode	Register
Dn*	000	register number	d(An, Xi)	110	register number
An	—	—	Abs.W	111	000
(An)	010	register number	Abs.L	111	001
(An) +	011	register number	d(PC)	111	010
− (An)	100	register number	d(PC, Xi)	111	011
d(An)	101	register number	Imm	111	100

*Long only; all others are byte only.

— Continued —

BTST

Test a Bit

BTST

Instruction Format (Bit Number Static):

15	14	13	12	11	10	9	8	7	6	5 4 3	2 1 0
0	0	0	0	1	0	0	0	0	0	Effective Address	
										Mode	Register
0	0	0	0	0	0	0	0	bit number			

Instruction Fields (Bit Number Static):

Effective Address field — Specifies the destination location. Only data addressing modes are allowed as shown:

Addressing Mode	Mode	Register	Addressing Mode	Mode	Register
Dn*	000	register number	d(An, Xi)	110	register number
An	—	—	Abs.W	111	000
(An)	010	register number	Abs.L	111	001
(An)+	011	register number	d(PC)	111	010
−(An)	100	register number	d(PC, Xi)	111	011
d(An)	101	register number	Imm	—	—

*Long only; all others are byte only.

bit number field — Specifies the bit number.

CHK

Check Register Against Bounds

Operation: If Dn<0 or Dn> (<ea>) then TRAP

Assembler
Syntax: CHK <ea>, Dn

Attributes: Size = (Word)

Description: The content of the low order word in the data register specified in the instruction is examined and compared to the upper bound. The upper bound
is a twos complement integer. If the register value is less than zero or
greater than the upper bound contained in the operand word, then the processor initiates exception processing. The vector number is generated to
reference the CHK instruction exception vector.

Condition Codes:

X	N	Z	V	C
—	*	U	U	U

N   Set if Dn<0; cleared if Dn> (<ea>). Undefined otherwise.
Z   Undefined.
V   Undefined.
C   Undefined.
X   Not affected.

Instruction Format:

15	14	13	12	11	10	9	8	7	6	5	4	3	2	1	0
0	1	0	0	Register			1	1	0	Effective Address Mode			Register		

Instruction Fields:

Register field — Specifies the data register whose content is checked.
Effective Address field — Specifies the upper bound operand word. Only
data addressing modes are allowed as shown:

Addressing Mode	Mode	Register	Addressing Mode	Mode	Register
Dn	000	register number	d(An, Xi)	110	register number
An	—	—	Abs.W	111	000
(An)	010	register number	Abs.L	111	001
(An)+	011	register number	d(PC)	111	010
−(An)	100	register number	d(PC, Xi)	111	011
d(An)	101	register number	Imm	111	100

CLR

Clear an Operand

Operation: 0 → Destination

**Assembler
Syntax:** CLR < ea >

Attributes: Size = (Byte, Word, Long)

Description: The destination is cleared to all zero bits. The size of the operation may be specified to be byte, word, or long.

Condition Codes:

```
X N Z V C
─ 0 1 0 0
```

N Always cleared.
Z Always set.
V Always cleared.
C Always cleared.
X Not affected.

Instruction Format:

15	14	13	12	11	10	9	8	7	6	5 4 3	2 1 0
0	1	0	0	0	0	1	0	Size		Effective Address Mode	Register

Instruction Fields:

Size field — Specifies the size of the operation:
   00 — byte operation.
   01 — word operation.
   10 — long operation.
Effective Address field — Specifies the destination location. Only data alterable addressing modes are allowed as shown:

Addressing Mode	Mode	Register	Addressing Mode	Mode	Register
Dn	000	register number	d(An, Xi)	110	register number
An	—	—	Abs.W	111	000
(An)	010	register number	Abs.L	111	001
(An) +	011	register number	d(PC)	—	—
− (An)	100	register number	d(PC, Xi)	—	—
d(An)	101	register number	Imm	—	—

Note: A memory destination is read before it is written to.

CMP

Compare

CMP

Operation: (Destination) – (Source)

**Assembler
Syntax:** CMP < ea >, Dn

Attributes: Size = (Byte, Word, Long)

Description: Subtract the source operand from the destination operand and set the condition codes according to the result; the destination location is not changed. The size of the operation may be specified to be byte, word, or long.

Condition Codes:

X	N	Z	V	C
—	*	*	*	*

N   Set if the result is negative. Cleared otherwise.
Z   Set if the result is zero. Cleared otherwise.
V   Set if an overflow is generated. Cleared otherwise.
C   Set if a borrow is generated. Cleared otherwise.
X   Not affected.

Instruction Format:

15	14	13	12	11	10	9	8	7	6	5	4	3	2	1	0
1	0	1	1	Register			Op-Mode			Effective Address Mode			Register		

Instruction Fields:

Register field — Specifies the destination data register.
Op-Mode field —

Byte	Word	Long	Operation
000	001	010	(< Dn >) – (< ea >)

Effective Address field — Specifies the source operand. All addressing modes are allowed as shown:

Addressing Mode	Mode	Register	Addressing Mode	Mode	Register
Dn	000	register number	d(An, Xi)	110	register number
An*	001	register number	Abs.W	111	000
(An)	010	register number	Abs.L	111	001
(An) +	011	register number	d(PC)	111	010
– (An)	100	register number	d(PC, Xi)	111	011
d(An)	101	register number	Imm	111	100

*Word and Long only.

Note: CMPA is used when the destination is an address register. CMPI is used when the source is immediate data. CMPM is used for memory to memory compares. Most assemblers automatically make this distinction.

426

CMPA   Compare Address   CMPA

Operation: (Destination) – (Source)

**Assembler
Syntax:**   CMPA <ea>, An

Attributes: Size = (Word, Long)

Description: Subtract the source operand from the destination address register and set the condition codes according to the result; the address register is not changed. The size of the operation may be specified to be word or long. Word length source operands are sign extended to 32 bit quantities before the operation is done.

Condition Code:

X	N	Z	V	C
—	*	*	*	*

N   Set if the result is negative. Cleared otherwise.
Z   Set if the result is zero. Cleared otherwise.
V   Set if an overflow is generated. Cleared otherwise.
C   Set if a borrow is generated. Cleared otherwise.
X   Not affected.

Instruction Format:

15	14	13	12	11	10	9	8	7	6	5	4	3	2	1	0
1	0	1	1	Register			Op-Mode			Effective Address Mode			Register		

Instruction Fields:

Register field — Specifies the destination address register.
Op-Mode field — Specifies the size of the operation:

011 — word operation. The source operand is sign-extended to a long operand and the operation is performed on the address register using all 32 bits.

111 — long operation.

Effective Address field — Specifies the source operand. All addressing modes are allowed as shown:

Addressing Mode	Mode	Register	Addressing Mode	Mode	Register
Dn	000	register number	d(An, Xi)	110	register number
An	001	register number	Abs.W	111	000
(An)	010	register number	Abs.L	111	001
(An) +	011	register number	d(PC)	111	010
– (An)	100	register number	d(PC, Xi)	111	011
d(An)	101	register number	Imm	111	100

CMPI Compare Immediate CMPI

Operation: (Destination) − Immediate Data

Assembler Syntax: CMPI #<data>, <ea>

Attributes: Size = (Byte, Word, Long)

Description: Subtract the immediate data from the destination operand and set the condition codes according to the result; the destination location is not changed. The size of the operation may be specified to be byte, word, or long. The size of the immediate data matches the operation size.

Condition Codes:

X	N	Z	V	C
—	*	*	*	*

N Set if the result is negative. Cleared otherwise.
Z Set if the result is zero. Cleared otherwise.
V Set if an overflow is generated. Cleared otherwise.
C Set if a borrow is generated. Cleared otherwise.
X Not affected.

Instruction Format:

15	14	13	12	11	10	9	8	7	6	5	4	3	2	1	0
0	0	0	0	1	1	0	0	Size		Effective Address Mode | Register					

Word Data (16 bits)	Byte Data (8 bits)

Long Data (32 bits, including previous word)

Instruction Fields:

Size field — Specifies the size of the operation:
  00 — byte operation.
  01 — word operation.
  10 — long operation.

Effective Address field — Specifies the destination operand. Only data alterable addressing modes are allowed as shown:

Addressing Mode	Mode	Register	Addressing Mode	Mode	Register
Dn	000	register number	d(An, Xi)	110	register number
An	—	—	Abs.W	111	000
(An)	010	register number	Abs.L	111	001
(An)+	011	register number	d(PC)	—	—
−(An)	100	register number	d(PC, Xi)	—	—
d(An)	101	register number	Imm	—	—

Immediate field — (Data immediately following the instruction):
  If size = 00, then the data is the low order byte of the immediate word.
  If size = 01, then the data is the entire immediate word.
  If size = 10, then the data is the next two immediate words.

CMPM

Compare Memory

CMPM

Operation: (Destination) – (Source)

**Assembler
Syntax:** CMPM (Ay) + , (Ax) +

Attributes: Size = (Byte, Word, Long)

Description: Subtract the source operand from the destination operand, and set the condition codes according to the results; the destination location is not changed. The operands are always addressed with the postincrement addressing mode using the address registers specified in the instruction. The size of the operation may be specified to be byte, word, or long.

Condition Codes:

X	N	Z	V	C
—	*	*	*	*

N   Set if the result is negative. Cleared otherwise.
Z   Set if the result is zero. Cleared otherwise.
V   Set if an overflow is generated. Cleared otherwise.
C   Set if a borrow is generated. Cleared otherwise.
X   Not affected.

Instruction Format:

15	14	13	12	11 10 9	8	7 6 5	4	3	2 1 0
1	0	1	1	Register Rx	1	Size	0	0	1 Register Ry

Instruction Fields:

Register Rx field — (always the destination) Specifies an address register for the postincrement addressing mode.
Size field — Specifies the size of the operation:
   00 — byte operation.
   01 — word operation.
   10 — long operation.
Register Ry field — (always the source) Specifies an address register for the postincrement addressing mode.

DBcc   Test Condition, Decrement, and Branch   # DBcc

Operation: If (condition false)
then Dn $- 1 \rightarrow$ Dn;
If Dn $\neq -1$
then PC $+ d \rightarrow$ PC
else PC $+ 2 \rightarrow$ PC (Fall through to next instruction)

**Assembler
Syntax:**   DBcc Dn, <label>

Attributes: Size = (Word)

Description: This instruction is a looping primitive of three parameters: a condition, a data register, and a displacement. The instruction first tests the condition to determine if the termination condition for the loop has been met, and if so, no operation is performed. If the termination condition is not true, the low order 16 bits of the counter data register are decremented by one. If the result is -1, the counter is exhausted and execution continues with the next instruction. If the result is not equal to -1, execution continues at the location indicated by the current value of PC plus the sign-extended 16-bit displacement. The value in PC is the current instruction location plus two "cc" may specify the following conditions:

CC	carry clear	0100	$\overline{C}$	LS	low or same	0011	$C + Z$
CS	carry set	0101	C	LT	less than	1101	$N \cdot \overline{V} + \overline{N} \cdot V$
EQ	equal	0111	Z	MI	minus	1011	N
F	false	0001	0	NE	not equal	0110	$\overline{Z}$
GE	greater or equal	1100	$N \cdot V + \overline{N} \cdot \overline{V}$	PL	plus	1010	$\overline{N}$
GT	greater than	1110	$N \cdot V \cdot \overline{Z} + \overline{N} \cdot \overline{V} \cdot \overline{Z}$	T	true	0000	1
HI	high	0010	$\overline{C} \cdot \overline{Z}$	VC	overflow clear	1000	$\overline{V}$
LE	less or equal	1111	$Z + N \cdot \overline{V} + \overline{N} \cdot V$	VS	overflow set	1001	V

Condition Codes: Not affected.

Instruction Format:

15	14	13	12	11	10	9	8	7	6	5	4	3	2	1	0
0	1	0	1	Condition				1	1	0	0	1	Register		
Displacement															

Instruction Fields:

Condition field — One of the sixteen conditions discussed in description.
Register field — Specifies the data register which is the counter.
Displacement field — Specifies the distance of the branch (in bytes).

Notes: 1. The terminating condition is like that defined by the UNTIL loop constructs of high-level languages. For example: DBMI can be stated as "decrement and branch until minus."

— Continued —

Notes: (Continued)

2.   Most assemblers accept DBRA for DBF for use when no condition is required for termination of a loop.

3.   There are two basic ways of entering a loop; at the beginning or by branching to the trailing DBcc instruction. If a loop structure terminated with DBcc is entered at the beginning, the control index count must be one less than the number of loop executions desired. This count is useful for indexed addressing modes and dynamically specified bit operations. However, when entering a loop by branching directly to the trailing DBcc instruction, the control index should equal the loop execution count. In this case, if a zero count occurs, the DBcc instruction will not branch causing complete bypass of the main loop.

DIVS

Signed Divide

DIVS

Operation: (Destination)/(Source) → Destination

**Assembler
Syntax:** DIVS <ea>, Dn

Attributes: Size = (Word)

Description: Divide the destination operand by the source operand and store the result in the destination. The destination operand is a long operand (32 bits) and the source operand is a word operand (16 bits). The operation is performed using signed arithmetic. The result is a 32-bit result such that:

1. The quotient is in the lower word (least significant 16-bits).
2. The remainder is in the upper word (most significant 16-bits).

The sign of the remainder is always the same as the dividend unless the remainder is equal to zero. Two special conditions may arise:

1. Division by zero causes a trap.
2. Overflow may be detected and set before completion of the instruction. If overflow is detected, the condition is flagged but the operands are unaffected.

Condition Codes:

X	N	Z	V	C
—	*	*	*	0

N Set if the quotient is negative. Cleared otherwise. Undefined if overflow.

Z Set if the quotient is zero. Cleared otherwise. Undefined if overflow.

V Set if division overflow is detected. Cleared otherwise.

C Always cleared.

X Not affected.

Instruction Format:

15	14	13	12	11 10 9	8	7	6	5 4 3 2 1 0
1	0	0	0	Register	1	1	1	Effective Address Mode | Register

Instruction Fields:

Register field — Specifies any of the eight data registers. This field always specifies the destination operand.

Effective Address field — Specifies the source operand. Only data addressing modes are allowed as shown:

Addressing Mode	Mode	Register	Addressing Mode	Mode	Register
Dn	000	register number	d(An, Xi)	110	register number
An	—	—	Abs.W	111	000
(An)	010	register number	Abs.L	111	001
(An)+	011	register number	d(PC)	111	010
−(An)	100	register number	d(PC, Xi)	111	011
d(An)	101	register number	Imm	111	100

Note: Overflow occurs if the quotient is larger than a 16-bit signed integer.

432

DIVU

Unsigned Divide

DIVU

Operation: (Destination)/(Source) → Destination

**Assembler
Syntax:** DIVU <ea>, Dn

Attributes: Size = (Word)

Description: Divide the destination operand by the source operand and store the result in the destination. The destination operand is a long operand (32 bits) and the source operand is a word (16 bit) operand. The operation is performed using unsigned arithmetic. The result is a 32-bit result such that:

1. The quotient is in the lower word (least significant 16 bits).
2. The remainder is in the upper word (most significant 16 bits).

Two special conditions may arise:

1. Division by zero causes a trap.
2. Overflow may be detected and set before completion of the instruction. If overflow is detected, the condition is flagged but the operands are unaffected.

Condition Codes:

X	N	Z	V	C
—	*	*	*	0

N   Set if the most significant bit of the quotient is set. Cleared otherwise. Undefined if overflow.
Z   Set if the quotient is zero. Cleared otherwise. Undefined if overflow.
V   Set if division overflow is detected. Cleared otherwise.
C   Always cleared.
X   Not affected.

Instruction Format:

15	14	13	12	11 10 9	8	7	6	5 4 3	2 1 0
1	0	0	0	Register	0	1	1	Effective Address Mode	Register

Instruction Fields:

Register field — specifies any of the eight data registers. This field always specifies the destination operand.

Effective Address field — Specifies the source operand. Only data addressing modes are allowed as shown:

Addressing Mode	Mode	Register	Addressing Mode	Mode	Register
Dn	000	register number	d(An, Xi)	110	register number
An	—	—	Abs.W	111	000
(An)	010	register number	Abs.L	111	001
(An) +	011	register number	d(PC)	111	010
− (An)	100	register number	d(PC, Xi)	111	011
d(An)	101	register number	Imm	111	100

Note: Overflow occurs if the quotient is larger than a 16-bit unsigned integer.

EOR

Exclusive OR Logical

EOR

Operation: (Source) ⊕ (Destination) → Destination

**Assembler
Syntax:** EOR Dn, <ea>

Attributes: Size = (Byte, Word, Long)

Description: Exclusive OR the source operand to the destination operand and store the result in the destination location. The size of the operation may be specified to be byte, word, or long. This operation is restricted to data registers as the source operand. The destination operand is specified in the effective address field.

Condition Codes:

X	N	Z	V	C
—	*	*	0	0

N   Set if the most significant bit of the result is set. Cleared otherwise.
Z   Set if the result is zero. Cleared otherwise.
V   Always cleared.
C   Always cleared.
X   Not affected.

Instruction Format:

15	14	13	12	11 10 9	8 7 6	5 4 3	2 1 0
1	0	1	1	Register	Op-Mode	Effective Address Mode	Register

Instruction Fields:

Register field — Specifies any of the eight data registers.
Op-Mode field —

Byte	Word	Long	Operation
100	101	110	(<ea>) ⊕ (<Dx>) → <ea>

Effective Address field — Specifies the destination operand. Only data alterable addressing modes are allowed as shown:

Addressing Mode	Mode	Register	Addressing Mode	Mode	Register
Dn	000	register number	d(An, Xi)	110	register number
An	—	—	Abs.W	111	000
(An)	010	register number	Abs.L	111	001
(An)+	011	register number	d(PC)	—	—
−(An)	100	register number	d(PC, Xi)	—	—
d(An)	101	register number	Imm	—	—

Note: Memory to data register operations are not allowed. EORI is used when the source is immediate data. Most assemblers automatically make this distinction.

434

EORI

Exclusive OR Immediate

Operation: Immediate Data ⊕ (Destination) → Destination

Assembler
Syntax: EORI #<data>, <ea>

Attributes: Size = (Byte, Word, Long)

Description: Exclusive OR the immediate data to the destination operand and store the result in the destination location. The size of the operation may be specified to be byte, word, or long. The immediate data matches the operation size.

Condition Codes:

X	N	Z	V	C
—	*	*	0	0

N   Set if the most significant bit of the result is set. Cleared otherwise.
Z   Set if the result is zero. Cleared otherwise.
V   Always cleared.
C   Always cleared.
X   Not affected.

Instruction Format:

15	14	13	12	11	10	9	8	7	6	5	4	3	2	1	0
0	0	0	0	1	0	1	0	Size		Effective Address Mode | Register					
Word Data (16 bits)								Byte Data (8 bits)							
Long Data (32 bits, including previous word)															

Instruction Fields:

Size field — Specifies the size of the operation:
00 — byte operation.
01 — word operation.
10 — long operation.

Effective Address field — Specifies the destination operand. Only data alterable addressing modes are allowed as shown:

Addressing Mode	Mode	Register	Addressing Mode	Mode	Register
Dn	000	register number	d(An, Xi)	110	register number
An	—	—	Abs.W	111	000
(An)	010	register number	Abs.L	111	001
(An) +	011	register number	d(PC)	—	—
− (An)	100	register number	d(PC, Xi)	—	—
d(An)	101	register number	Imm	—	—

Immediate field — (Data immediately following the instruction):
If size = 00, then the data is the low order byte of the immediate word.
If size = 01, then the data is the entire immediate word.
If size = 10, then the data is the next two immediate words.

435

EORI
to CCR

Exclusive OR Immediate to Condition Codes

EORI
to CCR

Operation: (Source) ⊕ CCR → CCR

Assembler
Syntax: EORI #xxx, CCR

Attributes: Size = (Byte)

Description: Exclusive OR the immediate operand with the condition codes and store the result in the low-order byte of the status register.

Condition Codes:

X N Z V C

*	*	*	*	*

N Changed if bit 3 of immediate operand is one. Unchanged otherwise.
Z Changed if bit 2 of immediate operand is one. Unchanged otherwise.
V Changed if bit 1 of immediate operand is one. Unchanged otherwise.
C Changed if bit 0 of immediate operand is one. Unchanged otherwise.
X Changed if bit 4 of immediate operand is one. Unchanged otherwise.

Instruction Format:

15	14	13	12	11	10	9	8	7	6	5	4	3	2	1	0
0	0	0	0	1	0	1	0	0	0	1	1	1	1	0	0
0	0	0	0	0	0	0	0	Byte Data (8 bits)							

EORI
to SR

Exclusive OR Immediate to the Status Register
(Privileged Instruction)

EORI
to SR

Operation: If supervisor state
then (Source) $\oplus$ SR $\rightarrow$ SR
else TRAP

Assembler
Syntax: EORI #xxx, SR

Attributes: Size = (Word)

Description: Exclusive OR the immediate operand with the contents of the status register and store the result in the status register. All bits of the status register are affected.

Condition Codes:

```
X  N  Z  V  C
```
*	*	*	*	*

N   Changed if bit 3 of immediate operand is one. Unchanged otherwise.
Z   Changed if bit 2 of immediate operand is one. Unchanged otherwise.
V   Changed if bit 1 of immediate operand is one. Unchanged otherwise.
C   Changed if bit 0 of immediate operand is one. Unchanged otherwise.
X   Changed if bit 4 of immediate operand is one. Unchanged otherwise.

Instruction Format:

15	14	13	12	11	10	9	8	7	6	5	4	3	2	1	0
0	0	0	0	1	0	1	0	0	1	1	1	1	1	0	0
Word Data (16 bits)															

EXG

Exchange Registers

EXG

Operation: Rx ⟷ Ry

**Assembler
Syntax:** EXG Rx, Ry

Attributes: Size = (Long)

Description: Exchange the contents of two registers. This exchange is always a long (32 bit) operation. Exchange works in three modes:
1. Exchange data registers.
2. Exchange address registers.
3. Exchange a data register and an address register.

Condition Codes: Not affected.

Instruction Format:

15	14	13	12	11 10 9	8	7 6 5 4 3	2 1 0
1	1	0	0	Register Rx	1	Op-Mode	Register Ry

Instruction Fields:

Register Rx field — Specifies either a data register or an address register depending on the mode. If the exchange is between data and address registers, this field always specifies the data register.

Op-Mode field — Specifies whether exchanging:
- 01000 — data registers.
- 01001 — address registers.
- 10001 — data register and address register.

Register Ry field — Specifies either a data register or an address register depending on the mode. If the exchange is between data and address registers, this field always specifies the address register.

EXT

Sign Extend

EXT

Operation: (Destination) Sign-extended → Destination

Assembler
Syntax: EXT Dn

Attributes: Size = (Word, Long)

Description: Extend the sign bit of a data register from a byte to a word or from a word to a long operand depending on the size selected. If the operation is word sized, bit [7] of the designated data register is copied to bits [15:8] of that data register. If the operation is long sized, bit [15] of the designated data register is copied to bits [31:16] of that data register.

Condition Codes:

X	N	Z	V	C
—	*	*	0	0

N   Set if the result is negative. Cleared otherwise.
Z   Set if the result is zero. Cleared otherwise.
V   Always cleared.
C   Always cleared.
X   Not affected.

Instruction Format:

15	14	13	12	11	10	9	8	7	6	5	4	3	2	1	0
0	1	0	0	1	0	0	Op-Mode			0	0	0	Register		

Instruction Fields:

Op-Mode Field — Specifies the size of the sign-extension operation:

010 — Sign-extend low order byte of data register to word.

011 — Sign-extend low order word of data register to long.

Register field — Specifies the data register whose content is to be sign-extended.

ILLEGAL   Illegal Instruction   ILLEGAL

Operation: PC→ – (SSP); SR→ – (SSP)
(Illegal Instruction Vector)→ PC

Attributes: None

Description: This bit pattern causes an illegal instruction exception. All other illegal instruction bit patterns are reserved for future extension of the instruction
set.

Condition Codes: Not affected.

Instruction Format:

15	14	13	12	11	10	9	8	7	6	5	4	3	2	1	0
0	1	0	0	1	0	1	0	1	1	1	1	1	1	0	0

JMP

Jump

JMP

Operation: Destination → PC

**Assembler
Syntax:** JMP <ea>

Attributes: Unsized

Description: Program execution continues at the effective address specified by the instruction. The address is specified by the control addressing modes.

Condition Codes: Not affected.

Instruction Format:

15	14	13	12	11	10	9	8	7	6	5 4 3	2 1 0
0	1	0	0	1	1	1	0	1	1	Effective Address Mode	Register

Instruction Fields:

Effective Address field — Specifies the address of the next instruction. Only control addressing modes are allowed as shown:

Addressing Mode	Mode	Register	Addressing Mode	Mode	Register
Dn	—	—	d(An, Xi)	110	register number
An	—	—	Abs.W	111	000
(An)	010	register number	Abs.L	111	001
(An)+	—	—	d(PC)	111	010
−(An)	—	—	d(PC, Xi)	111	011
d(An)	101	register number	Imm	—	—

JSR

Jump to Subroutine

Operation: PC→ – (SP); Destination→PC

**Assembler
Syntax:**   JSR < ea >

Attributes: Unsized

Description: The long word address of the instruction immediately following the JSR instruction is pushed onto the system stack. Program execution then continues at the address specifed in the instruction.

Condition Codes: Not affected.

Instruction Format:

15	14	13	12	11	10	9	8	7	6	5 4 3 2 1 0
0	1	0	0	1	1	1	0	1	0	Effective Address Mode | Register

Instruction Fields:

Effective Address field — Specifies the address of the next instruction. Only control addressing modes are allowed as shown:

Addressing Mode	Mode	Register	Addressing Mode	Mode	Register
Dn	—	—	d(An, Xi)	110	register number
An	—	—	Abs.W	111	000
(An)	010	register number	Abs.L	111	001
(An) +	—	—	d(PC)	111	010
– (An)	—	—	d(PC, Xi)	111	011
d(An)	101	register number	Imm	—	—

442

LEA   Load Effective Address   LEA

Operation: Destination → An

Assembler Syntax: LEA <ea>, An

Attributes: Size = (Long)

Description: The effective address is loaded into the specified address register. All 32 bits of the address register are affected by this instruction.

Condition Codes: Not affected.

Instruction Format:

15	14	13	12	11	10	9	8	7	6	5	4	3	2	1	0
0	1	0	0	Register			1	1	1	Effective Address Mode			Register		

Instruction Fields:

Register field — Specifies the address register which is to be loaded with the effective address.

Effective Address field — Specifies the address to be loaded into the address register. Only control addressing modes are allowed as shown:

Addressing Mode	Mode	Register	Addressing Mode	Mode	Register
Dn	—	—	d(An, Xi)	110	register number
An	—	—	Abs.W	111	000
(An)	010	register number	Abs.L	111	001
(An) +	—	—	d(PC)	111	010
– (An)	—	—	d(PC, Xi)	111	011
d(An)	101	register number	Imm	—	—

LINK

Link and Allocate

LINK

Operation: An → – (SP); SP → An; SP + d → SP

**Assembler
Syntax:** LINK An, #<displacement>

Attributes: Unsized

Description: The current content of the specified address register is pushed onto the stack. After the push, the address register is loaded from the updated stack pointer. Finally, the 16-bit sign-extended displacement is added to the stack pointer. The content of the address register occupies two words on the stack. A negative displacement is specified to allocate stack area.

Condition Codes: Not affected.

Instruction Format:

15	14	13	12	11	10	9	8	7	6	5	4	3	2	1	0
0	1	0	0	1	1	1	0	0	1	0	1	0	Register		
Displacement															

Instruction Fields:

Register field — Specifies the address register through which the link is to be constructed.

Displacement field — Specifies the twos complement integer which is to be added to the stack pointer.

Note: LINK and UNLK can be used to maintain a linked list of local data and parameter areas on the stack for nested subroutine calls.

LSL, LSR   Logical Shift   LSL, LSR

Operation: (Destination) Shifted by \<count\> → Destination

Assembler   LSd Dx, Dy
Syntax: LSd #\<data\>, Dy
            LSd \<ea\>

Attributes: Size = (Byte, Word, Long)

Description: Shift the bits of the operand in the direction specified. The carry bit receives the last bit shifted out of the operand. The shift count for the shifting of a register may be specified in two different ways:
1. Immediate — the shift count is specified in the instruction (shift range 1-8).
2. Register — the shift count is contained in a data register specified in the instruction.

The size of the operation may be specified to be byte, word, or long. The content of memory may be shifted one bit only and the operand size is restricted to a word.

For LSL, the operand is shifted left; the number of positions shifted is the shift count. Bits shifted out of the high order bit go to both the carry and the extend bits; zeroes are shifted into the low order bit.

LSL:

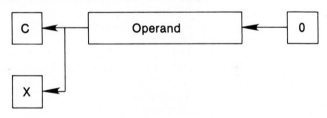

For LSR, the operand is shifted right; the number of positions shifted is the shift count. Bits shifted out of the low order bit go to both the carry and the extend bits; zeroes are shifted into the high order bit.

LSR:

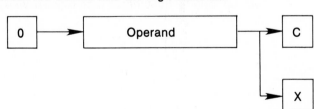

— Continued —

445

LSL, LSR   Logical Shift   # LSL, LSR

Condition Codes:

X	N	Z	V	C
*	*	*	0	*

N   Set if the result is negative. Cleared otherwise.
Z   Set if the result is zero. Cleared otherwise.
V   Always cleared.
C   Set according to the last bit shifted out of the operand. Cleared for a shift count of zero.
X   Set according to the last bit shifted out of the operand. Unaffected for a shift count of zero.

Instruction Format (Register Shifts):

15	14	13	12	11 10 9	8	7 6	5	4	3	2 1 0
1	1	1	0	Count/ Register	dr	Size	i/r	0	1	Register

Instruction Fields (Register Shifts):

Count/Register field —

If i/r = 0, the shift count is specified in this field. The values 0, 1-7 represent a range of 8, 1 to 7 respectively.

If i/r = 1, the shift count (modulo 64) is contained in the data register specified in this field.

dr field — Specifies the direction of the shift:

0 — shift right.

1 — shift left.

Size field — Specifies the size of the operation:

00 — byte operation.

01 — word operation.

10 — long operation.

i/r field —

If i/r = 0, specifies immediate shift count.

If i/r = 1, specifies register shift count.

Register field — Specifies a data register whose content is to be shifted.

— Continued —

LSL, LSR   Logical Shift   LSL,LSR

Instruction Format (Memory Shifts):

15	14	13	12	11	10	9	8	7	6	5 4 3 2 1 0
1	1	1	0	0	0	1	dr	1	1	Effective Address Mode | Register

Instruction Fields (Memory Shifts):

dr field — Specifies the direction of the shift:
0 — shift right.
1 — shift left.

Effective Address field — Specifies the operand to be shifted. Only memory alterable addressing modes are allowed as shown:

Addressing Mode	Mode	Register	Addressing Mode	Mode	Register
Dn	—	—	d(An, Xi)	110	register number
An	—	—	Abs.W	111	000
(An)	010	register number	Abs.L	111	001
(An)+	011	register number	d(PC)	—	—
−(An)	100	register number	d(PC, Xi)	—	—
d(An)	101	register number	Imm	—	—

MOVE
Move Data from Source to Destination
MOVE

Operation: (Source) → Destination

Assembler
Syntax: MOVE <ea>, <ea>

Attributes: Size = (Byte, Word, Long)

Description: Move the content of the source to the destination location. The data is examined as it is moved, and the condition codes set accordingly. The size of the operation may be specified to be byte, word, or long.

Condition Codes:

X	N	Z	V	C
—	*	*	0	0

N   Set if the result is negative. Cleared otherwise.
Z   Set if the result is zero. Cleared otherwise.
V   Always cleared.
C   Always cleared.
X   Not affected.

Instruction Format:

15 14	13 12	11 10 9	8 7 6	5 4 3	2 1 0
0 0	Size	Destination Register	Mode	Source Mode	Register

Instruction Fields:

Size field — Specifies the size of the operand to be moved:
01 — byte operation.
11 — word operation.
10 — long operation.
Destination Effective Address field — Specifies the destination location.
Only data alterable addressing modes are allowed as shown:

Addressing Mode	Mode	Register	Addressing Mode	Mode	Register
Dn	000	register number	d(An, Xi)	110	register number
An	—	—	Abs.W	111	000
(An)	010	register number	Abs.L	111	001
(An) +	011	register number	d(PC)	—	—
– (An)	100	register number	d(PC, Xi)	—	—
d(An)	101	register number	Imm	—	—

— Continued —

MOVE
Move Data from Source to Destination **MOVE**

Instruction Fields: (Continued)

Source Effective Address field — Specifies the source operand. All addressing modes are allowed as shown:

Addressing Mode	Mode	Register	Addressing Mode	Mode	Register
Dn	000	register number	d(An, Xi)	110	register number
An*	001	register number	Abs.W	111	000
(An)	010	register number	Abs.L	111	001
(An)+	011	register number	d(PC)	111	010
−(An)	100	register number	d(PC, Xi)	111	011
d(An)	101	register number	Imm	111	100

*For byte size operation, address register direct is not allowed.

Notes:
1. MOVEA is used when the destination is an address register. Most assemblers automatically make this distinction.
2. MOVEQ can also be used for certain operations on data registers.

MOVE
from CCR

Move from the
Condition Code Register

MOVE
from CCR

Operation: CCR → Destination

**Assembler
Syntax:** MOVE CCR, <ea>

Attributes: Size = (Word)

Description: The content of the status register is moved to the destination location. The source operand is a word, but only the low order byte contains the condition codes. The upper byte is all zeros.

Condition Codes: Not affected.

Instruction Format:

15	14	13	12	11	10	9	8	7	6	5	4	3	2	1	0
0	1	0	0	0	0	1	0	1	1	Effective Mode			Address Register		

Instruction Fields:

Effective Address field — Specifies the destination location.
Only data alterable addressing modes are allowed as shown:

Addressing Mode	Mode	Register
Dn	000	register number
An	—	—
(An)	010	register number
(An)+	011	register number
–(An)	100	register number
d(An)	101	register number

Addressing Mode	Mode	Register
d(An, Xi)	110	register number
Abs.W	111	000
Abs.L	111	001
d(PC)	—	—
d(PC, Xi)	—	—
Imm	—	—

Note: MOVE to CCR is a word operation. AND, OR, and EOR to CCR are byte operations.

MC68010

MOVE
to CCR

Move to Condition Codes

MOVE
to CCR

Operation: (Source) → CCR

Assembler
Syntax: MOVE < ea >, CCR

Attributes: Size = (Word)

Description: The content of the source operand is moved to the condition codes. The source operand is a word, but only the low order byte is used to update the condition codes. The upper byte is ignored.

Condition Codes:

X N Z V C

*	*	*	*	*

N   Set the same as bit 3 of the source operand.
Z   Set the same as bit 2 of the source operand.
V   Set the same as bit 1 of the source operand.
C   Set the same as bit 0 of the source operand.
X   Set the same as bit 4 of the source operand.

Instruction Format:

15	14	13	12	11	10	9	8	7	6	5	4	3	2	1	0
0	1	0	0	0	1	0	0	1	1	Effective Address Mode | Register					

Instruction Fields:

Effective Address field — Specifies the location of the source operand. Only data addressing modes are allowed as shown:

Addressing Mode	Mode	Register	Addressing Mode	Mode	Register
Dn	000	register number	d(An, Xi)	110	register number
An	—	—	Abs.W	111	000
(An)	010	register number	Abs.L	111	001
(An) +	011	register number	d(PC)	111	010
− (An)	100	register number	d(PC, Xi)	111	011
d(An)	101	register number	Imm	111	100

Note: MOVE to CCR is a word operation. AND, OR, and EOR to CCR are byte operations.

MOVE
to SR

MOVE
to SR

Operation: If supervisor state
then (Source) → SR
else TRAP

Assembler
Syntax: MOVE <ea>, SR

Attributes: Size = (Word)

Description: The content of the source operand is moved to the status register. The source operand is a word and all bits of the status register are affected.

Condition Codes: Set according to the source operand.

Instruction Format:

15	14	13	12	11	10	9	8	7	6	5	4	3	2	1	0
0	1	0	0	0	1	1	0	1	1	\multicolumn{3}{c}{Effective Address}			

Effective Address: Mode | Register

Instruction Fields:

Effective Address field — Specifies the location of the source operand.
Only data addressing modes are allowed as shown:

Addressing Mode	Mode	Register	Addressing Mode	Mode	Register
Dn	000	register number	d(An, Xi)	110	register number
An	—	—	Abs.W	111	000
(An)	010	register number	Abs.L	111	001
(An) +	011	register number	d(PC)	111	010
– (An)	100	register number	d(PC, Xi)	111	011
d(An)	101	register number	Imm	111	100

MOVE from SR

Move from the Status Register

MOVE from SR

Operation: SR → Destination

**Assembler
Syntax:** MOVE SR, <ea>

Attributes: Size = (Word)

Description: The content of the status register is moved to the destination location. The operand size is a word.

Condition Codes: Not affected.

Instruction Format:

15	14	13	12	11	10	9	8	7	6	5 4 3	2 1 0
0	1	0	0	0	0	0	0	1	1	Effective Address Mode	Register

Instruction Fields:

Effective Address field — Specifies the destination location. Only data alterable addressing modes are allowed as shown:

Addressing Mode	Mode	Register	Addressing Mode	Mode	Register
Dn	000	register number	d(An, Xi)	110	register number
An	—	—	Abs.W	111	000
(An)	010	register number	Abs.L	111	001
(An)+	011	register number	d(PC)	—	—
−(An)	100	register number	d(PC, Xi)	—	—
d(An)	101	register number	Imm	—	—

Note: A memory destination is read before it is written to.

MOVE
from SR

Move from the Status Register
(Privileged Instruction)

MOVE
from SR

Operation: If supervisor state
then SR → Destination
else TRAP

Assembler
Syntax: MOVE SR, <ea>

Attributes: Size = (Word)

Description: The content of the status register is moved to the destination location. The operand size is a word.

Condition Codes: Not affected.

Instruction Format:

15	14	13	12	11	10	9	8	7	6	5	4	3	2	1	0
0	1	0	0	0	0	0	0	1	1	Effective Address					

Effective Address: Mode | Register

Instruction Fields:

Effective Address field — Specifies the destination location. Only data alterable addressing modes are allowed as shown:

Addressing Mode	Mode	Register	Addressing Mode	Mode	Register
Dn	000	register number	d(An, Xi)	110	register number
An	—	—	Abs.W	111	000
(An)	010	register number	Abs.L	111	001
(An) +	011	register number	d(PC)	—	—
– (An)	100	register number	d(PC, Xi)	—	—
d(An)	101	register number	Imm	—	—

NOTE: Use the MOVE from CCR instruction to access the conditon codes.

MC68010

454

MOVE
USP

**Move User Stack Pointer
(Privileged Instruction)**

MOVE
USP

Operation: If supervisor state
          then USP → An;
              An → USP
          else TRAP

Assembler   MOVE USP, An
Syntax: MOVE An, USP

Attributes: Size = (Long)

Description: The contents of the user stack pointer are transferred to or from the specified address register.

Condition Codes: Not affected.

Instruction Format:

15	14	13	12	11	10	9	8	7	6	5	4	3	2	1	0
0	1	0	0	1	1	1	0	0	1	1	0	dr	Register		

Instruction Fields:

    dr field — Specifies the direction of transfer:
        0 — transfer the address register to the USP.
        1 — transfer the USP to the address register.
    Register field — Specifies the address register to or from which the user stack pointer is to be transferred.

MOVEA   Move Address   MOVEA

Operation: (Source) → Destination

**Assembler
Syntax:**   MOVEA <ea>, An

Attributes: Size = (Word, Long)

Description: Move the content of the source to the destination address register. The size of the operation may be specified to be word or long. Word size source operands are sign extended to 32 bit quantities before the operation is done.

Condition Codes: Not affected.

Instruction Format:

15	14	13 12	11 10 9	8	7	6	5 4 3	2 1 0
0	0	Size	Destination Register	0	0	1	Source Mode	Register

Instruction Fields:

Size field — Specifies the size of the operand to be moved:

11 — Word operation. The source operand is sign-extended to a long operand and all 32 bits are loaded into the address register.

10 — Long operation.

Destination Register field — Specifies the destination address register.

Source Effective Address field — Specifies the location of the source operand. All addressing modes are allowed as shown:

Addressing Mode	Mode	Register	Addressing Mode	Mode	Register
Dn	000	register number	d(An, Xi)	110	register number
An	001	register number	Abs.W	111	000
(An)	010	register number	Abs.L	111	001
(An) +	011	register number	d(PC)	111	010
− (An)	100	register number	d(PC, Xi)	111	011
d(An)	101	register number	Imm	111	100

456

MOVEC Move to/from Control Register MOVEC
(Privileged Instruction)

Operation: If supervisor state
  then Rc → Rn, Rn → Rc
  else TRAP

Assembler MOVEC Rc, Rn
Syntax: MOVEC Rn, Rc

Attributes: Size = (Long)

Description: Copy the contents of the specified control register to the specified general register or copy the contents of the specified general register to the specified control register. This is always a 32-bit transfer even though the control register may be implemented with fewer bits. Unimplemented bits are read as zeros.

Condition Codes: Not affected.

Instruction Format:

15	14	13	12	11	10	9	8	7	6	5	4	3	2	1	0
0	1	0	0	1	1	1	0	0	1	1	1	1	0	1	dr

| A/D | Register | | | Control Register | | | | | | | | | | | |

Instruction Fields:

dr field — Specifies the direction of the transfer:
  0—control register to general register.
  1—general register to control register.
A/D field — Specifies the type of general register:
  0—data register.
  1—address register.
Register field — Specifies the register number.
Control Register field — Specifies the control register.
Currently defined control registers are:

Binary	Hex	Name/Function
0000 0000 0000	000	Source Function Code (SFC) register.
0000 0000 0001	001	Destination Function Code (DFC) register.
1000 0000 0000	800	User Stack Pointer.
1000 0000 0001	801	Vector Base Register for exception vector table.

All other codes cause an illegal instruction exception.

MC68010

457

MOVEM   Move Multiple Registers   MOVEM

Operation: Registers → Destination
(Source) → Registers

Assembler MOVEM <register list>, <ea>
Syntax: MOVEM <ea>, <register list>

Attributes: Size = (Word, Long)

Description: Selected registers are transferred to or from consecutive memory location starting at the location specified by the effective address. A register is transferred if the bit corresponding to that register is set in the mask field. The instruction selects how much of each register is transferred; either the entire long word can be moved or just the low order word. In the case of a word transfer to the registers, each word is sign-extended to 32 bits (also data registers) and the resulting long word loaded into the associated register.

MOVEM allows three forms of address modes: the control modes, the predecrement mode, or the postincrement mode. If the effective address is in one of the control modes, the registers are transferred starting at the specified address and up through higher addresses. The order of transfer is from data register 0 to data register 7, then from address register 0 to address register 7.

If the effective address is in the predecrement mode, only a register to memory operation is allowed. The registers are stored starting at the specified address minus two and down through lower addresses. The order of storing is from address register 7 to address register 0, then from data register 7 to data register 0. The decremented address register is updated to contain the address of the last word stored.

If the effective address is in the postincrement mode, only a memory to register operation is allowed. The registers are loaded starting at the specified address and up through higher addresses. The order of loading is the same as for the control mode addressing. The incremented address register is updated to contain the address of the last word loaded plus two.

Condition Codes: Not affected.

Instruction Format:

15	14	13	12	11	10	9	8	7	6	5	4	3	2	1	0
0	1	0	0	1	dr	0	0	1	Sz	Effective Address Mode			Register		
Register List Mask															

458

— Continued —

MOVEM Move Multiple Registers MOVEM

Instruction Fields:

dr field:

Specifies the direction of the transfer:

0 — register to memory

1 — memory to register.

Sz field — Specifies the size of the registers being transferred:

0 — word transfer.

1 — long transfer.

Effective Address field — Specifies the memory address to or from which the registers are to be moved.

For register to memory transfer, only control alterable addressing modes or the predecrement addressing mode are allowed as shown:

Addressing Mode	Mode	Register	Addressing Mode	Mode	Register
Dn	—	—	d(An, Xi)	110	register number
An	—	—	Abs.W	111	000
(An)	010	register number	Abs.L	111	001
(An)+	—	—	d(PC)	—	—
−(An)	100	register number	d(PC, Xi)	—	—
d(An)	101	register number	Imm	—	—

For memory to register transfer, only control addressing modes or the postincrement addressing mode are allowed as shown:

Addressing Mode	Mode	Register	Addressing Mode	Mode	Register
Dn	—	—	d(An, Xi)	110	register number
An	—	—	Abs.W	111	000
(An)	010	register number	Abs.L	111	001
(An)+	011	register number	d(PC)	111	010
−(An)	—	—	d(PC, Xi)	111	011
d(An)	101	register number	Imm	—	—

Register List Mask field — Specifies which registers are to be transferred. The low order bit corresponds to the first register to be transferred; the high bit corresponds to the last register to be transferred. Thus, both for control modes and for the postincrement mode addresses, the mask correspondence is

15	14	13	12	11	10	9	8	7	6	5	4	3	2	1	0
A7	A6	A5	A4	A3	A2	A1	A0	D7	D6	D5	D4	D3	D2	D1	D0

while for the predecrement mode addresses, the mask correspondence is

15	14	13	12	11	10	9	8	7	6	5	4	3	2	1	0
D0	D1	D2	D3	D4	D5	D6	D7	A0	A1	A2	A3	A4	A5	A6	A7

Note: An extra read bus cycle occurs for memory operands. This amounts to a memory word at one address higher than expected being addressed during operation.

MOVEP Move Peripheral Data MOVEP

Operation: (Source) → Destination

Assembler MOVEP Dx, d(Ay)
Syntax: MOVEP d(Ay), Dx

Attributes: Size = (Word, Long)

Description: Data is transferred between a data register and alternate bytes of memory, starting at the location specified and incrementing by two. The high order byte of the data register is transferred first and the low order byte is transferred last. The memory address is specified using the address register indirect plus displacement addressing mode. If the address is even, all the transfers are made on the high order half of the data bus; if the address is odd, all the transfers are made on the low order half of the data bus.

Example: Long transfer to/from an even address.

Byte organization in register

31 24	23 16	15 8	7 0
hi-order	mid-upper	mid-lower	low-order

Byte organization in memory (low address at top)

15 14 13 12 11 10 9 8	7 6 5 4 3 2 1 0
hi-order	
mid-upper	
mid-lower	
low-order	

Example: Word transfer to/from an odd address.

Byte organization in register

31 24	23 16	15 8	7 0
		hi-order	low-order

Byte organization in memory (low address at top)

15 14 13 12 11 10 9 8	7 6 5 4 3 2 1 0
	hi-order
	low-order

Condition Codes: Not affected.

— Continued —

MOVEP   Move Peripheral Data   MOVEP

Instruction Format:

15	14	13	12	11	10	9	8	7	6	5	4	3	2	1	0
0	0	0	0	Data Register			Op-Mode			0	0	1	Address Register		
Displacement															

Instruction Fields:

Data Register field — Specifies the data register to or from which the data is to be transferred.

Op-Mode field — Specifies the direction and size of the operation:

100 — transfer word from memory to register.

101 — transfer long from memory to register.

110 — transfer word from register to memory.

111 — transfer long from register to memory.

Address Register field — Specifies the address register which is used in the address register indirect plus displacement addressing mode.

Displacement field — Specifies the displacement which is used in calculating the operand address.

461

MOVEQ   Move Quick   MOVEQ

Operation: Immediate Data → Destination

**Assembler
Syntax:**   MOVEQ #<data>, Dn

Attributes: Size = (Long)

Description: Move immediate data to a data register. The data is contained in an 8-bit field within the operation word. The data is sign-extended to a long operand and all 32 bits are transferred to the data register.

Condition Codes:

X N Z V C

—	*	*	0	0

N   Set if the result is negative. Cleared otherwise.
Z   Set if the result is zero. Cleared otherwise.
V   Always cleared.
C   Always cleared.
X   Not affected.

Instruction Format:

15	14	13	12	11	10	9	8	7	6	5	4	3	2	1	0
0	1	1	1	Register			0	Data							

Instruction Fields:

Register field — Specifies the data register to be loaded.
Data field — 8 bits of data which are sign extended to a long operand.

MOVES
Move to/from Address Space
(Privileged Instruction)
MOVES

Operation: If supervisor state
    then Rn → Destination <DFC>
    Source <SFC> → Rn
    else TRAP

Assembler   MOVES Rn, <ea>
Syntax: MOVES <ea>, Rn

Attributes: Size = (Byte, Word, Long)

Description: Move the byte, word, or long operand from the specified general register to a location within the address space specified by the destination function code (DFC) register. Or, move the byte, word, or long operand from a location within the address space specified by the source function code (SFC) register to the specified general register.

    If the destination is a data register, the source operand replaces the corresponding low-order bits of the that data register. If the destination is an address register, the source operand is sign-extended to 32 bits and then loaded into that address register.

Condition Codes: Not affected.

Instruction Format:

15	14	13	12	11	10	9	8	7	6	5	4	3	2	1	0
0	0	0	0	1	1	1	0	Size		Effective Address					
A/D	Register		dr	0	0	0	0	0	0	0	0	0	0	0	0

Instruction Fields:

    Size field — Specifies the size of the operation:
        00—byte operation.
        01—word operation.
        10—long operation.

    A/D field — Specifies the type of general register:
        0—data register.
        1—address register.
    Register field — Specifies the register number.
    dr field — Specifies the direction of the transfer:
        0—from <ea> to general register.
        1—from general register to <ea>.

MC68010

MOVES

**Move to/from Address Space
(Privileged Instruction)**

MOVES

Instruction Fields: (continued)

Effective Address field — Specifies the source or destination location within the alternate address space. Only alterable memory addressing modes are allowed as shown:

Addressing Mode	Mode	Register
Dn	—	—
An	—	—
(An)	010	register number
(An)+	011	register number
–(An)	100	register number
d(An)	101	register number

Addressing Mode	Mode	Register
d(An, Xi)	110	register number
Abs.W	111	000
Abs.L	111	001
d(PC)	—	—
d(PC, Xi)	—	—
Imm	—	—

ORI
to CCR

ORI
to CCR

Operation: (Source) v CCR → CCR

**Assembler
Syntax:** ORI #xxx, CCR

Attributes: Size = (Byte)

Description: Inclusive OR the immediate operand with the condition codes and store the result in the low-order byte of the status register.

Condition Codes:

X N Z V C

*	*	*	*	*

N   Set if bit 3 of immediate operand is one. Unchanged otherwise.
Z   Set if bit 2 of immediate operand is one. Unchanged otherwise.
V   Set if bit 1 of immediate operand is one. Unchanged otherwise.
C   Set if bit 0 of immediate operand is one. Unchanged otherwise.
X   Set if bit 4 of immediate operand is one. Unchanged otherwise.

Instruction Format:

15	14	13	12	11	10	9	8	7	6	5	4	3	2	1	0
0	0	0	0	0	0	0	0	0	0	1	1	1	1	0	0
0	0	0	0	0	0	0	0	Byte Data (8 bits)							

ORI
to SR

ORI
to SR

Inclusive OR Immediate to the Status Register
(Privileged Instruction)

Operation: If supervisor state
              then (Source) v SR → SR
              else TRAP

Assembler
Syntax: ORI #xxx, SR

Attributes: Size = (Word)

Description: Inclusive OR the immediate operand with the contents of the status
              register and store the result in the status register. All bits of the status
              register are affected.

Condition Codes:

X	N	Z	V	C
*	*	*	*	*

N   Set if bit 3 of immediate operand is one. Unchanged otherwise.
Z   Set if bit 2 of immediate operand is one. Unchanged otherwise.
V   Set if bit 1 of immediate operand is one. Unchanged otherwise.
C   Set if bit 0 of immediate operand is one. Unchanged otherwise.
X   Set if bit 4 of immediate operand is one. Unchanged otherwise.

Instruction Format:

15	14	13	12	11	10	9	8	7	6	5	4	3	2	1	0
0	0	0	0	0	0	0	0	0	1	1	1	1	1	0	0
Word Data (16 bits)																

476

PEA

Push Effective Address

PEA

Operation: Destination → − (SP)

**Assembler
Syntax:** PEA <ea>

Attributes: Size = (Long)

Description: The effective address is computed and pushed onto the stack. A long word address is pushed onto the stack.

Condition Codes: Not affected.

Instruction Format:

15	14	13	12	11	10	9	8	7	6	5 4 3	2 1 0
0	1	0	0	1	0	0	0	0	1	Effective Address Mode	Register

Instruction Fields:

Effective Address field — Specifies the address to be pushed onto the stack. Only control addressing modes are allowed as shown:

Addressing Mode	Mode	Register	Addressing Mode	Mode	Register
Dn	—	—	d(An, Xi)	110	register number
An	—	—	Abs.W	111	000
(An)	010	register number	Abs.L	111	001
(An) +	—	—	d(PC)	111	010
− (An)	—	—	d(PC, Xi)	111	011
d(An)	101	register number	Imm	—	—

RESET

Reset External Devices
(Privileged Instruction)

Operation: If supervisor state
  then Assert RESET Line
  else TRAP

Assembler
Syntax: RESET

Attributes: Unsized

Description: The reset line is asserted causing all external devices to be reset. The processor state, other than the program counter, is unaffected and execution continues with the next instruction.

Condition Codes: Not affected.

Instruction Format:

15	14	13	12	11	10	9	8	7	6	5	4	3	2	1	0
0	1	0	0	1	1	1	0	0	1	1	1	0	0	0	0

ROL
ROR

Rotate (without Extend)

ROL
ROR

Operation: (Destination) Rotated by <count> → Destination

Assembler
Syntax:
ROd Dx, Dy
ROd #<data>, Dy
ROd <ea>

Attributes: Size = (Byte, Word, Long)

Description: Rotate the bits of the operand in the direction specified. The extend bit is not included in the rotation. The shift count for the rotation of a register may be specified in two different ways:

1. Immediate — the shift count is specified in the instruction (shift range, 1-8).
2. Register — the shift count is contained in a data register specified in the instruction.

The size of the operation may be specified to be byte, word, or long. The content of memory may be rotated one bit only and the operand size is restricted to a word.

For ROL, the operand is rotated left; the number of positions shifted is the shift count. Bits shifted out of the high order bit go to both the carry bit and back into the low order bit. The extend bit is not modified or used.

ROL:

For ROR, the operand is rotated right; the number of position shifted is the shift count. Bits shifted out of the low order bit go to both the carry bit and back into the high order bit. The extend bit is not modified or used.

ROR:

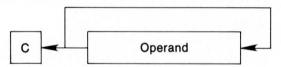

Condition Codes:

X	N	Z	V	C
—	*	*	0	*

N   Set if the most significant bit of the result is set. Cleared otherwise.
Z   Set if the result is zero. Cleared otherwise.
V   Always cleared.
C   Set according to the last bit shfited out of the operand. Cleared for a shift count of zero.
X   Not affected.

— Continued —

ROL
ROR

ROL
ROR

Instruction Format (Register Rotate):

15	14	13	12	11	10	9	8	7	6	5	4	3	2	1	0
1	1	1	0	Count/Register			dr	Size		i/r	1	1	Register		

Instruction Fields (Register Rotate):

Count/Register field —

if i/r = 0, the rotate count is specified in this field. The values 0, 1-7 represent a range of 8, 1 to 7 respectively.

If i/r = 1, the rotate count (modulo 64) is contained in the data register specified in this field.

dr field — Specifies the direction of the rotate:

0 — rotate right.

1 — rotate left.

Size field — Specifies the size of the operation:

00 — byte operation.

01 — word operation.

10 — long operation.

i/r field —

If i/r = 0, specifies immediate rotate count.

If i/r = 1, specifies register rotate count.

Register field — Specifies a data register whose content is to be rotated.

Instruction Format (Memory Rotate):

15	14	13	12	11	10	9	8	7	6	5	4	3	2	1	0
1	1	1	0	0	1	1	dr	1	1	Effective Address Mode			Register		

Instruction Fields (Memory Rotate):

dr field — Specifies the direction of the rotate:

0 — rotate right

1 — rotate left.

Effective Address field — Specifies the operand to be rotated. Only memory alterable addressing modes are allowed as shown:

Addressing Mode	Mode	Register	Addressing Mode	Mode	Register
Dn	—	—	d(An, Xi)	110	register number
An	—	—	Abs.W	111	000
(An)	010	register number	Abs.L	111	001
(An)+	011	register number	d(PC)	—	—
−(An)	100	register number	d(PC, Xi)	—	—
d(An)	101	register number	Imm	—	—

480

Rotate with Extend

Operation: (Destination) Rotated by < count > → Destination

Assembler
Syntax:
ROXd Dx, Dy
ROXd #<data>, Dy
ROXd <ea>

Attributes: Size = (Byte, Word, Long)

Description: Rotate the bits of the destination operand in the direction specified. The extend bit is included in the rotation. The shift count for the rotation of a register may be specified in two different ways:

1. Immediate — the shift count is specified in the instruction (shift range, 1-8).
2. Register — the shift count is contained in a data register specified in the instruction.

The size of the operation may be specified to be byte, word, or long. The content of memory may be rotated one bit only and the operand size is restricted to a word.

For ROXL, the operand is rotated left; the number of positions shifted is the shift count. Bits shifted out of the high order bit go to both the carry and extend bits; the previous value of the extend bit is shifted into the low order bit.

ROXL:

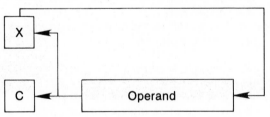

For ROXR, the operand is rotated right; the number of positions shifted is the shift count. Bits shifted out of the low order bit go to both the carry and extend bits; the previous value of the extend bit is shifted into the high order bit.

ROXR:

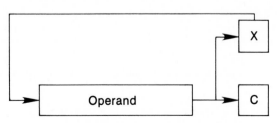

— Continued —

ROXL
ROXR

Rotate with Extend

ROXL
ROXR

Condition Codes:

X	N	Z	V	C
*	*	*	0	*

N   Set if the most significant bit of the result is set. Cleared otherwise.
Z   Set if the result is zero. Cleared otherwise.
V   Always cleared.
C   Set according to the last bit shifted out of the operand. Set to the value of the extend bit for a shift count of zero.
X   Set according to the last bit shifted out of the operand. Unaffected for a shift count of zero.

Instruction Format (Register Rotate):

15	14	13	12	11 10 9	8	7 6	5	4	3	2 1 0
1	1	1	0	Count/ Register	dr	Size	i/r	1	0	Register

Instruction Fields (Register Rotate):

Count/Register field:

If i/r = 0, the rotate count is specified in this field. The values 0, 1-7 represent range of 8, 1 to 7 respectively.

If i/r = 1, the rotate count (modulo 64) is contained in the data register specified in this field.

dr field — Specifies the direction of the rotate:

0 — rotate right.
1 — rotate left.

Size field — Specifies the size of the operation:

00 — byte operation.
01 — word operation.
10 — long operation.

i/r field —

If i/r = 0, specifies immediate rotate count.
If i/r = 1, specifies register rotate count.

Register field — Specifies a data register whose content is to be rotated.

— Continued —

ROXL
ROXR

Rotate with Extend

ROXL
ROXR

Instruction Format (Memory Rotate):

15	14	13	12	11	10	9	8	7	6	5 4 3	2 1 0
1	1	1	0	0	1	0	dr	1	1	Effective Address Mode	Register

Instruction Fields (Memory Rotate):

dr field — Specifies the direction of the rotate:

0 — rotate right.

1 — rotate left.

Effective Address field — Specifies the operand to be rotated. Only memory alterable addressing modes are allowed as shown:

Addressing Mode	Mode	Register	Addressing Mode	Mode	Register
Dn	—	—	d(An, Xi)	110	register number
An	—	—	Abs.W	111	000
(An)	010	register number	Abs.L	111	001
(An)+	011	register number	d(PC)	—	—
−(An)	100	register number	d(PC, Xi)	—	—
d(An)	101	register number	Imm	—	—

RTD

RTD

Return and Deallocate Parameters

Operation: (SP) + → PC; SP + d → SP

**Assembler
Syntax:** RTD #<displacement>

Attributes: Unsized

Description: The program counter is pulled from the stack. The previous program counter value is lost. After the program counter is read from the stack, the displacement value is sign-extended to 32 bits and added to the stack pointer.

Condition Codes: Not affected.

Instruction Format:

15	14	13	12	11	10	9	8	7	6	5	4	3	2	1	0
0	1	0	0	1	1	1	0	0	1	1	1	0	1	0	0
Displacement															

Instruction Field:

Displacement field — Specifies the twos complement integer which is to be sign-extended and added to the stack pointer.

MC68010

484

RTE

Operation: If supervisor state
then (SP) + → SR; (SP) + → PC
else TRAP

Assembler
Syntax: RTE

Attributes: Unsized

Description: The status register and program counter are pulled from the system stack. The previous status register and program counter are lost. All bits in the status register are affected.

Condition Codes: Set according to the content of the word on the stack.

Instruction Format:

15	14	13	12	11	10	9	8	7	6	5	4	3	2	1	0
0	1	0	0	1	1	1	0	0	1	1	1	0	0	1	1

RTE

**Return from Exception
(Privileged Instruction)**

Operation: If supervisor state
        then (SP) + → SR; (SP) + → PC
      If (SP) + = long format
        then full restore
      else TRAP

**Assembler
Syntax:**   RTE

Attributes: Unsized

Description: The status register and program counter are pulled from the system stack. The previous status register and program counter are lost. The vector offset word is also pulled from the stack and the format field is examined to determine the amount of information to be restored.

Condition Codes: Set according to the content of the word on the stack.

Instruction Format:

15	14	13	12	11	10	9	8	7	6	5	4	3	2	1	0
0	1	0	0	1	1	1	0	0	1	1	1	0	0	1	1

Vector Offset Word Format:

15	12	11	10	9	0
Format		0	0	Vector Offset	

Vector Offset Word Format Fields:

Format Field: — Specifies the amount of information to be restored.
    0000 — Short. Four words are to be removed from the top of the stack.
    1000 — Long. Twenty-nine words are to be removed from the top of the stack.
    Any Other
      Pattern — Error. The processor takes the format error exception.

MC68010

486

RTR

Operation: (SP) + → CC; (SP) + → PC

**Assembler
Syntax:** RTR

Attributes: Unsized

Description: The condition codes and program counter are pulled from the stack. The previous condition codes and program counter are lost. The supervisor portion of the status register is unaffected.

Condition Codes: Set according to the content of the word on the stack.

Instruction Format:

15	14	13	12	11	10	9	8	7	6	5	4	3	2	1	0
0	1	0	0	1	1	1	0	0	1	1	1	0	1	1	1

RTS

RTS

Operation: $(SP) + \rightarrow PC$

**Assembler
Syntax:** RTS

Attributes: Unsized

Description: The program counter is pulled from the stack. The previous program counter is lost.

Condition Codes: Not affected.

Instruction Format:

15	14	13	12	11	10	9	8	7	6	5	4	3	2	1	0
0	1	0	0	1	1	1	0	0	1	1	1	0	1	0	1

SBCD   Subtract Decimal with Extend   SBCD

Operation: $(Destination)_{10} - (Source)_{10} - X \rightarrow Destination$

Assembler
Syntax:
SBCD Dy, Dx
SBCD $-(Ay)$, $-(Ax)$

Attributes: Size = (Byte)

Description: Subtract the source operand from the destination operand along with the extend bit and store the result in the destination location. The subtraction is performed using binary coded decimal arithmetic. The operands may be addressed in two different ways:

1. Data register to data register: The operands are contained in the data registers specified in the instruction.
2. Memory to memory: The operands are addressed with the predecrement addressing mode using the address registers specified in the instruction.

This operation is a byte operation only.

Condition Codes:

X	N	Z	V	C
*	U	*	U	*

N   Undefined.
Z   Cleared if the result is non-zero. Unchanged otherwise.
V   Undefined.
C   Set if a borrow (decimal) is generated. Cleared otherwise.
X   Set the same as the carry bit.

NOTE
Normally the Z condition code bit is set via programming before the start of an operation. This allows successful tests for zero results upon completion of multiple-precision operations.

Instruction Format:

15	14	13	12	11 10 9	8	7	6	5	4	3	2 1 0
1	0	0	0	Register Rx	1	0	0	0	0	R/M	Register Ry

Instruction Fields:

Register Rx field — Specifies the destination register:
If R/M = 0, specifies a data register.
If R/M = 1, specifies an address register for the prececrement addressing mode.
R/M field — Specifies the operand addressing mode:
0 — The operation is data register to data register.
1 — The operation is memory to memory.
Register Ry field — Specifies the source register:
If R/M = 0, specifies a data register.
If R/M = 1, specifies an address register for the predecrement addressing mode.

Scc

Set According to Condition

Scc

Operation: If (Condition True)
then 1s → Destination
else 0s → Destination

**Assembler
Syntax:** Scc <ea>

Attributes: Size = (Byte)

Description: The specified condition code is tested; if the condition is true, the byte specified by the effective address is set to TRUE (all ones), otherwise that byte is set to FALSE (all zeroes). "cc" may specify the following conditions:

CC	carry clear	0100	$\overline{C}$		LS	low or same	0011	$C + Z$
CS	carry set	0101	C		LT	less than	1101	$N \cdot \overline{V} + \overline{N} \cdot V$
EQ	equal	0111	Z		MI	minus	1011	N
F	false	0001	0		NE	not equal	0110	$\overline{Z}$
GE	greater or equal	1100	$N \cdot V + \overline{N} \cdot \overline{V}$		PI	plus	1010	$\overline{N}$
GT	greater than	1110	$N \cdot V \cdot \overline{Z} + \overline{N} \cdot \overline{V} \cdot \overline{Z}$		T	true	0000	1
HI	high	0010	$\overline{C} \cdot \overline{Z}$		VC	overflow clear	1000	$\overline{V}$
LE	less or equal	1111	$Z + N \cdot \overline{V} + \overline{N} \cdot V$		VS	overflow set	1001	V

Condition Codes: Not affected.

Instruction Format:

15	14	13	12	11	10	9	8	7	6	5	4	3	2	1	0
0	1	0	1	Condition				1	1	Effective Address Mode | Register					

Instruction Fields:

Condition field — One of sixteen conditions discussed in description.
Effective Address field — Specifies the location in which the true/false byte is to be stored. Only data alterable addressing modes are allowed as shown:

Addressing Mode	Mode	Register	Addressing Mode	Mode	Register
Dn	000	register number	d(An, Xi)	110	register number
An	—	—	Abs.W	111	000
(An)	010	register number	Abs.L	111	001
(An)+	011	register number	d(PC)	—	—
−(An)	100	register number	d(PC, Xi)	—	—
d(An)	101	register number	Imm	—	—

Notes:
1. A memory destination is read before being written to.
2. An arithmetic one and zero result may be generated by following the Scc instruction with a NEG instruction.

STOP

Operation: If supervisor state
                   then Immediate Data → SR; STOP
                   else TRAP

Assembler
Syntax: STOP #xxx

Attributes: Unsized

Description: The immediate operand is moved into the entire status register; the program counter is advanced to point to the next instruction and the processor stops fetching and executing instructions. Execution of instructions resumes when a trace, interrupt, or reset exception occurs. A trace exception will occur if the trace state is on when the STOP instruction is executed. If an interrupt request arrives whose priority is higher than the current processor priority, an interrupt exception occurs, otherwise the interrupt request has no effect. If the bit of the immediate data corresponding to the S-bit is off, execution of the instruction will cause a privilege violation. External reset will always initiate reset exception processing.

Condition Codes: Set according to the immediate operand.

Instruction Format:

15	14	13	12	11	10	9	8	7	6	5	4	3	2	1	0
0	1	0	0	1	1	1	0	0	1	1	1	0	0	1	0
Immediate Data															

Instruction Fields:

Immediate field — Specifies the data to be loaded into the status register.

SUB

Subtract Binary

SUB

Operation: (Destination) – (Source) → Destination

Assembler SUB < ea >, Dn
Syntax: SUB Dn, < ea >

Attributes: Size = (Byte, Word, Long)

Description: Subtract the source operand from the destination operand and store the result in the destination. The size of the operation may be specified to be byte, word, or long. The mode of the instruction indicates which operand is the source and which is the destination as well as the operand size.

Condition Codes:

X N Z V C

X	N	Z	V	C
*	*	*	*	*

N   Set if the result is negative. Cleared otherwise.
Z   Set if the result is zero. Cleared otherwise.
V   Set if an overflow is generated. Cleared otherwise.
C   Set if a borrow is generated. Cleared otherwise.
X   Set the same as the carry bit.

Instruction Format:

15	14	13	12	11 10 9	8 7 6	5 4 3	2 1 0
1	0	0	1	Register	Op-Mode	Effective Address Mode	Register

Instruction Fields:

Register field — Specifies any of the eight data registers.
Op-Mode field —

Byte	Word	Long	Operation
000	001	010	(< Dn >) – (< ea >) → < Dn >
100	101	110	(< ea >) – (< Dn >) → < ea >

Effective Address field — Determines addressing mode:
   If the location specified is a source operand, then all addressing modes are allowed as shown:

Addressing Mode	Mode	Register	Addressing Mode	Mode	Register
Dn	000	register number	d(An, Xi)	110	register number
An*	001	register number	Abs.W	111	000
(An)	010	register number	Abs.L	111	001
(An) +	011	register number	d(PC)	111	010
– (An)	100	register number	d(PC, Xi)	111	011
d(An)	101	register number	Imm	111	100

*For byte size operation, address register direct is not allowed.

— Continued —

Subtract Binary

Effective Address field (Continued)

If the location specified is a destination operand, then only alterable memory addressing modes are allowed as shown:

Addressing Mode	Mode	Register	Addressing Mode	Mode	Register
Dn	—	—	d(An, Xi)	110	register number
An	—	—	Abs.W	111	000
(An)	010	register number	Abs.L	111	001
(An) +	011	register number	d(PC)	—	—
− (An)	100	register number	d(PC, Xi)	—	—
d(An)	101	register number	Imm	—	—

Notes:
1. If the destination is a data register, then it cannot be specified by using the destination <ea> mode, but must use the destination Dn mode instead.
2. SUBA is used when the destination is an address register. SUBI and SUBQ are used when the source is immediate data. Most assemblers automatically make this distinction.

SUBA

Subtract Address

SUBA

Operation: (Destination) − (Source) → Destination

**Assembler
Syntax:** SUBA <ea>, An

Attributes: Size = (Word, Long)

Description: Subtract the source operand from the destination address register and store the result in the address register. The size of the operation may be specified to be word or long. Word size source operands are sign extended to 32 bit quantities before the operation is done.

Condition Codes: Not affected.

Instruction Format:

15	14	13	12	11 10 9	8 7 6	5 4 3	2 1 0
1	0	0	1	Register	Op-Mode	Effective Address Mode	Register

Instruction Fields:

Register field — Specifies any of the eight address registers. This is always the destination.

Op-Mode field — Specifies the size of the operation:

011 — Word operation. The source operand is sign-extended to a long operand and the operation is performed on the address register using all 32 bits.

111 — Long operations.

Effective Address field — Specifies the source operand. All addressing modes are allowed as shown:

Addressing Mode	Mode	Register	Addressing Mode	Mode	Register
Dn	000	register number	d(An, Xi)	110	register number
An	001	register number	Abs.W	111	000
(An)	010	register number	Abs.L	111	001
(An)+	011	register number	d(PC)	111	010
−(An)	100	register number	d(PC, Xi)	111	011
d(An)	101	register number	Imm	111	100

SUBI

Subtract Immediate

SUBI

Operation: (Destination) – Immediate Data → Destination

**Assembler
Syntax:** SUBI #<data>, <ea>

Attributes: Size = (Byte, Word, Long)

Description: Subtract the immediate data from the destination operand and store the result in the destination location. The size of the operation may be specified to be byte, word, or long. The size of the immediate data matches the operation size.

Condition Codes:

X	N	Z	V	C
*	*	*	*	*

N   Set if the result is negative. Cleared otherwise.
Z   Set if the result is zero. Cleared otherwise.
V   Set if an overflow is generated. Cleared otherwise.
C   Set if a borrow is generated. Cleared otherwise.
X   Set the same as the carry bit.

Instruction Format:

15	14	13	12	11	10	9	8	7	6	5	4	3	2	1	0
0	0	0	0	0	1	0	0	Size		Effective Address Mode | Register					
Word Data (16 bits)								Byte Data (8 bits)							
Long Data (32 bits, including previous word)															

Instruction Fields:

Size field — Specifies the size of the operation.
  00 — byte operation.
  01 — word operation.
  10 — long operation.

Effective Address field — Specifies the destination operand. Only data alterable addressing modes are allowed as shown:

Addressing Mode	Mode	Register	Addressing Mode	Mode	Register
Dn	000	register number	d(An, Xi)	110	register number
An	—	—	Abs.W	111	000
(An)	010	register number	Abs.L	111	001
(An)+	011	register number	d(PC)	—	—
–(An)	100	register number	d(PC, Xi)	—	—
d(An)	101	register number	Imm	—	—

Immediate field — (Data immediately following the instruction)
  If size = 00, then the data is the low order byte of the immediate word.
  If size = 01, then the data is the entire immediate word.
  If size = 10, then the data is the next two immediate words.

SUBQ Subtract Quick SUBQ

Operation: (Destination) – Immediate Data → Destination

**Assembler
Syntax:**   SUBQ #<data>, <ea>

Attributes: Size = (Byte, Word, Long)

Description: Subtract the immediate data from the destination operand. The data range is from 1-8. The size of the operation may be specified to be byte, word, or long. Word and long operations are also allowed on the address registers and the condition codes are not affected. Word size source operands are sign extended to 32 bit quantities before the operation is done.

Condition Codes:

X	N	Z	V	C
*	*	*	*	*

N   Set if the result is negative. Cleared otherwise.
Z   Set if the result is zero. Cleared otherwise.
V   Set if an overflow is generated. Cleared otherwise.
C   Set if a borrow is generated. Cleared otherwise.
X   Set the same as the carry bit.

The condition codes are not affected if a subtraction from an address register is made.

Instruction Format:

15	14	13	12	11	10	9	8	7	6	5	4	3	2	1	0
0	1	0	1	Data			1	Size		Effective Address Mode | Register					

Instruction Fields:

Data field — Three bits of immediate data, 0, 1-7 representing a range of 8, 1 to 7 respectively.
Size field — Specifies the size of the operation:
00 — byte operation.
01 — word operation.
10 — long operation.
Effective Address field — Specifies the destination location. Only alterable addressing modes are allowed as shown:

Addressing Mode	Mode	Register	Addressing Mode	Mode	Register
Dn	000	register number	d(An, Xi)	110	register number
An*	001	register number	Abs.W	111	000
(An)	010	register number	Abs.L	111	001
(An)+	011	register number	d(PC)	—	—
–(An)	100	register number	d(PC, Xi)	—	—
d(An)	101	register number	Imm	—	—

*Word and Long only.

SUBX

Subtract with Extend

Operation: (Destination) – (Source) – X → Destination

Assembler SUBX Dy, Dx
Syntax: SUBX –(Ay), –(Ax)

Attributes: Size = (Byte, Word, Long)

Description: Subtract the source operand from the destination operand along with the extend bit and store the result in the destination location. The operands may be addressed in two different ways:
1. Data register to data register: The operands are contained in data registers specified in the instruction.
2. Memory to memory. The operands are contained in memory and addressed with the predecrement addressing mode using the address registers specified in the instruction.

The size of the operation may be specified to be byte, word, or long.

Condition Codes:

X	N	Z	V	C
*	*	*	*	*

N   Set if the result is negative. Cleared otherwise.
Z   Cleared if the result is non-zero. Unchanged otherwise.
V   Set if an overflow is generated. Cleared otherwise.
C   Set if a carry is generated. Cleared otherwise.
X   Set the same as the carry bit.

NOTE

Normally the Z condition code bit is set via programming before the start of an operation. This allows successful tests for zero results upon completion of multiple-precision operations.

Instruction Format:

15	14	13	12	11 10 9	8	7 6	5	4	3	2 1 0
1	0	0	1	Register Rx	1	Size	0	0	R/M	Register Ry

— Continued —

SUBX

Subtract with Extend

SUBX

Instruction Fields:

Register Rx field — Specifies the destination register:

If R/M = 0, specifies a data register.

If R/M = 1, specifies an address register for the predecrement addressing mode.

Size field — Specifies the size of the operation:

00 — byte operation.

01 — word operation.

10 — long operation.

R/M field — Specifies the operand addressing mode:

0 — The operation is data register to data register.

1 — The operation is memory to memory.

Register Ry field — Specifies the source register:

If R/M = 0, specifies a data register.

If R/M = 1, specifies an address register for the predecrement addressing mode.

SWAP

SWAP   Swap Register Halves   **SWAP**

Operation: Register [31:16] ↔ Register [15:0]

Assembler
Syntax: SWAP Dn

Attributes: Size = (Word)

Description: Exchange the 16-bit halves of a data register.

Condition Codes:

X	N	Z	V	C
—	*	*	0	0

N   Set if the most significant bit of the 32-bit result is set. Cleared otherwise.
Z   Set if the 32-bit result is zero. Cleared otherwise.
V   Always cleared.
C   Always cleared.
X   Not affected.

Instruction Format:

15	14	13	12	11	10	9	8	7	6	5	4	3	2	1	0
0	1	0	0	1	0	0	0	0	1	0	0	0	Register		

Instruction Fields:

Register field — Specifies the data register to swap.

TAS   Test and Set an Operand   TAS

Operation: (Destination) Tested → CC; 1 → bit 7 OF Destination

**Assembler
Syntax:** TAS <ea>

Attributes: Size = (Byte)

Description: Test and set the byte operand addressed by the effective address field. The current value of the operand is tested and N and Z are set accordingly. The high order bit of the operand is set. The operation is indivisible (using a read-modify-write memory cycle) to allow synchronization of several processors.

Condition Codes:

X	N	Z	V	C
—	*	*	0	0

N   Set if the most significant bit of the operand was set. Cleared otherwise.
Z   Set if the operand was zero. Cleared otherwise.
V   Always cleared.
C   Always cleared.
X   Not affected.

Instruction Format:

15	14	13	12	11	10	9	8	7	6	5 4 3	2 1 0
0	1	0	0	1	0	1	0	1	1	Effective Address Mode	Register

Instruction Fields:

Effective Address field — Specifies the location of the tested operand. Only data alterable addressing modes are allowed as shown:

Addressing Mode	Mode	Register	Addressing Mode	Mode	Register
Dn	000	register number	d(An, Xi)	110	register number
An	—	—	Abs.W	111	000
(An)	010	register number	Abs.L	111	001
(An) +	011	register number	d(PC)	—	—
– (An)	100	register number	d(PC, Xi)	—	—
d(An)	101	register number	Imm	—	—

Note: Bus error retry is inhibited on the read portion of the TAS read-modify-write bus cycle to ensure system integrity. The bus error exception is always taken.

TRAP   Trap   TRAP

Operation: PC→ − (SSP); SR→ − (SSP); (Vector)→ PC

**Assembler
Syntax:**   TRAP # <vector>

Attributes: Unsized

Description: The processor initiates exception processing. The vector number is
generated to reference the TRAP instruction exception vector specified by
the low order four bits of the instruction. Sixteen TRAP instruction vectors
are available.

Condition Codes: Not affected.

Instruction Format:

15	14	13	12	11	10	9	8	7	6	5	4	3	2	1	0
0	1	0	0	1	1	1	0	0	1	0	0	\multicolumn{4}{}{Vector}

Instruction Fields:

Vector field — Specifies which trap vector contains the new program
counter to be loaded.

TRAPV   Trap on Overflow   TRAPV

Operation: If V then TRAP

**Assembler
Syntax:** TRAPV

Attributes: Unsized

Description: If the overflow condition is on, the processor initiates exception processing. The vector number is generated to reference the TRAPV exception vector. If the overflow condition is off, no operation is performed and execution continues with the next instruction in sequence.

Condition Codes: Not affected.

Instruction Format:

15	14	13	12	11	10	9	8	7	6	5	4	3	2	1	0
0	1	0	0	1	1	1	0	0	1	1	1	0	1	1	0

TST

Test an Operand

TST

Operation: (Destination) Tested → CC

**Assembler
Syntax:** TST <ea>

Attributes: Size = (Byte, Word, Long)

Description: Compare the operand with zero. No results are saved; however, the condition codes are set according to results of the test. The size of the operation may be specified to be byte, word, or long.

Condition Codes:

X	N	Z	V	C
—	*	*	0	0

N Set if the operand is negative. Cleared otherwise.
Z Set if the operand is zero. Cleared otherwise.
V Always cleared.
C Always cleared.
X Not affected.

Instruction Format:

15	14	13	12	11	10	9	8	7	6	5	4	3	2	1	0
0	1	0	0	1	0	1	0	Size		Effective Address Mode			Register		

Instruction Fields:

Size field — Specifies the size of the operation:

00 — byte operation.
01 — word operation.
10 — long operation.

Effective Address field — Specifies the destination operand. Only data alterable addressing modes are allowed as shown:

Addressing Mode	Mode	Register	Addressing Mode	Mode	Register
Dn	000	register number	d(An, Xi)	110	register number
An	—	—	Abs.W	111	000
(An)	010	register number	Abs.L	111	001
(An)+	011	register number	d(PC)	—	—
−(An)	100	register number	d(PC, Xi)	—	—
d(An)	101	register number	Imm	—	—

UNLK

Unlink

UNLK

Operation: An → SP; (SP) + → An

**Assembler
Syntax:** UNLK An

Attributes: Unsized

Description: The stack pointer is loaded from the specified address register. The address register is then loaded with the long word pulled from the top of the stack.

Condition Codes: Not affected.

Instruction Format:

15	14	13	12	11	10	9	8	7	6	5	4	3	2	1	0
0	1	0	0	1	1	1	0	0	1	0	1	1	Register		

Instruction Fields:

Register field — specifies the address register through which the unlinking is to be done.

APPENDIX IVC: MC68000 INSTRUCTION FORMAT SUMMARY

C.1 INTRODUCTION

This appendix provides a summary of the first word in each instruction of the instruction set. Table C-1 is an operation code (op-code) map which illustrates how bits 15 through 12 are used to specify the operations. The remaining paragraph groups the instructions according to the op-code map.

Table C-1. Operation Code Map

Bits 15 through 12	Operation	Bits 15 through 12	Operation
0000	Bit Manipulation/MOVEP/Immediate	1000	OR/DIV/SBCD
0001	Move Byte	1001	SUB/SUBX
0010	Move Long	1010	(Unassigned)
0011	Move Word	1011	CMP/EOR
0100	Miscellaneous	1100	AND/MUL/ABCD/EXG
0101	ADDQ/SUBQ/Scc/DBcc	1101	ADD/ADDX
0110	Bcc/BSR	1110	Shift/Rotate
0111	MOVEQ	1111	(Unassigned)

Table C-2. Effective Address Encoding Summary

Addressing Mode	Mode	Register
Data Register Direct	000	register number
Address Register Direct	001	register number
Address Register Indirect	010	register number
Address Register Indirect with Postincrement	011	register number
Address Register Indirect with Predecrement	100	register number
Address Register Indirect with Displacement	101	register number
Address Register Indirect with Index	110	register number
Absolute Short	111	000
Absolute Long	111	001
Program Counter with Displacement	111	010
Program Counter with Index	111	011
Immediate or Status Register	111	100

Table C-3. Conditional Tests

Mnemonic	Condition	Encoding	Test
T	true	0000	1
F	false	0001	0
HI	high	0010	$\overline{C}\cdot\overline{Z}$
LS	low or same	0011	$C+Z$
CC(HS)	carry clear	0100	$\overline{C}$
CS(LO)	carry set	0101	C
NE	not equal	0110	$\overline{Z}$
EQ	equal	0111	Z
VC	overflow clear	1000	$\overline{V}$
VS	overflow set	1001	V
PL	plus	1010	$\overline{N}$
MI	minus	1011	N
GE	greater or equal	1100	$N\cdot V+\overline{N}\cdot\overline{V}$
LT	less than	1101	$N\cdot\overline{V}+\overline{N}\cdot V$
GT	greater than	1110	$N\cdot V\cdot\overline{Z}+\overline{N}\cdot\overline{V}\cdot\overline{Z}$
LE	less or equal	1111	$Z+N\cdot\overline{V}+\overline{N}\cdot V$

OR Immediate

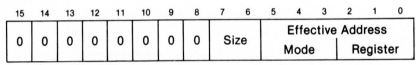

15	14	13	12	11	10	9	8	7	6	5	4	3	2	1	0
0	0	0	0	0	0	0	0	Size		Effective Address Mode			Register		

Size field: 00 = byte
01 = word
10 = long

OR Immediate to CCR

15	14	13	12	11	10	9	8	7	6	5	4	3	2	1	0
0	0	0	0	0	0	0	0	0	0	1	1	1	1	0	0

OR Immediate to SR

15	14	13	12	11	10	9	8	7	6	5	4	3	2	1	0
0	0	0	0	0	0	0	0	0	1	1	1	1	1	0	0

Dynamic Bit

15	14	13	12	11	10	9	8	7	6	5	4	3	2	1	0
0	0	0	0	Data Register			1	Type		Effective Address					
										Mode			Register		

Type field: 00 = TST
           01 = CHG
           10 = CLR
           11 = SET

MOVEP

15	14	13	12	11	10	9	8	7	6	5	4	3	2	1	0
0	0	0	0	Data Register			Op-Mode			0	0	1	Address Register		

Op-Mode field: 100 = transfer word from memory to register
                101 = transfer long from memory to register
                110 = transfer word from register to memory
                111 = transfer long from register to memory

AND Immediate

15	14	13	12	11	10	9	8	7	6	5	4	3	2	1	0
0	0	0	0	0	0	1	0	Size		Effective Address					
										Mode			Register		

Size field: 00 = byte
          01 = word
          10 = long

AND Immediate to CCR

15	14	13	12	11	10	9	8	7	6	5	4	3	2	1	0
0	0	0	0	0	0	1	0	0	0	1	1	1	1	0	0

AND Immediate to SR

15	14	13	12	11	10	9	8	7	6	5	4	3	2	1	0
0	0	0	0	0	0	1	0	0	1	1	1	1	1	0	0

SUB Immediate

15	14	13	12	11	10	9	8	7	6	5	4	3	2	1	0
										Effective Address					
0	0	0	0	0	1	0	0	Size		Mode			Register		

Size field: 00 = byte
01 = word
10 = long

ADD Immediate

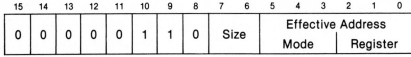

15	14	13	12	11	10	9	8	7	6	5	4	3	2	1	0
										Effective Address					
0	0	0	0	0	1	1	0	Size		Mode			Register		

Size field: 00 = byte
01 = word
10 = long

Static Bit

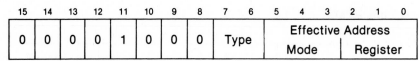

15	14	13	12	11	10	9	8	7	6	5	4	3	2	1	0
										Effective Address					
0	0	0	0	1	0	0	0	Type		Mode			Register		

Type field: 00 = TST
01 = CHG
10 = CLR
11 = SET

EOR Immediate

15	14	13	12	11	10	9	8	7	6	5	4	3	2	1	0
										Effective Address					
0	0	0	0	1	0	1	0	Size		Mode			Register		

Size field: 00 = byte
01 = word
10 = long

EOR Immediate to CCR

15	14	13	12	11	10	9	8	7	6	5	4	3	2	1	0
0	0	0	0	1	0	1	0	0	0	1	1	1	1	0	0

EOR Immediate to SR

15	14	13	12	11	10	9	8	7	6	5	4	3	2	1	0
0	0	0	0	1	0	1	0	0	1	1	1	1	1	0	0

CMP Immediate

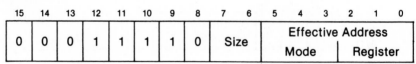

15	14	13	12	11	10	9	8	7 6	5 4 3	2 1 0
									Effective Address	
0	0	0	0	1	1	0	0	Size	Mode	Register

Size field: 00 = byte
01 = word
10 = word

MOVES   MC68010

15	14	13	12	11	10	9	8	7 6	5 4 3	2 1 0
									Effective Address	
0	0	0	1	1	1	1	0	Size	Mode	Register

Size field: 00 = byte
01 = word
10 = long

MOVE Byte

15	14	13	12	11 10 9	8 7 6	5 4 3	2 1 0
				Destination		Source	
0	0	0	1	Register	Mode	Mode	Register

Note register and mode locations

MOVEA Long

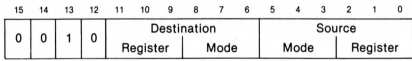

MOVE Long

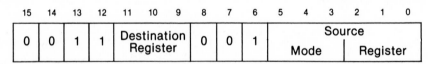

Note register and mode locations

MOVEA Word

15	14	13	12	11 10 9	8	7	6	5 4 3	2 1 0
0	0	1	1	Destination Register	0	0	1	Source — Mode	Register

MOVE Word

15	14	13	12	11 10 9	8 7 6	5 4 3	2 1 0
0	0	1	1	Destination — Register	Mode	Source — Mode	Register

Note register and mode locations

NEGX

15	14	13	12	11	10	9	8	7	6	5	4	3	2	1	0
0	1	0	0	0	0	0	0	Size		Effective Address Mode			Register		

Size field: 00 = byte
01 = word
10 = long

MOVE from SR

15	14	13	12	11	10	9	8	7	6	5	4	3	2	1	0
0	1	0	0	0	0	0	0	1	1	Effective Address Mode			Register		

CHK

15	14	13	12	11	10	9	8	7	6	5	4	3	2	1	0
0	1	0	0	Data Register			1	1	0	Effective Address Mode			Register		

LEA

15	14	13	12	11	10	9	8	7	6	5	4	3	2	1	0
0	1	0	0	Address Register			1	1	1	Effective Address Mode			Register		

CLR

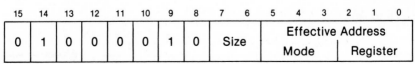

15	14	13	12	11	10	9	8	7	6	5	4	3	2	1	0
0	1	0	0	0	0	1	0	Size		Effective Address Mode			Register		

Size field: 00 = byte
01 = word
10 = long

MOVE from CCR   MC68010

15	14	13	12	11	10	9	8	7	6	5	4	3	2	1	0
0	1	0	0	0	0	1	0	1	1	Effective Address					

Effective Address — Mode | Register

NEG

15	14	13	12	11	10	9	8	7	6	5	4	3	2	1	0
0	1	0	0	0	1	0	0	Size		Effective Address					

Effective Address — Mode | Register

Size field: 00 = byte
01 = word
10 = long

MOVE to CCR

15	14	13	12	11	10	9	8	7	6	5	4	3	2	1	0
0	1	0	0	0	1	0	0	1	1	Effective Address					

Effective Address — Mode | Register

NOT

15	14	13	12	11	10	9	8	7	6	5	4	3	2	1	0
0	1	0	0	0	1	1	0	Size		Effective Address					

Effective Address — Mode | Register

Size field: 00 = byte
01 = word
10 = long

MOVE to SR

15	14	13	12	11	10	9	8	7	6	5	4	3	2	1	0
0	1	0	0	0	1	1	0	1	1	Effective Address					

Effective Address — Mode | Register

NBCD

15	14	13	12	11	10	9	8	7	6	5	4	3	2	1	0
0	1	0	0	1	0	0	0	0	0	Effective Address					
										Mode			Register		

SWAP

15	14	13	12	11	10	9	8	7	6	5	4	3	2	1	0
0	1	0	0	1	0	0	0	0	1	0	0	0	Data Register		

PEA

15	14	13	12	11	10	9	8	7	6	5	4	3	2	1	0
0	1	0	0	1	0	0	0	0	1	Effective Address					
										Mode			Register		

EXT Word

15	14	13	12	11	10	9	8	7	6	5	4	3	2	1	0
0	1	0	0	1	0	0	0	1	0	0	0	0	Data Register		

MOVEM Registers to EA

15	14	13	12	11	10	9	8	7	6	5	4	3	2	1	0
0	1	0	0	1	0	0	0	1	Sz	Effective Address					
										Mode			Register		

Sz field: 0 = word transfer
 1 = long transfer

EXT Long

15	14	13	12	11	10	9	8	7	6	5	4	3	2	1	0
0	1	0	0	1	0	0	0	1	1	0	0	0	Data Register		

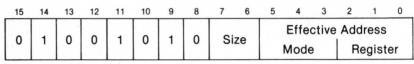

TST

15	14	13	12	11	10	9	8	7	6	5	4	3	2	1	0
0	1	0	0	1	0	1	0	Size		Effective Address Mode			Register		

Size field: 00 = byte
01 = word
10 = long

TAS

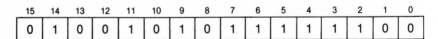

15	14	13	12	11	10	9	8	7	6	5	4	3	2	1	0
0	1	0	0	1	0	1	0	1	1	Effective Address Mode			Register		

ILLEGAL

15	14	13	12	11	10	9	8	7	6	5	4	3	2	1	0
0	1	0	0	1	0	1	0	1	1	1	1	1	1	0	0

MOVEM EA to Registers

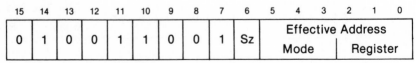

15	14	13	12	11	10	9	8	7	6	5	4	3	2	1	0
0	1	0	0	1	1	0	0	1	Sz	Effective Address Mode			Register		

Sz field: 0 = word transfer
1 = long transfer

514

TRAP

15	14	13	12	11	10	9	8	7	6	5	4	3	2	1	0
0	1	0	0	1	1	1	0	0	1	0	0	Vector			

LINK

15	14	13	12	11	10	9	8	7	6	5	4	3	2	1	0
0	1	0	0	1	1	1	0	0	1	0	1	0	Address Register		

UNLK

15	14	13	12	11	10	9	8	7	6	5	4	3	2	1	0
0	1	0	0	1	1	1	0	0	1	0	1	1	Address Register		

MOVE to USP

15	14	13	12	11	10	9	8	7	6	5	4	3	2	1	0
0	1	0	0	1	1	1	0	0	1	1	0	0	Address Register		

MOVE from USP

15	14	13	12	11	10	9	8	7	6	5	4	3	2	1	0
0	1	0	0	1	1	1	0	0	1	1	0	1	Address Register		

RESET

15	14	13	12	11	10	9	8	7	6	5	4	3	2	1	0
0	1	0	0	1	1	1	0	0	1	1	1	0	0	0	0

NOP

15	14	13	12	11	10	9	8	7	6	5	4	3	2	1	0
0	1	0	0	1	1	1	0	0	1	1	1	0	0	0	1

STOP

15	14	13	12	11	10	9	8	7	6	5	4	3	2	1	0
0	1	0	0	1	1	1	0	0	1	1	1	0	0	1	0

RTE

15	14	13	12	11	10	9	8	7	6	5	4	3	2	1	0
0	1	0	0	1	1	1	0	0	1	1	1	0	0	1	1

RTD   MC68010

15	14	13	12	11	10	9	8	7	6	5	4	3	2	1	0
0	1	0	0	1	1	1	0	0	1	1	1	0	1	0	0

RTS

15	14	13	12	11	10	9	8	7	6	5	4	3	2	1	0
0	1	0	0	1	1	1	0	0	1	1	1	0	1	0	1

TRAPV

15	14	13	12	11	10	9	8	7	6	5	4	3	2	1	0
0	1	0	0	1	1	1	0	0	1	1	1	0	1	1	0

516

RTR

15	14	13	12	11	10	9	8	7	6	5	4	3	2	1	0
0	1	0	0	1	1	1	0	0	1	1	1	0	1	1	1

MOVEC   MC68010

15	14	13	12	11	10	9	8	7	6	5	4	3	2	1	0
0	1	0	0	1	1	1	0	0	1	1	1	1	0	1	dr

dr field: 0 = control register to general register
1 = general register to control register

JSR

15	14	13	12	11	10	9	8	7	6	5	4	3	2	1	0
0	1	0	0	1	1	1	0	1	0	Effective Address Mode			Register		

JMP

15	14	13	12	11	10	9	8	7	6	5	4	3	2	1	0
0	1	0	0	1	1	1	0	1	1	Effective Mode Mode			Register		

ADDQ

15	14	13	12	11	10	9	8	7	6	5	4	3	2	1	0
										Effective Address					
0	1	0	1	Data			0	Size		Mode			Register		

Data field: Three bits of immediate data, 0, 1-7 representing a range of 8, 1 to 7 respectively.

Size field: 00 = byte
01 = word
10 = long

Scc

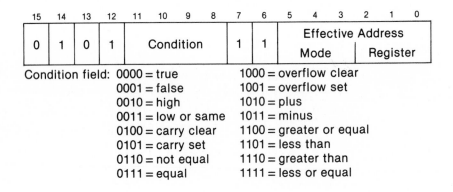

15	14	13	12	11	10	9	8	7	6	5	4	3	2	1	0
										Effective Address					
0	1	0	1	Condition				1	1	Mode			Register		

Condition field: 0000 = true   1000 = overflow clear
0001 = false   1001 = overflow set
0010 = high   1010 = plus
0011 = low or same   1011 = minus
0100 = carry clear   1100 = greater or equal
0101 = carry set   1101 = less than
0110 = not equal   1110 = greater than
0111 = equal   1111 = less or equal

DBcc

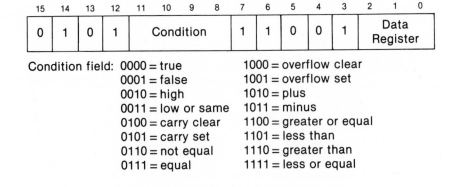

15	14	13	12	11	10	9	8	7	6	5	4	3	2	1	0
0	1	0	1	Condition				1	1	0	0	1	Data Register		

Condition field: 0000 = true   1000 = overflow clear
0001 = false   1001 = overflow set
0010 = high   1010 = plus
0011 = low or same   1011 = minus
0100 = carry clear   1100 = greater or equal
0101 = carry set   1101 = less than
0110 = not equal   1110 = greater than
0111 = equal   1111 = less or equal

SUBQ

15	14	13	12	11	10	9	8	7	6	5	4	3	2	1	0
0	1	0	1	Data			1	Size		Effective Address					

15	14	13	12	11 10 9	8	7 6	5 4 3	2 1 0
0	1	0	1	Data	1	Size	Mode	Register

Data field: Three bits of immediate data, 0, 1-7 representing a range of 8, 1 to 7 respectively.

Size field: 00 = byte
01 = word
10 = long

Bcc

15	14	13	12	11 10 9 8	7 6 5 4 3 2 1 0
0	1	1	0	Condition	8-Bit Displacement

Condition field: 0010 = high   1001 = overflow set
0011 = low or same   1010 = plus
0100 = carry clear   1011 = minus
0101 = carry set   1100 = greater or equal
0110 = not equal   1101 = less than
0111 = equal   1110 = greater than
1000 = overflow clear 1111 = less or equal

BRA

15	14	13	12	11	10	9	8	7 6 5 4 3 2 1 0
0	1	1	0	0	0	0	0	8-Bit Displacement

BSR

15	14	13	12	11	10	9	8	7 6 5 4 3 2 1 0
0	1	1	0	0	0	0	1	8-Bit Displacement

MOVEQ

15	14	13	12	11	10	9	8	7	6	5	4	3	2	1	0
0	1	1	1	Data Register			0	Data							

Data field: Data is sign extended to a long operand and all 32 bits are transferred to the data register.

OR

15	14	13	12	11	10	9	8	7	6	5	4	3	2	1	0
1	0	0	0	Data Register			Op-Mode			Effective Address					
										Mode			Register		

Op-Mode field:

Byte	Word	Long	Operation
000	001	010	(<Dn>)v(<ea>)→Dn
100	101	110	(<ea>)v(<Dn>)→ea

DIVU

15	14	13	12	11	10	9	8	7	6	5	4	3	2	1	0
1	0	0	0	Data Register			0	1	1	Effective Address					
										Mode			Register		

SBCD

15	14	13	12	11	10	9	8	7	6	5	4	3	2	1	0
1	0	0	0	Destination Register*			1	0	0	0	0	R/M	Source Register*		

R/M field: 0 = data register to data register
            1 = memory to memory
*If R/M = 0, specifies a data register.
 If R/M = 1, specifies an address register for the predecrement addressing mode.

DIVS

15	14	13	12	11	10	9	8	7	6	5	4	3	2	1	0
1	0	0	0	Data Register			1	1	1	Effective Address Mode			Register		

SUB

15	14	13	12	11	10	9	8	7	6	5	4	3	2	1	0
1	0	0	1	Data Register			Op-Mode			Effective Address Mode			Register		

Op-Mode field:

Byte	Word	Long	Operation
000	001	010	$(<Dn>) - (<ea>) \rightarrow Dn$
100	101	110	$(<ea>) - (<Dn>) \rightarrow ea$

SUBA

15	14	13	12	11	10	9	8	7	6	5	4	3	2	1	0
1	0	0	1	Data Register			Op-Mode			Effective Address Mode			Register		

Op-Mode field:

Word	Long	Operation
011	111	$(<ea>) - (<An>) \rightarrow An$

SUBX

15	14	13	12	11	10	9	8	7	6	5	4	3	2	1	0
1	0	0	1	Destination Register*			1	Size		0	0	R/M	Source Register*		

Size field: 00 = byte
01 = word
10 = long

R/M field: 0 = data register to data register
1 = memory to memory

*If R/M = 0, specifies a data register.
If R/M = 1, specifies an address register for the predecrement addressing mode.

CMP

15	14	13	12	11 10 9	8 7 6	5 4 3	2 1 0
						Effective Address	
1	0	1	1	Data Register	Op-Mode	Mode	Register

Op-Mode field:

	Byte	Word	Long	Operation
	000	001	010	(<Dn>) – (<ea>)

CMPA

15	14	13	12	11 10 9	8 7 6	5 4 3	2 1 0
						Effective Address	
1	0	1	1	Data Register	Op-Mode	Mode	Register

Op-Mode field:

	Word	Long	Operation
	011	111	(<ea>) – (<An>)

EOR

15	14	13	12	11 10 9	8 7 6	5 4 3	2 1 0
						Effective Address	
1	0	1	1	Data Register	Op-Mode	Mode	Register

Op-Mode field:

	Byte	Word	Long	Operation
	100	101	110	(<ea>) ⊕ (<Dn>) → ea

CMPM

15	14	13	12	11 10 9	8	7 6	5	4	3	2 1 0
1	0	1	1	Destination Register	1	Size	0	0	1	Source Register

Size field: 00 = byte
01 = word
10 = long

AND

15	14	13	12	11	10	9	8	7	6	5	4	3	2	1	0
1	1	0	0	Data Register			Op-Mode			Effective Address					
										Mode			Register		

Op-Mode field:	Byte	Word	Long	Operation
	000	001	010	$(<Dn>)\Lambda(<ea>) \rightarrow Dn$
	100	101	110	$(<ea>)\Lambda(<Dn>) \rightarrow ea$

MULU

15	14	13	12	11	10	9	8	7	6	5	4	3	2	1	0
1	1	0	0	Data Register			0	1	1	Effective Address					
										Mode			Register		

ABCD

15	14	13	12	11	10	9	8	7	6	5	4	3	2	1	0
1	1	0	0	Destination Register*			1	0	0	0	0	R/M	Source Register*		

R/M field: 0 = data register to data register
1 = memory to memory
*If R/M = 0, specifies a data register.
 If R/M = 1, specifies an address register for the predecrement addressing mode.

EXG Data Registers

15	14	13	12	11	10	9	8	7	6	5	4	3	2	1	0
1	1	0	0	Data Register			1	0	1	0	0	0	Data Register		

EXG Address Registers

15	14	13	12	11	10	9	8	7	6	5	4	3	2	1	0
1	1	0	0	Address Register			1	0	1	0	0	1	Address Register		

EXG Data Register and Address Register

15	14	13	12	11	10	9	8	7	6	5	4	3	2	1	0
1	1	0	0	Data Register			1	1	0	0	0	1	Address Register		

MULS

15	14	13	12	11	10	9	8	7	6	5	4	3	2	1	0
1	1	0	0	Data Register			1	1	1	Effective Address					
										Mode			Register		

ADD

15	14	13	12	11	10	9	8	7	6	5	4	3	2	1	0
1	1	0	1	Data Register			Op-Mode			Effective Address					
										Mode			Register		

Op-Mode field:

Byte	Word	Long	Operation
000	001	010	$(<Dn>) + (<ea>) \rightarrow Dn$
100	101	110	$(<ea>) + (<Dn>) \rightarrow ea$

ADDA

15	14	13	12	11	10	9	8	7	6	5	4	3	2	1	0
1	1	0	1	Data Register			Op-Mode			Effective Address					
										Mode			Register		

Op-Mode field:

Word	Long	Operation
011	111	$(<ea>) + (<An>) \rightarrow An$

ADDX

15	14	13	12	11	10	9	8	7	6	5	4	3	2	1	0
1	1	0	1	Destination Register*			1	Size		0	0	R/M	Source Register*		

Size field: 00 = byte
             01 = word
             10 = long
R/M field: 0 = data register to data register
             1 = memory to memory
*If R/M = 0, specifies a data register.
 If R/M = 1, specifies an address register for the predecrement addressing
          mode.

SHIFT/ROTATE — Register

15	14	13	12	11	10	9	8	7	6	5	4	3	2	1	0
1	1	1	0	Count/ Register			dr	Size		i/r	Type		Data Register		

Count/Register field: If i/r field = 0, specifies shift count
                      If i/r field = 1, specifies a data register that contains the
                                shift count
dr field: 0 = right
          1 = left
Size field: 00 = byte
             01 = word
             10 = long
i/r field: 0 = immediate shift count
          1 = register shift count
Type field: 00 = arithmetic shift
             01 = logical shift
             10 = rotate with extend
             11 = rotate

SHIFT/ROTATE — Memory

15	14	13	12	11	10	9	8	7	6	5	4	3	2	1	0
1	1	1	0	0	Type		dr	1	1	Effective Address Mode			Register		

Type field: 00 = arithmetic shift
             01 = logical shift
             10 = rotate with extend
             11 = rotate
dr field: 0 = right
          1 = left

APPENDIX IVD: INSTRUCTION EXECUTION TIMES

D.1 INTRODUCTION

This Appendix contains listings of the instruction execution times in terms of external clock (CLK) periods. In this data, it is assumed that both memory read and write cycle times are four clock periods. A longer memory cycle will cause the generation of wait states which must be added to the total instruction time.

The number of bus read and write cycles for each instruction is also included with the timing data. This data is enclosed in parenthesis following the number of clock periods and is shown as: (r/w) where r is the number of read cycles and w is the number of write cycles included in the clock period number. Recalling that either a read or write cycle requires four clock periods, a timing number given as 18(3/1) relates to 12 clock periods for the three read cycles, plus 4 clock periods for the one write cycle, plus 2 cycles required for some internal function of the processor.

NOTE

The number of periods includes instruction fetch and all applicable operand fetches and stores.

D.2 OPERAND EFFECTIVE ADDRESS CALCULATION TIMING

Table D-1 lists the number of clock periods required to compute an instruction's effective address. It includes fetching of any extension words, the address computation, and fetching of the memory operand. The number of bus read and write cycles is shown in parenthesis as (r/w). Note there are no write cycles involved in processing the effective address.

Table D-1. Effective Address Calculation Times

Addressing Mode		Byte, Word	Long
	Register		
Dn	Data Register Direct	0(0/0)	0(0/0)
An	Address Register Direct	0(0/0)	0(0/0)
	Memory		
(An)	Address Register Indirect	4(1/0)	8(2/0)
(An) +	Address Register Indirect with Postincrement	4(1/0)	8(2/0)
− (An)	Address Register Indirect with Predecrement	6(1/0)	10(2/0)
d(An)	Address Register Indirect with Displacement	8(2/0)	12(3/0)
d(An, ix)*	Address Register Indirect with Index	10(2/0)	14(3/0)
xxx.W	Absolute Short	8(2/0)	12(3/0)
xxx.L	Absolute Long	12(3/0)	16(4/0)
d(PC)	Program Counter with Displacement	8(2/0)	12(3/0)
d(PC, ix)*	Program Counter with Index	10(2/0)	14(3/0)
#xxx	Immediate	4(1/0)	8(2/0)

*The size of the index register (ix) does not affect execution time.

526

D.3 MOVE INSTRUCTION EXECUTION TIMES

Tables D-2 and D-3 indicate the number of clock periods for the move instruction. This data includes instruction fetch, operand reads, and operand writes. The number of bus read and write cycles is shown in parenthesis as (r/w).

Table D-2. Move Byte and Word Instruction Execution Times

Source	Destination								
	Dn	An	(An)	(An)+	−(An)	d(An)	d(An, ix)*	xxx.W	xxx.L
Dn	4(1/0)	4(1/0)	8(1/1)	8(1/1)	8(1/1)	12(2/1)	14(2/1)	12(2/1)	16(3/1)
An	4(1/0)	4(1/0)	8(1/1)	8(1/1)	8(1/1)	12(2/1)	14(2/1)	12(2/1)	16(3/1)
(An)	8(2/0)	8(2/0)	12(2/1)	12(2/1)	12(2/1)	16(3/1)	18(3/1)	16(3/1)	20(4/1)
(An)+	8(2/0)	8(2/0)	12(2/1)	12(2/1)	12(2/1)	16(3/1)	18(3/1)	16(3/1)	20(4/1)
−(An)	10(2/0)	10(2/0)	14(2/1)	14(2/1)	14(2/1)	18(3/1)	20(3/1)	18(3/1)	22(4/1)
d(An)	12(3/0)	12(3/0)	16(3/1)	16(3/1)	16(3/1)	20(4/1)	22(4/1)	20(4/1)	24(5/1)
d(An, ix)*	14(3/0)	14(3/0)	18(3/1)	18(3/1)	18(3/1)	22(4/1)	24(4/1)	22(4/1)	26(5/1)
xxx.W	12(3/0)	12(3/0)	16(3/1)	16(3/1)	16(3/1)	20(4/1)	22(4/1)	20(4/1)	24(5/1)
xxx.L	16(4/0)	16(4/0)	20(4/1)	20(4/1)	20(4/1)	24(5/1)	26(5/1)	24(5/1)	28(6/1)
d(PC)	12(3/0)	12(3/0)	16(3/1)	16(3/1)	16(3/1)	20(4/1)	22(4/1)	20(4/1)	24(5/1)
d(PC, ix)*	14(3/0)	14(3/0)	18(3/1)	18(3/1)	18(3/1)	22(4/1)	24(4/1)	22(4/1)	26(5/1)
#xxx	8(2/0)	8(2/0)	12(2/1)	12(2/1)	12(2/1)	16(3/1)	18(3/1)	16(3/1)	20(4/1)

*The size of the index register (ix) does not affect execution time.

Table D-3. Move Long Instruction Execution Times

Source	Destination								
	Dn	An	(An)	(An)+	−(An)	d(An)	d(An, ix)*	xxx.W	xxx.L
Dn	4(1/0)	4(1/0)	12(1/2)	12(1/2)	12(1/2)	16(2/2)	18(2/2)	16(2/2)	20(3/2)
An	4(1/0)	4(1/0)	12(1/2)	12(1/2)	12(1/2)	16(2/2)	18(2/2)	16(2/2)	20(3/2)
(An)	12(3/0)	12(3/0)	20(3/2)	20(3/2)	20(3/2)	24(4/2)	26(4/2)	24(4/2)	28(5/2)
(An)+	12(3/0)	12(3/0)	20(3/2)	20(3/2)	20(3/2)	24(4/2)	26(4/2)	24(4/2)	28(5/2)
−(An)	14(3/0)	14(3/0)	22(3/2)	22(3/2)	22(3/2)	26(4/2)	28(4/2)	26(4/2)	30(5/2)
d(An)	16(4/0)	16(4/0)	24(4/2)	24(4/2)	24(4/2)	28(5/2)	30(5/2)	28(5/2)	32(6/2)
d(An, ix)*	18(4/0)	18(4/0)	26(4/2)	26(4/2)	26(4/2)	30(5/2)	32(5/2)	30(5/2)	34(6/2)
xxx.W	16(4/0)	16(4/0)	24(4/2)	24(4/2)	24(4/2)	28(5/2)	30(5/2)	28(5/2)	32(6/2)
xxx.L	20(5/0)	20(5/0)	28(5/2)	28(5/2)	28(5/2)	32(6/2)	34(6/2)	32(6/2)	36(7/2)
d(PC)	16(4/0)	16(4/0)	24(4/2)	24(4/2)	24(4/2)	28(5/2)	30(5/2)	28(5/2)	32(5/2)
d(PC, ix)*	18(4/0)	18(4/0)	26(4/2)	26(4/2)	26(4/2)	30(5/2)	32(5/2)	30(5/2)	34(6/2)
#xxx	12(3/0)	12(3/0)	20(3/2)	20(3/2)	20(3/2)	24(4/2)	26(4/2)	24(4/2)	28(5/2)

*The size of the index register (ix) does not affect execution time.

D.4 STANDARD INSTRUCTION EXECUTION TIMES

The number of clock periods shown in Table D-4 indicates the time required to perform the operations, store the results, and read the next instruction. The number of bus read and write cycles is shown in parenthesis as (r/w). The number of clock periods and the number of read and write cycles must be added respectively to those of the effective address calculation where indicated.

In Table D-4 the headings have the following meanings: An = address register operand, Dn = data register operand, ea = an operand specified by an effective address, and M = memory effective address operand.

Table D-4. Standard Instruction Execution Times

Instruction	Size	op<ea>, An†	op<ea>, Dn	op Dn, <M>
ADD	Byte, Word	8(1/0) +	4(1/0) +	8(1/1) +
	Long	6(1/0) + **	6(1/0) + **	12(1/2) +
AND	Byte, Word	—	4(1/0) +	8(1/1) +
	Long	—	6(1/0) + **	12(1/2) +
CMP	Byte, Word	6(1/0) +	4(1/0) +	—
	Long	6(1/0) +	6(1/0) +	—
DIVS	—	—	158(1/0) + *	—
DIVU	—	—	140(1/0) + *	—
EOR	Byte, Word	—	4(1/0) ***	8(1/1) +
	Long	—	8(1/0) ***	12(1/2) +
MULS	—	—	70(1/0) + *	—
MULU	—	—	70(1/0) + *	—
OR	Byte, Word	—	4(1/0) +	8(1/1) +
	Long	—	6(1/0) + **	12(1/2) +
SUB	Byte, Word	8(1/0) +	4(1/0) +	8(1/1) +
	Long	6(1/0) + **	6(1/0) + **	12(1/2) +

NOTES:

+ add effective address calculation time

† word or long only

* indicates maximum value

** The base time of six clock periods is increased to eight if the effective address mode is register direct or immediate (effective address time should also be added).

*** Only available effective address mode is data register direct.

DIVS, DIVU — The divide algorithm used by the MC68000 provides less than 10% difference between the best and worst case timings.

MULS, MULU — The multiply algorithm requires 38 + 2n clocks where n is defined as:

MULU: n = the number of ones in the <ea>

MULS: n = concatanate the <ea> with a zero as the LSB; n is the resultant number of 10 or 01 patterns in the 17-bit source; i.e., worst case happens when the source is $5555.

528

D.5 IMMEDIATE INSTRUCTION EXECUTION TIMES

The number of clock periods shown in Table D-5 includes the time to fetch immediate operands, perform the operations, store the results, and read the next operation. The number of bus read and write cycles is shown in parenthesis as (r/w). The number of clock periods and the number of read and write cycles must be added respectively to those of the effective address calculation where indicated.

In Table D-5, the headings have the following meanings: # = immediate operand, Dn = data register operand, An = address register operand, and M = memory operand. SR = status register.

Table D-5. Immediate Instruction Execution Times

Instruction	Size	op #, Dn	op #, An	op #, M
ADDI	Byte, Word	8(2/0)	—	12(2/1) +
	Long	16(3/0)	—	20(3/2) +
ADDQ	Byte, Word	4(1/0)	8(1/0) *	8(1/1) +
	Long	8(1/0)	8(1/0)	12(1/2) +
ANDI	Byte, Word	8(2/0)	—	12(2/1) +
	Long	16(3/0)	—	20(3/1) +
CMPI	Byte, Word	8(2/0)	—	8(2/0) +
	Long	14(3/0)	—	12(3/0) +
EORI	Byte, Word	8(2/0)	—	12(2/1) +
	Long	16(3/0)	—	20(3/2) +
MOVEQ	Long	4(1/0)	—	—
ORI	Byte, Word	8(2/0)	—	12(2/1) +
	Long	16(3/0)	—	20(3/2) +
SUBI	Byte, Word	8(2/0)	—	12(2/1) +
	Long	16(3/0)	—	20(3/2) +
SUBQ	Byte, Word	4(1/0)	8(1/0) *	8(1/1) +
	Long	8(1/0)	8(1/0)	12(1/2) +

+ add effective address calculation time
* word only

D.6 SINGLE OPERAND INSTRUCTION EXECUTION TIMES

Table D-6 indicates the number of clock periods for the single operand instructions. The number of bus read and write cycles is shown in parenthesis as (r/w). The number of clock periods and the number of read and write cycles must be added respectively to those of the effective address calculation where indicated.

Table D-6. Single Operand Instruction Execution Times

Instruction	Size	Register	Memory
CLR	Byte, Word	4(1/0)	8(1/1) +
	Long	6(1/0)	12(1/2) +
NBCD	Byte	6(1/0)	8(1/1) +
NEG	Byte, Word	4(1/0)	8(1/1) +
	Long	6(1/0)	12(1/2) +
NEGX	Byte, Word	4(1/0)	8(1/1) +
	Long	6(1/0)	12(1/2) +
NOT	Byte, Word	4(1/0)	8(1/1) +
	Long	6(1/0)	12(1/2) +
S$_{CC}$	Byte, False	4(1/0)	8(1/1) +
	Byte, True	6(1/0)	8(1/1) +
TAS	Byte	4(1/0)	10(1/1) +
TST	Byte, Word	4(1/0)	4(1/0) +
	Long	4(1/0)	4(1/0) +

+ add effective address calculation time

D.7 SHIFT/ROTATE INSTRUCTION EXECUTION TIMES

Table D-7 indicates the number of clock periods for the shift and rotate instructions. The number of bus read and write cycles is shown in parenthesis as (r/w). The number of clock periods and the number of read and write cycles must be added respectively to those of the effective address calculation where indicated.

Table D-7. Shift/Rotate Instruction Execution Times

Instruction	Size	Register	Memory
ASR, ASL	Byte, Word	6 + 2n(1/0)	8(1/1) +
	Long	8 + 2n(1/0)	—
LSR, LSL	Byte, Word	6 + 2n(1/0)	8(1/1) +
	Long	8 + 2n(1/0)	—
ROR, ROL	Byte, Word	6 + 2n(1/0)	8(1/1) +
	Long	8 + 2n(1/0)	—
ROXR, ROXL	Byte, Word	6 + 2n(1/0)	8(1/1) +
	Long	8 + 2n(1/0)	—

+ add effective address calculation time
n is the shift count

D.8 BIT MANIPULATION INSTRUCTION EXECUTION TIMES

Table D-8 indicates the number of clock periods required for the bit manipulation instructions. The number of bus read and write cycles is shown in parenthesis as (r/w). The number of clock periods and the number of read and write cycles must be added respectively to those of the effective address calculation where indicated.

Table D-8. Bit Manipulation Instruction Execution Times

Instruction	Size	Dynamic		Static	
		Register	Memory	Register	Memory
BCHG	Byte	—	8(1/1) +	—	12(2/1) +
	Long	8(1/0) *	—	12(2/0) *	—
BCLR	Byte	—	8(1/1) +	—	12(2/1) +
	Long	10(1/0) *	—	14(2/0) *	—
BSET	Byte	—	8(1/1) +	—	12(2/1) +
	Long	8(1/0) *	—	12(2/0) *	—
BTST	Byte	—	4(1/0) +	—	8(2/0) +
	Long	6(1/0)	—	10(2/0)	—

+ add effective address calculation time
* indicates maximum value

D.9 CONDITIONAL INSTRUCTION EXECUTION TIMES

Table D-9 indicates the number of clock periods required for the conditional instructions. The number of bus read and write cycles is indicated in parenthesis as (r/w). The number of clock periods and the number of read and write cycles must be added respectively to those of the effective address calculation where indicated.

Table D-9. Conditional Instruction Execution Times

Instruction	Displacement	Branch Taken	Branch Not Taken
B$_{CC}$	Byte	10(2/0)	8(1/0)
	Word	10(2/0)	12(2/0)
BRA	Byte	10(2/0)	—
	Word	10(2/0)	—
BSR	Byte	18(2/2)	—
	Word	18(2/2)	—
DB$_{CC}$	CC true	—	12(2/0)
	CC false	10(2/0)	14(3/0)

+ add effective address calculation time
* indicates maximum value

D.10 JMP, JSR, LEA, PEA, AND MOVEM INSTRUCTION EXECUTION TIMES

Table D-10 indicates the number of clock periods required for the jump, jump-to-subroutine, load effective address, push effective address, and move multiple registers instructions. The number of bus read and write cycles is shown in parenthesis as (r/w).

Table D-10. JMP, JSR, LEA, PEA, and MOVEM Instruction Execution Times

Instr	Size	(An)	(An) +	– (An)	d(An)	d(An, ix) +	xxx.W	xxx.L	d(PC)	d(PC, ix) *
JMP	–	8(2/0)	–	–	10(2/0)	14(3/0)	10(2/0)	12(3/0)	10(2/0)	14(3/0)
JSR	–	16(2/2)	–	–	18(2/2)	22(2/2)	18(2/2)	20(3/2)	18(2/2)	22(2/2)
LEA	–	4(1/0)	–	–	8(2/0)	12(2/0)	8(2/0)	12(3/0)	8(2/0)	12(2/0)
PEA	–	12(1/2)	–	–	16(2/2)	20(2/2)	16(2/2)	20(3/2)	16(2/2)	20(2/2)
MOVEM M → R	Word	12 + 4n (3 + n/0)	12 + 4n (3 + n/0)	–	16 + 4n (4 + n/0)	18 + 4n (4 + n/0)	16 + 4n (4 + n/0)	20 + 4n (5 + n/0)	16 + 4n (4 + n/0)	18 + 4n (4 + n/0)
	Long	12 + 8n (3 + 2n/0)	12 + 8n (3 + 2n/0)	–	16 + 8n (4 + 2n/0)	18 + 8n (4 + 2n/0)	16 + 8n (4 + 2n/0)	20 + 8n (5 + 2n/0)	16 + 8n (4 + 2n/0)	18 + 8n (4 + 2n/0)
MOVEM R → M	Word	8 + 4n (2/n)		8 + 4n (2/n)	12 + 4n (3/n)	14 + 4n (3/n)	12 + 4n (3/n)	16 + 4n (4/n)	–	–
	Long	8 + 8n (2/2n)	–	8 + 8n (2/2n)	12 + 8n (3/2n)	14 + 8n (3/2n)	12 + 8n (3/2n)	16 + 8n (4/2n)	–	–

n is the number of registers to move

* is the size of the index register (ix) does not affect the instruction's execution time

D 11 MULTI-PRECISION INSTRUCTION EXECUTION TIMES

Table D-11 indicates the number of clock periods for the multi-precision instructions. The number of clock periods includes the time to fetch both operands, peform the operations, store the results, and read the next instructions. The number of read and write cycles is shown in parenthesis as (r/w).

In Table D-11, the headings have the following meanings: Dn = data register operand and M = memory operand.

Table D-11. Multi-Precision Instruction Execution Times

Instruction	Size	op Dn, Dn	op M, M
ADDX	Byte, Word	4(1/0)	18(3/1)
	Long	8(1/0)	30(5/2)
CMPM	Byte, Word	–	12(3/0)
	Long	–	20(5/0)
SUBX	Byte, Word	4(1/0)	18(3/1)
	Long	8(1/0)	30(5/2)
ABCD	Byte	6(1/0)	18(3/1)
SBCD	Byte	6(1/0)	18(3/1)

D.12 MISCELLANEOUS INSTRUCTION EXECUTION TIMES

Tables D-12 and D-13 indicate the number of clock periods for the following miscellaneous instructions. The number of bus read and write cycles is shown in parenthesis as (r/w). The number of clock periods plus the number of read and write cycles must be added to those of the effective address calculation where indicated.

Table D-12. Miscellaneous Instruction Execution Times

Instruction	Size	Register	Memory
ANDI to CCR	Byte	20(3/0)	—
ANDI to SR	Word	20(3/0)	—
CHK	—	10(1/0) +	—
EORI to CCR	Byte	20(3/0)	—
EORI to SR	Word	20(3/0)	—
ORI to CCR	Byte	20(3/0)	—
ORI to SR	Word	20(3/0)	—
MOVE from SR	—	6(1/0)	8(1/1) +
MOVE to CCR	—	12(2/0)	12(2/0) +
MOVE to SR	—	12(2/0)	12(2/0) +
EXG	—	6(1/0)	—
EXT	Word	4(1/0)	—
EXT	Long	4(1/0)	—
LINK	—	16(2/2)	—
MOVE from USP	—	4(1/0)	—
MOVE to USP	—	4(1/0)	—
NOP	—	4(1/0)	—
RESET	—	132(1/0)	—
RTE	—	20(5/0)	—
RTR	—	20(5/0)	—
RTS	—	16(4/0)	—
STOP	—	4(0/0)	—
SWAP	—	4(1/0)	—
TRAPV	—	4(1/0)	—
UNLK	—	12(3/0)	—

+ add effective address calculation time

Table D-13. Move Peripheral Instruction Execution Times

Instruction	Size	Register → Memory	Memory → Register
MOVEP	Word	16(2/2)	16(4/0)
MOVEP	Long	24(2/4)	24(6/0)

D.13 EXCEPTION PROCESSING EXECUTION TIMES

Table D-14 indicates the number of clock periods for exception processing. The number of clock periods includes the time for all stacking, the vector fetch, and the fetch of the first two instruction words of the handler routine. The number of bus read and write cycles is shown in parenthesis as (r/w).

Table D-14. Exception Processing Execution Times

Exception	Periods
Address Error	**50**(4/7)
Bus Error	**50**(4/7)
CHK Instruction	**44**(5/4) +
Divide by Zero	**42**(5/4)
Illegal Instruction	**34**(4/3)
Interrupt	**44**(5/3) *
Privilege Violation	**34**(4/3)
RESET**	**40**(6/0)
Trace	**34**(4/3)
TRAP Instruction	**38**(4/4)
TRAPV Instruction	**34**(4/3)

+ add effective address calculation time

* The interrupt acknowledge cycle is assumed to take four clock periods.

** Indicates the time from when RESET and HALT are first sampled as negated to when instruction execution starts.

APPENDIX IVE: MC68008 INSTRUCTION EXECUTION TIMES

E.1 INTRODUCTION

This Appendix contains listings of the instruction execution times in terms of external clock (CLK) periods. In this data, it is assumed that both memory read and write cycle times are four clock periods. A longer memory cycle will cause the generation of wait states which must be added to the total instruction time.

The number of bus read and write cycles for each instruction is also included with the timing data. This data is enclosed in parenthesis following the number of clock periods and is shown as: (r/w) where r is the number of read cycles and w is the number of write cycles included in the clock period number. Recalling that either a read or write cycle requires four clock periods, a timing number given as 18(3/1) relates to 12 clock periods for the three read cycles, plus 4 clock periods for the one write cycle, plus 2 cycles required for some internal function of the processor.

NOTE
The number of periods includes instruction fetch and all applicable operand fetches and stores.

E.2 OPERAND EFFECTIVE ADDRESS CALCULATION TIMES

Table E-1 lists the number of clock periods required to compute an instruction's effective address. It includes fetching of any extension words, the address computation, and fetching of the memory operand. The number of bus read and write cycles is shown in parenthesis as (r/w). Note there are no write cycles involved in processing the effective address.

Table E-1. Effective Address Calculation Times

Addressing Mode		Byte	Word	Long
	Register			
Dn	Data Register Direct	0(0/0)	0(0/0)	0(0/0)
An	Address Register Direct	0(0/0)	0(0/0)	0(0/0)
	Memory			
(An)	Address Register Indirect	4(1/0)	8(2/0)	16(4/0)
(An) +	Address Register Indirect with Postincrement	4(1/0)	8(2/0)	16(4/0)
− (An)	Address Register Indirect with Predecrement	6(1/0)	10(2/0)	18(4/0)
d(An)	Address Register Indirect with Displacement	12(3/0)	16(4/0)	24(6/0)
d(An, ix)*	Address Register Indirect with Index	14(3/0)	18(4/0)	26(6/0)
xxx.W	Absolute Short	12(3/0)	16(4/0)	24(6/0)
xxx.L	Absolute Long	20(5/0)	24(6/0)	32(8/0)
d(PC)	Program Counter with Displacement	12(3/0)	16(4/0)	24(6/0)
d(PC, ix)	Program Counter with Index	14(3/0)	18(4/0)	26(6/0)
#xxx	Immediate	8(2/0)	8(2/0)	16(4/0)

*The size of the index register (ix) does not affect execution time.

E.3 MOVE INSTRUCTION EXECUTION TIMES

Tables E-2, E-3, and E-4 indicate the number of clock periods for the move instruction. This data includes instruction fetch, operand reads, and operand writes. The number of bus read and write cycles is shown in parenthesis as: (r/w).

Table E-2. Move Byte Instruction Execution Times

Source	Destination								
	Dn	An	(An)	(An) +	− (An)	d(An)	d(An, x) *	xxx.W	xxx.L
Dn	8(2/0)	8(2/0)	12(2/1)	12(2/1)	12(2/1)	20(4/1)	22(4/1)	20(4/1)	28(6/1)
An	8(2/0)	8(2/0)	12(2/1)	12(2/1)	12(2/1)	20(4/1)	22(4/1)	20(4/1)	28(6/1)
(An)	12(3/0)	12(3/0)	16(3/1)	16(3/1)	16(3/1)	24(5/1)	26(5/1)	24(5/1)	32(7/1)
(An) +	12(3/0)	12(3/0)	16(3/1)	16(3/1)	16(3/1)	24(5/1)	26(5/1)	24(5/1)	32(7/1)
− (An)	14(3/0)	14(3/0)	18(3/1)	18(3/1)	18(3/1)	26(5/1)	28(5/1)	26(5/1)	34(7/1)
d(An)	20(5/0)	20(5/0)	24(5/1)	24(5/1)	24(5/1)	32(7/1)	34(7/1)	32(7/1)	40(9/1)
d(An, ix) *	22(5/0)	22(5/0)	26(5/1)	26(5/1)	26(5/1)	34(7/1)	36(7/1)	34(7/1)	42(9/1)
xxx.W	20(5/0)	20(5/0)	24(5/1)	24(5/1)	24(5/1)	32(7/1)	34(7/1)	32(7/1)	40(9/1)
xxx.L	28(7/0)	28(7/0)	32(7/1)	32(7/1)	32(7/1)	40(9/1)	42(9/1)	40(9/1)	48(11/1)
d(PC)	20(5/0)	20(5/0)	24(5/1)	24(5/1)	24(5/1)	32(7/1)	34(7/1)	32(7/1)	40(9/1)
d(PC, ix) *	22(5/0)	22(5/0)	26(5/1)	26(5/1)	26(5/1)	34(7/1)	36(7/1)	34(7/1)	42(9/1)
#xxx	16(4/0)	16(4/0)	20(4/1)	20(4/1)	20(4/1)	28(6/1)	30(6/1)	28(6/1)	36(8/1)

*The size of the index register (ix) does not affect execution time.

Table E-3. Move Word Instruction Execution Times

Source	Destination								
	Dn	An	(An)	(An) +	− (An)	d(An)	d(An, ix) *	xxx.W	xxx.L
Dn	8(2/0)	8(2/0)	16(2/2)	16(2/2)	16(2/2)	24(4/2)	26(4/2)	20(4/2)	32(6/2)
An	8(2/0)	8(2/0)	16(2/2)	16(2/2)	16(2/2)	24(4/2)	26(4/2)	20(4/2)	32(6/2)
(An)	16(4/0)	16(4/0)	24(4/2)	24(4/2)	24(4/2)	32(6/2)	34(6/2)	32(6/2)	40(8/2)
(An) +	16(4/0)	16(4/0)	24(4/2)	24(4/2)	24(4/2)	32(6/2)	34(6/2)	32(6/2)	40(8/2)
− (An)	18(4/0)	18(4/0)	26(4/2)	26(4/2)	26(4/2)	34(6/2)	32(6/2)	34(6/2)	42(8/2)
d(An)	24(6/0)	24(6/0)	32(6/2)	32(6/2)	32(6/2)	40(8/2)	42(8/2)	40(8/2)	48(10/2)
d(An, ix) *	26(6/0)	26(6/0)	34(6/2)	34(6/2)	34(6/2)	42(8/2)	44(8/2)	42(8/2)	50(10/2)
xxx.W	24(6/0)	24(6/0)	32(6/2)	32(6/2)	32(6/2)	40(8/2)	42(8/2)	40(8/2)	48(10/2)
xxx.L	32(8/0)	32(8/0)	40(8/2)	40(8/2)	40(8/2)	48(10/2)	50(10/2)	48(10/2)	56(12/2)
d(PC)	24(6/0)	24(6/0)	32(6/2)	32(6/2)	32(6/2)	40(8/2)	42(8/2)	40(8/2)	48(10/2)
d(PC, ix) *	26(6/0)	26(6/0)	34(6/2)	34(6/2)	34(6/2)	42(8/2)	44(8/2)	42(8/2)	50(10/2)
#xxx	16(4/0)	16(4/0)	24(4/2)	24(4/2)	24(4/2)	32(6/2)	34(6/2)	32(6/2)	40(8/2)

*The size of the index register (ix) does not affect execution time.

Table E-4. Move Long Instruction Execution Times

Source	Destination Dn	An	(An)	(An)+	−(An)	d(An)	d(An, ix)*	xxx.W	xxx.L
Dn	8(2/0)	8(2/0)	24(2/4)	24(2/4)	24(2/4)	32(4/4)	34(4/4)	32(4/4)	40(6/4)
An	8(2/0)	8(2/0)	24(2/4)	24(2/4)	24(2/4)	32(4/4)	34(4/4)	32(4/4)	40(6/4)
(An)	24(6/0)	24(6/0)	40(6/4)	40(6/4)	40(6/4)	48(8/4)	50(8/4)	48(8/4)	56(10/4)
(An)+	24(6/0)	24(6/0)	40(6/4)	40(6/4)	40(6/4)	48(8/4)	50(8/4)	48(8/4)	56(10/4)
−(An)	26(6/0)	26(6/0)	42(6/4)	42(6/4)	42(6/4)	50(8/4)	52(8/4)	50(8/4)	58(10/4)
d(An)	32(8/0)	32(8/0)	48(8/4)	48(8/4)	48(8/4)	56(10/4)	58(10/4)	56(10/4)	64(12/4)
d(An, ix)*	34(8/0)	34(8/0)	50(8/4)	50(8/4)	50(8/4)	58(10/4)	60(10/4)	58(10/4)	66(12/4)
xxx.W	32(8/0)	32(8/0)	48(8/4)	48(8/4)	48(8/4)	56(10/4)	58(10/4)	56(10/4)	64(12/4)
xxx.L	40(10/0)	40(10/0)	56(10/4)	56(10/4)	56(10/4)	64(12/4)	66(12/4)	64(12/4)	72(14/4)
d(PC)	32(8/0)	32(8/0)	48(8/4)	48(8/4)	48(8/4)	56(10/4)	58(10/4)	56(10/4)	64(12/4)
d(PC, ix)*	34(8/0)	34(8/0)	50(8/4)	50(8/4)	50(8/4)	58(10/4)	60(10/4)	58(10/4)	66(12/4)
#xxx	24(6/0)	24(6/0)	40(6/4)	40(6/4)	40(6/4)	48(8/4)	50(8/4)	48(8/4)	56(10/4)

*The size of the index register (ix) does not affect execution time.

E.4 STANDARD INSTRUCTION EXECUTION TIMES

The number of clock periods shown in Table E-5 indicates the time required to perform the operations, store the results, and read the next instruction. The number of bus read and write cycles is shown in parenthesis as: (r/w). The number of clock periods and the number of read and write cycles must be added respectively to those of the effective address calculation where indicated. In Table E-5 the headings have the following meanings: An = address register operand, Dn = data register operand, ea = an operand specified by an effective address, and M = memory effective address operand.

Table E-5. Standard Instruction Execution Times

Instruction	Size	op <ea>, An	op <ea>, Dn	op Dn, <M>
ADD	Byte	−	8(2/0) +	12(2/1) +
	Word	12(2/0) +	8(2/0) +	16(2/2) +
	Long	10(2/0) + **	10(2/0) + **	24(2/4) +
AND	Byte	−	8(2/0) +	12(2/1) +
	Word	−	8(2/0) +	16(2/2) +
	Long	−	10(2/0) + **	24(2/4) +
CMP	Byte	−	8(2/0) +	−
	Word	10(2/0) +	8(2/0) +	−
	Long	10(2/0) +	10(2/0) +	−
DIVS		−	162(2/0) + *	−
DIVU		−	144(2/0) + *	−
EOR	Byte	−	8(2/0) + ***	12(2/1) +
	Word	−	8(2/0) + ***	16(2/2) +
	Long	−	12(2/0) + ***	24(2/4) +
MULS		−	74(2/0) + *	−
MULU		−	74(2/0) + *	−
OR	Byte	−	8(2/0) +	12(2/1) +
	Word	−	8(2/0) +	16(2/2) +
	Long	−	10(2/0) + **	24(2/4) +
SUB	Byte	−	8(2/0) +	12(2/1) +
	Word	12(2/0) +	8(2/0) +	16(2/2) +
	Long	10(2/0) + **	10(2/0) + **	24(2/4) +

NOTES:
- \+   Add effective address calculation time
- *   Indicates maximum value
- **   The base time of 10 clock periods is increased to 12 if the effective address mode is register direct or immediate (effective address time should also be added).
- ***   Only available effective address mode is data register direct

DIVS, DIVU — The divide algorithm used by the MC68008 provides less than 10% difference between the best and worst case timings.

MULS, MULU — The multiply algorithm requires 42 + 2n clocks where n is defined as:

MULS: n = tag the <ea> with a zero as the MSB; n is the resultant number of 10 or 01 patterns in the 17-bit source, i.e., worst case happens when the source is $5555.

MULU: n = the number of ones in the <ea>

E.5 IMMEDIATE INSTRUCTION EXECUTION TIMES

The number of clock periods shown in Table E-6 includes the time to fetch immediate operands, perform the operations, store the results, and read the next operation. The number of bus read and write cycles is shown in parenthesis as: (r/w). The number of clock periods and the number of read and write cycles must be added respectively to those of the effective address calculation where indicated. In Table E-6, the headings have the following meanings: # = immediate operand, Dn = data register operand, An = address register operand, and M = memory operand.

Table E-6. Immediate Instruction Clock Periods

Instruction	Size	op#, Dn	op#,An	op#, M
ADDI	Byte	16(4/0)	—	20(4/1) +
	Word	16(4/0)	—	24(4/2) +
	Long	28(6/0)	—	40(6/4) +
ADDQ	Byte	8(2/0)	—	12(2/1) +
	Word	8(2/0)	12(2/0)	16(2/2) +
	Long	12(2/0)	12(2/0)	24(2/4) +
ANDI	Byte	16(4/0)	—	20(4/1) +
	Word	16(4/0)	—	24(4/2) +
	Long	28(6/0)	—	40(6/4) +
CMPI	Byte	16(4/0)	—	16(4/0) +
	Word	16(4/0)	—	16(4/0) +
	Long	26(6/0)	—	24(6/0) +
EORI	Byte	16(4/0)	—	20(4/1) +
	Word	16(4/0)	—	24(4/2) +
	Long	28(6/0)	—	40(6/4) +
MOVEQ	Long	8(2/0)	—	—
ORI	Byte	16(4/0)	—	20(4/1) +
	Word	16(4/0)	—	24(4/2) +
	Long	28(6/0)	—	40(6/4) +
SUBI	Byte	16(4/0)	—	12(2/1) +
	Word	16(4/0)	—	16(2/2) +
	Long	28(6/0)	—	24(2/4) +
SUBQ	Byte	8(2/0)	—	20(4/1) +
	Word	8(2/0)	12(2/0)	24(4/2) +
	Long	12(2/0)	12(2/0)	40(6/4) +

+ add effective address calculation time

E.6 SINGLE OPERAND INSTRUCTION EXECUTION TIMES

Table E-7 indicates the number of clock periods for the single operand instructions. The number of bus read and write cycles is shown in parenthesis as (r/w). The number of clock periods and the number of read and write cycles must be added respectively to those of the effective address calculation where indicated.

Table E-7. Single Operand Instruction Execution Times

Instruction	Size	Register	Memory
CLR	Byte	8(2/0)	12(2/1) +
	Word	8(2/0)	16(2/2) +
	Long	10(2/0)	24(2/4) +
NBCD	Byte	10(2/0)	12(2/1) +
NEG	Byte	8(2/0)	12(2/1) +
	Word	8(2/0)	16(2/2) +
	Long	10(2/0)	24(2/4) +
NEGX	Byte	8(2/0)	12(2/1) +
	Word	8(2/0)	16(2/2) +
	Long	10(2/0)	24(2/4) +
NOT	Byte	8(2/0)	12(2/1) +
	Word	8(2/0)	16(2/2) +
	Long	10(2/0)	24(2/4) +
S_{CC}	Byte, False	8(2/0)	12(2/1) +
	Byte, True	10(2/0)	12(2/1) +
TAS	Byte	8(2/0)	14(2/1) +
TST	Byte	8(2/0)	8(2/0) +
	Word	8(2/0)	8(2/0) +
	Long	8(2/0)	8(2/0) +

+ add effective address calculation time.

E.7 SHIFT/ROTATE INSTRUCTION EXECUTION TIMES

Table E-8 indicates the number of clock periods for the shift and rotate instructions. The number of bus read and write cycles is shown in parenthesis as: (r/w). The number of clock periods and the number of read and write cycles must be added respectively to those of the effective address calculation where indicated.

Table E-8. Shift/Rotate Instruction Clock Periods

Instruction	Size	Register	Memory
ASR, ASL	Byte	10 + 2n(2/0)	—
	Word	10 + 2n(2/0)	16(2/2) +
	Long	12 + 2n(2/0)	—
LSR, LSL	Byte	10 + 2n(2/0)	—
	Word	10 + 2n(2/0)	16(2/2) +
	Long	12 + 2n(2/0)	—
ROR, ROL	Byte	10 + 2n(2/0)	—
	Word	10 + 2n(2/0)	16(2/2) +
	Long	12 + 2n(2/0)	—
ROXR, ROXL	Byte	10 + 2n(2/0)	—
	Word	10 + 2n(2/0)	16(2/2) +
	Long	12 + 2n(2/0)	—

+ add effective address calculation time
n is the shift count

E.8 BIT MANIPULATION INSTRUCTION EXECUTION TIMES

Table E-9 indicates the number of clock periods required for the bit manipulation instructions. The number of bus read and write cycles is shown in parenthesis as: (r/w). The number of clock periods and the number of read and write cycles must be added respectively to those of the effective address calculation where indicated.

Table E-9. Bit Manipulation Instruction Execution Times

Instruction	Size	Dynamic		Static	
		Register	Memory	Register	Memory
BCHG	Byte	—	12(2/1) +	—	20(4/1) +
	Long	12(2/0) *	—	20(4/0) *	—
BCLR	Byte	—	12(2/1) +	—	20(4/1) +
	Long	14(2/0) *	—	22(4/0) *	—
BSET	Byte	—	12(2/1) +	—	20(4/1) +
	Long	12(2/0) *	—	20(4/0) *	—
BTST	Byte	—	8(2/0) +	—	16(4/0) +
	Long	10(2/0)	—	18(4/0)	—

+ add effective address calculation time
* indicates maximum value

E.9 CONDITIONAL INSTRUCTION EXECUTION TIMES

Table E-10 indicates the number of clock periods required for the conditional instructions. The number of bus read and write cycles is indicated in parenthesis as: (r/w). The number of clock periods and the number of read and write cycles must be added respectively to those of the effective address calculation where indicated.

Table E-10. Conditional Instruction Execution Times

Instruction	Displacement	Trap or Branch Taken	Trap or Branch Not Taken
B_{CC}	Byte	18(4/0)	12(2/0)
	Word	18(4/0)	20(4/0)
BRA	Byte	18(4/0)	—
	Word	18(4/0)	—
BSR	Byte	34(4/4)	—
	Word	34(4/4)	—
DBCC	CC True	—	20(4/0)
	CC False	18(4/0)	26(6/0)
CHK	—	68(8/6) + *	14(2/0) +
TRAP	—	62(8/6)	—
TRAPV	—	66(10/6)	8(2/0)

+ add effective address calculation time
* indicates maximum value

E.10 JMP, JSR, LEA, PEA, AND MOVEM INSTRUCTION EXECUTION TIMES

Table E-11 indicates the number of clock periods required for the jump, jump-to-subroutine, load effective address, push effective address, and move multiple registers instructions. The number of bus read and write cycles is shown in parenthesis as: (r/w).

Table E-11. JMP, JSR, LEA, PEA, and MOVEM Instruction Execution Times

Instruction	Size	(An)	(An) +	− (An)	d(An)	d(An, ix) *	xxx.W	xxx.L
JMP	−	16(4/0)	−	−	18(4/0)	22(4/0)	18(4/0)	24(6/0)
JSR	−	32(4/4)	−	−	34(4/4)	38(4/4)	34(4/4)	40(6/4)
LEA	−	8(2/0)	−	−	16(4/0)	20(4/0)	16(4/0)	24(6/0)
PEA	−	24(2/4)	−	−	32(4/4)	36(4/4)	32(4/4)	40(6/4)
MOVEM M → R	Word	24 + 8n (6 + 2n/0)	24 + 8n (6 + 2n/0)	− −	32 + 8n (8 + 2n/0)	34 + 8n (8 + 2n/0)	32 + 8n (10 + n/0)	40 + 8n (10 + 2n/0)
	Long	24 + 16n (6 + 4n/0)	24 + 16n (6 + 4n/0)	− −	32 + 16n (8 + 4n/0)	32 + 16n (8 + 4n/0)	32 + 16n (8 + 4n/0)	40 + 16n (8 + 4n/0)
MOVEM R → M	Word	16 + 8n (4/2n)	− −	16 + 8n (4/2n)	24 + 8n (6/2n)	26 + 8n (6/2n)	24 + 8n (6/2n)	32 + 8n (8/2n)
	Long	16 + 16n (4/4n)	− −	16 + 16n (4/4n)	24 + 16n (6/4n)	26 + 16n	24 + 16n (8/4n)	32 + 16n (6/4n)

n is the number of registers to move

* is the size of the index register (ix) does not affect the instruction's execution time

E.11 MULTI-PRECISION INSTRUCTION EXECUTION TIMES

Table E-12 indicates the number of clock periods for the multi-precision instructions. The number of clock periods includes the time to fetch both operands, perform the operations, store the results, and read the next instructions. The number of read and write cycles is shown in parenthesis as: (r/w).

In Table E-12, the headings have the following meanings: Dn = data register operand and M = memory operand.

Table E-12. Multi-Precision Instruction Execution Times

Instruction	Size	op Dn, Dn	op M, M
ADDX	Byte	8(2/0)	22(4/1)
	Word	8(2/0)	50(6/2)
	Long	12(2/0)	58(10/4)
CMPM	Byte	−	16(4/0)
	Word	−	24(6/0)
	Long	−	40(10/0)
SUBX	Byte	8(2/0)	22(4/1)
	Word	8(2/0)	50(6/2)
	Long	12(2/0)	58(10/4)
ABCD	Byte	10(2/0)	20(4/1)
SBCD	Byte	10(2/0)	20(4/1)

E.12 MISCELLANEOUS INSTRUCTION EXECUTION TIMES

Tables E-13 and E-14 indicate the number of clock periods for the following miscellaneous instructions. The number of bus read and write cycles is shown in parenthesis as: (r/w). The number of clock periods plus the number of read and write cycles must be added to those of the effective address calculation where indicated.

Table E-13. Miscellaneous Instruction Execution Times

Instruction	Register	Memory
ANDI to CCR	32(6/0)	—
ANDI to SR	32(6/0)	—
EORI to CCR	32(6/0)	—
EORI to SR	32(6/0)	—
EXG	10(2/0)	—
EXT	8(2/0)	—
LINK	32(4/4)	—
MOVE to CCR	18(4/0)	18(4/0) +
MOVE to SR	18(4/0)	18(4/0) +
MOVE from SR	10(2/0)	16(2/2) +
MOVE to USP	8(2/0)	—
MOVE from USP	8(2/0)	—
NOP	8(2/0)	—
ORI to CCR	32(6/0)	—
ORI to SR	32(6/0)	—
RESET	136(2/0)	—
RTE	40(10/0)	—
RTR	40(10/0)	—
RTS	32(8/0)	—
STOP	4(0/0)	—
SWAP	8(2/0)	—
UNLK	24(6/0)	—

+ add effective address calculation time

Table E-14. Move Peripheral Instruction Execution Times

Instruction	Size	Register → Memory	Memory → Register
MOVEP	Word	24(4/2)	24(6/0)
	Long	32(4/4)	32(8/0)

+ add effective address calculation time

E.13 EXCEPTION PROCESSING EXECUTION TIMES

Table E-15 indicates the number of clock periods for exception processing. The number of clock periods includes the time for all stacking, the vector fetch, and the fetch of the first instruction of the handler routine. The number of bus read and write cycles is shown in parenthesis as: (r/w).

Table E-15. Exception Processing Execution Times

Exception	Periods
Address Error	94(8/14)
Bus Error	94(8/14)
Interrupt	72(9/6) *
Illegal Instruction	62(8/6)
Privileged Instruction	62(8/6)
Trace	62(8/6)

* The interrupt acknowledge bus cycle is assumed to take four external clock periods.

APPENDIX IVF: MC68010 INSTRUCTION EXECUTION TIMES

F.1 INTRODUCTION

This Appendix contains listings of the instruction execution times in terms of external clock (CLK) periods. In this data, it is assumed that both memory read and write cycle times are four clock periods. A longer memory cycle will cause the generation of wait states which must be added to the total instruction time.

The number of bus read and write cycles for each instruction is also included with the timing data. This data is enclosed in parenthesis following the number of clock periods and is shown as: (r/w) where r is the number of read cycles and w is the number of write cycles included in the clock period number. Recalling that either a read or write cycle requires four clock periods, a timing number given as 18(3/1) relates to 12 clock periods for the three read cycles, plus 4 clock periods for the one write cycle, plus 2 cycles required for some internal function of the processor.

NOTE

The number of periods includes instruction fetch and all applicable operand fetches and stores.

F.2 OPERAND EFFECTIVE ADDRESS CALCULATION TIMES

Table F-1 lists the number of clock periods required to compute an instruction's effective address. It includes fetching of any extension words, the address computation, and fetching of the memory operand if necessary. Several instructions do not need the operand at an effective address to be fetched and thus require fewer clock periods to calculate a given effective address than the instructions that do fetch the effective address operand. The number of bus read and write cycles is shown in parenthesis as (r/w). Note there are no write cycles involved in processing the effective address.

Table F-1. Effective Address Calculation Times

	Addressing Mode	Byte, Word		Long	
		Fetch	No Fetch	Fetch	No Fetch
	Register				
Dn	Data Register Direct	0(0/0)	—	0(0/0)	—
An	Address Register Direct	0(0/0)	—	0(0/0)	—
	Memory				
(An)	Address Register Indirect	4(1/0)	2(0/0)	8(2/0)	2(0/0)
(An)+	Address Register Indirect with Postincrement	4(1/0)	4(0/0)	8(2/0)	4(0/0)
−(An)	Address Register Indirect with Predecrement	6(1/0)	4(0/0)	10(2/0)	4(0/0)
d(An)	Address Register Indirect with Displacement	8(2/0)	4(0/0)	12(3/0)	4(1/0)
d(An, ix)*	Address Register Indirect with Index	10(2/0)	8(1/0)	14(3/0)	8(1/0)
xxx.W	Absolute Short	8(2/0)	4(1/0)	12(3/0)	4(1/0)
xxx.L	Absolute Long	12(3/0)	8(2/0)	16(4/0)	8(2/0)
d(PC)	Program Counter with Displacement	8(2/0)	—	12(3/0)	—
d(PC, ix)	Program Counter with Index	10(2/0)	—	14(3/0)	—
#xxx	Immediate	4(1/0)	—	8(2/0)	—

*The size of the index register (ix) does not affect execution time.

544

F.3 MOVE INSTRUCTION EXECUTION TIMES

Tables F-2, F-3, F-4, and F-5 indicate the number of clock periods for the move instruction. This data includes instruction fetch, operand reads, and operand writes. The number of bus read and write cycles is shown in parenthesis as (r/w).

Table F-2. Move Byte and Word Instruction Execution Times

Source	Destination								
	Dn	An	(An)	(An)+	-(An)	d(An)	d(An, ix)*	xxx.W	xxx.L
Dn	4(1/0)	4(1/0)	8(1/1)	8(1/1)	8(1/1)	12(2/1)	14(2/1)	12(2/1)	16(3/1)
An	4(1/0)	4(1/0)	8(1/1)	8(1/1)	8(1/1)	12(2/1)	14(2/1)	12(2/1)	16(3/1)
(An)	8(2/0)	8(2/0)	12(2/1)	12(2/1)	12(2/1)	16(3/1)	18(3/1)	16(3/1)	20(4/1)
(An)+	8(2/0)	8(2/0)	12(2/1)	12(2/1)	12(2/1)	16(3/1)	18(3/1)	16(3/1)	20(4/1)
-(An)	10(2/0)	10(2/0)	14(2/1)	14(2/1)	14(2/1)	18(3/1)	20(3/1)	18(3/1)	22(4/1)
d(An)	12(3/0)	12(3/0)	16(3/1)	16(3/1)	16(3/1)	20(4/1)	22(4/1)	20(4/1)	24(5/1)
d(An, ix)*	14(3/0)	14(3/0)	18(3/1)	18(3/1)	18(3/1)	22(4/1)	24(4/1)	22(4/1)	26(5/1)
xxx.W	12(3/0)	12(3/0)	16(3/1)	16(3/1)	16(3/1)	20(4/1)	22(4/1)	20(4/1)	24(5/1)
xxx.L	16(4/0)	16(4/0)	20(4/1)	20(4/1)	20(4/1)	24(5/1)	26(5/1)	24(5/1)	28(6/1)
d(PC)	12(3/0)	12(3/0)	16(3/1)	16(3/1)	16(3/1)	20(4/1)	22(4/1)	20(4/1)	24(5/1)
d(PC, ix)*	14(3/0)	14(3/0)	18(3/1)	18(3/1)	18(3/1)	22(4/1)	24(4/1)	22(4/1)	26(5/1)
#xxx	8(2/0)	8(2/0)	12(2/1)	12(2/1)	12(2/1)	16(3/1)	18(3/1)	16(3/1)	20(4/1)

*The size of the index register (ix) does not affect execution time.

Table F-3. Move Byte and Word Instruction Loop Mode Execution Times

	Loop Continued			Loop Terminated					
	Valid Count, cc False			Valid Count, cc True			Expired Count		
	Destination								
Source	(An)	(An)+	-(An)	(An)	(An)+	-(An)	(An)	(An)+	-(An)
Dn	10(0/1)	10(0/1)	—	18(2/1)	18(2/1)	—	16(2/1)	16(2/1)	—
An*	10(0/1)	10(0/1)	—	18(2/1)	18(2/1)	—	16(2/1)	16(2/1)	—
(An)	14(1/1)	14(1/1)	16(1/1)	20(3/1)	20(3/1)	22(3/1)	18(3/1)	18(3/1)	20(3/1)
(An)+	14(1/1)	14(1/1)	16(1/1)	20(3/1)	20(3/1)	22(3/1)	18(3/1)	18(3/1)	20(3/1)
-(An)	16(1/1)	16(1/1)	18(1/1)	22(3/1)	22(3/1)	24(3/1)	20(3/1)	20(3/1)	22(3/1)

*Word only.

Table F-4. Move Long Instruction Execution Times

Source	Destination								
	Dn	An	(An)	(An)+	-(An)	d(An)	d(An, ix)*	xxx.W	xxx.L
Dn	4(1/0)	4(1/0)	12(1/2)	12(1/2)	14(1/2)	16(2/2)	18(2/2)	16(2/2)	20(3/2)
An	4(1/0)	4(1/0)	12(1/2)	12(1/2)	14(1/2)	16(2/2)	18(2/2)	16(2/2)	20(3/2)
(An)	12(3/0)	12(3/0)	20(3/2)	20(3/2)	20(3/2)	24(4/2)	26(4/2)	24(4/2)	28(5/2)
(An)+	12(3/0)	12(3/0)	20(3/2)	20(3/2)	20(3/2)	24(4/2)	26(4/2)	24(4/2)	28(5/2)
-(An)	14(3/0)	14(3/0)	22(3/2)	22(3/2)	22(3/2)	26(4/2)	28(4/2)	26(4/2)	30(5/2)
d(An)	16(4/0)	16(4/0)	24(4/2)	24(4/2)	24(4/2)	28(5/2)	30(5/2)	28(5/2)	32(6/2)
d(An, ix)*	18(4/0)	18(4/0)	26(4/2)	26(4/2)	26(4/2)	30(5/2)	32(5/2)	30(5/2)	34(6/2)
xxx.W	16(4/0)	16(4/0)	24(4/2)	24(4/2)	24(4/2)	28(5/2)	30(5/2)	28(5/2)	32(6/2)
xxx.L	20(5/0)	20(5/0)	28(5/2)	28(5/2)	28(5/2)	32(6/2)	34(6/2)	32(6/2)	36(7/2)
d(PC)	16(4/0)	16(4/0)	24(4/2)	24(4/2)	24(4/2)	28(5/2)	30(5/2)	28(5/2)	32(6/2)
d(PC, ix)*	18(4/0)	18(4/0)	26(4/2)	26(4/2)	26(4/2)	30(5/2)	32(5/2)	30(5/2)	34(6/2)
#xxx	12(3/0)	12(3/0)	20(3/2)	20(3/2)	20(3/2)	24(4/2)	26(4/2)	24(4/2)	28(5/2)

*The size of the index register (ix) does not affect execution time.

Table F-5. Move Long Instruction Loop Mode Execution Times

Source	Loop Continued			Loop Terminated					
	Valid Count, cc False			Valid Count, cc True			Expired Count		
				Destination					
	(An)	(An) +	− (An)	(An)	(An) +	− (An)	(An)	(An) +	− (An)
Dn	14(0/2)	14(0/2)	—	20(2/2)	20(2/2)	—	18(2/2)	18(2/2)	—
An	14(0/2)	14(0/2)	—	20(2/2)	20(2/2)	—	18(2/2)	18(2/2)	—
(An)	22(2/2)	22(2/2)	24(2/2)	28(4/2)	28(4/2)	30(4/2)	24(4/2)	24(4/2)	26(4/2)
(An) +	22(2/2)	22(2/2)	24(2/2)	28(4/2)	28(4/2)	30(4/2)	24(4/2)	24(4/2)	26(4/2)
− (An)	24(2/2)	24(2/2)	26(2/2)	30(4/2)	30(4/2)	32(4/2)	26(4/2)	26(4/2)	28(4/2)

F.4 STANDARD INSTRUCTION EXECUTION TIMES

The number of clock periods shown in Tables F-6 and F-7 indicate the time required to perform the operations, store the results, and read the next instruction. The number of bus read and write cycles is shown in parenthesis as (r/w). The number of clock periods and the number of read and write cycles must be added respectively to those of the effective address calculation where indicated.

In Tables F-6 and F-7 the headings have the following meanings: An = address register operand, Dn = data register operand, ea = an operand specified by an effective address, and M = memory effective address operand.

Table F-6. Standard Instruction Execution Times

Instruction	Size	op<ea>, An***	op<ea>, Dn	op Dn, <M>
ADD	Byte, Word	8(1/0) +	4(1/0) +	8(1/1) +
	Long	6(1/0) +	6(1/0) +	12(1/2) +
AND	Byte, Word	—	4(1/0) +	8(1/1) +
	Long	—	6(1/0) +	12(1/2) +
CMP	Byte, Word	6(1/0) +	4(1/0) +	—
	Long	6(1/0) +	6(1/0) +	—
DIVS	—	—	122(1/0) +	—
DIVU	—	—	108(1/0) +	—
EOR	Byte, Word	—	4(1/0) **	8(1/1) +
	Long	—	6(1/0) **	12(1/2) +
MULS	—	—	42(1/0) + *	—
MULU	—	—	40(1/0) +	—
OR	Byte, Word	—	4(1/0) +	8(1/1) +
	Long	—	6(1/0) +	12(1/2) +
SUB	Byte, Word	8(1/0) +	4(1/0) +	8(1/1) +
	Long	6(1/0) +	6(1/0) +	12(1/2) +

NOTES:

+ add effective address calculation time
* indicates maximum value
** only available addressing mode is data register direct
*** word or long only

Table F-7. Standard Instruction Loop Mode Execution Times

Instruction	Size	Loop Continued — Valid Count cc False op <ea>, An*	op <ea>, Dn	op Dn, <ea>	Loop Terminated — Valid Count cc True op <ea>, An*	op <ea>, Dn	op Dn, <ea>	Expired Count op <ea>, An*	op <ea>, Dn	op Dn, <ea>
ADD	Byte, Word	18(1/0)	16(1/0)	16(1/1)	24(3/0)	22(3/0)	22(3/1)	22(3/0)	20(3/0)	20(3/1)
ADD	Long	22(2/0)	22(2/0)	24(2/2)	28(4/0)	28(4/0)	30(4/2)	26(4/0)	26(4/0)	28(4/2)
AND	Byte, Word	—	16(1/0)	16(1/1)	—	22(3/0)	22(3/1)	—	20(3/0)	20(3/1)
AND	Long	—	22(2/0)	24(2/2)	—	28(4/0)	30(4/2)	—	26(4/0)	28(4/2)
CMP	Byte, Word	12(1/0)	12(1/0)	—	18(3/0)	18(3/0)	—	16(3/0)	16(4/0)	—
CMP	Long	18(2/0)	18(2/0)	—	24(4/0)	24(4/0)	—	20(4/0)	20(4/0)	—
EOR	Byte, Word	—	—	16(1/0)	—	—	22(3/1)	—	—	20(3/1)
EOR	Long	—	—	24(2/2)	—	—	30(4/2)	—	—	28(4/2)
OR	Byte, Word	—	16(1/0)	16(1/0)	—	22(3/0)	22(3/1)	—	20(3/0)	20(3/1)
OR	Long	—	22(2/0)	24(2/2)	—	28(4/0)	30(4/2)	—	26(4/0)	28(4/2)
SUB	Byte, Word	18(1/0)	16(1/0)	16(1/1)	24(3/0)	22(3/0)	22(3/1)	22(3/0)	20(3/0)	20(3/1)
SUB	Long	22(2/0)	20(2/0)	24(2/2)	28(4/0)	26(4/0)	30(4/2)	26(4/0)	24(4/0)	28(4/2)

*Word or long only.
<ea> may be (An), +(An), or −(An) only. Add two clock periods to the table value if <ea> is −(An).

F.5 IMMEDIATE INSTRUCTION EXECUTION TIMES

The number of clock periods shown in Table F-8 includes the time to fetch immediate operands, perform the operations, store the results, and read the next operation. The number of bus read and write cycles is shown in parenthesis as (r/w). The number of clock periods and the number of read and write cycles must be added respectively to those of the effective address calculation where indicated.

In Table F-8, the headings have the following meanings: # = immediate operand, Dn = data register operand, An = address register operand, and M = memory operand.

Table F-8 Immediate Instruction Execution Times

Instruction	Size	op #, Dn	op #, An	op #, M
ADDI	Byte, Word	8(2/0)	—	12(2/1) +
ADDI	Long	14(3/0)	—	20(3/2) +
ADDQ	Byte, Word	4(1/0)	4(1/0) *	8(1/1) +
ADDQ	Long	8(1/0)	8(1/0)	12(1/2) +
ANDI	Byte, Word	8(2/0)	—	12(2/1) +
ANDI	Long	14(3/0)	—	20(3/1) +
CMPI	Byte, Word	8(2/0)	—	8(2/0) +
CMPI	Long	12(3/0)	—	12(3/0) +
EORI	Byte, Word	8(2/0)	—	12(2/1) +
EORI	Long	14(3/0)	—	20(3/2) +
MOVEQ	Long	4(1/0)	—	—
ORI	Byte, Word	8(2/0)	—	12(2/1) +
ORI	Long	14(3/0)	—	20(3/2) +
SUBI	Byte, Word	8(2/0)	—	12(2/1) +
SUBI	Long	14(3/0)	—	20(3/2) +
SUBQ	Byte, Word	4(1/0)	4(1/0) *	8(1/1) +
SUBQ	Long	8(1/0)	8(1/0)	12(1/2) +

+ add effective address calculation time.
* word only

F.6 SINGLE OPERAND INSTRUCTION EXECUTION TIMES

Tables F-9, F-10, and F-11 indicate the number of clock periods for the single operand instructions. The number of bus read and write cycles is shown in parenthesis as (r/w). The number of clock periods and the number of read and write cycles must be added respectively to those of the effective address calculation where indicated.

Table F-9. Single Operand Instruction Execution Times

Instruction	Size	Register	Memory
NBCD	Byte	6(1/0)	8(1/1) +
NEG	Byte, Word	4(1/0)	8(1/1) +
	Long	6(1/0)	12(1/2) +
NEGX	Byte, Word	4(1/0)	8(1/1) +
	Long	6(1/0)	12(1/2) +
NOT	Byte, Word	4(1/0)	8(1/1) +
	Long	6(1/0)	12(1/2) +
Scc	Byte, False	4(1/0)	8(1/1) + *
	Byte, True	4(1/0)	8(1/1) + *
TAS	Byte	4(1/0)	14(2/1) + *
TST	Byte, Word	4(1/0)	4(1/0)
	Long	4(1/0)	4(1/0) +

+ add effective address calculation time
* Use non-fetching effective address calculation time.

Table F-10. Clear Instruction Execution Times

	Size	Dn	An	(An)	(An) +	− (An)	d(An)	d(An, ix) *	xxx.W	xxx.L
CLR	Byte, Word	4(1/0)	—	8(1/1)	8(1/1)	10(1/1)	12(2/1)	16(2/1)	12(2/1)	16(3/1)
	Long	6(1/0)	—	12(1/2)	12(1/2)	14(1/2)	16(2/2)	20(2/2)	16(2/2)	20(3/2)

* The size of the index register (ix) does not affect execution time.

Table F-11. Single Operand Instruction Loop Mode Execution Times

		Loop Continued			Loop Terminated					
		Valid Count, cc False			Valid Count, cc True			Expired Count		
Instruction	Size	(An)	(An) +	− (An)	(An)	(An) +	− (An)	(An)	(An) +	− (An)
CLR	Byte, Word	10(0/1)	10(0/1)	12(0/1)	18(2/1)	18(2/1)	20(2/0)	16(2/1)	16(2/1)	18(2/1)
	Long	14(0/2)	14(0/2)	16(0/2)	22(2/2)	22(2/2)	24(2/2)	20(2/2)	20(2/2)	22(2/2)
NBCD	Byte	18(1/1)	18(1/1)	20(1/1)	24(3/1)	24(3/1)	26(3/1)	22(3/1)	22(3/1)	24(3/1)
NEG	Byte, Word	16(1/1)	16(1/1)	18(2/2)	22(3/1)	22(3/1)	24(3/1)	20(3/1)	20(3/1)	22(3/1)
	Long	24(2/2)	24(2/2)	26(2/2)	30(4/2)	30(4/2)	32(4/2)	28(4/2)	28(4/2)	30(4/2)
NEGX	Byte, Word	16(1/1)	16(1/1)	18(2/2)	22(3/1)	22(3/1)	24(3/1)	20(3/1)	20(3/1)	22(3/1)
	Long	24(2/2)	24(2/2)	26(2/2)	30(4/2)	30(4/2)	32(4/2)	28(4/2)	28(4/2)	30(4/2)
NOT	Byte, Word	16(1/1)	16(1/1)	18(2/2)	22(3/1)	22(3/1)	24(3/1)	20(3/1)	20(3/1)	22(3/1)
	Long	24(2/2)	24(2/2)	26(2/2)	30(4/2)	30(4/2)	32(4/2)	28(4/2)	28(4/2)	30(4/2)
TST	Byte, Word	12(1/0)	12(1/0)	14(1/0)	18(3/0)	18(3/0)	20(3/0)	16(3/0)	16(3/0)	18(3/0)
	Long	18(2/0)	18(2/0)	20(2/0)	24(4/0)	24(4/0)	26(4/0)	20(4/0)	20(4/0)	22(4/0)

F.7 SHIFT/ROTATE INSTRUCTION EXECUTION TIMES

Tables F-12 and F-13 indicate the number of clock periods for the shift and rotate instructions. The number of bus read and write cycles is shown in parenthesis as (r/w). The number of clock periods and the number of read and write cycles must be added respectively to those of the effective address calculation where indicated.

Table F-12. Shift/Rotate Instruction Execution Times

Instruction	Size	Register	Memory*
ASR, ASL	Byte, Word	6 + 2n(1/0)	8(1/1) +
	Long	8 + 2n(1/0)	—
LSR, LSL	Byte, Word	6 + 2n(1/0)	8(1/1) +
	Long	8 + 2n(1/0)	—
ROR, ROL	Byte, Word	6 + 2n(1/0)	8(1/1) +
	Long	8 + 2n(1/0)	—
ROXR, ROXL	Byte, Word	6 + 2n(1/0)	8(1/1) +
	Long	8 + 2n(1/0)	—

+ add effective address calculation time
n is the shift or rotate count
* word only

Table F-13. Shift/Rotate Instruction Loop Mode Execution Times

Instruction	Size	Loop Continued			Loop Terminated					
		Valid Count, cc False			Valid Count, cc True			Expired Count		
		(An)	(An) +	– (An)	(An)	(An) +	– (An)	(An)	(An) +	– (An)
ASR, ASL	Word	18(1/1)	18(1/1)	20(1/1)	24(3/1)	24(3/1)	26(3/1)	22(3/1)	22(3/1)	24(3/1)
LSR, LSL	Word	18(1/1)	18(1/1)	20(1/1)	24(3/1)	24(3/1)	26(3/1)	22(3/1)	22(3/1)	24(3/1)
ROR, ROL	Word	18(1/1)	18(1/1)	20(1/1)	24(3/1)	24(3/1)	26(3/1)	22(3/1)	22(3/1)	24(3/1)
ROXR, ROXL	Word	18(1/1)	18(1/1)	20(1/1)	24(3/1)	24(3/1)	26(3/1)	22(3/1)	22(3/1)	24(3/1)

F.8 BIT MANIPULATION INSTRUCTION EXECUTION TIMES

Table F-14 indicates the number of clock periods required for the bit manipulation instructions. The number of bus read and write cycles is shown in parenthesis as (r/w). The number of clock periods and the number of read and write cycles must be added respectively to those of the effective address calculation where indicated.

Table F-14. Bit Manipulation Instruction Execution Times

Instruction	Size	Dynamic		Static	
		Register	Memory	Register	Memory
BCHG	Byte	—	8(1/1) +	—	12(2/1) +
	Long	8(1/0) *	—	12(2/0) *	—
BCLR	Byte	—	10(1/1) +	—	14(2/1) +
	Long	10(1/0) *	—	14(2/0) *	—
BSET	Byte	—	8(1/1) +	—	12(2/1) +
	Long	8(1/0) *	—	12(2/0) *	—
BTST	Byte	—	4(1/0) +	—	8(2/0) +
	Long	6(1/0) *	—	10(2/0)	—

\+ add effective address calculation time
* indicates maximum value

F.9 CONDITIONAL INSTRUCTION EXECUTION TIMES

Table F-15 indicates the number of clock periods required for the conditional instructions. The number of bus read and write cycles is indicated in parenthesis as (r/w). The number of clock periods and the number of read and write cycles must be added respectively to those of the effective address calculation where indicated.

Table F-15. Conditional Instruction Execution Times

Instruction	Displacement	Branch Taken	Branch Not Taken
B$_{CC}$	Byte	10(2/0)	6(1/0)
	Word	10(2/0)	10(2/0)
BRA	Byte	10(2/0)	—
	Word	10(2/0)	—
BSR	Byte	18(2/2)	—
	Word	18(2/2)	—
DB$_{CC}$	CC true	—	10(2/0)
	CC false	10(2/0)	16(3/0)

\+ add effective address calculation time
* indicates maximum value

F.10 JMP, JSR, LEA, PEA, AND MOVEM INSTRUCTION EXECUTION TIMES

Table F-16 indicates the number of clock periods required for the jump, jump-to-subroutine, load effective address, push effective address, and move multiple registers instructions. The number of bus read and write cycles is shown in parenthesis as (r/w).

Table F-16. JMP, JSR, LEA, PEA, and MOVEM Instruction Execution Times

Instr	Size	(An)	(An)+	–(An)	d(An)	d(An, ix)+	xxx.W	xxx.L	d(PC)	d(PC, ix)*
JMP	—	8(2/0)	—	—	10(2/0)	14(3/0)	10(2/0)	12(3/0)	10(2/0)	14(3/0)
JSR	—	16(2/2)	—	—	18(2/2)	22(2/2)	18(2/2)	20(3/2)	18(2/2)	22(2/2)
LEA	—	4(1/0)	—	—	8(2/0)	12(2/0)	8(2/0)	12(3/0)	8(2/0)	12(2/0)
PEA	—	12(1/2)	—	—	16(2/2)	20(2/2)	16(2/2)	20(3/2)	16(2/2)	20(2/2)
MOVEM M → R	Word	12+4n (3+n/0)	12+4n (3+n/0)		16+4n (4+n/0)	18+4n (4+n/0)	16+4n (4+n/0)	20+4n (5+n/0)	16+4n (4+n/0)	18+4n (4+n/0)
	Long	12+8n (3+2n/0)	12+8n (3+2n/0)	—	16+8n (4+2n/0)	18+8n (4+2n/0)	16+8n (4+2n/0)	20+8n (5+2n/0)	16+8n (4+2n/0)	18+8n (4+2n/0)
MOVEM R → M	Word	8+4n (2/n)	—	8+4n (2/n)	12+4n (3/n)	14+4n (3/n)	12+4n (3/n)	16+4n (4/n)	—	—
	Long	8+8n (2/2n)	—	8+8n (2/2n)	12+8n (3/2n)	14+8n (3/2n)	12+8n (3/2n)	16+8n (4/2n)	—	—

n is the number of registers to move
*is the size of the index register (ix) does not affect the instruction's execution time

F.11 MULTI-PRECISION INSTRUCTION EXECUTION TIMES

Table F-17 indicates the number of clock periods for the multi-precision instructions. The number of clock periods includes the time to fetch both operands, perform the operations, store the results, and read the next instructions. The number of read and write cycles is shown in parenthesis as (r/w).

In Table F-17, the headings have the following meanings: Dn = data register operand and M = memory operand.

Table F-17. Multi-Precision Instruction Execution Times

			Loop Mode		
			Continued	Terminated	
		Non-Looped	Valid Count, cc False	Valid Count, cc True	Expired Count
Instruction	Size	op Dn, Dn	op M, M*		
ADDX	Byte, Word	4(1/0)	18(3/10)	22(2/1)	28(4/1)	26(4/1)
	Long	6(1/0)	30(5/2)	32(4/2)	38(6/2)	36(6/2)
CMPM	Byte, Word	—	12(3/0)	14(2/0)	20(4/0)	18(4/0)
	Long	—	20(5/0)	24(4/0)	30(6/0)	26(6/0)
SUBX	Byte, Word	4(1/0)	18(3/1)	22(2/1)	28(4/1)	26(4/1)
	Long	6(1/0)	30(5/2)	32(4/2)	38(6/2)	36(6/2)
ABCD	Byte	6(1/0)	18(3/1)	24(2/1)	30(4/1)	28(4/1)
SBCD	Byte	6(1/0)	18(3/1)	24(2/1)	30(4/1)	28(4/1)

*Source and destination ea is (An)+ for CMPM and –(An) for all others.

F.12 MISCELLANEOUS INSTRUCTION EXECUTION TIMES

Table F-18 indicates the number of clock periods for the following miscellaneous instructions. The number of bus read and write cycles is shown in parenthesis as (r/w). The number of clock periods plus the number of read and write cycles must be added to those of the effective address calculation where indicated.

Table F-18. Miscellaneous Instruction Execution Times

Instruction	Size	Register	Memory	Register → Destination**	Source** → Register
ANDI to CCR	—	16(2/0)	—	—	—
ANDI to SR	—	16(2/0)	—	—	—
CHK	—	8(1/0) +	—	—	—
EORI to CCR	—	16(2/0)	—	—	—
EORI to SR	—	16(2/0)	—	—	—
EXG	—	6(1/0)	—	—	—
EXT	Word	4(1/0)	—	—	—
	Long	4(1/0)	—	—	—
LINK	—	16(2/2)	—	—	—
MOVE from CCR	—	4(1/0)	8(1/1) + *	—	—
MOVE to CCR	—	12(2/0)	12(2/0) +	—	—
MOVE from SR	—	4(1/0)	8(1/1) + *	—	—
MOVE to SR	—	12(2/0)	12(2/0) +	—	—
MOVE from USP	—	6(1/0)	—	—	—
MOVE to USP	—	6(1/0)	—	—	—
MOVEC	—	—	—	10(2/0)	12(2/0)
MOVEP	Word	—	—	16(2/2)	16(4/0)
	Long	—	—	24(2/4)	24(6/0)
NOP	—	4(1/0)	—	—	—
ORI to CCR	—	16(2/0)	—	—	—
ORI to SR	—	16(2/0)	—	—	—
RESET	—	130(1/0)	—	—	—
RTD	—	16(4/0)	—	—	—
RTE	Short	24(6/0)	—	—	—
	Long, Retry Read	112(27/10)	—	—	—
	Long, Retry Write	112(26/1)	—	—	—
	Long, No Retry	110(26/0)	—	—	—
RTR	—	20(5/0)	—	—	—
RTS	—	16(4/0)	—	—	—
STOP	—	4(0/0)	—	—	—
SWAP	—	4(1/0)	—	—	—
TRAPV	—	4(1/0)	—	—	—
UNLK	—	12(3/0)	—	—	—

+ add effective address calculation time.
* use non-fetching effective address calculation time.
** Source or destination is a memory location for the MOVEP instruction and a control register for the MOVEC instruction.

F.13 EXCEPTION PROCESSING EXECUTION TIMES

Table F-19 indicates the number of clock periods for exception processing. The number of clock periods includes the time for all stacking, the vector fetch, and the fetch of the first two instruction words of the handler routine. The number of bus read and write cycles is shown in parenthesis as (r/w).

Table F-19. Exception Processing Execution Times

Exception	
Address Error	126(4/26)
Breakpoint Instruction*	42(5/4)
Bus Error	126(4/26)
CHK Instruction**	44(5/4) +
Divide By Zero	42(5/4)
Illegal Instruction	38(4/4)
Interrupt*	46(5/4)
MOVEC, Illegal Cr**	46(5/4)
Privilege Violation	38(4/4)
Reset***	40(6/0)
RTE, Illegal Format	50(7/4)
RTE, Illegal Revision	70(12/4)
Trace	38(4/4)
TRAP Instruction	38(4/4)
TRAPV Instruction	40(5/4)

+ add effective address calculation time.
* The interrupt acknowledge and breakpoint cycles are assumed to take four clock periods.
** Indicates maximum value.
*** Indicates the time from when $\overline{RESET}$ and $\overline{HALT}$ are first sampled as negated to when instruction execution starts.

APPENDIX IVG: MC68010 LOOP MODE OPERATION

The MC68010 has several features that provide efficient execution of program loops. One of these features is the DBcc looping primitive instruction. The DBcc instruction operates on three operands, a loop counter, a branch condition, and a branch displacement. When the DBcc is executed in loop mode, the contents of the low order word of the register specified as the loop counter is decremented by one and compared to minus one. If equal to minus one, the result of the decrement is placed back into the count register and the next sequential instruction is executed, otherwise the condition code register is checked against the specified branch condition. If the condition is true, the result of the decrement is discarded and the next sequential instruction is executed. Finally, if the count register is not equal to minus one and the branch condition is false, the branch displacement is added to the program counter and instruction execution continues at that new address. Note that this is slightly different than non-looped execution; however, the results are the same.

An example of using the DBcc instruction in a simple loop for moving a block of data is shown in Figure G-1. In this program, the block of data 'LENGTH' words long at address 'SOURCE' is to be moved to address 'DEST' provided that none of the words moved are equal to zero. When the effect of instruction prefetch on this loop is examined it can be seen that the bus activity during the loop execution would be:

1. Fetch the MOVE.W instruction,
2. Fetch the DBEQ instruction,
3. Read the operand where A0 points,
4. Write the operand where A1 points,
5. Fetch the DBEQ branch displacement, and
6. If loop conditions are met, return to step 1.

```
         LEA      SOURCE, A0      Load A Pointer To Source Data
         LEA      DEST, A1        Load A Pointer To Destination
         MOVE.W   #LENGTH, D0     Load The Counter Register
LOOP     MOVE.W   (A0) + , (A1) + Loop To Move The Block Of Data
         DBEQ     D0, LOOP        Stop If Data Word Is Zero
```

Figure G-1. DBcc Loop Program Example

During this loop, five bus cycles are executed; however, only two bus cycles perform the data movement. Since the MC68010 has a two word prefetch queue in addition to a one word instruction decode register, it is evident that the three instruction fetches in this loop could be eliminated by placing the MOVE.W word in the instruction decode register and holding the DBEQ instruction and its branch displacement in the prefetch queue. The MC68010 has the ability to do this by entering the loop mode of operation. During loop mode operation, all opcode fetches are suppressed and only operand reads and writes are performed until an exit loop condition is met.

Loop mode operation is transparent to the programmer, with only two conditions required for the MC68010 to enter the loop mode. First, a DBcc instruction must be executed with both branch conditions met and a branch displacement of minus four; which indicates that the branch is to a one word instruction preceding the DBcc instruction. Second, when the processor fetches the instruction at the branch address, it is checked to determine whether it is one of the allowed looping instructions. If it is, the loop mode is entered. Thus, the single word looped instruction and the first word of the DBcc instruction will each be fetched twice when the loop is entered; but no instruction fetches will occur again until the DBcc loop conditions fail.

In addition to the normal termination conditions for a loop, there are several conditions that will cause the MC68010 to exit loop mode operation. These conditions are interrupts, trace exceptions, reset errors, and bus errors. Interrupts are honored after each execution of the DBcc instruction, but not after the execution of the looped instruction. If an interrupt exception occurs, loop mode operation is terminated and can be restarted on return from the interrupt handler. If the T bit is set, trace exceptions will occur at the end of both the loop instruction and the DBcc instruction and thus loop mode operation is not available. Reset will abort all processing, including the loop mode. Bus errors during the loop mode will be treated the same as in normal processing; however, when the RTE instruction is used to continue the execution of the looped instruction, the three word loop will not be re-fetched.

The loopable instructions available on the MC68010 are listed in Table G-1. These instructions may use the three address register indirect modes to form one word looping instructions; (An), (An) +, and − (An).

Table G-1. MC68010 Loopable Instructions

Opcodes	Applicable Addressing Modes	
MOVE [BWL]	(Ay) to (Ax)	− (Ay) to (Ax)
	(Ay) to (Ax) +	− (Ay) to (Ax) +
	(Ay) to − (Ax)	− (Ay) to − (Ax)
	(Ay) + to (Ax)	Ry to (Ax)
	(Ay) + to (Ax) +	Ry to (Ax) +
	(Ay) + to − (Ax)	
ADD [BWL] AND [BWL] CMP [BWL] OR [BWL] SUB [BWL]	(Ay) to Dx (Ay) + to Dx − (Ay) to Dx	
ADDA [WL] CMPA [WL] SUBA [WL]	(Ay) to Ax − (Ay) to Ax (Ay) + to Ax	
ADD [BWL] AND [BWL] EOR [BWL] OR [BWL] SUB [BWL]	Dx to (Ay) Dx to (Ay) + Dx to − (Ay)	

Opcodes	Applicable Addressing Modes
ABCD [B] ADDX [BWL] SBCD [B] SUBX [BWL]	− (Ay) to − (Ax)
CMP [BWL]	(Ay) + to (Ax) +
CLR [BWL] NEG [BWL] NEGX [BWL] NOT [BWL] TST [BWL] NBCD [B]	(Ay) (Ay) + − (Ay)
ASL [W] ASR [W] LSL [W] LSR [W] ROL [W] ROR [W] ROXL [W] ROXR [W]	(Ay) by #1 (Ay) + by #1 − (Ay) by #1

NOTE
[B, W, or L] indicate an operand size of byte, word, or long word.

APPENDIX IVH: MC68000 PREFETCH

H.1 INTRODUCTION

The MC68000 uses a two-word tightly coupled instruction prefetch mechanism to enhance performance. This mechanism is described in terms of the microcode operations involved. If the execution is defined to begin when the microroutine for that instruction is entered, some features of the prefetch mechanism can be described.

1. When execution of an instruction begins, the operation word and the word following have already been fetched. The operation word is in the instruction decoder.

2. In the case of multiword instructions, as each additional word of the instruction is used internally, a fetch is made to the instruction stream to replace it.

3. The last fetch from the instruction stream is made when the operation word is discarded and decoding is started on the next instruction.

4. If the instruction is a single-word instruction causing a branch, the second word is not used. But because this word is fetched by the previous instruction, it is impossible to avoid this superfluous fetch. In the case of an interrupt or trace exception, both words are not used.

5. The program counter usually points to the last word fetched from the instruction stream.

H.2 INSTRUCTION PREFETCH

The following example illustrates many of the features of instruction prefetch. The contents of memory are assumed to be as illustrated in Figure H-1.

```
            ORG        0                      DEFINE RESTART VECTOR

            DC.L       INISSP                 INITIAL SYSTEM STACK POINTER
            DC.L       RESTART                RESTART SYSTEM ENTRY POINT

            ORG        INTVECTOR              DEFINE AN INTERRUPT VECTOR
            DC.L       INTHANDLER             HANDLER ADDRESS FOR THIS VECTOR

            ORG                               SYSTEM RESTART CODE
RESTART:
            NOP                               NO OPERATION EXAMPLE
            BRA.S      LABEL                  SHORT BRANCH
            ADD.W      D0,D1                  ADD REGISTER TO REGISTER
LABEL:
            SUB.W      DISP(A0),A1            SUBTRACT REGISTER INDIRECT WITH OFFSET
            CMP.W      D2,D3                  COMPARE REGISTER TO REGISTER
            SGE.B      D7                     Scc TO REGISTER
            ...
            ...
INTHANDLER:
            MOVE.W     LONGADR1,LONGADR2      MOVE WORD FROM AND TO LONG ADDRESS
            NOP                               NO OPERATION
            SWAP.W                            REGISTER SWAP
```

Figure H-1. Instruction Prefetch Example, Memory Contents

The sequence we shall illustrate consists of the power-up reset, the execution of NOP, BRA, SUB, the taking of an interrupt, and the execution of the MOVE.W xxx.L to yyy.L. The order of operations described within each microroutine is not exact, but is intended for illustrative purpose only.

Microroutine	Operation	Location	Operand
Reset	Read	0	SSP High
	Read	2	SSP Low
	Read	4	PC High
	Read	6	PC Low
	Read	(PC)	NOP
	Read	+(PC)	BRA
	<begin NOP>		
NOP	Read	+(PC)	ADD
	<begin BRA>		
BRA	PC = PC + d		
	Read	(PC)	SUB
	Read	+(PC)	DISP
	<begin SUB>		
SUB	Read	+(PC)	CMP
	Read	DISP(A0)	<src>
	Read	+(PC)	SGE
	<begin CMP>	<take INT>	
INTERRUPT	Write	−(SSP)	PC Low
	Write	−(SSP)	PC High
	Read	<INT ACK>	Vector #
	Write	−(SSP)	SR
	Read	(VR)	PC High
	Read	+(VR)	PC Low
	Read	(PC)	MOVE
	Read	+(PC)	xxx High
	<begin MOVE>		
MOVE	Read	+(PC)	xxx Low
	Read	+(PC)	yyy High
	Read	xxx	<src>
	Read	+(PC)	yyy Low
	Read	+(PC)	NOP
	Write	yyy	<dest>
	Read	+(PC)	SWAP
	<begin NOP>		

Figure H-2. Instruction Prefetch Example

H.3 DATA PREFETCH

Normally the MC68000 prefetches only instructions and not data. However, when the MOVEM instruction is used to move data from memory to registers, the data stream is prefetched in order to optimize performance. As a result, the processor reads one extra word beyond the higher end of the source area. For example, the instruction sequence in Figure H-3 will operate as shown in Figure H-4.

			MOVE TWO LONGWORDS INTO REGISTERS	Assume Effective Address Evaluation is Already Done			
	...			Microroutine	Operation	Location	Other Operations
	MOVEM.L	A,D0/D1			...		
	...			MOVEM	Read	A	
A	DC.W	1	WORD 1				Prepare to Fill D0
B	DC.W	2	WORD 2		Read	B	A → DOH
C	DC.W	3	WORD 3		Read	C	B → DOL
D	DC.W	4	WORD 4				Prepare to Fill D1
E	DC.W	5	WORD 5		Read	D	C → D1H
F	DC.W	6	WORD 6		Read	E	D → D1L
							Detect Register List Complete

Figure H-3.
MOVEM Example, Memory Contents

Figure H-4.
MOVEM Example, Operation Sequence

Appendix V

Design Module Memory Map

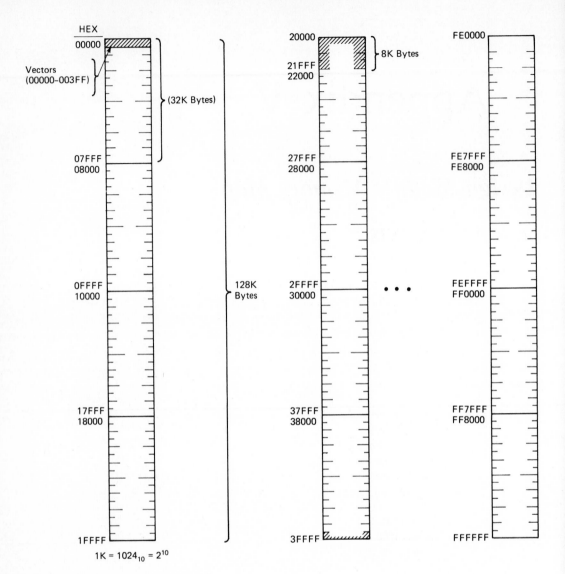

HEX

Vectors
(00000–003FF)

(32K Bytes)

00000
07FFF
08000
0FFFF
10000
17FFF
18000
1FFFF

128K
Bytes

1K = 1024₁₀ = 2¹⁰

20000
21FFF
22000

8K Bytes

27FFF
28000
2FFFF
30000
37FFF
38000
3FFFF

FE0000
FE7FFF
FE8000
FEFFFF
FF0000
FF7FFF
FF8000
FFFFFF

Notes:
(1) Shaded area at $20 000 is MACSbug ROM area.
(2) Shaded area at $3F FF0 is I/O space.

Figure V.1 Design module memory map.

560

Answers to

Selected Exercises

Chapter 2

2.1.1. Reference to periodicals such as *Electronics* is suggested. Manufacturer's literature could also be helpful.

2.1.2. (a) 0.75 microseconds
(b) 0.6 microseconds
(c) 0.48 microseconds

2.1.3. The memory would require 32 chips, typically arranged in 4 rows of 8 each.

2.2.1. (a) Bytes 1000, 1001,—1007
(b) Words 1000,1002,—1006
(c) Longwords 1000, 1004

2.2.2. (a) 12
(b) 16
(c) 24

2.2.3. (a) 65,536
(b) 1,048,576
(c) 16,777,216

2.2.4. 23 lines

2.3.1. The trap is caused by some condition occurring in the program and it is synchronous with the execution of the program. An interrupt is due to an external cause.

2.3.2. The results of an illegal instruction execution are unpredictable unless an "illegal instruction" trap is available.

2.3.3. (a) Time for R3 is 20 microseconds + 4.4 microseconds = 24.4 microseconds.

(b) R2 is executed in a minimum of 34.4 microseconds to a maximum of 24.4 + 34.4 = 58.8 microseconds.

(c) R1 is executed in a minimum of 24.4 microseconds to a maximum of 83.2 microseconds. The worst case occurs when R1 must wait for R3 and then R2 to complete.

2.3.4. A two-operand instruction using 32-bit direct addresses is 5 words in memory. The shortest instructions occupy one word if no extension words are required.

2.3.5. An operating system executes in the supervisor mode and controls all the resources of the system available to a program, i.e., interrupt handling, I/O as well as controlling the user program execution.

Chapter 3

3.1.1.1. 4.375

3.1.1.2. 255.99998

3.1.1.3. (a) 108

(b) 35

(c) 0.975098

(d) 61450

3.1.1.4. $x = 5$

3.1.1.5. 4,294,967,295

3.1.2.1. (a) $1111\ 1001\ 1011\ 1001_2$

(b) $1111\ 1111\ 1111\ 0101_2$

(c) 11010.010_2

3.1.2.2. $100 \cdots 0_2$

3.1.2.3. (a) Extend 0's to left.

(b) Extend 1's to left.

3.1.2.4. (a) 346.27

(b) 8223_{16}

(c) 1.1001111

3.1.2.5. (a) $-127, +127; -127, +127; -128, +127$

(b) $-32767, 32767; -32767, 32767; -32768, +32767$

(c) $-2{,}147{,}483{,}647, +2{,}147{,}483{,}647;$
$-2{,}147{,}483{,}647, +2{,}147{,}483{,}647;$
$-2{,}147{,}483{,}648, +2{,}147{,}483{,}647$

3.1.2.6. -1 to -1000

3.1.3.1. (a) $0100\ 0000\ 0000_2$

(b) $CF08_{16}$

(c) 4,294,967,295

(d) 120_5

3.1.3.2. 0.428571428

3.1.3.4. -0.0078125

3.1.3.5. $10.00, 10.01 \cdots 11.11, 00.00, 00.01, \cdots 01.11$

3.2.1.1. (a) $0000\ 0111_2$
   (b) $0001\ 0011_2$
   (c) $1001\ 1001_2$

3.2.1.2. (a) 1970
   (b) Invalid

3.2.1.3. (a) 99
   (b) 9999
   (c) 9999 9999

3.2.1.4. Error if sum $\geq 10^L$

3.2.2.1. 128 (BCD)

3.2.2.2. $0001\ 1111\ 1101_2$; multiply Lth digit by 10^L in binary and sum.

3.2.2.3. Multiply Lth digit by multiplier and then by 10^L; convert partial result to BCD and sum into result.

3.2.3.1. (a) $0000\ 0001\ 0010\ 0100_2$
   (b) $1001\ 1001\ 1001\ 1001_2$
   (c) $1001\ 0000\ 0000\ 0000_2$
   (d) Invalid

3.2.3.2. (a) $-10;\ +9$
   (b) $-1000;\ +999$
   (c) $-10,000,000;\ +9,999,999$

3.3.1.2. $0\ 0111\ 1100\ 0000 \cdots_2$

3.3.1.3. (a) $4160\ 0000_{16}$
   (b) $BFA0\ 0000_{16}$

3.3.2.1. (a) $3F00\ 0000_{16}$
   (b) $BF00\ 0000_{16}$
   (c) $0080\ 0000_{16}$

3.3.2.2. 2×10^{38} (approximately)

3.3.2.3. (a) $401C\ 0000 \cdots 00_{16}$
   (b) $C03E\ 0000 \ldots 00_{16}$

3.4.1. 500,000 bytes or 2.98% of memory

3.4.2. 54 48 45 20 'THE'
   4D 4F 54 4F 52 4F 4C 41 20 'MOTOROLA'
   4D 43 36 38 30 30 30 'MC68000'

3.4.3. (a) $1111\ 1111_2$
   (b) 02 55
   (c) 32 35 35

3.4.4. (a) $0010\ 1101_2$

(b) 34 35

(c) 2D 30 34 35

3.4.5. No, the morse code is ternary (dot, dash, space).

Chapter 4

4.1.1. 10^{-5} watt; 5×10^3

4.1.2. $S = 1.49$

4.2.1. (a) Mask level 4 interrupt

(b) Supervisor mode

(c) $Z = \{1\}$ condition code

(d) Trace in supervisor mode

4.2.2. $(SR) = 2400_{16}$

4.2.3. SR, PC, SSP; USP

4.2.4. The stack changes as follows:

Address	After level 1 interrupt		After level 2 interrupt	
$007FF4_{16}$			2100_{16}	(SR_1)
$007FF6_{16}$			0000_{16}	
				(PC_1)
$007FF8_{16}$	(Free)		$200C_{16}$	
$007FFA_{16}$	0000_{16}	(SR0)	0000_{16}	(SR0)
$007FFC_{16}$	0000_{16}		0000_{16}	
		(PC0)		(PC0)
$007FFE_{16}$	$101C_{16}$		$101C_{16}$	

In the level 1 interrupt $(SR) = (2100)$; in the level 2 interrupt $(SR) = (2200)$. Addresses and contents are given in hexadecimal.

4.3.1. $(1000) = 00$

$(1001) = 00$

$(1002) = 00$

$(1003) = 00$

4.3.2. (a) $(D2)[15{:}0] = 0801_{16}$

(b) $(1000) = 1901_{16}$

(c) $(1000) = 0000$

(d) $(D2)[15{:}0] = 0806_{16}$

(e) $(D1)[15{:}0] = 1F14_{16}$

4.4.1. (a) (7D0)[W] = (3E8)
  (b) (D1)[W] = (1000)
  (c) (D1)[B] = (3E8)
  (d) (FF FFFC) = 0000 0000

4.4.2. (a) (D1)[W] = 3E8
  (b) (D1)[W] = FFE0
  (c) (D1)[W] = FFE0
  (d) (D1)[W] = 03E8

4.4.3. (a) (D1)[W] = 4142
  (b) (D1)[W] = 00C1
  (c) (D1)[W] = 03E8

4.4.4. MOVE.W D1, TEMP
  MOVE.B TEMP,1001
  MOVE.B TEMP + 1,1002
  (TEMP is the address of a word location). Values are in hexadecimal except in Exercise 4.

4.5.1. MOVE.W VAL1,D0
  ADD.W   VAL2,D0
  MOVE.W D0,RESULT

4.5.2. (a) (1000) = 00
  (b) (1000,1001) = 00 00
  (c) (1000) = 1000
  (d) (D1)[15:0] = 0010
  (e) (D1)[15:0] = 1000
  (f) (D1)[7:0] = 10

4.5.3. (a) CLR.W D1
  (b) MOVE.L A3,D0
  (c) MOVE.B #$2E,D0

4.5.4. (a) 4240
  (b) 2008
  (c) DA00
  (Values are in hexadecimal.)

4.6.1. 16,777,216 bytes; 8,388,608 words; 4,194,304 longwords

4.6.2. (a) (1000) = 1020 (BCD)
       (1002) = 3040 (BCD)
  (b) (1000) = 0200
       (1002) = 00FC
  (c) (1000) = 4142
       (1002) = 4344

4.6.3. (1002) = 0002
  (1004) = FFF0
  (Values are in hexadecimal in Exercises 2 and 3 unless otherwise noted.)

Chapter 5

5.2.3. (a) 4E 20 49 53 (hexadecimal)
   (b) 14_{16}
   (c) HERE = (LC)
   (d) Reserve 4 bytes
   (e) Location of "LABEL" + 2

5.2.4. (a) $0FFE
   (b) $1000
   (c) $800
   (d) $555 (integer division)
   (e) $4000

5.3.1. The PC references instructions, which, according to the MC68000 designers, should not be modified.

5.3.2. Use MOVEA.L #0, <An> to clear <An>.

5.3.3. Operands defined by absolute addressing cannot have their addresses changed after assembly. Indirect and relative addresses can be changed during execution since the effective address is calculated as the instruction executes.

5.3.4. Short addresses require only one extension word but the range is restricted to 16 bits.

5.3.5. (a) $0FFF
   (b) $1000
   (c) $0FFE

5.3.6. (a) ((A0)) ← ((A0) + 4)
   (b) (D1)[W] ← ($FF9000); sign extended source address
   (c) (D1)[B] ← ((A0) + (D1))

5.3.7. Both modes sign extend the value to $FF8000.

Chapter 6

6.1.1. The condition code bits C and V should be cleared after a data transfer so that the conditional tests will work properly.

6.1.4. Using MOVEM results in a shorter program if several registers are saved.

6.1.5. SWAP allows access to most significant byte in a word. A rotate instruction is needed to access individually all bytes in a longword.

6.2.1. The jump table (held in read/write memory) allows modification of entry addresses in ROM.

6.2.3. (a) BEQ
   (b) BGT
   (c) BLT

6.3.1. The offset is $000E_{16}$. The instruction is
$610E_{16}$

6.3.3. Nesting is limited by the length of the stack.

Chapter 7

7.1.3. The result represents -16384; $V = \{1\}$ indicating an error.

7.2.1. (a) $FF00; $C=\{1\}$, $V=\{0\}$, $Z=\{1\}$
(c) $FFFE: $N=\{1\}$
(e) $0000; $Z=\{1\}$

7.3.1. (a) $0002, $0000
(c) $FFFE, $0000
(d) $FFFE, $FFFF

7.5.1. (a) $00 37
(b) $99 63

Chapter 8

8.2.1. Six bits are used to specify the shift count.
8.2.3. $+40$ with $V = \{1\}$.

8.3.1. (a) Bit $0 = \{0\}$
(b) Bit $m = \{1\}$
8.3.2. (a) BCLR #15,D2
(b) BSET #15,D2
8.3.5. An interrupt occurring between a TST and BNE instruction could allow a routine to execute that tests the flag before it is modified by the interrupted program. Thus a false indication is given to the interrupting routine.

Chapter 9

9.1.1. (a) $3000
(b) $0000 A000
9.1.3. $FFFF A000

9.2.1. Use MOVE.W #1,D1 to initialize (D1). Also, "RESULT" as a destination cannot be relative.
9.2.2. The pointer (A0) is modified each time the program is loaded and executed.

9.4.2. No address need be passed to the subroutine since (PC) is the base address of the parameter area in-line. The values are fixed, however.

9.4.5. The instruction sequence accomplishes the same thing as the LINK instruction.

Chapter 10

10.1.1.–10.1.4. See text for discussions.

10.2.1. (a) Trace off; user mode; disable level 4 and lower level interrupts.
(d) Change to user mode.

10.2.2. (a) C = {0}; V = {0}; X = {0}; set N, Z
(c) Trap (privilege violation)

10.2.4. In the MC68000, the MOVE from SR allows user access to the CCR. The MC68010 has a separate instruction to accomplish this.

10.3.1. Circuitry external to the CPU must recognize address $0000 0000 when requested by the CPU. The circuitry then translates the address to $20000.

10.3.2. The sequence shown puts the CPU in user mode before the JMP is executed. The JMP instruction is in the supervisor memory space.

Chapter 11

11.3.2. An illegal instruction might occur if a program terminated improperly or otherwise caused a transfer of control to an area of memory containing data values. A memory failure might cause illegal instructions to be fetched.

11.4.1. A nonmaskable interrupt could be used to abort a program caught in an infinite loop situation. Pushing the "ABORT" button on the Motorola design module causes this interrupt, for example. The interrupt could also be used to begin a power down sequence.

Chapter 12

12.1.1. Memory mapped I/O allows all instructions to reference I/O operations and there is no limit on the number of I/O ports within the addressing capability of the CPU. However, memory space is used for I/O. Isolated I/O is typically faster.

12.2.2. (a) Interrupt
(b) Interrupt or DMA
(c) DMA

12.3.1. (a) 7.35 microseconds
(c) 3.52 microseconds

12.3.2. If a DIVS instruction is executing, up to 202 cycles could be taken to respond to the interrupt or about 25.3 microseconds in an 8-MHz version of the MC68000.

12.4.2. (a) User data
(b) User program
(c) Supervisor program

Index